MINDFULNESS REDESIGNED FOR THE TWENTY-FIRST CENTURY

MINDFULNESS REDESIGNED FOR THE TWENTY-FIRST CENTURY

Let's Not Cage the Hummingbird
A Mindful Path to Resilience

Amit Sood, MD
Professor of Medicine

© 2018 Amit Sood, MD

All rights reserved. No part of this publication may be transmitted, stored in a retrieval system, copied, reproduced or distributed in any form or by any means, mechanical, electronic, recording, photocopying, or otherwise, without the prior written permission of the publisher.

Disclaimer: The information in this book is intended only as an informative guide about health and wellbeing. In no way is this book intended to substitute, conflict or countermand with a physician or other health care provider's advice or medical care. Please consult your physician or other health care provider if you are experiencing any symptoms or have questions pertaining to the information contained in this book. The ultimate decision about your care is between you and your physician or other health care provider. DO NOT DISREGARD PROFESSIONAL MEDICAL ADVICE OR DELAY SEEKING MEDICAL TREATMENT BECAUSE OF SOMETHING YOU HAVE READ IN THIS PUBLICATION.

The information in this book is complete and true to the best of our knowledge. The information in this book is general and offered with no guarantees, representations or warranties on the part of the author or the Global Center for Resiliency and Wellbeing. The author and the Global Center for Resiliency and Wellbeing disclaim all liability in connection with the use of this book. Except for the names of specific scientists and author's personal relatives and friends, the names of people associated with the events described in this book have been changed and are fictionalized. Any resemblance to an actual person is purely coincidental.

The contents of this book represent the personal opinions of the author and are not endorsed by Mayo Clinic.

ISBN-13: 9780999552506
ISBN-10: 0999552503
Library of Congress Control Number: 2017916299
LCCN Imprint Name: Global Center for Resiliency and Wellbeing, Rochester, MN

To all the world's children

Dear friend,

My gratitude to you for your interest in this book and for trusting me with your time. I share "*Mindfulness Redesigned*" in the spirit of one student sharing some exciting information that he chanced upon, with a fellow student.

I invite your enthusiasm, patience, and open-minded skepticism as you journey through the pages and explore the deeper recesses of your brain, to grasp and, if you wish, embrace mindfulness.

I will love to learn from you and hear your stories. You can contact me at amit@stressfree.org or @amitsoodmd on Twitter. If you wish, check out stressfree.org for more information.

Take care,
Amit

Homo sapiens come in two varieties: the effortlessly mindful, and the rest of us, who struggle with being in the moment. If you belong to the second group, welcome to the club!

This book will help you access the depths of mindfulness even if you can't sit like a pretzel, appreciate the raisin for an hour, or silence the committee that meets daily inside your head.

Hummingbirds are a powerful flying machine; they perish when caged. The self in me also wants to fly. Presently though, I sit in a cage—of my brain's negative traits, my past wounds, present chaos, future fears, and the finiteness of time.

This book tracks my effort to uncage me, a striving to reach my highest potential, and a passion to empower you.

Contents

She Loves to Fly xiii
Fireside Chat #1 xv
Mindfulness v2: A Taster xx

Part I. Into the Yesteryears 1
1   Setting the Stage 3
2   In the Mountains 11
3   Uncle Ad 13
4   Yoga 16
5   Siddhartha Gautama 21
6   Mindfulness 500 BC 25
7   Modern Mindfulness 27
8   A Lonely Night in Denver 30
9   Struggling *Sapiens* 33
10 Guilty and Back 42
11 A Dialogue with His Holiness the Dalai Lama 45
12 The Seven Tenets 50

Part II. The First Tenet: Insight 53
13 Fireside Chat #2 55
14 I Don't Know 57
15 Why We Suffer 61
16 The Neural Traps 63
17 Neural Trap #1: Continually Distracted
    (Mind Wandering) 65
18 Neural Trap #2: Drawn by Negativity
    (Negativity Bias) 71

19	Neural Trap #3: Emotionally Sensitive (Emotional Vulnerability)	76
20	Neural Trap #4: Stuck in Our Imaginations (Imaginary Feels Real)	80
21	Neural Trap #5: Always Comparing (Compares and Competes)	84
22	Neural Trap #6: Can't Suppress the Thoughts (The Mental Itch)	90
23	Neural Trap #7: Designed to Be Dissatisfied (Programmed Dissatisfaction)	93
24	Neural Trap #8: Addicted to Short-Term Gratification (Deficits in Self-Regulation)	97
25	Neural Trap #9: Caught in the Habit Loop (The Habit Trap)	101
26	Neural Trap #10: Conflicted (To Be or Not to Be)	106
27	Neural Trap #11: Vulnerable to Dishonesty (Liar, Liar)	109
28	Neural Trap #12: Not Designed to Forgive (The Avenger)	116
29	Neural Trap #13: Tired Beyond Imagination (Fatigued)	120
30	Uncertainty	126
31	Complexity	129

Part III. The Second Tenet: Presence ... 133

32	Fireside Chat #3	135
33	Inspiring Adrian	140
34	Presence: Two Modes	142
35	Time	144
36	The Evolving Brain	148
37	Instinctive Presence: People	151
38	Intentional Presence: People	153
39	Instinctive Presence: Things and Events	161
40	Intentional Presence: Things and Events	164

Part IV. The Third Tenet: Attention ... 169

41	Fireside Chat #4	171
42	The Two Inputs	175
43	Meditation and the Brain	178
44	Curiosity	181

45	Building Curiosity	186
46	Meaning	191
47	In Search of Meaning	198
48	How to Handle a Bad Day	205
49	Engagement	209
50	Flow	214
51	Flexible Presence	219

Part V. The Fourth Tenet: Perspective — 221

52	Fireside Chat #5	223
53	Three Depths of Doing	226
54	Neural Zoom	228
55	Stuck in Between	230
56	When in Doubt, Zoom Out	233
57	ZIZO: The Flexible Zoom	242

Part VI. The Fifth Tenet: Attitude — 245

58	Fireside Chat #6	247
59	A Practical Alternative	249
60	Patience	253
61	Cultivating Patience	258
62	Compassion	261
63	What Limits Our Compassion?	265
64	Four Steps to Compassion	272
65	Compassion Fatigue	280
66	Self-Compassion	284
67	Humility	290
68	How to Be Humble	294
69	Forgiveness	299

Part VII. The Sixth Tenet: Practice — 311

70	Fireside Chat #7	313
71	Rethinking Meditation	316
72	What Is Meditation?	319
73	The Informal Practice	325
74	Cultivating Healing Presence	327

Part VIII. The Seventh Tenet: Anchor **331**
75 Fireside Chat #8 333
76 Hope 338
77 Inspiration 343
78 Courage 347

Part IX. Integration **355**
79 Fireside Chat #9 357
80 A Nod to Resilience 359
81 My Personal Practice 372

    Appendix 1: Curious or Serious? 379
    In Gratitude 385
    Notes 387
    About Dr. Sood 447

She Loves to Fly

Her heart beats a thousand times a minute; her brain remembers where to find every flower she has ever visited and when it will be ready with the nectar again. Lighter than a nickel and smaller than your little finger, she can flap her wings fifty times a second, as she lurches forward, pauses, goes down, climbs up, moves backward, and then hovers—all within one blink of your eye.

She has trimmed her body, bulked up her pectorals, shortchanged her feet, and turbocharged her metabolism—all so she could be fast and free. She loves to fly. If you trap her now, confine her to comfort and captivity, she will perish.

Let's not cage the hummingbird. Let's free her to fly.

My inner hummingbird also likes to fly. Nature has delicately carved my mind so I can rethink the past and query the future as I attend to the present. I want to soar high—higher than my fear and regrets, toward hope and light—with my wings of inspiration and courage. I want to touch, taste, hear, and feel, and I want to think about what I touched, tasted, heard, and felt. I want to imagine, dream, and create so that my children can imagine, dream, and create instead of spending their days fighting evil ogres, outer or inner.

Inspire me to embrace my vulnerabilities, transcend my negativities, and dodge the spears the world flings at me every single day. As I do that, please do not ask me to empty my thoughts, trap me into the present moment, or stone me into nonjudgmental acceptance. My ancestors made countless sacrifices, outsmarted beasts and big cats, and thus evolved a hardware (a brain) that likes to fancy, fantasize, and flow. I deciphered the world so I could know myself and, through knowing myself, know you, deeper than my eyes can show. If you deprive me of these joys, I will become morose, dull, and apathetic. I might perish.

Let's not cage my mind. Let's free my mind to fly.

Fireside Chat #1

We are about to start the first of nine fireside chats I will have with Mike to discuss *Mindfulness Redesigned* in a more conversational, informal setting. We are sitting before an audience of about twenty people.

A brief introduction to Mike: *He is single, in his twenties, and a third-year engineering student from New York. He calls himself a lifelong learner who loves reading children's books that have a touch of wisdom. He is cynical about anything groundbreaking or too good. He is an avid runner, likes to eat healthy, and has dabbled in meditation. He is a straight shooter. He wants to be an entrepreneur.*

I have mostly been interviewed by polished journalists seeking well-planned stories. I know where they want me to go. I don't know where Mike will take me. I haven't met him before. I am a bit nervous. This will be a good test of my mindfulness skills.

Mike walks in. He is a little taller than I am, with sharp eyes, thin hair, and a symmetrical face. Mike looks like a computer programmer whom you can trust at first glance. I realize I am making a quick judgment here, but this is a positive one.

"How shall I pronounce your name? I want to say it right." Mike asks as he shakes my hand. He has a warm confident handshake.

I smile. "Sood like food, Amit like dammit. Just remove the *D*!"

Mike chuckles. "Amit, why redesign mindfulness?" He isn't one to beat around the bush.

I follow his lead, saying, "I understand you tried your hand at meditation?"

"How do you know?"

"It was on your bio. Do you still meditate?"

"Off and on."

"Which form?"

"I combine mindfulness with my own mantra."

"Would you call meditation super easy or difficult?"

"You are being silly, aren't you?"

"No, I am serious."

"Of course, difficult. Some days are better than others." Mike confesses.

"That's the point. I don't know five people who can claim they're excellent at meditation."

"Why is that?" Mike's forehead furrows.

"Meditation feels difficult because meditation *is* difficult. We haven't innovated enough to make it easier."

"What do you mean?"

"Do we farm the way we did twenty-five hundred years ago?" I ask.

"Nope. We have automated our farming; present day farmers are much more productive."

"Precisely. Then why do we meditate like it is 2000 BC? The old models were created when the average life span was in the mid-twenties. We didn't know the earth was round. We considered the brain to be irrelevant. Thankfully, we worked hard, discovered and invented, and created new paradigms. Shouldn't we apply the same ingenuity to meditation and move forward rather than stay stagnant?" I feel my ears getting warm with energy.

"Hmm. Interesting. What do you propose?"

"Recognize that in this millennium we have new and unique stressors compared to the ancient times. Discover and invent ideas that align with our current challenges. Learn from the older ideas, interpret them from the modern perspective, and leverage twenty-first-century scientific wisdom to help our condition. I propose we think deeper and rediscover meditation. I suggest we offer simpler, clearer, and easier practices that make us stronger. A totally fresh approach is in order."

"What is that fresh approach?" Mike is engaged. I think I am gaining his trust. Too soon to tell, though.

"Sure. I suggest seven tweaks, which I call the seven tenets. Although these tenets apply to most other forms of meditation, my focus here is on mindfulness."

"I am all ears."

"As a first step, bolster philosophy with science."

Mike raises his chin. Perhaps he wants to ask a question. I choose to continue.

"Most traditional practices are grounded in thousand-year-old philosophies. I think science, particularly twenty-first-century neuroscience is essential to understand our struggles now. **Everybody should know how the human brain works, particularly about the glitches in our brain's operations.**"

"Glitches?"

"**Our brain struggles with weak attention, gets tired easily, inflates the bad, discounts the good, is addicted to short-term gratification, and wasn't designed to be in the moment.**"

"That's my brain!" Mike smiles with his lips and his eyes.

"That's my brain too! Have you tried to be in the moment?" I ask.

"Sure."

"Keep going."

Mike says, "I succeeded a few times, but pretty soon mind wandering took over. Why is that?"

"Because you are human. The prefrontal cortex in your brain that is phenomenal at imagining can think of an infinite future. You'll have to silence your prefrontal cortex if you want to be in the moment for any length of time. And that will take tens of thousands of hours of training."

"Is it a good idea, to silence the prefrontal cortex?"

"For a few seconds, maybe. For hours and days, likely not. Without curiosity and imagination, we all would still be hunting and gathering in a forest in Africa. And that is also the reason we can't be in the moment. If my wife asks me our plans for Friday evening, I can't tell her, 'Honey, I am in the moment right now. Can we talk about this later?'"

"That's funny. What will happen if I try harder to be in the moment? Will my head explode?"

"Your head won't explode, I don't think. You'll only transiently succeed, that's all. You might also waste a lot of time. Undistracted present-moment awareness can be occasionally visited but is very difficult to sustain. Asking your brain to stop imagining is like asking your heart to stop beating."

"What alternative do you propose?"

"**I believe instead of trying to be in the present moment, it's more important and easier to be intentional about what fills the moment.** Cultivate curiosity for the ordinary, find meaning in the familiar, look for novelty, feel grateful for the simple, expand your zone of compassion, and experience moments of flow. **Live your meditation instead of thinking about meditation as a practice.** Seek freedom for your mind and not more rules to constrict it."

"I see what you mean." Mike looks convinced. I don't know yet if he truly believes me or is just being polite.

I continue, this time with a question. "Which part of your body hosts meditation?"

"I presume the brain."

"That's right. Here is an important insight. Research shows you engage the same brain network when you notice the world with your eyes open as you do when you think about the world with your eyes closed."

"How is that important?"

"Meditation with eyes open or eyes closed engages the same brain areas."

"Are the two practices the same, then?"

"For your brain, yes. And since projecting attention outward is much easier than going inward, I suggest starting with externally focused meditation. **Get out of your head and into the world.**"

"Why is it easier to project outside than inside?"

"We have hundreds of open files in our head. There is so much to think about. When you project inward, you get lost in these thoughts. In our minds, the past, the present, and the future blend with each other. It's like the rapids in a river. You can't write on the rapids or expect that your boat will stay steady. That is the reason most of us struggle with going inwards. Not so with the world. Unlike the mind that has no speed limit, the world, particularly nature, still marches at sixty seconds a minute. I will explain more when we discuss the neuroscience."

"OK. Here is my concern. How practical will it be to project outward and stare at my keyboard for forty-five minutes?"

"The idea isn't to stare at something for forty-five minutes. Instead, notice a little more novelty and find a little more meaning than you would do otherwise."

"Can you give an example?"

"Sure. When was the last time you dined outside?"

"Like, yesterday."

"How did you look at the waiter?"

"Didn't pay much attention."

"Nothing wrong with that. But you could have considered that your waiter is also a father and a brother, and he's supporting a family of four. Most waiters have lots of wisdom to share. He was the most important person in your life at that time. Your entire dinner experience depended on his physical and mental health."

"Won't I get exhausted if I pay attention to everyone like this?"

"You don't have to do it all day long. **Just spend a few moments in which you experience life at a deeper level.** Each of those moments will fill you with energy. With practice, you'll effortlessly engage in the world with complete presence."

"Is that mindfulness?"

"It is. You have a choice in how you access mindfulness. You can pick the existing approaches, or if you wish to dabble in something new, try the redesigned program that is simpler, easier, quicker, and deeper. The ideas are also more aligned with how our twenty-first-century minds operate. I like to call this approach, mindfulness *v2*."

"Cool! That's a modern name, and easy to remember. How else is mindfulness *v2* different?"

"I don't suggest a non-judgmental stance. That isn't possible either."

"What do you suggest instead?"

"**Instead of removing judgments, create positive judgments. Try compassion, gratitude, humility, patience, and forgiveness.**"

"What else?"

"I don't believe in emptying the mind. I believe in filling the mind with hope, inspiration, and courage. **Better than noise is silence; better than silence is melody. Melody for the mind is hope, inspiration, and courage.**"

"Hmm. I need to do some thinking. How long does it take to learn this program?"

"A couple of hours."

"That's it?" Mike doesn't believe me this time.

"I believe the practices should be so simple and intuitive that they can be learned in a jiffy. They should also be enjoyable."

"I struggle with focusing on the breath; it becomes boring."

I can't believe Mike seems firmly in my camp already. I offer a generalization. "**Unless a practice is enjoyable in the short term, it won't work for the long term.** My goal is to put greater joy into the practices."

Mike doesn't disagree but has a comeback. "If it's that simple, why do you need 81 chapters and two-hundred-thousand words to explain it?" Mike shows me the hummingbird cover.

Mike's comment throws me off balance. I try to quickly recover.

"I didn't want to shortchange science. I have put a lot of science, stories, and skills in one volume. The book has over twelve hundred references. I am taking you on a journey across two continents. We will meet my ancestor, Uncle Ad, walk with Buddha, spend an evening in Denver, chat with His Holiness the Dalai Lama, and peek into the brain of neuroscientists. That's a bit of a journey."

"Sounds like it. We are almost out of time. Any last-minute thoughts?"

"My worry is that you might see me as a mindfulness rebel, which I am not. This isn't a criticism of mindfulness, its teachers, or its students. I admire them deeply. This is a striving to make mindfulness more accessible, using a different, more modern path. My goal is to deepen and simplify our understanding of mindfulness and while preserving the core essence, make it more relevant to our times."

"Got it. One last question. Do you practice what you preach?"

"I'm definitely a work in progress. But this I can promise: I strive every single day to live by the principles I have presented in this book."

"Good luck, Amit."

"Thanks, Mike. You pronounced 'Amit' just right!"

"Dammit!"

Mindfulness v2: A Taster

It's Tuesday morning, 5:38 a.m. to be precise. Each of my eyelids weighs twenty pounds. But I am already eight minutes behind. I sigh as I bid my comforter goodbye.

First stop: I check on my kids to make sure their noses aren't covered by pillows and they haven't fallen out of bed. A flurry of activities follows: checking e-mails, getting ready, helping kids get ready, preparing breakfast, dropping kids off at school while dodging tardy tickets, and more.

A different universe waits at work: students, manuscripts, patients, colleagues, research projects, e-mails, write-ups, meetings, and interviews—all mired in expectations, deadlines, and occasional disappointments. The more predictable evenings are punctuated by spikes of turbulence fashioned by the specific tantrum, homework, or bill that needs the most immediate attention.

Friends, I have given up on the ideal of living in the now. **I believe any intelligent, imaginative species that has preferences and has to raise kids is bound to struggle with living in the present moment.** It would be a different thing if you were a fish who could lay eggs and move on.

It is extremely difficult, if not impossible to constantly live in the present moment.

Perhaps it was never about the present moment. I heal myself with the thought. *Aren't most animal brains in the present moment? To the best we know, none have yet found "freedom" or have self-actualized.*

As I think more, several questions bubble up.

- What is more important and practical—to be in the present moment or to be intentional about what fills the moment?
- Should I focus more on the short-term or the long-term?
- What is easier and more pragmatic—to be nonjudgmental or compassionate?
- Shall I prioritize meditating forty-five minutes a day or embody a kind presence all day long?
- Should I try to empty my mind or to fill it with hope, inspiration, and courage?

A larger question is: Shall I embrace the mind-body techniques that were developed thousands of years ago or modify them so they will fit well with how my twenty-first-century brain operates?

I'd love for you to read this entire book. But if you don't have the time or patience, here are some answers I have arrived at after a few decades of reading, thinking, experimenting, teaching, and living:

- Living in the present moment can provide profound peace but is difficult to attain and sustain because of the way our brains are designed. For those unable to succeed, the effort can be wearisome and frustrating. A more accessible practice is to focus on what fills the moment.
- Short-term and long-term perspectives are complementary; *flexibly* shifting between the short term and the long term provides a perfect blend for peace and joy.
- A non-judgmental stance can be comforting, but it is difficult if not impossible. It is also passive and doesn't leave a clear direction for the mind. If you don't make judgments, what do you do? Being kind and compassionate is an easier, more freeing, and more immediately accessible solution.
- A long, sitting meditation is a wonderfully relaxing practice. But for those who struggle with meditation, an equally powerful and perhaps more liberating practice is to carry an intentional, grateful, and compassionate presence all day long.
- Emptying the mind sounds great but is impractical. The mind can't be emptied, just as the heart can't be stopped. A more accessible practice is to free the mind by filling it with hope, inspiration, and courage.

Easier (and perhaps more useful) than living in the present moment is to be intentional about what fills the moment.

This book is divided into two parts. Part 1 describes the evolution of mindfulness from Buddha's time to today. After setting the stage with my two core realizations and a short visit to a monastery, I will introduce you to one of my ancestors, Uncle Ad. Buddha's and Uncle Ad's stories and struggles will help you grasp the state of the world that gave rise to the noble eightfold path and mindfulness as one of its key ingredients. Part 1 will also include a peek into mindfulness research, the story of my meeting with His Holiness the Dalai Lama, and will lay the foundation for the seven tenets that describe the redesigned mindfulness (mindfulness *v2*).

Part 2 will share the core tenets of mindfulness *v2*. Starting with neuroscience, I will discuss the neural traps that are programmed in our brains and prevent us from living fulfilled lives. We will then dive deeper and find a twenty-first-century alternative to present-moment awareness, a sitting meditation, a non-judgmental stance, and the emptying of the mind. I will end the book introducing you to the very important construct of resilience and connect mindfulness *v2* with living a resilient life. My humble hope is that you'll find the ideas fresh, novel, freeing, and inspiring. Through all this, I will steer clear of clichés and share concepts and skills that aren't only for a select few who have lots of free time to ponder and pontificate.

The book offers a pragmatic approach toward mindfulness for those who find meditation daunting (because of difficulty in slowing their minds) or impractical (because of resource or time constraints), and it offers a template for deepening personal practice for the select few who are truly able to meditate. It also offers a credible approach for those dealing with difficult life circumstances (such as health or relationship crises) in which being told to "just breathe" simply isn't enough.

Every generation has its stress, but the specific stressors change every few generations. The solutions then also need to adapt to the change.

Our stress solutions must adapt to the changing needs of the generations.

I believe that the mind-body techniques of yesteryear can teach us a lot. I also believe that the older concepts and practices need to be tweaked so they fit better with how our brains now operate. **If we don't farm the way we did thousands of years ago, should we not revisit how we meditate?**

—⁂—

If we do not modify mindfulness practices to adapt to the societal changes (with the resulting changes in our brains' networking) that have happened since mindfulness was first conceived, we risk losing relevance for vast segments of our society. Spending fifteen minutes focusing on the breath can provide some help, but it won't be enough if the next twelve hours are filled with pure adrenaline. Hence the need to reformulate older ideas into a new theme—Mindfulness *v2*.

Part I
Into the Yesteryears

1

Setting the Stage

It is easy to talk about mindfulness or resilience in a lunch-and-learn session with twenty graduate students whose minds are preoccupied with a previous disappointment or the next grade. But how do I offer a meaningful solution to a forty-year-old grocery clerk with metastatic colon cancer who is trying to figure out which chemo will give her a few extra months? What words do I use to support, validate, and comfort a sixty-year-old who, after twenty-eight years of marriage, has just discovered that her husband is gay? Can I in any way help the citizens of a country that stands in the crosshairs of ego fights between two immature leaders, with residents who aren't sure whether the family hug they share tonight will be their last one? How do I converse with the parents of a child in the ICU who don't know whether the morning sun will bring falling blood pressure, a positive blood culture, or hope for a cure? I think about these and many more struggles, as I worry about the world and its inhabitants (you, me, and our children) and wonder what we can do to make it a better place.

Our current state isn't acceptable. We must do better. We can do better.

We have to change the world until, even in my pain, I think about yours. We have to change ourselves so we never give up on hope, have the courage to accept our failings, and live each day inspired to make the world a better home for our children. We have to create a world in which fear isn't necessary, greed isn't cool, envy is extinct, and hatred isn't a recognized word. In this effort, we don't have infinite time. I am in a hurry to help us transform, before the collective powers of ignorance and selfishness destroy our innocence and plunder our precious planet.

That is the mandate for mindfulness—a hefty mandate. We have a lot of work to do, because we aren't there yet. Let's start this work with talking about the little legged creatures for whom our hearts beat: our kids.

LITTLE WORKSHOP

On a late-summer Friday evening, I spoke at a stress-management workshop for middle and high schoolers. Clouded by my bias, I anticipated that ten or twelve kids might come, and stay for half the session while updating their social-media posts. Over one hundred twenty showed up, in a standing-room-only presentation. After the talk and the Q&A session, we had to literally turn off the lights to let them know it was time to go. Every single kid raised his or her hand when asked, "Do you have a lot of stress?" Many raised both their hands. It broke my heart to see so many kids struggling, but it also inspired me to do more.

Our children are hurting. They are lonely, anxious, stressed, confused, and overwhelmed. They have few role models. Their attention is weak. Their principles are shaky. They lack meaning. They don't know whom to trust. Ditto for the grown-ups. In almost all of the thousands of workshops I have taught, I have been struck by the universality of silent suffering.

Until a few years ago, I couldn't make sense of the stress and struggles I saw. I thought that well-paved roads, manicured lawns, single-digit unemployment, and the highest GDP in the world should add up to lasting happiness. Why should affluence, cutting-edge technology, and military might keep the company of depression, chronic pain, fatigue, suicide, violence, and toxic stress? I had no idea that my curious search would propel me on a lifelong expedition to understand and help the human condition. I also had no idea this search would transform my own life. My journey started over two decades ago, the day I landed at JFK Airport in New York City.

THE UNHAPPY MAGIC KINGDOM

I arrived in New York in June 1995, at the age of twenty-seven, carrying in my heart the love of my family and friends, but also memories of my early-life struggles. From worrying as a small child that I had been picked up from the street and didn't belong to my family to developing a neurologic illness in adolescence to witnessing, in person, one of the all-time worst industrial disasters (the Bhopal gas tragedy) at age seventeen, I remember desperately wanting to grow up and for once feel that I was in control.

To prepare for coming to the United States, I saw a few movies and read some articles about life in the nation. From what I saw and read, I expected to find this world full of fun and endless celebration—a wealthy, carefree, utopian society. I imagined that as kids people here played in Disneyland, as adults they played slots in Las Vegas, and they all retire playing bingo in Florida.

Boy was I wrong! The reality, as you can imagine, didn't match my expectations, particularly since I started my life here in the inner-city Bronx of the 1990s. The drugs, HIV, violence, and poverty were painful to watch. Even wealthier places didn't seem happy. Missing were smiles for strangers, random acts of kindness, and people looking relaxed and happy just because they were together. Families seldom talked to each other at thirty-six thousand feet, except for the essentials, such as asking each other to pass a drink. Instead, most people, including kids, watched angry, violent videos.

I was struck by the disconnect between material and emotional well-being. I could have believed that "USA" stood for "Unhappy States of America."

I hope one day I can do something about it, I thought.

But at that time, I was an insecure immigrant on an exchange visa with a negative bank balance and a pleasant but not always understandable Indian accent. Every protocol here was so different. I had to get used to driving in the right lane, lack of vegetarian options, buying milk by the gallon (and not liter), resisting jaywalking, speaking in metaphors, rolling my tongue, calling biscuits "cookies," and remembering that the smallest cup of coffee is called "tall."

Eventually, I found friendships, job security, good veggie sandwiches, a decent credit card, and I could correctly pronounce the word *entrepreneur*. Taking the oath of citizenship in 2008 was a surreal moment. I was surrounded by thousands of kindred spirits from sixty-seven different countries, all with funny accents like mine. "This is the *United* States of America that we are proud of," the articulate judge remarked to a standing ovation. *I now belong. This is my land. These are my people*, I thought, with tears in my eyes.

I had already moved to the Mayo Clinic by then, realizing a long-cherished childhood dream. A few years prior, I had begun the pursuit of my original endeavor: to find an answer for human angst. I read, traveled, noticed, perceived, and spent a lot of time thinking. I became a deeper observer of human nature. Along the way, I ran into tremendous complexity in many disciplines: psychology, philosophy, neuroscience, spirituality, behavioral economics, anthropology, mindfulness, and more. I remember once getting frustrated and yelling into my head, "Simplify, simplify!" Gradually, a theme emerged. I was able to connect a large portion of our struggles with two main challenges—*my two core realizations*.

First, I realized the dizzying speed with which the world, particularly the United States, was whizzing by. I believe this phenomenon is a recent one in our species' evolution. I can best put this in perspective by first talking about an eternal tug-of-war that is waged by every life-form on our planet.

AN ETERNAL TUG-OF-WAR

Every single day of every single life-form is a tug-of-war between two forces: the forces of change and the forces of adaptation. When adaptation keeps pace with change, individuals and species thrive. No matter how big or strong, animals that lag in adaptation—the mammoths, the saber-toothed cats, the Neanderthals—fade into oblivion. As *Homo sapiens*, we dominate the earth's ecosystem today because we are masters of adaptation.

> ***Humans and not Neanderthals populate this planet because our speed of adaptation has kept pace with the speed of change.***

Until very recently, nature was the primary driver of change. Nature-driven change, although not always predictable, was slow, and it integrated the past as it created the future. Our brains comfortably jogged in sync with or ahead of the change and were handsomely rewarded. We learned to cage the tigers and build brick houses instead of getting mauled or living in caves.

For most of our existence, the two hypothetical lines tracking the speed of change and our brain's ability to adapt have likely had roughly similar slopes, something like this:

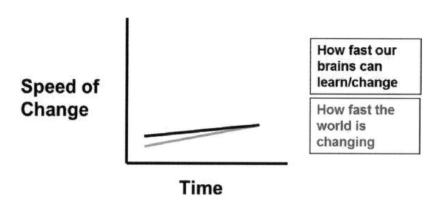

Unfortunately, these two innocent lines show life in the rearview mirror. In the twenty-first century, one of these lines has become a curve with a strong upslope, causing widespread angst and chaos. Let's look at which one.

A LINE BECOMES A CURVE

It took me thirteen years of training to learn how to take care of my patients. Today I still hit the curb when parallel parking. I am terrible at helping our seven-year-old put bobby pins in her hair. I believe it is easier to do endoscopy than to place bobby pins perfectly (at least for dads). The bottom line—my brain is a slow learner.

The pace of change, however, has taken off. An average executive in 1970s handled about a thousand communications in a year. That number is now fifty to three hundred thousand. But our brain hasn't become fifty to three hundred times smarter or faster. It might actually be the opposite. A few months ago, I changed two passwords on the same day. It was a disaster!

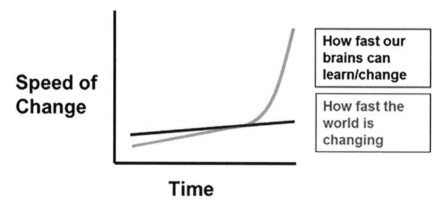

This disconnect is unprecedented. Our adaptation ability has always been ahead of change. Not so now.

Our adaptations are now lagging behind change.

Further, this change is unique, unlike anything our planet has ever seen before.

A NEW KIND OF CHANGE

Change in twenty-first century downtowns is very different from change in rain forests or arctic tundra. Instead of integrating, change now decimates the past as it creates the future. This is because the primary driver of change now is no longer nature. It is the innovative spirit of humans, almost eight billion of us. As a result, what used to be a slow tide of change has morphed into a tsunami of disruption.

A convergence of innovations—capitalism, globalization, technology, medicine, democracy, credit, communication, travel—has made our lives rich, complex, and interesting. Greater opportunity, however, has created greater uncertainty. The ever-increasing gap between line A and curve B has overloaded the most important organ of the body: the brain.

OUR OVERLOADED BRAINS

If only the bricklayers get backaches, then you can ascribe backaches to hard manual work. But if backaches happen to attorneys, chaplains, investment bankers, real-estate agents, and county clerks, then perhaps they aren't an individual's problem. They are a human problem. Back pain affects 80 percent of us.[1] This is because when we became erect, an unnatural stance for an earth dweller, we overloaded our lumbar spine. Blaming a single person for his or her back pain speaks of ignorance and completely misses the point.

The same is true for excessive stress. Research shows 80 percent of us now feel stressed.[2] Almost the same percent of employers say stress is their number one healthcare concern.[3] This is because when we accelerated the pace of our world, we overloaded another body part: the brain. Most of our day, our brain holds multiple simultaneous ideas or tasks, often at its maximum capacity. Blaming a single person for his or her excessive stress also speaks of ignorance and completely misses the point.

A large body of research across several disciplines shows that much of our daily stress is because of brain overload that comes from excessive demands placed on us, lack of control, and an inability to find meaning. Further, this overload happens to a brain that is remarkably ill-equipped to handle that load—my second realization.

THE VULNERABLE BRAIN

My second realization brought me face to face with a humbling reality: I am phenomenally ignorant and imperfect. And I have lived my entire life unaware of my ignorance and imperfections. As I studied human suffering, I learned about human imperfections, about my own imperfections and resilience deficits.

If you don't respond to my text in a few minutes, don't acknowledge my phone message in a few hours, and don't reply to my e-mail within a day, I will take it personally. Ice cream, pizza, doughnuts, mango lassi, crème brûlée, dark chocolate—I have a long list of food cravings. I am greedier than I'd like to be. I have irrational fears I can't shed, have caught myself exaggerating, and wish I was more patient. I can't listen to two kids at the same time, I regularly forget items on the grocery list, and would rather bite my nails than get bored. All these traits, that are a product of my imperfect brain, make me weaker.

Before I trash myself with an ignominious rant, here is the uplifting reality: most of our neural vulnerabilities aren't present because we want or choose to be that way. Instead, they originated in our ancestors' evolutionary struggle for survival. Our ancestors had to make many compromises to defeat the Neanderthals, outsmart the big cats, and survive the elements so they could live long enough to pass on and protect their genes. A whole host of our neural vulnerabilities—negativity bias, hedonic adaptation, tendency to compare, addiction to short-term gratification, and more—are a product of these compromises. (I will talk about all these in part II: The First Tenet.) We can't blame anyone for our brain's vulnerabilities. But that doesn't mean we can't find solutions for them.

To sum up, the core realization that helped me understand our collective angst is this: **In the twenty-first century, our brains are trapped under an excessive load that they are ill-equipped to carry.** This is akin to carrying a hundred pounds of weight uphill, with a broken back.

Our brains are overloaded and ill-equipped to carry that load.

With the problem identified, the obvious next question was, how do we solve it?

THE TWO OPTIONS

The solution seemed twofold: decrease the load and increase the brain's capacity to lift the load.

The two overload solutions: Decrease the load & increase the capacity to lift the load.

Better time management, simplifying life, intelligently delegating, improving work efficiency, prioritizing, increasing productivity—all of these can help us. Take it easy, sleep more, take more vacations, carry no guilt if you have to say no—you can find these and many more ideas inside wellness magazines.

The problem is that even though we have known these solutions for a long time, I don't know many people who are successful at decreasing their load. Almost no invention that has promised to save boatloads of time has delivered on its promise. Very likely, at this time next year, you'll have more user IDs and passwords, more bills, and more regrets and hurts than you have today. I have never heard a CEO say, "Let's do less with more." The targets keep going up. Pressed by their boards, leaders in every industry are pushing for bigger numbers while, in at least some cases, ignoring the pain and burnout they are causing. If that were not so, then four-fifths of workers wouldn't have excessive stress, one-sixth wouldn't be taking psychiatric drugs, and one-third of us wouldn't be taking prescription opioids—a modern pharmaceutical crisis.[4]

The same challenge affects our children. Our children are more stressed, and they struggle with more attention issues than any other generation. We lose many precious lives to drugs and alcohol, gangs, and violent crimes. One is too many. It breaks my heart to see that most large hospitals now have pediatric sleep-apnea clinics in which obese ten-year-olds are being prescribed CPAP masks so they can sleep better. Kids who are lucky enough to dodge these demons get trapped in bullying, school politics, social-networking sites, and mountain of homework.

If we can't succeed with decreasing the load, then where do we find hope? I believe it is in the second solution: increasing the capacity to lift the load, by giving our brain a long overdue upgrade.

Increasing our capacity is the low-hanging fruit.

Capacity enhancement is an untapped and immediately accessible solution. This is where it starts to get exciting.

INCREASING THE CAPACITY

For thousands of years, passionate healers and scientists in a variety of disciplines have been developing techniques to help our brains better lift their loads. Spirituality, psychotherapy, social support, culture, philosophy, literature—these and several other constructs inspire hope and infuse strength and courage. Authentic practices in each of these disciplines have helped and continue to help billions of people. One immensely popular practice that touches all these disciplines, which was conceptualized thousands of years ago, is mindfulness.

I learned of and embraced mindfulness several decades ago, and I have benefited from the practice both personally and professionally. The practice of mindfulness offers an effective solution to improve attention, enhance well-being and decrease emotional pain. But after years of learning, practicing, researching, and teaching, I have realized that the current models of teaching mindfulness are helping only a fraction of the people. This isn't because mindfulness and its practitioners are wrong. It is because the core concepts and the key ideas that support the current models of training were devised for brains that lived in 500 BC. Further, despite all the good intentions, we may have made some tweaks to the original practices, that decreased their value and instead of simplifying, made the practices even more trying.

I particularly struggled with three ideas that are the basis of the practices: tethering my presence to the construct of time (the present moment), cultivating a mindset of nonjudgmental acceptance, and emptying the mind into silence.

I am a human hummingbird. My mind likes to visit cherished memories and inviting imaginations, must make quick judgments to be safe and effective, and can't be silenced or emptied. The harder I tried to silence my mind and tether it to the present moment, the more stifled I felt. This bird wanted freedom, not shackles.

Perhaps I am just a terrible meditator or was taking it too literally, I thought. But when I looked around, the majority struggled. In my consults and workshops, I found that more than 95 percent of the people struggle with meditation and aren't able to maintain a successful meditation practice. *Perhaps I am just working with a select sample*, I thought. But when it was safe to vent, even the mindfulness teachers shared their challenges in practicing the skills. For many, the practices helped in the short term, but only the most committed could sustain them for the long term.

Dissatisfied, I started looking for simpler, more practical, effective, deeper, modern, engaging, and uplifting solutions that would appeal to twenty-first-century brains. Finding none that satisfied me, I immersed myself in science, listened to stories, and experimented with countless practices. During the journey, I made several detours and gained many insights. These detours and insights gave birth to the redesigned mindfulness (*v2*).

MINDFULNESS V2

Mindfulness *v2* is a compilation of science, stories, skills, and inspirations that will give you a glimpse into the human condition, the traps that prevent us from realizing our potential, and the solutions. Mindfulness *v2* leverages many of the constructs of the original mindfulness traditions, but reinterprets them from a twenty-first-century perspective, in the form of seven tenets. It is an effort to expand the reach of mindfulness to the brains that struggle with impatience, contend with constant distractions, and feel frustrated when they can't experience sustained stillness on the mat.

Humanity is hurting and overloaded, and we don't have an effective solution. Given the global headlines that worsen each week, we urgently need solutions that are effective and can help us relatively quickly.

The ideas I am about to share with you have helped close to half a million people with whom I have connected so far, and they have been proven effective in over twenty research studies. I consider it a personal responsibility and privilege to bring these concepts to many more. I strongly believe that **mindfulness (and more broadly, meditation) programs need innovation and a fresh look so that they have a powerful effect on resilience and can help the majority relatively quickly**, and not just the rare few who have the patience and resources to go on silent retreats or can spare forty-five minutes every day to meditate.

This is a humble attempt to narrow the gap between the line (of adaptation) and the curve (of change), a gap that threatens our peace and happiness, even our very existence.

Our survival depends on narrowing the gap between the line of adaptation and the curve of change.

Our collective struggles are pushing us into disruption. From here, we can spiral either up or down. Where we go depends on us, all of us, for we are in this together. I invite you to give mindfulness *v2* a chance, so you stop the downward spiral of sadness, fear, hurts, and regrets, and instead, spiral up with hope, inspiration, courage, and resilience.

The first stop in our journey is at a monastery—taking a step away from the world, to fully immerse in it.

2

In the Mountains

Several years ago, I spent a week in a monastery. We were amid rolling hills, fruit trees, panoramic views, and fresh air. We woke up to the chirping of birds, walked barefoot on dew, ate *sattvik* food, and were surrounded by Duchenne smiles. We sat on the floor all day long, grateful that, after a few hours of sitting cross-legged, our legs stopped hurting because the nerves stopped conducting.

This world was full of humility, discipline, environmental awareness, silence, and frugality. People had sensitivities—to cell-phone towers, energy fields, low-*prana* foods, and frivolous talk. Away from the headline news, Wall Street gyrations, deadlines, and utility-disconnect notices, we spent most of the day learning ancient philosophies, meditating, and practicing yoga.

After a few days at the monastery, my mind stopped wandering, sleep became deeper, food tasted more flavorful, and thoughts became clearer. I was able to learn and flawlessly recite hymns and poems, as I did four decades ago. A fog was lifted.

As I look back, I realize what had changed was the depth and sustainability of my focus. The quiet, peace-filled world fostered the most basic human ability: to pay undivided attention.

Attention is the gateway into the brain. Strong attention creates a more expanded workspace in our brain to better process our thoughts and sensory input.

Strong attention helps you better observe, think, and thus speak and act.

Of the billions of bytes of data that strike your sensory system, you can consciously experience only a few hundred. Your attention picks the most salient (of immediate survival value) information and takes it to the brain's foyer, where the information is mixed with your context and preferences to enable a conscious experience.

Salience comes in three flavors: *threatening, novel, and pleasant*. For most animals, information that alerts them to threats is the most salient. The same is true for us humans. Unlike all the other species, however, we can choose to separate salience from threat, freeing our attention for creative pursuits and joy. **The most progressive companies and enlightened parents foster creativity by freeing talent from the fear of failure.**

You can see such "attentional freedom" among children playing with the jets in a water park or blowing and catching bubbles in the backyard, with no worries about their retirement savings or future supervisor's attitude.

Creativity flourishes when our attention is freed from fear.

Unfortunately, in several parts of the world, human attention is mired in fear. In these—mostly war-torn nations, poverty-stricken lands, or places of civil unrest—the daily struggle for survival stifles creativity. These places are reminiscent of how we lived for tens of thousands of years. (Seeing the global headlines and everyday geopolitical drama, some days I get very concerned that we might be regressing toward the same chaos that we thought we had left far behind.)

It'll help for us to travel back to ancient times to understand the challenges that were rife in the world then. Knowing that world will help us understand ourselves and give our modern-day tendencies a better context. It'll also provide a deeper perspective into contemplative practices, since most of the modern-day meditations find their roots thousands of years ago. The tour guide on this part of our journey will be one of my gentle ancestors—Uncle Ad.

3

Uncle Ad

NORTHERN INDIA, 3000 BC

Uncle Ad hadn't even turned one when he lost his mother from a fall she sustained while carrying a pile of firewood on her back. His aunt, Mina, who belonged to a wealthy aristocratic family, adopted Ad. Mina couldn't conceive because of tubercular scarring of her internal organs, and she desperately needed a son to continue her heritage. Otherwise, she risked being evicted from her clan.

Adopting a foster child, however, wasn't enough for her husband and in-laws. Ad's clef lip didn't help either. Despite receiving a fortune in dowry, Mina's husband found another bride, and in a few years, he had three children. Unfortunately for dear uncle Ad, two of them were sons. In a few years, the family's entire wealth was bequeathed to Ad's two half brothers, leaving Ad poor and disillusioned.

Misfortunes do not strike alone. By age fifteen, Ad had lost the majority of his childhood friends, mostly to external injuries and infections such as typhoid, malaria, and rabies. Ad desperately needed a caring adult, but the only help available came from a local shaman who was overwhelmed with helping the recently bereaved, of whom there were plenty. Depressed, desperate, and feeling unloved, Ad ran away from home in search of someone who could pull him out of the rubble. No one came looking for him.

After a few weeks of searching, Ad found an ashram, where he landed a small job as a kitchen assistant, hardly satisfying for a wannabe aristocrat but enough for him to avoid heatstroke and mosquitoes and to gain access to shelter, food, and somewhat clean toilets. The ashram also protected Ad from thugs and pedophiles.

Unlike the polite monasteries of the twenty-first century, ashrams in those times were tougher than the modern Navy SEAL training program. Ad's morning started with pulling dozens of buckets of water from the old well that was the ashram's only source of drinking water. Ad then swept the floor, washed the compound, cleaned the dishes, made tea for all the students, and prepared breakfast. Every chore, however simple, had a protocol. These protocols were orally transmitted. The ashram didn't have any books. Ad had heard rumors of a fascinating new invention called papyrus, on which one could write and preserve those writings, but he hadn't seen it firsthand. People stored information in their brains, certainly not on CDs, on DVDs, or in clouds. To maintain high fidelity of transmission, everything had to be learned—memorized.

AMBITIOUS AD

Ad had bigger plans for his life than living at the bottom of the ashram hierarchy. A few months after settling in, instead of taking a nap every afternoon, Ad would sneak into the students' quarters and watch the students rehearse their lessons. Until then, Ad had secretly envied these students since they spent little time doing menial work and were busy learning new and exciting things. But his envy morphed into empathy when he saw their lives up close and personal.

The students lived under great pressure. Their every waking moment was preoccupied with mastering the course work. They had to memorize and repeat, in the evening, every detail of the lesson.

In those days, negative feedback wasn't sugarcoated or delivered in private.[5] In class, students had to lock their eyes with the teacher's for hours on end, not letting their attention waver even once. A few strikes of distraction and the student would be dismissed. There were no catch-up classes, no helicopter parents challenging the curriculum. Failing a class meant a dead end with no remediation and no possibility of succeeding at a career, finding a bride, or raising children. Relegated to a life of inconsequence, the students would bring disgrace to themselves and their families. Suicide was a common sequel. Some students would just wander off into oblivion. Understandably, paying complete, undivided attention wasn't an optional skill; it was critical for survival.

> ***For our ancestors, strong attention was essential for survival, more so than it is for us.***

Even in daily life, strong attention was as essential as breathing. With no GPS to guide travel and with broken dirt roads, one had to mark and remember the milestones. Stray rabid dogs, robbers, swarms of mosquitoes, muddy puddles, and unmarked wells kept travelers' minds from wandering. **I believe attention-training techniques must have first emerged as survival skills before they became part of the spiritual traditions.**

Strong attention alone, however, wouldn't have been enough for Ad. Ad's world, both inside and outside of the ashram, but particularly outside, was extremely hierarchical and nepotistic. He lived in a time of contrasts; sensual indulgence and extreme deprivation were next-door neighbors. One's fate was often decided by one's last name. A skinny boy with an awkward name could never rise to the top. Exorcism, a caste system, and child labor were the norm. Unexplained illnesses, mostly infections, were coupled with a lack of medical insurance and a very fragmented medical system. There was no social security, police, or 911. Dacoits would commonly loot the few possessions people had in their straw houses.

HEALING: THE FIRST STEPS

Misery gets multiplied when it afflicts intelligent beings. I sincerely hope that mice, gazelles, wildebeests, cows, chickens, bunnies, and turkeys do not have insight into their suffering. A deep-thinking gazelle with good memory and imagination might continue to have nightmares for years after a single chase by a lion.

Lacking any scientific construct, people in the insecure world in which Ad lived naturally turned to myths and rituals for comfort. Often, these rituals were prescribed by fear mongers whose main credentials were their abilities to manipulate the spirits and visit the netherworld.

It was in this milieu that countless paths were developed to help heal the human condition. Many of these paths, steeped in mysticism, promoted angry gods as the cause of nature's wrath: volcanoes were ascribed to an angry volcano god, earthquakes to an angry earth god, and monsoons to an angry rain god. (As a kid, I heard and believed several such stories.)

Suffering and struggle, however, don't have just a dark side. **Suffering is a potent force that, given the scaffold of time, tills the mind to grow wisdom and love.**

Many transformations start with suffering.

The suffering and struggles in the old world spawned many philosophers and spiritual luminaries. Their strong attention partnered with their passion to improve the life of the common man. They cried not from personal pain but from seeing innocence in pain. The paths that emerged from their wisdom and love offered hope through kindness and forgiveness.

Depending on the specific local constraints and demands, and the realizations of these awakened souls, the wisdom and love in these paths were wrapped and expressed in philosophies, books, symbols, rituals, beliefs, myths, sacred places, and more. Several of these paths, that have survived the attrition of time, are now integrated as holistic systems of living (often called religions). These systems of living inspire billions of us today.

A few of the paths evolved practices that can be interpreted both within the traditional religious/spiritual context and within a secular framework. These practices broke free of rituals and dogmas (to a large extent), became less rigid, and received a thumbs-up from science and celebrities. For all these reasons, they have now become wildly popular globally. These are the approaches of yoga and mindfulness—both developed as eightfold paths.

4

Yoga

BHOPAL, INDIA, SUMMER OF 1972

A thirty-eight-year-old mother of four, weak and recovering from recent lung tuberculosis, developed severe back pain radiating to the legs. Not knowing whether this was an ordinary mechanical low-back pain, herniated disc, or something more sinister, she sought help from a local physician.

The physician prescribed complete bed rest for two months, the standard recommendation in the pre-MRI era. She was told if she bent forward, she might never be able to walk straight. Despite frailty and unremitting pain, bed rest wasn't an option for her. She was raising four kids; running her entire home, from cooking to cleaning to grocery shopping; and working full time as an elementary-school teacher. Her husband, a caring man, was mostly unavailable because his job was about a hundred miles away, an enormous distance to travel in those days. Thus, instead of rest, she enrolled in the only physical-therapy program available to her at that time: yoga.

Yoga turned out to be just the right medicine for her. Her pain improved faster than anticipated. In less than six weeks, she had more energy than she had before developing the pain. She fell in love with yoga.

In a few years, she became a yoga teacher. Then she became a master and, finally, a grand master. Today, at age eighty-three, she runs a large yoga center and has taught tens of thousands of students and trained hundreds of teachers in her lifetime. She stands straight, walks several miles each day, and is more flexible than people ten or twenty years younger. That's because, when confronted with an illness, she chose a path of wellness, of resilience.

> ***Choose a path of resilience and wellness, to prevent, confront, and vanquish illness.***

She also successfully raised her four children with values, dedication, and love. The youngest of those children happens to be me.

This is the story of my mother, Shashi, whose life was transformed by yoga. I don't wish to speculate what would have happened to my siblings and I had she taken to bed at that time. No wonder she introduced me to yoga and related contemplative practices when I was at the ripe old age of twelve.

YOGA: A BRIEF HISTORY

Early Greek and French philosophers tried to understand the world by breaking it into parts. Plato's theory of forms in the *Phaedo*, which Aristotle later refined, was followed by Descartes's dualism of two separate entities: immaterial mind and material body.[6, 7]

Early Eastern sages tried to understand the world by uniting those entities into one, the classic philosophy being the *Advaita*.[8] While Western reductionism fostered material science, and its pragmatic applications created technological advances, Eastern holism offered a more accessible solution for the mind. Both yoga and mindfulness emerged as an offshoot of holism.

Yoga was developed as a discipline, philosophy, and spiritual practice for controlling the mind's instinctive and maladaptive predispositions. The word *yoga* connotes union—a practice that brings about union of body with the mind and union of body and mind with the spirit. Critics argue that this union already exists so we don't really need a practice to effect such a union. The counterargument is that yoga doesn't really bring about the union; it makes us aware of the timeless union.[9] Each yoga practice (summarized below) is designed to help the seeker move closer to that awareness.

While it is widely accepted that yoga emerged from the Indian subcontinent, no single person is credited with developing the entire yoga system. Yoga was anchored in an ancient Indian philosophy called *Samkhya*, which is particular to a faith and time but is not theistic.[10, 11] Both God and teacher are equally revered in the yoga philosophy, freeing it from faith.

YOGA MEETS SCIENCE

In its westward journey, yoga received a much-needed boost when it received a thumbs up from the primary arbitrator of the modern world—science. Science has strongly supported the value of yoga in hundreds of research studies. Clinical trials and systematic reviews, despite limitations in research design, show promising results for a number of outcomes, including chronic pain, balance, mobility, anxiety, depression, hypertension, diabetes, asthma, fatigue, sleep disturbance, cardiovascular risk factors, inflammatory conditions, control of cancer symptoms, weight loss, executive functions, and others.[12-44] A few studies have also been done in children. In most studies, yoga has been found to be as safe as usual care or exercise.[45]

But even the best evidence-based ideas can languish and remain undiscovered in the attic if they aren't marketed well. To complement the research studies, yoga received strong celebrity endorsements. The result: instead of being looked down upon as an unnecessary side effect of globalization and outsourcing, yoga is seen more as a wellness-promoting activity that also helps the mind.

Yoga has something for all: fitness, disease prevention, disease control, coping, positive mood, sports performance, moral living, self-care, attention control, and spiritual growth. Yoga is now seen as a flexible recipe; one can pick the ingredients to one's liking and modify them to one's taste. This recipe has eight ingredients.

THE EIGHT COMPONENTS OF YOGA

Sage Patanjali (ca. AD 400) is widely credited with consolidating a large body of yoga knowledge into a single volume, *Patanjali Yoga Sutras*, which describes eight components of yoga.[46]

1. *Yama*—Moral and ethical guidelines for living. The five *yamas* are nonviolence, truthfulness, non-stealing, self-control, and non-coveting.
2. *Niyama*—Internal practices that extend the moral guidelines. The five *niyamas* are purity of body and mind, contentment, self-discipline, self-study, and devotion.
3. *Asana*—Physical postures that prepare the body for meditation by enhancing flexibility and strength, and promoting health and wellness.
4. *Pranayama*—Breathing practices that enhance and balance energy and decrease the activity of the sympathetic nervous system.
5. *Pratyahara*—Attention training through focusing attention inward with the ability to develop deeper awareness of senses and free one's thought processes from the senses.
6. *Dharana*—Attaining one pointed focus of the mind (inner or outer focus).
7. *Dhyana* (Meditation)—Sustained flow of awareness toward the object of attention, active engagement, and immersion while maintaining individual identity.
8. *Samadhi*—Complete immersion in the object of contemplation with loss of personal identity.

These eight components have been stitched together in several ways, the most common of which can be captured in three metaphors.

THE THREE METAPHORS

Over the years, three metaphors have been used to describe the eight components of yoga.

- A ladder—Each of the eight components represents a rung on the ladder. Students climb the ladder as they develop deeper states of the mind through understanding and practice.
- A tree—Each component represents a branch of a tree. The progress doesn't have to be as rigid as in climbing the rungs of the ladder. One can be more flexible about scaling the branches.
- A rope—Each component is a strand in a rope. They are fully intertwined, and they strengthen and support each other.

In the 1980s, I learned yoga using the ladder and the rope metaphors, in a series of steps that followed the eight components, while knowing that each component strengthens and supports all the others. After basic grounding in *yamas* and *niyamas*, we learned the physical postures (*asanas*), breathing practices (*pranayamas*), and relaxation.[47] Only after we attained finesse with the *asanas* and *pranayamas* and could effortlessly sit cross-legged were we taught the deeper contemplative practices that involved progressively refined attention. The premise was that we needed to stabilize and strengthen our attention using the physical body and breath as anchors before we could direct our attention toward a single point of focus for a sustained period.

Further, yoga was seen not just as a practice but as a way of life. After food and the very loud neighbors, yoga was the third most discussed topic in our home. A lot has changed since then.

YOGA JUMPS THE OCEANS

A number of factors colluded to dismantle the eight strands as yoga jumped the oceans. These included the pace of life, the relative inexperience of teachers, the need to separate yoga from its philosophy (to remove the jargon), and the view of yoga as a physical therapy instead of as a way of life. Yoga became fragmented as it globalized. Here is what happened to the original eight components.

- *Yamas* and *niyamas* were largely eliminated. Contentment can't thrive when the mantra "greed is good" is celebrated in the movies, news channels and talk shows. Many of the neural traps that I will present in the next section contributed to this trend.
- *Asanas* and *pranayamas* became the defining features of yoga but not in their innate form. Some teachers tried to patent their sequences; others gave the practices their last name (and ego). The result was many varieties of yoga.
- *Pratyahara, dharana,* and *dhyana* melded (and were simplified) into one as a stand-alone meditation practice.
- *Samadhi* all but disappeared, as it was considered too mystical, esoteric, and unreachable.

Although these changes expanded access to the physical postures and breathing practices, they also caused a loss of depth. Practicing meditation without going through the first steps is like driving on the highway without training on the slower roads. The changes led to a high failure rate and attrition.

Yoga lost some of its core essence when we tried to lighten and simplify the practice.

When the holistic system of yoga interacted with scientific reductionism and restless minds, it was dismantled to meet the immediate needs of the world. It went from being embraced as a way of life to being a three-times-a-week practice. As a result, attention and attitude on the yoga mat became disconnected from attention and attitude during the rest of the day.

And a single petal isn't the flower. In a high-pressure start-up in downtown San Francisco, entrepreneurs aren't embracing the full repertoire of yoga when they practice sun salutations or the downward-dog posture. They only taste one of its limbs. I am not sure whether Sage Patanjali would have been utterly frustrated, overjoyed, or amused with this transformation, but the change is here to stay.

A part of me finds the good in this change. The fusion of generations, technologies, and cultures changes everyone involved. The present question is this: Now that we have taken the first steps in yoga, are we ready to dig deeper? I believe a deeper exploration is inevitable, because the curiosity of the human spirit can't be doused. **With science as our guide, we can fearlessly explore further, going from known to unknown, ready to transform ourselves as well as the age-old traditions.**

Thoughtful progress is important because yoga isn't the only ancient practice that was subjected to randomized controlled trials or functional MRI scans. The same fate awaited the second eightfold path, which spawned the mindfulness movement. Let's travel back a few thousand years again to understand the birth of mindfulness. This time we will walk in the steps of a prince named Siddhartha Gautama in northeast India.

5

Siddhartha Gautama

It warms my heart to write this chapter since as a child I lived and traveled very close to the places where Siddhartha (aka Buddha) lived and traveled.

EARLY YEARS

Siddhartha Gautama traveled the earth between the sixth century and the fourth century BC in northern India.[48-50] The futurists of his time predicted that he would either consolidate the sixteen kingdoms into which India was divided at the time or become an ascetic. Suddhodana, his ambitious father, a king in eastern India, naturally wanted his son to expand the empire. Hoping to quell the ascetic instincts of his son, he raised Siddhartha in extreme luxury, away from life's pains and struggles.

As fate would have it, at age twenty-nine, Siddhartha ventured outside his palace, and in his travels, for the first time, he saw an old man, a sick man, and a corpse. These sights of suffering made him realize that the life he was leading was unreal. The common man outside faced a much harsher existence. Siddhartha finally encountered an ascetic, who sought a path of austerity and deprivation to overcome suffering. Young and restless and now driven by passion to find a solution for suffering, Siddhartha decided to pursue the path of the ascetic. After shaving his head, he left his wife, his son, and the palace and embraced the vulnerability of being an impoverished commoner.

ON HIS OWN

Soon after leaving the prison of his palace, he recognized the other prison that had caged the society: the prison of rituals. In those times, rituals were more important than values or faith. The society was rife with predatory wealthy; kindness was rare and often construed as weakness.

Seeking the company of a master who could help him traverse the path to freedom, he traveled south and found two gurus who were immersed in yoga and meditation. A quick learner, he soon realized that the trance states of yogis were only temporary blissful escapes from reality that didn't lead to lasting transformation. He traveled farther and joined a group of five ascetics who, assuming the physical body obstructed enlightenment, practiced ways to torture and subdue their bodies to transcend them. They exposed themselves to the elements, experienced prolonged starvation, and inflicted pain on their physical body. Embracing these practices, Siddhartha became sunken eyed, with a scalp like a "gourd" and a spine like a "string of seeds."

Nearing death but still unrealized and filled with angst, he remembered a moment from his childhood when, feeling compassion for the ants in the ground, he spontaneously sat in meditation. As he remembered that childhood moment, a maid offered him rice pudding, which he ate. Slowly he nursed his body back to health. He quit the path of self-torture, realizing the wisdom of living in balance. His five ascetic companions left him, blaming him for becoming a weakling and succumbing to a life of indulgence.

SIDDHARTHA BECOMES BUDDHA

At this point, Siddhartha sat down in meditation under the bodhi tree and resolved not to get up until he fully understood the root cause of suffering and its solutions. As legend has it, Mara (the mythical demon who tempts the seekers away from the virtuous path) challenged him with fear and desire and asked him to verify the authenticity of his practice, and when he passed all the tests, he saw the cosmic vision of the workings of the universe. The tree is believed to have rained down flowers at that moment. Siddhartha Gautama, at age thirty-five, had become self-realized—the Buddha.

He stayed near the bodhi tree for several weeks, unsure whether his teachings would be understood or be of use to the world. According to myth, the gods implored him to teach, so out of compassion for the world, he started teaching, first to his five previous companions. He shared that the path to enlightenment lies neither in indulgence nor in asceticism, but in balance—just like the strings of a well-tuned sitar. Offering wisdom through four core truths, he acknowledged the reality of suffering, named the causes of suffering, promised that suffering has a cure, and offered the noble eightfold path for the cure.[51]

THE FOUR TRUTHS

First, he recognized and accepted the reality of physical and mental suffering. He noted that physical suffering often has an external cause but can also start within the body. Similarly, mental suffering may come from an external event (often related to failed relationships or unmet expectations) or arise spontaneously from inner predispositions.

> ***Both physical and mental suffering can be from an external cause or an inner predisposition.***

Second, he explained the origins of suffering. He had been exposed to yoga (which, through *yamas* and *niyamas*, emphasized ideas around moral living and lowering one's cravings) and to *Advaita* philosophy, which denied the existence of a discrete self. But none of these disciplines directly tackled the issue of suffering. Buddha declared the root cause of suffering to be craving and ignorance (*avidya*). Humans crave pleasure and immortality, and we invariably cannot satisfy these cravings, certainly not forever. Buddha lived in a time when we had little control over nature, illnesses, and crops. Since his model was focused on actionable wisdom, he interpreted the problem in a way that would lend itself to immediate action.

Third, Buddha promised a solution. Quite simply, **relinquish craving and see reality as is, and your suffering will end**, he promised. Reality to him meant fully realizing the unsatisfactoriness of life, the impermanence of every experience and entity, and the lack of a discrete self. This was a brilliant solution when humans had little control over the elements and when medicine was rudimentary, because the loosening of the identification with the self also disconnects one from the self's pain.

Finally, Buddha detailed the solution for suffering. He described this as the middle path, the path of balance. Here Buddha described eight parts: right view, intention, speech, action, livelihood, effort, mindfulness, and concentration. He promised that a concerted eightfold practice would lead to insight into suffering, impermanence, and the nature of self (or non-self)—a state of enlightenment, filled with perfect wisdom and love.

Many or most of these principles may seem obvious today to someone who has access to the wealth of wisdom collected over the last two thousand years through psychiatry, psychology, neuroscience, and other disciplines. But Buddha's lessons were cutting edge in his times. He was an innovator.

BUDDHA THE INNOVATOR

Buddha proved his genius and courage by deviating from the prevailing customs. He saw the limitations of the religions of his time and focused on considering the wisdom of teachings from the instructor rather than from a particular godhead. He avoided dogmas or rituals. **It didn't matter whether you took three or four circles around the altar. What mattered was that you were kind toward others and yourself.**

> *Practicing kindness in the littlest of activities is more important than most rituals.*

He directed his students to wisely choose their focus of concentration so they could negate their maladaptive predispositions. He invited people to feel the normal human emotions instead of trying to escape them. He helped them learn to experience grief and invited them to find meaning in it. **He reminded them that having a relationship with life included losing it.** Noticing the wars that ravaged the world he lived in, he advised people to renounce inner violence to stop outer violence.

Since he was teaching a philosophy—a better way of living—and not religion, Buddha openly welcomed people of every caste to his congregation. Women were welcome in his group, unlike what was in vogue in his time. Buddha asked his students to replace greed, anger, and ignorance with generosity, compassion, and wisdom. He repeatedly emphasized impermanence and carefully avoided discussing details about life after death. He spoke of expressing compassion, of experimenting with one's beliefs, and of helping his students awaken to interconnectedness. These thoughts were revolutionary in his time, because the world then was mired in rituals, myths, and mysticism.

IF YOU BUILD

As he built, they came, in throngs. A monastery developed around him. He sent his monks far and wide to teach his message. He himself traveled across northeast India, teaching wherever he went. Stories spread about his miracles: taming the wild elephant, creating a walkway in the air, spontaneously separating wood splinters, and more. He was, however, unaffected by the stories, and he didn't seek miracles.

Buddha traveled and taught for more than forty years. At about age eighty, then old and feeble, he became very ill after eating a bad meal near Kushinagara in Nepal. Lying in a quiet grove of *sal* trees, he reminded his students to strive on untiringly, to be their own light, and remembering impermanence, to embrace a path of morality, wisdom, and contemplation. It is believed he died with his head pointed north, face to the west.

6

Mindfulness 500 BC

Buddha searched for the root cause of suffering long before the term *neuroscience* was coined. At about the same time, in ancient Greece, Aristotle (fourth century BC) wrote that the brain served as a radiator (cooling agent) for the heart, dissipating all the extra heat.[52, 53] Darwin was still more than two millennia away. There were no graduate students, think tanks, or NIH-funded laboratories. Buddha was alone. He had to rely on his own intuition. He thus went inward, into the laboratory of his mind.

During these times rife with rituals and mysticism, Buddha didn't create a model with invisible forces, such as the gods of suffering or pain. Instead, he crafted a simple four-part message based on four noble truths to help people understand and cure suffering. The final part of that message was the noble eightfold path.[51]

THE NOBLE EIGHTFOLD PATH

Buddha's noble eightfold path offered a prescription for peace, wisdom, and moral living:

1. Right view—See life, nature, and the world the right way, as they really are, focusing on the truth rather than on individual biases. Right view culminates in removing ignorance and developing wisdom that guides all future efforts.
2. Right intention—Renounce attachment and intend goodwill and harmlessness. Let go of desire, not by repression but by wisdom; express goodwill toward all through loving kindness.
3. Right speech—Speak the truth, use kind words, and avoid idle chatter. Speak words that connect and do not divide people. Avoid mystical or ethereal language.
4. Right action—Practice ethical living, abstaining from violence, theft, and immoral relationships.
5. Right livelihood—Earn one's living by engaging in prosocial occupations.
6. Right effort—Persist in the wholesome effort to cultivate right view, intention, speech, action, and livelihood.
7. Right mindfulness—Develop optimal attention and memory so one embodies undistracted presence to what is important and meaningful, both in the world and in the mind. Cultivate an open, quiet, and alert presence.
8. Right concentration—Develop and deepen meditation practice focused on breath, image, or word and anchored by wisdom, leading to tranquility, equanimity, and bliss.

BUDDHA'S MINDFULNESS

Buddha recognized the central importance of strong attention. Recall that undistracted presence was essential for high-fidelity transmission of information before paper was invented. Also, not paying such attention incurred a heavy cost on the student; it was also critical for procuring food and safe travel. Attention, conceptualized as mindfulness, was thus indispensable for survival and success long before it became a practice for emotional and spiritual growth.

The original term for mindfulness in the noble eightfold path was *sati* or *smriti*, which roughly translates to the concept of awareness, remembrance, discernment, and alertness. (By way of history, in 1881, Pali language scholar Thomas William Rhys Davids translated *sati* into "mindfulness" ["that activity of mind and constant presence of mind"] for the first time. But the word "mindfulness" was used by John Palsgrave as early as 1530.)[54]

A mindful mind was originally described as one with no distracted wanderings, no biases, and no confusion. Further, clear comprehension and memorization accompanied authentic presence. Mindfulness—described as a combination of undistracted presence, comprehension, and memorization—was essential to learning.

In a commonly taught metaphor, ordinary attention was considered akin to seeing the moon through the clouds or looking at the horizon on a foggy day, while mindful attention cleared the clouds and fog to show reality as it was. Buddha recognized the need to free attention from interpretation in order to see reality as is, and cultivate deeper wisdom.

Further, Buddha's mindfulness sat in an ecosystem that was geared for developing morality and wisdom and, through those, freedom. Training in mindfulness sat within the context of the eight-fold path. Mindfulness contributed to the emergence of wisdom and eventually a state of *Samatha*—absorption.

Buddha's mindfulness nourished, and was nurtured by morality and wisdom.

Mindfulness was a conduit to serenity and insight. Mindfulness supported the larger goal of enlightenment. It was a means to an end, not the end itself. Mindfulness was like the foot of a stool, supported by and in turn supporting the other limbs of the eightfold path. Silence was a step forward from noise, but silence wasn't the ultimate destination. The ultimate destination was melody, which for the mind was wisdom and love.

Buddha's mindfulness was humble, and it helped to decrease the focus on the self. In partnership with the other seven limbs of the eightfold path, mindfulness placed self in the context of the infinite. Several changes occurred in the intervening millennia, as humans reimagined mindfulness.

7

Modern Mindfulness

I work with many scientists whom I consider modern sages. They devote just about every single day of their lives to one goal: seeking solutions for human afflictions. Sometimes, however, we scientists oversimplify. A perfect example of science's misstep is the story of vitamins. That experience is particularly contextual, so I will summarize it here.

AN APPLE A DAY

Multiple research studies have shown that people who eat more fruits and vegetables are healthier; have lower risk of heart attack, stroke, and cancer; and enjoy greater longevity.[55-64] An apple a day really does its job.

Knowing what is right, however, doesn't mean we will do what is right. On most days, less than 10 percent of us eat enough veggies, and less than 15 percent eat enough fruits.[65] The entrepreneurs found a solution by encapsulating wellness in a pill. Concluding that the benefit of fruits and vegetables must be in the vitamins, manufacturers, supported by a few scientists, flooded the market with high-potency vitamins. Some holistic-health leaders cheered the movement. Apples and oranges in the pantry were replaced by multivitamins in the drug cabinet. This was the first mistake.

The second mistake was to supersize it. If 100 percent of daily intake is good, then 1,000 percent must be better. Dangerous doses of vitamins, touted as "cancer-fighting chemicals" or "healthy aging potions," can still be bought over the counter. Thankfully, several astute and justifiably cynical researchers questioned this practice. They launched large-scale clinical trials to find the truth.

The results were surprising. **The clinical trials showed that the high doses of "innocuous" vitamins and antioxidants provided no benefit. Worse, they increased the risk of cardiovascular events, cancer, and even death.**[66-69]

Vitamins—when served in combination with fiber, flavonoids, healthy fatty acids, amino acids, fruit sugars, natural colors, and water (the key ingredients in a fruit)—are nature's gift to us. When we separate those vitamins from their home and serve them in a pill, we lose most of the benefits.

Vitamins condensed in capsules are no match to natural nutrients in fruits.

How does this relate to mindfulness? I believe we have treated mindfulness the same way we treated the vitamins in fruits. We separated mindfulness from the other folds and offered it as a stand-alone package. We paid little attention to the right view, intention, speech, action, livelihood, and effort, and jumped straight to mindfulness and concentration. Further, in designing the current programs, we interpreted mindfulness based on the prevailing culture in the previous millennium, when terms like internet, computer, terrorism, and artificial intelligence were alien to us.

I believe this pursuit was well intentioned. One of the leaders of mindfulness movement shared with me that their effort was to free mindfulness from culturally unpalatable constructs that would have limited its spread. They were unsure how the eastern practices would be received in the west. They thus "cleaned" mindfulness as much as they could and offered it a stand-alone status, separated from its family of the eight folds.

DEFINITIONS

As mindfulness achieved a stand-alone status, it was paired with new partners, perhaps to enrich the experience and bolster its benefits. Mindfulness and yoga practices were merged. All the mindfulness retreats I have sampled so far spend roughly a third or more of the time with yoga *asanas*, *pranayamas*, and *shavasana* (that often includes body scan).

New definitions were developed. Currently, mindfulness has as many definitions as there are people defining it. There is considerable difference among teachers about what mindfulness truly means, which makes it difficult to compare results across different research studies.[70-75]

Three well-known definitions that encapsulate the present-day understanding of mindfulness are:

- paying attention in a particular way: on purpose, in the present moment, and nonjudgmentally;[76]
- an open and receptive attention to and awareness of what is occurring in the present moment;[77] and
- the awareness that comes from intentionally attending in an open and discerning way to whatever is arising in the present moment.[78]

The two best-known mindfulness programs are MBSR (mindfulness-based stress reduction) and MBCT (mindfulness-based cognitive therapy). Several other programs have been developed, including mindfulness-based eating-awareness therapy, relapse prevention, childbirth and parenting, art therapy, and mental-fitness training. In addition, dialectical behavioral therapy and acceptance-and-commitment therapy have integrated mindfulness concepts within their structures.

Modern contemplatives and teachers have gone a step further and used a variety of terms and ideas to capture the essence of modern mindfulness:[74] lucid awareness, bare presence, no elaboration, pure awareness, bare attention, suspending judgments, prior to duality, preconceptual/prelogical, non-judgment awareness, non-conceptual awareness, awareness of the presence as it unfolds, prior to thoughts, egoless awareness, non-reactive awareness, awareness of all: observer, observed, and observation, non-dual experience, experience bereft of the self, and non-egotistic alertness.

Three common themes emerged from these and other definitions and descriptors: the central importance of attention, receptivity and engagement with the present moment, and non-judgmental disposition.

MODELS AND SCALES

Several different models have been developed to understand how mindfulness works, with the more recent models increasingly focused on neuroscience.[79, 80] The simplest approach emphasizes attention training, with the more complex models integrating multiple processes (attention, intention, emotion, motivation, non-attachment, pro-sociality), to explain improvements in self-awareness, self-regulation and self-transcendence.[81]

Researchers have developed several mindfulness scales to capture the essence of the practice and measure changes in research studies.[82] Some of the most well-known scales are the Mindful Attention and Awareness Scale (MAAS), Kentucky Inventory of Mindfulness Skills (KIMS), Five Facet Mindfulness Questionnaire (FFMQ), Toronto Mindfulness Scale (TMS), Freiburg Mindfulness Inventory (FMI), and Cognitive and Affective Mindfulness Scale, Revised (CAMS-R). The core components assessed in these scales are present-moment awareness, acceptance, non-judging, and observing.

Mindfulness training is presently offered as an attention-centric approach. Engagement with the now and nonjudgmental disposition combine to form an excellent short-term strategy to quiet the restless mind. Further, the yoga *asanas*, *pranayamas* and relaxation (*shavasana*) added to the mix have created a rich and comprehensive package that has been reported to be effective in several research studies.[83-98]

Mindfulness promises a solution for a wide variety of problems, from performance anxiety to irreconcilable loss, which contributes to its popularity. Reported changes in genetic expression,[99, 100] inflammatory markers,[101, 102] and telomere size[103-105] capture imagination of learners fascinated by the genomic revolution. From large global companies to school children, mindfulness is now seen as part of the answer, sometimes universal panacea, for a plethora of human afflictions, occasionally even as part of the business model.[106, 107]

When you are able to talk to a cab driver about mindfulness while munching on a mindful burger, you can rest assured that mindfulness has gone mainstream. For many, the word mindfulness is now synonymous with all types of meditations.

I worry that such broad application and dissemination could be premature. Despite the potential usefulness of some of the currently available programs, the majority aren't able to fully benefit from the contemporary approaches for the reasons I describe in the next section. This is particularly true over the long term. Some people could even get hurt.

Let's delve into this a little deeper to look at the facts. Allow me to share my experience with practicing and teaching meditation as a way to better manage stress and enhance resiliency. I will share my chest-pain episode on a lonely night in a Denver hotel, an objective survey of mindfulness/meditation research, and then an enlightening meeting with His Holiness the Dalai Lama—three reasons that gave me the final push to write this book.

8

A Lonely Night in Denver

During a trip to Denver, Colorado, I experienced a slight burning deep in my chest. At first, I didn't think much of it. About an hour before, I had gorged on a thousand-calorie spicy dinner. *This is the price I must pay for the tamarind chutney*, I thought. A glass of cold water helped. Just before I went to sleep around midnight, however, the burning returned.

I pressed on the chest—no local tenderness. I moved around; nothing changed. Very soon I was thinking heart attack, blood clots in the lungs, pericarditis, and a few other sinister possibilities that my physician brain could surmise. But alone in the hotel room, I was too lazy and too cozy to do anything.

My thoughts went to my family; I saw my kids' little faces. *What if I have fatal arrhythmia and sudden cardiac death in my sleep? An innocent world out there needs me. I am not ready to die yet*, I catastrophized, which I am good at.

I took a few deep breaths. No change. Next, I did a quick diagnostic test. I got out of the bed and did ten push-ups. The burning didn't get any worse, and soon went away, not to return. I am not suggesting that push-ups are a new treatment for chest pain. I am just sharing how irrational I can be at 12:15 a.m.

I woke up foggy headed after a few hours. My attention immediately returned to my heartburn. My chest was quiet. *It was the chutney after all*, I thought. With this big worry behind me, I reached out to my new surrogate body part: my smartphone. I smiled. I was reminded of my friend Sam, whom I recently met at a birthday party.

SAM'S E-MAILS

Sam is a brilliant physician and an even better philosopher. He is about forty, is perfectly tanned, has a thick crop of hair (which I secretly envy), and has big, bright brown eyes guarded by silver-framed glasses that rest on his sharp nose. Sam doesn't mince words, which can sometimes be embarrassing.

While we were chatting about everything from corn to compassion, Sam stopped me halfway through the conversation and, with a serious physician face, said, "Amit, this has nothing to do with you. I like you. What you are saying is interesting. But I have a tremendous urge to check my e-mails right now. I just can't focus on your words." Next, he took off to check his e-mails. He came back after a few minutes, looking more relaxed, as though he had puffed a few blue breaths to calm his nicotine withdrawal.

Sam is hooked to his smartphone, like many of us are. In just a few years, smartphones have become our surrogate body parts, drawing our attention fifty to a hundred times during the day.[108]

HUMBLING INSIGHTS

Back to Denver. Remembering Sam, I put the smartphone away without checking e-mails. Instead, I turned to a different morning ritual that I have cultivated the last few years: sending silent gratitude to five people in my life who I know care about me. Near the end of the gratitude practice, I drifted off into a sweet, refreshing sleep.

That morning, I had a few humbling insights about myself:

- I have an irrational, restless mind.
- Despite years of practicing and teaching stress-management and resilience skills, I catastrophize.
- I believe my irrational, catastrophizing thoughts.
- **I can't stop my mind from thinking.**
- **If I choose to, I can change my thoughts.**

An irrational mind believes its irrational catastrophizing.

The last two are very important. My mind wasn't created to be stilled. It was created to think. My mind won't stop thinking as long as I am alive. That choice I don't have. I do, however, have another choice: to think differently, until the new thoughts become habitual.

Until a few years ago, I was training my mind to redirect its attention with a time-tested technique I learned as a teenager: meditation. I was born in India. I like meditation. What's not to like about meditation? It is relaxing, health improving, brain enhancing, and free of side effects. There is only one problem. After decades of learning and practicing, I have a confession to make: I find meditation a difficult practice. On many days, I don't know what I am doing when I'm meditating. I can count on my fingers the number of people I know who have a consistent and effective meditation practice.

A comforting truth: even the most skilled meditators struggle with their practice.

If, after years of practice, this is my state, I have no doubt others must be struggling too, I thought.

I need not go any further than my own memory lane. To help people with excessive stress, I would often start with meditation. Everyone loved it. But after a few months, almost every single person would say something like this: "I really enjoyed my time with you, but when I try on my own, it is difficult. I ended up quitting."

Maybe I am not good at teaching the skills, I thought. But when I looked around, I found everyone struggled with this problem. In my talks and group sessions, I started asking these two questions (I have asked them of more than fifty thousand people): "How many of you have tried meditation?" and "How many of you find meditation easy?"

Generally, in response to the first question, almost all the hands would go up, while less than 1 percent would raise their hands to report that they found meditation easy.[109] This particular struggle was so ubiquitous that it merited further inquiry.

9

Struggling *Sapiens*

As I looked deeper, more stories emerged. A concerned mom asked me to see her eighteen-year-old daughter, who was developing progressively worsening anxiety from meditation. When I met her, the daughter said, "The more I try to meditate, the more anxious I get. I feel constricted. That doesn't make any sense."

An entrepreneur from Arizona remarked, "Please don't ask me to be in the present moment. I can't keep my mind steady for a minute."

A monk from New Zealand stressed, "You have to meditate ten thousand hours before you become good at it."

A manager from Idaho said, "Meditation is so boring. Can you make it interesting?"

An attorney from Montana said, "My mind closes the moment I hear about this soft stuff."

A physician from Colorado sighed. "There is only so much I can focus on the breath. I need something else, something deeper."

A migrant worker from rural Illinois said, "You can only meditate if you have lots of money. It ain't for people like us."

These and other stories didn't sound like the voice of freedom. These voices were of the people desiring freedom, still struggling, many trapped by their twenty-first-century struggles.

TWENTY-FIRST CENTURY STRUGGLES

The world has changed a lot in the last 2,500 years. The commonest causes of death aren't external injuries and infections; they are cardiovascular illness and cancer. People's lives are packed. Perceived loneliness, a risk factor for a wide variety of chronic illnesses, is an increasingly significant problem as we get busier in our minds.

(Research shows that up to 80 percent of children below age eighteen and 40 percent of adults above age sixty-five feel lonely.[110, 111] In today's world, most elephants, lions, hyenas, wildebeests, buffalo, geese, ants, and honeybees have richer social connections than the average human.[112] Loneliness can increase sympathetic activity, worsen immunity, increase inflammation, and cause sleep disturbance and several chronic illnesses.[113, 114] Loneliness and social isolation in particular increase the risk of death in both the elderly[115] and the general population.[116] In one study, **social isolation was found to be as risky as smoking and diabetes in its effect on adverse health outcomes**.[116])

Loneliness is the new smoking.

We now suffer as much if not more from emotional pain as we do from physical pain.[117] Psychological threats hurt us even more than do real threats.

Emotional pain feels as painful as physical pain.

Our challenges now aren't systematic persecution, the caste system, or high infant mortality; our challenges are job insecurity, financial pressures, family responsibilities, and health concerns. We are burdened by electronic toxicity and fear of terrorism. Even though we are wealthier than we have ever been, the disparities in wealth and the programmed dissatisfaction of our brains (more on this in chapter 23) keep us preoccupied with financial struggles.[118]

(The richest 1 percent hold about 40 percent of the wealth; the richest 10 percent hold greater than 75 percent of the wealth.[119, 120] The average employee earns in a month what the average CEO earns in an hour.[121] Greater wealth, through its asymmetry, has thus paradoxically created greater perceived poverty. "USA" has been cynically interpreted to mean "the Unequal States of America."[122])

As we will soon see, our brains are comparison machines. Our brains don't look at our absolute progress or net worth. Instead, they compare. I compare what I have with what Peter has, particularly if Peter and I went to the same high school and competed for the same prom date. **The positive effects of the country's financial success on happiness evaporate if the financial rewards are patchy and limited to a select few.** Such growth worsens our stress, as it has.

This brings me to an important question—will we always continue to struggle? Will a day arrive when every human being will be happy, peaceful, and content?

HERE IS THE REALITY

The sooner we accept this reality, the better: Our world will never be perfect. Even if all our current problems are solved, we will discover or invent newer struggles. For as long as we live on this planet, we will face stressors for which we won't have solutions. Because we love, have preferences, have pain receptors on our body, and emotional centers in our brain, we will experience fear, sadness, regret, pain, and angst. Many of these feelings will visit us daily.

The minds of the present and every future generation will thus need help, including help for the problems that have no rational basis and exist only in our imaginations.

Another dose of reality is that the solutions will never be perfect. We will forever be looking for newer and better ideas to help our mind. It is because once we learn and adapt to a new idea, its effect fades and we start seeking something else (more on this in the next section).

Presently, many therapists, celebrities, high-profile newspapers, and magazines promote mindfulness to help us with these struggles. Many find mindfulness a perfect solution, even a panacea for the human mind. An important rationale they use is the extent of research that supports mindfulness. But is that rationale really sound?

Wearing my physician-researcher-professor hat, I decided to dig deeper to understand the research supporting the effectiveness of mindfulness, beyond the promising headlines and glossy magazine covers. In this quest I had help, from many scientists who have started asking this very important question—does mindfulness really work as we believe it does?

MINDFULNESS RESEARCH

A large body of research attests to the value of mindfulness, particularly for stress, symptoms of anxiety and depression, and chronic pain.[83-98] But when I scratched the surface, I found several details worthy of attention, particularly in light of the recent concerns about integrity and reproducibility of research findings in the psychology world.[123, 124] (Please look at Appendix: Curious or Serious? for a deeper dive and additional insights into this discussion.)

Let's explore now a few reasons that made me wonder if the enthusiasm about mindfulness is a bit disconnected from its demonstrated benefits in research studies. Please note that although my review here focuses mostly on mindfulness, I am also including studies with other forms of meditation.

(You can skim this section quickly if you aren't interested in the subtleties of research designs. Here is the bottom line: Most of mindfulness research findings are still inconclusive.)

1. **Weak benefit.** To my surprise, when I looked more closely at the absolute benefit (presented in systematic reviews and meta-analyses) from the currently available programs, I found it was either inconclusive or mild to moderate at best, [92, 94, 97, 94, 125-149] with unclear or no benefit for children.[150, 151] (I have provided additional studies here based on a more recent literature search.) In many situations, the benefits were short term and faded over time.[152, 153] One of the largest studies to assess the value of meditation-based practices (including mindfulness) found that the benefit was limited for anxiety, depression, and pain, small for stress and quality of life, and an inconclusive or no effect for positive mood, attention, substance abuse, eating habits, sleep, and weight loss.[153] I was also concerned by reports of potential harm (more below).[154-156]

(Consider reading an excellent review article by Nicholas T. Van Dam and colleagues that methodically outlines some of these issues.[82] This article grew out of a series of conferences and workshops funded by the Mind and Life Institute. An eloquent response to this article, authored by Dr. Richard Davidson and

Cortland Dahl, two prominent leaders of the mindfulness movement, agreed with the premise of the article and offered additional insights into research challenges.[82a] I find both the articles written by influential leaders of the mindfulness movement strongly supporting several of the arguments I am making here. That is the beauty of science: the ability to test its own veracity. I am grateful for the humility of these modern sages.)

Bulk of the mindfulness research shows weak benefit.

2. **Biased reporting.** A group of respected researchers did an in-depth analysis of the way mindfulness research is reported.[127] They raised concern that a high proportion (62 percent) of the studies weren't reported, giving a biased view of the literature. In general, the unreported studies are much more likely to be negative because both researchers and journals are less enthusiastic about these studies. Further, many of the study plans didn't specify the primary outcome and time of assessment, thus increasing the risk of biased reporting. Despite these concerns, none of the positive systematic reviews (which synthesize many studies and are the gold standard of research evidence) noted that biased reporting could have affected their results.

Researchers commonly do not publish negative studies.

Often, the conclusions were biased to be positive without noticing the nuances that can undermine the outcomes.[157] Even the negative trials have been reported with much fanfare using language such as "non-inferior to treatment as usual" (which in simple language means the program didn't work).[158]

In research, a common mistake is to confuse "statistically significant result" for clinically or practically meaningful change. A p value less than 0.05 (the common threshold used for statistical significance) might not mean much if after intensive training and practice the participants improved only by 3 percent. This has affected mindfulness research also.

With all of the above biases, in a headline-driven world, the unsuspecting public and even some experts might look at the positively tilted wording in the conclusions, and take home the message that the intervention works, when in reality the study was negative or inconclusive.[159]

3. **Different types of programs.** Meditation programs are of various types of which mindfulness is one.[160] Mindfulness itself is a family of many different programs. Zen mindfulness is different from Tibetan. An established yogi's practices are a class apart from a curious beginner's (Please look at the Appendix for more details about the practice of Ananda and Andy). Given that substantial difference among experts about what

mindfulness truly means affects the structure of different programs, comparing research findings from different studies is often technically flawed even if attempted with great rigor.

Focused attention on breath or mantra, body scan, walking meditation, open-awareness, and loving kindness are just a few types of meditation. Research shows different meditation types have unique effects on the brain and behavior.[161] However, it is not uncommon for the same analysis to compare and combine results of four or more different types of programs. This level of variability increases the risk of biased results, making it difficult to estimate the true benefit of any program.[162] Further, it isn't accurate to extrapolate results from one meditation type to another, as has often been done. More universally accepted definitions and greater precision in our understanding of the concepts will greatly help advance the research.

4. **Low-quality studies.** The studies performed are often of low quality, with weak design and poor justification for the number of participants and without an appropriate comparison group. Many of the studies have problems with the way deviations are handled and data is analyzed.[163] The trainers could be masters in mindfulness or novices with less than one year of experience, affecting the results.[164] Concerns have been raised about the validity of self-reports, lack of blinding, lack of optimal control, inadequate description of the interventions, validity of study measures, lack of registration of the studies, and credibility of data analyses.[165, 166] In a review that assessed 18,753 meditation studies (including mindfulness meditation, mantra meditation, and transcendental meditation), only 47 studies (0.25%) were found to be of good quality.[127] Another review that specifically assessed mindfulness research estimated that more than 90 percent of mindfulness research is of questionable quality with only 1 percent of research performed in the real-world setting.[167] Thus we have little to no information about how well the current mindfulness training programs perform outside of research studies.

A study published in October 2017 by the Davidson group showed that the quality of research has barely budged between the years 2000 and 2016.[167b]

(To be fair, the lack of high quality studies often isn't intentional. The challenge with mindfulness research is the inability of anyone to own the resulting product. That takes away the incentive for any group to make substantial investment in this research, impacting the study quality. I have struggled with the same challenges doing research.)

Another quality issue is disregarding the complexity of measurement and statistical challenges when interpreting neuroscience studies and taking an overly simplistic view of the brain changes. Researchers also tend to pool studies evaluating the brain changes with very different meditation programs, akin to counting apples and oranges together.[168, 169]

Finally, the existing tools to measure mindfulness (and other self-reported outcomes), are a work in progress. Since mindfulness is a complex concept with many definitions, there are countless ways to describe and interpret mindfulness. This creates tremendous subjectivity in its assessment. There isn't a "gold standard" tool for measuring mindfulness (like we have for measuring blood glucose or serum sodium). As a result, sometimes with the existing tools, the duration and frequency of practice isn't related to change in mindfulness scores.[82]

Bulk of the mindfulness research is of low quality.

5. **Short follow-up duration.** Many studies have a short-term follow-up, making it difficult to assess the long-term benefit of the program.[170] Further, currently we have no good data about how many people stick with their formal mindfulness practice over the long term after the initial eight weeks of training. Based on my informal assessment of asking people in the workshops and individual visits, that number is low, likely in single or low double digits.

6. **Yoga as an add-on.** Mindfulness is seldom tested as a stand-alone approach. Many mindfulness programs have yoga *asanas* (postures), *pranayamas* (breathing exercises), and *shavasana* (relaxation) as an integral part of the training. Since **yoga has an independent benefit for almost every condition for which mindfulness has been tested**, it is difficult to dispel the argument that the benefit of the mindfulness programs is driven mostly by the yoga component. Yoga has also been independently shown to improve mindfulness.[171]

Yoga provides the same benefit as mindfulness.

7. **Placebo effect.** In research studies, people improve for many reasons. One reason is the placebo effect.[172] When we get attention from others and participate in a group activity that involves a lot of support, our stress level goes down. Could the benefits of mindfulness programs arise from attention and group participation and not really from the specific practices? Several studies with a good comparison arm showed muted or no benefit.[153, 173]

One of the world's premier research groups (University of Wisconsin—Madison) carefully designed a matched control (called HEP—Health Enhancement Program) to one of the best-known mindfulness programs (MBSR) to take away the placebo effect. They matched the control for the duration of training, exposure to the study, and other aspects. The study disappointingly showed no difference between MBSR and the control group.[166, 174, 175] Here is how the researchers summarized their results in one of the studies: "Participant-reported outcomes (PROs) replicate previous improvements to well-being in MBSR, but indicate that MBSR is no more effective than a rigorous active control in improving these indices."[176] (I was a visiting Professor at this campus in March 2010 when the team was designing and conducting the studies, had the privilege of meeting the researchers, and was truly impressed with their academic rigor and attention to details.)

Researchers and entrepreneurs have developed different online programs and smartphone apps to enhance dissemination. However, online programs show similar mixed results when compared to a credible control intervention.[177]

Researchers have also raised concern about the "popularity effect." Since many of the mindfulness programs are fashionable, participants might feel better simply by virtue of participating in something trendy.[93] Finally, people practicing meditation are likely to embrace other healthy life styles such as physical activity and healthy diet that can influence the study outcomes.[178]

8. Excessive self-focus. I don't know how to say this mildly. Here's what I feel: modern mindfulness programs have excessive self-focus. Body scan, walking meditation, sitting meditation, breathing practices—the majority of the practices tested in research studies and offered in training programs drive a person inward. In some programs, in addition to the formal practice, participants are asked to notice their body, breath, and stance and to examine their mind throughout the day. But inside my head isn't where the party is happening!

I can understand how inward focus may have helped Uncle Ad when he wanted to relax because his outside world was treacherous. But these days, we cry more often from emotional pain than we do from physical pain. When we go inward we risk getting lost in our regrets, hurts, concerns, fears, and all the open files—a perfect and powerful trap.

In older times, when mindfulness kept the company of the other seven folds, training in altruism and kindness often preceded or accompanied attention training. In fact, greater emphasis was on altruism and kindness. Mindfulness was just a conduit. Same for yoga. This is particularly important because several research studies suggest that our society may be getting increasingly self-centered and materialistic (Generation Me),[179, 180] while at the same time, at least some of its members are shunning hard work for the material gains they desire.[181] A few studies report that individualistic traits such as narcissism and assertiveness are on the rise.[182] I was shocked to read one research study's findings that 40 percent of us, given the choice, would save our own pet over a foreign tourist.[183] Could the internally focused practices of mindfulness increase this propensity? This is a legitimate concern raised by some researchers that I will visit again later.

> ***The growing narcissism in our society can be better helped by greater focus on compassion than on breathing practices.***

9. Adverse effects. I started my research career with the assumption that mindfulness programs (and broadly all forms of meditation programs) have no risk of adverse effects. That was a naive assumption, given that relaxation has been associated with anxiety in previous reports.[184, 185] Presently we don't know the frequency of adverse effects since less than 25 percent of research studies collect that information, a problem well recognized among psychotherapy researchers.[186-188] Instead of actively asking participants to check from a list of anticipated adverse effects, we passively rely on their spontaneous reporting of adverse effects, an approach that can decrease the prevalence of reported adverse effects over 20-fold.[189]

Over the years now, I have read isolated reports of meditation linked with increase in anxiety, dizziness, precipitation of hallucinations, and other symptoms.[190] Additional studies have reported memory impairment, false-memory susceptibility, asociality, panic attacks, psychosis, mania, recurrence of traumatic-memories, depersonalization, and impaired reality testing.[191, 184, 192-199] Two reports have even suggested higher prevalence of substance use among people who score high on mindfulness![178, 200] Researchers have compiled a list of mental, physical, and spiritual side effects with suggestions to collect that information from research studies.[201] But this is seldom followed.

(Personally, I have noticed only minor adverse effects among participants, such as light headedness, palpitations, occasional headache, and irritability, and haven't noticed any significant serious adverse effects from meditation. It may be partly because we are careful about excluding participants with conditions where meditation can be harmful including most patients with risk factors for psychosis, schizophrenia spectrum disorder, and patients with uncontrolled severe mental health issues including severe depression, bipolar disorder and others, unless the study is specifically designed to help these patients and has the resources and protocols to monitor them.)[201, 202]

A recent study reported greater correlation between mindfulness and criminogenic tendency.[203] This was related to "nonjudgment of self." Researchers noted that some degree of judgment of the self is necessary, particularly among people in the criminal justice system.

An older study with twenty-seven long-term practitioners showed that almost two-thirds of the participants had side effects from meditation with a few having "profound adverse effects."[204] A small study that tracked participant diaries reported that during the first eight weeks almost everyone experienced some distress related to the practice.[205] A larger recent online survey has found that about a quarter of the people develop side effects, usually mild and transient.[206] Interestingly, greater side effects were noted with focused attention practice and practices that lasted longer than twenty minutes.

An important consideration is the "opportunity costs"—the risk of people abandoning credible proven therapies in favor of the more "natural" approaches, particularly for the more severe conditions. Reports concluding that brain imaging favors meditation for depression, and thus the suggested approach should be—"meditate don't medicate," might capture a few headlines but can hurt someone who starts treating his or her severe psychotic depression with subscribing to a meditation app.[207]

The bottom line: the lukewarm benefits in research studies, the possibility that most of the benefits could be coming from yoga, the inability to control for the placebo effect, biased reporting, inward focus of attention, potential for adverse effects, combined with my own and others' struggles with meditation, seeded doubts in my mind. I also read reports that raised concerns that at work places, the stripped-down versions of mindfulness (sometimes called McMindfulness) might be used as a Band-Aid to cover larger issues by increasing docility among employees.[208] Mindfulness was not designed to make us numb; it was developed for personal transformation.

Are the media representations of the purported benefits exaggerated?[107] This isn't the first time the press has gotten prematurely excited about a novel technology or idea. (Interestingly, of late, several mass media, trade/weekly journals, practitioner journals, and academic journals have begun to host debate about the pros and cons of mindfulness.[191] I believe this is the beginning of a new trend that will likely accelerate.)

(This section of the book may provoke a quick judgment from some readers. If you are an ardent believer in mindfulness, you might strongly disagree; if you do not believe, you might strongly agree. The truth is somewhere in between. The truth also depends on your personal experience. For some, the current practices might work perfectly. The research findings, good or bad, then would be a moot point for them. Unfortunately, they are in the minority, less than 10 percent. Most of us would love a simpler, more accessible approach. My suggestion is to withhold judgment for now, go over the seven tenets and the appendix, and then decide for yourself.

Also, please note that most of my comments here are related to mindfulness research and not to the original concept of mindfulness per se. The problem isn't with mindfulness, the problem is with our understanding and how we apply that understanding in the training programs and daily life.)

The problem isn't with mindfulness; the problem is with how we hyped less than conclusive results of some impractical practices.

The above thoughts brought me face to face with a personal concern. I was concerned that I had violated a moral standard. I went through a period of tremendous personal guilt.

10

Guilty and Back

FEELING GUILTY

Challenging an age-old practice was extremely difficult for me. If you understand my background, it will make sense to you.

Meditation practices and teachers are highly respected in Asian Indian families. Many teachers are revered as spiritual leaders of the society. Their images are placed in each room. In daily prayer, people bow to the images, decorate them with flowers, and light incense sticks in front of them. People see their teachers in dreams to solve personal problems. In families with a faith-based practice, these teachers are considered a conduit to God. Annoying or disbelieving them or their instructions could be considered worse than heresy.

I have met several teachers who indeed deserve a high pedestal, but some do not. Nevertheless, if a teacher is caught committing nefarious practices, as has happened numerous times, instead of lowering the pedestal, the unsuspecting students often reframe by saying that the teacher is testing their spiritual resolve by creating this drama.

With this cultural perspective etched within me, my guilt, conflict, and anxiety grew along with the doubts I shared in the previous chapter. I felt vulnerable. *Will these doubts bring bad luck, illness, or curse to my family?* I thought. The scientist in me conflicted with myths and rituals I had learned as a child. A master at overthinking, I did what I do best with such conflicts: I stopped thinking about it and tabled the idea.

OVERCOMING GUILT

I didn't stay put with the idea for very long. My return journey started when I heard about people with no meditation experience who were perceiving the deepest *samadhi* states as a result of acute stroke. I read about brain tumors and seizures causing sacred visions and spiritual experiences.[209-214]

Could these states and visions just be a product of our brain's electrical activity? I asked myself. If that is the case, will it be worthwhile to spend my entire life seeking such experiences?

Some neurological disorders can provide "deeply spiritual"
experiences without much "spiritual effort".

Then I read about swamis who had obtained these experiences but were doing very bad things. I heard stories about self-styled gurus who claimed to be adept at awakening people's *kundalini* (and many of their followers felt their "energy" and saw the "light" with their help) but were nothing but greedy, immoral charlatans. They were illegally usurping money and property, abusing women and children, and committing other unspeakable crimes. I saw a few of them getting caught, was amazed at how low they could go in trying to defend themselves, and could clearly see the selfish psychopath beneath the long hair and saffron color. My uninformed faith in some of these traditions began to crack. That worked wonders on my guilt. (I should mention here that not all swamis are fake. I have personally met several masters of meditation who I deeply respect, who are humble, selfless, and kind, and are truly living each day to help the world.)

LOOKING DEEPER

With my blind faith unblinded, the more I studied, the deeper I looked and the more learners I worked with, the more convinced I became that most mindfulness programs in their current form need editing before they can optimally help twenty-first-century brains.

In our effort to make mindfulness simpler, despite our good intentions, we have misrepresented some of its constructs.[215] Further, some of the language and philosophy is 2,500 years old. It simply needs to be refreshed. What is old and practiced for thousands of years doesn't always have to be perfect or even right. After all, they anointed cow dung on umbilical cords that caused tetanus, didn't believe in pasteurization, practiced child labor, and bad-mouthed any woman who stepped outside the house to join the workforce. (Unfortunately, all of these are still happening in some parts of the world.)

The result of my deeper search was freedom. While I still revere the timeless wisdom of many scriptures, I have largely escaped my childhood blinders, partly because I feel confident in the new tool we now have to study the truth: science. Using the scientific lens polished with common sense, I came up with a few key ideas for how to better align our understanding of mindfulness with twenty-first-century challenges so it can better serve resilience.

FEW IDEAS

Here is what I thought was needed:

- Integrate twenty-first-century neuroscience to help better understand the human condition. Philosophy alone isn't enough.
- Offer skills that emphasize uplifting emotions and not just attention training.
- Have more explicit focus on compassion, gratitude, and forgiveness.
- Abbreviate the training time.
- Offer practices that are shorter and more relevant to people's lives.
- Enhance focus on relationships to decrease perceived loneliness.
- Integrate hope, inspiration, and courage in the program.

In addition to above, I felt adding humor to the program (and life) was vital. Fun and laughter are great sources of bonding and inspiration, and if we keep the training and the skills dry, then they will remain inaccessible, particularly to the younger generation.

I debated and doubted these thoughts for months but couldn't negate any one of them. As a next step, I considered a three-part solution:

1. Educate people about their brains, emphasizing how our neural traps generate negative emotions and hurt our attention.
2. Offer different (briefer and deeper) attention practices that are easier to practice and adopt, that provide uplifting emotions, and that center on relationships.
3. Return mindfulness to its ecosystem in the company of compassion, gratitude, forgiveness, relationships, hope, inspiration, and courage.

I strongly believed I was moving in the right direction, but received pushback from some old colleagues in the field. Pushbacks often demoralize me and they worked their magic this time also. But each time I saw someone struggling whom I couldn't optimally help, the thoughts creeped up again. I needed one final push. Then His Holiness the Dalai Lama came to my rescue.

11

A Dialogue with His Holiness the Dalai Lama

The first of the final two straws for me was when a student, not unlike my friend Sam, said, "Can we try something else? Meditation has become one more thing to feel bad about." That made me pause.

And the second straw came when I got an opportunity to dialogue with His Holiness the Dalai Lama for a few hours.

When I was asked to speak with the Dalai Lama, an excited panic coursed through my body. What if I froze or uttered something dumb that annoyed him? How could I speak with someone so much wiser than I? What if I were excommunicated because of all these doubts about mindfulness?

The day prior to the conversation, I had a preparatory meeting with a preeminent teacher of meditation and positive emotions. I laid my heart bare to him. This is the gist of the discussion we had that day over a cup of coffee.

"I am worried about the conversation tomorrow."

"Why?" he asked.

"I am worried because I have a slightly different take on mindfulness. I believe we are teaching difficult-to-impossible practices. I believe we should mingle joy in the practices and offer approaches that are more relationship centric and have a direct focus on compassion. I have seldom heard the words *gratitude*, *forgiveness*, or *meaning* in the retreats. The greatest focus is on nonjudgmental acceptance, which is so difficult and impractical. I am concerned the Dalai Lama will read my mind and will get annoyed." I surprised myself with my candor. I poured it all out even though I risked being pulled out of the dialogue.

He smiled, and, after a mile-long pause, said, "You're going to have a great time with the Dalai Lama. He totally believes in what you're saying." I looked at him in disbelief. When it was clear he wasn't kidding, I couldn't contain my joy. I felt validated. I was in a state of high that evening.

The next day, Dr. Daniel Goleman, who helped coordinate the event, was as gracious and kind as any human being can be. He gave me free rein and time for me to ask any question I pleased. On the stage, I was joined by my dear friend Carla Paonessa and a respected colleague, Dr. Sherry Chesak.

It was a dramatic ninety minutes. I found the Dalai Lama to be kind, gentle, encouraging, fun, and wise. Spending time with him was like learning from my very sweet, very loving grandpa.

I asked the Dalai Lama lots of questions—about human struggles, compassion, his childhood, and more. Then, in his presence, I asked these two questions to the audience of about five hundred people, the who's who of the meditation world: (The answers would truly shock me and steer me forward in my path.) "How many of you have practiced meditation?" and "How many of you have found meditation a piece of cake, very easy?"

As expected, the majority of the participants raised their hands in response to the first question. In response to the second question, barely one or two hands went up.

At that point, the Dalai Lama, in all his humility, shared his insights about meditation. I have watched this clip several times on YouTube. He described two types of meditation: analytical and single pointed. Analytical meditation cultivates a sense of curiosity—an alert mind that is busy exploring the nature of the body, world, humanity, and mind. Such a mind analyzes all it sees and connects different experiences to learn about the world. Analytic meditation helps develop a holistic view. It decreases the gap between appearance and reality. This form of meditation he found easy, and he thought it was more important than the second form of meditation—focused attention.

For the second form of meditation, which creates a single-pointed mind (in which you focus on a single object of attention), the word Dalai Lama used was *impossible*. It needed a lot of time—four, five, or six hours every day.

Here are some of his words (transcribed from the video recording).

"Meditation…basically two types. Analytical meditation and single-pointed meditation. Analytical meditation I consider more important. Curiosity…Alert mind…Analyze Analyze Analyze…nature of the body, of the world, humanity…my mind not dull…my mind sharp…because of analytical meditation…"

Next, he said a few words about single-pointed meditation that were to change the direction of my career. He said, *"Single-pointed…for me, up to now, impossible…because you need lot of time…at least every day 4, 5, 6 hours continuously concentrate on it…"*

He said he wouldn't compromise his sleep to meditate. For this reason, he hasn't had the deepest meditation experience *(Samatha)*.

Here is the link to that video. Watch the interesting ten-minute conversation that is between 1:05:45 and 1:14:30 at https://www.youtube.com/watch?v=ca7faWkfmwc. (If the provided link doesn't work, type "Dalai Lama Mayo Clinic 2012" in the YouTube search box. The first link that is 1:31:11 long is the video. Advance to 1:05:00 to watch the related segment.)

The word I heard the Dalai Lama say for creating a single-pointed mind was "impossible".

🕊

It was clear to me that the Dalai Lama was emphasizing the importance of cultivating deeper insights and wisdom through intentional attention and thinking. I assumed this was his take on where mindfulness should take us. Further, he was sharing the difficulty with single-pointed meditation and perhaps downplaying its value (the last point is my extrapolation).

AHA!

Talking to the Dalai Lama was a moment of great realization for me. I felt uplifted, absolved, freed. My cage had been opened. This hummingbird was ready to fly.

If the Dalai Lama struggles with single-pointed meditation and promotes a more wisdom-seeking analytical process, why was I seeking single-pointed meditation as a first step? Why were many other programs doing the same?

I realized my folly. I was copying and pasting practices I had learned without much thinking. I had picked clichés. I was talking about the "now" without knowing what it meant. I was evangelizing about being in the present moment without knowing how difficult it was. I was sharing practices that didn't work for the majority of the people for the long term. They were just too polite to tell me. I was setting them up for failure, swapping one trap for the other. This wasn't right, and I needed to fix it.

If the basic concepts of diet and exercise are simple and can be learned in a very short time, why shouldn't mindfulness, resilience, happiness, and stress management be equally simple and accessible? I thought.

I went back to the drawing board; immersed myself deeper in science, particularly in neuroscience and evolutionary biology; traveled overseas and within the United States; and talked to countless fellow citizens, scientists, and spiritual luminaries. I heeded the Dalai Lama's advice and sat down to think deeply. I checked the notes I had taken earlier. After several months of effort, a few themes emerged. (Recall the three core features of the current mindfulness practices as a reference: the central importance of attention; receptivity and engagement with the present moment; and nonjudgmental disposition.)

A FEW THEMES

Here are the seven themes that emerged from my exploration. These themes synthesize the different concepts I have presented in this book so far:

1. A focus on attention is a good first step; attention, however, is just one part of the solution. It is good to clearly see beneath the lake, but what if the bottom of the lake is dirty? Settling into the breath is good, but what if the breath is painful? **Mindfulness can help us more if it offers a construct not just to see but also to see the beauty beneath the perceived ugliness and the meaning behind the pain. Mindfulness is but a tool that allows wisdom to sprout. It is really about wisdom, not bare attention.**

2. In both of the eightfold paths (yoga and the noble eightfold path), a complete prescription for the mind has three components: ethical conduct (morality), the right view of the world and self (wisdom), and contemplation (attention). The noble eightfold path of Buddha prescribes a combination of wisdom (right view, right intention), ethical conduct (right speech, right action, right livelihood), and deeper presence (right effort, right mindfulness, right concentration). Most authentic yoga programs integrate these three components. Meditation (*dhyana*) is a reward for sustained practice in focused attention, moral living, and insight into the nature of reality.

All the masters of the noble eightfold path and yoga I have met emphasize the value of wisdom and ethical conduct as much as, if not more than, attention. The reason is simple. Training attention is like sharpening the edge of the saw. But the purpose of the saw, its direction and intention, has to be strong and guided by deeper values.

A complete prescription for the mind has three parts: morality, wisdom, and contemplation.

People with strong attention but evil intention have been very destructive to the world. In fact, a diagnosis of psychopathy is considered a no-no for meditation (you don't want relaxed psychopaths). Attention is thus an enabler, not an end in itself. **Attention that isn't built on the foundation of morality and wisdom remains vulnerable. Attention needs an altruistic intention and meaning to sustain its depth and for it to transform the entire being.**

3. Repeatedly, I find myself struggling with two central tenets: present-moment awareness and non-judgmental stance. **After connecting with close to half a million people now, I haven't met a single person (other than a few monks) who can consistently anchor his or her attention in the present moment. Inability to access and stay in the present moment isn't a human weakness; it is scripted in the basic design of our nervous system** (more on this in chapter 17). Teaching a skill that almost everyone is likely to fail at isn't a good way to inspire people. This is one reason majority of the people I meet, despite their good intentions, eventually give up on meditation.

I also find that most learners struggle with a non-judgmental stance. The mind's nature is to be curious. Non-judgmental stance leaves nothing tangible to anchor our attention. We are constantly busy foraging for information that enhances survival value. We use this information to create our model of the world and the people who live in it. We have been doing this for our entire existence. How easy, then, will it be to try practicing bare attention with no judgment? Will it not be going backward?

Trying to attain present-moment awareness and non-judgmental stance is impractical and can take away energy from easier and more powerful practices.

4. In the twenty-first century, many more people ask why before they ask what or how. Sharing with them some of the scientific underpinnings (particularly those of neuroscience) isn't optional anymore. It is mandatory, validating, and freeing. Philosophy alone isn't enough. Further, the training time (and thus the cost) has to be considerably brought down for the programs to reach a broader population. Otherwise, a few will sit in the ivory tower of peace while most others will be left behind.

5. Despite all the research and media coverage, less than 10 percent of us meditate,[216] while 50 percent exercise regularly[217] and about 71 percent pray daily or weekly.[218] One of the reasons the exercise world has succeeded is innovation. We have made exercise fun. From ballet to basketball, dancing, hopscotch, Zumba, Hula-Hooping, and more, there are literally hundreds of different fun exercises to choose from.[219, 220, 221]

Innovation in the exercise world enhances dissemination. I wish I could say the same about the meditation world. Some innovation has happened, such as EEG and heart-rate-variability feedback, and some high-tech gadgets and apps, but not enough to move the needle.[222-224]

Meditation needs innovation.

6. After spending several years studying behavior-change literature, I have arrived at this conclusion: **for any practice to work for the long term, it has to feel pleasurable in the short term**. If you wish to lose weight, replacing most of your meals with steamed broccoli might work in the short term. But by the end of the week, you will likely start an anti-nausea pill. **A good diet is not only nutritious but also delicious. Similarly, mind-body practices of the future shouldn't feel heavy or burdensome.** Good and effective mind-body practices will feel nourishing, freeing, and uplifting. A hint of humor will also help. Only then will they reach the masses.

7. **Engaging emotions is a powerful way to cement a lifelong practice**. A transformative change is much more likely if contemplative practices positively engage our deep-seated emotions and offer a path to stronger relationships with self, others and what we consider sacred. The single most important source of our joy and sorrow is relationships. Practices that directly enhance relationships will likely have the greatest long-term benefit.

I applied these ideas in my own life, tested the resulting programs in research studies, and offered the skills in clinical practice. The result was truly transformative—for my personal practice and for my patients and learners.

In research studies, we tested the benefits of the program for improving stress, anxiety, happiness, quality of life, mindfulness, resilience, and burnout. While I cannot exclude the possibility of a placebo effect, the positive outcomes (with large effect sizes) in multiple clinical trials with long-term follow-up, corroboration of research findings with participant comments, replication in multiple studies, feedback from hundreds of workshops, and use in clinical and nonclinical settings with tens of thousands of people every year add strength to the conclusions. (Some of our studies have been published in peer-reviewed journals; many are in different stages of review.)[225] A synthesis of this approach is now available both online, in in-person courses (see chapter 80 for details) and in three published books, two from the Mayo Clinic.[226-230]

With the background information covered so far, we are now ready to dive into the seven tenets of mindfulness *v2*.

12

The Seven Tenets

I believe we have seen only the beginning of where mindfulness and other forms of meditation can take us. The practices are bound to evolve, as will the core concepts.

Every good product or idea that has helped us humans has been helped in turn by our ingenuity and transformed beyond its original version. Almost everything good comes with a promise that it can be made better. The earliest computers weighed nearly thirty tons and had eighteen thousand vacuum tubes.[231] The first airplane flew for only twelve seconds and covered 120 feet.[232] We thankfully didn't stop there. The same innovation and growth will and must happen to contemplative practices, including mindfulness.

We continue to innovate and improve upon our every product and idea. That must include mindfulness.

Mindfulness will continue to be rediscovered by every generation. In parts 2–10 that follow, I present the seven tenets of mindfulness *v*2, in my effort to help us reclaim a simpler, clearer, easier, and deeper version of mindfulness.

THE TENETS

The version of mindfulness I offer here integrates the original ideas of the noble eightfold path; the approaches currently in vogue; the more recent advances in science; and the prevailing societal needs related to our present-day challenges, lifestyles, and opportunities. This approach is a modification of the older ideas about how we access mindfulness along with updating our understanding of mindfulness itself.

The ideas I offer may work better for some but not for others. You don't have to agree with every premise noted here. Take what you like and recycle the rest.

Mindfulness *v*2 has seven tenets. Let's compare them with the current mindfulness practices (which for the sake of simplicity I will call mindfulness *v*1).

Tenet	Mindfulness v1	Mindfulness v2
1. Insight	Focused on ancient philosophy	Focused on science
2. Presence	Anchored by time	Anchored by intentionality
3. Attention	Internally focused meditation	Externally focused meditation
4. Perspective	Zoomed in	Zoomed in and out at will
5. Attitude	Nonjudgmental	Compassionate
6. Practice	The majority of the practice is formal	The majority of the practice is informal
7. Anchor	Empty the mind; anchor it in breath	Fill the mind with hope, inspiration, & courage

SEVEN TWEETS

Here are the seven tenets presented as seven tweets. Please sit with the following seven ideas for a few moments before you proceed further in the book:

1. Ancient wisdom relied on philosophy; modern wisdom increasingly consults twenty-first-century science.
2. Time is fleeting and untethered. Anchor presence by intentionality instead of time.
3. Intentional attention, external or internal, engages the same brain network. Focus your meditation on the world if you struggle with the mind.
4. If the short term is challenged, think about the long term; if the long term is challenged, live for the next moment. Keep a flexible zoom.
5. A non-judgmental stance can be comforting but is unachievable. Being grateful and compassionate is an easier and more accessible solution.
6. Mindfulness isn't a practice; it is a way of life.
7. Instead of emptying the mind, fill it with hope, inspiration, and courage.

These tenets/tweets converge to the following definition of mindfulness *v2*:

Living with intentionality, kindness, and gratitude.

Thus, the greatest emphasis is on the following: living the principles, being intentional, cultivating kindness (to self and others), and being grateful.

Definition of mindfulness v2: Living with intentionality, kindness, and gratitude.

To these elements are added the following— greater insight into the scientific findings, externally focused practices, flexibility in attention, and nurturing hope, inspiration, and courage.

Let's dive into each of these tenets on a mindful path to resilience! We'll start with science.

Part II
The First Tenet: Insight

Tenet	Mindfulness v1	Mindfulness v2
Insight	Focused on ancient philosophy	Focused on science

—⁂—

Ancient wisdom relied on philosophy; modern wisdom increasingly consults twenty-first-century science.

13

Fireside Chat #2

"That was a fascinating journey, from Uncle Ad to Buddha to Denver to research to the Dalai Lama," Mike remarks, and then he asks, "Was Uncle Ad your real ancestor?"

"I am sure I had an uncle who lived in 3000 BC, but I don't know his name."

"Then how do you know all the details about Uncle Ad's times?"

"When I was younger, I hung around yogis quite a bit. They still live like it's 3000 BC. It's amazing, the simplicity. I visited many ashrams and read stories that go back thousands of years. Many places where technology hasn't yet penetrated are quite like what I described in Uncle Ad's times."

"Fascinating. Did you travel to any of the places Buddha visited?"

"I was about fourteen when we traveled to Bodhgaya and saw the bodhi tree where he achieved enlightenment. My family home is thirty miles from Sanchi, one of the oldest and most well-known Buddhist stone structures that houses many sacred relics."

"What did it feel like in Bodhgaya?"

"Not much at that time. I was young. I didn't walk away enlightened!"

"What would Buddha think of modern mindfulness?"

"He would be proud. He would be proud to see mindfulness on the cover of *Time* magazine and as a published article in *JAMA*. He would be fascinated by neuroscience, psychoneuroimmunology, and genomics. I believe if he came back now, Buddha would be a neuroscientist."

"Would he disagree with you?"

I thought for a moment and then heard myself say, "Hard to say but don't think so. He was all about practicality, simplicity, and relevance. He might disagree with some of the details but would agree with adapting the ideas to the current challenges. That's what he did in his times."

"Switching gears, what was it like speaking with the Dalai Lama?"

"It was one of the most memorable experiences of my life. I was first fearful and anxious, but the Dalai Lama has a way of comforting you. I was struck by his humility, kindness, and authenticity."

"Were you surprised by what he shared about his struggles with meditation?"

"I was totally taken aback. He freed me with his humility. His integrity gave me the courage and inspiration to go forward with my intuition. I believe the Dalai Lama is more about morality and wisdom than about contemplation."

"And that is missing in modern mindfulness?"

"I shouldn't say missing, but it's not emphasized enough. Also, some of the practices are not as relevant for our modern struggles and for how twenty-first-century brains are wired. When we fail a few times, we give up. That's a loss."

"What next?"

"The first tenet will help you know the three traps that constrain our minds. Before we go there I wish to share with you the story of a king who sought the counsel of a monk to learn how best to rule his kingdom. It has an important message. I don't know though if this is a true story or a made-up one."

"Doesn't matter as long as it is interesting!" Mike laughs.

Encouraged, I continue. "Once they settled across the royal table, the monk said to the king, 'I will share three ideas that'll help you. First, consider yourself a servant of your kingdom.'

"'Yep, that's what I do every single day. What else?' the king replied.

"'Treat everyone who depends on you as your close relative.'

"The king interrupted. 'Everyone here shares my ancestral lineage. I do that too. What else?'

"The monk kept his patience. 'Do not yield to greed, lust, or sloth.'

"'Sure, I wake up early and work hard all day, and nobody can call me greedy or lustful.'

"At this point, the monk stopped teaching and asked the king to order two empty cups and a teakettle. The monk first filled his cup with tea. Next, when filling the king's cup, he kept pouring until the tea started to spill on the table and onto the king's clothes.

"The king was infuriated. 'Please stop pouring the tea. My clothes are getting spoilt. Don't you see the cup is already full?'

"'That's the point,' the monk admonished. 'Your cup is already full. I can't teach you anything because you already know everything. Come back to me when your cup is empty.' Saying such, the monk left.

"What was the king lacking?" I ask Mike.

"Humility. He thought he knew everything."

"Precisely. Even though the king sought the monk's counsel, he wasn't really listening. Instead of reflecting deeply on the monk's words, the king was busy showing off his wisdom. He was ignorant, and he was ignorant about his ignorance. **It is easier to wake up someone who wants to awaken than to wake up a person who isn't aware he is asleep or is pretending to be sleeping**. The first step in acquiring wisdom is to recognize our ignorance, to know that we don't know, and accept it. That's where we are going now."

14

I Don't Know

The three most powerful and freeing words that have spurred every major advance known to mankind are "I don't know." The greatest progress in our understanding of the world happened when we truly realized the power of not knowing.[233]

The three most transformative words that can help you grow are: "I Don't Know".

PRIOR TO NOT KNOWING

Before we knew that we didn't know, we were practicing witchcraft and exorcism and ascribing our ills—ranging from smallpox and cholera to volcanic eruptions and earthquakes—to angry gods and evil spirits. During my training in biostatistics, I learned about a physician who experimented with a cutting-edge treatment of his time for yellow fever: bloodletting. When several of his patients didn't die, he confidently concluded that every patient with yellow fever ought to be treated with bloodletting. (George Washington died as a result of this treatment when more than half of his blood was removed in just a few hours to treat an infection.)

Our individual sampling of space and time is infinitely small compared to the totality of space and time. When we don't question and test the validity of our biases, we remain stuck in the dense fog of ignorance. We get trapped in the assumption that our inferences based on our biases and limited observation reflect reality. This combination of ignorance and confidence hurts us as individuals and everyone else whose lives we touch.

The first step to enter the gateway of wisdom is to realize the mantra "I don't know." Once you internalize this reality, you start finding better answers and, more importantly, start asking better questions.

Knowing you don't know starts the path toward knowing.

Once we collectively knew that we didn't know, we began our search, so we could know, at least a little. That search has a name: science.

Science is a systematic study of the truth. **Honest, unbiased scientific pursuit is truly a spiritual exercise.** Science and spirituality are one, both seeking the truth to better the human condition. Further, spiritual practices will be well served and more widely adopted if they are informed by science. Although philosophy formed the basis for many older traditions, **I believe in the modern times, science and philosophy together will do a better job to inform us about our place and purpose in the world**.

Science and spirituality have the same goal: the pursuit of truth.

PHILOSOPHY

The following three questions aren't fully answerable by any modern discipline: Who are we? Why are we here? What is this world? Throughout humankind's history, three disciplines have tried to answer these three questions: spirituality, science, and philosophy.

Philosophy is the pursuit of wisdom through deep thinking. I love deep thinking. But deep thoughts, despite their tremendous value, are still a reflection of the thinker's inner life, family, and culture as well as of the prevailing milieu of the world and the ambient causes of suffering. Humans couldn't think of the earth as round and tides as a product of lunar activity. They also couldn't envision how the heavens would look until the Hubble telescope opened our eyes.

As a result, over the millennia, philosophers have contradicted each other, have been proven wrong, and have condoned, in their time, practices that today we find despicable.

While science isn't foolproof by any measure, practices and lifestyles not backed by science are riskier. One of my patients with chronic lung disease told me that when he was in high school, his mother would keep four cigarettes in his lunch box so he could focus better after taking a few puffs. This was before we knew the adverse effects of smoking. If it wasn't for science, more than 50 percent of the people would still be smoking like they did in the early 1960s, when the surgeon general first issued the report linking smoking to cancer (in 1964).

Many despots were deep thinkers, but their twisted philosophies took millions of lives. Unfortunately, that history continues to repeat itself.

For all these reasons, philosophy is a body of knowledge that is relevant to its time, but it can't be called timeless wisdom.

A literal and rigid application of older philosophies in modern times can be counterproductive. Beliefs and biases, in older times, were enough to sway opinions, and if the individuals were charismatic and powerful, those opinions became guiding principles for large populations. Such beliefs and biases, if they emerged from fears and selfish interests, often weren't prosocial; many good people got hurt in the process. This phenomenon is less common now, although it hasn't been totally eliminated. We have improved because many of today's thoughts are refined by science, a different discipline that is bringing us closer to the truth. Deep thought informed by science is the way of the present and the future. But let's play ignorant for a moment and ask an important question: What is so special about science? Why science?

WHY SCIENCE?

Science offers a rare ability to pursue the truth, independent of ego. **Science is objective, is humble despite being direct, and in good hands, is largely unbiased.** Science is uniquely able to test its own veracity by checking whether it can predict objective phenomena of the observable world. Einstein became a household name not when he published his general theory of relativity in 1915 but when it was proven right by Sir Arthur Eddington through his observation of the bending of light during the solar eclipse of May 29, 1919.[234]

You are as likely to find modern-day sages in white coats in university labs as you are in places of worship.

These scientific sages drive our understanding of the world. We now rely on the Hubble telescope to spy on the stars, the Hadron Collider to tell us about the stuff our world is made of, advanced genomic sequencing to show us the Neanderthal hidden within us, and sophisticated brain scans to tell us what happens in our brains when we have compassionate thoughts.[235-237] We don't just imagine these details. We arrive at them with careful scientific experimentation.

Science also has a way of simplifying things and making them more compact. You can see the evolution of cell phone that felt like a large heavy brick in the 1970s to a sleek handheld gadget now, to see how hard work, intelligent insights and careful experimentation can transform an idea. I hope to keep science on our side as we explore the deeper recesses of our mind.

Luckily, a surge in science has paralleled a thirst for the truth. A twenty-first-century seeker won't be satisfied with ethereal and idealistic imaginations about the creation of the universe. Explanations like "the meeting of consciousness and energy effected the big bang because consciousness felt lonely and needed to love itself" would draw eye rolls from an audience of millennials.

Today's seeker finds comfort walking in step with science, particularly the aspects of science that teach us about who we are and what is our place in the world. I find experiments and observations in cosmology, evolutionary biology, anthropology, behavioral economics, quantum mechanics, and other related disciplines spiritually uplifting—as uplifting as the meditations of ancient sages and spiritual luminaries. (I must confess, however, that I don't always fully understand concepts like quantum entanglement or rank-dependent utility theory.)

None of the scientific disciplines tries to teach us the truth about the afterlife or claims to know the ultimate meaning of life. Science also doesn't postulate whether there is a true self within me, whether my thoughts are real or unreal, or what ultimately causes human suffering. These are all wonderful questions, but they are presently unanswerable in the scientific realm. We will lose a lot of people if we prioritize exploring these questions as the first step. Further, I have read stuff written by people and met a few people who claimed to know the answers to all these questions but offered mostly disappointing assertions based on their own limited world view. Talking to them, I was amazed to see how ignorance and overconfidence often coexist in the same space.

Ignorance and overconfidence often coexist in the same space.

I believe having a very strong view about questions that are unanswerable by science and letting ourselves be offended because others have a different view are markers of ignorance. Such ignorance not uncommonly seeds conflicts, some of them global.

I have, however, been informed by science that we sit in an unimaginably massive universe that produces over three hundred million new stars every single day (and that may be an underestimate).[238] Science has also taught me important details about our neural system. I know that many of us struggle with fatigued brains that spend the bulk of the day with wandering attention.[239, 240] Most people experience fear every single day, partly because of our brains' negativity bias, which starts at a very young age, as early as three months.[241-243] Nothing completely satisfies our brains for long because of our tendency to quickly adapt to all that we recently found spectacular.[244, 245] Our brain's pleasure center is a conflicted tool; it activates when we contemplate revenge and also when we experience compassionate thoughts and actions.[235, 246] True altruistic happiness activates anti-inflammatory genes, while predominantly hedonistic happiness activates pro-inflammatory genes.[247] Mindfulness that teaches this kind of insight to curious minds will stay relevant for a very long time.

ON AN UNSTOPPABLE JOURNEY

The pursuit of truth, bereft of individual ego or bias, has put us on an unstoppable journey to learn it. I hope we stay this way, aware of our ignorance, for a very long time, until we figure it all out, if we ever do. **We become more aware each day that we wake up humble and willing to accept our ignorance.** Insight in mindfulness *v*2 is thus insight into our ignorance, our preciousness, our finiteness, our vulnerabilities, and our suffering.

This brings us to a question: Why do we suffer? Buddha's journey started with the quest to understand human suffering and its solutions. If Buddha were to start his journey afresh in the twenty-first century, what would he find? I have no doubt he would explore twenty-first-century neuroscience as much as he explored the inner corners of his mind through meditation.

Although the three main questions—who am I, why am I here, and what is this world—aren't definitively answerable, science has made phenomenal progress in our understanding of the root causes of suffering. Let's listen to what science tells us about the origins of our suffering, information I believe every *Homo sapiens* should know.

15

Why We Suffer

As a child growing up, I heard the following allegory.

"I want peace and happiness," an old lady told a realized master.

"Remove the word *I*," he said with a smile. "What are you left with?"

"Want peace and happiness." She looked puzzled.

"Now remove the word *want*," he said. "What remains now?"

"Peace and happiness," she said.

"That's the point." He beamed. "Remove *I* (ego) and *want* (cravings), and you'll claim peace and happiness."

THE THREE FACTORS

We live in a world in which we change our jobs twelve to fifteen times or more, and run our lives with several dozen user IDs and passwords.[248, 249] More efficient farming, automation, industrialization, and better division of labor have freed countless minds to explore creative ideas. The resulting deluge of choices and the decisions we have to make every day creates complexity in our lives. Added to this complexity is the uncertainty of what the tomorrow might bring, and how long we get to live on this planet.

Our brain comforts in predictability and control. The combination of complexity and uncertainty is too much for our brain to handle. Further, our brain has several predispositions that trap us into negativity. This trio (Complexity + Uncertainty + Neural traps) in combination with our illnesses, losses, regrets and hurts, keep our attention in a trap. They are the proximate cause of our suffering. Our focus in this section and book is on emotional suffering, hence we will discuss further the three causes of emotional suffering: complexity, uncertainty, and neural traps.

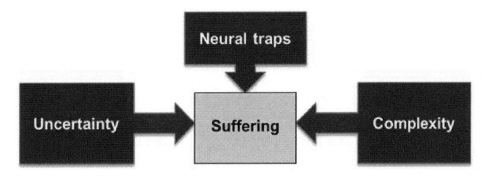

In chapters 16-31, I present to you the science and stories that will help you understand the root cause of our pain and suffering, and leverage that understanding to learn ways to better handle our pain and bypass our suffering.

We will spend most of our time together talking about the neural traps. One of the main goals of mindfulness *v2* is to help you understand the strengths and weaknesses of our brain, the most complex information processor known to mankind.

16

The Neural Traps

Of the twelve major organ systems that make up our body, the king that sits on the throne, in charge of it all, is the brain. The brain perceives, processes, and prescribes every conscious experience by collecting information, interpreting it, and generating output that maximizes our survival and success.

The specific behaviors that optimize these goals have changed over the millennia. Finding a buried juicy tuber would have been tremendously helpful for a tribal in the sub-Saharan desert. Discovering an undervalued stock or cryptocurrency is the skill of the day.

Our Stone Age ancestors evolved several neural traits that helped them survive the treacherous world. The same traits (that I like to call traps), particularly when out of balance, now predispose us to physical and emotional pain and, in some instances, early death.

> ***The neural traits that helped our ancestors survive are the very traits that produce angst and suffering today.***

After years of studying, I believe the following thirteen traps together conspire to capture and corrupt our thoughts, words, and actions. These traps cause us to be—

- Continually distracted (mind wandering)
- Drawn by negativity (negativity bias)
- Emotionally sensitive (emotional vulnerability)
- Stuck in our imaginations (imaginary feels real)
- Always comparing (compares and competes)
- Ineffective at suppressing our thoughts (the mental itch)
- Dissatisfied (programmed dissatisfaction)
- Addicted to short-term gratifications (deficits in self-regulation)
- Caught in the habit loop (the habit trap)
- Conflicted (to be or not to be)
- Vulnerable to dishonesty (liar, liar)

- Unforgiving (the unforgiveness instinct)
- Tired beyond imagination (the fatigued brain)

By supporting and strengthening each other, these thirteen traits have created a tremendous force that traps our inner hummingbird.

Friends, fasten your seat belts and put your seatbacks and tray tables in the upright and locked position, because we are now ready to take a sixty-page flight into a synthesis of science (particularly neuroscience) and stories that will help you understand why we struggle and what we can do to transcend our vulnerabilities. I suggest you savor and digest this information instead of rushing through it.

I hope the synthesis of the scientific studies that I will share with you next fascinates you as much as it fascinates me. It will help you understand our collective present state of being. This understanding is critical to freeing ourselves and cultivating more intentional brains—those of our choosing.

17

Neural Trap #1: Continually Distracted (Mind Wandering)

Are you concerned that you are becoming forgetful?
Do you struggle to keep your attention on your loved ones for more than ten seconds?
Have you tried to skip pages while reading a book to your child?
Do you arrive home some days with no recollection of anything you saw on the road?
Do you feel the urge to check your e-mails within a few seconds of waking up?
Do you multitask while brushing your teeth in the morning?

My brain has struggled with all of the above. If you answered yes to any, you likely have experienced excessive mind wandering.

The heaviest load we carry is invisible. It is the load of all the open files in our heads.

The heaviest load we carry are the invisible open files in our head.

Most of us walk around with hundreds of unresolved issues that suck up our attention.[250] You likely have more than a dozen user IDs and passwords. I'm certain you pay bills now to vendors that you wouldn't have recognized a decade ago. Unless you are very organized, perhaps you missed paying a bill or two last quarter (if it helps you feel any better, research shows roughly one in four don't pay bills on time.).[251] Life has become busy for all of us. We have a lot of stuff to think about. As a result, we spend at least half of our day in our heads—mind wandering.[240]

MIND WANDERING

Wandering attention that was focused on the outside world must have been very helpful for our ancestors—to continually screen for predators, quicksand, ditches, and more. Uncle Ad didn't have the luxury of getting lost in his mind because he had little dispensable attention (and mind wandering is typically associated with attention that is decoupled from the external world).[252, 253] With sidewalks paved and most predators either roaming the Serengeti or locked up in zoos, the same wandering attention is freed to meander inside our heads, jostling with hurts, regrets, concerns, fears, and all the open files.[240, 254]

Researchers have assigned a variety of names to this form of thinking: spontaneous thoughts, stimulus-independent thoughts, task-unrelated thoughts, fantasy, self-generated thoughts, undirected thoughts, unconscious thoughts, absentmindedness, zoning out, daydreaming, and more.[255] I will call it mind wandering (MW) in this book.

In my workshops, I have asked tens of thousands of participants what proportion of the day they spend with a wandering mind. The average answer is 60 to 80 percent. As you read these pages, about two to three billion people are walking around the planet with no idea where they are. One of the reasons this happens so often is that a network in the brain hosts our MW—the default network. The issue at hand is complex since the default network likely has many different roles and many different brain areas collaborate to generate MW. Nevertheless, it is safe to say that activity in the default network strongly correlates with MW.[256-259]

DISTRACTED (DEFAULT) VERSUS FOCUSED STATES

The name default network implies that it is the baseline we default to when we are not fully or intentionally engaged with our sensory experiences, either because we have a lot to think about, the experiences are uninteresting, or because such engagement isn't needed, as when we are driving on familiar roads, for example.[260, 261] Since we have grazed forests, chased away wild beasts, and built safer neighborhoods, a state of distraction has become the default state of our brains.

Your brain's undistracted (focused) state is engaged when you find something worthy of your attention.[254] Four-year-olds are immersed in the world; everything is novel to them. They find novelty because they seek novelty. That's one reason they're happy. But as we grow up, we seek safety and get easily bored as things become familiar and loved ones become borderline boring. **Our brain dreads getting bored and will do anything to get out of boredom.** In fact, in a research study, investigators found that people would rather give themselves painful electric shocks than just sit and get bored.[262] In a state of boredom, we check out when we can be safe without paying full attention.

We dread boredom. People would rather give themselves electric shock than just sit and get bored!

In such a state, you'll find little reason to attend to the world unless something is truly engaging. The consequence is increased time spent MW with resulting attention lapses.[263] This is a catch-22 because the more time you spend MW, the stronger the brain networks that host MW. **Unlike our shoes and sandals, which wear out with repeated use, brain networks become stronger with repeated use.**[264, 265] Over time, MW becomes a way of life.

Our physical brain isn't that smart. When you use a certain network, the brain says, "Aha! My owner wants to use this network. Let me make it stronger." As a result of MW strengthening the MW apparatus (the basis for which is neuroplasticity—our brain's ability to change with experience), people get trapped in their heads. This trap has caught many of us. Later we will talk about how we can free ourselves using the same neuroplasticity that got us handcuffed.[266]

The more you use a brain network, the stronger it gets.

UNHAPPY WANDERER

This mental trap increases negative emotions. Research shows **we're less happy when we mind wander than when we have an intentional presence**. Further, the less happy we are, the more our minds wander, creating a circular loop.[267] Emerging research has connected abnormalities in default-network activity and connectivity with increased symptoms of depression,[268-270] anxiety,[271-273] posttraumatic stress disorder,[274-276] fatigue,[277, 278] chronic pain,[279, 280] insomnia,[281-283] and even dementia.[284-287] I have no doubt as we do more research, this list will grow longer.

Excessive MW has also been associated with memory lapses, poor attention, lower reading comprehension, worse academic performance, and even lower IQ and SAT scores.[255, 288, 289] In an interesting study, researchers monitored brain activity and errors while participants performed a task.[290] Just by looking at the brain scans, researchers could predict when the errors would happen. About thirty seconds before the error, the brain scans showed increased activation of the default network and lower activity in the task-focused network. This is important to know for high-risk repetitive jobs, in which the cost of error is prohibitive. You wouldn't want a distracted neurosurgeon, airline pilot, train engineer, or Oscars host.

Wandering mind is an unhappy and unproductive mind.

DESIGNED AS A WANDERER

You might be asking yourself how we can mind wander while doing complex things like driving or assembling a toy or how professionals like dentists or auto mechanics can mind wander while doing a skilled job. The answer is simple. When people become good at their trade, the cerebral real estate they need to do that work becomes minimal, particularly for repetitive work like tooth cleaning. Here is how the brain divides its labor:

- Automatic activities that need little effort (like loading a dishwasher while listening to music) are hosted by distinct brain areas. Thus, your brain can run these parallel operations easily (because it has two different assigned areas, like two different rooms to host two parties).
- Activities that are effortful are hosted by strongly overlapping brain areas. The two activities crowd the same network, bumping into each other. That is the reason your brain can't run these operations simultaneously.[291] Try planning your retirement in your head while skiing for the first time. You will likely fail at both.

Because you have finite resources for intentional attention, you can't run two engaging simultaneous activities and perform well at both. Further, research shows that while MW, your brain can still attend to unusual sensory events (such as a car swerving into your lane).[292] This is the reason you can arrive safely at home without remembering anything you saw on the road.

The brain has limited resources to run tasks that need conscious attention.

(It took me a few readings of the research to understand the above concepts. So feel free to read it one more time if you struggled with fully understanding in the first read.)

DEFAULT ISN'T ALL BAD

Now for the contrarian view. You might say, "I need my MW. It makes me creative." And you are right. There is reason why the brain's default activity has been preserved. Let's dig a little deeper.

MW can be of three types. So far, we have talked about the MW that occurs because of weak attention and excessive world demands (referred to as cognitive-control failure). This is often associated with negative emotions, inattention, and all the adverse effects noted above. Such MW is more likely to be focused on the past.

The second, **more positive form of MW is called positive constructive daydreaming**. Positive constructive daydreaming is associated with a rich mental life. It gives relief from boredom, helps with constructive planning and creativity, provides breaks from external tasks, and correlates with an ability to delay gratification.[252, 293] Such MW is more likely to be focused on the future. It allows us to connect the past with the future, helping us plan and rehearse possible future scenarios. Creativity and productive problem-focused thinking is associated with good cooperation and coordination between the focused (executive and salience networks) and default areas of the brain.[294-297]

Thus, MW is not all bad, particularly when it's adaptive wandering that connects past with future and helps you plan and rehearse for what is to come.[298] It helps you think deeper thoughts, develop a wider perspective, derive meaning, cultivate compassion, think of others, and develop moral reasoning.

A third, also helpful form of MW is intentional wandering. Here you choose what to think based on your deeper values. You develop newer insights and travel into past and future to connect them both, find deeper meaning, and thus understand the world. For this to happen, you should be able to free your brain from needing to attend to the world (i.e. locate yourself in a safe place, and away from responsibilities and deadlines).[299] It is a form of meditation.

The ability to intentionally switch between internal and external streams of consciousness is a capacity you can build. Such thinking involves the cooperation of multiple networks in the brain.[300]

I dream of a day when the focused (hosted by the executive and salience networks) and default (hosted by the default network) modes of our brains collaborate and cooperate all day long, guided by gratitude and compassion. I have no doubt that will happen someday, sooner than we all believe. Unfortunately, presently, because of our ability to decouple our attention from the outside world and a very complex inner world, we spend the bulk of the day inside our heads with wandering attention.

OUR KIDS LOSE

Our kids are the biggest losers because of our wandering minds. When we live our lives a mile wide and an inch deep, we barely register the moments as our kids walk out of the crib and transform into grown-ups ready for college. When we don't nurture our moments with our partners, they don't find the energy to be fully present for the family.

Our children are the biggest losers when we have weak attention.

When we check out, our kids check out. They glue themselves to screens. They grow up with weak attention. Their emotional intelligence is underdeveloped. They have poor inhibitory control and are more vulnerable to eating dysregulation, addictions, learning disabilities, and more. I have met more than a few parents who have lost their kids to suicide, regretting that they hadn't taken the time to talk about deeper issues. Perhaps they would have heard the cry sooner, when the pain was reversible.

With lack of attention, our memories get foggy, not in our seventies or eighties but in our thirties, forties, and fifties. (Weak memory is more often because of weak attention than dementia.) The worst form of MW is when someone forgets a toddler in a hot car. Such a tragedy happens once about every ten days, and not just to negligent parents; it also happens to the kindest, most caring ones.[301] Some published reports suggest that hot car deaths are on the rise. What could be a sadder fact to share?

ESCAPE THE DEFAULT TRAP

We got into this default trap not by choice but as an unintended consequence of our technological and financial success. We need to get out of this trap, or we will squander the benefit of all our hard work. Mindfulness *v2* strives to get us out of this trap.

The problem is that when we are mind wandering, we're seldom aware that we are doing it. We register few conscious memorable moments in this state. Hence, the first step is to become aware of how much your mind wanders by understanding the science behind our neural traps.

The second step is to cultivate intentionality, so you live most of the day guided by your core values instead of passively drifting in a partially aware state.

We shouldn't fight battles we can't win. Just as the ocean has tidal waves, our minds have flows of thoughts. We can't stop those flows. But we can tame and harness them. Our goal is to avoid the tsunami of negative thinking and think more purposeful, productive and positive thoughts. (If your blood pressure is 160/100, you won't decide to decrease it to 0/0. Reducing it only by 10 to 15 percent will get you to the desired target. That is our goal: not to eliminate MW but to decrease it by just 10 to 15 percent. That will be enough.)

We don't need to stop mind wandering. Just decrease the wanderings by 10 to 20 percent.

Intentionality, the key skill necessary to decrease MW, makes sure your experience is governed by your values and not by external contingencies or automatic actions. Those intentional moments enlist cooperation from multiple brain networks so that you consider the past, plan for the future, think of your values, as you engage with the present.

In essence, the key question is this: **Are you thinking your thoughts, or is thinking happening to you? In most situations, the former is healthier and the latter not as much.**[302] Our goal is to preserve the healthiest aspects of MW, which help us with future planning and creativity, while minimizing errors, absentmindedness, and inattention.[289]

When such intentionality becomes a habit, a transformed mind will emerge that spontaneously thinks constructive, creative positive thoughts, visits past and future with ease, pays deeper attention to the world, and flexibly switches between different domains, thus carving out a fulfilling life for self and others.

We could overcome excessive, uncontrolled, spontaneous mind wandering if this were our only neural trap. Unfortunately, that isn't the case. Our weak, wandering attention meets the next neural trap, the negativity bias, which mires us deeper in dirt instead of prompting us to admire the lilies.

18

Neural Trap #2: Drawn by Negativity (Negativity Bias)

IT'S ALL BAD

We have been hurt. We have been hurt by those we knew could hurt us: the greedy, the violent, the envious, the angry, and the vengeful. We have also been hurt by those we trusted to love and care for us: the spiritual, the influential, caregivers, loved ones, friends, and even the meek and the vulnerable. **Research shows everyday aggression is less likely from strangers and more likely from the people closest to us.**[303]

The people most likely to hurt us are
the ones closest to us.

❧

Aggression can be direct, such as yelling and hitting, or indirect, such as spreading rumors or breaking someone's favorite possession. Aggression can be sinister. High-school shootings; money laundering after major tragedies; blatant lies under oath; abusive parents, spouses, or grandparents; and predatory clergy—once we see all this, we stop trusting anyone. We begin to paint the world with a dark brush and see dishonesty, greed, and selfishness as the norm.

This is compounded by the fact that **trust in our society is at an all-time low**. A full 82 percent of us do not trust big business, 80 percent do not trust newspapers, and 71 percent do not trust the medical system. Trust in the US Congress is down to 8 percent.[179, 304]

We are constantly surrounded by information about whom we shouldn't trust. And that includes everybody. I have no doubt that just as you are part of one person's in-group, you are also part of another person's out-group. A significant proportion of our worry relates to the safety and well-being of our children. The young in our society run a high risk of being victims of violent crime.[305]

We worry not because we want to but because we have to. Recently, while visiting one local school, I saw a sign that read, "Safety is our first priority." Although the safety focus is appropriate, the need to emphasize that safety from violent crimes instead of education is the first priority in places of learning should make us pause and ask, "Where did we go wrong?" I hope we do not reach a point where, as a physician, I have to think about protecting patients from violent crimes in the hospital as my first priority. This isn't far from the experience of many physicians in war-torn parts of the world.

IT'S NOT THAT BAD

The world, however, hasn't suddenly become bad. In fact, by many measures, the world is much safer, almost the safest it has ever been. There has never been a safer, more secure time to be a kid in America.[306, 307]

So where is the disconnect? Our perception is erroneous because our awareness of the mishaps has dramatically increased. We have developed a constant awareness of the happenings of the entire globe. Most likely, as you are reading this book, you are connected with the world by emails, phone calls, text messaging, and a few social media accounts. News, particularly bad news can come from any of these sources. Likely, you monitor your accounts fairly frequently, to make sure nothing new and concerning (or exciting) needs attention. This is your attention in the prey mode: constantly monitoring the world for inauspicious signals. How can you relax and be in the moment?

Further, we add about two hundred thousand babies to the world's population every day; the world is the most populous it has ever been. With so many of us walking on the planet, it is highly likely that somewhere in the world, at least a few people are thinking destructive thoughts right at this moment.

Research shows that threats caused by humans create much more fear than natural disasters.[308] This particularly applies for threats such as terrorism or robbery. Even the stock market reacts more negatively to manufactured disasters than to natural ones.[309] Given that manufactured events occupy headline news almost every day, spending even a little time with the media can unnerve our hearts and brains.

Intentional threats caused by humans cause greater angst than natural disasters.

One reason for the fear of intentional threats is their unlimited potential. Because of the widespread and sometimes thoughtless dissemination of technology, including our ability to harness the energy of the atom, own extremely destructive weapons, encrypt and mass communicate a sinister message, and more, a single person with destructive thoughts can hurt a large number of people. Tools and technology do not pay attention to the emotional state or maturity of the person owning them. Every few weeks I hear about a child who mistakenly unloaded a gun on himself or herself, or someone else.

For all the above reasons, even though we live longer and are more prosperous than we have ever been, we feel extremely insecure.[308, 310] (Our longevity numbers, however, may be cracking. Data just published as this book was about to go to print showed that for two years in a row now, our longevity, for the first time in several decades, has shown a slight downward trend.)[311, 311b]

The result of this insecurity is excessive stress. **About a third of us are doing well, a third are struggling, and a third are drowning in stress.**[312, 313] No wonder WHO declared stress to be the "global health epidemic of the 21st century." At work, about 80 percent of professionals experience significant work-related stress that adversely affects their health, engagement, and loyalty.[2, 314]

The above numbers may be a conservative estimate because many of us are stressed but aren't aware of how stressed we are until we feel better. A considerable number suffer in silence. For example, of the people with severe depressive symptoms, two out of three (65 percent) do not receive help from mental-health professionals, partly because they sulk alone in a quiet corner, too fatigued and too mortified to seek help.[315, 316]

Two out of three people with depression do not get the help they need.

SNAKE VERSUS BLENDER

The stressed brain is an active participant in perpetuating the negative. The dark input goes into a brain that selectively attends to the imperfect and the threatening. For example, research shows that the brain sees a snake much sooner than it sees a blender and remembers more details about the snake than the blender.[317] Infants start preferentially looking at a fearful face (compared to a neutral face) by the time they are seven months old.[318, 319]

The amygdala, our fear-processing center, constantly scans sensory input for the threatening.[320-322] The amygdala is busy protecting not only your physical body but also your emotional body (I will return to this shortly). It is the amygdala's job, along with a few other areas in the brain, to keep you safe and alive.[323] If it experiences ongoing, intense emotional or physical hurts (such as in a crime-prone neighborhood or a war zone), it becomes more active and better networked, a change that predisposes our veterans to posttraumatic stress disorder (PTSD), a severe form of anxiety.[324, 325] **Many veterans who come back with emotional injuries are hurt as badly as or far worse than those who come back emotionally intact but physically injured.** Both kinds of injuries are real—the visible (physical) and the invisible (emotional).

NEGATIVE VELCRO

Further, negative events (associated with threat or disgust) stick in our heads much longer, as though we have Velcro that attracts them.[326-328] Pause for a second and try to remember the last time you saw a police car. Perhaps it was sometime this week. But do you remember seeing a red Chevy? Probably not (unless you own one). You remember the police car because at that moment your heart rate went up from, let's say, seventy-two to eighty-four. **The brain more often remembers moments when your heart accelerates (counting out physical workouts of course).** This is because during these moments the brain tells itself, "I better remember this event or person because this information might protect me from a future threat." The brain releases CRH, norepinephrine, and other chemicals that increase the memory of the moment.

Similarly, compared with accolades, insults stick deeper and stay longer. Go back twenty years and recall the names of every person who made you feel small. Perhaps you can create that list pretty quickly. Kids tell me it is much easier to make a list of whom not to invite to a birthday party than whom to invite.

Moments of vulnerability and people who make us feel unworthy occupy a disproportionate real estate in our head.

A SILLY QUESTION

Let's say you step on a nail. What is your initial response—do you withdraw your foot or dig deeper? I suppose that is a silly question. Now let's say you turn on the television and see the news of a terrorist attack. What is your response—do you pull yourself away or try to uncover all the details? You uncover the details, don't you? Even if the event happened thousands of miles away. See how the senses and the mind work differently? Our senses withdraw from the pain; our mind goes toward the pain. Both are trying to protect you. Senses do a good job of it; the mind often overshoots.

Our sensory system is designed to withdraw from pain; our mind is designed to go deeper into pain.

This is a neural trap, which starts with the rational need to be safe but mires us in a whirlpool of negativity and drains away happiness. A good reminder here is that happier people don't have more positive and fewer negative events; they pay more attention to positive events and less to negative ones.

Unfortunately, however, research shows that by design, the negative information sticks like superglue in our brain. Negative feedback is more difficult to forget than is positive feedback; faces that look startled draw greater attention than do calm, happy ones; and losses hurt more than gains feel good.[328] These predispositions start even before we begin to crawl.[241, 242, 329]

Some researchers have actually quantified our negativity bias. They report that it takes three units of positive to neutralize one unit of negative.[330, 331] As an example, in a relationship, you want to hear at least three positives to be able to absorb one negative. Five is even better than three.[332]

This concept has been challenged by other researchers, not the basic premise of the desirability of greater positivity in life but the idea of confining it to rigid equations and specific ratios.[333, 334]

ANOTHER CATCH-22

Over time, the brain sculpts itself around the most attended input. When the brain repeatedly sees threats, its fear circuits become stronger because it assumes it will preferentially need these circuits.[335] **Personal hurts multiply when we revisit them too often; personal hurts heal when we attend to others who are hurting.**

This is another catch-22: strong fear circuits increase your threat perception; increased threat perception strengthens the fear circuits. Do you see how we can get stuck experiencing the shady side of life? **It is akin to living in a beautiful home but spending all your time in the dark attic full of spiders and dirt and not experiencing the joy of the kitchen, the living room, and the bedroom. It is a tremendous missed**

opportunity for a species that has worked so hard to build this beautiful world. Constantly living in fear, with the resulting activity in our fear center (amygdala), predisposes us to inflammation and risk of heart attack and stroke.[336] Every input that reminds us of our insecurities matters.

I NEED MY FEAR

You might be thinking that you need your negativity bias and threat focus to be safe. And I agree with that. One patient, labeled SM, who damaged both her amygdalae, has been known to play with spiders and snakes and has no fear of visiting haunted houses that would evoke fear in most.[337] She has put herself in situations in which she could have been seriously injured or killed.

You don't swim with alligators or jump into a polar-bear enclosure, because you have a healthy amygdala. We need our amygdala, but we don't need brains that are ruled by the amygdala. **We don't need our amygdala to be so busy protecting our emotional body that we forget to sing the song of our life worried someone might laugh at us.** You want to think about the people who could hurt you, **but don't let someone who shouldn't be in the story of your life write more than a line. Certainly, do not let that person write the title of your story.**

Don't let someone who shouldn't be in the story of your life, write the title of your story.

༺

We need to modulate our fears and keep them rational so we don't spend our entire lives just trying to be safe. Keeping rational fears and, once we secure our safety, experiencing uplifting emotions and motivation along with the positive perceptions of others, is key to success, long-term well-being, and a fulfilled life. **Once we shed the fear of negative emotions we start experiencing authentic positive emotions.**

Consider negative thoughts to be a waste product of the brain's activity. Unlike every other system in the body, we have no system to excrete the negative thoughts. They pile up, contaminating our inner environment. Hence the need to develop a discipline to identify and neutralize them with the timeless principles of gratitude, compassion, meaning, and forgiveness. (In chapter 80, I will share with you the gist of a structured approach that I and my colleagues have found successful in integrating these principles in daily life.)

—⚜—

Our negativity bias is fed and fueled by four powerful predispositions: emotional sensitivity, imagination, comparison, and the paradox of thought suppression.

19

Neural Trap #3: Emotionally Sensitive (Emotional Vulnerability)

HURTS GALORE

I started off being allergic to books. My childhood was all about soccer, cricket, and hockey. Physical hurts were an everyday event. Most days I was nursing a cut, scratch, bruise, or sprain. Every physical injury has healed and is all but forgotten. The few I remember were particularly bad (for instance, my Achilles tendon avulsed when it got jammed in a bicycle wheel that was running at thirty miles per hour on a downslope). But the details are foggy and the healed scars are largely pain-free. In contrast, the scars carved out by previous emotional hurts endure; some are still painful.

I vividly remember my math teacher thrashing me for not doing my homework (I don't remember the physical pain as much as I remember the humiliation in front of the entire class). I remember slipping and falling from my scooter in front of a large crowd (I quickly got up and drove a mile farther, away from anyone who had seen the fall, before taking stock of my cuts and bruises). I remember being teased by fellow students for refusing to say curse words. I remember being called an introvert. I remember the day I discovered my best friend's desire to see me fail. I carry countless memories of feeling helpless while trying to save my patients. It has taken years of labor to tone down my emotional sensitivity. I suppose this is true for you too. Recently, neuroscience has validated our collective experience. **Human brains light up as strongly and in the same places for emotional hurts as they do for physical hurts.**[338]

EMOTIONAL PAIN = PHYSICAL PAIN

Pain comes in various shapes, sizes, and colors. The brain economizes by hosting a variety of physical pains in the same area. Paper cut and stubbed toe activate the same pain matrix. Similarly, emotional pains of different kinds, such as social rejection and the emotional aspects of back pain, also share overlapping areas.[339]

But here is the surprise: our brains make less of a distinction between physical and emotional pain than we do. Many areas that activate with physical pain also activate with emotional pain.

Thus, the scans of those in physical pain and those suffering from social rejection look strikingly similar. **Emotional hurts have hijacked the brain pathways that were designed to host physical injury.**

Emotional and physical hurts activate the same areas of the brain.

Rejection truly hurts. This may be the biological reason that physical pain flares up when patients experience excessive stress.[340-344] Although some researchers have contested these findings,[345, 346] an interesting study provides strong evidence that supports the connection between physical and emotional pain.

In this study, researchers gave participants either acetaminophen (the active ingredient in Tylenol) or a placebo for three weeks. **Researchers found that acetaminophen decreased reports of social pain and decreased brain changes associated with social rejection.**[347] In other words, acetaminophen decreased the emotional pain. I haven't yet taken Tylenol when my seven-year-old thinks less of me for not making a perfect pony tail; perhaps I should!

Since the senses forget but the mind remembers, the memory of emotional injury lasts longer than that of physical injury. This is the reason we spend more time and resources these days protecting our emotional bodies than our physical bodies.

We spend greater energy protecting our emotional body than our physical body.

This is also true for young children; repeated yelling leaves lasting wounds on children's psyches. Research shows that yelling and expressing disappointment increase children's risk of aggression symptoms.[348] **Forces that hurt the heart are stronger than ones that break a bone.** A tree that resists sixty-mile-per-hour winds can become hollow when attacked from the inside by wood beetles.

Another reason for the nuisance of emotional hurt is the relative frequency. Look back at your previous ten years. Have you cried more from emotional hurts or physical hurts? I have asked this question countless times in my workshops. People uniformly report more emotional pain than physical pain.

EMOTIONAL PIRANHAS

It is rare to experience only an occasional emotional hurt. Commonly, we experience multiple negative emotions every day, from either real or imaginary events. These are like emotional piranhas, which alone may be inconsequential but in a school, are deadly. Anyone who has hurt you in the past and hasn't been forgiven continues to hurt you again and again.

Our pain fibers forget the hurt of a broken bone once the bone heals. But our emotional circuits keep simmering in response to the memory. With so many connections and our innate drive to compete and judge, we experience an emotional hit-and-run every month, if not every week or every day.

Although we need our negative emotions to experience the full range of our humanity and to be safe, we don't need a daily dose of intense negative emotions or a constant feeling of vulnerability. The repeated ricocheting of painful memories in our emotional circuits crowds us with hurtful feelings even on days we aren't injured.

We also don't need to feel guilty about our negative emotions or to carry a desire to always be positive. That is also unreal and undesirable. **Excessive positive thinking can be negative.**[349]

Instead, we can try to find ways to accept, flow with, and learn from our negative emotions; discover meaning in them; and thus, experience a potpourri of positive and some negative emotions. **I am OK with encountering an occasional piranha as long as I am playing mostly with clown fish.**

YOUR INJURY IS MINE

If, by a stroke of luck, you have escaped personal physical and emotional injury in your life, there is one more trap waiting for you. **The brain can't tell the difference between self-injury and injury to others, particularly those we care about and strive to protect.** Every loving parent of a sick child would rather be personally sick than see his or her child hurting. Three of my own hearts beat outside my physical body—one is of my wife and the other two of our two daughters.

In a research study, investigators found that areas of the brain that respond to the emotional experience of pain (the anterior insula and part of the anterior cingulate cortex) were activated not only when volunteers experienced a painful stimulus but also when they saw a signal indicating that their loved one received the same painful stimulus.[350] Further, your close loved one's injury feels more painful than your own injury.[351] These findings have now been replicated in multiple studies.[352] Even people who are born with a rare disorder of insensitivity to personal physical pain feel other people's pain.[353]

> *Our brain can't tell personal hurts from the hurts of those closest to us. Both the hurts activate the same brain areas.*

Research further shows that the more intensely we see the other person's pain, particularly in facial expressions, the greater the activation of our own pain networks.[354] Since children are masters of overreaction (at least from an adult's perspective), seeing them in pain will activate our pain network more than seeing a stoic adult hurting. This is one of the reasons that your child going through a difficult medical experience feels worse than your own illness. Turning your head the other way won't help, since hearing someone's pain response has a similar effect as seeing it.[355]

If you overdose on empathy, all of this can wreak havoc on your emotional well-being. The more vulnerable your loved ones are, the more vulnerable you feel. This is the basis of the old saying that you are as happy as your saddest child.

There is hope. Although you can't stop your pain network from activating with personal or empathic pain, you can train another part of the brain—your prefrontal cortex—to help cool the embers. Research shows that in people experiencing social pain, the greater the activation of their prefrontal cortex, the lower their personal distress.[356] Fortunately, we now know of several activities that trigger the prefrontal cortex, ideas that we will explore in the coming chapters and sections.

Let's summarize what we have discussed so far. **We spend most of the day with superficial wandering attention, inflate the negative, can't tell emotional from physical pain, feel others' pain as though it were our own, and can't tell the difference between what's imaginary and what's real.** This can help or hurt us based on where we direct our imagination, as we shall see next. If you are already wondering about the depth of our human imperfections, let me remind you that so far, we have covered only the first three neural traps!

20

Neural Trap #4: Stuck in Our Imaginations (Imaginary Feels Real)

MESSED UP IN MY HEAD

In my early thirties, I had my first heart attack. Since then I have had several small attacks but fortunately have done well. I have also had at least three cancers. Our house has burned down a few times, and I have been mugged twice. All of this is in my head. None of it actually happened; I have only imagined these mishaps. **My mind knows how to be miserable.**

Thankfully, most of my worst experiences have been in my imagination, but that hasn't helped my emotional health or happiness. This is because of the fourth neural trap: **when thinking about an event, the areas of the brain that activate are the same ones that light up when the event actually happens**.

For your brain, the imaginary is real.

This can help, for example, in training for piano; imagining playing the notes activates similar brain areas as those activated when playing the notes.[357] Athletes and patients alike use this phenomenon. For example, in patients with stroke, research shows that imagining motor activity improves recovery.[358] In patients with chronic pain, imagining pain-free movements can decrease pain and disability and improve quality of life.[359] Guided imagery is a simple and effective tool to decrease stress, fatigue, pain, and depressive symptoms in a variety of settings.[360-362] Visualizing comforting sights can even improve wound healing.[363]

Our creativity and innovation depend on our imaginations. Human imagination is largely the reason that our dinner menu is so varied and includes animals ten or a hundred or thousand times our size instead of us being their menu. But when our imaginations are taken to the dark side, they create and perpetuate suffering.

HURTFUL IMAGINATIONS

Just as thinking of a loved one can decrease the stress response,[364] traumatic imagery can worsen mood, increase anxiety, and change metabolism in the brain.[365] The brain hurts not just on feeling a needle pierce the skin but on seeing a needle pierce the skin in a virtual setting.[366]

Words are equally hurtful. Thinking about positive and negative words is powerful; both activate the brain's emotional centers, but negative words uniquely activate the pain-processing areas.[367] Although pain-related images, descriptions of pain, and environmental cues related to pain all reliably activate the pain matrix in the brain, even the processing of pain-related words is enough to activate this matrix.[368]

All these changes are more prominent if you already have ongoing stress or a mental-health issue. For example, anticipating that you'll see spiders and snakes causes greater activation of the insula (the area of the brain that processes negative anticipatory emotions) in anxiety-prone patients than in those with no anxiety.[369] Terrorist events have a much greater impact on patients with mental-health disorders than on those with no mental-health issues.[370]

Our imaginations work in collaboration with the world around us. Events happening around us have a tremendous impact on our brain processes, even during sleep. For example, the attack on 9/11 changed the contents of people's dreams.[371, 372] Physical attacks, sexual assaults, major fires, and other such adverse events also change our dreams; in general, the stronger the emotion, the greater its impact on the movie we see while sleeping.[373] Perhaps evolution has conserved this movie so we can imagine threats, simulate a response, and thus be better prepared (called the threat-simulation theory).[374]

But constantly dwelling on threats can be counterproductive when you want to enjoy restorative sleep. Many of these imaginations are irrational and provide minimal to no help for our threat preparedness.[375] Such experiences may have helped us adapt in older times, but now they worsen sleep and adversely affect daily life, predisposing us to greater psychological suffering.[376, 377]

Even pleasurable fantasies often aren't driven by altruism. Search online for "what are our commonest fantasies" and see the results. Many fantasies are healthy. Perhaps we wouldn't have five babies born every second on our planet if fantasies were totally absent. But fantasies in a troubled mind can lead to antisocial behavior or even heinous crimes.[378, 379] Before we start calling names, however, we should recognize that we all have had fantasies that we would rather not own. How comfortable would you be with having all your desires and fantasies broadcast on a billboard? I would be embarrassed if the world knew all my thoughts.

Most humans experience embarrassing imaginations. Stop them at source, work on your outlook, and most definitely, don't act on them.

LET'S BE REALISTIC

I wish I could live a passionate, successful life and keep everyone safe without swimming in embarrassing imaginings. I cannot. I wish I could stop judging, completely let go of envy, experience no unhealthy wants, and avoid overreacting to irrational fears, but I can't help it. Given that my mind is mired in the drive to eat, avoid being eaten, and reproduce, my imaginations and dreams revolve around these three goals. These are essential goals for survival serving the animal within me (and all of us). But if life served only these instinctive goals, then we would live like better-clad chimpanzees, not the most evolved species to have ever roamed the earth.

Most of us struggle with keeping in check our fantasies that serve these essential goals. And many fail. If that were not so, pornography, infidelity, and pedophilia would not be well-recognized words. A casual search of the Internet will give you more links to these words than to altruism.

Thus, as with many of the brain's other capabilities, **imagination is a double-edged sword**. I wish we could create an Archimedes, Newton, and Einstein in every generation without creating despots, tyrants, and abusers. But we can't if we let our imaginations take a free ride.

THE RIGHT TETHER

Given our strong tendency for spontaneous mind wandering, innate negativity bias, and emotional sensitivity, we will not all wake up tomorrow with positive thoughts and healthy imaginations. We will always have a few minds that are imaginative, brilliant, selfish, and cruel all at the same time, resulting in effective tyrants supported by their minions of like-minded opportunists. Given the right (or wrong) set of conditions, they will stir up so much dust that we will all lose hope. But nothing is constant except change. **Love and compassion are the most powerful forces, and they will eventually prevail.** We can access these forces by tethering our imaginations to the wisdom that is innate to us: our conscience.

The more we tether our imaginations to our conscience, the more creative and prosocial our thinking. This transformation won't happen spontaneously. Intentionality—the power to intentionally refocus your imagination toward a higher meaning—is important.

> *When you tether your imaginations with your conscience, your thoughts,*
> *words and actions serve greater prosocial purpose.*

The smartest minds on the planet shouldn't be thinking about how to get you to click ads or backdate options.[380] They should focus on how to eliminate teenage suicide and drug abuse and how to raise happier, more resilient kids. We need to prioritize kindness and prosocial thinking. Building self-driving cars, living to age 120, developing molecular recycling, printing 3-D organs, and uploading our brains into a computer won't help us unless we build our world around integrity and kindness.[381] **Technology that doesn't deepen relationships and kindness hurts us in the long term. Every entrepreneur's brain needs a heart.**

Without kindness and integrity, in a few decades we might have close to ten billion people living long lives on a hot, crowded, fuel-deprived, and happiness-starved planet. That will be sad.

We need to create a society in which dishonesty surprises us—a society in which we do good for the sake of good and are kind for the sake of kindness, not because it helps us bulk up our CVs so we can get into a better college or get rich and famous and gain access to more beautiful partners. Such progress will require that we focus on our deeper core values, allow our consciences to speak, and stop unhealthy comparisons.

This brings us to the fifth neural trap of mindfulness *v2*: our tendency to compare. **Imagination flies on the wings of comparison.**

21

Neural Trap #5: Always Comparing (Compares and Competes)

My wife and I witness an entertaining scene playing out at our home every day. Sia, our seven-year-old, intensely competes with Gauri, our thirteen-year-old. If Gauri has a round white plate for dinner, that's what Sia wants. If Gauri takes a pink plastic fork with a broken tip, Sia wants a pink plastic fork, and its tip had better be broken. Hair clips, pens, shoes, jackets, dresses—everything has to be the same as her older sister. At Sia's age this seems endearing, but it won't be if it continues into adulthood.

Some comparisons are helpful. The golden rule of diagnosis in medicine is comparison. Comparing test results with the expected norm has served me well in making diagnoses and planning treatment. A swollen knee looks clearly swollen when compared to the normal knee. But such comparison is valid only for entities that are expected to be similar. Over the years, I have realized that I've overgeneralized this rule.

INSTINCT TO COMPETE

When I meet other people, I instinctively compare their success or attractiveness with mine. I feel threatened by those who, in my mind, score higher than I do. I struggle with feeling proud of those who at one point were my colleagues or classmates but now are more accomplished. I don't want to hear or think about them (there is a name for it—envy). Recently a friend of mine got a much-desired promotion with a hefty raise. Nonetheless, I found him gloomy. His colleague had gotten a bigger raise.

We usually compete with a limited number of people we define as competitors. They often start at the same or lower level as we do. I wouldn't care if the entire world got richer than me, but Adam, my schoolmate? His success breaks my heart. I don't think of the hard work he put in. Sometimes, unwillingly, I do see his efforts, but only as a way to escape from the prison of despair that I put myself in with the bars of comparison. Let's see what science says about these predispositions.

In an interactive game of chance in which participants could win or lose money, those who lost money were actually happier if their competitors lost more money than they did. On brain scans, the reward area (the ventral striatum) of their brains became much more active when information about their competitor's loss was added, to the point that the loss looked like actual gain. Conversely, gaining money did little to increase their happiness once they knew that a competitor had gained more money.[382] This is the classic demonstration of social-comparison theory, which describes how we compare ourselves with others.[383]

MISERABLE COMPARING

We compare ourselves with others and compete in every imaginable domain: physical attractiveness, strength, intelligence, the looks of our partners, success (fame, money, meaning), children, and more. The brain doesn't have just one comparison center. Depending on the specifics, different areas activate. For example, in several interesting studies, researchers evaluated comparisons made based on judgments about moral beauty versus physical beauty. Some brain areas showed shared activation for both the judgments, but moral-beauty judgments activated additional areas of the brain.[384, 385] In another study, when a comparison was made between two very different characteristics, such as height and intelligence, different areas of the brain were activated.[386] Our instinct to compare is deeply etched in multiple areas of our brain.

Comparisons are of two kinds: upward and downward. We get miserable by making upward comparisons (with those more accomplished) or try to heal ourselves with downward comparisons (with those less fortunate). **In general, happier people are very good at downward comparison.** For example, happier students more heavily weighed a slower peer's evaluations in their self-assessments.[387] You could argue that a downward comparison will lower standards, but happier people are also more comfortable spending time with those who have superior skills, compared to the less happy people who are more likely threatened by them.[388] This is a good place to be—**inspired by someone more skilled, comforted by someone less skilled**. I so wish we all were that rational. Unfortunately, we are not.

Comparison can seed envy and hubris or inspiration and humility. The choice is yours.

We compare our physical appearance not only with others but also with career models whose job is to look good. We forget that our core identity is not in our physical appearance. Such comparison hurts our self-esteem.[389] We make these comparisons in person as well as online, opening us up to infinite possibilities for misery.[390]

In companies, employees often compare their closeness to the leadership with that of other employees. If we feel we are not as close as others, our job performance goes down.[391] We develop envy, and worse, schadenfreude (deriving pleasure in witnessing someone's misfortunes). True to the feeling, while envy activates the anterior cingulate cortex of the brain (not a source of pleasure), schadenfreude activates the reward (pleasure) center.[392]

Such pleasure is particularly strong when those hurt are higher-status people whom we believe to be our competitors. We are more willing to endorse harming those people.[393] Envy not only leads to minor scuffles but can seed mass genocide of millions of people.

Be wary of hurtful comparisons that are part of the brain's design. This is particularly important because a new form of social comparison has now taken birth: comparison that originates on social networking sites (SNS). Some researchers call it social comparison 2.0.

SOCIAL COMPARISON 2.0

SNS provide a snapshot into our lives. We post the most attractive pictures and show our lives in the best light.[394] We upload selfies with celebrities, with exotic zoo animals, and from mountaintops. Such depictions, we believe, will attract the most followers. This can backfire. Some people have even lost their lives when they put themselves in dangerous situations trying to take selfies they think might go viral.

Although the positive impact of SNS on connectivity and communication is truly impressive, their value in enhancing societal happiness and well-being is iffy at best. If anything, some research points in the other direction.

In one research study, investigators tracked people's happiness over time and correlated it with their use of SNS. Usage correlated with a decrease in moment-to-moment happiness (SNS usage at one moment correlated with feeling worse subsequently) and with a drop in life satisfaction.[394] One obvious reason for this finding is that seeing others' Facebook pages can make you feel that your life is boring.[395] Looking at all the cool things happening in others' lives causes envy and fear of missing out (FOMO).[396] Also, looking at the profile of a successful person worsens one's own perception of career success, and looking at the profile of an attractive person worsens one's body image and might predispose one to eating disorders.[397]

Part of this relates to what we remember. When we look at the accounts of others on SNS, we recall the most positive examples instead of taking the average of all we saw.[395] Anguish created by excessive SNS is thus often irrational. Positive emotional expression on SNS doesn't mean subjective well-being.[398] For this reason, not uncommonly, we might be envious of someone whose life is much more difficult than ours.

We are often envious of someone who may have greater difficulties and pain than us.

To be fair, thoughtful use of SNS has helped us in many ways, including in the areas of mental health and happiness. Assessing the mood of society using social-media communications can predict health and disease. For example, in one study that analyzed 148 million tweets, the psychological content of the tweets (anger, disengagement, and negative relationships versus engagement and positive emotions) was a better predictor of heart disease than were the well-known risk factors (smoking, diabetes, hypertension, and so on).[399] In another study, using SNS as a targeted intervention (rather than self-reported use) showed a benefit for improving anxiety, self-esteem, loneliness, depression, and health behaviors.[400-402] Thus, the effects of SNS has a lot to do with how we use this tool; the technology itself isn't evil.

TATTLETALE

I am not done yet with my tattletale of our instinct to compare and compete. Several other comparison frames can make us miserable. For example, we can become sad when thinking about what we had or could have had but didn't. I have met several investment bankers and stock traders who remain obsessed with how much they left on the table. They forget that **every time you buy a stock, it invariably goes down, and every time you sell the stock, it invariably goes up**. That is investing 101. But it is easier to preach than to practice.

Investing 101: A stock you purchase will always go down; a stock you sell will always go up.

Even positive memories can be hurtful if they push us into thinking about our current sorry state. Thus, people who are predisposed to depression get more depressed when they think of the good old days.[403, 404]

Similarly, we compare our anticipated future with the desired future. We don't learn from our past, which teaches us that most of our fears won't come true and that we can't predict the precise future. We also can't predict how we will react to the future (these are called errors in affective forecasting).[405] The last point is important. **Even if all your future dreams are realized, you may find them dissatisfying when you meet them.**[406] Experts have a name for this: miswanting.[407]

This holds particularly true for extrinsic goals (such as money, fame, and image).[408] These comparisons will become even more important in affecting our well-being if we continue to shift from Generation We to Generation Me.[409]

The same errors in forecasting hold true for our fears. **Even if your future fears turn out to be realized, you might be better prepared to meet them at that point than you are today.** There's no point obsessing over them at this moment.

Unfortunately, our tendency to compare meets two multipliers that feed our comparison instinct: inequality and attribution error.

ALL MEN AND WOMEN AREN'T CREATED EQUAL

We live in a world that has created inequality on a massive scale. Incomes are soaring for the top few percent and lagging for the bottom 90 percent.[410, 411]

A large percentage of people are earning no more than they were twenty-five years ago. They also have no hope for a better tomorrow. Frustration is a natural consequence. In many societies, hunger and abject poverty are coupled with the sight of a few buying expensive homes and yachts. How can such a society promise happiness to its masses? This inequality creates a sense of unfairness. **The brain is designed to catch unfairness, particularly intentional unfairness, very quickly, and it strongly reacts to it, sometimes irrationally.**[412-414] Every time I have stood in the rental car line, someone jumping ahead of me has challenged my commitment to kindness and self-control!

Economists and social scientists believe that one of the reasons our productivity and economic gains have made little to no impact on our happiness is because of this inequality, which is real.[415, 416] Our society will remain in significant unrest until we find a way to decrease its inequalities.

ATTRIBUTION ERROR

The second multiplier is our tendency to judge the actions of others based on their internal characteristics and our own based on external situations.[417, 418]

Because of this error, I find my quirks and missteps justifiable based on my constraints, but I expect perfection from all others. I am particularly harsh on the younger generation, totally forgetting my own tantrums and silliness when I was sixteen. Further, I judge others based on their worst moments. I compare their worst moments with my best without knowing their pressures in those moments.

ESCAPING THE COMPARISON TRAP

An important question, then, is how we escape our comparison trap. As a first step, we must recognize its workings. Just as two sides of a scale naturally compare with each other, our brain is designed to compare expectation with reality. You can't stop it. The question is whether you can be wiser and more flexible in changing your expectations to look at reality differently and to soften your comparison instinct. Can you convert unhealthy comparisons into healthy ones? The answer is a definite yes.

For example, do not tell elderly people with poor control over their routine about people ten years older than them who can still tango. Research shows that providing them with downward social comparison will better help their well-being.[419] Patients with HIV on the other hand, love to hear stories of someone with the same diagnosis doing well physically, because that inspires them.[420] In an area such as intelligence, in which one person is clearly better than the other, giving the better person a label of genius was shown to protect self-esteem and perceived personal competence among those not so gifted.[421]

***In general, people with no hope prefer downward comparison;
people who are hopeful prefer upward comparison.***

Comparisons have the potential to inspire us to become better. Smokers who choose to be with a group that has successfully quit are more likely to succeed than are smokers who choose failing groups.[422] We admire people we find braver than us. We admire those who have overcome adversities that would have crushed us. Anyone living a virtuous life with a deeper focus on principles and with greater discipline becomes worthy of admiration. I have met countless patients whom I admire for their fortitude and grit amid severe illness. Every story of grit fills me with hope, inspiration, and courage, which we will talk about in chapters 76–78.

Research indicates that admiration of someone better than us can inspire us to do better.[423] The same study showed that **a small dose of envy can actually do us good**. From that perspective, researchers draw a distinction between benign and malicious envy. The former is healthy and inspiring, while the latter fills us with negative emotions, is uninspiring, and leads to schadenfreude.[393]

As with mind wandering, negativity bias, emotional sensitivity, and imagination, we can neither totally suppress nor let go of the brain's tendency to compare. A more practical alternative is to preserve comparison's most inspiring aspects while letting go of toxic comparisons that can make our lives and the lives of others miserable.

Specifically, here is what I try to do. I try not to compare the worldly success of others with my success. Instead, I focus on how much good another person is doing. I try my best to use my comparison instinct to inspire me to become a better person. Instead of fearing that I might be left behind, I fear that I will leave my skills unused and not help as many. Near my last breath, I want to feel that I have fully used my energy and mortal frame to serve the world.

If you are greedy to do as much good as you can, then you might help a few more than you would otherwise. If you use your tendency to compare to admire others' good work and thus inspire yourself and gain more courage, then perhaps it will be a healthy comparison. Since research shows that others' choices impact our own, cultivating inspiring comparisons can help you grow.[424] It might help bring out the best in you. If we can be happy watching a stranger win thousands of dollars in a game show, why should we not feel the same about our cousins and competitors?[425]

Be greedy about helping as many as you can.

I hope you are enjoying learning a few details about the brain so far. Let's keep going and talk about the itch that afflicts us all. This is an itch that dermatologists can do nothing about. Like other vulnerabilities noted here, it could stop behaving like a trap once you understand and use its best parts.

22

Neural Trap #6: Can't Suppress the Thoughts (The Mental Itch)

The itch—it creates that irresistible urge to scratch your skin. Resisting an itch can be very unpleasant, while scratching a mild itch is often pleasurable. I remember meeting a depressed patient who didn't want his itchy skin rash treated. "This is the only source of pleasure in my life," he said. You might try to forcefully suppress your itch, but during moments of introspection or distracted attention, when you aren't in control, your hands find the spot and rub the skin. Scratching relieves momentary discomfort but doesn't heal the skin. Scratching actually is part of the problem. It keeps the rash angry and inflamed.

Itching never cures the itch.

Thoughts, particularly the ones that focus on unresolved fears or unfulfilled wants, are like mental itches. The mind visits and revisits them, hoping for a solution. After a while, the mind gets tired and wants to give up. But the thoughts won't go away. So, the natural next reaction is to get rid of the thoughts by suppressing them. But it isn't that easy.

THE SPRING RECOILS

A large body of research shows that thought suppression is an ineffective strategy to eliminate your thoughts.[426] Suppressed thoughts don't go away. Instead, like a spring, they recoil. Multiple studies show that when you suppress your thoughts instead of allowing them to flow, you experience more of the same thoughts.[427-431] Sometimes they come back as dreams.[432]

The classic study to test this process was done by asking participants to stop thinking about a white bear, which, as you might expect, didn't stop their thoughts of the white bear. They had a rebound of those thoughts.[433]

Have you ever woken up to a rhythm stuck in your head? What happens when you try to suppress it? It keeps coming back, doesn't it? That's the nature of the human mind. You can throw away a rotten banana and forget about it, but you can't throw away a rotten thought. Here is how it works: when you try hard to stop thinking about the parking ticket, you have to keep thinking about the parking ticket so you don't think about it. You start a monitoring process for that thought, which keeps it alive and available.[434]

Although research is early and sparse, functional MRI studies show that thought suppression engages specific areas of the brain, including the dorsolateral prefrontal cortex when the thought is suppressed and the anterior cingulate cortex when the thought emerges.[435-437] Interestingly, in one study, investigators found that the brain network hosting thought suppression showed significant fluctuation, which the researchers interpreted was compatible with difficulty in maintaining thought suppression.[438]

SHORT-TERM FIX

We keep attempting thought suppression despite its failure because the approach works in the short term, particularly in people with better self-regulation, high working-memory capacity, greater intelligence, and lower stress.[439, 440]

We don't realize that this strategy is bound to eventually fail, it prevents us from accessing more adaptive strategies (such as gratitude, finding meaning, and acceptance), and it isn't an innocent process. In the last two decades, researchers have linked thought suppression with several adverse outcomes, including depressive symptoms, anxiety,[441] obsessive-compulsive disposition,[442, 443] opioid craving among patients with chronic pain,[444, 445] eating disorders and posttraumatic stress disorder in patients who had experienced sexual assault,[446, 447] problem gambling,[448] body-image dissatisfaction and eating psychopathology,[449] greater spider-related thoughts in arachnophobes,[450, 451] failure at smoking cessation,[452] binge eating and food craving,[453] greater recall of negative memories,[454] and persistent suicidal ideation.[455] That's a long list.

In trauma-exposed individuals, thought and emotion suppression were associated with greater posttraumatic stress disorder.[456, 457] Thought suppression combined with hopelessness and catastrophizing mediates the relationship between pain and depressive symptoms.[458] In one study, emotion suppression (a close cousin of thought suppression) was associated with a 35 percent increase in mortality.[459] In another study, being moved to tears, and thus expressing emotion, was associated with better immunity (lower cortisol and inflammatory cytokines) and better control of rheumatoid arthritis compared to just feeling the emotions without crying.[460] **Being tough doesn't mean being callous and uncaring. It means allowing yourself to cry and finding a smile as the tears dry.**

Authentic emotional expression, including crying is healing, better than bottling up feelings.

In terms of focus, one would think that thought suppression might free up mental space and enhance our ability to focus. It actually does the opposite. In a research study, thought suppression, when compared to the alternative practice of acceptance, was associated with decreased ability to focus on mental imagery.[461]

When you are hungry, you might stall your hunger for the short term if you eat two candies. But then you become hungry again. The transient satisfaction might fool you and distract you from eating a full meal. Similarly, thought suppression works for the short term. But the mind can't fool itself. Blanket optimism postpones suffering but doesn't bypass or heal it. The reality eventually catches up with us. When a pigeon closes its eyes after seeing a fox, that action doesn't make the fox go away.

NEGOTIATING THE QUICKSAND

As discussed previously, it's important to realize that the human thought train can't be stopped. Instead, we can direct it toward more productive and adaptive thoughts. Negating thoughts won't help (because it won't appeal to your intellect), but deepening our thinking will.

Although thought suppression seems like an obvious solution to the mind, it's like quicksand; greater struggle takes you deeper. The way out of quicksand—to lie flat and inch toward the edge so that your weight is more evenly distributed—isn't instinctively obvious to the mind, partly because that solution entails bringing your head closer to the ground. Many alternatives can help the mental itch: distraction, thought postponement, exposure, focused breathing, willingness to accept the situation, a feeling of gratitude for what is right, self-expression in journaling, hypnosis, self-affirmation, discovering meaning, forgiveness, and when feasible, a change in the situation.[462]

These strategies work in two ways: they take away the mind's need to keep thinking about the particular thoughts to suppress them, and even if the thoughts aren't suppressed, they become less bothersome.[463, 464]

Until the above approaches (some of which I will elaborate further in later sections) become habitual and your mind develops the finesse to thwart its tendency to suppress its activity, try the old and simple exercise of deep breathing when facing thoughts you wish to suppress. Research shows deep breathing can help and is better than trying to take your attention away with distracting images.[465]

I hope by now I am beginning to convince you of the limitations of the brain's innate wiring and workings. I can't wait to hear what Mike thinks about all this science in the forthcoming fireside chat.

The next set of neural traps might amuse you further. We will talk about how we discount the good, are addicted to short-term gratification, get caught in the habit loop, walk around loaded with conflicts, play the dishonesty game, are wired to fail at forgiveness, and to top it all off, experience the world all day long with a tired brain.

23

Neural Trap #7: Designed to Be Dissatisfied (Programmed Dissatisfaction)

I recently witnessed my seven-year-old's interaction with cupcakes. Her first bite was frenzied. The fifth bite was much calmer. By the time she finished the second cupcake, she couldn't have cared less. She moved on to the next excitement. Her response isn't very different from that of a grown-up.

Think about the last promotion you got. How long did you enjoy it? Not one of my fulfilled dreams—getting into medical school, becoming a doctor, working at a prestigious medical center, becoming a published author—has provided lasting happiness. This was as true in the times of Uncle Ad as it is today. Like a wildfire that is forever hungry to grow, my desires sit at the leading edge of achievement. My mind constantly seeks the next big excitement. The goal post gets pushed back as soon as I reach close to it. Why is that?

WANTING VERSUS LIKING

It will help us to understand the difference between wanting and liking (drawing from the incentive sensitization theory of drug addiction).[466] Wanting is the desire to experience or acquire something. It has a significant motivational element. Wanting is classically mediated by the neurotransmitter dopamine.[467] We want experiences, things, and relationships that cause a dopamine release in the reward areas of the brain. The good news is that many (but not all) experiences that cause a dopamine release also enhance our chances of success and survival.[466]

These experiences are pleasurable; we like them. Liking is mediated by a complex soup of chemicals, including dopamine, endorphins, serotonin, adrenaline, oxytocin, endocannabinoids, GABA, and more.[468] Pleasure has many flavors—hence all these different mediators. The pleasure of bonding and trust hosted by oxytocin[469] might feel very different from the bliss mediated by endocannabinoids.[470]

In experiencing wanting and liking, we have two challenges. First, the brain isn't a passive participant as is, say, an automated dispensing machine, where four quarters will get you an identical bag of potato chips the first time as well as the fiftieth time. The brain, being an active participant, changes in response to its experience.[471] This is best studied in the context of drugs of addiction. The two outcomes of repeated drug use are a higher drug requirement and a loss of liking with regular exposure. Here is how this happens.

Higher drug requirement. With repeated use, the brain turns down the volume—just as you would turn down the TV volume if it was too loud. The same drug now releases less dopamine and other rewarding chemicals (scientists call this phenomenon tachyphylaxis). Further, even if the same amount of dopamine were released, it wouldn't stimulate the reward area as much because the brain decreases receptors for dopamine in response to previous stimulation. This leads to escalation of the drug dose.[467] These changes happen not just with drugs of abuse but also with many other life experiences that engage the same brain areas (for example, food, money, intimacy, gambling, and fame).[470]

Loss of liking with repeated exposure. Since wanting and liking are hosted by different brain areas, they do not always go together.[472] Thus, you may want something, but you may not like it once you have it. This classically happens for drugs of abuse. The addict craves the drug but, after a period of use, stops enjoying it. With full-blown addiction, drugs do not produce joy; they just release angst and discomfort.[471] The disconnect between wanting and liking can happen with most other sensory pleasures once they lose their novelty. This is one reason people feel dissatisfied while continuing to crave more. **Perhaps this is also the reason we miss people when they are away but start arguing the moment they arrive.**

What we want we do not always like, once we have it.

The outcome of these phenomena is that the brain's reward center gets strongly excited by anticipation. If the anticipation meets disappointment, we get distraught. If the anticipation meets success, we initially get pleasure. With repeated success, we discount that pleasure and start seeking something else, because the value of the accomplishment fades and becomes a basic expectation.

REWARD LOSES REWARD

For these reasons, our reward systems can provide only transient happiness, not sustained joy. If we aren't aware of this neural trap, we will constantly look into the future for something better to deliver lasting happiness. That something better, though, doesn't exist (for most of us). Nothing in the material world, no matter how good it is, can provide lasting happiness. Experts call this phenomenon hedonic adaptation (a state of programmed dissatisfaction).[244] This is the reason that winning the lottery provides little lasting pleasure.[473, 474] This is also the reason that our infatuation with someone becomes dull over time and in some instances, may degenerate into boredom or even annoyance.

The amazing fact is that none of us believes or imagines that such a change can happen to us. If you ask the bride and groom whether they ever expect to get a divorce, a full 0 percent will say yes to that question.

Did you notice the double whammy in the brain's design? **The reward center *fatigues* with repeated exposure to pleasurable stimuli, while our fear center gets *sensitized* with repeated exposure.** Further, once sensitized, the fear center starts firing on its own, just from us imagining the fearful. Doesn't sound like a happy design, does it?

Our brain's default is to discount the good and inflate the bad.

Our discounting the good and inflating the bad is expensive. It keeps us dissatisfied, always wanting more. **In our constant effort to make things better, we seldom enjoy how good they already are.** We also plunder the planet. This is one reason relationships cool off after a few years. This is also the reason that many millionaire corporate executives are in jail.

OUT OF AFRICA

You might wonder why evolution allowed this system to survive. The answer is simple: if we were totally satisfied with the status quo, we would still be rubbing stones to produce fire. Our dissatisfaction nudges us out of our comfort zone. Our impatience and drive for novelty helped us populate the entire planet and become the dominant species. It is this dissatisfaction that helps entrepreneurs work hard and innovate even when they have earned enough to feed five generations.

Given this long-term value of programmed dissatisfaction, its assault on our ability to sustain happiness and relationships, and its push to promote splurging, a natural question arises: What is the appropriate strategy to partner with this quirk? I believe we can work to keep novelty alive and choose a reward that doesn't easily exhaust. Here is how.

PAUSE, PERCEIVE, AND PRAISE

When was the last time you paused and looked at the color of your loved one's eyes? What five trees are closest to your home? Can you find a new detail in your kitchen you haven't noticed before? Count the number of colors you see in the body of a monarch butterfly. Meet at least one person during the day with full presence; assume that he or she is the nicest person on the planet.

There are countless ways you can find novelty in the world, just like you did as a four-year-old building a paper plane. The key is to pause your planning and problem solving and just perceive. Once you find novelty within the ordinary and allow yourself to be pleased with the simple, you will start getting more out of life. We will talk about this in greater detail in the next section.

The second way to avoid dissatisfaction is to pick rewards that can feed your mind (and soul) over and over again. Biologically, our senses fatigue very fast (the third mango tastes nothing like the first one). Further, senses provide only transient happiness, carrying little or no memory. So sensory pleasures can't provide lasting joy. The most memorable moments come when we experience deep positive emotions. That happens when we feel worthy.

How does one feel worthy? **You feel transient worthiness when you get special treatment. You feel sustained worthiness when you help someone else feel special.** If you wish to feel worthy today, help someone else feel worthy. One of the most precious gifts you can give to others is to help them believe in themselves.

The easiest way to feel special is to help someone else feel special.

The joy of remembering a good deed is almost as strong the tenth time as it is the first time. Such experiences and memories can infuse positivity even in the most difficult situations. Research shows that caregivers of patients with advanced illness commonly experience positive emotions, particularly when they feel useful to the patient and can make their loved ones happier.[475]

Given the biological restraints in our system, you might think we should have learned by now how to invest time in altruistic activities that provide lasting joy. Unfortunately, that isn't the case. We are still prisoners in our minds, fighting little, ordinary battles, because of our next predisposition: addiction to short-term gratification.

24

Neural Trap #8: Addicted to Short-Term Gratification (Deficits in Self-Regulation)

I have an impatient brain. I seldom brush my teeth for the recommended two minutes. I struggle when it takes too long for the water to turn hot in the shower. The ninety seconds it takes to warm my cereal in the microwave feels painful. I rarely wait for the car engine to warm up on a day when it is twenty below zero outside. Traffic lights are agonizing, particularly the long ones that keep me waiting for more than a minute while every car from the other three directions seems to be moving. The slow elevators test my patience. I give up on a video if it doesn't load in a few seconds. I have to work hard to not interrupt others in a meeting, and sometimes I fail. I dread meeting people who take more than thirty seconds to come to their point. I could go on. I think I am not alone in my impatience.

SWIMMING IN IMPATIENCE

Research shows people start abandoning a website at about the two-second threshold; if the video they want to watch doesn't start in two seconds, they quit, and they are less likely to come back to the site.[476]

Also, people with faster Internet connections abandon sooner. I have asked over ten thousand people in workshops if they invest the full two minutes in the morning brushing their teeth. Less than 5 percent do. More than 80 percent multitask while brushing their teeth. Dentists and dental assistants have secure careers.

We are ten times more likely to multitask while brushing our teeth, than brush for the full two minutes.

Occasionally this lack of patience turns sinister, as when a person with a boiling temper empties a gun on a car that was too slow at a stop sign. **Impatience is wired into our brain, and the efficiencies in our society are fueling it.**

Our impatience originates in the phenomenon called delay discounting (also called time discounting or temporal discounting).[477] The brain values immediate gain over long-term gain. A dollar today is worth more than a dollar in a month or perhaps even two dollars in a month. Our brain discounts the gain, adjusting for the value of time. Thus, most of us would be willing to forgo a dollar today in favor of a million dollars in a month. As you decrease the value, a point comes when people aren't willing to wait for the delayed reward. This threshold is different in different people. In general, the less we discount the delayed reward, the better off we are. People with steep delay discounting have higher stress[478] and are at increased risk of addictions,[479] weight gain,[480, 481] and other conditions.

Impatience is here to stay as the brain plays catch-up with internet search engines. Rising stress, 24/7 connectedness, and even the kinds of food we eat (hint: fast food) can increase our impatience. Further, research shows that a high proportion (up to 50 percent) of our impatience is genetically coded.[482, 483] Outsmarting our genes will take a long time.

ILL WITH IMPATIENCE

Impatience breeds many different kinds of rage in our society (more on this in chapter 60). One of the biggest risks of impatience is that the resulting lack of self-control can lead to different forms of addiction. Tobacco, alcohol, cocaine, meth, opiates, sleeping pills, calorie-dense food, sex, gambling…there is a long list of chemicals, behaviors, and hobbies to which we get addicted.[484-487] Addiction isn't just about spending a little time and money. It can become an obsession, leading to an entire life invested in seeking the addictive agent. It can lead to death. Drug overdose is now the leading cause of mortality in people younger than fifty.[488]

Addicted people aren't the stupid or the weak. Just as often, the smartest people, leaders of our society and businesses, get caught in the whirlpool. Why would they surrender their life's work to some chemicals? It is because these chemicals are very powerful. They stimulate the reward center—the core machinery that drives our sense of pleasure. When lacking patience, we want the reward center stimulated ASAP and can't wait for any future moment.

The studies in mice are instructive. The mice continue pressing the lever to stimulate their reward center, quit all eating, and eventually die of exhaustion.[489] Such is the power of these agents to which we are vulnerable because of our predisposition to get addicted to short-term gratification.

> *The addicting chemicals are so strong and the reward center they activate so powerful, that the smartest most wonderful people can get hooked.*

Although the addictive agents carry the headline news and devastate a section of society, **the cumulative effects of daily cravings have an even larger impact.** These effects include the desire for calorie-dense food, the obsession with screens big and small, and the propensity for philandering. They can lead to lying, cheating, and distracted focus—all serving short-term pleasure while sacrificing long-term goodness.

SELF IN CONTROL

Scientists have discovered that our ability to self-control (scientifically called self-regulation) is associated with all sorts of good outcomes, ranging from higher SAT scores to better jobs, healthier habits, lower risk of divorce, lower addiction, better emotional health, higher self-worth, better physical health, and even longer life.[490-493] Patient children are more socially competent, achieve better academic performance, cope better with stress and frustration,[494] are less likely to be overweight,[495] and get higher SAT scores.[496] They also make good baby sitters! You are more likely to trust people who demonstrate better self-control.[497]

The key connection is between self-control and the ability to make good decisions. Research shows that **half of the premature mortality in the United States is because of poor choices.**[498]

The single most important cause of early death is making poor choices.

When we are stressed, self-control is very difficult. For example, research shows that **the same calorie-dense food that may look uninteresting to a peaceful brain looks highly appetizing to a stressed-out brain.**[499, 500]

One of the early effects of excessive stress on the brain is loss of self-control.

Empowering people to make good decisions and better handle their stressors so they can cultivate good habits can save millions of lives every year.

As a first step, recognize that impatience and addiction to short-term gratification are part of who we are. A variety of strategies can train our self-control. Distraction is the simplest way; just look away from the doughnut or look toward something that you find compelling.[501] But distraction alone isn't enough. Another option is to look at the appetizing aspect of the experience in a different light. For example, if you consider a potato chip to be a square yellow object, it might look slightly less attractive.[494] (I once heard someone say this about potato chips: "Two seconds in your hands, two minutes in your mouth, two hours in your stomach, and always on you!") Another approach is to train your attention so you aren't as vulnerable to the inducement. In children, attention training has been shown to improve patience.[502]

The stronger your attention, the greater your patience.

Sprinkling moments of patience in daily life—during a meal, with a child, at the traffic light, in a meeting—can build your patience muscles. Resist the urge to jump the yellow light, wait until everyone is seated at the table before starting to eat, listen with patience, watch slower-paced TV shows, or pick some other idea that makes the most sense to you.

You can further strengthen these muscles by filling the dull moments with something else, such as music, kind attention, or another practice. Hum your favorite song at the traffic light or while waiting for the water to turn hot in the shower.

Most importantly, be patient with yourself. I am reminded of an interesting expression: "God give me patience…but please hurry up!"

It takes time to build the patience habit—or, for that matter, any habit, to which we turn next.

25

Neural Trap #9: Caught in the Habit Loop (The Habit Trap)

A cousin of mine works at an international company as a new-projects manager. His team picks the projects; thinks about the infrastructure, marketing, budgetary, and other needs; and then brings the project to execution. Once a project is executed, it goes to a different team. As the project matures, becomes part of the ecosystem, and is refined to a science, fewer and fewer personnel are needed. Further, those working on a mature project often aren't the masters of innovation. Their expertise is in diligently following an established protocol. The brain works the same way.

SKILLFUL DELEGATOR

Go back to the first time you played piano or violin (or any other skill you learned). Would you have appreciated a phone call at that time? No, because your attention was used up in figuring out the details of playing the instrument. But now you can effortlessly play while talking, singing, or even watching a movie. Playing the instrument takes much less attention now than it did when you started. As you go from novice to expert, the neural real estate needed to host the activity goes down dramatically.[503-505]

If I am skiing or driving a race car, my entire brain will turn red and purple on a functional MRI compared with an expert, whose MRI will show minimal activity. Here is the tactical shift that happens in the brain: the conscious action during training needs a lot of cerebral-cortex activity, but when the behavior becomes programmed, the cerebral cortex delegates the workload to the automatically driven subcortical parts of the brain (the basal ganglia).[506, 507] When you are driving your car, you consciously control the steering wheel, but a lot is happening simultaneously; the engine is running, the fan is cooling the engine, the tire gauge is sensing tire pressure, the inside temperature is regulated to your comfort, and more. Similarly, our brains have evolved to run several simultaneous operations.

This has been tremendously advantageous for our species. Because of this shift, when you repeat a behavior enough times, it needs minimal conscious resources. That frees your attention to do other things. You can look out for predators, hold the baby and pick the berries—all at the same time.

Given that we have finite attention and willpower, we welcome anything that can increase efficiency.[508] If that were not so, every activity would feel like going through an airport security check, from brushing teeth in the morning to switching off the lamp at night. Behaviors repeated enough times become automatic. They become habits.

HABITS

Habits are automatic behaviors triggered by cues. We swim in our habits. **About half of what we do on most days is driven by habit.** How much attention do you pay to washing your hands after using the restroom, changing clothes, or turning on the lights at night?

Our actions during the day can be classified into two broad types: intentional and habitual. Intentional actions need conscious attention. Driving in a new neighborhood, assembling a dollhouse, playing chess—all need intentional focus. Actions driven by habits need little conscious attention. They are initiated by prior events (cues).[508]

We form these habits over a lifetime. We repeat patterns of behaviors that help us reach our goals. Often repeated, such behaviors become automatic, need minimal conscious effort, and they are triggered by cues. The resulting reward (pleasure, relaxation, success, gain, or win) keeps it going. This is the automatic cycle in which we spend half our day.

The automation of the habit circuits comes with two costs. The first is that during habitual activity, we are less likely to pay attention and more likely to mind wander.[509] The second is that it creates serious vulnerability if your reward comes from an activity or chemical that can be destructive in the long term. The cue (stress), when linked with the habit (smoking) that gives the reward (a relaxed feeling), will lock you into a lifetime of smoking. You won't even know when you light up the cigarette. Prolonged sitting, multitasking, comfort foods, angry outbursts—all of these and many more behaviors become habitual because they feed our hunger for short-term gratification. Try swapping smoking for a relaxing book, music, deep breathing, or prayer when you feel stressed. That'll be much more adaptive. I wish it was that simple and easy.

First you make good habits. Then your good habits make you.

Habits are powerful. Once formed, they are difficult to break. In a study on habitual popcorn eaters, participants showed clear preference for fresh popcorn over stale popcorn. But when given stale popcorn in a movie theater, they ate as much as participants who received fresh popcorn. Hunger had minimal influence on how much they ate.[510]

Any effort to change an ingrained behavior has to cross the habit hump. This hump can't be crossed just through education. Educational programs provide strategies and change short-term intentions, but they aren't enough to change the behavior.[511, 512]

HOPPING OVER HABITS

To overcome the habit trap, we need a well-thought-out approach. Look at the following seven tactics to break a habit, keeping in mind that the overriding theme is to keep it simple.[513, 514]

1. Work on the triggers (cues) that launch the behavior. Decrease the old cues in your life. For example, with smoking, decrease the time you spend with buddies who smoke or who goad you to smoke, minimize conflicts and other stressful situations, and eliminate the breaks in your calendar that you had assigned to smoking.[515] Sometimes a change in life situation, such as relocation or a new job, provides the perfect opportunity to remove the old cue and insert a new cue that guides you to a new behavior.[516] Take advantage of that opportunity. Also, when you choose a new cue, pick something that you experience most days in your normal daily life. For example, **connect flowing water in the tap with the feeling that blessings are coming into your home. Connect your first awareness in the morning of being alive, with the word** *gratitude*. **Let go of a few negative thoughts the day you empty the trash can.** You can't eliminate all the negative thoughts, but you can choose to smile at them and let them go with gratitude, knowing that they too served a purpose.

> *Take out a few negative thoughts from your mind the day*
> *you take out the trash from the garbage can.*

2. Try to replace the behavior with something else that gives you the same reward. In the case of smoking, the reward of relaxation can be attained by deep breathing, talking to a trusted friend, listening to music, coloring, watching a short video, going for a walk, taking a short nap, writing creatively, practicing tai chi or yoga, or doing something else that makes sense to you. Try to **pick an activity that is simple, short, doable, and pleasant**.

3. Increase the difficulty of smoothly executing the habitual behavior. In the popcorn study I shared above, forcing participants to eat with their non-dominant hand made a difference.[510] At the same time, decrease the difficulty of executing the new behavior. Try to find ways to save time while performing the new behavior and make it easier. Changing plate sizes, lighting, layout, color, and convenience can all help you change what and how much you eat.[511]

4. Repeat the new behavior until your brain makes fresh connections that automatically host the new behavior. There isn't a magic number of thirty, sixty, or two hundred days for which the behavior should be

repeated for it to become habitual. It is individual. It'll be good to remember that the old circuits in the brain won't disappear. You'll have to monitor with diligence to avoid slipups that can lead back to old patterns.[517]

Don't water the seeds you'd rather not sprout.

5. Perhaps most importantly, add meaning to the change. I remember a grandma who told me the story about her smoking. She had smoked for about fifty years and had failed every treatment. One day, she leaned forward to kiss her four-year-old grandson. He took two steps back and said, "Grandma, you stink." That was the day. She stopped smoking so she could kiss her grandson. **Add a deeper meaning to your behavior change. That'll give you strength in your weaker moments.**[518]

Change inspired by meaning lasts longer.

6. Train your muscle of intentionality. **Do things differently so you become accustomed to trying new things.** Take a new route to work, park on a different floor, rearrange your furniture, try a new restaurant, listen to a completely different kind of music, or eat a new cuisine with your non-dominant hand. Also, exercise self-control in little daily activities. Sit for no more than an hour at a stretch, skip dessert, say no to seconds, avoid parking at the closest ramp. Sprinkling self-control throughout the day will help you strengthen the willpower muscle so you can resist more sinister temptations. In this world filled with "supernormal" stimuli, against which our senses are defenseless once exposed (think doughnuts or porn),[519] living with intentionality guided by your values and creating a distance between you and such stimuli will help shield you from the myriad attractants.

7. Keep it simple and pleasant. **The simpler and easier the change and the greater the pleasure it gives, the more likely you will be able to sustain it.**

Changing and sustaining behaviors is hard work. We can't rely on the individual to do it all alone. Bringing about change at the city, state, or national level will require policy changes as well as enlightened and caring leaders.[520]

Recognize that the world around you isn't so innocent and gullible. Right this moment, as I write these lines and you read them, thousands of individuals and companies are figuring out how to separate you from your money and quality time with loved ones by getting you addicted to some reward-producing behavior that may seem exciting in the short term but could hurt you in the long term. They are finding ways to get you hooked to their product or idea, no matter its true benefit to you.[521]

The daily livelihood of many people depends on getting you hooked to destructive habits and separating you from your money and loved ones.

As I said earlier, it is sad that the most brilliant minds aren't thinking about how to enhance forgiveness and compassion in our society; they are innovating so you click more ads and their products go viral.

Why do we fall for the trap laid by people who don't mean us well? Why can't we see their ruse? There are many reasons; one of them goes back to the design of the brain—the ease with which it gets conflicted—our brain's tenth trap.

If you have read nonstop so far, it might be a good idea to take a short break before reading about our conflicted brain.

26

Neural Trap #10: Conflicted (To Be or Not to Be)

Should I be soft with our kids or become a tiger parent? If I have fifteen extra minutes, should I exercise or take a nap? Should I pick up the clutter or insist my kids pick up their own mess? Should I always stick to the highway or once in a while take the side roads (not only while driving but also in life, particularly when I see others reaching their destinations faster by taking the short cuts)? Countless work- and life-related conflicts create forks in my life that confuse and overwhelm me. Why does that happen? It is because **the human brain by design is a conflicted organ.**

THE TWO CONSULTANTS

The brain has two consultants that provide two different inputs based on what they are charged to do. Consider a doughnut (or a slice of pizza, bowl of ice cream, or cookie) in front of you. The central reward (limbic) part of the brain asks you to eat the doughnut. This part recognizes that the doughnut is tasty and calorie dense and might provide survival benefit in a matchup with a Neanderthal that can happen at any moment. Evolutionarily, this is the older part of the brain that sits deep inside. It is fully integrated in our psyche. Wrapping around the central part of the brain is the new cortex, which is more rational; it asks you to avoid the doughnut or at least eat only one doughnut today because it can think about the long term. Since this is the newer part of the brain and produces less drama, we don't always trust or listen to it readily.[522-525]

The forces of temptations are older and more familiar to us than the power of self-control.

A doughnut is a benign example. How about other, more sinister short-term gratifications, such as lying to advance a personal cause, cheating on a spouse or partner, backstabbing a friend, planning disproportionate revenge, watching pornography, stealing money, engaging in research misconduct, usurping intellectual property, or forcing oneself on someone?[526, 527]

Why do we, the wisest, most compassionate species on the planet, fall into these traps? Why do we even consider the possibility of taking advantage of a fellow human's vulnerabilities, while we risk getting caught, destroying our (and their) life, even spending the rest of our life behind bars? Why do we assume that someone attractive whose career depends on our favors is fair game? Why can't we wake up tomorrow and become instinctively kind? It is because **within us we have both a sage and a savage, who are in a constant tug-of-war.** Any species that has such a conflicted information processor is bound to struggle.

The sage and savage within us are in a constant tug of war.

Most other animals don't struggle like we do. They don't have such mature prefrontal cortices.[528, 529] They live guided by the instincts generated by the central part of the brain, without much long-term thinking or compassion. Male lions don't look conflicted when they capture another pride and then go about killing all the cubs so the females are ready to mate. A wildebeest pup, if separated from its mother, won't be fed by other moms. They actually chase the pup away lest it steal energy from their own pups. Such cruel action creates no conflicts in these moms. Not so for us. When I read statistics about hunger half a world away, I feel guilty taking a bite of my taco salad.

Some of the core high-level conflicts I face on most days involve whether I should care for myself or others, stick to my values or let fears take over, focus on money or chase meaning, speak up or be quiet, or think about the short term or the long term. These conflicting thoughts also conflict with each other. I want to help a stranded motorist at two o'clock in the morning, but I have heard bad stories. If I wish to help, how do I overcome fear? If I don't help, how do I bear the guilt?

CHOICE OVERLOAD

Our conflicts are compounded by the number of choices accessible to us, creating an ocean of indecision. Researchers estimate that we make more than two hundred food-related decisions every day.[530] Work and travel also offer many decision points. Each e-mail offers a decision: read, delete, flag, reply, forward, or do nothing. This process of deciding fatigues and stresses us; **ambiguity activates the stress-producing parts of the brain.**[531]

Too many choices stress our brain. Stressed brains make poor choices.

Not infrequently, I see patients with serious diagnoses feeling relieved, even jubilated, once they decide on a course of action. Nothing may have changed—they may have even received bad news—yet they feel better. This is because they have been relieved of the burden of indecision. Decisional conflicts, intrinsic to the design of the brain, produce extreme stress. It doesn't help that we have created a world in which we are faced with countless choices.[532]

Choices enhance our well-being up to a point; the relationship is like an inverted U. A lack of choice is stressful, but excessive choice is equally stressful. Too many choices leave us feeling that we have settled for the second best or been cheated. And our brains are exquisitely sensitive to feeling cheated. The brain feels threatened when it feels taken advantage of.

The little daily conflicts, added together, become a big deal. Slowly, as we come under the influence of the savage and the greedy within us, the selfless sage goes silent. This can happen to the finest, most well-meaning people. If that were not so, we would not have witnessed, and continue to witness, repeated instances of human cruelty and greed on an individual, national, and global scale. Many more would have been saved when the *Titanic* sank.

Most of the conflicts the brain faces arise between an easy, likely pleasurable and somewhat sinful action that is rewarding in the short term and a more difficult, less enjoyable action for which the reward is postponed (think brownie versus broccoli). It would be easy for us to come out virtuous most of the time, if it were not for the next neural trap: our vulnerability to dishonesty.

27

Neural Trap #11: Vulnerable to Dishonesty (Liar, Liar)

Getting little kids to eat healthy foods takes tremendous negotiating skills. Several years ago, I was helping my then two-year-old drink her milk. She wouldn't relent. I was late for work, so I tried a little trick. I told her that if she drank her milk, five hungry kids in a poor part of the world would get milk that morning. The entire cup disappeared in a few gulps. I was happy, but I soon realized my folly. I had just cheated. I resolved not to do that again.

BEWARE THE CHEATER

As I take an honest look at my life, I realize I have cheated many times. I copied a friend's answer in fifth grade (on the moral-science exam!). I once stole a handful of chickpeas from a vendor when I was about ten. I have driven over the speed limit, parked in a restricted area, lied to hang up the phone on an unsolicited caller, and kept the tooth fairy and Santa Claus alive for my girls as long as I could. I have no doubt I have made many exaggerations to impress my friends, exaggerations that I don't even remember.

Lest I drown in guilt, I draw comfort from the realization that cheating and **lying are universal traits of intelligent life forms**. Camouflage is a form of cheating. Chimpanzees hide their food and play a ruse by taking their tribe to a different place.[533] They can even deceive human competitors by using a route hidden from human view.[534]

> *All intelligent life forms come with the cheating software installed in them.*

CONS ARE US

Humans are particularly deft at cheating. Between 50 and 80 percent of us show ourselves in a better light (a polite way of saying we lie) on online dating sites.[535] We portray ourselves as wealthier, more successful, taller, thinner, younger, and better built than we actually are.[536]

Some of the most inspiring athletes have doped to enhance their performances, disappointing millions.[537] In a survey of 2,500 managers, 56 percent reported catching applicants lying on their résumés.[538]

The commonest lies were exaggerating skills, padding previous responsibilities, and claiming employment with companies they never worked for.

In experiments conducted with university students who could cheat on a math test in return for a monetary award, about two-thirds cheated. The same result has been found in surveys of researchers.[539, 540] The comforting finding is that most cheated only by small amounts, perhaps so they would not get caught.[540]

GUILT-FREE CHEATING

When are we likely to cheat more? When many individuals are involved in a transaction, they are more likely to cheat because of decreased personal responsibility.[541] Cheating also increases when something separates the action and the reward. For example, participants who received tokens (which they later exchanged for money) rather than a direct monetary award were more likely to cheat.[540]

Lying is also a social phenomenon. **Seeing others lie normalizes the habit.** We are more likely to lie if our friends and loved ones also lie.[542] In fact, we might feel compelled to lie to conform to our social milieu. This is particularly so if lying becomes accepted as a social norm.[543] The psychological safety of a group encourages unethical behavior, particularly if the group is more "practical" than principled.[544]

Lying is infectious. You can catch the lying bug from a dishonest friend.

Finding meaning in dishonest actions is a perfect trap. We are more apt to cheat and feel morally justified in it if we are made to believe that our dishonest actions are likely to help others, particularly many others.[545] I grew up reading the story of a hunter who comes to an intersection while chasing a mama deer with a baby in tow. If the hunter asks you where the mama deer went, would you tell him? The moral of the story is that it is appropriate to lie to save someone's life. We sometimes use the same logic, though, to justify our selfish lies.

We use excuses, saying that we are sparing unnecessary details, don't want to hurt anyone, need the money for the family, and so on. Our leaders claim to act in the national interest, in a political party's interest, or for the world, or plead ignorance or double down, when they are caught deceiving. Barring rare exceptions, this is a slippery slope.

A relatively innocent activity that increases our risk of lying is wearing counterfeit items.[546] Research shows we are more likely to lie and judge others to be unethical when we carry a Louis Vuitton bag that we bought for eight dollars. Further, we are blissfully unaware that our innocent but fake sunglasses are influencing how we think.

CREATIVE CONS

Dishonesty has one positive correlation: with creativity. Dishonesty and creativity both involve breaking the rules. Creative people find more creative justifications for their cheating.[547] No wonder researchers have found **that the more creative the mind, the greater and more complex its ability to cheat.**[548] You can't create a Bernie Madoff with an IQ of 70.

The more creative you are, the more effort you'll have to put in to remain honest.

Power makes it worse. If Bernie Madoff feels powerful and in control, he will cheat even more. Research shows that **power inflates asymmetry in our judgments**.[549] People who feel powerful are much more likely to bad-mouth others' cheating while at the same time cheating themselves. They also are harsher in judging others' moral transgressions compared to their own.

CAN'T HELP IT
Finally, we are more liable to cheat when our self-control resources are depleted. We are also more likely to expose ourselves to the temptations that make us cheat when our self-control resources are depleted.[550] Hunger and thirst can cause self-control resources to be depleted, and sure enough, **the hungrier and thirstier we are, the more likely we are to cheat**.[551] Feeling anxious also decreases our honesty. Any time we feel threatened, our self-focused, unethical behavior gets an uptick.[552] The same phenomenon happens when we anticipate personal losses, particularly if we have a more selfish disposition.[553]

We descend into our primal instincts on days we feel vulnerable.

You may have noticed that **dishonesty generally starts with small, inconsequential actions**. These accumulate and escalate into larger actions over time.[554] Most high-profile smugglers, robbers, and corporate swindlers start with petty thefts. They practice, master their skills, become comfortable with it, and then go pro. You can prevent more serious infractions by committing yourself to honesty even in the inconsequential aspects of life.[555] The fascinating neuroscience of cheating, that I will mention next, provides a good window into how we go down this slippery slope.

THE HONEST DISHONEST BRAIN
Both truthfulness and deception can activate large-scale brain areas depending on the situation.[556, 557] The brain knows it is doing something wrong when it gets into the deception business. Deception thus activates the amygdala and the sACC, two brain areas associated with negative emotions.[557, 558] When lying, we feel uneasy and also get aroused and hypervigilant.[559]

Interestingly, in many people, lying also increases reward-center activity.[560] The extent of this activation depends on individual wiring. I think it is fair to speculate that those around you who get a kick out of fooling others have much greater reward-center activation when they lie. Some researchers call it the "cheater's high."[561] On top of this, one critical switch occurs in the brain that can change a person from occasional cheaters to maestro liars.

With repeated lying, the brain adapts to dishonesty. The amygdala, which was turning red hot early on, stops reacting to repeated lying.[554] I speculate that **those among us who rapidly downregulate their amygdala response to lying and who have strong activation of the reward area are more likely to become habitual liars**.

The selective nature of the memory amplifies this phenomenon. **Our memory of personal dishonest actions is much foggier compared to that of honest actions.** Researchers call this phenomenon "unethical amnesia."[562] Interestingly, even though we forget our personal moral failures, we still remember the failures of others.[563] Further, after dishonest actions, we forget the moral rules we learned before cheating (but we don't forget morally irrelevant information).[564]

Some brains enjoy lying. Most brains forget they lied.

As a result, **by the time people become habitual liars, they lose self-awareness**. When they score well because they cheated, they ascribe their good scores to their intelligence, not to cheating. They also overestimate their future performance based on the current scores that they got by cheating.[565] It is this neuroscience of cheating (our eleventh neural trap) that gives birth to the likes of Enron.

CHEATING ISN'T FREE

Cheating in all its variations is very expensive to our society. Cheating leads to loss of trust, which results in divorce, bankruptcies, wars, degradation of sport, and potential economic collapse. Dishonest employees engage in more harmful and less helpful behaviors than do their more honest counterparts.[566] The higher up in an organization dishonesty starts, the more widespread its effect. The United States annually loses $1 trillion because of bribes, $270 billion to $345 billion in taxes from unreported income, and $42 billion due to shoplifting and employee theft.[567, 568] Insurance fraud costs tens of billions of dollars every year.[569]

In an interesting study, researchers found that unethical acts increased one's perception of body weight.[570] **You can literally feel physically heavy (in addition to emotionally heavy) from the burden of dishonesty.**

Parts of the world where trust has collapsed become riddled with crime and abuse. The vulnerable, particularly children, suffer the most in these regions.

Dishonest societies short-change their vulnerable, particularly the children.

Every little effort you, I, and others can make to live with integrity and values helps us, our families, and the larger world.

RX FOR CHEATING

Here are ten ideas to help you become more honest.

1. Remind yourself of your true honorable nature and make sure to listen to those reminders before you have traveled too far down the path of dishonesty. For example, in a research study, signing the form at the beginning instead of at the end significantly increased honest reporting.[571] Reminding students of their honor code or the Ten Commandments increased their honesty, even if their university had no formal honor code.[563, 572]

> *Rise in your own eyes and in the eyes*
> *of the noble and the humble.*

2. Fill your environment with subtle cues that remind you of your morality.[567] In your living space, sprinkle around writings of Proverbs, Shlokas, and Tora as well as memorabilia that take you to a beautiful moment in life. Listen to uplifting music that connects you with values. We have a sacred corner in our home in which my wife and I go to sit if we are feeling disturbed. Keep a sacred corner in which you can sit and remind yourself of your life's purpose.

3. Practice honesty in little daily actions to strengthen your self-control muscles.[555] A previous colleague of mine, Karen, whom I greatly respect for her integrity, taught me a valuable lesson. Once, I was discussing a project with her. After I showed her a few slides and shared some ideas, she looked like she was lost. I asked her what the matter was. She said, "I am hungry. I was thinking about food. I barely heard anything you said." After an awkward moment, we both laughed and proceeded to lunch. I know that I can trust her to always speak the truth. Admit you overslept (assuming you did) and that's why you were late for the meeting instead of claiming that the elevator got stuck on the twelfth floor. This will take courage, that we will visit in chapter 78.

4. Never lie to kids. I have come to dislike the idea of "just kidding." Many children are too literal to catch metaphors and a sense of humor. They take an adult's lying as silent approval to speak the untruth.

> *Decrease the dose of "just kidding," particularly with the kids.*

5. Be kind behind the veil of anonymity. We often behave the worst under the veil of anonymity. Visit any online chat group that allows anonymity. You'll recognize how mean and unkind we can be when we think no one is watching. We spare no one—the recently bereaved, the flood victims, the injured, the sick, the dying. We forget that **we are always being watched—by ourselves**. Every time we deride someone, we deride ourselves. **Be your kindest when you know no one is watching—in the silence of your mind. Be particularly kind when posting under a pseudonym; every sharp comment hurts.**

The sacred within us knows, registers, and feels all the words our pseudonyms post anonymously.

If you can, provide a more transparent feedback. Honesty is best served where peer observation is likely.[567] It might feel uncomfortable sometimes, but it is better than the alternative.

6. Be compassionate. The more altruistic and compassionate you are and the more you think of others, the less likely you will be dishonest.[566] We will spend a fair bit of time talking about compassion in chapters 62 through 66.

7. Pay attention to the words you use. In one study, when researchers gave different instructions to the students ("Please don't cheat" versus "Please don't be a cheater"), the second instruction was much more effective at preventing dishonesty.[573] People like to maintain a good self-image. Engage others in thoughts, words, and actions that help them enhance their self-image. Elevating their perception of who they are will make morality easier.

8. Take good care of yourself. When we are hungry, thirsty, stressed, or threatened, we are more likely to cheat. **Keep yourself hydrated, nourish your body with healthy food, and believe in those who believe in you.**[550, 551]

9. Value time more than money. Research shows that a focus on money increases cheating, while a focus on time decreases cheating.[574] I believe your main energy resource is the number of heartbeats still left in your life. That depends on your heart rate and the amount of time you have. The more you focus on finite time, the greater the likelihood that you will focus on values.

10. Avoid partial confessions. When wanting to come clean, partial confessions seem attractive because, without giving away the whole thing, we feel we can build trust. While it is true that we are more likely to be seen as honest when we confess at least partially as compared to not confessing at all, research shows that emotionally we are worse off from giving a partial confession.[575] Perhaps, if the world believes our partial confession, we feel guilty about deceiving the world one more time.

I hope this chapter provided you with interesting insights into the science and art of cheating. With this knowledge, when I see someone lying, I can more easily look past the action, think about its neural basis, and get to the bottom of where it is coming from. It has allowed me to be kinder. Before that, I felt the whole world was out to cheat me. I couldn't trust anyone, and I doubted everyone's intentions. I felt very vulnerable, believing everybody was out to get me. I internalized and personalized minor insults. I couldn't forgive, which is our twelfth neural trap.

28

Neural Trap #12: Not Designed to Forgive (The Avenger)

It is 1856. A teenage boy from tribe A falls in love with a girl from a rival tribe (tribe B). Tribe B elders take offense and stage an attack past midnight. They kidnap, torture, and kill the boy. They load his dead body on a donkey and send it back to tribe A. Tribe A plans a counterattack. They kidnap the girl and sell her as a slave in a distant land.

After that, each subsequent generation of the two tribes continues the ritual of revenge. They raise children in fear, lose young men and women, and celebrate when drought or malaria strikes the other tribe.

Nobody now remembers how it all started. All they know is that they have to hate and hurt each other. Mutual hatred defines their lives.

This is happening right now in many parts of the world. With my own eyes, I have seen this playing out in families and dynasties.

Why don't we give reconciliation a chance when revenge is so harmful for everyone and seems to serve no useful purpose? Let's try to answer that question.

HELLO AGAIN, UNCLE AD!

Let's go back to Uncle Ad's time to answer this question. In Uncle Ad's days, kindness and politeness were luxuries. Resources were scarce; people struggled for food, cattle, and land to support their families. There were no grocery stores with bakery aisles or whole sections devoted to cereals. If one child ate, that meant someone else's child was going hungry, not unlike what you still see among lions and hyenas in National Geographic videos. Autocracy was widespread. A disgruntled king could destroy an entire family with one immature utterance. Tribes attacked other tribes, destroyed homes, stole cattle, and hurt women, children, and the elderly just because their leaders had bad dreams.

The response to such attacks couldn't have been forgiveness. Revenge was the language of the brave. Revenge acted as a deterrent to future or previous aggressors by showing that the targets were not small and vulnerable.[576] People needed to broadcast this to the whole world to prevent future attacks. Research shows when two people argue on the street, the presence of a third person doubles the possibility that the argument will expand into a brawl. This is because each wants to show that he isn't vulnerable to getting trampled.

Forgiveness—the opposite of revenge—was the language of the weak, or at least it was perceived that way. The top leaders of most ancient civilizations were ruthless and evil schemers.

No wonder the brain evolved mechanisms so that we never forget those who don't mean us well. Our survival depended on whom we could trust when we were sleeping at night.

WIRED FOR REVENGE

Here is how the brain keeps revenge alive. **Contemplating revenge activates our pleasure center.**[246, 577, 578] As you know, we are likely to repeat experiences that activate the brain's reward (pleasure) center. Planning revenge to exact justice and prevent a future assault is thus distinctly pleasing.[579] Retaliatory aggression also activates the pleasure center.[580] Giving up an activity that provided pleasure and secured survival and safety made no sense to our ancestors. I believe many of our ancestors who prioritized forgiveness may have been eliminated prematurely.

Contemplating revenge feels like eating dark chocolate: both activate the brain's pleasure center.

The same rules, however, don't apply to the modern world. The world has changed now. Hurts are more often psychological. The consequences of not forgiving minor slurs are often disproportionate. I hear about people shooting others because they bumped into each other and refused to apologize. I hear about someone getting shot because one person honked at the person ahead. We are less patient, less tolerant, and more armed.

Why do we forget that our main goal of travelling is to have a good time with the person we are traveling with and reach our destination, and not pick a fight with a co-traveler who might have cut across us because he or she was rushing to the emergency room?

Revenge has other problems. Unlike what we believe, **revenge provides only temporary relief and, paradoxically, can increase anger**.[581] Revenge causes us to continue to ruminate on the insult. Further, the way the neural system operates, if A punches B and then B counterpunches A (to make it even), A will not connect B's counterpunch with his or her own initial punch.[582] A will assume B is wrong and punch B again. B will do the same, and on it goes for generations. No wonder Mahatma Gandhi said, "An eye for an eye leaves the whole world blind."

Revenge begets revenge, not healing or satisfaction.

"I am sorry" and "No worries; I understand" are such powerful words. A brain that thinks, speaks, and lives these words will understand that most people struggle with their vulnerable selves, will be compassionate, will have gratitude for life's gifts, will be able to find meaning even in hurts, and thus will develop pragmatic acceptance. Only when the mind is enriched with these values can forgiveness sprout. Research shows that forgiveness is associated with activation of the brain network involving empathy, the understanding of the mental state of others, and better emotional regulation using the frontoparietal areas of the brain.[583]

FIT AND FORGIVING

What does the research show about the benefits of forgiveness? Forgiveness is inversely related to stress and mental illness, with cause and effect pointing from lack of forgiveness to stress and mental illness and not the other way around.[584] A national survey found that, while unforgiveness is associated with poor self-reported physical health,[585] forgiveness is associated with better physical and mental health and better work productivity.[586]

In the elderly, forgiveness and depression are anticorrelated: the more they forgive, the less depressed they feel.[587] In people with difficult life situations, those with greater forgiveness continue to do well physically and mentally despite higher levels of stress.[588]

A distinct form of forgiveness is self-forgiveness. Forgiving oneself, like forgiving others, is associated with better physical and mental health.[589] Further, even if you feel unforgiven by others, self-forgiveness can protect you from depression.[590] **Forgive yourself if you don't have a PhD in human relationships or life's struggles. Your mistakes reflect the reality that you are and will always be a student of life.**

*Forgiving someone at work improves
your relationship at home.*

Since forgiveness isn't for the faint of heart, you might ask: Will all these benefits accrue if you intend to forgive but can't fully commit yet? The answer is yes. **Just an intention to behave better toward the transgressor is enough**, although a deeper commitment with positive emotions toward the transgressor will likely help more.[591]

If you can't forgive yet, just nurture the desire to forgive. That'll be enough for now.

PICK YOUR INSTINCT

We have instincts for both revenge and forgiveness. Both instincts serve a purpose. In general, the revenge instinct prevails when we are hurt intentionally by someone who will likely repeatedly hurt us, who is not part of our inner circle, and whose relationship isn't worth maintaining. Forgiveness prevails for people who didn't mean us harm, who are unlikely to hurt us in the future, and whom we care about the most.

We will continue to need both instincts. The key is to exercise the right judgment and prioritize one instinct over the other. In general, with greater interdependence and with a higher proportion of hurts being emotional and unintended, the forgiveness instinct will be more likely to help. **The key to forgiveness is to expand the circle of people we are willing to consider meaningful and for whom we can separate action from intentionality.**

With this in mind, experts have developed multiple structured programs to enhance forgiveness. Most of these programs enhance forgiveness, and in turn decrease anxiety and depression, and increase hope.[592] In general, forgiveness programs intervene at four levels; they help you to do the following: (I will come back to this topic in chapter 69.)

- Find the other person more forgivable
- Rise in your own eyes
- Find forgiveness meaningful
- Practice the forgiveness process

Almost every society has capital punishment and the desire for blood revenge.[582] Every society also has a mechanism for forgiveness. Even nonhuman primates find a path of reconciliation after a fight.[593] It is really up to us which behavior we feed and allow to germinate.

FREE UP HEADSPACE

Each of the above traps—combined with the uncertainty of life and the complexity of the world, which I will discuss soon—overloads the brain. You'll need a lot of brainpower to handle future uncertainty. **Forgive if you can; storing old hurts isn't a good use of headspace.**

> *Storing old hurts isn't a good use of headspace.*

The stuff our brain has to deal with occupies memory slots in the brain's processor. Inside the brain is working memory similar to RAM for a computer; it is the memory we use to run our lives. We have finite working memory; some experts believe we have just seven slots.[594]

With even a few open files running in our heads, the slots get occupied, crowding the space that could otherwise be used for running more useful and enriching programs.

A crowded working memory is like a computer with multiple windows open. Eventually the windows freeze the computer. In the brain, so many options cause decisional fatigue. This is one of the many ways our brain gets fatigued—the final neural trap.

29

Neural Trap #13: Tired Beyond Imagination (Fatigued)

Have you sometimes said or done something that clearly seems stupid in retrospect and had to ask yourself, "What was I thinking?" Have there been days when you felt so wiped out by six o'clock in the evening that you just wanted to be left alone to hibernate? After working for a few hours on a project, have you struggled maintaining your focus? If so, during each of those times, you probably were experiencing brain fatigue.

TWO KINDS

With respect to fatigue, we have two kinds of organs in our body. The first type can work constantly and doesn't need formal rest—the kidneys, for example. You don't have to plan your day around the need to rest your kidneys. The brain is the second type. After some time, it gets tired and needs rest.

If you are doing your favorite activity—such as playing golf, reading a page-turner, watching a movie, or playing with children—the brain can go on for many hours. But if you are reviewing documents, filling out forms, or studying for an exam, the brain gets fatigued in about an hour.[595, 596] If the task is intense (such as seeing a series of letters and matching each letter with the one seen two letters prior), then fatigue and related errors can appear in thirty minutes.[597, 598] If the task is very intense (such as reading a paragraph while trying to understand the meaning and counting the number of vowels all at the same time), fatigue can start in as little as four minutes.[599]

The more intense and boring the task,
the faster the brain gets tired.

WHY BRAIN FATIGUE?

When you maintain focus on a particular topic, you do two things: focus on the topic and inhibit distractions. These inhibitory pathways get particularly exhausted. With time, the brain loses its ability to suppress irrelevant information.[595] Once fatigue has set in, increasing the motivation can temporarily restore the focus, but only temporarily.[600]

Fatigue, like pain, is a protective mechanism that prevents damage. Fatigue of the body occurs when muscles are overused. This is peripheral fatigue. Mental or brain fatigue occurs from brain overuse. **Mental fatigue isn't just about brain overload. It is also related to your motivation and emotions.** Anticipated reward is matched against perceived effort. When this equation is favorable, we experience less fatigue, and when it's unfavorable, we experience more.[601, 602]

The precise mechanism of mental fatigue isn't currently established. Some researchers believe the brain contains facilitation and inhibitory systems. When the brain thinks it has overexerted itself, the facilitation systems slow down and the inhibitory systems activate.[239] Researchers believe that inaccurate sensing in this system can cause fatigue with minimal exertion or, conversely, dangerous levels of fatigue without timely warning.

With repeated activity, the overused areas of the brain also accumulate neurotransmitters and other chemicals in the space between neurons. This gunk needs to be cleared for efficient nerve transmission. Scientists have recently discovered channels that clear the brain's gunk, called the glymphatic channels.[603] I speculate that when the clearing is inefficient, our focus suffers.

SUFFER IN SILENCE

The brain experiences the bulk of its fatigue in silence. Here is the reason. If you walk around lifting fifty pounds, in a very short time your back and shoulders will start to hurt, a signal for you to stop. Pain and fatigue are good feedback signals that keep us safe so we don't exhaust ourselves to death. The problem with the brain is that it doesn't have any pain receptors for itself. **A neurosurgeon can operate on the brain in a conscious patient without the patient feeling any pain.**

The brain lacks pain receptors for itself.

So how does the brain tell you that it is tired (or hurting)? Among other things, you might have weakened focus, lower creativity, lower engagement and performance, more errors, a desire for coffee, greater irritability, and tired eyes. These are nonspecific forms of feedback.

When our muscles fatigue, we give them rest. What do you do when your brain can't focus because it is tired at 3 p.m. in the afternoon? Do you stop and give yourself some rest or try to muscle through? You try to muscle through, don't you? We push ourselves more just when we need the rest.

A cup of coffee provides a short-term boost.[604-606] But this is akin to flogging a tired horse. Fatigue and its metabolic effects continue to build up until you are totally spent.[604] And this isn't innocuous.

THE REAL DEAL

Fatigue impairs attention, predisposes you to errors, lowers engagement, and increases the risk of accidents.[607-609] **Tired brains get irrational, depleted of willpower, inefficient, less creative, illogical, and impulsive, and they experience a higher risk for mood disorders.**[610] For example, if you are driving with a tired brain, you're likely to make more errors and have greater stress, and you will be less aware of performance impairment.[611] Fatigue more strongly affects complex tasks that involve planning and thinking through a lot of different options.[612] All of the twelve neural traps we have reviewed so far become worse with brain fatigue.

Several studies have shown that **mental fatigue decreases physical endurance and performance**. When the brain is tired, the body goes into self-preservation mode. The same exertion feels much more intense, so we stop sooner than we would have otherwise.[613-615] Mentally fatigued soccer players don't do as well with running, passing, and shooting.[616] Elite cricket players also show worse performance after developing mental fatigue.[617]

A tired brain is an unhappy, unproductive, disengaged brain.

It doesn't end there. Mental fatigue increases adrenaline (increased sympathetic activity), predisposing one to abnormal heart rhythms.[618] Such changes can start in as little as a few minutes, predisposing the individual to potentially fatal rhythm abnormalities, heart disease, stroke, and even death.[599] Work-related death, which is partly mediated by brain fatigue and its adverse consequences, is recognized as a significant health hazard in Japan, where it is called *karoshi*.[619, 620]

When the brain gets tired, the eyes also silently get spent.

TIRED EYES

Embryologically, eyes are an offshoot of the brain. A tired brain and tired eyes go together. **Our eyes weren't designed to stare for ten hours at a flashy screen few inches away.** In the past, we were accustomed to seeing landscapes in nature with different depths of perception. When you stare at a screen for more than two hours, your tear film dries up.[621] You blink less often than needed, and even individual blinks become less efficient.[622] As a result, you experience symptoms of eye burning, dryness, visual blurring, merging lines and words, grittiness, headache, light sensitivity, and a desire to close the eyes.[623] This symptom complex is called the computer-vision syndrome.

You can make a few simple changes to decrease eye fatigue. Color, contrast, brightness, viewing angle, distance, and font size—all of these can be adjusted on our screens to comfort the eyes. Wearing computer glasses, installing antireflective screens, and keeping the screen about two feet away and slightly below eye level can help too. I also recommend avoiding very bright light, exposing the eyes to different depths of perception, and resting for twenty seconds every twenty minutes.

Brain and eye fatigue are unintended consequences of our technological success. I am sure this isn't what we were seeking when we first built fires and discovered the wheel at the beginning of our journey to become the most brilliant and well-adapted species on the planet.

THE BRAIN LIKES RUM

How can you prevent brain fatigue? One obvious answer is to decrease the brain's load. But that isn't easy or feasible for many. Fortunately, we have two additional options. Let's talk about each of them.

The first option is to sprinkle brain breaks multiple times throughout the day so your brain has time to rejuvenate itself. We can't prevent the brain from getting tired. But we can recharge it before the battery is down to 2 percent. But how practical would it be to take forty-five minutes of rest every two hours? I have a better solution, which I like to call creative rest. Here is its basis.

Our brain needs two kinds of food to be fully nourished. First comes the physical nourishment of oxygen-glucose that is provided by blood flow to the tune of four hundred gallons per day. The second kind of nourishment is subtler. Answer this question before you read further: What is your brain hungry for?

_____

_____

The most common answers I get are rest, sleep, and new, interesting experiences. Those are all good, but they do not truly capture our core hunger. Here is what I believe is the correct answer: **uplifting emotions**.

The brain works much better if it keeps feasting on uplifting emotions every couple of hours. Uplifting emotions can come from reading an inspiring passage, watching an entertaining video, talking to someone who cares about you, a simple gratitude practice or even exchanging a positive text. (One text that uplifted me a few years ago read – "She did it!!" It was my wife texting me about our three-year-old daughter who had been struggling with constipation for a few days.)

The second important nourishment is motivation. I forget my "why" very easily and have to remind myself every week, if not more often. In my office at work is an image of a little girl who died from a bomb blast. I don't know her, but any day I feel low or am motivated by fear or greed, I look at her. My life's purpose is to help build a world in which we treat our little ones better than we treated her. She has never failed in motivating me to work harder and do the right thing.

Our brain needs a combination of Rest, Uplifting emotions, and Motivation, a different kind of RUM.

Our brain is energized by uplifting emotions and motivation.

How do you add RUM moments during the day? Build brain brawn.

BUILDING BRAIN BRAWN

As with muscles, you can exercise your brain networks to strengthen them. Here are nine research-supported ideas:

1. Increase perceived control. Research shows that, for the same task, the greater our perception of control, the lower our fatigue.[624] In fact, **lack of perceived control at work interferes with recovery at home over the weekend.**[625] Involve yourself in the decisions that affect you; involve others in the decisions that affect them.

2. Make friends. We feel vulnerable when we feel lonely. Research shows that the higher your perceived social support, the lower your mental fatigue.[626] Invest in relationships; connect with people; help them feel worthy. **Let others associate you with feeling good about themselves. They will return the gift.**

If you want others to like you, let them know you like them.

---

3. Healthy self-talk. Your words are heard by others; your thoughts are heard by you. Research that shows healthy positive self-talk enhances endurance and delays fatigue.[627] When you speak positive words to yourself, your perception of exertion is lower for the same level of effort. Thinking good, uplifting thoughts is inexpensive but invaluable.

4. Use happy faces. Emojis increase the quality of the texts my thirteen-year-old sends. Images of happy faces, inspiring words, and honorable people are great as decorations. Research shows that **sprinkling positive emotion cues, such as happy and content faces and words that point toward action and energy, into your messages can enhance performance.**[628] Surround yourself with these images and words.

5. Challenge yourself. It is fair to assume that most of us are driven by external motivators. Research shows that the higher the potential gain, the lower the fatigue. This affects both subjective and objective fatigue measures.[629]

6. Be prepared. The better prepared you are, the greater your courage and lower your fatigue. Research shows that **the effect of fatigue on errors is less pronounced among those who are better prepared.**[630]

7. Engage in self-care. Do not shortchange sleep. Insufficient sleep is a major source of fatigue.[631] Sleep deficiency causes negative thinking and disrupts your attention.[632] Train yourself physically. The stronger you are physically, the better off you are mentally.[633] And **if you feel you are low on energy, conserve your energy so you will be at your best for the tasks that are the most meaningful to you.**[634]

Physical health improves mental health; mental health improves physical health.

---

8. Surround yourself with meaning. Keep images, words, artifacts, and audio or video recordings around you that have a deeper story and that remind you of your role on this planet. Let them appeal to your emotional side and not just to your rational side.

9. Take multiple breaks. The cornfields can improve their yield with fertilizer, but they eventually have to rest in the winter to sprout again in the spring. Recognize that uplifting emotions and motivation can go only so far in replenishing your energy. Research shows that positive experiences at work significantly decrease fatigue only on days you experience a lot of negative events or have a high level of personal stress.[635] But on days with not too many negative events, positive experiences have only a marginal effect on fatigue. At some point, you'll need to give your brain a rest, just as you would rest a heated engine.

I totally believe in taking small "snacks" of breaks. Multiple research studies support my personal practice; taking multiple breaks enhances performance.[636-645] I call it putting my brain in the airplane mode! During this time give your brain a break from planning and problem solving.

When you are not flying the plane, let your brain rest in the airplane mode.

If you are not someone who can relax in the airplane mode, then do something that you enjoy doing. If you truly, deeply enjoy your work, then your work will feel like a break and will engender much less fatigue. This happens when you find greater curiosity and meaning in your work.

You can add several additional RUM moments during the day by doing simple things. Spend two minutes sending silent gratitude to a few people who care about you, take a stroll and send silent good wishes to everyone you see, watch an uplifting video, read a few pages from a good book, do something you find meaningful, savor humor, or practice deep breathing for a few minutes. I will share several additional ideas throughout this book.

Phew! That was a long, detailed map of how our brain's instinctive workings can trap us! I hope you found it as fascinating as I do. I wish I knew this information as a teenager. I believe mindfulness that enhances our self-awareness by teaching us the neuroscientific basis of our struggles will better engage our imagination. Mindfulness that teaches unbiased authentic understanding of the human condition through neuroscience will future proof itself.

Knowing that our brain's default design pushes us to be distracted, threat focused, sensitive, dreamy, envious, conflicted, ungrateful, dissatisfied, dependent, habit driven, dishonest, unforgiving, and tired has helped me become a kinder person. The brain's default design is a serious problem. Put seven and a half billion such brains on a planet, give them free will, arm them with creativity and imagination, inequitably distribute resources, and fire them up with competition and aggression, and you have the perfect recipe for the chaos that surrounds us.

Even with all these vulnerabilities, the brain might still be OK if left alone in a Zen world. How I wish that were the case! The brain is put to rigorous tests every single day. The two tests, related to the uncertainty of life and complexity of the world, together create the load we have to lift each day. Let's look at these tests next.

(At this point I invite you to pause for a bit, perhaps take a stroll or enjoy a cup of coffee, before proceeding to the next chapter.)

30

Uncertainty

I love watching sunsets, particularly the ones in which the sun softens its glow and the sky has ample clouds to absorb and reflect the fading photons, which assume shades of mango, orange, and ripe papaya.

"Where do people go when they die?" my seven-year-old asked me one day.

"They become stars."

"Like the ones in the sky?"

"Sort of."

She looked contemplative. I sensed that her little mind needed more explanation.

"When the sun sets here, it rises in a different world. It has to set here to rise there. Same with people. They have to leave this world to show up somewhere else."

"I get it," she says.

I wonder whether she really gets it. Because I don't get it. My brain is limited and has no way of sampling information from the other side of the curtain.

The brain has the momentous task of preserving the spark of life that inhabits it. Destined to eventually fail in this task, the brain struggles with every situation, real or imaginary, that increases its risk of failure. Add to that all the imperfections that prompt it to inflate the bad and discount the good, no wonder we sometimes feel burned out.

***Every single day, our brain shows up for a task
in which it is eventually bound to fail—keeping us alive. That's gotta be difficult.***

FINITENESS, UNCERTAINTY, AND LACK OF CONTROL

The brain faces three challenges: finiteness, uncertainty, and lack of control. The very nature of life is *finiteness*. Every day about 150,000 people pass away. Where they go and what happens to them, no one knows for certain. We're all like the salmon swimming upstream. In a hundred years, almost everyone around you will have been replaced, including yourself. We visit here for a short period. This dream will eventually end. But we don't know when and where we will wake up or how painful the transition will be. Sometimes our mortality disturbs us less than the fear of pain and suffering we might have to endure during the transition.

> ***Often, a greater fear than the fear of death is the fear of pain and suffering during the transition.***

Life would be much different if we knew our fate and liked what we saw and, without having to go through a near-death experience, could see the light, meet the angelic beings, and experience universal love. But the powers that be have kept the curtain closed. We create our versions of truth, read books, listen to sermons, and yet we can't overcome our lingering doubt. Hence, we struggle, with finiteness and the uncertainty of our fate.

Uncertainty is the nature of life. Imagine flying a single-engine plane with a broken fuel gauge. Life is a bit like that. No one knows for certain how much fuel is left in the tank. Yet optimists tell us that all is well. Self-help experts tell us to focus only on the now. **How can I anchor in the now when it can't promise it will stand by me in the next now?** We have three choices: fight this uncertainty, accept it, or believe in an eternal savior.

As much as you hate uncertainty, fighting with a force a million times stronger than you won't help. Nevertheless, intolerance of uncertainty strongly correlates with anxiety and depression.[646] Acceptance is the second option and is almost as difficult. Faith is the third choice. It is a powerful option, but without anything tangible to hang on to, the vast majority of the faithful still have doubts.

The problem with acceptance is that we don't know what we are accepting. How can I accept my future when I don't even know what it is? Every fiber of my being tells me to choose, drive carefully, focus, and steer my vehicle myself. But the road into the fog of the future, particularly the future beyond the curtain, is unseen. **Living feels like driving a vehicle I can't control on a road that doesn't exist.**

Even if I can accept my mortality, how do I accept the suffering that might precede my death without knowing anything about it? I have no control over how much pain I will have before my mortal frame is put to rest, and I hate lack of control. I also hate that I can't keep my loved ones safe in a bubble. They have to carve their own destiny.

That's the third challenge of human life: *lack of control*. When flying a plane, you can't do anything about the wind gusts or lightning or the state of mind of the air-traffic controller who is guiding you. **Illusion of control is a great trick to borrow short-term peace.** In reality, though, we don't get to choose the most important aspects of our lives: our parents, country of birth, race, genes, children, or children's genes. As we get wiser, the illusion ends, and if it ends before true wisdom sets in, we suffer.

Lack of control inflames our insides. Trying to control the outcome of a soccer game when you are watching your own team play not only causes adrenaline to go up but also more than doubles your risk of heart attack.[647] In a Canadian study, watching a live hockey game doubled the heart rate, equivalent to vigorous physical stress. The increase was particularly strong during overtime and scoring opportunities.[648] Perception of lack of control at work worsens almost every health measure, including risk of heart disease and chance of survival among British civil servants.⁶⁴⁹

In many situations, you can't do much about uncertainty and lack of control other than changing your own perspective.

Finiteness, uncertainty, and lack of control are difficult problems with imperfect solutions.

Life indeed throws complex, unsolvable challenges at the little brains we have. We swim in an ocean of uncertainty. Just as birds can't afford to fear flying and fish can't fear water, we can't live in peace if we are afraid of uncertainty. The sooner we develop a healthier relationship with finiteness, uncertainty, and lack of control, the better it is for us.

Sometimes I feel we would have been happier if we were a little less intelligent. Nevertheless, the brain has done pretty well despite the odds against it. But in its effort to accommodate and control the phenomena, the brain has created one more assault on itself by carving nature into a chaotic space that is complex and rapidly changing—our dynamic, high-tech world.

31

Complexity

My family and I had a pet dog named Mikki, whom we lost a few years ago. Mikki lived in psychological heaven his entire life. All he needed to be happy was a full stomach and a playmate. A bouncy ball would do too. Although at times he struggled with acceptance, such as when we left him alone for the whole day, he was an expert at forgiveness.

Mikki taught me the value of simplicity, of not overthinking, of not getting caught in catastrophizing, and of letting go. But I haven't fully internalized the lessons yet. For example, I totally believe in being grateful to Mother Nature, but when I see innocent lives lost in tornadoes, hurricanes, earthquakes, volcanoes, tsunamis, floods, and fires, I feel lost. Why does Mother Nature at times behave like a callous and unconcerned parent? Are those suffering just caught in a play of chance, or are there underlying reasons for those disasters, that we will ultimately understand but currently do not?

Do we matter to the universe? Are we an experiment, an afterthought, or the very purpose of creation? How special are we after all? Who can provide conclusive answers to these questions? Why don't we have access to the answers? Why should so many of us feel so lonely when seven and a half billion of us inhabit the planet?

ILLITERATE AGAIN

As if nature's fury wasn't unsettling enough, you and I are caught in an increasingly complex and restless world of our own creation. **The world today generates over 2.5 Exabyte of data every day** (one Exabyte is approximately a hundred thousand times the printed material in the entire Library of Congress, which includes over thirty-six million books).[650]

After having spent over fifteen years in college, I feel illiterate again. Every day I hear an acronym I haven't heard before. I haven't yet cracked the texting code of teenagers.[651] The choices my brain confronts every day and the number of decisions it has to make when sifting through these choices overwhelm me. Try to buy a cell phone and get a deal on a calling plan, and you'll know what I mean. I don't know half of what the sales agent says. I just smile and politely nod. The complexity is accelerating because of the rapidity of change that I talked about in the preface (remember how the line became a curve).

The world around me changes faster than I can blink. Just when I become comfortable with one version of the software, the next version arrives. Delay the decision by ten minutes, and my airline ticket might be fifty dollars costlier. I can't keep up with the gyrations in gas prices, stock-market volatility, valuations of cryptocurrency, rapidly changing national and international politics, and multivitamin recommendations.

The economic fate of an entire country sometimes changes in a matter of a few hours. Uncle Ad would be dizzy all day if he visited our planet now.

DOUBLE-EDGED SWORD

Change draws attention. The more immediately relevant the change, the more it ruffles us. Nowhere else is the Refresh button more familiar and impactful than with headline news. Headline news is now a greater source of entertainment than is quality time with loved ones. Next time you travel, notice which is more common in the airports—having a good time with loved ones or watching headline news. Our obsession with the news is affecting our well-being, increasing our levels of stress.[652] Turning off the television in disgust, my father said yesterday "No channel is good. All they talk about is crime."

Change is essential to growth. We need change. But what used to be an enjoyable surfing wave of change has become a tsunami of information. The information overload generates open files for the default mode, provides fodder for fear-based thinking, increases cynicism, takes us away from attending to relationships with self and others, and usurps the space that should be occupied by creative insights and thoughts about timeless principles.

> ***We allow worthless information to crowd the priceless space in our brain.***

The need to adapt to change makes us hurry. Everyone seems so rushed these days. Most of my hellos are hurried, with my attention already on what I need to do next. **As I am saying hello, I often hope the other person doesn't stop me from my rushing.** I might as well be saying to him or her, "I like you and will miss you when you aren't around, but when you're with me, I would rather pay attention elsewhere."

Like a mirror, the brain reflects the world it sees. You can easily imagine what could happen when an unpredictable, uncontrollable, sometimes furious, rapidly changing, and complex world interacts with a brain that loves predictability and control and is designed to discount the good and inflate the bad.

> ***We have successfully created a world full of material pleasures and emotional misery.***

The destructive habits that play out on the national stage arise from this triangle of causation: our neural predispositions, our lack of control, and the increasing complexity of the world.

INSIGHT

Insight in mindfulness *v2* is becoming fully aware of what traps our mind, instead of or in addition to the philosophical concepts that address whether we have a self within us, a detail that may or may not appeal to a curious mind that is hungry for objective facts. I believe every person in the world should know about how the thirteen human neural traps collude with our world and life's realities to create suffering.

It is validating to know that we all are a little crazy—each one of us. I wish I had known all this thirty years ago. I would have faced fewer struggles. Every time I faced failure or struggled with envy, I blamed myself. I thought I was a bad and selfish person.

Further, it has taken me a long time to realize and accept that **bad things can happen to good people**. Sometimes the best of people experience pain, illness, and failure. I have also realized that my success isn't rooted in my wealth or fame; it is about the values I embody.

It is my life's mission to share this knowledge with as many as I can. I believe we all will better understand one another's angst and will be more compassionate once we wake up to the reality of the struggles we all face. Knowing our vulnerabilities will make us wiser.

Knowledge that fosters compassion is true wisdom.

Once we realize that a high proportion of a person's stress is driven by individual biology, current societal norms, and the world's situation, we will become kinder. That will do wonders to our stress. **Stress is a biological problem with a psychological solution.**

We have landed now! This completes the first tenet of mindfulness *v*2, a scientific review of the reasons behind our suffering. I have shared with you a synthesis of what I have learned in the previous twenty years. I provided this information in some detail to fully engage your intellect. I am grateful to you for staying with me.

The tenets that follow provide a perspective and approach geared to help you escape the default state of the brain by cultivating an intentional brain—one that is better equipped to handle the challenges that it faces now instead of the challenges Uncle Ad's brain faced thousands of years ago. This approach aims to accomplish the dual task of achieving freedom and increasing resilience—freedom from negativity and resilience to transcend adversity.

Tenet 2 will offer a pragmatic alternative to being in the present moment: **instead of being in the present moment, be present for your moments.**

Part III
The Second Tenet: Presence

Tenet	Mindfulness *v1*	Mindfulness *v2*
Presence	Anchored by time	Anchored by intentionality

―∿―

Time is fleeting and untethered. Anchor presence by intentionality instead of time.

We don't need to be in the present moment; we need <u>freedom</u> from the need to be in the present moment.

32

Fireside Chat #3

"What did you think about the first tenet?" I ask Mike.

"I appreciated how we get trapped today by the same neural traits that helped us survive in the past. I loved the focus on science. A twenty-first-century citizen is more likely to be convinced by MRI scans than philosophical speculations."

"I have no doubt that the contemplatives who shared inspired philosophies would have used this science if they'd had access. Scientific understanding doesn't invalidate their assertions; it builds on them. Were you surprised by any of the findings?"

"I can't believe we humans have come so far, given how messed up we are in our head!"

"We sure are a work in progress. The interesting reality is that most of us aren't aware of our collective imperfections. We don't see our multiple blind spots. Because of this ignorance about our ignorance, we get hurt, and we hurt each other. My personal passion is to share this knowledge with the whole world. I believe once we understand our collective quirks, we will become kinder. We will become more compassionate, in pleasure and in pain. The day we become truly, deeply compassionate toward each other, we will transform. We will have transcended suffering. **Suffering that inspires kindness and love transforms you**."

"You know how I applied what I learned about the brain?"

"How?"

"I lowered expectations from my teenage nephew last night. We hung out together and had more fun than we have had in a long time."

"**Happiness equals reality minus expectations. You seldom can change the reality, but you can always play with the expectations**."

"Which one is your favorite neural trap?" Mike asks.

"You mean the least favorite?" I tease Mike.

"That's what I mean."

"I like, I mean dislike, them all." I speak as I think. "I don't have one. My top three are distracted by default, tired beyond imagination, and drawn by negativity. Those three traps are what I share in our resilience program. I call them our struggle with focus, fatigue and fear. Which ones are yours?"

Mike is ready with the answer. "Designed to be dissatisfied and vulnerable to dishonesty. I can forgive pretty easily."

"Good for you. Our dissatisfied design is one reason our happiness level hasn't budged, despite a multifold rise in income over the past sixty years."

"Could you expand on that?"

"With the way the brain operates, yesterday's dream becomes today's norm and tomorrow's disappointment. Many of us also feel lonely and could be wiser about how we use our resources. Most material objects and experiences provide little pleasure when experienced alone. Yet once we collect more resources, we seek greater privacy and thus become lonelier. The more we value happiness, the lonelier we get, which decreases happiness.[653]

"You may have read of research that shows money and material gains give little lasting pleasure, particularly when spent on the self.[654] Indeed, research shows that when we have a lot to spend, we stop enjoying the little daily pleasures. If you are, or believe you are, a world traveler, you stop enjoying your neighborhood's community park.[655] Even imagining being fabulously wealthy takes away the joy of dark chocolate.[656] **Money can give much more pleasure if it is used to savor experiences rather than to collect goods, and if your spending is aligned with your personality.**[657-660] **Experiences are often shared and not owned; indeed, spending money for the collective and sharing the pleasure gives the greatest joy.**[661, 662] **Savoring is in sharing.**"[660]

"How are the different neural traps related to each other?"

"They are all interconnected, and they feed each other. Mind wandering feeds negativity bias, and deficits in self-regulation get the habit loop going."

"Are they just a nuisance now, or do they serve a purpose?"

"They do serve a purpose. Mind wandering helps you think about the future. Negativity bias helps you lock the door and be safe. Architects use imagination to design our world. Comparison inspires you; programmed dissatisfaction nudges you; habits make your life simpler. And I am sure you want to indulge your short-term gratifications once in a while!"

"You got that right. Tell me something. If we have all these neural traps, why don't we all go crazy? Why don't we jump like chimps all day long or call nine-one-one when we see a dead ladybug?"

"Because we aren't just our neural traps or instincts. We are also self-control, compassion, and wisdom. A part of the brain is designed to brake our primal instincts."

"You mean the prefrontal cortex."

"Yep! One of the main roles of the prefrontal cortex is inhibitory control. You don't shoplift, chase giraffes in a zoo, or jump the checkout line, even though part of you may have fantasized about all this. The prefrontal cortex slams the brakes by helping us think of the consequences."

"Is the prefrontal cortex unique to us humans?"

"It's not. Most other animals have it, but it isn't as developed. Animals have other areas that are better developed. Dogs are masters of aromas; eagles are masters of movement; dolphins echolocate. We are masters of thinking—the crown achievement of the human brain. We can think, rationalize, imagine, and create. We can choose to let go of personal gain in favor of the collective. We aren't just a bunch of instincts. We are also a collection of well-thought-out choices."

"At least we can be."

"You are right; at least we can be. **Most of us aren't aware of the power of our thoughtful choices**—hosted by the prefrontal cortex. You can look at the entire mindfulness *v2* program as a system to train the prefrontal cortex."

"Sounds like training the brain is empowering the prefrontal cortex."

"Yes, it is. We all experience negative events and negative emotions. The question is how quickly we can recover from them. The instinctive brain takes the bait and can't disengage attention from the negative, making us anxious and depressed.[663-667] A strong attention and a trained prefrontal cortex break free of the negative quickly, eliminating much optional suffering. Wouldn't it be nice if we could rid the world of depression and anxiety?"

"Is that possible?"

"I believe so; most of it, anyway. My grandparents lost all their teeth; they never flossed, didn't have vibrating toothbrushes, and never got their teeth cleaned. But our generation will get to keep our teeth into very old age. This is simply because we floss and brush away all the debris. What if we learned to floss away all the mental debris? Couldn't we then keep the curiosity and joy we had as children? We might still have genetic predispositions but a kinder world will cushion us so they don't become uncontrolled mental health diagnoses."

"Sounds promising to me."

"Think about this. How do you feel on days you are constipated?"

Mike smiles.

"Elimination is as important as nourishment. We can use oxygen only if we eliminate carbon dioxide. We depend on our kidneys and liver to keep our bodies fresh. Unfortunately, our brains aren't very efficient at eliminating waste while we are awake. **Every night when we sleep, a system of channels opens up, called the glymphatic system, which is like a garbage truck for the brain.**[668, 669] These channels drain away waste products, helping you wake up fresh.[670] Researchers speculate that partial failure of this system, from genetic abnormalities or lack of good sleep, could cause an accumulation of toxins in the brain, leading to disorders like dementia.[668] In fact, researchers have even found that the brain's waste-disposal system works best when we sleep on our sides, as opposed to on our backs or stomachs.[671]"

"Do you think I should start sleeping on my side?"

"That's what I've done since I learned this science."

"Is your sleep better now?"

"Can't say for sure. Perhaps."

"How is this related to stress?"

"We have one more elimination system that's subtler than the physical channels—our thought-disposal system. By forgetting and reframing, we discard toxic thoughts. But most of us do a terrible job of discarding our thoughts. We are good at generating thoughts but not eliminating them."

"We are thought constipated!" Mike has a laugh.

I giggle too. "Or thought hoarders. And chronically so. We stack away these thoughts, particularly the negative ones, thinking they might come in handy someday. But like unhealthy food that doesn't stay unattended in the pantry and always finds a way into our mouths, these toxic thoughts do not sit unattended. We spend inordinate amounts of time revisiting them. This awareness can be very empowering, because you can start to fix the problem only when you become aware of it. If I never knew about mice in my basement, I wouldn't catch them."

"How long will it take for us to learn to catch our mice early, before they even enter our home?"

"Not very long. In a few generations, we stopped littering, started driving in lanes, and eliminated weeds from our yards. Why shouldn't we now use science to take care of our brains?"

"We should."

"The single most important skill we can use to take care of our brains is the topic of the second tenet. Could you summarize the entire field of healthy eating for me in one line?" I ask Mike.

After a brief pause, Mike says, "Cut down calorie-dense food?"

"That's pretty good. I might add to that to eat more fruits and veggies. Of course, you can add many subtleties to this core idea. In fact, some people find healthy eating more difficult than filing taxes."[672]

"Interesting."

"Many complex fields are driven by one or a few algorithms. You can capture the essence in just a few lines. The other day I was thinking about what two words capture the essence of mind-body practices."

"Kindness and gratitude?"

"That's pretty close. I was actually thinking—kindness and intentionality."

"How so?"

I clear my throat for a monologue.

"Most animal brains spend the bulk of their day in the instinctive mode, searching for food or a mate, marking their territory, or trying to be safe. Unfortunately, as you know, many human brains are also busy doing the same, with wandering minds. Since wandering minds often focus on concerns, regrets, and hurts, they make us live in a prey mode. We are the only species that sits at the apex of the evolutionary pyramid yet experiences daily fears. You wouldn't hear of lions having panic attacks or sharks swimming around with generalized anxiety. We can do better, much better, by being intentional.

"Intentionality helps you fully engage the brain's central executive—the salience and executive networks. With the central executive fully engaged, you effortlessly attend to what is important and meaningful, both in the world and in the mind, and in the domains of the past, the present, and the future.

"Being intentional is being flexible. Intentionality doesn't lock you in the present moment. It flows. Intentionality encourages an open, quiet, and alert presence. When you are intentional, you can perceive and think deeper; transcend the limited, instinctive way of living; and thus fully experience the gift of being human.

"At core, most mind-body practices guide you to be intentional—about how and what you attend to, what you think, and how you interpret. You choose your thoughts instead of letting thinking happen to you. Once you are intentional and intentionally kind, then you'll engage your conscience and values and will integrate the short term and the long term. You'll be less reactive and will spend more time focusing on what truly matters."

I pause to see if Mike has a question. Sensing none, I continue, now pouring a bit more energy into my words. "Presence isn't the present moment. Presence is being intentional about what fills your moments. Once you are intentional, it doesn't matter whether you are in the past, the present, or the future. Intentionality empowers you to take a step back behind the drama of life, see it from a place of poise, and then choose which character you want to play and which dialogue you wish to speak or hear. Intentionality is empowering."

"What about kindness?"

"Kindness provides the direction and purpose to intentionality. Without kindness intentionality can lead you astray, into unethical, immoral, even criminal activities. Kindness provides the banks to the river of your attention, so it is prosocial and altruistic. Your kindness is a marker of your strength, not weakness. Our babies need us to be kind. We can survive lack of gratitude, we can survive distractions. But if you take away kindness, we will become brutes. We will burn each other's homes, destroy cities, plunder our planet. We will cease to exist. Hence the need to pair intentionality with kindness."

"Bravo!" Mike claps.

"Is that all you have to say? I exhaled both of my lungs out in that monologue!" I wasn't sure if Mike was serious or making fun of me.

"For now, that's it."

"All right! Let's start with a brief encounter I had with Adrian, an inspiring colleague of mine who embodies intentionality and kindness."

33

Inspiring Adrian

A few years ago, as I was leaving work after a long day, I received an important lesson in presence from my colleague, Adrian. Adrian usually comes to work late in the afternoon when everyone is about to leave, since he is a janitor at our workplace. He has bright, intelligent eyes and a welcoming smile. I often see him darting across the hallways right when we are ready to leave work. That day, as I walked toward the elevator, I saw him approaching from the other end. We exchanged silent nods. Next, he pressed the elevator buttons, both Up and Down. I had never seen anyone simultaneously pressing both elevator buttons.

He clearly doesn't know where he is going. Wonder if his head is in the right place, I thought. Concerned, I decided to check his mental status.

"You haven't decided where you wish to go. Have you?" I joked, hoping for a response.

He looked at me, smiled, and said, "I'm going up to clean the upper floors. You must be going down since it's the end of the day and you look kind of tired. I pressed the Down button for you."

I could have melted. *This guy is a master in kind presence,* I thought. He was so far ahead of me. Here I was judging and making a negative conclusion about him, while he, during his busy workday, was anticipating another's needs, above and beyond his call of duty. *He should be teaching a course in mindfulness,* I thought.

Later that day I asked my wife, Richa, what she thinks when she first sees me at home at the end of the workday. After a long and deep sigh, she dropped her shoulders and gave this depressing reply: "Chores! What can I get you to do in the garage!" We both started laughing at her response. To me, that was a true compliment, indicating her trust in my capabilities, and also proof that we have been married twenty-five years.

After years of togetherness, partners can become borderline boring!

I asked the same question to our then five-year-old. Without a moment's hesitation, she answered, "Play. What I can play with you!"

That day was a great lesson in human nature. **Our short-term needs and concerns dictate how we consciously experience the world, including our closest loved ones.** Our thoughts have a strong influence on how we see the world—our presence.

34

Presence: Two Modes

Presence is your conscious experience at any moment. Presence among humans swings between two modes: instinctive and intentional. At any time, you can be in one of these but not both.

INSTINCTIVE

Untrained attention is driven by instincts (instinctive), focusing on the most interesting, engaging, or threatening part of the sensory experience. As I walk on the Magnificent Mile in downtown Chicago, countless sensory experiences draw my attention: shops, tourists, cars, performers, pets, a bronze man, traffic lights, and more. But a flashing, speeding police car immediately puts everything else in the background. A claim on our attention (our presence) is the ultimate victory for the myriad inputs that compete for it (more on this in the next chapter). I have enjoyed every visit to the Magnificent Mile because the novelty and richness of sensory experience there entertains me.

But when washing dishes in the kitchen sink or walking from my office to the cafeteria, I have seldom felt entertained. And the day I pulled my back, I could focus on nothing but the sharp jabs. This is my instinctive attention, drawn toward novelty and pain, with very little focus on the familiar and the ordinary. **Instinctive, untrained attention is vulnerable to external contingencies.** Some researchers call it the bottom-up attention.

INTENTIONAL

Most attention-regulating practices help you develop intentional attention that's guided by your core values so you are more empowered to regulate your conscious content. I can best describe it the way an F-16 airline pilot taught me. While landing the plane, myriad inputs crowd his attention—a gauge showing an error, a beeping sound, his plan for the day. But at that moment, he shuts everything out and focuses on landing the plane. He fills his attention with the information of his choosing. This is intentional attention that researchers call the top-down attention.

Intentional attention is driven by inner meaning not outer novelty or threat.

Some people are born with strong intentional attention. If they find a vocation or hobby that challenges and engages them, they blossom and become maestros of their field. They become outliers. The good news is that we can strengthen our intentional attention by training. Strong intentional attention is essential for any professional who wishes to excel in her or his chosen job. Such attention also comes in handy when listening to your spouse, talking to your child, driving safely, or enjoying your soup or a glass of wine. **Mindfulness training hones intentional attention.**

We can approach intentional attention by defining it from two different perspectives: time and content (what fills your attention).

Defining presence by time (the present moment versus the past or future) seems like an obvious solution but for reasons I will discuss next, is more difficult, less helpful, and less practical.

—⚡—

Time is an elusive and unsteady concept that science is actively reevaluating presently. Further, while anchoring awareness in the present moment can provide short-term respite, it can't offer a cure for our neural vulnerabilities. As I will argue in the following pages, a much stronger anchor for our presence is becoming intentional about what fills our moments, the second tenet of mindfulness *v*2. Let's start with time.

35

Time

BURIED BY BRILLIANCE

The only human creation I can think of that has no downside is dark chocolate! Everything else has unintended consequences. (That was an obvious exaggeration!)

Our species has a unique ability to enslave itself with its own inventions. Every new technology has a short-term positive impact on our productivity, but eventually it becomes a burden. An average executive today gets more than fifty thousand communications every year, compared to about a thousand a year in the 1970s. **Most people I know are barely keeping up and have little to no uninterrupted time.**[673]

When hunter-gatherers became farmers, they became dependent on a limited few crops, got glued to the land and livestock, and became vulnerable to diseases.[674] The discovery of farming helped us produce more children, but that came at the cost of individual wellbeing. Farming also led to loss of novelty; hunter-gatherers experienced a new landscape every day, whereas farmers see the same boring fields day after day after day. The same history has repeated itself with the technological revolution.

Modern technology has given us a remarkable ability to manufacture comfort, to communicate, and to save lives, but it has come at a price.

Technology has phenomenally increased an individual's ability to inflict harm. Technology has crowded our memory, increased the speed of life, and made us more impatient. There are days I wish the internet had not gone any faster than what the 56k modem provided. Many of these unintended consequences converge to one outcome— brain overload.

Every technological advance comes loaded with unintended consequences.

Many of us now are too busy to savor food, get a good night's sleep, or enjoy undistracted quality time with family. The outcome is a loss of meaningful connection with the world.[675, 676] **We have become materially wealthier but emotionally depleted.** An invaluable product of the technology that has caged us is time.

WHAT IS TIME?

You can tell what time it is but not what time itself is. **We know time, until we start deeply thinking about it.** Then we don't know time. Time can be considered a real entity essential to the fabric of the universe (Newton) or just an intellectual concept that enables us to describe and catalog a succession of events (Kant).[677]

We know what time it is, but we don't know what is time.

Galileo's pendulums were the first to tame time; his astute observation that pendulums take the same time to swing irrespective of the amplitude gave us an objective way to measure time. This was followed by balanced-spring watches, quartz crystal vibrations, and the time it takes for a cesium atom to vibrate (one second is defined as 9,192,631,700 cycles of the radiation that causes the cesium atom to vibrate between its two energy states). For most daily experiences, counting ("One Mississippi…two Mississippi…"), as my daughters have taught me, will suffice.

A good way to look at time is to consider it a dimension that describes and enables the sequence of events. **The arrow of time irreversibly moves toward the future, not the past.** Babies are born and then get older, oranges ripen, and eggs turn into omelets. Other than in the movies, we can't get younger, travel back into the past, or convert omelets into eggs. Time also moves from order to disorder (or as scientists call it, from lower to higher entropy).

Time inserts discipline in life. Time creates causality, experience, and memory. Time enables life by providing it with a scaffold of predictability. Time creates the past, present, and future. Time, however, can bind us and produce unease, in two ways.

UNHAPPY WITH TIME

First, time binds us when we experience time deficiency, commonly felt as time pressure or too little time. **Time pressure is a perception that you have less time to accomplish a task than is necessary.** Time pressure isn't related just to the absolute amount of time. The more you connect time with money, the greater your perception of time pressure and the lower your patience.[678] The longer your to-do list, the greater your time pressure. (I believe even more important than a to-do list is a not-to-do list.)

The more we connect time with money or tasks, the more time constrained we feel.

Time pressure is now a way of life.[679] I find myself hurrying when I'm late; I find myself hurrying even when I am early. Hurrying has become a habit. This hurrying comes at a cost. Hurried physicians become bad diagnosticians.[680] Time pressure decreases creative solution seeking, worsens mood,[679, 681] and increases stress[682] and impulsivity.[683]

Second, time concern also comes from the realization of the finiteness of our time and the uncertainty of what awaits us when our time is (literally) up. The mind, as you know, abhors finiteness and uncertainty. When the mind tries to grab time, fails to do so, and cannot accept this reality, we suffer.

There is a third way time can feel painful: when your time is filled with the undesirable and hurtful, against your wishes, and beyond your ability to tolerate or accept. A long meeting and a boring meeting are both hurtful. They often go in combination.

Given our inability to parse pleasant from good, our negativity bias, and our programmed dissatisfaction, the present moments get crowded with the neutral or undesirable. Further, **when the past and future trespass into the present, they often arrive with regrets and concerns**. The result is our default state of struggle with the present.

BUDDHA'S TIME CURE

Buddha offered an ingenious cure for our unhealthy relationship with time—by denying time. He considered time an illusion.[684] Nirvana entailed transcending time by recognizing that the entire creation breathes in unison in only one moment—the eternal present. With such awareness, the movement of time and the illusion of the world would stop. The resulting peace was considered a reward for a lifelong practice in moral living, wisdom, and meditation.

Nirvana, however, is an unrealized dream for most of us, and thus timelessness isn't a perceived reality for our senses. Over the centuries, however, physicists have been busy systematically dismantling the concept of time as a real entity. For instance, time slows when you move fast. At 87 percent of the speed of light, time slows to half its normal rate, and at 99.999 percent, it slows to 224 times its normal rate.[685]

Newton's gravity, Einstein's relativity, and quantum mechanics—none of them need time to solve their equations. Perhaps one day, timelessness will be a part of everyday understanding, but for now, I need to know the time to avoid tardy tickets, missed flights, and angry patients. Hence, there is the need for an interim solution.

THE TIMELESS PRESENT

A surrogate of freedom from time is the freedom of your mind from the past and the future by anchoring your awareness in the timelessness of the present moment. We live life in the present moment. **The past was and the unlived future will also be experienced in the present.** (Some neuroscientists and physicists might opine that the past and the future both exist only in the neural circuits of our brains.) Recall the essential need for present-moment awareness during Uncle Ad's time. Uncle Ad didn't have the luxury of mind wandering if he hoped to learn as a student and survive as a human. Thus, mindfulness became equated with bare presence. The present moment, however, doesn't work for me.

I have spent several years training myself to access present-moment awareness. It entails letting go of all fear, greed, ego, and selfishness, completely surrendering to the happenings of the now, and becoming an observer of the flow of life. During the moments I succeeded, the experience filled me with joy and imbued a sense of ethereal lightness in my being. Accessing such moments, however, takes tremendous effort and entails a significant time commitment (recall the Dalai Lama's experience that I shared in chapter 11). Further, such moments last for a very brief period, with the inevitable return of attention (and life) to its default state of wandering. Also, with the amount of time such practice consumes, I risk annoying my wife and completely missing our children's innocent antics.

> ***In the mind, the past, the present, and the future exist in a continuum because of our memory and ability to imagine.***

Buddha's original intent of freedom from time through negating it was reintroduced as the idea of focusing on the present moment. Although this might help for brief periods, it is not only difficult (or near impossible) but also counterproductive. The reason goes back to the very design of the human brain. Let's explore this interesting science.

36

The Evolving Brain

The reason we struggle with accessing and anchoring in the present moment goes back to the purpose and design of our brains. Our brains evolved because of our need to integrate information, process multiple inputs, and create a coherent output. Information needed to be communicated, and conflicts needed to be avoided. The left hand needed to know what the right hand knew. This led to the evolution of the complex structure of the brain.

The brain is the most complex biological information processor known to us.

THREE BRAINS IN ONE

The human brain has three key parts: hindbrain, midbrain, and forebrain. It's like having three brains woven together in a single space. The hindbrain makes sure you breathe without thinking about it and ensures that your heart beats and automatically changes its beat based on your body's needs. Consider the alternative. If every time you exercised, you had to mechanically readjust your heartbeat, wouldn't that become mentally exhausting? The hindbrain also makes sure your intestines digest, you maintain balance, and you receive information from the face, ears, and taste buds.

The midbrain influences hearing and vision and helps with arousal, temperature regulation, sleep cycle, and body movement.

The forebrain, which has gone through three expansions, has expanded the most. The first expansion was for enhancing the sense of smell. The second expansion was for processing other inputs, including visual, balance, and sensory. The third and most recent expansion involves thinking, imagining, and planning.

We have three brains in one.

Most animal brains have little forebrain or have experienced only the first or the first two expansions. Most animals are thus immersed in their sensory and motor worlds with three key goals: eat, do not get eaten, and reproduce.

They have little imagination and little foresight and are mostly driven by instincts. Instincts force them to live in the present. **A lifetime of living in the present moment, however, doesn't lead them to self-actualization.**

Most animals are in the present moment but they haven't yet self-actualized.

When a lion chases a wildebeest, the wildebeest either escapes or becomes a meal. If the wildebeest escapes, then within a few minutes it will be munching grass and doing normal wildebeest things, as though it had just gone on a particularly thrilling roller coaster and now it was time for the food court.

Imagine what would happen if any of us escaped the lion chase. We would hyperventilate, live in fear for days, might need professional help, could develop PTSD, and might be scarred for life. And if you knew that the lion could come at any moment from any direction and you didn't have the protection of a secure home, you would never relax enough to explore creative pursuits. You'd live in fear, in the prey mode.

Such fear protects us but comes at a cost—emotional suffering. The neural mechanisms that produce angst are the very mechanisms that have helped us survive. This is the reason you can't trust toddlers' ability to protect themselves—they have limited imagination, have irrational fearlessness, and are anchored in the present. The brain pathways that help them escape danger aren't mature yet.

That provokes the question: What is the key neural difference between us and the wildebeest and many other animals? The differences are many, but the key difference is the third expansion of our forebrain. **We humans are unique in having a prefrontal cortex that empowers us to imagine by traveling into the past and the future.** This ability has helped us create the wonderful world around us. Our prefrontal cortex helps us plan and problem solve. It helps us avoid future dangers and respond to current danger.

THERE'S NO GOING BACK

Given that we have a fully developed prefrontal cortex, there is no going back. We can't escape our rich imaginations. We also can't divorce the insecurities lodged in our memories. Do you see how our neural system is designed to keep us thinking about the past and the future?

Any species that is intelligent, is imaginative, has preferences, and has to take care of babies can't live in the present moment. An average person these days has 150 undone tasks that entail juggling many issues at the same time. Asking us to completely stop multitasking is unachievable.

Asking our brain to stop thinking and imagining is like asking
our heart to stop beating and pumping.

Further, the present moment isn't always the best time zone to be in, as can happen when reclining in the dentist's chair. I do not carry particularly fond feelings toward my dentist's sharp instruments rubbing and manipulating my gum margins. I know I eat more sweets than I should and don't floss as much as I should, yet that doesn't help me embrace the pain and scratchy sounds of a dental exam. In one such exam, I tried to settle into the breath, which helped some. Then I took my attention out of the present and into my high-school days. I thought about my favorite teachers, my naughty moments, and the times I felt worthy and loved. These rich imaginings numbed the discomfort and helped me endure the procedure. Escape from the present moment provided the necessary respite to allow me to better handle the present moment.

Thus, the answer can't be to always live in the moment. An effort to go back into the confines of the present moment would be akin to living like other animals. It wouldn't be fun. It would also fail. **Limiting the hummingbird to just one flower would be the same as keeping her trapped in a cage.** Wouldn't it be more useful to let the bird fly and spend more time on the flowers that are safe and have plenty of nectar?

I have realized that if I strive to chase a particular span of time, I will spend the bulk of my life just chasing. **We don't need freedom from past or future; we need freedom from our negative predispositions. We don't need to anchor ourselves in the present moment; we need freedom from the need to anchor ourselves in the present moment.** Buddha achieved this by negating time. We can achieve this by choosing what fills our time. Both are good options, but I believe the latter is an easier and more realistic option for the mind of a twenty-first-century go-getter.

Freedom from our negative predispositions will free us from the past and the future.

When you go to a restaurant, you don't tell the waiter to just get whatever. You look at the menu and carefully pick selections based on your palate and wallet. You can do the same with your mind.

The world is a giant canvas. You can't take it all in. Whatever you choose to shine the flashlight of your attention on becomes your reality. Similarly, your mind is also a giant canvas, and you have a choice in how you direct your thoughts. Unfortunately, many of us aren't aware we have that choice, and thus we let our default instincts control our attention. If our default was fulfilling, purposeful, and values driven, we wouldn't be collectively struggling, as we are right now. Hence the need to take charge, by being intentional.

We don't have to remain in the confines of our default state. We have a tremendous ability to direct our attention using our core values and consequently transform our sensory experiences and thought processes. Let's see how.

37

Instinctive Presence: People

It was June 1994. I was taking the final test before being awarded board certification in internal medicine from one of the most prestigious medical centers in India, All India Institute of Medical Sciences, New Delhi.

In the oral MD exam, I was asked to evaluate four different patients. The most complex patient was a lady with paralysis of all four limbs secondary to neuropathy (nerve damage). I focused on getting the key elements of her history and eliciting the pertinent physical signs. I am embarrassed to confess that I was so focused on doing well on the exam that I didn't think about her for a moment. At that moment, she was nothing more than an object. She wasn't a sentient being; she was a means to an end. I so much wish I could find her and apologize.

That is the first instinctive way of looking at people: *as a means to an end*. We can't help it, stuck as we are with wants filling most of our day. In that state, we splurge and sometimes do things that could seed hurts and regrets. This is particularly true for some selfish and foolish leaders who believe everyone who works for them is within their sphere to satisfy their fantasies. **As long as we aren't content with what we have and who we are, we seek from others whatever we think will make us whole at that moment.**

> *Treating people as a means to an end may help us hit short-term targets, but risks sacrificing relationships and forgoing long-term meaning.*

In my childhood, I heard a story about Mahatma Gandhi, who championed nonviolence and truth to secure freedom for India. Once he was invited to a dinner. He showed up in his traditional attire of an inexpensive dhoti. The gatekeeper, judging him to be an underdressed, undernourished commoner, refused admission, even though Gandhi told him that the banquet was in his honor. Gandhi went back home and returned dressed in a suit and tie. He was immediately let in. At the banquet, he started smearing food on his clothes instead of eating. When people asked him why he was doing that, he said (paraphrased), "At this banquet it isn't me; it is my clothes that are invited."

That is the second instinctive way we look at people: *judgmentally*. **We make quick judgments about others, including their competence, based on what they are wearing or how they look.** Sometimes it can be embarrassing. Several years ago, a good friend of mine was training at the prestigious Fred Hutch

Medical Center in Seattle. He was attending a lecture on bone-marrow transplantation. A few minutes into the lecture, an older gentleman, perhaps a little hard of hearing, came and sat in the back. Later he asked my friend about what he had missed in the lecture. My friend gave him a nice little talk about the basics of bone-marrow transplantation, thinking he was a retired community physician needing some attention in his senior years. My friend later learned that the person was the humble Dr. E. Donnall Thomas, the pioneering Nobel laureate who had developed the bone-marrow transplant.

The third instinctive way we look at others is by perceiving them *with suspicion*. Our almond-sized amygdala, whose job is to keep us alive and safe, screens all our sensory input for potential threats. The amygdala is like the chief security officer; when it starts yelling, the entire rest of the brain listens. The brain suspends all other conscious operations and does what the amygdala wants it to do. There's a good reason we are this way.

Let's speculate about two potential ancestors standing in the middle of a thick forest fifty thousand years ago. One had a hypervigilant amygdala, whereas the other was a happy-go-lucky type. Hearing a rustle in the bushes, the hypervigilant ancestor feared a tiger and took cover, while the more laid-back ancestor assumed it was a hedgehog, so he kept munching on tubers. Guess what? Sometimes, it was a tiger, a hungry one. As a result, within a few generations we lost the most laid-back ancestors, leaving only the anxiety prone! This is one reason, I speculate, that the anxious and the stressed have survived the evolutionary guillotine.

Further, multiple research groups have noted that our amygdala selectively lights up when we see people we consider different or unfamiliar.[686] **Within thirty-three milliseconds of seeing someone we decide whether we are going to trust that person or not, even before we have recognized the face**.[687] We have a stronger empathic response to people who have the same faith as us[688] or belong to the same race.[689] The tribal within us is alive and kicking.

We are biologically designed to notice dissimilarities, and see others who look different as threatening.

The other extreme of this phenomenon is an interesting condition called Williams syndrome. People afflicted with this condition are hypersocial, gregarious, quick to approach and connect with strangers, and not as sensitive to fear.[690] This is partly related to lower activity of the amygdala in these people.[691] The balance is somewhere between Williams syndrome and our current state.

In summary, these are the three default ways we look at others: *as means to an end*, *judgmentally*, and *with suspicion*. The final default way is to not even notice. Our instinctive way of looking at people isn't peaceful and can harm our health. Research shows the greater your amygdala activity, the greater your risk of autoimmune diseases, heart attack, and stroke.[336] There is indeed a better way accessible to us humans—a way that entails being intentional about how we perceive others.

38

Intentional Presence: People

I have been blessed to have come across some of the finest teachers in the world. Several years ago, I wrote a research grant to test an innovative approach to help breast-cancer patients. My mentor sent me back the grant with one major edit: in every instance, he changed my phrase "breast-cancer patients" to "patients with breast cancer." It was a subtle but important edit. I learned to stop defining my patients by their diagnoses. As an intern and then resident, I had picked up the habit of looking at patients based on their predominant diagnoses and the length of time they would stay on my service. "I have two acute hepatitis, one pneumonia, one back pain, and one retroperitoneal tumor," I would hear myself say. It worked to convey the information but dehumanized the precious beings who had entrusted their care to us. Fortunately, I learned from my teachers in both India and the United States that **I must care for my patients as though they are my loved ones and friends**. After all everyone is worth trillions for someone.

Everyone is worth trillions for someone.

PHENOMENALLY INTERESTING

I can choose to look at a patient as either a female with strep throat or a forty-two-year-old woman with strep throat who's also a mother of three, an over-worked accounts manager, and a caregiver for a mother with early-onset dementia. The former is more "efficient," the latter more holistic and healing. I feel sad when the medical field of today rewards my colleagues and me for being more efficient than more healing. It might save a dollar today, but it will cost ten dollars tomorrow. A study conducted among patients with upper-respiratory infection showed that **more compassionate care eventually decreases the cost of care**. In this study, patients treated by a physician providing compassion-enhanced care had one less day of illness and had a significant reduction in repeat visits.[692]

I have never met a compassionate person who lacked competence.
When we preserve compassion, we preserve it all.

In another interesting study that evaluated the impact of paying intentional attention, researchers found that participants cued to pay better attention to a face started to find it more attractive.[693] Many of us who have had the same partner for a long time stop noticing each other. A simple practice of paying better attention to each other more often can grow greater fondness. Here is what I have found: Just as novelty draws greater attention, when you pay deeper intentional attention, you start finding greater novelty.

In a meeting with work colleagues, by choosing to focus on the people for at least a few moments, I can unlock the little universes they are carrying in their minds by asking them about their families, hobbies, birthplaces, favorite foods, favorite sports teams, or even more engaging details, such as their happiest or most interesting days, childhood aspirations, or inspirations. I have learned through personal experience that I am able to better work with the people I find fascinating (in a good way).

I also find it beneficial to respect children as though they're little grown-ups and to remember when engaging with grown-ups that there is a little child in each of us.

Find the child in a grown-up and a grown-up in a child.

That's the first way to be intentional about people: **assume the person in front of you is phenomenally interesting and has a story worth hearing.**

CIRCLE OF LOVE

The second intentional way of looking at people is to **see them in their circle of love**, in their full context. This isn't instinctive to us, even with children. A few months ago, my family was shopping for clothes in a mall, and I gradually wandered into the men's section. A few minutes later, from a distance I heard the loud cry of a child who sounded like our six-year-old. I rushed to where our kids were and was relieved to see our younger daughter playfully trying on different dresses. Then I paused for a moment and thought, *It's interesting that I feel relieved that the child who is crying is not my daughter. It is still a child crying, and I should be just as concerned, even though she isn't biologically related to me.* A quick investigation revealed that it was a little girl who had thrown a tantrum about some trivial want. It made me think, however, of our basic biological design: **we are most compassionate toward those who are biologically related to us.** Extending care beyond that circle takes effort. But the effort is handsomely rewarding.

When I remember to look at the airline agent as someone's mother, the coffee server as someone's daughter, the volunteer as a loving grandfather, and the cab driver as the father of a family of four, I savor the otherwise mundane transaction with that person. When I add meaning to people, they become special and worthy of deeper attention. It makes me kinder. It has also made me lose some money by helping me become a generous tipper. But that is a worthwhile investment because **the well of kindness invariably gets filled with the water of happiness.** The deeper your kindness, the greater joy you'll find in life.

Remember that no one struggles with being appreciated too much. Two thirds of the people feel discriminated on any given day.

Most people we meet each day feel discriminated.

Also, **you feel worthy for a few moments when you're treated in a special way, but you feel worthy for a long time when you help someone else feel special. People, particularly the elderly, fear becoming inconsequential and being forgotten. Help others feel they will always matter and never be forgotten.**

This is a good way to summarize the first two intentional ways of looking at others: **consider strangers as neighbors, think of friends as loved ones, and treat loved ones as friends.**

Think of friends as loved ones, and treat loved ones as friends.

SACRED

The third and even more intentional way of looking at everyone is to **consider every person sacred**. The dollar value of the physical elements in the human body has been estimated at $4.50.[694] But the person, as a whole, is priceless. What gives us that value? Is it the love you share with others, the intelligence that has put it all together, the spark of life within, or the spiritual core? Perhaps it's all of those things. No matter how you define it, when you connect with others, you can choose to focus more on that essence and less on the physical body. The larger the number of people you believe have that essence, the deeper and more enjoyable your connection with the world. It helps steer you toward the one attribute that can capture all the different elements of intentionality: kindness.

KINDNESS

As we mature and evolve, eventually, all forms of intentionality converge to kindness. Three insights have helped me bring kindness to daily life.

First, several years ago, walking the corridors of my workplace, I did a thought experiment. I assumed that in that sea of humanity, a self-realized master was walking among us. I then imagined how this person would be looking at others. Would he or she be mind wandering, lost in thought, barely noticing anyone? Would he or she be looking at people judgmentally, noticing perceived physical imperfections, or observing the color of their clothing? Would he or she be focusing on his or her breath or immersed in a mantra? Would he or she be piercing into the soul, trying to assess who is pure and who is less so? Or would he or she be silently blessing every person, honoring the human imperfections and struggles of each and wishing everyone a path to healing? The answer I got was that a spiritually evolved person would be silently wishing everyone well.

Why shouldn't I try to look at others with the same eyes? I thought. Over the next few minutes, I experimented with this kind presence. My moments were transformed. I saw purity and beauty and suffering and grace, all at the same time. I carry the memory of that moment to this date. It has been life changing to practice looking at others with kindness.

The second insight emerged from my asking this question to thousands of people over the last few years: "Anyone here related to or know someone who is worth trillions?" The only people who don't raise their hands are the ones too tired to move! I believe every person on the planet is worth trillions for someone. Before you read any further, **I want you to be completely convinced that you are worth trillions.** You may not value yourself that much, but others do, at least silently.

The third insight came from hearing this when talking to people about their personal struggles: "I am the only one who seems to be hurting. Everyone else in the lobby seems OK." I realized that if everyone feels this way, then perhaps everyone is hurting, because everyone has a story. Most people have a less exciting life than is portrayed on their social-media accounts.

So, my life has become infinitely simple. Throughout the day, at work or in my personal life, I try my best to keep this at the forefront of my mind: **everyone I meet is special and struggling, and everyone is worth trillions.**

Every person you meet every day is special and struggling.

With this awareness, I have a choice in how I look at and connect with people. The default option is to judge others or feel judged by them. The intentional option is to send them a silent good wish. The silent good wish, even for perfect strangers, helps me more than it does anyone else. When I look at others with kindness, my oxytocin surges, I feel more benevolent, and my heart rate slows, all helping me be healthier, happier, and in better control of my attention.[695]

A wall has bricks and mortar to keep it together. Although the mortar is invisible, it is the part that keeps the wall strong. **Kindness is the mortar that keeps all the bricks of your life together. This mortar has to be made fresh every day,** requiring you to actively bring kindness to your life. Let kindness, particularly kind attention, become as natural to you as your breath. Send your silent good wishes to most people you meet every day, knowing that they have struggles too. **When you wish someone well, you wish two people well. The first is the other person and the second is yourself.**

When you wish someone well, you wish two people well. The first is the other person and the second is yourself.

You can practice kind attention over the phone or even when you are alone, in your thoughts. A few years ago, I was in the ER for a medical evaluation. As I lay in the hospital bed waiting for the blood-test results, my thoughts went to all the people who had used that bed in the past. Some may have received good news and gone home; others may have been prompted to start planning for the last phases of their lives. I spent some time sending them silent good wishes. Next, I thought about all those who would be using that bed after me. I wished them luck for what would undoubtedly be a stressful phase filled with uncertainty and fear. The practice took my attention away from my own pain, creating a positive memory of the experience of being in the ER.

KIND TOUCH

Kind attention expressed as kind, well-meaning touch is even more powerful. Your warm touch can lower blood pressure, increase oxytocin, and positively influence several biological markers.[696] Spending a few minutes holding hands with someone you trust and love can decrease the acceleration of your heart rate and rise in blood pressure during public speaking.[697] **Even holding a warm object can help; a warm object activates the same part of the brain that is activated when holding the hand of someone who cares.**[698] Whenever you can, feel the warmth around you—warm water in the faucet, warm air from heating, the warmth of the fireplace, warm food, or a warm smile.

Touch is a powerful communication tool. Scientists have found that you can communicate eight different emotions using different types of touch; these emotions include anger, fear, disgust, love, gratitude, sympathy, happiness, and sadness.[699] In a study that assessed touch in NBA players, researchers found that early-season touch predicted late-season success, independent of player status and preseason expectations.[700] **Your kind touch can work magic and speak volumes; your hands are a tool of healing.**

Hugging, when appropriate, is another tremendously healing exchange. A hug is a perfect act of sharing where both the parties are givers and receivers. Of late, I have started practicing what I like to call, virtual hugs. It is just imagining hugging people who I feel close to but are far away. Try sending a virtual hug to your mother, father, children, siblings, and old friends, and see how you feel. It's a simple way to push away loneliness and experience uplifting emotions in the middle of the day.

> *Give virtual hugs to people who are emotionally close but physically distant.*

CREATIVITY WITH KINDNESS

You can be creative with your kind attention. When you walk down an empty hallway, you can send kind attention to all those who have walked through that space. When you hold a doorknob, you can send a good wish to every other person who has touched that doorknob. As you get into this habit, you send blessings to yourself in the process of wishing others well. Looking at another human will become an uplifting experience. I believe that's a better way of looking at each other, and a skill worth teaching in every school and college.

We teach our kids how to talk, eat, dress, write, and do so much more, but we never teach them how to see. Seeing is one of the most important skills. Don't you think that if we all committed to looking at others with kindness, it would change the flavor of every meeting, every party, and literally every encounter with another person?

> *Teaching students to look at each other with kindness should be a standard part of the K-12 curriculum.*

Next time you have a family reunion, commit to kind attention. Your moments together will be filled with more laughter and less judgment. The day you send silent good wishes to many will feel like a good day, even if it wasn't as productive as you would have desired.

Kindness to others will spawn another important habit: kindness to yourself. **Practice looking at yourself through the eyes of someone who loves and trusts you. Believe in those who believe in you. You are who your pet thinks you are.** I will emphasize self-kindness more than once in this book since we are instinctively judgmental of ourselves, as Tabatha's story will teach us at the end of this chapter.

YOUR MAKEUP

I can't leave my face unattended for more than a day. If I don't apply a moisturizer, my skin becomes dry. I start looking unkempt. We all have to take care of our faces so we look pleasant and attractive. Some use light makeup, others heavy. The other part of our beings that needs daily makeup is the mind.

I need to attend to my mind several times during the day to keep my disposition pleasant. Doing so entails being flexible, easygoing, and focusing on the presence I embody and the energy I am giving out.

This is particularly important with people close to me. I have to make a special effort to remember that **the more I learn about someone, the more imperfections I will find**. Preemptively preparing yourself for this discovery and adjusting your expectations will help you preserve kindness and nurture deeper relationships.

It helps me to be aware that when I struggle with hopelessness and apathy, others around me also begin losing hope.[701] Further, my personal happiness travels up to three degrees of separation (to my friend, my friend's friend, and the friend of my friend's friend).[702] If we assume that an average person is connected to about 150 people (known as the Dunbar number),[703] that means that your personal happiness could eventually reach hundreds of millions of people!

The more authentic your smile, the greater its effect on your ability to cope with negative life situations[704] and the more it elicits positive feelings in others, including their compassion for you.[705] Further, the happier you are, the better your physical health.[706] Isn't that a good enough reason to gift yourself happiness every single day? That is the true power of your intentional, kind, and cheerful presence.

Decorate your mind with kindness before you start your day, just as you decorate your face.

Others, even little ones absorb your feelings more than you think or can know. Even before they have learned to speak, infants as young as six months old prefer people they see interacting with and helping others compared to those who are neutral or hindering.[707-709] No wonder we can quickly tell the airline agent who is extra helpful from another one who didn't sleep well last night or is missing her coffee this morning.

KINDNESS TO SELF

Tabatha was a social worker for the county. Within a few minutes of our meeting, I could see the dew drops in her eyes. A few months ago, she was diagnosed with stage-one breast cancer. It was curable. But Tabatha was inconsolable. "I constantly worry about my two young children," she said. Sensing there was something more, I gently probed further. Slowly, Tabatha opened up. A week ago, she discovered some suspicious texts on her husband's cell phone. Just yesterday she had found out that he was seeing another woman. This had devastated Tabatha. He was her high school sweetheart.

Amidst all this, the one person Tabatha blamed the most was herself. She blamed herself for skipping the mammogram, for taking oral contraceptives, for being less intimate with her husband, for gaining some weight, for not saving enough for her kids, and more. The self-blame was squeezing out any remaining vitality from her.

For no fault of hers, Tabatha was drowning in self-blame. Many of us are like Tabatha. We struggle with kindness to the self. We aren't taught how to be gentle and delicate with the self. I firmly believe that good people are very good at feeling bad about themselves.

Good people are very good at feeling bad about themselves.

The solution is self-kindness. Self-kindness isn't lowering your standards. Self-kindness is treating yourself with the same gentleness with which you care for a young child. It is recognizing your constraints, honoring your good intentions, valuing your effort, and giving yourself a break. Removing yourself from the pedestal of perfection, delaying acceptance of the blames hurled at you, and opening yourself to the love and care of others, is all self-kindness. How can anyone argue with that?

I will talk about self-kindness (self-compassion) further in chapter 66.

To recap, **intentional presence with people means paying undistracted attention to them, keeping in mind that every person is phenomenally interesting and has a story, that every person is surrounded by a circle of love (and you can choose to see them in that circle), that every person is struggling, and that every person is sacred.** Intentional presence is kind presence.

39

Instinctive Presence: Things and Events

I remember the day my family got our first refrigerator. It was 1979. We celebrated the cool three-foot-tall magic for over six months. We treated it with the same care as we would have a pet. We kept it cleaner than the living-room sofa and listened to (and overinterpreted) every sound it made. We read the instruction manual cover to cover and treated the manual with the same respect we'd have given to a spiritual text. If our refrigerator had died prematurely, we would have had to save for five more years to get another one.

Before we got the refrigerator, ice cream was a once-a-quarter affair, and we made it with a manual machine that mixed ice with salt. It was mostly a partially frozen mix of milk and sugar, but it tasted like heaven. Now, in the twenty-first century, with several ice-cream shops in every mall selling a decent cup for a reasonable price, ice cream has lost its novelty. Recently, I was amazed when my kids showed little interest in eating ice cream, an unthinkable possibility when I was their age. **Abundance keeps company with loss of appreciation.**

Having a lot takes away the joy of enjoying the little.

🕊

This phenomenon has affected the rest of my life. I recently noticed the quick loss of novelty on my family's only trip to Hawaii.

EXPERIENCING HAWAII

We went to Hawaii for a medical conference. The first day it felt like the entire place was hand carved by the divine, with every inch meticulously planned. The second day we drove by the ocean, paying attention to the waves. By the third day, we had gotten used to the place. While driving by the Pacific, we were mostly chatting and focusing on arriving at the restaurant rather than admiring the expansive blue sage.

The same thing happens when you move into a new home. After the first few months of noticing, we stop paying attention. I'm sure you haven't paid a whole lot of attention to the design of your kitchen sink or garbage can in the previous week.

I once met a successful commercial builder who was fabulously wealthy but totally bored with life, to the point of getting depressed, because all he had built in the previous decade was a series of identical hotels. He wanted to build a new design, even for lower profit. Many of us don't find our work engaging when it is totally driven by protocols. Protocols, however, ensure quality control and error-free operation. **A tension exists between novelty and familiarity.** Your brain wishes to feast on variety, while your supervisor's brain wants the usual predictable product.

Our experience of novelty versus familiarity is intimately related to the mix of attention and interpretation in an experience.

ATTENTION AND INTERPRETATION

Our every experience is a mix of attention and interpretation. For novel objects, attention claims a greater proportion of our experience. This helps us seek novelty, since the greater the attention (assuming the object is nonthreatening), the greater the joy. Over time as familiarity develops, the experience becomes dominated by interpretations (or quick judgments). This is how the brain conserves its attention resources.

In contrast to hunter gatherers, in the modern world of our creation, we spend most of our time in the same home, at the same workplace, and drive on the same route. Our experience is thus crammed with interpretations. There's little room for attention, which creates too few excitements in a routine day.

Our instinctive way of experiencing, with little attention and lots of interpretation, creates dissatisfaction; almost no material goods or experiences offer lasting happiness. The good that becomes familiar no longer feels good. In this state, we remain forever hungry for positive emotions and lasting joy. The loss of novelty feeds into one negative experience all humans dread: boredom.

BORED TO DEATH

We get bored very easily and actually dread it. **Boredom is not only boring but also risky. Bored brains become inattentive and drowsy, lack self-control, and are likely to do something unwise to amuse themselves.**

Boredom can lead to inattention, and immoral, illegal, even criminal actions.

In a research study, untrained participants who were forced into boredom by having to spend six to fifteen minutes alone doing nothing chose to give themselves painful electric shocks rather than sit with their own thoughts.[262] They preferred the pain of the shock to the pain of the boredom.

My mother used this loss of novelty for good measure with my elder brother Kishore, who, as a child, used to secretly steal sugar each day, not to the delight of his teeth. One day my mother took a big bowl, filled it with sugar, and put it in front of him. She asked him to eat all of it in one go. Flooded with so much sugar, he found the allure of it faded after a few spoons. Secretly eating a spoonful of sugar excited him; eating eighty spoons in one sitting in front of our mother didn't. He never stole sugar again after that and has kept all his teeth!

The bottom line is that with instinctive presence, the familiar becomes boring. Since you are likely to have the same job, same house, same partner, and same neighborhood tomorrow as you have today, you run a high risk of descending into boredom, with its downstream effect of disengagement and loss of joy. Let's now discuss a few cures for boredom—by intentionally finding novelty. Novelty can also help us hone our attention and get a little more out of life.

40

Intentional Presence: Things and Events

NOVEL WITHIN ORDINARY

Several years ago, my family and I were touring the Taj Mahal and its surrounding historic sites in Agra, India. We decided to hire a tour guide. He was about thirty, spoke several languages, and was a master at humor, timing, and details. I was fascinated by his fund of knowledge and presence. Intrigued, I asked him how many times he had given this tour.

"Ten thousand," he replied.

"Don't you get bored, then? The same jokes, the same details," I questioned.

"Nope," he said. "It isn't about the details; it's about the people listening to the details."

He drew passion from giving people the best experience possible. I have taken his lesson to heart. When I give a talk, I try my best to think about the people who are participating and not the fact that I have presented the topic a few thousand times. Recently I was feeling low on energy while addressing an audience of about a thousand people. Thinking that two hundred of these people may have experienced depression, a few would have been suicidal, and some may have a sick child, immediately helped me focus on them rather than me. I also thought about the Baseball legend Joe DiMaggio. When asked about the secret of his consistent performance, he said, "There is always some kid who may be seeing me for the first time. I owe him my best."

The more you get out of your own head and the less it is about you, the more you will enjoy the experience. It could be any experience—from watching Broadway theater to brushing your teeth. **Intentionally finding novelty is thus a simple yet profound way to remain engaged with what might otherwise seem ordinary and mundane.** That is the first step toward intentional presence: **to find or create novelty within the ordinary**.

SPECIAL AND PRECIOUS

Another way to intentionally engage with things and events is to convince yourself that **this experience is special and precious like none other**. When I remember to tell myself that each pancake is special because there is only so much mix in the bowl and I will only *get to* eat two pancakes, then each bite becomes special. I have a finite number of Thanksgiving, Independence, and New Year's Days that I will *get to* celebrate increases the importance of the current experience.

Mark the use of the expression "get to" rather than "have to." **Whenever you can, use "get to" instead of "have to." For example, I get to work, I get to shovel snow, I get to load the dishwasher, I get to walk the dog, and so on.**

Update your vocabulary. Replace your "have to" with "get to".

TRANSIENCE

The realization of transience is a powerful and potentially transformative force when you can integrate the related wisdom and use it to become inspired rather than depressed. Extrapolated to the whole day, transience means that **if you live this day assuming this is all you have and try to make the most of it, then you might say "I love you" more often and truly, deeply appreciate the beauty that surrounds you**.

How many times will you get to: admire the tulips in the garden, boat in the lake in your town, savor ice-cream sundaes, hold your child's hand while crossing the street? All of these are finite experiences, the realization of which will make them special.

SAVOR NATURE

There is a reason we call nature "Mother Nature." Nature isn't just the source of physical energy for us; nature also nourishes our minds and spirits. All you have to do to relax is to be in nature and let nature work its magic.

Nature is never judgmental. You can be yourself in nature, even on a bad hair day!

In an interesting study that tested the effect of nature on thinking, researchers found that spending time in nature decreases mind wandering compared to spending time in the city.[710] The decreased mind wandering leads to improvement of mood, even in a hospital setting. Patients with depression improve faster in sunny hospital rooms than in dreary rooms.[711] No wonder people who feel more connected to nature experience more positive emotions and have greater vitality and life satisfaction.[712]

In a most remarkable demonstration of the power of nature, researchers found that patients admitted to a sunny room after a heart attack had better chances of survival than did the patients admitted to a dark room.[713] Increase the dose of nature in your life, to be happier, healthier, and to even live longer.

CHALLENGE YOURSELF

Challenging yourself to new experiences is the next way to live with intentionality. When was the last time you planted a planter, sketched a portrait, wrote a poem, baked a brownie, visited a sporting-goods store, took a selfie with your pet, bought something from a street vendor, ate with your non-dominant hand, or watched a silent movie or *I Dream of Jeannie*?

Challenge yourself to new activities that force you to sharpen your old skills or create a new set of skills. **The mind needs challenge to find an experience interesting.** It will put you into a transient state of "flow," which I'll talk about in the next section.

A little challenge is better than no challenge, for your brain health as well as overall wellbeing.

Even if you can't find new things to do, you can try to find freshness in the familiar by looking at it from a different angle. Looking at the sky today, you can see the same dull clouds or a formation never seen before. You have the same choice with your work.

DETAILS, DETAILS

Intentional attention to details is another way to more fully engage. Try to do one thing to perfection today, such as driving, loading the dishwasher, ironing clothes, cooking, or getting your children ready—anything. Once you choose to savor the experience of cooking, you will see more life in lettuce and vegetables, become amazed by the brilliant shine of tomatoes, discover a work of art inside a watermelon, and notice intricate grains on the skin of an apple.

The same goes for driving. Choose to drive with the utmost care without breaking any rules. Be aware of all the white and yellow lines, slow appropriately for the turns, and be mindful of the distance from the other cars. You might enjoy that drive a little more. Extend this attention to details to other activities.

One day I was watching my then eight-year-old play tennis, and I kept tracking the movement of the ball instead of answering e-mails or wanting her to hit the right shots. After about five minutes, I felt a sense of lightness and bliss that lasted for several minutes, just as one feels in deep meditation after years of practice.

MEANING

Finding greater meaning in what you are doing is a great way to be more intentional. **Meaning provides the answer to the important question: why?** Gone are those hierarchical days when the team becomes fully engaged, blindly trusting and following the leader's vision and mandate. **For the team to produce excellence, you want them to be inspired, not just motivated. For that inspiration, meaning is most important.**

Ask why before how or when or what.

Let's take the example of medical students. Every one of them starts medical school inspired. It's wonderful to see fresh faces full of hope and possibilities. But a full 50 percent of students experience burnout by their fourth year—a state of apathy, cynicism, low self-esteem, and depersonalization. And this isn't just in medical students. Burnout is an epidemic among all professions. Two-thirds of attorneys are burned out, along with half of nurses, school principals, social workers, journalists, and more. There are many reasons for burnout, but I believe one major reason is loss of meaning.

I often ask medical students to keep their personal statements, which summarize why they chose medical careers, on their study table and re-read those statements once in a while. **It's a good idea to re-read the personal statement you wrote decades ago. It'll remind you of your innocence and might reconnect you with your purpose.**

I also remind medical students that in their careers, they will touch ten million lives (about three thousand patients a year for thirty years, with each patient connected to between a hundred and a hundred fifty people). It is often comforting for them to know that no patient ever questions his or her doctor's grades in anatomy. **Patients want a competent and compassionate physician who feels enthusiastic about serving in the role of a physician.**

The importance of preserving compassion increases as powerful guidelines and algorithms are quickly replacing individual physician judgment creating industrial healthcare. In industrial healthcare, rules are mindlessly applied and rigid protocols replace common sense. Providers and patients alike are seen as cogs in the wheel. Building a compassion-impoverished culture diminishes self-compassion, predisposing to burnout.

When we treat workers like light bulbs (dispensable), they burn out. Dehumanizing customers and employees will hollow our companies, culture, and country.

Medicine delivers three things: knowledge, technology, and compassion. The delivery of knowledge and technology is getting increasingly automated in a world driven by artificial intelligence and robotics. Hence the need to remind ourselves of this definition of health care: **health care is using knowledge and technology to deliver compassion.** Thankfully many leading health researchers of the world are recognizing the importance of compassion and kindness in health care.[713b]

CRY AS YOU PERFORM

I had the pleasure of listening to a riveting concert in my hometown by a world-renowned devotional singer from India, Anup Jalota. Later, during an informal chat, he shared the secret of his melody. He said, "I truly immerse myself in what I am doing. I don't plan any concert; it spontaneously happens." His most moving words were, "I cry as I sing. If I don't cry during my devotional song, how can I expect my audience to cry?"

Anup reflects a perfect integration of intentionality that has now become his instinct. **Intentionality practiced over time becomes ingrained as an instinct.** Excellence then isn't the goal; it becomes the path. You experience deeper depths. You feel lighter, freer. That is where the principles and practices of mindfulness *v*2 will take you.

By focusing on novelty, recognizing the value of each encounter, attending to details, challenging yourself to excellence, finding greater meaning, and giving your all to your performance, you can more deeply engage with anything you do.

Find novelty within the familiar to keep life interesting, and find familiarity within the novel so you don't get overwhelmed.

Find novelty within familiarity and familiarity within novelty.

Binding the mind to time can stifle its creativity. **The mind needs time as a construct to run its life, but it doesn't relish getting shackled by time.** In past eras, people denied time to achieve freedom. It is a difficult and often impractical path for modern minds. Intentionality in attention and interpretation offers one way of accessing the same freedom. Intentionality reorganizes your brain. Research shows that intentionally choosing your thoughts activates the attention controlling areas of the brain and quiets the stress-producing hubs (the amygdala).[714]

I have just discussed some of the aspects of intentionality with people, things, and events. One additional way to help your mind is to cultivate flexibility in mental projection—whether you are focusing inward or outward or thinking about the short term or the long term. The third and fourth tenets leverage the idea of intentionality and explore it deeper, so that you can train and deepen your attention. These tenets increase your flexibility by directing your attention externally (the third tenet) and also develop an ability to flexibly shift your perspective between the short term and the long term (the fourth tenet).

Part IV
The Third Tenet: Attention

Tenet	Mindfulness *v1*	Mindfulness *v2*
Attention	Internally focused meditation	Externally focused meditation

—ₘ—

Intentional attention, external or internal, engages the same brain network. Focus your meditation on the world if you struggle with the mind.

41

Fireside Chat #4

"I liked your focus on kindness. Kindness is the language that the deaf can hear and the blind can see." Mike says.

"Isn't that Mark Twain?"

"It is."

"Anger, particularly seething rage, blows out the lamp of the mind. Kindness preserves your energy. Kindness doesn't seek attention, but eventually brings you greater respect. Kindness helps you believe in yourself and teaches self-restraint. I believe the purpose of human life isn't just to develop strong attention. It is to cultivate universal kindness. A world in which even 10 percent of humans practice universal kindness will be a transformed world."

"I agree. Let's talk about intentionality for a moment. You shared so many different ideas around intentionality. Where do I start?" Mike asks.

"Pick only one or, at the most, two ideas that make the most sense to you. My all-time favorite is the morning-gratitude practice."

"I have heard you mention that. Could you remind me of the specifics?"

"**Do not leave the bed until you have thought about five people in your life who you know care about you, and send them your silent gratitude.** The idea is to wake up in control of your brain and think of the good people in your life at least once a day. The alternate is to cede control of your attention right away to the worldly concerns and wake up mind wandering."

"I have one or two people I can think about first thing in the morning. Do I get an F if I can't come up with five?"

"Then start with one. Here is what I do—Right after I wake up, I bring my wife's face in front of my eyes and think about one good thing she has done or said recently, preferably in the previous twenty-four hours. She also gifts the same practice to me. Try this tomorrow morning for someone close to you. That will get you an A+!"

"What will that do to me?"

"You'll wake up with better control of your attention and not give back control to the world first thing in the morning. You'll feel connected. You'll wake up visiting a happy area of your brain. You'll feel more nurtured and less lonely. Because of this little practice, the moment my wife and I connect in the morning, we start our day with humor and positive energy. That wasn't the case ten years ago."

"Won't I get bored, thinking about the same person and the same thing?"

"Unlikely. I have seen a change in me. When I wake up thinking about one good thing my wife has said or done in the previous twenty-four hours, I spend the day noticing the good things. Earlier I used to remember the disagreements; now I remember the kindness. It is like picking a good first song to start the playlist. The first song sets the tone for the entire playlist.

"Also, I could think about my father's eyes a million times and not get bored. I could think about my grandmother and give her a virtual hug every day of my life and not get bored. I could remember holding my girls right after they were born an infinite number of times and not get bored. If you are running out of ideas, you can get creative. You can think about all the ladies who came for your mother's baby shower before you were born."

"Many people pray very soon after they wake up. What do you suggest to them?" Mike asks.

"If they are happy with their practice, it's just fine to continue it. Perhaps they can send gratitude while brushing their teeth or at the end of the day. One possibility is to add their loved ones to their prayers. **Research shows your relationship improves when you start praying for your partner**."[715]

"I worry that I will start worrying about my loved ones if I think about them first thing in the morning."

"Here is my suggestion for that. When you send them your gratitude, assume you are protecting them for the week with the practice. It will decrease your worry, and also create a subliminal guilt the next day if you forget the practice, helping you continue with it."

"What if I want to start with paying intentional attention to things?"

"Two advantages of focusing on the people are that in addition to training attention the practice also uplifts emotions and decreases perceived loneliness. You'll lose that advantage with things. Having said that, as long as you can stick with the practice, if you wish to start with things, that's fine. It depends on your personality and life situation. The practice, over the long term, helps train your intentionality muscles. You are choosing what fills your moment. You are taking charge of your brain by working on your attention."

"I keep hearing about how our kids struggle with attention these days. How can we help our kids?"

"**The first step in helping our kids is to help ourselves.** They notice when you eat a pizza slice in three hurried bites. They notice when your entire evening was nothing but a date with a screen. They notice if you lie to lower your insurance premium. They also notice when you are more present and truthful. When you are present, you'll become more creative about helping them experience their world. Help them discover the space they inhabit. While reading books, point out details they might skim over. While you're driving, show them the world instead of talking on the phone. When our daughters were younger, I would take them on a scientific tour of the home. We would walk through different rooms and notice and talk about all the little things, like a hair clip, the carpet, the sofa, a lamp, a toothbrush, and more. Each trip was an adventure for both them and me. Let them see the world as you see it, and let them show you the world as they see it."

"What about social media? What influence is it having on us and our kids?"

"I wish I had an easy answer. Here is the bottom line for me: the problem isn't social media; the problem is us. We have given outsized importance to our virtual presence, sometimes at the cost of our real presence. Treat social media like you treat breakfast cereal: taste it only once or, at the most, twice a day. Do not snack on social media all day long. I consider my smartphone to be an addictive toy. A good way to avoid smartphone addiction is to make accessing the internet slightly cumbersome. For instance, resist the urge to unlock your phone with a fingerprint scanner. Type a password instead. Let your home page be something that reminds you of your values rather than a website that provides access to headline news right away. **Our most used body part shouldn't be our right thumb to unlock our phone; it should be our eyes to wish others well and our ears to truly listen.**"

"How do you personally handle the barrage of negative news every day?"

"I keep its dose at a minimum, less than ten minutes during the day. I also believe in creating positivity in my little world in response to the negativity I see in the larger world. I do not let the negative news dishearten me. It inspires me to find even more energy to spread goodness since so much needs to be done."

"Like many, I am sure you multitask to get through the day. Don't tell me you don't! What are your thoughts about multitasking?"

"Think about the last time you went through an airport security check. Was your TSA agent screening four people at the same time?"

Mike nods and then smiles.

"Tasks that need conscious attention can't be multitasked. But thanks to technology, you can do several parallel things by intelligent sequencing. While you heat up your soup in the microwave, you can toast the bread and water two plants. Our brains are designed for efficiency. **Your brain can run tasks that don't need conscious attention in parallel, and sequence the tasks that need conscious attention**. The problem occurs when you parallel run tasks that need conscious attention. This problem occurs in two instances: relationships and high-risk situations. First, **do not multitask in relationships**. Whenever you can, even for the most mundane conversations, try to bring your full presence. When you give partial presence, you send the message that others aren't worthy of your full presence. **Your partial presence could be worse than absence.** Second, do not multitask in high-risk situations that need your full attention, such as driving. Also keep in mind that heavy multitasking might weaken your attention and memory, increase your impulsivity, and up your sensitivity to irrelevant thoughts and stimulations. Multitask only when you have to."[716-719]

"You shared multiple ideas about the concept of time. What is your personal take on time?"

"Thinking about time makes me anxious. Instead of thinking about time, I focus more on what fills my time. I believe less in time management and more in priority management. **More important than making a to-do list is making a not-to-do list.** Give a haircut to your inbox. Focus on the most meaningful messages and tasks, and snip away the rest. **Fill your past with gratitude, your present with meaning, and your future with hope.** That will take away time anxiety."

Mike closes his eyes, pauses for a few seconds, takes a deep breath, and then asks, "Where is mindfulness *v*2 headed now?"

"We will talk about a worthy target for our intentionality muscles: the world that hugs us. Do you know what percentage of workers come to work wanting to do something other than what they are doing?"

"I would guess 10 or 20 percent?"

"It is 70 percent!"

"What?" I can see the whites of Mike's eyes.

"Yes, 70 percent of workers aren't engaged or are actively disengaged. They aren't interested in, committed to, or enthusiastic about their work. They don't enjoy giving discretionary time."

"Why is that?"

"They didn't start out that way. You don't work hard in school and college, get degrees, and land your dream job only to disengage or, worse, burn out. We are doing something wrong that is destroying curiosity and meaning, the two ingredients that foster engagement. On the menu next is the science and art of curiosity and meaning so we can reengage. The work you do to serve others is a spiritual activity. It is prayer. I can't think of a more powerful meditation than full immersion in work and the experience of flow during that process. We will explore ways we can live our days engaged and in flow."

"Let's flow!"

42

The Two Inputs

FROZEN IN TIME

A few years ago, I visited my hometown—Bhopal, India. Standing in the bangle bazaar in inner-city Bhopal, I could see a few hundred people in each visual field. Gracing the show, while playing tag with each other, a few roosters darted across the road. Cars traveled slower than pedestrians, honking every few seconds—not in an irritable manner warning people to get out of their way, but in a social manner, as if speaking, "howdy." Hundreds of small roadside vendors were busy selling glittery attractions to little girls. The smells of roasted peanuts and chickpeas filled the air. This world never slept, and it seemed to be frozen in time. It was exactly the same as I had left it in June 1995 when I'd left for the United States. This is where I grew up, fascinated by latex balloons molded into myriad shiny shapes, cotton candy, and boxes running on wheels, all immersed in eighty-decibel cacophony.

As I left the bangle bazaar that day, it struck me that amid such rich sensory indulgence, I had experienced no moments of mind wandering. I had been immersed in the world parading before my senses.

Another instance that halted my train of thoughts happened a few years ago when a rumor went out that some exotic animals had escaped in northern Rochester. When my wife and I went to pick up our elder daughter after an activity at Assisi Heights (a fairly wooded area in northern Rochester), we experienced no mind wandering because our attention was absorbed in monitoring the external environment.

A few thousand years ago, when our threats were mostly external, training attention would have meant pushing it inward toward the depths of the mind, the basis of most meditation practices. A lot has changed since then, such that the **definition of escape isn't escaping *into* the mind but escaping *from* the mind**. Let's explore that now.

TWO INPUTS AND TWO BODIES

At any moment when you are awake, your attention, the gateway into your conscious experience, brings information to the brain from two sources: the senses and the mind. The senses collect input from the outer world and from the body and the breath. The mind's input comes in the form of thoughts, spontaneously generated or created at will.

The sensory input from the world constantly competes with the thought input from the mind. Eventually the input perceived as the most threatening or novel wins the trophy of your attention.

🕊

These inputs collectively gather in the foyer of your brain (also called the working memory). Only an extremely small fraction (perhaps a billionth) of the information that enters the foyer passes deeper, into the house (conscious perception). As far as conscious perception is concerned, it allows through only one car on green, no more. Generally, information about safety and survival receives top priority.

Not long ago, most of the brain's information came from the external world. We were busy protecting our physical bodies, since external injuries and infections were the primary cause of mortality until a few hundred years ago. Average life expectancy was less than half of what it is today.

Statistically speaking, many areas of the world are now quite safe. Average life expectancy is pushing into the eighties in many countries, and cardiovascular disease and cancer (diseases of lifestyle and not injuries and infections) are the top causes of mortality. If you are sitting in your bedroom behind three locked doors and a security alarm, you are probably as physically safe as you will realistically get. In this state, your attention can shift from current physical vulnerability to possible future physical vulnerability or, more likely, present and future emotional vulnerability. That is the reason we now have the luxury of investing our time in protecting our second body—the emotional body.

These days, we spend much more time protecting our sense of self-worth, evading emotional predators, rethinking past slurs, and recovering from emotional hit and runs. Naturally, our brains' foyers have a higher proportion of mind-generated input, and we spend significant time, sometimes most of the day, with our thoughts.

We spend more time protecting our emotional body than our physical body.

🕊

Our days have changed from noticing the outside to thinking on the inside. If this change truly protected us, then it would be adaptive. But only in rare situations are our negative thoughts and self-doubt helpful. Mostly, the resulting stress from these thoughts peels away the fragile scab of healing from old hurts, pushes compassion and forgiveness into the attic, and predisposes us to many chronic medical conditions, including diabetes, hypertension, cardiovascular disease, inflammatory conditions, chronic infections, addictions, and perhaps even early mortality.[720-723] Neuroplasticity, our brain's ability to change with experience, worsens the toxic effects of unhelpful ruminations.

Our negative thoughts and self-doubt are seldom helpful.

🕊

NEUROPLASTICITY

Unlike car tires that are worn with repeated use, **the brain networks you frequently use get more resources and thus become stronger and better connected**. It doesn't matter whether these networks host fear or reason, harm or help. The more you use them, the greater their dominance in the brain. For this reason, the brain real estate that hosts negative emotions and mind wandering is particularly well connected in modern humans, locking us in a perpetual cycle of mind wandering and negativity.

We get locked into this cycle because of a unique aspect of brain biology. Most feedback loops in the body are negative feedback loops—eating sates your hunger, drinking quenches your thirst, the rise of thyroid hormone sends a signal to the thyroid gland to stop its production. Many illnesses occur from a break in this healthy negative feedback loop.

The feedback loop in the brain is different. It is a positive feedback loop. That is the reason why using a particular area of the brain makes it stronger. Imagine if eating made you hungry. Then the more you ate, the hungrier you'd get!

Because of this positive feedback loop in the brain, the more our minds wander, the greater the strength of our mind-wandering apparatuses, which fuels more mind wandering. It also makes fear difficult to forget, particularly in people predisposed to stress and anxiety.[724-726]

The positive feedback loops in the brain are helpful for learning and adaptation but create unintended vulnerabilities. They trap us in negativity and biases, and multiply our innate predispositions. Mindfulness *v2* breaks this cycle with practices that pull your attention externally, instead of letting yourself be passively pulled internally. A speculative thought related to the neuroscience of meditation further supports this idea.

43

Meditation and the Brain

MEDITATION NETWORK?

Meditation has several benefits but isn't essential for survival. Presently only 8 percent of Americans meditate,[727] compared to greater than 70 percent who pray daily or weekly.[728]

Further, best we know, humans have been meditating only for the last few thousand years, a very small time frame from the evolutionary perspective. The brain thus doesn't have a committed meditation network (as we have for other essential functions, like fear, sight, pain, and so on). Likewise, we have no committed soccer network, chess network, or tooth brushing network. We would need brains ten or a hundred times the current size if each of our activities needed a dedicated network. Nature solved this problem in a simple way: **most novel activities piggyback on existing brain networks**.

Researchers have documented structural brain changes with acquiring many novel physical and mental skills, such as learning to reason or playing musical instruments.[729-731] The resulting brain changes associated with mindfulness and other forms of meditation (although fascinating to many), aren't too surprising to neuroscientists.

The key networks trained in meditation are related to focusing, becoming aware when the mind wanders, shifting focus, maintaining sustained focus, and in some practices, experiencing positive emotions, compassion or other feelings. All of these are done while silencing the mind-wandering apparatus,[732] an effort common to most meditations.[733, 734]

Areas of the brain that host executive functions get better connected during meditation.[735] An important question for which we do not yet have a perfect answer is whether these changes are transient or permanent. Research so far shows that barring some caveats, lasting changes need years of intensive practice. (See Appendix for more details)

Lasting meditation induced brain changes accrue from years of intensive practice.

Such lasting effects are often reflected in change in brain structure. Although the specifics differ among studies, partly related to different study designs and practices, many areas of the brain become thicker and better networked with a disciplined meditation practice.[736-746] A review of these studies reported up to eight different areas of the brain affected by meditation practice.[747] The specific areas affected are likely related to the psychological and behavioral aims of each meditation style.

__Different meditation styles produce different brain changes.__

An important aspect of the brain is that **thinking about an activity engages similar brain areas to those engaged in actually practicing the activity**. Thus, research shows that imagining playing piano or violin or imagining dancing can help you improve your piano, violin, or dance performance.[357, 748, 749]

When I read all this research, I speculated that the same networks should be engaged whether you focus externally or internally (playing piano versus thinking about playing piano). Thus, meditation with eyes closed (internally directed) or eyes open (externally directed) should engage the same or similar parts of the brain. I was excited to see that an interesting study supported precisely this speculation.

AN IMPORTANT REALIZATION

In this study, investigators evaluated which brain areas activate based on two variables: external versus internal focus, and intense versus low-grade attention.[291] Researchers found that **the intensity of focus had much greater effect on the activation than did the direction of focus**. Thus, very similar areas were activated when the participants were intensely focusing, whether looking out at an object externally or thinking about the details of the object internally. An additional research team has recently corroborated these findings.[749a]

__External or internal focus, both activate the same brain network.__

Realizing this has freed me. I meet so many colleagues and learners who find the internally focused meditation practice very difficult. I have similarly struggled with sitting meditation. I feel comfortable now in suggesting externally focused meditation, in which you experience your world with full attention. Because from the brain's perspective it doesn't matter whether you are focusing externally or internally. Therefore, **in addition to or in lieu of sitting with the eyes closed, you could meditate immersed in the world, with your eyes open**. It will activate the same or similar areas of the brain.

Since we spend most of the day in the world and not sitting on a cushion, we could get ten thousand hours of training (which some but not all experts suggest is needed to become really good at anything) in just a few years.

The third tenet builds on intentionality and emerging research, offering you a different way to meditate: **instead of meditating with eyes closed, you meditate with eyes open by intentionally projecting your attention externally**.

Let's explore a few more details specific to meditating with your eyes open. The general theme is to notice details, discover novelty, and challenge yourself, all the while keeping a kind intention and attention. The desirable outcome of such a pursuit, in both personal and professional life, is captured in a familiar word: engagement.

When you are engaged, you are interested, committed, and enthusiastic about what you are doing or with whom you are interacting. Two ingredients contribute to engagement: *curiosity* and *meaning*. Curiosity provides the initial impetus. Once you start enjoying the process, a meaning takes shape and pulls you along the path toward a worthy goal. Let's start with getting curious.

44

Curiosity

A few years ago, when my wife and I were landing in Rochester, we got rerouted so that the airplane was flying directly above our neighborhood. We were so excited to see the different houses from up above—the mailboxes, the yards, the rooftops, the chimneys, the play areas, and more. After we landed and drove home, we found the same old plain neighborhood. So why did it look so exciting from up above? It was because we were looking at it from a different angle. The same thing seen with a fresh perspective or viewpoint can engage you by tickling awake your curiosity. Your observation and joy in observing are less related to the specifics of the object or event and more related to the quality of the attention and curiosity you bring.

What you see depends not only on what it is but also on how you see it.

SIX QUESTIONS

Who, what, where, when, where, and how—these are the six questions we ask every day to keep learning and to jog our attention and thinking networks of the brain. For Tesla, Farnsworth, Darwin, Einstein, Newton, Curie, Fleming, and so many more, curiosity was the primary force that fueled their scientific pursuits. While others were eating apple pie, Newton got curious about falling apples. Alexander Fleming worried less about the failed experiment and more about the fungus around which the bacteria simply couldn't grow. All of these **curious observations have transformed our world**.

Curiosity is a natural human tendency to make sense of the world; it is our desire for information. Cicero called it passion for learning. William James called it the impulse toward better cognition.[750] It is our intense and intrinsic need to know. **Curiosity is a recognition of a gap in our knowledge and a desire and passion to fill that gap.**

NATURE OF CURIOSITY

The spectrum of curiosity ranges from automatic bias toward novelty in infants to intentional seeking of something interesting among inventors.[751] In general, information seeking is more likely to be labeled curiosity when it represents an intrinsic drive rather than a focus on a tangible reward.[752] **Curiosity exists for the**

sake of curiosity. Researchers identify four attributes of curiosity: intensity, transience, impulsivity, and lack of satisfaction on resolution.[753]

Curiosity is an intense—sometimes irrationally intense—desire to know. Some researchers consider it one of the primary human drives, but unlike other primary drives, such as thirst and hunger, curiosity unattended often doesn't grow with time; it fades when the attention gets distracted. This makes biological sense, because thirst is a primary survival drive, and you don't want it to fatigue and give you an inaccurate signal when you are dehydrated. Curiosity often takes a backseat in the presence of more pressing drives, such as hunger, that are of immediate survival value.

Curious people can do crazy, impulsive things. They might climb a wall, get into a gutter, take pictures they shouldn't be taking, or snoop into records and files they shouldn't be snooping into. Many people get into trouble because of unchecked curiosity. Thus, we need to **couple curiosity with meaning (and common sense) to deploy it for a prosocial purpose**.

Curiosity needs meaning to channel its intensity toward the greater good.

Finally, curiosity satisfied spawns fresh curiosity. I know of no research colleagues who felt their research hunger was satisfied once the experiment was completed. After describing gravity and developing calculus, Isaac Newton continued throughout his life to seek a deeper truth that could explain the universe. So did Nikola Tesla, who kept experimenting to send high levels of energy wirelessly. **In the research world, every conclusion is the beginning of a new hypothesis.**

TYPES OF CURIOSITY

We all are curious but in different ways. **Our differences create the phenomenal variety on our planet.** Curiosity has been described as good (such as one that initiates scientific inquiry or exploration of new lands) or bad (such as neighborhood gossip, voyeurism, and drug use). Bad curiosity can lead to drug addiction, dishonest actions, and even crime.

Curiosity can also be categorized into perceptual or epistemic.[754] Perceptual curiosity seeks novel sensations and stimuli; epistemic curiosity expands knowledge and understanding of the world. Epistemic curiosity makes us travel into space, read heavy books (like this one), watch PBS documentaries, and visit history museums, to the irritation of our kids. Epistemic curiosity is unique to us humans.

Curiosity also depends on one's core areas of interest—physicists are curious about how the universe works, while biologists are curious about how life works.

WHY ARE WE CURIOUS?

You can't help but be curious. **Curiosity helps you acquire that most prized yet weightless commodity—information.**[753, 755]

Information isn't a substance you can hold in your hands. But information is priceless. Our entire sensory system and large parts of our brain are committed to acquiring and interpreting information. Our survival depends on efficient acquisition of information. Amazingly, the scanning movements of our eyes in a complex environment are almost as good as an ideal laboratory scanner that works off of complex algorithms.[756] No wonder you can spot your child in a nanosecond among dozens of children at day care. You can also quickly spot the checkout counter with the shortest line.

> *We are still hunter gatherers, hunting and gathering information.*

Curiosity may have been evolutionarily selected because information enhances survival, particularly in complex societies. Our newborns come with very little knowledge of the ways of the world. If they weren't feverishly collecting information, they wouldn't make it. They also have to be selective since they can process only a very small fraction of what touches their sensory systems. They naturally prioritize sights with greater contrast, movement, and faces.[757]

Curiosity thus evolved as a natural drive. Perceived lack of information produces an unpleasant sensation that is resolved by seeking and knowing.[758] This resolution is only temporary and also doesn't generalize to other aspects of life (knowing who came to the Smiths' party doesn't take away the desire to know about the Martins)—keeping the curiosity alive and kicking.

Beyond its extrinsic role, curiosity is also its own reward. It emerges from our motivation to master our environment.[759] We love to know more than we need to know, even if the information doesn't have the remotest chance of being helpful. The brain is a complex information-processing system, and curiosity provides the fodder for this processor so that it keeps going. No wonder Einstein said, "Curiosity has its own reason for existing."

NEUROSCIENCE

Let's revisit two key areas of the brain that guide many of life's decisions: the reward network and the hippocampus. Most moments of excitement and joy increase activity in the reward network. When dopamine surges in the reward network, you feel good. This is a powerful part of the brain. In lab experiments, mice keep pressing a lever to stimulate the reward network to the point of exhaustion and death from starvation. Drugs of addiction have the same effect on our brain.

The hippocampus, the second important area, is the master of the memory orchestra. It directs the formation and storage of new memories. Patients with bilateral hippocampal damage are locked in the perpetual present; they stop forming new memories and forget whom they greeted, sometimes just a minute ago.[760]

Curiosity increases activity in the reward network, which explains why healthy curiosity helps us feel good.[761] Resolving curiosity, such as revealing the answer to a trivia question or removing the blur from an image, activates the hippocampus, the reward network and related areas.[758] Curiosity thus enhances memory and learning.

Research shows that **curiosity that we believe will be satisfied increases the feeling of reward**; that's the reason millions of people enjoy watching *Jeopardy*.[757] But experiencing curiosity from insufficient information or impaired information (such as from seeing a blurred picture on TV or dealing with a weak signal on a cell phone), which we don't know will be resolved, activates areas of the brain associated with annoyance and aversion.[758] Even the latter curiosity, however, when resolved, activates the reward network. Thus, playing peekaboo with babies is a good exercise that increases happiness, as long as your face shows up in good time from behind your hands. If you delay reappearing, you'll frustrate the little one.

WHY INCREASE CURIOSITY?

The two sparks for creativity are curiosity and meaning. You work to quench your curiosity appetite and to fulfill meaning. Add brilliance, diligence, opportunity, and luck in the mix, and you have the perfect ingredients for every remarkable career that has helped us move forward. Curiosity is an important contributor to our movement from Africa to populate the entire Earth and, in the future, perhaps Mars and other planets.

A moderate level of curiosity is a pleasant, low-calorie way to amuse yourself. It is one of the driving forces in child development.

Curiosity keeps your brain happy and young.

Curiosity enhances attention, memory and learning, and in observational studies, it has even been shown to improve health and increase longevity. The curious have greater vitality; curiosity enhances intimacy and relationship satisfaction.

Curiosity, however, follows an inverted U curve. Very low curiosity makes life uninteresting and often unaccomplished, and it is a marker of depression. Very high curiosity can get you in trouble, particularly if it is coupled with suboptimal judgment. Excessive curiosity can lead to shifty attention and an annoying, intrusive nature.

The curious need prosocial meaning to stay out of trouble.

We need the novel as well as the mundane. After an hour of curious seeking, infants and children like to go back to their moms and dads to emotionally refuel.

The mundane is comforting, the novel is exciting; we need an optimal mix of both.

The authentically and pro-socially curious are also humble. They accept their ignorance and work hard to remove it so they can be more useful. Their curiosity serves a larger meaning.

As long as curiosity is coupled with good judgment and is harnessed to serve a higher meaning, increasing curiosity in our children and ourselves promises to take us to a better and brighter future. The good news is that curiosity, like the planters in your home, can be watered and nurtured with the right fertilizers to help it grow. You can build your curiosity.

45

Building Curiosity

A few months ago, my wife and I were at an ice-cream shop with our girls. Once we bought the ice cream, we scanned the place and found an empty table. Four tables down was a family with a little girl, about six. Immediately, our then six-year-old became interested in her. Within minutes, she and the little girl disappeared into the play area, and by the end of our visit, they had already become best friends. I realized that adults try their best to stay away from the other adults they don't know, whereas little kids try their best to connect with the other little kids they don't know. Our juniors definitely aren't little adults from Lilliput.

Our natural curiosity as a child is replaced by caution, a sense of propriety, and mind wandering. But you can take several positive and enjoyable steps to increase your curiosity. Some of these are perspectives, and others are practices.

KNOWLEDGE GAP

Reading a summary of a book, visiting a local museum or a website about a topic you're unfamiliar with (such as how the circulation war between Joseph Pulitzer and William Randolph Hearst gave birth to yellow journalism), or watching an educational documentary or *Jeopardy* will make you aware of the knowledge gap. **Awareness of the knowledge gap and the knowledge that you can fill it, enhance motivation** to know more. In general, the optimal situation is when you know a little bit about something but not a lot. We get bored by repetition and mildly threatened by something entirely unfamiliar.

Awareness of ignorance is essential to acquiring knowledge, that
with time and experience, becomes wisdom.

Such motivation is healthy since its pursuit enhances happiness. A common bias that hurts our curiosity is that we believe we know more than we actually do. We can enhance curiosity by being willing to let go of this bias and being inspired rather than annoyed when we learn that someone else knows much more than we do.

SPRINKLES OF CURIOSITY

Curiosity drives many aspects of daily life. What is the headline news today? What is in the mail? Who called when I was away? What are people saying about me on social media? Who won the primary? These are natural, simple external drivers of our daily lives. You can also add on some simple, interesting exercises that I have tried. For example, often when I am waiting for the elevator with someone, I make a bet with that person as to which of the elevators will come first. That often starts a lighthearted conversation.

On Halloween, I keep a count: will we entertain fewer or more than forty trick-or-treaters? Intentionally sprinkling curiosity throughout the day makes for a more interesting day even when nothing truly rewarding happens. It certainly keeps the kids excited.

The greater your curiosity, the happier your kids.

My hope is that **if we get ourselves and our children to crave curiosity, it will start them on a path of lifelong learning. It might also keep them out of trouble.**

INCREASING THE A-I GAP

We have previously discussed that the two core ingredients of every experience are attention (*A*) and interpretation (*I*). We will keep revisiting this concept because of its central importance. The more you can fill your experience with attention, the greater your curiosity and joy. For example, you can look at a hibiscus as another hibiscus or notice the details so you get to know this particular hibiscus. You can look at your loved one, a friend, or a known client as someone familiar or meet him assuming there is an opportunity to discover something new.

When spending time with a friend or family member, spend a few seconds looking at the color of that person's eyes. When looking at a tree in your neighborhood, notice its branching pattern. When watching a movie, consider it a work of art and notice the details of the sets. When watching a dance, notice the expressions of the supporting performers in the background. When listening to your parents, feel the depth of their voices. Each of these experiences will take you deeper into a new world.

Live deeper.

JUST WATCH THE GAME

Think about this. It is the World Cup semifinals. Germany is playing Italy in a high-stakes game. You are Marcus, glued to the TV in Berlin, watching your team play. What will happen to your heart rate? Won't it accelerate?

Here is the outcome of that acceleration: an intriguing study published in 2008 showed that Germans watching their own team play had a two- to threefold increased risk of acute cardiovascular events. The risk was much higher in men within two hours of the start of the game.[647] Although the home team has the advantage of playing in front of their crowd, the crowds watching have a disadvantage because they have no sense of control.[762] They want to tilt the odds in their team's favor, and struggle when they can't.

We side with one of the teams very quickly when we start watching the game. Even in a game in which we aren't emotionally attached to either team, we pick a favorite and start rooting for them. If things don't go our way, we get a little anxious. I have experienced this while watching my thirteen-year-old and seven-year-old play tennis. It seems silly to want your seven-year-old to score a point by hitting the ball over the net and to get your adrenaline going if she doesn't.

You can either enjoy the game or obsess over who might win.

I think in this instance it is best to just watch the game. I have now learned to let go of my preference. Just enjoy the moves and the finesse of the players, and side with both teams. Be curious about the tactics the teams use and anticipate the moves they make. **Carry the mindset that every game is a social event and not a competition.** I enjoy the game much better with that attitude.

SAVOR THE STORIES

We love to listen to stories. We also love to tell stories. Let's play a little game. Write a story that has these six characters: a bunny, a carrot, a panda bear, a tennis racket, a radio, and a cup of coffee. Next, ask someone else to write a story using the same characters.

Most likely, their story will be a little or a lot different. You can play this game with your loved ones and friends. Once you get into the habit of listening to and telling stories (like the very wise Forrest Gump) with kindness and care, you will discover the hopes and concerns of many who surround you. You may not be able to do anything tangible to help them, but when their stories are heard, they will heal. Remember that **we have two ears and one mouth; listen at least twice as much as you speak**.

SOLICIT A GUIDE

Several years ago, my family visited the redwood forests in California. The tall redwoods looked like giant sages. For the first forty-five minutes, we randomly roamed around. Then we had the help of a tour guide. The whole forest lit up with the guide's words. We started seeing the little saplings at the roots of the trees. We came to know how some of the forest fires have been helpful. We were taken to a tree that was so big that about fifteen of us could crawl into its hollowed core. I have come to completely believe in asking someone who is more experienced than me. **Assume that everyone has a domain of expertise, a particular hobby or skill that you will find fascinating.** People are willing to tell you; you just have to ask. One of my neighbors knows everything about dogs; another builds miniature ships; a third is an expert in architecture.

The more I ask, the more experts I find, ranging from expert handymen to experts in jewelry design, construction, cosmology, farming, poetry, dance, bee farming, carpentry, and singing. I have learned that the single most important step in revealing the wealth of talent that others are hiding is to just ask and then enjoy listening to them singing the songs of their lives.

Better to ask for directions than take an expensive detour.

FIND ONE NEW DETAIL (FOND)

Have you counted the colors on a monarch butterfly, noticed in an elevator that the edges of the carpet are cleaner than the central area, and seen that the screws in your home are most likely not aligned with each other? Have you paused to notice whether your ring finger or pointer finger is longer? How about your spouse's? Have you noticed that every chimney in your town is slightly different? How about the ponytails of the cars (the antennas)—have you noticed that some are long, some short, some stiff, some mobile, and some cars have none? I try to notice these silly little details and many more in the world around me, and I show them to others, particularly to little children.

I am always on the lookout for new details in a familiar object. Try to do this in your own life. Every day find one new detail in the world around you. If you feel up to it, share it with someone, perhaps someone in your family. Write about it. Make it a game. Let everyone in your family or your office find one new detail. Finding new details will make you all genuinely fonder of those objects, and also each other. It is a great team-building practice. It will keep you curious and learning and keep your brain young.

EAT WITH THE EARTH

Not all of us are surrounded by nature every single day, particularly if we live in a high-rise downtown or spend a lot of time traveling. **Eating is one of the best times to connect with nature.** As you admire the bowl of soup or salad, the bread, or the veggies, connect with the fields; imagine where they came from. Read about the details of that vegetable or fruit from Wikipedia. Think of the farmer and his family, the skies above the fields, and the sun that baked the fruits. Savor at least the first few bites, eat slowly (chew each bite as many times as the number of your teeth), take small bites, and eat smart (nourishing, fresh food that isn't very calorie dense). Those are the four *S*s of eating: savor, slow, small, and smart.

Spending time studying the history of your food will help you appreciate and enjoy it more. This slows my eating. I have found that **if I can be slow during the first few minutes of eating, I end up eating less and feeling more satisfied.**

Knowing the history of your food can help you enjoy it more.

❦

REDEFINE ANATOMY

One of the best ways to live and learn is to ask lots of whys and so-whats. I suggest medical students not simply memorize their anatomy but **ask lots of whys**. Why does the windpipe sit in front of the esophagus? Why do veins sit on top of the arteries and not the other way around? Why do eyes sit on top of the head? Why are wisdom teeth shaped the way they are? Why is the appendix vestigial? Why is the stomach acidic and intestines alkaline? Why does the brain's surface have folds? Why is the heart not placed perfectly in midline? The practice of asking whys and so-whats can apply to any field. This Socratic inquiry helps you reach a depth of understanding that makes you innovative so that you move your field forward.

If you struggle with forgetting, start asking lots of whys and so-whats.

❦

As you get more curious and use your curiosity to understand the world around you, your attention deepens, and you start making connections you hadn't made before. You start looking deeper—both externally in the world and internally in your thoughts. **The ability to go deeper and stay there is the essence of the meditation practice.**

An average person lives about thirty thousand days on this planet. In that much time, we have a lot to figure out and do; in the process, we increase our knowledge and wisdom. Ask yourself: What will you regret—spending 50 or 80 percent of the day mind wandering or cultivating curiosity to make the most of your earthly journey? In this situation, there's no harm in cultivating FOMO (fear of missing out). Fear of loss is often a more powerful motivator than the allure of gain.

Let curiosity enrich your life and keep you young. You will find that as you become more knowledgeable, the field itself will become more accessible. It often starts with awareness of a small knowledge gap.

Intentionally sprinkling greater curiosity throughout your life eventually kindles within you a fire of internally driven curiosity to know how the world operates and how you can make it better. Such **curiosity empowers you to acquire the knowledge that helps you live a life filled with meaning**.

46

Meaning

THE WHY

Meaning is the why of our life's driving force. **Just as gravity powers the rivers, meaning powers the flow of our lives.** For most nonhuman life-forms, the underlying substance of meaning converges to these two drives: survive and reproduce.

Plants and animals go to great lengths to serve this meaning. They are obsessed with collecting and storing energy. In some instances, their devotion and sacrifice make anything we humans can do pale in comparison (more on this later in this chapter). Many of these admirable behaviors, however, are instinctive and embodied by every member of their species. Animals don't have to think or duel with conflicting ideas to do what they do.

Procreation and child-rearing are instinctive for us humans also. When it comes to the children in our lives—our own kids and grandkids, friends' kids, nephews, nieces, neighborhood children—we want to protect them all. **Our children are like our own hearts beating outside our bodies.** It gives us great meaning to help raise them and protect them, often at the cost of our own comfort and well-being. Many parents I know, if they could, would willingly take their children's pain, illness, or misfortune on themselves. Our meaning, however, isn't limited to our instincts. Humans have two additional meanings.

UNIQUELY HUMAN

Many of us are searching for something larger than ourselves. It could be serving the country, saving the bees, preventing global warming, or spreading the gospel. Poets, philosophers, and contemplatives have used flowery and inspirational words to describe this purpose for which we are willing to invest substantial time and money, even sacrifice our dear lives. At no time is this more evident than when soldiers march onto the battlefield, willing to die to protect their country. Parents have been known to willingly sacrifice their children's lives to protect something larger than themselves, an action that goes against their every instinct. This meaning is intentional and unique to us humans.

Serving something larger than us brings out the best in us.

A second unique aspect of humanity is our ability to assign meaning to random events, particularly the unpleasant ones. Such meaning often relates to how the bad could have prevented something worse or created something good. An annoying person in your family could be the uniting force for everyone else. A forgotten job interview could have saved you from a potentially toxic work environment. A missed exit could be an accident avoided. A series of viral illnesses could be food allergies averted. **Finding the good in bad, the gains in losses, and the lessons in reversals can be extremely empowering.**

A negative event assigned a positive meaning starts feeling less negative.

A human life deprived of meaning drifts like driftwood, easily jostled by waves of desires or adversity. Unfortunately, most of us haven't resolved this very important question: What is the ultimate meaning of life? This question doesn't have an easy answer. Searching for it is a bit like looking through dense fog; you can't see clear to the horizon. Until we know what precedes and follows our earthly existence, we won't be able to convincingly and completely answer the question about what it means. **A better question with respect to the meaning of life is, what is the meaning of *my* life? How can I make my life more meaningful?** Those are answerable questions that provide a good intermediate meaning, which might suffice for most of us.

What is the ultimate meaning of life is a difficult question to answer. How can I make my life more meaningful is an easier and a more useful question.

In general, the more thoughtful you are about living your life with meaning (serving the planet's children, thinking about something larger than yourself, finding positive meaning amid adversities), the more connected you feel with the world. **When you get busy helping the world, the world gets busy helping you. The only caveat is that it takes time for the world's actions to become visible.**

Most of what is meaningful in the world around us can be captured in four overlapping domains.

THE FOUR DOMAINS
Four domains capture the essence of our meaning: belonging, building, becoming, and believing.

Belonging (relationships)
Emperor penguins are known for extreme devotion to their offspring, braving the cold and starvation for months. Octopus mothers go even further. After they lay eggs, these hardy little ladies spend the rest of their lives close to the eggs, protecting them and sending fresh water so they get enough oxygen. They never leave the brood, not even to feed. Just when the eggs hatch, with the job done, the mothers die—of

starvation. Instinctive devotion to offspring is common in the animal kingdom. Mama bears, elephants, buffalo, lions, leopards, whales, and humans all fiercely protect their young. They'll take on an adversary twice their size to save their children. We do that because nothing in life has greater meaning than protecting our children.

I have been protected and nurtured by many. My eldest sister, Rajni, worked harder than I did to help me study for admission into medical school, even though she didn't get into medicine. This was despite my phenomenal ability to annoy her with my innately naughty disposition. My elder sister Sandhya spoilt me the entire time I was in medical school. She tended to every little need. When my father, Sahib, was working away from home, which was most of his career, my elder brother Kishore became the father figure for the family and made many sacrifices to his career to support us all. I cannot recall any wants that my father and brother didn't meet.

Several decades ago my mother, Shashi, and I once fell from our scooter after being hit by a pig that suddenly emerged from a side bush as we were driving. Having sustained a concussion and only partially conscious, my mother kept repeating one question: "Are you OK, Amit? Are you OK?" When I said yes, she would lie down, reassured. In a few minutes, she would wake up asking the same question. This went on for about fifteen minutes. Every time I revisit these memories, I feel warm and nurtured.

Refresh kind memories by revisiting them often.

Beyond my immediate family, I have seen countless selfless actions that fill me with hope and pride for humanity. My friend and colleague Sam recently donated a kidney to his brother. When I asked how long it took him to decide, he said, "Less than thirty seconds. My brother needed a kidney, and I had a spare one. What was there to think?" Another colleague of mine, a woman from Japan, when asked what makes her happiest, replied, "I am most happy when I see my husband happy." I wish we all had such brothers, spouses, and friends.

Personally, there are many in the world who are more precious to me than I am to myself. In fact, every child, including your child/children, grandkids, nephews and nieces are more precious to me than I am to myself. If you find greater meaning than yourself in the young, then you are aligned with the way nature operates. For example, during pregnancy, nature ensures that the fetus gets enough iron and calcium, even if that entails depleting the mother of these essential minerals. *Ubuntu*, an ethical concept of South African origin, beautifully captures the essence of meaning: **we are because we belong. The best way to live for yourself is to live for the world. The people and purpose you serve power all your efforts.**

We are because we belong.

Building (working)

Many of us across different species invest large chunks of our lives, even putting our lives on the line, in the service of what we build and protect. Take the example of honeybees and ants. The life of a honeybee is completely devoted to maintaining the home, raising the young, and serving the queen. They willingly sacrifice their lives to save the queen. Ants are very similar. So are squirrels, tucking away nuts for the winter. You can do few activities (other than sleep) eight hours a day, week after week, for thirty to forty years of your life, other than work.

Our identities are often related to our core contributions to the world. We don't define an apple tree by its leaves or stem. We call it honeycrisp or red delicious based on the apple it produces. **Together, we are (or, I believe, should be) involved in just one business: building a better, kinder, happier, and more hope-filled world for our planet's children.** Each of us uniquely contributes toward this job. Society provides different financial rewards based on the perceived difficulty and value of the job. Yet each job is of value. In a hospital, a janitor, volunteer, chef, nurse, lab technician, administrator, and medical provider are all doing just one thing: serving the patients. The same applies to every company, government office, nonprofit, or other organization. **Honor the meaning (how one serves the world), not just the means (the skills one uses).**

The more we can identify with our core business (building a better world), the greater meaning it will provide. A farmer could see himself as feeding the nation, a library assistant as educating the nation, a journalist as informing the nation, and an actor as entertaining the nation. **A meaning larger than oneself can be a beacon of light for journeying into the future and a reliable source of strength in difficult times.**

Every job that serves mankind (or animals or nature) is honorable.

A friend of mine shared this story of Tim, one of his mentors. Tim was part of a team involved in a three-year education project that he was passionate about. Halfway into the project, he received an ominous diagnosis that gave him only six months to live. He called an urgent meeting. Everyone was thinking that Tim would withdraw from the project. To their surprise, here is what he said: "We have got only six months now to deliver this baby. Let's triple our effort. I won't allow myself to be buried without this being done." They all worked hard, and Tim lived to see his project go live. I feel inspired by his passion and commitment.

Becoming

Someone wants to have a building named after him; another wants to be surrounded by people seeking her autograph. The Nobel Prize fascinates some; others desire to become president of their neighborhood unions. Some want to have a baby girl, some want to have a boy, and some want to adopt. We carry a concept of what will make us complete, and that is what guides our lives.

When I lived in a four-hundred-square-foot home with no decent play area outside and no defined bedroom inside, I dreamed of a neighborhood with a play area and a home with a personal bedroom. Working at a primary health center overseas at which the only available antibiotic was ampicillin, I aspired to be at a place where I could practice medicine the way it should be practiced. Both these aspirations guided a significant part of my initial efforts in life; I am grateful to have lived to see them satisfied.

The challenge with the human mind is that what you aspire to become or acquire often stops being satisfying once you achieve it. For most of the first two decades of my life, I seldom had access to hot water. Taking a shower in the winter was pure torture. A few years into having hot water, I found myself complaining that the water pressure wasn't strong enough. This revision of expectations would continue unless I choose to give it a pause. Hence the need for becoming altruistic—focused on others.

We stop being miserable the day we decide to live our life helping others.

Have high altruistic aspirations. My personal two-word mission for this life is "eliminate suffering." We can't eliminate pain; in fact, if we lose pain receptors in our feet, we risk losing our feet. Similarly, if we lose the ability to experience emotional pain, we risk losing compassion for others' pain. But we can always help provide comfort to others hurting and, when feasible, help them find meaning in their pain. You can craft your own short mission that aligns with your worldview and skill set. Bringing kindness to fellow beings, eliminating loneliness, curing cancer, ending poverty, removing discrimination, helping everyone gain access to safe water—working toward these or other such goals can continue to inspire you all your life.

Believing (spirituality or a belief system)

Belonging, building, and becoming all depend on the external world. They are vulnerable to the shifting priorities of individuals and corporations, geopolitical issues, the whims of human minds, and the sheer uncertainty of the world. One aspect of meaning that isn't vulnerable to worldly uncertainties and that can support all the other meanings comes from spirituality or a belief system. Because of the sheer strength of the meaning that spirituality provides, those of us anchored in this meaning become deeply invested in it, are protected by it, and go to great lengths to protect it.

In support of an ideology or faith, people can march on rocks or fire despite all sorts of physical discomfort. From prolonged fasting to forest dwelling, giving away all possessions, burning one's skin, and practicing other extreme forms of self-mortification, people act in all kinds of physically painful ways because they believe the spiritual gain is a good bargain. I personally saw many such actions during the first twenty-seven years of my life living in India.

Practicing one's faith and observing the rituals aligned with the faith can unite large swaths of humanity into cohesive groups. The more your spiritual meaning (believing) can support the other three meanings (belonging, building, and becoming), the better for you and the world. Spiritual meaning that forces us to reject others or pick up arms against each other can be a very destructive force, particularly because individuals feel totally justified and inspired, even exhilarated, in defending such meaning. The owner of such meaning sees nothing wrong with it, unlike others at the receiving end of the spears.

A truly spiritual idea unites us instead of dividing us.

Often such spiritual meaning begins to form early in life. The earlier we can help anchor the next generation in a more altruistic way of believing and the more this can be done globally, the greater chance we have of surviving on this planet long enough to truly figure out the answer to the question of the ultimate meaning of life.

Our relationships, actions, desired identities, and spirituality are the four constructs that are like the four dimensions (space and time) defining our place in this world. These four constructs provide us a strong scaffold with which to build our lives. The greater our engagement with these areas, the more we get pulled into the world around us. They can, however, also tie us down, pushing us into a darker abyss of hatred, envy, and crime. A healthy integration of vertical meaning (believing) with horizontal meaning (belonging, building, and becoming) can provide you a lifelong recipe for peace and excellence.

The more meaning centric your day is, the greater your efficiency, happiness, health, and longevity—the meaning in finding meaning.

MEANING IN FINDING MEANING

Let me say in one breath the different benefits of finding meaning. In one's personal life, having a sense of meaning improves physical health, enhances self-care (better diet and exercise), decreases risk of infections, lowers pain, enhances emotional well-being, lowers mental-health issues, enhances coping, and increases longevity.[763, 764] Several of these changes, such as improvement in diet and physical activity, have positive effects on many other aspects of life. **For example, in an interesting Australian study, increasing fruits and veggies increased happiness to the same extent as moving from unemployment to employment.**[765]

Healthier food nurtures a happier mood.

Having a sense of meaning decreases the risk of heart attack by as much as 25 percent.[766] At work, meaning improves focus, performance, and job satisfaction, leading to lower turnover. In fact, with respect to career success, the more people focus on healthy sharing and giving, the higher they rise compared with those who focus only on taking.[767]

Finding meaning is an effective analgesic for both physical and emotional pain. In an interesting study, researchers found that the same area of the brain helps with the search for meaning, the placebo response to pain, and the activation of descending analgesic pathways in the brain.[768] This provides the physiological explanation for how finding meaning can tangibly decrease the severity of both emotional and physical pain.

The pain for which you can find meaning becomes less painful.

Shared meaning also improves relationships. People perceive their best days at work to be when they rejoice in professional relationships and spend several hours in quality social time. In research, the optimal amount of social time was about six hours each day.[769] Social time includes talking on the phone, interacting with clients, attending group meetings, and participating in online chats. Enjoyable social time not only improves the quality of the days but also preserves memory and can even increase longevity.[770, 771]

Jobs that nurture quality relationships enhance your wellbeing and may even improve your longevity.

An important recent observation was that **having a sense of meaning and purpose can completely reverse the adverse effects of loneliness on inflammatory gene expression**.[772] We cannot always eliminate loneliness, but we can help give people a sense of meaning that resonates with their worldview, which may be a useful interim solution.

Meaning improves work performance. People perform better on days they feel motivated and feel good about their work and their team. Interestingly, research shows that their best days at work are when two conditions are met: they make progress and are appropriately praised. **Progress without recognition and praise without progress are both unhelpful**.[773] Meaning is a motivator and is the culmination of the integrated physical, emotional, and cognitive efforts that drive one to excellence.[774, 775]

Lack of praise and false praise, both are demoralizing and hurtful.

Despite all these benefits of finding meaning, a high proportion of us either do not think about meaning or struggle with it. In a survey of over twelve thousand employees, 50 percent felt they lacked meaning and significance at work.[776] This is unfortunate because, **not uncommonly, our meaning is right in front of us. We just can't see it**. I have no doubt that if you search, you'll find a deeper meaning both for your efforts and also for many (but not all) of your adversities.

47

In Search of Meaning

When we can't see our North Star, we struggle with finding direction, moving more like driftwood and not like the focused Jet Ski. Such a journey also produces angst. A full 50 percent do not find work satisfying, 50 to 80 percent have moderate to high levels of work-related stress, and 70 percent are not engaged or are actively disengaged at work.[777-779] Clearly, finding a deeper meaning can serve us and our society well. Here are a few ideas.

DEPTH OF INQUIRY

The deeper you look, the more meaning you will find. If you look deep enough, even the most mundane activities might start looking meaningful. When I was about ten years old, I watched a Hindi movie named *Boot Polish*, which was about a little boy and girl who were orphans. They were raised by an unkind aunt, but they found a good-hearted albeit unkempt mentor on the street. He taught them to live with dignity and not spend their lives panhandling. The little boy (who was about my age in the movie) worked hard and collected enough money to buy a kit for setting up a street-side boot-polish shop. The boy was extremely excited about his future as a boot-polish boy. I remember crying while watching the scene in which he told his sister, "I will be the best boot-polish boy ever. I will polish people's boots so well that they can see their face in their boot." That movie left a deep impact on me about the dignity of work. **No work is too small or too large. As long as you serve with passion and joy, your work can provide you a deeper meaning.**

What you do is important. How you do it is sometimes even more important.

Often, you just have to spend some time exploring the depth. Think about how your software code is helping an end user, your teaching is raising future citizens, your social work is bringing hope and homes to families, or your taxi is providing safe commutes to many.

Meaning more often needs to be discovered, than invented.

Do not peg your self-worth on the dollars society provides you; peg your self-worth on the people you serve and the values you live by. If you don't make an effort to find deeper meaning, then even the deepest thoughts and actions will look superficial. Carl Jung aptly said, "The least of things with meaning is worth more in life than the greatest of things without it."

BE FLEXIBLE

Meaning is individual and changes with context and time. Fulfilling an essential need, providing comfort, bringing pleasure, educating, helping relationships, tending to nature, innovating cost-effective solutions, enhancing beauty, spreading good values, creating legacy—all of these and many more are worthy pursuits. The world needs all of them.

No need to be biased against someone, as long as he or she does not seek meaning in harming others. Pushing elevator buttons was tremendously meaningful to my five-year-old. If I accidentally forgot to let her do that, she would invariably press many buttons, and I would end up apologizing to smiling co-passengers. Like many people, I am sure I am stuck in some elevator-button equivalent today that I will grow out of, once I start looking for higher meaning.

Picking trivial squabbles shortchanges the infinitely precious self within you.

TIME AND MEANING

Past, present, and future are all meaningful. The past gives us context and is a great teacher, life happens in the present, and we look forward to the future. We tend to get stuck in one time zone, often the most hurtful one. I have an elderly family member stuck in the past, mostly in regrets; a young cousin stuck in the future, mostly in concerns; and another cousin stuck in the present, mostly frustrated with the daily grind. Intentionality and strong attention can help you overcome this instinct so you focus more on where joy is rather than where hurt resides.

About the hurtful past, ask yourself, "Can I find gratitude in this? Is this the tuition I had to pay?" Remember that **the more painful the hurt, the longer it takes for us to find meaning**.

The more painful the hurt, the longer it will take for you to find meaning.

About the concerning future, ask yourself, "Will it matter in five years? Is my pain likely to help someone else in pain? What is my future concern teaching me about who I am?"

About the unsatisfactory present, ask yourself, "Is this a step back that will eventually be a move forward? Can I see the good in what seems bad? Are my expectations realistic, or do they need to be tweaked?"

It isn't so much where you are focusing, whether it's the past, present, or future; more important for your well-being is the attitude you carry when you focus, and the flexibility with which you can shift your perspective from the past to the present to the future.

Where you are focusing (the past, the present, or the future) is less important than the attitude you carry as you focus.

SELF VERSUS OTHER

Who is your primary customer? Is it just the self or the collective? They do not have to conflict. **You can serve the self to serve the collective.** When Mother Teresa started her work, she would often give away her lunch to hungry children. How can one eat if one is seeing hunger and malnutrition all around? A few days into her daily routine, she passed out. Her mentor, understanding her compassionate disposition, advised her to take care of herself so that she could better serve others.

In order to integrate self and other, build your eulogy and resume simultaneously.[780] Building only one or the other may not be enough. **Your resume will help you grow professionally; your eulogy will help you grow as a human being.** Eventually the two will become integrated and mutually supportive, like the two wheels of a bicycle; building one builds the other.

As you build your resume, do not forget to build your eulogy.

CHOOSE MEANING

Subjectivity rules most aspects of life. I used to sit on study sections for the National Institutes of Health (NIH) and editorial boards of journals, and I have thus participated in some of the most rigorous reviews of research grants and papers. I was amazed at how subjective some of the evaluations can be. Often, one person's opinion changed the direction of the conversation and swayed every other expert in the room.

On a trip, I once bought a refurbished iPad for my then eight-year-old. I called her on the phone from the Minneapolis airport to tell her I was getting a gift for her. Thinking she might be happy to hear it, I told her I was getting an iPad. She started crying, not happy tears but sad ones. I was confused; I thought an iPad would be a pretty awesome gift for her, way beyond her expectations.

"Why are you crying?" I asked.

She replied, "Why did you tell me what you're getting? It's not a surprise anymore." For her the surprise element was more meaningful than the gift itself!

When you give someone a birthday gift, that person can interpret it so many ways. The best interpretation is gratitude that you remembered and made the effort. But the possibilities for interpretation are many: what a cheap gift (you don't care about me), what an expensive gift (you're trying to show off), what a good choice, what a poor choice, now I have to remember to give you something on your birthday, this seems like something that was regifted, and more. **The same gift can have many meanings depending on the person receiving it.**

One person may be grateful receiving a fistful of dirt; another may whine receiving a fistful of diamonds. Guess who is likely to be happier!

There are some events, however, that can't be interpreted in many different ways. An unspeakable act of human aggression is perhaps one of them. But in most situations, the meaning you make out of the experience is completely up to you. Recognize its tremendous power in influencing your feeling of how well your life is going.

THE THREE QUESTIONS

On an introspective day, meditate on these three questions: Who am I? Why do I exist? What is this world? I have spent some time pondering these ideas to come up with a construct that is believable (in my mind) and practical yet deep enough to be solid. **I believe that we are agents of service and love, that we exist to make a kinder and happier world for our planet's children, and that this world is a giant school of learning.**

I try not to define who I am with narrower titles, such as physician, attorney, librarian, teacher, grocery clerk, or others. That has the potential for creating judgments, since our society doesn't reward every profession equally. Service and love connect all these themes. **We are all agents of service and love**, making our unique contributions based on our skills and capacity.

You are an agent of service and love, helping build a kinder and happier world for our planet's children.

Whenever in doubt, I ask myself which of my actions is most likely to help the planet's children? The answer to that question almost always points me in the right direction. **I believe our evolutionary responsibility is to create a better world for our children.** Thoughts, words, and actions that serve this purpose are less likely to go astray.

Serving our children is serving the sacred.

The world isn't for plundering while pursuing pleasure. We are because the world is. The world is our teacher. Through each experience, we gain wisdom in how to better express love as compassion, connection, attention, and caring. **I believe the best job in the world is that of being a student.** It helps you to be humble and accept your vulnerability. A learning brain remains plastic and young, which helps with future learning.[781] These changes in the brain can be seen on sophisticated scans with as little as one week of training.[782] **Never give up your job of being a student.**

If you take up the job of being a lifelong student, you will never get bored and can never be fired!

SHORT TERM VERSUS LONG TERM

You likely have at least a rough idea of what you want to do in life. Perhaps a clear idea. The challenge is to **align your daily actions with long-term meaning**. Very likely, you want to be healthier, happier, and more successful, and you want to have better relationships, be more respected, and touch many lives. All of this requires hard work, because you'll need self-control. You will have to say no to desserts, get out of bed when you would rather snooze, work on projects and with people you would rather avoid, cultivate patience, better respond to others' annoyances, go the extra mile to help others, and work on boring assignments day after day after day.

Align short-term actions with long-term meaning.

Creating long-term meaning is easier than implementing it. But you have to start somewhere. Perhaps pick one or two activities that contribute to your long-term meaning and act on them. You can incrementally add individual activities as your capacity allows.

CELEBRATE THE PROCESS

Most researchers live in the future. Often, the first time they pause to celebrate a research project is when the project is completed and the manuscript written, accepted, and published. Until then, it is just the grind. Such an approach can lead to quicker burnout, particularly if the grants come in slowly and rejections come fast, which is the reality for almost every researcher.

I believe in celebrating the milestones. Not the extravagant all-night-party kind of celebration, but a simple one like a celebration with ice cream when the grant is submitted, a pizza party with a favorable review (with healthy pizza), or a social in the office when the participants start enrolling. The same can be applied to a software project or any other endeavor. **Waiting to celebrate at the finish line is too late.**

Celebrate the steps instead of waiting for the ultimate outcomes.

Like celebration, the more meaning you can find in the process done well rather than the outcome achieved, the better your focus will be, with potentially better outcome. **Your effort and intentions, and not the outcome, are in your control. Peg your self-worth on your effort and intentions, not on the outcome.**

TEN-MINUTES TEST

How do I prioritize? What is important? What is incredibly important? I have come to realize the value of each letter after I opened a Twitter account. With limited characters at my disposal to convey an idea, each character is precious. Since I send no more than one tweet on most days, I wish for them to be meaningful. Sometimes a 200-word blog post takes the same time to write as a 200-character tweet. The same applies to prioritizing in life.

When you are faced with little time to pack all the important stuff, then you get to the essence. Let's say you have only ten minutes to wrap up your entire life. In that time, you're allowed to write a few messages and call a few people. What will you write, and whom will you call? This exercise might give you insight into what is most meaningful to you.

Realize that each of the meanings is particular to your present mortal life. The human mind cannot access the ultimate meaning that connects all our individual meanings. Instead of asking, "What is the meaning of life?," it is better to ask, "What is the meaning of *my* life?"

WORK-RELATED MEANING: THREE STEPS

Work provides a strong sense of meaning for many. To find out what would be most meaningful to me, I took three key steps that I think are applicable to most pursuits.

Step 1: Is this a big idea? You want to pursue something that has significant societal impact. Your chance of helping many, attracting resources to your work and success are higher if you pick a big idea. For example, in health care, think about decreasing costs, finding a treatment for conditions with poor outcomes, or decreasing patient burden. There are a few questions to ask regarding this: Does the society care about this? Is this problem going to get worse in the years to come? Are there no effective solutions for this? If I find a solution, will people be willing to invest in it? Does the problem I am tackling affect many different aspects of life? The more yeses you get to these questions, the more certain you can be that this problem is worth exploring.

Think big to reach high.

Step 2: Do I have personal passion for this? I tried my hand at interventional cardiology and surgery. I was terrible at both. I constantly worried that I might hurt my patients while doing a procedure. With deep admiration for those who can do it, I changed my course. We are all cut out for different things. It is best to align your work with your natural skill set. Ask questions like these: Can I devote my life to this? Is it worth thinking about for sixteen hours a day? Can this be my legacy? Is this aligned with my core values? Am I a natural at this? Again, the more yeses, the better.

Step 3: Do I (or can I) have the resources to pull this off? Some careers require the right networking, some ask you to pull all-nighters, some need large capital, and some require a significant workforce. Ask yourself these questions: Can I arrange the capital needed? Can I arrange the workforce needed? Is the technology ripe to support my plan? Are my skill set and personal strengths appropriate for my goal?

Take your already successful idea or an idea that is germinating through the three steps I outlined above. The process will give you insight into how far you would want to explore that idea. If it's a big idea for which you feel passionate and have resources, then your brain will experience a deeper connection with it. You'll engage with it—on good days as well as bad days.

48

How to Handle a Bad Day

Bad days are a weekly event for most of us. These are the days when we wake up tired, feel physically sick, snap at our loved ones, make little progress at work, feel unworthy, do something stupid, aren't creative or productive, and have to spend time with someone who gives us hives. About three to four out of seven days in a week we experience such moments. The annoying stress on these days predisposes us to chronic inflammation.[783-786]

Although you cannot avoid every bad day, you do have the ability to prevent a mistake from becoming a catastrophe and to keep a bad day from becoming a disastrous day. Four simple steps can help you better handle a bad day: investigate, eliminate, negotiate, and celebrate.

1. INVESTIGATE: WHY IS THIS A BAD DAY?

Most bad days are bad because of one or more of these four features (and most bad days have at least two of them):

- Demand-Resource Imbalance—When you have to clock in twenty hours worth of work every day, day after day, your brain can't it take any more. If you add time pressure to this, it becomes particularly toxic. Given that no one urges us to do less with more, demand-resource imbalance is here to stay for the foreseeable future.
- Lack of Control—On most days, something is happening around me that I can't control. When that something becomes unpleasant, undesirable, and personal, I have a bad day.
- Lack of Meaning—Why am I doing this? How will this help anyone? If we do not have a good answer to these questions, then we don't savor our work. A negative meaning—for example, working for someone you find repulsive or spending time with a relative who lacks basic human decency—can predictably seed a bad day.
- Low self-worth—There are days when everything is going well but we feel crummy because we feel unworthy. We feel unworthy because we remember a failure or a previous insulting comment, are in the company of someone who is arrogant, or sometimes we just feel unworthy for no good reason. You can call it brain colic, like the random colic infants have. If in our negative mood we say or do

something that annoys others and the negativity echoes back, then we put ourselves in a downward spiral that might culminate in a migraine, a binge, or a panic attack.

Once you know the underlying reason for the bad day, you can next go about fixing it.

2. ELIMINATE: CAN I FIX THE PROBLEM?
Some problems can be fixed. You can install antivirus software, get the broken taillight fixed, take ibuprofen for back pain, and sleep in over the weekend to shake off your fatigue.

Take out the thorn from your finger before asking how it got there.

But many problems are like a chronic rash that gets worse with each scratch. You can't change your neighbor, improve the memory of your colleagues, eliminate drug abuse from our country, or easily "unbully" your narcissistic supervisor. In all these situations, and even those that are fixable, finding a way to negotiate reality might help.

3. NEGOTIATE: CAN I THINK ABOUT THIS DIFFERENTLY?
If I were to act on all my initial impulses, I would be either jailed or dead. The reptile in me is obsessed with safety and survival. It also wants to collect energy—calories, money, and fame—and distribute its genes. Taming it has been the work of a lifetime.

Instead of reacting, recover faster from adversity by asking these questions:

- Can I be grateful for what went right within what went wrong?
- Can I be grateful that there is a whole lot that is still right?
- Does this situation remind me to be more compassionate?
- Am I uniquely hurting, or does stuff like this happen to many people?
- Was this the tuition I had to pay for one of the lessons of life?
- Can this help me long term?
- Did this prevent something worse?
- Will forgiveness help heal the hurt?

You don't have to secure a good answer to every single question. Any one of them can help you rethink the situation and renegotiate the challenge. Science can help. For example, research shows that **previous social rejection increases your chances of creative success**.[787] The point of this study isn't that you get yourself socially rejected to be more creative, but if you find yourself socially rejected, reframe it by believing that it will help you in ways you can't even imagine. Instead of catastrophizing, if you can, celebrate.

4. CELEBRATE: CAN I DILUTE THE BAD WITH THE GOOD?

You have a tough day that involves a verbal brawl in a meeting, road rage, bad coffee, and a stubbed toe. You come home bruised. Greeting you is your eight-month-old, all excited, clean, and happy. What happens to your frowns? Don't they melt right away? The mind is like a giant, complex mural. We experience the mural based on where the flashlight of our attention is projected. Project the flashlight on a happy image, at least a few times during the day.

Let the good dilute the bad, not the other way around.

Dilute a bad experience with good thoughts, not a good experience with bad thoughts.

Celebrate when you wake up in the morning, run into an old friend, meet your family at the end of the day, or get to nap in the afternoon. When you get in the habit of micro-celebrations, you will find ways to recover from a bad day by diluting it with something festive. You might also have fewer bad days.

Achieving emotional equilibrium stops the energy drain, providing you the bandwidth to be more creative on what could be a bad day. Such equilibrium will also help prevent a bad day from becoming a very bad day.

Very bad days with catastrophic events happen to 70 percent of us in our lifetimes, with one out of three people experiencing four or more such events.[788] Some of them are unavoidable. You can't prevent a deadly tornado from ripping through your town. But some bad days, we create by ourselves.

A few years ago, a previous colleague of mine was standing at a bus stop to drop off his daughter for school. About half a mile away, on a quiet road, a truck swerved into the wrong lane and hit a car. The truck driver panicked. Instead of stopping and helping, he accelerated, lost control, and hit my colleague, taking his life in front of his little girl. This is the bad turning into the catastrophic. I hope and pray such catastrophic days never knock at anyone's door.

Many modern catastrophes are a product of our own creation, and are thus preventable.

Even during these extraordinarily difficult circumstances, keeping your head together can help you survive and find balance that might limit further damage. Using any of the above ideas can prevent a bad day from becoming a very bad or catastrophic day. Working on your attention and mindset on days when all is good will help you preserve your energy and sanity on days that are challenging, likely saving you much grief.

The trees don't make roots the night of the storm. They strengthen their roots little by little every single day. That is how they are able to withstand category four hurricanes.

Curiosity and meaning both entail projecting attention externally and looking deeper into your sensory world. Each of these brings your presence into a meditative state. This is the reason mindfulness *v2* guides you to immerse yourself in your world. With practice, you can be meditative all day long—sprinkling curiosity about the simplest things and doing work that is meaningful (or finding greater meaning in what you are presently doing). The resulting intentional presence is captured in a business buzzword: engagement.

49

Engagement

When I think about engagement, I go back to a summer many years ago. One of the rooms in our home had a large window with a prominent ledge on the top. A pair of birds (most likely robins) decided to build a nest on top of the ledge. I had a month off, so I had all the time in the world to watch, while the robin couple was the busiest little pair on the planet.

Right at sunrise they would fly in with small sticks (and sometimes grass and mud) in their beaks. From sunrise to sunset, they would go to eat worms and then bring in sticks, mud, and grass. In a matter of days, I saw a small home attached to our home. I remember wanting to sleep in it.

Then one day I saw an egg in the nest and then another and another, until there was a clutch of four. The next few weeks were frantic for the robin mom. She would incubate the eggs the entire day. She would jump up to the edge and then use her bill to rotate the eggs. She would turn the eggs multiple times daily, not leaving them for more than a few minutes, for two weeks in a row. Just when I thought their job was done, they actually had the busiest two weeks of all. I woke up to the chirping sounds of a little baby bird. The next day, a second one arrived, and then two more followed.

The robin mom and dad must have made at least a hundred trips a day to soothe their babies' hunger cramps. This feeding frenzy lasted for many days, by which time the babies were almost as big as their parents. Then one day, to my disappointment, the nest was empty. The fledglings had flown away. I am told the robin mom immediately got busy preparing for the next clutch.

Now that is engagement!

Experts define engagement as a combination of being involved, committed, and enthusiastic while giving discretionary effort.[789] **Engagement is emotional commitment to the work.** A robin's life fits every single descriptor here, as do the lives of most birds and perhaps most animals in general (but we might exclude drones, and people who act like drones).

TWO KINDS OF ENGAGEMENT

Engagement can be automatic or intentional. Automatic engagement depends on the experience being naturally entertaining or meaningful, preferably both. My six-year-old, when she is making a bead bracelet, and my mother, when she is teaching yoga, find great joy and meaning in those activities. I wish everything we did was as entertaining and meaningful as making bead bracelets and teaching yoga, but it is not. Reviewing research papers isn't as engaging. Trying to learn new software, buying groceries, preparing taxes—none of these is naturally engaging for most of us. But these activities need good attention anyway, hence the need for intentionality in engagement.

Intentional engagement actively seeks meaning and novelty. It is a discipline. When you are doing an activity that you repeat day after day after day (driving on the same road, performing the same surgery, exercising on the same treadmill, cooking the same dish, or teaching the same topic), you will need to intentionally find meaning and novelty to preserve engagement and thus quality and freshness. One way to maintain engagement is to focus on how you are touching people's lives instead of letting the repetitiveness of the activity push you into boredom.

Every time I give a talk, I truly feel grateful and sometimes overwhelmed by the trust and commitment people bring to the presentation.

Those taking your help are truly helping you.

On the days I need greater motivation, I assume someone in the audience has a sick child or has lost a child, or recently had suicidal thoughts. I try to help that person. This perspective has never failed me in keeping stress, mind wandering, and self-doubt to a minimum, thereby improving my performance.

It is less about what you do and more about who you are serving.

MULTIPLE BENEFITS

In a large study by Gallup involving 1.4 million employees, employee engagement was associated with positive outcomes in nine areas:[790]

- Customer ratings
- Profitability
- Productivity
- Turnover
- Safety incidents
- Shrinkage (theft)
- Absenteeism
- Safety incidents
- Quality (defects)

Research shows that companies with good engagement have four times the earnings-per-share growth rate than companies without good engagement. Disengagement costs US businesses north of $300 billion every year.[791]

With all these wonderful benefits and insights, we might think that most workers would be engaged in their work. That is far from true. In several interesting studies, researchers have found a consistent drop since the 1950s in the percentage of people who say yes to this question: Would you work if you won the lottery?[792] The global level of engagement is a mere 13 percent. **It is stunning that about 90 percent of workers spend most of their week doing an activity they really do not care much about.**[793] Undoubtedly, we can do better.

SUSTAINING ENGAGEMENT

Most workers start their jobs with the intention of full engagement. Early on, curiosity, meaning, and optimal challenge help them engage, as long as they have ample cognitive and emotional energy. Engagement, however, fades as novelty fades, fatigue sets in, distractions crop up and the meaning that was important to begin with stops being the driving force. A senior leader of a successful startup in San Francisco recently shared with me her firm's internal data which showed that employees remain very passionate for the first eighteen months and then there is a steep drop off. After a few attempts at recovery, the downtrend continues into year four or longer. This is natural and expected, but unfortunate.

Loss of novelty and meaning are the core reasons that global engagement metrics are so disappointing. **Meaning fades faster when employees have poor relationships with their managers and when there is toxic workplace politics.** This is true not just at work but also in personal relationships. Loss of engagement from disagreements, annoyances, and fading away of novelty leads to families falling apart.

Good relationships at work preserve novelty and meaning, and thus engagement and performance.

It is also true for parenting. After the initial enthusiasm, when novelty fades, parents start seeing children as a burden. No wonder having a teenager at home is an independent predictor of excessive stress.[794] I am sure you have heard of horrible stories in which some of the most selfish and least enlightened parents have tried to take the lives of their children so they could reclaim the freedom and independence they had earlier. I was recently contacted by a pediatrics unit looking for solutions to help violent parents who abuse their children because they are sick. Every time I hear this, I lose a little bit of hope.

Sustaining engagement in our personal and professional lives is not only profitable but essential to the survival of our species. To sustain engagement, we need to reaffirm novelty and continue to strive for a deeper meaning. We also will be helped by having flow experiences during work as well as play. Flow is an important concept that I will briefly discuss in the next chapter.

Novelty

You can look at the people in front of you in two ways: as means to an end or an end in themselves. When you look at them as means to an end, you have an agenda. In this way, you objectify other people. When that agenda is fulfilled, they lose their value. I have felt used many times, in both personal and professional situations. I am sure you have too. Once you delivered the goods that others wanted, they stopped caring. That's not the way to nurture long-term relationships.

A much better way is to **look at others in their circles of love**. See them in the full context of their lives; assume that context if you don't know it. Such perspective helps bring out the best in you while serving and connecting with people, both those you know and strangers.

Similarly, you can look at the objects in front of you as mundane and boring or as miraculous and spectacular. The gold in your ring was formed in a supernova explosion billions of years ago; the pear is a product of millions of years of evolution; the photon in the sunlight today was born in the core of the sun a hundred thousand years ago; the wooden table in your home was the stem of a tree on a hilly slope a few decades ago. **The more you think about the profound history of what seems mundane in front of you, the more special it will look.**

> *What seems mundane is actually special and spectacular. We just don't know it.*

Even chewing gum has a long Wikipedia page devoted to it that describes its six-thousand-year history. Keep your curiosity alive but remain patient, for you can't fast-track a caterpillar into a butterfly or a two-year-old into opening the ketchup-bottle lid that she is committed to opening as your pizza slice is getting cold.

Meaning

When I make a few trips from Rochester, Minnesota, to Minneapolis, two things are happening. One is that I am visiting Minneapolis (and for our family, Minneapolis is just one place—the Mall of America). But that is only part of the story. The deeper story, the second thing that is happening, is that I am becoming a better driver. The same is true about life. You fulfill many roles: parent, spouse, child, sibling, friend, colleague, neighbor, professional. Fulfilling these roles is one part of the story. **The deeper story is that you are becoming a better human being.** (I will come back to this at the very end of the book.)

> *Every experience has superficial facts and a deeper reality. Finding or imagining an uplifting deeper reality transforms the experience.*

If you anchor your thoughts in the deeper story, then every little task you perform will become more meaningful. This is what Brother Lawrence practiced; he washed dishes and cleaned the floor, all for God, his God. That gave him peace, which he liberally shared with others.[795]

Novelty and meaning are the two most important ingredients in engagement. Just as your smartphone starts discharging the moment you stop charging it, novelty and meaning also fade with time. You will need to purposefully seek them out, remind yourself of their presence, and continue to challenge yourself. It is in this milieu that you will experience flow.

50

Flow

Your daily moments can be grouped into three categories: dragging, sprinting, and flowing.

THREE CATEGORIES

I dread those days when I'm dragging. I drag if I am asked to review a research grant about the pattern of glucose uptake by rabbit muscles under different isometric loads. Talking to someone who takes five deep breaths between two words, attending a presentation in which the speaker has twenty-four lines of text on each PowerPoint slide, chatting on an international call with a weak cell-phone signal—during all these activities, time passing at sixty seconds per minute seems too slow. In general, three scenarios make me drag: one, when the work is too difficult or too easy (cooking a multicourse gourmet dinner or peeling potatoes); two, when the work is boring and/or repetitive (reading the same story to a five-year-old for the fifth time in two days); and three, when I struggle to find meaning.

Thankfully, not all the days feel like a drag. Many activities make me sprint—for example, making a difference in someone's life, having *Aha!* or *Wow!* moments during the day, or working through a variety of interesting projects. The brain loves novelty, worthy challenges, and meaningful learning. An optimal mix of these helps you sprint at work. Sprinting is great, but it eventually leads to fatigue. Even better than sprinting is flowing.

When you are in flow, you feel and perform at your best. You forget yourself, pay little attention to your body sensations (discomfort), and become immersed in what you are doing. The rest of the world falls away. Time either expands or shrinks—minutes may feel like hours, and hours may go by in a minute. One action effortlessly merges into the next.

Let's explore flow more deeply. If you can create this immersive presence even for a brief period during the day, you'll find every aspect of your life much more engaging, not to mention more efficient and productive.

AMIABLE MIHALY

I had the unique privilege of hosting Professor Mihaly Csikszentmihalyi, the father of the flow experience, as a keynote speaker at one of our conferences. Mihaly is a kind, humble, and brilliant human being with a deep presence and extraordinary sense of humor. It is easy to see how he sprints and flows through every day.

(In case you were wondering, it took me some time to figure out how to say his last name correctly! He takes this struggle in great stride.)

Growing up in Europe, he was caught in World War II at the age of eight. When he saw the behavior of the adults around him—cribbing, squabbling, and struggling—Mihaly realized that humans haven't yet figured out how to live happily. He sought refuge in art, philosophy, and religion but wasn't satisfied. He made his life's mission to find states of consciousness that would help people flourish.

A chance encounter with Carl Jung fueled his interest. While studying psychology he was perplexed by the asymmetry of findings: a lack of resources caused unhappiness but the presence of resources, after a minimal threshold was met, caused no increase in happiness. In looking for answers, he explored moments in everyday life when people were very happy. He interviewed different professionals who were excellent at what they were doing: musicians, farmers, butchers, assembly-line workers, blind nuns, Dominican monks, Himalayan yogis, Navajo shepherds, and many more.[796]

They all described reaching an optimal state of immersion in their tasks when nothing else mattered. They had no fear, could work for hours, and experienced minimal fatigue. They felt their existence suspended. Often, people achieved such a state in a moderately difficult but worthwhile (as opposed to easy) activity that they wanted to do, in which both the challenge and the skills involved were higher than average. Many people described themselves as flowing, so he coined the term *flow*. Mihaly described flow as "a state in which people are so involved in an activity that nothing else seems to matter." His research has shown that **your quality of experience depends less on whether it is work or leisure and more on whether you are in flow.**[797]

> *The quality of your attention has greater effect on the quality of your experience than the details of your task.*

In flow, attention is focused. You have high motivation to do what you are doing, and you experience positive emotions. Some of the attributes of the flow experience are as follows.

- **Challenge-skill balance**—An optimal balance between the challenge and your skill fosters flow. Flow jobs are just a bit more difficult than what you are accustomed to doing.
- **Complete immersion of attention**—Your attention is completely taken by the activity until you have no residual attention left for mind wandering.
- **Lack of self-awareness**—With little residual attention, your mind-wandering apparatus is silenced.
- **Loss of awareness of time**—The perception of flow of time depends on what fills the time. Time may stretch or compress when you are in flow.
- **Positive emotions**—In flow, the process becomes enjoyable, bordering on blissful. Minimal mind wandering combined with the feeling that you are doing something worthwhile creates a sense of inner joy.

- **Internally rewarding activity**—The pleasure comes from the activity itself rather than from a specific external reward. The outcome becomes secondary when you are flowing. A perfect example is children drawing with chalk outside the house. They might spend two hours drawing, but once it is done, they will very easily cross it out and move on.

NEUROSCIENCE OF FLOW

Neuroscientists describe two systems for information processing: explicit and implicit. The explicit system involves thinking-based action. The implicit system is more skills based and efficient, and it is hosted by the lower parts of the brain.[798, 799]

As you develop mastery, the implicit system can manage most of the operations, supported by an efficient explicit system. You stop micromanaging your actions. This has been demonstrated in jazz musicians,[800] people performing extreme rituals,[801] and those engaged in vigorous exercise.[802-806] Not every study, however, has corroborated these findings regarding exercise[807, 808] or playing computer games.[809]

Researchers believe that a soup of chemicals hosts the flow state. Dopamine enhances alertness and reward, norepinephrine enhances concentration, and a combination of neurotransmitters (endorphins, serotonin, and anandamide) enhances mood and positivity. On the EEG, the waves associated with distracted thinking (beta chatter) become quiet, and we experience the waves associated with calm and deep presence (greater alpha and theta waves).[810]

The neural state in flow leads to a merger of attention and awareness and a state of self-forgetfulness.

Forgetting the self is the first step toward finding the self.

This leads to peak performance, great joy, and high energy and creativity. In one study, **achieving flow helped people become five times more effective at what they were doing.**[811]

No matter the activity—coding, music, art, dance, sports, writing, learning—you can do it better when you flow. Such flow can sometimes be artificially created through transcranial magnetic stimulation,[812] but wouldn't it be nice to make some tweaks in living and work styles to achieve greater flow on most days?

GETTING INTO FLOW

Many activities can bring you in full flow. They can be planned activities, like yoga, tai chi, exercise, and prayer, or they can be part of ordinary daily living. **Flow typically happens with externally oriented attention, when you are giving your best to a moderately difficult challenge that is meaningful.** Research shows **flow can be spontaneous but also can be created at will.**

Most spontaneous experiences and feelings can be intentionally recreated.

In the following list, I summarize some of the key aspects of experience that can be manipulated to generate flow.

- **Goals**—Remove vagueness about your goals. When you don't know what the expectations are, part of your attention is absorbed in the uncertainty of what you are doing and whether it will be appreciated or not. **The clearer and more measurable the goals, the more likely you will flow.**
- **Feedback**—Getting feedback about your performance keeps you on track and continues to challenge you. Honest feedback decreases the need of the wondering and wandering mind to spend time thinking about how it is doing. **Knowing you will receive honest feedback frees your attention to focus on the task.**
- **Optimal skill for challenge**—For flow, you want to **be challenged just a tad bit above your current capacity**. Playing chess with someone much worse or better than you won't bring flow. Creating a marketing solution for a very simple or very complex product also won't bring flow. Flow occurs when you play chess with someone just a bit better than you or when you create a solution for a product just slightly more complex than what you have handled before.

Clear goals, honest feedback and
optimal challenge, promote flow.

- **Intense focus**—Removing distractions or annoying interruptions helps. Minimizing negative emotions at the start, choosing your preferred environment (music, temperature, color, and so on), and keeping the amygdala (fear) quiet can all help with flow.
- **Don't think about failure**—**The more people think about the process rather than the ultimate outcome, the more likely they are to flow.** When astronauts were hanging upside down repairing the Hubble telescope, the entire billion-dollar project depended on their efforts at that moment. If they had brought all that to their heads, they would have lost their focus and flow and would have more likely made a mistake. In that instance one dropped screw hitting the lens could have been the most expensive dropped screw ever. The same happens to gymnasts, tennis players, and race-car drivers. The more they focus on their steps and not on the outcome, the more likely they are to flow. At that level of competition, flow through muscle memory is critical to success. Research supports what someone very aptly said that **the best way to break people's golf swing is to ask them to show their best swing.**[813]
- **Don't think about time**—One of the biggest killers of joy, quality, and flow is time pressure. With time pressure, attention shifts from the task at hand to a future point. Time pressure also keeps the stress networks active and reward networks quiet. One of the ways to avoid time pressure is to prioritize wisely and let go of the opportunities and engagements that aren't meaningful to you, by keeping a healthy Not-to-do list.

Avoid time pressure by keeping your To-do list small, and the Not-to-do list long.

It's important to be realistic when approaching flow. We can't eliminate drag completely and can't flow all day long. It would also be exceptional to add every flow ingredient into the equation. Pick one or, at the most, two aspects that you can easily bring. That will be enough as a start.

    I believe the simplest way to find flow is to challenge yourself to perfect your skill. It could be work related, such as writing software code, performing a procedure, or serving a client, or it could involve simple, mundane skills such as driving, loading the dishwasher, vacuuming, ironing clothes, or peeling an apple. I have tried all of these (except writing software code). When peeling an apple, an activity I used to abhor, I started challenging myself with trying to remove the thinnest possible skin and taking out the entire skin in one piece. Once I challenged myself so, I started enjoying the practice.

Doing it right is not only good, but also enjoyable.

The key is to **keep challenging yourself to do better**. The purpose isn't to become obsessive; the intention is to keep improving so the practice remains interesting.

Once you become good at something, flow disappears, and it becomes boring. Amp up the challenge to reclaim the flow. And if the magic just won't happen, then let it be. Try it again the next morning. Be flexible, for flexibility is a sign of health.

51

Flexible Presence

In the third tenet, we explored ways to develop meditative attention by cultivating curiosity and focusing on meaning in the outside world. This helps us with engagement and flow. These externally oriented practices are not only easier but also more effective than trying to see the light in an inwardly focused meditative trance. The pursuit also makes you a more engaged spouse, parent, employee, and citizen. Attention so strengthened loses its rigidity. It becomes supple and flexible. Flexibility gives you freedom. In most situations, **flexibility is a sign of health**.

Take the example of the heart. The heart pumps two thousand gallons of blood every day. **The commonest cause of heart failure isn't the heart's inability to squeeze; it is its inability to relax.** Heart muscles that become stiff do a poor job of receiving blood. Poor relaxation creates backward pressure, causing different parts of the heart to enlarge, irregular rhythms to develop, and fluid to accumulate in the lungs.

Your joints also rely on flexibility. Most diseases that damage the joints eventually cause pain and stiffness. Even structures in our body that don't move, such as the liver and skin, become stiffer as they become diseased.

In nature, bamboo is stronger than concrete when wet and stronger than steel when dry, partly because of its flexibility. Modern buildings boast design flexibility so they can adapt to changing needs over the decades and withstand earthquakes by gently swaying instead of collapsing. Generally, flexibility is a sign of health, rigidity a sign of illness.

The strongest structures in nature derive their strength from flexibility.

This rule also applies to the mind and the attention.[814] Psychological and attentional flexibility help you adapt your mindset to the need of the hour, shift your perspective across different time domains, and maintain balance between different aspects of life.

In tenet 3 you have taken the next step of mindfulness *v2*—used the power of intentionality to project your attention externally. Since we are presently so much in our heads, externalizing our attention is the first step in freeing ourselves so we can cultivate greater curiosity, find deeper meaning, and enter flow. Attention so strengthened naturally acquires flexibility. With strong and flexible attention, you can effortlessly project inward or outward, depending on what is most meaningful at any moment.

Strength and flexibility help overpower unhealthy and maladaptive instincts. **Flexibility provides the space for you to process your reactions based on your values.** Developing strong and flexible attention opens up different and yet unexplored possibilities in life.

The ultimate goal with attention practices is to develop an effortlessly flowing attention that is intentional, strong, and flexible. With such attention, you sample life at deeper depths and think deeper thoughts. You still mind wander, but your wanderings are much more intentional. You recognize that the better your binoculars, the more pockmarks you will see on the moon. **The closer you get to someone, the more imperfections you will find in that person. This awareness adjusts your expectations so you don't treat the people closest to you by discounting their good and inflating their bad, which is our default instinct.**

Lower your expectations of the people closest to you, so they remain close to you.

An attention that is intentional, strong, and flexible helps you look past the annoyance so you can see the value. It helps you eliminate the noise and focus on your core meaning, the pursuit of which fosters creativity and engagement. That's how you create excellence.

—ɯ—

Another aspect of intentionality and flexibility is choosing whether to focus on the short term or the long term by training your zoom. Let's now see how mindfulness *v2* can help you train your zoom so your perspective can flow across the span of life and you find healing even when faced with a mountain of adversity—a tall order but eminently achievable.

Part V
The Fourth Tenet: Perspective

Tenet	Mindfulness v1	Mindfulness v2
Perspective	Zoomed in	Zoomed in and out at will

―⁂―

Engagement in the very short term (this moment) can provide a temporary escape from uncertainty and lack of control; thinking of the very long term can provide respite from worries, hurts, and regrets related to short-term losses. Being able to flexibly shift between the short term and the long term provides an optimal recipe for living a busy life while remaining peaceful and happy.

If the short term is challenged, think about the long term; if the long-term is challenged, live for the next moment. Keep a flexible zoom.

52

Fireside Chat #5

"I enjoyed the vivid description of your hometown, Bhopal. Is it really the same as it was a decade ago?"

"Some of it has changed. More people wear jeans now. Instead of holding each other's hands, they hold cell phones. Pop has replaced water; shampoo has replaced hair oil. You can pay hawkers by credit card."

"I sensed joy and energy in your voice when you were describing that experience."

"It reminded me of times my mind didn't wander much. **Any time you can decrease mind wandering or think about moments when your mind didn't wander much, you'll be happier.**"

"Anytime? How about if I am being chased by a rabid dog?"

"That would be an exception! We don't savor moments when our attention is monitoring for threat. That applies to both the outer physical world and the inner mental world."

"How are the outer world and the inner world related? Are they distinct or a continuum?"

"They are a continuum. Most days, our attention flows from the outer to the inner world and back depending on the need of the moment. A perfect example is driving on a familiar road. You notice, mind wander, and then notice again. But what happens when a police car shows up in the rearview mirror?"

"You don't mind wander anymore!"

"Your brain gets a shot of adrenaline. It wakes up. Your heart rate accelerates. You start noticing. All mind wandering stops. That is not the time to think about why Steve slurps while drinking coffee. You also lose your sense of humor for a few seconds. The accelerated heart rate settles the moment you take an exit and aren't being followed anymore. But for some, the hypervigilance continues much longer, for the next five, ten, even hundred miles. It isn't their fault; they have a predisposed biology. Their amygdala is on steroids because they inherited that predisposition, acquired it from childhood experience or previous trauma, or all three."

"Is that predisposition rare or common?"

"What do you think?"

"Pretty common."

"That's right. Every news of a shooting, robbery, terrorist act, atrocity, abuse, war, famine, or accident causes our amygdala to react. Watching a movie that shows the mind of a cruel psychopath does the same. Our brain is designed to better remember a negative event.[815] After multiple such reactions, a basal angst persists that causes it to overreact."

"Neuroplasticity at work?"

"Yes, neuroplasticity at work. Neuroplasticity is how your brain changes itself with experience. When nature was carving our brains for adaptation, nature had no idea that we would invent the internet, nuclear bombs, headline news, and genetic engineering. Our brains were crafted to thwart an enemy tribe and figure out the emotions of the one hundred fifty people in our tribe. We weren't prepared to see the destruction wreaked by a MOAB (Mother of All Bombs). Neuroplasticity is still working like it is 3000 BC. When you see fear and pain, your fear and pain networks become stronger. That can lock you in a perpetual cycle of fear and pain. Have you ever driven on a road that is under construction?"

"Sure, all the time."

"We joke in Rochester that our roads go through two seasons: snow and under construction. It is painful to drive during construction—slow traffic, blocked roads, bumps, diversions, and so on. Our brains are like that, still under construction. **We have to live the best life possible in an imperfect world using a brain that has the drywall, windows, flooring, and cables done but needs a lot of interior detail.** That's why we hurt."

"But we can't live in a bubble."

"Agreed. We can't. But we can train ourselves so our angst doesn't last for the next hundred miles. Instead, we can choose to feel comforted upon seeing a police car. A better feeling is that of gratitude for that cop (and every professional) working hard to keep us comfortable and safe. With a perspective like this, you feel free and know you have the tools to handle most life situations."

"How can we learn to default to that perspective?"

"The first step is developing strong attention. When our attention is weak, we can't pull it out of fear-based thoughts. We are caught in the whirlpool of negativity. **Strong attention isn't sucked into the negative, and it can free itself quickly.** Getting curious, like you were as a kid, is a great first step."

"You shared some ideas earlier. Could you remind me, like neuroplasticity, could curiosity also backfire?"

"What do you mean?"

"Could I get way too curious?"

"That's possible, if your curiosity isn't coupled with good judgment. Health-care providers can get a pink slip if they look at the medical records of a friend out of curiosity. **Couple curiosity with good moral judgment, and you will be safe. Add meaning to the mix, and you will be golden.**"

"I assume you have spent some time thinking about meaning. What meaning drives your own personal life?"

"Kids. Ever since my wife and I became parents, our lives have revolved around helping our girls develop the right values. I am curious about every technology, policy, idea, and perspective that will help us build a better world for all our children. This meaning prevents me from thinking, speaking, or doing anything immoral or utterly selfish. If I ever have a weak moment when my short-term-gratification instinct challenges me, I think about children. It helps a lot."

"Can meaning also drive creativity?"

"To a great extent. I see people driven by two core motivations: to *approach* something desirable or to *avoid* something undesirable. People are still reeling from the images of 9/11 and the 2008 financial crisis.

For every person living with an approach mindset, I see four driven by avoidance. Research shows that **avoidance-motivated people get very tired very quickly when they exercise their creativity muscles.**[816] If you add time pressure to the mix, performance remarkably deteriorates.[817] What do you think is the perfect solution to building their stamina?"

"What?" Mike asks.

"As you said, give them meaning. When they have explicit goals, when they feel they are making progress, when they believe they are doing something worthwhile, they will do much better. They will also do better when they are rewarded for their creativity and effort and not just for the outcome or completion of the task.[818] The more the organization's leaders can look past this quarter or the next quarter, the better their employees will perform."

"I assume this applies to parenting as much as it does to running a company."

"It does. Although I get salary from my primary employer, I see my main employer as all the children of the world. I serve at their pleasure. It helps me remain centered and zoomed out.

"**Your ability to quickly zoom out can help you negotiate difficult and high-stakes situations.** A few years ago, I was giving an interview to NPR. The previous night I had slept only a few hours because our elder daughter had to make a balloon-powered car as an assignment, and for an A grade, that car had to travel at least fifteen feet. We spent many hours figuring out the mechanics, until we finally succeeded. As I was sitting in the media room waiting for the interview to start in two minutes, a sense of anxious fatigue coursed through my body. I got concerned, thinking, 'What if my brain freezes and I start speaking gibberish?' I only had two minutes to regroup myself.

"I closed my eyes and lifted my awareness. I sensed the presence of the room, then the building, then our city, then the state, country, earth, solar system, Milky Way, and the Universe. As I zoomed out, I realized that in the context of the Universe, this little interview was inconsequential. That realization relaxed me and gave me the stamina to conduct the full hour with much better energy.

"I call this process zooming out. That's what we will talk about."

"What if I zoom out but can't find a peaceful perspective?" Mike is always two steps ahead of me.

"That is where reframing helps. **Think gratitude: can you think of what went right within what went wrong? Think compassion: is someone's frustration coming from an inner hurt or insecurity? Think acceptance: is this worth spending your time and energy on? Think meaning: can this adversity help you in the long term in ways you can't even imagine? Think forgiveness: can you take the high road and choose to forgive in honor of all those who have forgiven you or are hurt even more than you?**"[226, 819]

"I wish I could remember this when I experience adrenaline hijack."

"You will. Practice, practice, and then practice some more!"

53

Three Depths of Doing

This is an adaptation of a story I heard many years ago:

A student once visited a farm on which lived a three-generation family. The student's capstone project was to understand what motivates our farmers to work so hard to feed our nation. It was spring. The son, the father, and the grandfather were working together, planting seeds.

The student asked the teenage son what he was doing. Wiping the sweat from his forehead, the farmer boy shrugged and said, "Sowing the seeds." He had been working all day long doing the same thing over and over.

With a busy look, the father answered the same question. "Planting a crop," he said. He was working against a deadline to finish the seeding.

When the grandfather was asked the same question, he said with a cheerful look, "Feeding the planet."

The son was zoomed in, the grandfather was zoomed out, and the father was somewhere in between. While the son was intermittently focused on the immediate activity, he hadn't accessed the meaning of it. He wanted to be somewhere else, and thus his attention wavered all day long. He hadn't yet balanced the checkbooks.

The farmer saw an intermediate-level meaning that was focused on his immediate needs. His attention wavered because while doing one activity, his mind was busy planning the next; he had to keep it all together.

The grandfather had seen it all. He was a natural with the steps, and he intuitively connected what he did with its larger meaning. He also knew that meaning and effort had to go together: **meaning plays out in the long term, while the effort is invested in the short term**.

Zooming is your ability to shift your perspective from the very short term to the very long term. The greater your ability to zoom, the greater the repertoire of perspectives available to you, which frees your attention to access multiple ways to heal.

Over the past few decades, we have gone overboard in celebrating the now. Zooming in and engaging with the now alone isn't enough. Zooming out alone isn't enough either. **An optimal disposition is to have a combination of zoomed-out perspective, which provides the larger meaning to what you are doing and what life is about, and of zoomed-in presence, so you fully engage with what is.**

The best cameras can rapidly and flexibly zoom in and zoom out. So can the healthiest minds.

Perspective and meaning, when combined with intentionality and engaged presence, can convert a mundane job into a flow-generating activity that becomes enjoyable and memorable even though it's repetitive.

It'll help us to share a word about the neural zoom before we learn ways to manipulate it.

54

Neural Zoom

The brain and eyes mature in parallel. A newborn can't see farther than one foot. As our eyes and the neural pathways that host vision mature, we start seeing greater expanse of the world. Further, as the rest of the brain matures, our mental projection expands.

Early on, we aren't at all shy about crying. We cry when hungry, wet, sleepy, unwell, or in pain. As we get older, our thresholds change. Five-year-olds could cry if deprived of candy or the right hair clip. They are quite limited in postponing rewards; a lollipop in hand is better than two tomorrow. These are cute traits in a kid, but the equivalent adult traits would be impatience, frustration, quick reaction, and selfishness. Often the instinct to take revenge also fits in this category.

Most animal brains remain locked in the perpetual present—able to zoom out to only the next few minutes at the most.

Most animal brains are locked in the perpetual present.

The animals that behave as though they are planning for the future (such as when squirrels hide nuts) do it instinctively rather than because of a well-thought-out strategy after a series of committee meetings. Human brains are different.

As we mature and acquire wisdom, we learn to zoom out, like the wise owl that is born blind but in a matter of months develops the ability to scan through space and peer through the dark. We can take in the perspective and ask, "Will it matter five years from now? Ten years? Twenty years? Can this adversity help me long term in ways I can't even imagine? **Does my partner's annoying behavior reflect inner vulnerability and thus merit my compassion and not my reaction? Is this person who cut me off on the road struggling with low prefrontal dopamine level?**" (I will share the science behind this in chapter 60.)

Only the humans have the ability to zoom out.

With the ability to change the perspective, we look deeper and become less reactive. These moments of zooming out, however, stay with us only for the short term. Mind wandering quickly takes over, restoring the status quo.

—※—

Instead of being totally zoomed in like animals or optimally zoomed out like exceptionally wise humans, most of us live stuck between the present moment and eternity, not a happy place to be.

55

Stuck in Between

Does this sound familiar? All these years you have gone out of the way to help a certain someone. But a few days ago, you weren't able to meet his or her expectations since you were super busy. Perhaps you delayed responding to e-mails and forgot an anniversary. That was enough for that person to discount you from his or her life. Everything you did all these years didn't matter.

This is extremely common. What happened yesterday is much more powerful in influencing opinions than what has happened over the last fifteen years. People can't zoom out and take a broader perspective.

__Years of friendship and sacrifice can evaporate in the fire of few angry words.__

THE IN-BETWEEN PLACE

In general, we humans live like the farmer dad in the story in chapter 53—somewhere between zoomed in and zoomed out. **By developing a prefrontal cortex, humans have acquired the ability to imagine, and have thus escaped the present moment. But we haven't yet claimed eternity, since to fully nurture a zoomed-out perspective, we need a stronger prefrontal cortex than we have right now.**

We thus live most of our lives thinking about something other than what we are doing. Some researchers call it "nexting." **We like to predict what will make us happy, are bad at making such predictions, and aren't aware how bad we are.** Not precisely a recipe for a happy life.[820]

The in-between place isn't the most desirable abode. **Peace is in the present moment; peace is also in having a real long-term perspective. The greatest misery is in between, which is precisely where we are much of the time.**

__Our instinctive attention is quite skilled at keeping us miserable.__

Most humans spend the bulk of their lives unable to access the joy of being in the moment (a skill they had as a child), and the peace that comes from a fully zoomed-out perspective. Mindfulness *v*2 invites you to develop a flexible zoom by learning to zoom in and zoom out at will. Here is how this works.

THE THREE FUTURES

Since for most people, the greatest amount of time is spent thinking about the future, we will focus on the future for now. The figure below shows your three futures. Zone A is your immediate future, usually measured in hours, zone B is your intermediate future measured in days, and zone C is the long term, spanning from months to years to decades or even longer.

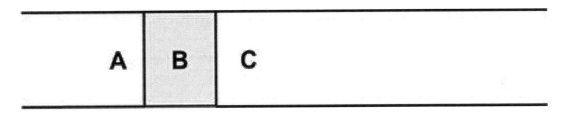

Let's say you anticipate a difficult meeting this afternoon. You are prepared for it, but you are anxious. This anxiety can cause hyperventilation, thirst, and stomach cramps, which can leave you cranky and tired. The more you think about this meeting the worse you feel, but every instinct of yours pulls you toward thinking about this meeting.

A good strategy now is to think about this meeting in the perspective of your entire life (zone C). Likely, it isn't that important. **Things become only as big as you allow them to become.** You can swap meeting for an annoying email, an unanswered text, less than courteous service, a delayed flight, and more. In this situation, focusing on the plans for the weekend or for an upcoming trip (zone B) might be helpful too.

Another example: Next week (Zone B), you have to undergo one of the most despised medical procedures of all time: a colonoscopy. If you don't have a disciplined mind, you'll likely think of the procedure twenty times every day, which will be exhausting. In this situation, either zoom in (into zone A) or zoom out (into zone C). Lift only the load of the next hour. A very simple way to do this is to notice more by projecting your attention externally and noticing novelty. Fill your time with work, read a comforting book, watch a funny movie, go to the theater, savor your food, or visit with friends. Most meditation and mindfulness approaches are geared to bringing you into the present. Zoom out by thinking about your vacation for next year, planning the next steps in your career, and asking yourself whether it will bother you in five or ten years. You can also find meaning in it: you're lucky that you are healthy and have the resources to screen for cancer by getting a colonoscopy (I know I am pushing it!), this procedure could save your life by preventing cancer, and you only need it once every ten years (Some patients with genetic predisposition to aggressive colon polyps need a colonoscopy once every year, and their screening starts at age fifteen. Perhaps this realization may fill you with compassion for them and gratitude for your good luck that you don't have the abnormal genes.).

Next example: Each day about forty-one thousand people in the world get a new diagnosis of cancer. Some are early stage, but many are advanced-stage cancers. Most patients with advanced cancer that limits their longevity go through a tough phase of adaptation. This high-stress situation increases the risk of cancer progression and death.[821-828] Braking the stress response not only enhances well-being over the long term[829-834] but also might impact cancer progression and recurrence (although this isn't yet fully proven).[835] In such a situation, **zooming in by living your life one hour at a time can significantly decrease the load, enhance quality of your moments, and improve sleep and relationships.** Setting the right priorities, finding the right mindset in which to reframe (with gratitude, compassion, and meaning), lowering your threshold to forgive, and faith can all help.

The final example: Some very unfortunate people are stuck in a situation where they can't find comfort anywhere. Bethany, a forty-five-year old mother of three, very active and gregarious, developed abdominal pain that in a few days led to a diagnosis of metastatic ovarian cancer. She has six to twelve months. Now after three rounds of chemotherapy, she is fatigued, nauseous and barely able to take care of herself. Her present moment and intermediate zone are both full of pain, and she has no long-term to talk about. For people like Madeline, zooming in or out alone won't work. Her strongest resilience factors are support from friends and family, and faith.

A MOMENT IS TOO LITTLE

The present moment is too evanescent for the mind to capture. It is like the butterfly that is always a step ahead of you. The rich neural package within the prefrontal cortex that is wonderful at imagining and time traveling can be given a time-out for a bit, but it can't be silenced.

Further, like it is for Madeline, the present moment isn't always easy to embrace. I don't want to be in the present moment when undergoing a medical procedure. I have to raise two kids, send them to college, decide whom to vote for, and so much more. All of this needs thinking, planning, and mental time travel. Hence, a mind that can flow across time zones, and focus attention on the zone with the greatest meaning and joy can serve us the best. The present moment for such a mind expands to include the past and the future, and is better defined by intentionality rather than time zone. Such a mind achieves authentic mindfulness.

> *A mind that can easily flow across different time zones is more mindful than a mind stuck in the present moment.*

Interestingly, when you are flexibly flowing with time, you will find it much easier to access the present moment.

Right when you give up and get busy with life, the butterfly comes and sits on your shoulder.

The current mindfulness practices provide wonderful skills for zooming in, but the need of the hour is for skills in zooming out. Let's talk about that next.

56

When in Doubt, Zoom Out

Zooming out isn't just a meditation or a transient state. It is a perspective; it is wisdom to be able to look at things more broadly. It is like having the sight of an eagle, able to scan the vast vistas. Zooming out expands the possibilities available to you in rethinking your challenges. With greater variety available to you, you can pick the more desirable explanations, tracks, and solutions to better negotiate life's challenges. Here are some ideas to help you zoom out.

WILL IT MATTER FIVE YEARS FROM NOW?

The simplest and most straightforward zooming-out skill is to pause and ask yourself, **will it matter five years from now?** Try to recall everything that stressed you on this very day five years ago. Perhaps your memory will fail you. You'll agree that most likely it wasn't a week when you had no worries or negative thoughts. **If what matters today likely won't matter in five years, then perhaps we can be more stoic about how we handle it.** Why wait five years for the sting to soften when we can change our perspective right here, right now.

If five years seem too short, expand to ten years or more. The purpose is to find a peaceful place in your mind in which you can steady your focus to put energy toward meaningful action.

Allow only those things to bother you that will continue to bother you in five years.

Whatever the stressors, uncertainty, and chaos, nothing is worth having a heart attack over. Take care of yourself, since you are all you've got.

Failure and success often seesaw in life. Success is often preceded and followed by failure. **If you're successful today, be humble for you'll likely fail; if you're failing, keep the hope and courage, for you'll succeed.** This realization will prevent you from inflating and deflating yourself with each rise and fall, preserving your energy and helping you succeed more often.

CONTROL THE CONTROLLABLE

Three strikes integrate to generate today's stress: genetic predisposition, childhood adversity, and present-day stressors.[836]

Researchers have identified many genes that can predispose us to lower resilience.[837-840] People with vulnerable genes have a tendency to ruminate and have a low happiness reserve in their brains, predisposing them to depression and other mental-health issues. A person with healthier variant of the gene will easily brush off the stressor, while one with the vulnerable variant might perseverate for months or develop PTSD. That is the first strike.

The second strike is childhood adversity. This can present in many forms: poverty, illness, parental neglect, abuse, war, bullying (including cyberbullying), and more.

> *The annoying person at your office or in your neighborhood most likely has vulnerable genes and had to endure childhood abuse.*

Many children facing these difficulties still thrive.[841, 842] Here is the most important reason. **The single most important resilience factor for a child is a caring adult.**[843] Children who have at least one caring adult who loves and trusts them are able to withstand adversity much better than those who feel they are alone in the world. That adult can be a parent, teacher, grandparent, distant relative, friend's parent, neighbor, counselor, or someone else.

The brains of children with kind adults become structurally healthier when they grow up.[844, 845]

> *Your kindness carves a resilient brain in the children whose lives you touch.*

Unfortunately, the abuse of children at the hands of those who should love them is extremely common and is often the second strike. **Childhood adversity gets under the skin and affects genetic expression, predisposing children to inflammation, low self-regulation, mistrust of others, and poor relationships.**[846-849] All of these increase the risk and impact of the third strike: adult stressors.

Adult stressors come in many flavors: work, money, relationships, responsibilities, health, home, and many more. The impact of adult stressors depends not only on the severity of the stressor but also on our perception of how bad it is, how many resources we believe we have to overcome it, whether we believe those resources will be effective, and what it all means.[850-852]

If you are already a grown-up, you have little control over the first two strikes. Even stressors that come to us from the world are often not in our control. You can exercise your vote, but you can barely nudge others to pick the nominee you feel is the worthiest. **What you can control is how you process your stressors, how much meaning you find in them, whether you can find right within wrong, and of course, whether you are willing to forgive.**

Taking control, even planning to take control, is comforting. So, it is wise to invest your energy in the controllable. Bemoaning, catastrophizing, and blaming, usurp your energy. Instead, put more energy on effecting the change. **Take control of your mind, even if you can't take control of the world.**

Take control of your mind, even if you can't take control of the world.

It is helpful to **believe that the smaller daily annoyances give us useful emotional workouts so we can better swim through and vanquish, the tsunami of adversity when it arrives.**

COULD MY ADVERSITY HAVE PREVENTED SOMETHING WORSE?

This story may sound silly to you. I fully participated in the year 2000 stock-market crash. Over a period of a painful few days, I lost almost all my investments. As I was watching triple-digit drops in the Dow, I couldn't help but imagine how wonderful it would have been had I sold my holdings a week earlier. I am sure I wasn't alone in that fantasy.

I wanted to recover fast. So here is how I convinced myself. I said, "Had I sold all my stocks, I would have bought a flashy car with the money, crashed, and died. I am glad I don't have that money." In a few hours, I was actually feeling pretty good for having survived!

You can always tell yourself a better, more healing story.

Ask yourself, "Can this short-term loss somehow help me in the long term? Is this pink slip somehow protecting me? Could this annoying supervisor have helped my career in some way? Was this missed flight a blessing in disguise?" I personally know two people who are alive today because they missed a flight.

I don't believe in being a Pollyanna. I also don't believe in negating the truth. **I believe in looking at the truth in its most optimistic version. That is wisely zooming out.**

HEALTHY COMPARISON

Here is my instinct: when I do well, I get haughty; when others do well, I get envious. I ascribe my success to my hard work and natural gifts; I ascribe the success of others to luck and unreasonable favors. I lived the first twenty-five years of my life blissfully unaware I had this instinct and have been fighting it ever since.

Unhealthy comparison is a perfect way to decimate happiness. It's best to choose otherwise. **Be humble when you succeed and inspired when you see others succeed.** Such change takes effort, often decades of effort, but is totally worthwhile. It gives you peace, inspiration, and friendship.

Let your success fill you with humility and others' success fill you with inspiration.

When others share their success, do not compare their success with yours. Also, do not ascribe it to just good luck or consider it unfair. Don't downplay it either. Instead, celebrate their success. When you celebrate their success, they will show up to celebrate yours.

IT COULD HAVE BEEN WORSE

I once met a person who had been traumatized by an abusive relationship while living in a crowded inner city in the Northeast. She was surrounded by crime, drugs, and HIV. Her boyfriend, bad as he was, wasn't into drugs. He was also clean with respect to chronic infections. Although I validated her concern and shared that what she went through was pure misery, she found some comfort when she focused on the fact that she escaped that hell physically unharmed. It could have been worse, much worse.

This too shall pass, and it could have been much worse.

I use this approach almost every week, telling myself that it could have been worse. Recover by thinking that it isn't as bad as it could have been. Once your energy drain is plugged, use your energy to fix what is still bad. **The intention isn't to say it is all good; it's to recognize that it needs fixing and that fixing will take time, and it's to decide not to allow yourself to be miserable during that time.**

WILL IT BE FAIR?

Suffering comes in two forms: visible and invisible. Visible suffering is in many places, including emergency rooms, outpatient clinics, attorney's offices, courts, funeral homes, and police stations. Nearly one out of two people develop cancer, almost everyone has experienced back pain, and the majority experience a traumatic event at some point.[853]

Invisible suffering is even more ubiquitous. Two out of three professionals experience burnout, 60 percent of people feel discriminated against, half of us feel lonely every week, one out of five experiences depression, and about eight hundred thousand people worldwide commit suicide every year. That is about one every forty seconds.[854] For each person completing suicide, about twenty try.[855]

Think about this: as you are reading this, about forty-four thousand people around the world are so desperate that they will try suicide today. The number of people who are severely depressed and have suicidal thoughts is multifold higher. If you and I are not among them, **if we have the privilege of being grateful today, then we have the responsibility to be compassionate.**

If you are privileged to be grateful, then you have a responsibility to be compassionate.

A good assumption: Every person you have met and will ever meet experiences silent suffering.

With so many people struggling, it wouldn't be fair if I never had back pain, never experienced financial loss, and was never deceived by a friend or badmouthed by a loved one. This awareness and its preemptive acceptance empowers me to better engage with what is instead of fighting myself or living in fear of adversity.

Further, research shows that the happiest people aren't those who have faced either no adversity or overwhelming suffering. Moderate lifetime adversity correlates with the lowest distress and posttraumatic symptoms and with higher life satisfaction. Your resilience also is likely to be highest if you have faced some adversity. With this awareness, **look at the adversity today (but not the overwhelming kind) as seeding happiness tomorrow.**[856]

Today's adversities seed tomorrow's happiness.

NEURAL BASIS

Enron, WorldCom, Tyco, and Lehman Brothers are just a few companies in which highly accomplished intelligent people made truly dumb and unethical choices. They forgot ethics, shareholder interest, the need to tell the truth, and so much more. They allowed the promise of short-term reward to dominate their brains at the cost of potential long-term consequences.

Our reward and fear centers are both strongly influenced by the potential for short-term gains and losses, respectively. The nearer the reward, the greater its potency. Some economists call it delay discounting. (We discussed this in chapter 24 and will talk some more about it in chapter 61.) Animals have little to no defense against this bias. We humans also struggle with it. If that were not so, there would be no divorces because of infidelity. Concepts like tax fraud, shoplifting, cybercrime, and wire fraud wouldn't exist. We discussed previously that given the opportunity, 70 percent of us lie and cheat. That predisposition somehow got into our DNA. As a first step, it helps to be aware of this predisposition. Then train yourself to think of the long term, of the broader consequences of our greed and cheating. One way to do this is to store a few algorithms in your head.

ALGORITHMS

Algorithms are simple steps to solving a problem, particularly a mathematical problem. Algorithms also work in daily life. When you see a red traffic light, your brain signals you to stop. You follow three simple steps: remove your foot from the accelerator, plant your foot on the brake, and slowly press the brake until your car stops. You do the reverse when the light turns green. I am sure it took some time for these steps to become fluid and effortless. You can create the same algorithms for your mind. Let's look at two of them.

When someone is upset, you can see that person in two different lights: unreasonable versus hurt. Both may be true at times. The default algorithm for most of us is this:

Upset = Unreasonable = Call for reaction.

I have used this many times. It doesn't take me or the other person to a good place. Here is the alternative algorithm based on the simple idea that "an expression other than love is a call for help." The simple algorithm is this:

Upset = Hurt = Call for help.

I have personally never regretted assuming that **a person who is upset is actually hurt**. I know that if most of us live by this assumption, the world will be a better place for all of us. Try to be a peacemaker rather than picking a fight. Do not take the bait.

Another example: I spilled milk on the dining table because my daughter didn't cap the carton tightly. The default algorithm is:

Spilled milk = Find who is at fault = Blame/get upset/react.

Of late, I have been asking these two simple questions of myself that I mentioned earlier: "Will it matter five years from now? Did I do this (or something like this) when I was a thirteen-year-old?" If it won't matter in five years and I did or could have easily done the same mistake, why stress out and react about it today? Here is my new algorithm, which has removed 90 percent of my stressors:

Spilled milk = Won't matter in five years/It could have been me/It could have been worse = Keep my calm.

You can swap spilled milk with a lot of different things: slow drivers, unreturned e-mails, flat tires, delayed flights, forgotten birthdays, and so much more.

Create and rehearse values-based "thinking algorithms" that can help you better handle everyday annoyances.

Here are a few additional ideas that have helped me craft new algorithms:

- Think about what went right within what went wrong.
- Assume positive intent.
- Forgiveness is for me, not for the other person.

- It is difficult to dislike someone who you know likes you.
- No one struggles with being appreciated too much.
- Remind people of their strengths.
- Everyone is special and struggling.

My amygdala is a work in progress. It notices the slightest insults. It gets ruffled by the least bit of unfairness. But with these algorithms, I recover much faster, sometimes within a few seconds. Earlier, I would perseverate for days if I heard someone bad-mouthing me or not paying attention to my preferences. But now I tell myself a more healing story. Perhaps the other person has a different perspective; perhaps he or she is going through a tough time; perhaps he or she may have meant differently. The result of this thinking is that I avoid hurting myself over trivial issues. I am kinder to myself, which empowers me to be kinder to others.

REMEMBER FINITENESS

My brother lives in Princeton, New Jersey. We get to meet about twice a year. If I assume that I will leave the planet at about age eighty, quick math tells me that I will meet him probably only sixty more times in this life. That's it.

You can do that math for any of your relationships. **We have finite time with each other, less than we think.** This awareness inspires me to make the most of this day. It also helps me be kinder. I need this perspective to remind me almost every single day about what truly matters.

When I don't remind myself about finiteness, I get lost in the mundane. I spend too much time attending to dead screens even when surrounded by sentient beings.

I don't stew on finiteness. I get inspired by it. I don't wish to regret at age eighty that I didn't say "I love you" enough and that I carried grudges I really didn't need to.

Empty yourself of the unforgiven grudges so love can find enough room to grow.

I personally believe the vast majority of people are good. Sometimes they forget how good they are; other times they are stuck in situations that prevent them from expressing their goodness. If I had infinite time to spend on this planet, it would be fine to squander it in grudges. But I am getting older by sixty seconds a minute. This awareness helps me enjoy the roses as I am weeding the yard.

CLOSE THE ROADS YOU WON'T TAKE

Sometimes **it helps to close the roads you won't take**. I will not spank my children. I will not be unfaithful in my marriage. I will not steal. I will not bare personal details of anyone that could embarrass that person. I will not breach the trust my patients place in me. I will not take advantage of anyone's vulnerability. These and a few more roads, I have decided, do not exist for me.

It helps to think through some scenarios and tell yourself that those aren't places you will go. The transient pleasure of a short-term reward is too trivial for the lifelong regret such moments can seed.

> ***Close the mental roads that have quicksand of greed and potholes of selfishness and cruelty. Instead, take your mind through the scenic highway of kindness, patience, and humility.***

When we are faced with a tempting situation, the brain is designed to yield. If we do not yield, we run the risk of temporarily feeling miserable. One way to not yield and not feel miserable is to avoid the circumstances that put you in a tempting situation. If you don't wish to eat potato chips, just don't buy them; don't even look at them in the store. Once they are in your home or office, I guarantee you they'll find a place in you.

The second way is to plan your action ahead of time, not just for tempting situations but also the challenges. What will you do when someone prods you to spill the beans about someone at a party? How will you respond to your child's temper tantrum? How will you deal with an insult hurled by a relative? What words will you use to shut a colleague who tries to bully you? How will you thwart unwelcome advances? The better prepared you are, the more likely you will not succumb to temptations or take the role of a prey to the unkind and predatory elements of the world.

FOCUS ON LONG-TERM MEANING

Think of why you arrived on this planet. Did you come to satisfy the unappeasable sensory wants, or did you come as a student to learn the lessons of wisdom and love? If it's the former, then you'll live in fear of death and will leave the world dissatisfied. If it's the latter, you will likely experience authentic love and become wiser as you grow older.

It is good to remember that the more life you add to your years, the more years you add to your life. The less vitriol of anger, envy, hatred, resentment, and greed, and the more gifts of kindness, gratitude, patience, humility, and forgiveness you bestow to yourself, the longer you will live.

> ***You add years to your life when you add life to your years.***

We get what we seek. If you seek sensory pleasures, you'll get them. But given that time is a zero-sum game for all of us, you'll spend the bulk of your life seeking and not finding. Also, once you get those pleasures, they will quickly stop pleasing you. Our senses carry no memory and quickly habituate. We also get past our happy moments quickly.

Excessively valuing personal happiness is associated with lower happiness and higher risk of depression.[857, 858]

Chasing happiness pushes it away.

Conversely, if you seek to make others happy and if you find joy in meaning and contentment, then you are in for a treat in this world.

Seeking happiness for others makes you happier.

I have no doubt that **because of the way the brain operates, the pursuit of gratitude and compassion will make you happier than the pursuit of happiness.** Try to seek long-term meaning for long-term joy. **The best way to be happy is to be a source of happiness; the best way to be a source of happiness is to seek it for someone else.**

You can consider yourself to be a human being having a human experience, a spiritual being having a human experience, a human being having a spiritual experience, or a spiritual being having a spiritual experience. I like the fourth option the best. It gives me an inspiring perspective about who I am and what is important. If you have that perspective, align your short-term actions with your long-term meaning.

The greater the number of people your long-term meaning serves, the greater its positive effect on you. Consider this world your home, and assume what you do touches every person, to the farthest corner of the world. A chef or a janitor in the hospital is as busy saving patients' lives as a physician. Such perspective will give you the home-team advantage, no matter where you play.

Hold yourself in high regard. Get up each day and tell yourself, "I am a good person. A bad thought, hurtful word, or unethical action is unbecoming of me." **The day we all wake up feeling good about ourselves will be the day that, despite having pain, we will have overcome suffering.**

57

ZIZO: The Flexible Zoom

ZIZO

ZIZO stands for zoom in, zoom out. The best cameras have an adjustable zoom that can cover a wide range as well as use a narrow focus. That's what our minds need. Limiting ourselves to any one domain won't satisfy the curious hummingbird.

The good news is that you can find peace by both zooming into the present moment and zooming out to the very long-term perspective—the ZIZO practice. It's in the intermediate zone, in the worries of tomorrow and the day after, that our greatest stress resides. Mindfulness *v2* guides you to develop a flexible zoom by zooming in and zooming out at will, whichever is most appropriate for the situation.

Here is a simple approach:

- When the present moment is challenged, zoom out.
- When the long term is challenged, zoom in.
- When the intermediate term is challenged, zoom in or zoom out, depending on your preference and skill set.
- When you can't find peace anywhere, search for what went right or find meaning in what went wrong. If you can't find meaning, keep the faith that the meaning will present itself in due course.

ZIZO isn't Pollyanna or an escape from reality. It is intelligently preserving your energy to effect the change. If you are busy all day fighting emotional demons, you'll exhaust yourself. We can learn from our physical body. Our body has enough bacteria in our colon and mouth to kill us with sepsis, we have enough enzymes in the pancreas to auto-digest our physical frame. The body intelligently keeps them contained, so our bacteria and enzymes serve their purpose without harming us. Containing negative emotions uses the same principles. Use your negative emotions to inspire you and comfort others' hurts, rather than simmering in them all day long.

Remember that the deeper the hurt, the longer it will take you to find meaning. Also, for those with faith-based practices, the choice of surrender provides great comfort. None of this means you won't solve the problem when you can. **If you have a thorn in your finger, first take the thorn out and then think about how it got there.**

APPLYING ZIZO

Flexibility allows you to change how you approach your challenges. Flexibility is freeing. Some goals, such as discarding a rotten apple, are easy to handle. Some, such as completely eliminating cancer, are presently unachievable. Most challenges fall in between; you can make a difference yet not eliminate the problem.

I am reminded of how we handle snow on the driveway. We shovel the snow. Shoveling the snow doesn't melt it; it just pushes it aside. Often, that's all we can do for many problems, and that may be enough. A useful perspective can keep snow from annoying us: **snow is the water we will get to drink in the summer**. This perspective softens the stress for me if I have to shovel for the third time in two days.

> ***When shoveling snow remember that snow is the water you'll get to drink in the summer.***

Flexibility allows us to adapt solutions to the problems at hand and be comfortable with imperfect solutions in our current state of technological development.

I was recently chatting with a student who had failed a test and was preparing to retake it. He felt angry and sad, and he had low self-worth. Being forced to study the same material again made him feel like a failure. Here I saw the perfect application of zoom gone wrong.

This is how he was approaching it: while studying, his mind zoomed out into zone B (see Chapter 55) and thought about all that could go wrong. He could fail the test, disappoint everyone, lose his scholarship, and fail in life. When thinking about his situation, he was too zoomed in into zone A, worrying about its immediate impact.

I asked him to reverse this process. When studying, zoom in and focus only on the goals of the next hour. When thinking about his situation during the rest of the day, zoom out into zone C, and look at it from the perspective of his whole life, without catastrophizing. We also considered this experience to be meaningful, as it was teaching him patience and helping him handle disappointment. He did much better with this strategy. It stopped his fight with himself, which helped him save his energy for preparation. As I write these lines, I just heard that he passed.

In general, if you were to ask me for one simple skill, I would say to practice zooming out. That is the direction we are evolving in as a species. We are maturing, seeking freedom from our lower predispositions, and becoming wiser than most other animals, who are too zoomed in. Such growth will help free our attention to discover our compassionate selves.

> ***When in doubt, zoom out.***

Many of the contemplative practices ask us to zoom in, which may work fine if your present moment transcends time, by including the past, the present, and the future. Mindfulness *v2* invites you to zoom out, which I believe is easier, and more useful these days.

By zooming out you declutter your head and create some extra space so you can think deeper thoughts and develop an attitude of your choosing, one filled with humility, gratitude, forgiveness, and the crown jewel of all the mindfulness practices—compassion.

Part VI
The Fifth Tenet: Attitude

Tenet	Mindfulness *v1*	Mindfulness *v2*
Attitude	Nonjudgmental	Compassionate

—⁓—

A non-judgmental stance can be comforting but is unachievable. Being compassionate is an easier and more accessible solution.

58

Fireside Chat #6

"What was your takeaway from the farmers' story?" I ask Mike.

"**Effort plays out in the short term; meaning presents in the long term.** But if I can keep the meaning in my mind, then even a repetitive, boring activity might become enjoyable."

"That's a great conclusion. You are a fast learner, Mike!" Mike nods and smiles.

"How do you apply the idea of the flexible zoom in your own life?"

"Like many, I don't do well under high stress. I lose focus, can't make good decisions, get physically exhausted, and risk saying something I would regret later. Here is how I work with my zoom: If today's realities are painful, I think long term. If the long term is insecure, I lift only the next hour's load, living my life one hour at a time."

"How do you handle hurts and losses?"

"Hurts and losses are unavoidable, but I call them by different names. If you carefully study your life, you'll realize that healed hurts transform into wisdom, and healed small losses seed big successes. When hurting or losing, I try to remember that someday I'll call them by a different name. This attitude keeps my stress contained and saves me a lot of energy."

"Isn't stress sometimes good, though?"

"Stress is a bit like salt in your soup. You need some salt but not four spoons in a cup. Good stress challenges but does not overwhelm. It is meaningful and provides some level of control. I like good stress. Work is good stress, but twelve-hour shifts for six months in a row in a toxic work environment create bad stress. I want to keep my good stress and push away the bad stress as much as I can."

"What if you are stuck in a toxic work environment and can't get out of it? What do you do then?"

"Here is what I do: I stop thinking about tomorrow or next week. I think of either the next hour or the next five years. I live my day one hour at a time and think about what decisions I should make so I am not doing the same thing five years from now. I also remind myself that there is meaning in imperfections. **Birds with asymmetric feathers are the ones that can fly; symmetry looks pretty and perfect but doesn't provide the lift.**"

"Is this where you use the algorithms?"

"Yes, algorithms come in very handy. They provide a quick escape, a way to reframe."

"Could you recap a few?"

"First, **feel grateful for the simple and ordinary**, such as a glass of water, blue sky, an apple, and the ability to chew and taste an apple. Second, **assume that someone upset is actually hurt**; it's a call for help. Third, **consider that most of your short-term adversities and losses are serving a long-term gain, even if you can't see it.** Fourth, **remember that we have one primary employer we are committed to serving: all the world's children.** Fifth, **the main beneficiary of forgiveness is you, not the person you are forgiving**. The perspectives I shared as ways to zoom out—such as asking whether it will matter in five years, realizing it could be worse, understanding it wouldn't be fair if I experienced no adversity, and remembering finiteness—all support these five core ideas."

"Hmm. What about if I am stuck in a toxic relationship? If I forgive, am I not enabling?"

"That's an important point. Each of these algorithms sits within a context. Life is complex, and you have to think about many things. There are times when unbridled optimism, positivity, or forgiveness can be counterproductive.[859] You have to exercise good judgment and perhaps get help from someone you trust. This is where experience comes into play. You also have to think about the short term versus the long term."

"I can see how it can get complex."

"One of the challenges and joys of the human brain is its ability to hold simultaneous opposing thoughts. We can be happy and sad at the same time. We can be both confident and insecure, fearful and courageous, perfection seeking yet accepting, even angry yet forgiving. **The more comfortable you are keeping contrasting thoughts in your head, the richer and more peaceful your life.** Most things in life aren't black or white; they are different shades of gray."

"Is that the reason you don't like the non-judgmental stance either?"

"It's not that I don't like the non-judgmental stance. For those who can embody a nonjudgmental perspective, it works great. But I find it impractical. I will present my case for why I believe nonjudgment, at least in its literal application, isn't feasible. It leaves no anchor for the mind. Instead, compassion is much more accessible and equally, if not more, powerful. Patience creates the space in our mind for compassion to find a home. Humility and forgiveness help us save energy, which we can give out in compassion. All of these are on the menu next."

"I have one more lingering question. How do you know that the approach you're suggesting works?"

"Fair question. Using this approach, we and others have completed over twenty clinical trials across a broad spectrum of populations using a variety of outcomes. Within their limitations, most studies show strongly positive results with a small time commitment.[225] In clinical trials, we have followed participants for a year, and they have continued to do well. We reach close to fifty thousand people every year with the in-person programs and many more through online and other channels. With the core program having been tested, we are now adapting it to other demographic groups, including children. Science is our friend as well as judge, sometimes a harsh judge!"

59

A Practical Alternative

DAY-CARE PICKUP

I went to pick up my then five-year-old daughter at day care. It was a sunny day in Rochester, and all the kids were outside. I stood at the side of the yard admiring the controlled chaos. It looked like a dozen little twins playing—running around, going down the slide, and sitting on the swing. In a few years, they will be headed in different directions, but that day they all looked so alike, particularly when playing. My eyes searched for a purple top since that's what my daughter had put on that morning. I spotted it behind the slide. She was in flow, carving her little universe on the sand. I waited for her to complete her artwork, and then we walked away, holding hands for a few moments until she remembered she was a big girl who didn't need to hold my hand anymore.

I spotted my little one by the purple color. My eyes instinctively scanned for that color. In scientific terms, the purple color at that moment was salient for me. Because several billion bytes of information competed for my attention at that time, my attention system had to prioritize what was important at that moment. We do such screening for the salient all the time. Otherwise you wouldn't find that one empty parking space among two hundred cars and wouldn't spot your car from as many. Our attention is busy serving our present-moment needs.

Human interpretations and preferences are the same. We can't be nonjudgmental. We don't go to a restaurant and tell the server to get whatever. We choose. Complete equanimity is an unachievable ideal, given that we have to raise, protect, and feed our children. When we see people, we have to make judgments about how safe they are, how competent, and more.

Please don't ask me to be nonjudgmental. It will make me and my family vulnerable.

One of my friends who has a daughter with severe peanut allergies has avoided several potentially life-threatening reactions by judging the competence of the chef based on his or her body language, facial expressions, and hesitancy in speaking, combined with that indescribable, infinitely precious skill called mother's intuition. She is vigilant when they travel, watching for the littlest crumbs on airline tray tables and cafeteria benches. An inconsequential little scrap can threaten her daughter's life. How could I ask her to be nonjudgmental?

At the neural level, the moment we see someone, we start to judge his or her attractiveness, trustworthiness, and competence. The **judgment of trustworthiness happens in thirty-three milliseconds, even before we recognize the person**.[687] These judgments, hosted by the primitive parts of the brain, particularly the amygdala, are difficult to stop.[860]

It took millions of years for us to develop our ability to judge. How can we let go of that? The brain can't help but judge a book by its cover, even if that judgment turns out to be wrong. *Harry Potter* received a dozen rejections before it was accepted. Thankfully, we have an alternative to the non-judgmental stance.

A PRACTICAL ALTERNATIVE

A practical alternative to the non-judgmental stance is to delay judgment, recover quickly from a negative judgment, and choose compassion. Judge only after deeper deliberation; judge with a bias toward kindness. To understand the difference, let's look at two meditation styles, one nonjudgmental and the other compassionate (with the added flavor of gratitude). We will start with the nonjudgmental meditation. It goes something like this:

"Just be," the teacher gently suggests. "Focus on the flow of your breath, this moment, and the emptiness of now."

After a few minutes, the student says, "I can feel my breath."

"Stay there. Remain aware of your breath and your aliveness."

"What should I do with my thoughts?"

"When thoughts come, just watch them come and go without getting attached to them."

"OK."

"Make no judgments. How do you feel now?"

"Relaxed."

"Stay there for the next two minutes. I will let you know when our session ends."

Here is another version, one filled with gratitude and compassion:

"Think of someone you know who truly cares about you. Let me know when you have settled on that person."

"I am thinking about my mother, Debra."

"Try to recall her smiling face at this moment. Look at the color of her eyes."

"I can see her face; her eyes are hazel green."

A one minute silence follows.

"Now send Debra silent gratitude for being in your life, for all she has done for you."

Another minute of silence follows.

"Bring within you the feeling of compassion for her. Think of the struggles she has gone through. Wish and pray that her pain be healed. Stay with your mother for the next two minutes."

"When you are ready, you may open your eyes."

Both practices engage the brain's focusing networks. I have tried both. While the first practice may be more relaxing over the short term, I find the second one more engaging since it has social and emotional elements to it. It also has the advantage of improving my relationship with the person I am thinking about, and it gives me a greater uplift. I can also keep it novel by thinking about new people in this light every day. I don't get easily bored with this practice and am more likely to continue it over the long term.

With a non-judgmental stance, I don't have anything to hold on to. **With compassion, I have a construct that can anchor my mind and prevent its wandering.**

A better alternative than being nonjudgmental is being compassionate.

Having said that, I should make one clarification, lest I sound or become unreasonably cynical.

ONE CLARIFICATION

I don't loath the non-judgmental stance. I just find it difficult and impractical. For those who can cultivate a radical non-judgmental stance, it can be very helpful. But it is difficult to run our complex lives with this stance. We have to make judgments to survive. We have to call a spade a spade and a diamond a diamond. I tried having a non-judgmental stance for many years but couldn't go far with it. I felt I was leaving no one in charge of my mind. I was creating silence that was suffocating.

Here's the other issue. When we say "nonjudgmental," we actually do not mean nonjudgmental. We mean no negative judgment. By "non-judgmental stance," we mean giving the benefit of the doubt and assuming positive intent. This attitude is a mixture of acceptance and compassion.

Now, acceptance is a very heavy load to lift. In my years of teaching and living, acceptance has been one of the most difficult practices for me and others. Bare acceptance asks us to step out of the fight without the reassurance that we will be the winners. Those who can embrace acceptance find it beneficial. But not many are ready, at least not for the long term. I struggle with acceptance on most days.

Further learners often make a literal interpretation. As a young student of mindfulness and resilience, I wanted lucid and direct instructions. If the teacher said nonjudgmental, I had my marching orders to remove all judgments, good or bad. I struggled. "If I don't judge, what should I do? What should I think?" "Just be," the teacher said. "You'll get your answer."

But I didn't get the answer. I got disappointed. I blamed myself. Thankfully I didn't stop there. I searched for an alternative that my mind could grab and feel. I was lucky to have found the perfect solution: Compassion.

Compassion is much easier and every bit as powerful. In relationships, compassion doesn't leave you in the neutral gear. My car can't move in neutral. Compassion drives you to be kind to yourself and others. **Kind doesn't mean weak. Kind means caring, even if you have to show anger and give time-outs.**

The grittiest people find their greatest strength in kindness.

You will have judgments; the question is how you structure your judgments. I find the anchor of compassion most empowering. Interestingly, as you go deeper in compassion, you will find acceptance and a nonjudgmental attitude emerging on their own.

The first step in helping compassion flourish is cultivating patience. This is because compassion needs space to land its feet and grow. **Patience creates space between information and response, a cognitive gap.** Only when you have an available space can you fill it with intentional thoughts, words, and actions guided by compassion. Let patience create that space in your mind before we go about filling it, with compassion.

60

Patience

We arrive in the world very impatient, with an extraordinarily narrow zone of comfort. A little change here or there—whether that means becoming wet, cold, hungry, overfed, overstimulated, bored, or alone—and we launch in to loud, attention-seeking exhalations (grown-ups call them crying). Despite a crammed schedule during the first few days after arrival, every day we still find two hours for these loud exhalations.

Crying works. It buys immediate attention and helps us vent our frustration. Our me-first attitude, however, can last for only so long. Eventually we have to learn to be willing to wait, to postpone gratification, and to develop self-control. We have to learn to be patient.

Although patience is decidedly desirable, **impatience is our genetic default**. Ever met anyone who loves inching traffic, forgetful servers, slow internet connections, an elevator that stops at every floor, or long checkout lines? A bird in hand is my bird. Ten dollars in six months have half the value of ten dollars today. This instinct creates impatience.

Impatience is our genetic default.

IMPATIENT? YOU CAN BLAME YOUR GENES

Patience (or impatience) is often scientifically described as "individual steepness of delay discounting." This is your ability to tolerate delays and postpone gratification.[477] The greater the steepness (which means you steeply decrease the value of delayed reward), more impatient you are. This trait is seen in most animal species, whether they're humans or pigeons.[861] Interestingly, this is part genetic and part acquired, just like our personalities. In fact, up to 50 percent of delay discounting is genetic.[482, 483] Researchers are now finding specific impatience genes that might explain why one infant frets every hour while another lets you watch your favorite TV show even when he or she has a wet diaper.

The amount of dopamine in the prefrontal cortex correlates with our patience. Scientists have discovered an enzyme that breaks up dopamine, called COMT. This can be more or less active depending on your genetic makeup. When COMT is more active (Val type), you have lower dopamine in the prefrontal cortex and thus lower patience.[862] The guy who honked at you at the traffic light likely has Val-type COMT and is trapped in impatience because of lower prefrontal cortex dopamine. When someone cuts you off on the road, instead of calling him jerk, label him "the low prefrontal dopamine guy." It will make forgiveness easier! This can apply to many life situations.

> *That guy who cut you off on the road most likely has low prefrontal cortex dopamine. This realization will help you contain your anger.*

I find it very empowering that we are able to connect genetic patterns with brain structure and function and our behaviors.[863, 864] There is a scientific term for this connection: brain-based endophenotypes. **Understanding each other is an early step in becoming more compassionate.** The same is true for understanding our children. I used to be more impatient with my daughters when I was late for an important meeting and they were arguing about pink versus purple hair clips. Now, having read studies that show that the prefrontal cortex matures only late into adulthood,[865] I have become more patient—and also more hopeful.

You can use the fifty-fifty division of nature versus nurture for patience to your advantage. **Blame your genes for your impatience; pat yourself on the back for your patience**. Now, that's freeing! As an aside, a lot of different aspects of our lives—well-being, happiness, risk of depression—follow this fifty-fifty rule. I choose to feel both validated and empowered by it. Why not?

> *Fifty percent of our impatience is encoded in our genes. Blame your genes for your impatience, pat your back for your patience!*

HAZARDS OF IMPATIENCE (BENEFITS OF PATIENCE)

The opposite of patient isn't impatient; it's anxious, angry, injured, unwell, or even dead. You know the hazards of impatience if you have shared the road with a few impatient drivers. The outcome can range from annoying to life threatening. Impatience increases the speed of life and interferes with deep thinking. Impatience keeps attention superficial. Superficial attention predisposes us to quick judgments, which often have a negative bias. Impatience hurts every aspect of our lives: health, happiness, relationships, lifestyle, and work.

> *The opposite of patience isn't impatience. It is anxious, angry, injured, unwell, even dead.*

Impatience and health. An impatient mind hurts the physical body in which it resides. If you have diabetes, then the lower your patience, the poorer the control of your blood sugars and lower your adherence to the treatment.[493] Hypertension, migraine, and ADHD are other conditions associated with impatience.[490, 866-868] Through its association with diabetes and hypertension, impatience is connected to adverse cardiovascular health. Impatience even affects us at the level of our chromosomes. In a study involving 1,158 university students, impatience was found to be associated with shorter telomeres, a marker of accelerated aging.[869] **The only thing impatience speeds is our aging.** Patience works just the opposite. For example, **in patients with heart disease, nurturing greater patience decreased coronary reinfarction rates by 44 percent.**[870]

Impatience slows the speed of progress and accelerates the speed of aging.

Impatience and happiness. Patience correlates with mental well-being, whereas impatience is associated with depression, anxiety, and stress.[478] Moment-to-moment patience is associated with greater life satisfaction and well-being.[491]

Impatience and relationships. Impatience has been associated with relationship infidelity.[871] In a study involving medical practitioners, impatience was associated with the spouse's marital dissatisfaction, while achievement striving was not.[872] Impatience and intolerance are the hidden factors behind many senseless crimes that seed regrets and sorrows of a lifetime every single day.

Impatience and lifestyle. Impatience and its cousin, impulsiveness, are associated with many bad habits that plague our well-being: overeating,[480, 481] substance use and abuse,[479, 485] and pathological gambling.[486] In several studies, impatience has also been associated with road-traffic accidents.[873, 874]

Impatience and success. Although time pressure may look like pure adrenaline, **impatience is associated with worse academic and financial outcomes.**[492, 494] Further, the impatient, even if they hold rewarding jobs, are less likely to be satisfied with them.[875]

Ask any fabulously successful businessman, and he or she will tell you that a good way to lose money is to be impatient.

For all the above reasons, patience is a tremendous gift. Gifting patience to others is gifting healthier hearts and brains to them and to yourself.

WHY SUCH IMPATIENCE?

Everyone seems to be in such a hurry these days. Most of us have so little time to pause, notice, or think deeply. **Patience-deficit disorder isn't a known diagnosis, but it should be.** Many factors contribute to the impatience epidemic. Perhaps the most important reason is the invasion of technology in every aspect of our life.

Our pace of life is governed by the speed of internet search engines. And they keep getting faster. People will prefer a competitor's website if yours is 250 milliseconds slower. Excessive competition makes us feel vulnerable.

The world is rife with competition. When I was younger, we kept the same phone for at least a decade. Not so now. Product cycles for many items have shortened to a few months. Software and designs quickly become obsolete. Most workers have to constantly learn new skills to keep up. Companies have to constantly innovate to survive. All of this crowds our schedules, leaving little room for error and patience, and provides plenty of fodder for stress.

Rising stress in the world wreaks havoc on the brain networks that host deep thinking, focusing, and reframing. Stress predisposes us to seeking short-term gratifications, an important contributor to impatience (this can be partially reversed by training in gratitude).[876]

The other problem is that impatience breeds impatience. One online retailer found that for each extra second its website takes to load, it risks losing close to $2 billion in yearly revenue.[877] The natural response is to develop the technology that speeds the website, which leads to our expectation for the website to be fast. When the websites are faster, we start expecting our spouses, kids, parents, friends, and clients to operate with the speed of a search engine.

Every business I know rewards speed. Everything else being the same, you'll be less likely to visit a slower restaurant, grocery store with slower checkout line, slower mail career, or slower anything. What is rewarded influences our behavior. A society that in the short-term rewards impatience is going to breed impatience.

Our world rewards speed and multi-tasking, making us impatient and unfocused.

An interesting study showed that our way of eating, specifically fast food, increases impatience. In this study, researchers found that **subconscious exposure to fast-food symbols increased participants' reading speed even when they had no need to hurry**. The more participants thought about fast food, the greater their preference for time-saving products. Further, exposure to fast-food symbols decreased participants' preference to save. Instead, they chose immediate gains while forfeiting future returns, hurting their overall profits.[878] I hope investment bankers are familiar with this research. It might improve their eating habits. This is particularly important, because we have reached a point at which research shows that **chimpanzees can exercise greater self-restraint than we can when it comes to eating**.[879]

How and what we eat changes how and what we think.

Impatience has created new forms of rage. I first heard of road rage when I was in my twenties. Then came air rage. Now we have a plethora of rages: sports rage, parking-lot rage, vending-machine rage, computer-crash rage, low-cell-phone-battery rage, and more. We are innovating new forms of rage while doing little to innovate new ways to be patient or compassionate. We need to take charge and reverse this trend.

A society that rewards speed and *busi-ness* cultivates impatience and angst. Such a society locks itself in high stress and low happiness. Investing in technologies and ideas to increase our patience can balance our appetite for speed. Let's look at five simple ideas to cultivate patience.

61

Cultivating Patience

An interesting study compared patience between two monkey species—marmosets and tamarins.[880] Both these monkeys have comparable body and brain sizes, mating systems, and life-history trajectories. By all measures, their levels of patience should be similar. Investigators assessed how long a delay monkeys will tolerate, the point beyond which they won't wait to get the six pellets but instead will eat the two pellets available right away. That wait time was about eight seconds for tamarins and almost fifteen seconds for marmosets—a large difference that can't be explained by their evolutionary development or biology. What made the marmosets a role model of patience? The answer came from their eating habits.

Tamarins are mostly insectivorous—they have to act fast to catch moving prey. Marmosets are mostly gummivorous—they punch holes in trees and then sit around watching a long World War II documentary, waiting for the gum to exude. This difference in feeding habits translated into a difference in patience.[880]

I find this hopeful because it means that if we live more thoughtfully, we can strengthen the patience muscles. The more you choose patience, the greater your patience will be. **Once you create the patience habit, the patience habit will create you.** Here are five ideas to cultivate patience.

1. PRACTICE PATIENCE

Insert intentional delays (that you can afford) during the day. Train your mind to get used to emptiness and a slower pace. Here are some suggestions:

- Prepare a hot meal from scratch.
- Wait until every family member is at the table before taking the first bite.
- Chew your food well.
- Enjoy every sip of your coffee.
- Assemble your own furniture or toys.
- Stand in the longer line at the checkout.
- Drive in the slower lane.
- Iron your clothes.
- Load the dishwasher as though it were a jewelry box.

- Take your time peeling your orange or apple.
- Play tennis with a five-year-old.
- Plant a garden and watch it grow.
- Delay checking your e-mails after your flight lands.
- Let children take the lead in which game to play.
- Listen with no desire to speak (listening isn't waiting to speak).
- Do not jump the orange light.

Some days load the dishwasher as if it were your jewelry box!

2. SHIFT YOUR ATTENTION

Empty, unproductive moments such as standing in the checkout line, waiting for a large video file to upload, or waiting for a cab often feel painful. Filling that time with active engagement will decrease the pain. Here are a few ideas for when you're at the grocery-checkout line: listen to the random clicks of the scanner; notice the items the person ahead of you has bought (The average person samples a miniscule percentage of the forty thousand items that an average grocery store carries. Noticing others' carts will be educational and amusing.); listen to the music playing in your environment; silently wish people around you well; feel grateful for the breadth of the items available for sale; count your breaths; bring a smile to your eyes; notice the different hairstyles of all the people around you; notice all the colors in your environment.

3. TRAIN YOUR ATTENTION

Train your attention so it isn't as vulnerable to disruptions. A strong attention guided by your core values can help enhance your patience.

Assume that your clients and colleagues know much less than you in your area of expertise, and be willing to give them full attention. If they ask something that is too obvious to you, remember that what isn't obvious to them today wasn't obvious to you when you were learning. They are brilliant (in their own unique way), just with a little less experience.

Teach attention skills to the kids in your life. **In research studies, children with trained attention show increased patience.**[502]

Strong patience needs strong attention.

4. SEE DIFFERENTLY

Give your mind a little workout by choosing to see the annoying differently. Your creative mind can find infinite perspectives and coat a sour experience with sweet wrappers.

For example, a gentleman I met had multiple work responsibilities and was constantly interrupted. The nature of his job was such that interruptions were inevitable. After a good discussion, he started looking at interruptions as an essential part of his job. He considered that he went to work to be interrupted. Now he embraces the interruptions rather than withdrawing from them. This shift in perspective has decreased his stress level and that of his colleagues and has made him much more effective at work.

Embrace your interruptions so you aren't interrupted by them.

5. SHIFT FROM SIMPLE TO DIFFICULT

Just as biking progresses from training wheels to a small bike and then a bigger bike, your patience will play out in three domains of life in increasing order of difficulty: daily hassles, interpersonal affairs, and life hardships. It would be extremely difficult to embody perfect patience if your basement floods with storm water. Start with something simple.

Consider being a perfectly patient driver on Monday, a perfectly patient parent on Tuesday, a perfectly patient spouse on Wednesday, and a perfectly patient employee/employer on Thursday. On Friday, be perfectly patient with yourself. Give yourself a break on Saturday and Sunday (you might be exhausted by then!).

Work out your patience muscle with someone who currently gets on your nerves. It could be a colleague who slurps while drinking coffee, a teenager who likes to shower only once a week, a spouse whose snores risk cracking your home's foundation, or a neighbor who doesn't believe in recycling. Pick only one person and promise patience only for one day of the week. Gradually work your way up.

These perspectives and practices will help you reach a point at which your worldview will change. You will become calmer, deeper and will have more working space in your head. In addition to seeing others' imperfections, you'll start seeing their constraints. You will become more compassionate.

62

Compassion

The practice of compassion is healing. The presence of a compassionate person is equally healing. In fact, reading, thinking, writing, or talking about compassion or a compassionate person is healing in its own right. I truly feel happy and healed to be writing about compassion at this moment.

Empathy is a closely related word. Empathy is recognizing and feeling another person's pain. Compassion is recognizing and feeling another person's pain *with an active desire to help and heal.*

Watching your child struggle with a difficult medical diagnosis, living with an older pet in his or her final few days, trying to help a close friend stranded in an abusive relationship—all naturally evoke compassion. The question is, how do we expand our compassion to a larger world without getting overwhelmed? Let's seek some answers. Our first stop is the brain.

YOUR BRAIN ON COMPASSION

Here is a summary of compassion neuroscience: **When you see someone hurting, your pain network lights up; when you help someone who is hurting, your reward network lights up. Compassion thus simultaneously activates both the pain and reward networks.** Now for some details.

Pain network. Every life-form is familiar with the experience of pain. Pain hurts us, but it secures our survival by sounding an alarm. This alarm jogs widespread areas of the brain. As a result, we drop the hot skillet or evade the narcissistic bully before either can hurt us.

Interestingly, **with respect to physical and emotional pain, our definition of self extends beyond us**. When we observe or even imagine others (particularly those we care about), in a painful physical or emotional state, our brains behave as though we were experiencing that state ourselves.[881] Observing someone else in pain thus activates our own pain matrix.[350, 882, 883] Several other areas activate depending on the kind of pain—physical pain areas when the other person is in physical pain[882, 884] and areas that host the understanding of another's emotional state when the other person is in emotional pain.[350, 352]

When we are designed to feel others' pain as our own, how can we stop ourselves from acting to secure their healing?

Your pain is mine, and mine is yours. When you heal I heal, and when I heal you heal.

Compassion is so hardwired within us that even people with a rare disorder that makes them insensitive to their own physical pain nevertheless experience activation of their pain matrix when they see someone else in pain.[353]

Reward network. The reward area of the brain activates (and makes us feel good) when we do something good, or something good happens to us that might enhance our probability of survival. Delicious food, good company, large sums of money, promotions, social-media attention, and acceptance into a college of choice all activate the reward area of the brain. We love to revisit experiences that activate our reward areas.

Compassion is a powerful stimulator of the reward area.[236] **Empathy alone can decrease happiness by activating the pain network, while compassion that extends empathy into healing intention and action increases happiness by activating the reward network.**[885] (See Appendix (*A Meditation Secret*) for more details)

Empathy activates the pain network while compassion activates the reward network of the brain. Convert your empathy into compassion. The switch will make you happier.

When observing others' pain, we can feel either distressed or compassionate. The more we train ourselves to help, the greater our likelihood of feeling other people's feelings without getting distressed.[886]

We have developed several strategies to numb our emotional pain. Suppression and distraction are two weak options that work in the short term but eventually fail. Reappraisal and compassion are two stronger and longer-lasting options. **Reappraisal decreases negative feelings, whereas compassion enhances positive feelings** by activating the reward areas.[235]

During a meeting with His Holiness the Dalai Lama, an audience member asked for the solution to compassion fatigue. The Dalai Lama shared that **true compassion is actually energizing and doesn't lead to fatigue.** I suppose he was hinting at this line of research that connects compassion with feeling energized.

True compassion seldom causes fatigue.

In practice, particularly in health care, compassion fatigue is widespread due to seeing unimaginable suffering day after day, particularly when you see the finest of people experience bad outcomes. I will share with you shortly how you can strengthen your compassion muscles without getting fatigued.

WHY COMPASSION?

Compassion isn't just a good idea. **Compassion is the oxygen for the soul. Lack of compassion is *the* problem that is causing many other problems in the world. Without compassion, we will perish as a species.** Let me tell you why.

Human newborn brains don't arrive ready to take on the world. They need years of care—care that is often taxing and annoying. Such care needs cooperation and sharing of resources. Most social animals thrive on cooperation. Fascinating research shows that consensus decision making and democracy are the rule rather than the exception among animals.[887-890] In his classic, *The Descent of Man*, Darwin, spoke of love many more times than he did the idea of the survival of the fittest. Our essential nature is thus of cooperation, consensus decision making, connection, sympathy, and compassion. That is the reason compassion is so hardwired within us.

Given our greater focus on science than philosophy in mindfulness *v2*, let us look at what research shows about the benefits of compassion.

- **Compassion is associated with lower sympathetic and greater parasympathetic activity.**[891, 892]
- **Compassion is associated with lower inflammatory response in adults as well as in adolescents.**[893, 894]
- Compassion training enhances altruistic behavior.[236]
- **Patients who perceive their physicians as more compassionate have shorter duration of the common cold and better immune response.**[895]
- Medical students trained in compassion become better at interviewing their patients.[896]
- Training in compassion toward one member expands compassion toward the group as a whole.[897]
- Low levels of compassion predict higher levels of bullying among adolescents.[898]
- **More compassionate weight-loss discussions lead to greater attempts by patients to lose weight and change exercise patterns.**[899]
- Adolescents receiving compassion training have lower aggression, anger, hostility, and personal distress than do those not receiving the training.[900]
- **Compassion-appeal messages are more effective for regular smokers than fear-appeal messages.**[901]
- Brief compassionate statements that validate patients decrease their intention for litigation.[902]
- Compassion is associated with better sleep.[903]
- Learning compassion helps lower depressive symptoms.[904]

A compassionate mind carves a healthy
body and a thriving society.

Compassion is a simple and powerful way to access authentic happiness in life. When we move from no food to bread and soup, we become happy. The jump from bread to cake creates little incremental happiness. Going from a have-not to a have causes a large jump in well-being, but going from a have to have-lots causes minimal incremental jump. Countless times I have found that the compassionate haves are much happier than the uncaring have-lots.

In many parts of the world, we have overcome basic survival needs. **If we wish for greater happiness, acquiring more material wealth is a much less efficient solution than is boosting compassion.**

Compassion is also more easily accessible. In a study, watching just a forty-second "enhanced compassion" video clip decreased viewers' anxiety and elicited a feeling that the caregiver was more sensitive and kind.[905]

Compassion is also critical to competence. Those who become compassionate start caring and become motivated to learn the necessary skills. I believe that **in today's world, a compassionate spirit is even more important than a competitive spirit.** A truly caring professional is more difficult to find than one who is brilliant. Further, **if you start caring, you become brilliant. I haven't ever met a worker who is compassionate yet incompetent.**

Enhancing compassion is a powerful way to enhance competence.

If you agree with the foregoing, the natural question is, why aren't we more compassionate than we are? Why do we need reminders and training? Why is compassion not as natural to us as breath? What limits our compassion?

63

What Limits Our Compassion?

Every beating heart has the song of compassion programmed in its beat. The problem is that it sings compassion only for a few that it chooses. Fascinating research shows that trees care for their kind in a group. They live as a family, supporting and nurturing each other.[906] Ants and bees care for their whole colonies. So do many other animals. What about humans?

Many humans are kind, but unfortunately, many are not. Some commit unspeakable horrors. Hiding behind pseudonyms some of us celebrate others' pain, shame them and laugh over their losses. I believe the technology that allows pseudonyms and encrypted communications also enables cruelty, hatred, and broadcasting words that go against the golden rule.

We have created many constructs to justify our actions—from older tribes to modern companies, cities, and countries, not to mention gangs, mobs, and more. It saddens me to also include religious fervor in this group. Unfortunately, a small percentage of us try to hijack pious and sacred constructs with greed, fear, and ignorance, and soil the pond.

If we all could live with the sincerity of the trees, helping our kind while intending to harm none and expanding our zone of care to at least everyone who breathes in our shouting distance, we would transform the world.

The selfless life of a tree is truly inspiring.

We must expand our perimeters of compassion. We must move from centering on the individual and the family, to include the city, the country, and eventually the world.

Five human predispositions limit our compassion: fear, anger, envy, hatred, and pity.

FEAR

Three types of fear hurt our compassion. The first fear is that our compassion will stretch us too far. How can I help the whole world or absorb its suffering? Won't it deplete me and drain my limited resources? What is the point, then, of thinking about the world and developing compassion fatigue? I will visit this topic shortly in chapter 65.

The second fear is of the world. If we act carelessly, travel to the wrong place, fight with the wrong people, or say the wrong things, we can get physically and emotionally hurt. News channels preferentially broadcast such events since they know our amygdala can't resist paying attention to the threatening. Reminded constantly of the threats, how can we be compassionate toward a world that we dread?

Our fears fuel our cruelty and demolish our compassion.

Individuals with the third type of fear struggle with receiving compassion. They have greater self-coldness and self-criticism and are insecure in their attachments. They are so uncomfortable receiving compassion that they start fearing it.[907] This fear may reach a point at which they are uncomfortable experiencing any positive emotion, a trait that increases their risk of depression.[908] They also struggle with self-compassion (an important topic that we will discuss in chapter 66).

When our brain worries that compassion will get us too stretched or put us in harm's way, we fashion a much weaker empathic neural response toward others, particularly people of other races,[689] and those we believe have been unfair.[577, 909] Seeing them hurt activates our reward area, pushing compassion out of the room.[577]

Notice that these predispositions are programmed within us. We don't choose to think or live this way. These fears are thus legitimate. Trashing them won't help. Acceptance of these fears is a good first step toward overcoming them.

With the first fear (that you will be overstretched), draw a distinction between compassionate intentions and compassionate actions. **Try to carry compassionate intentions for everyone while performing compassionate actions only to the extent you are able. Expand your good wishes and prayers to include as many as you can, recognizing that we are all related to each other.**

While your compassionate actions may touch only your neighbor, your compassionate intentions can travel every corner of the globe.

I touch my heart every time I see or hear about someone struggling. At times, I deprive myself of a small pleasure in honor of those hurting. Although it may not change anything in the world, it helps me express solidarity with those who might be struggling half a world away. (There are days I wish I could win a series of Powerball lotteries and do much more than I am currently able to do.)

Trying to be compassionate toward someone you fear is almost superhuman. My only suggestion is to keep your fears rational. **Do not fear the trivial, the implausible, or the uncontrollable. There isn't much you can do about in-flight turbulence. Hope is believing it will stop; caution is sitting with your seat belt on; fear is having a panic attack. Keep an abundance of hope and caution while skirting fear.**

Keep rational fears. Do not worry about in-flight turbulence, be fearful of texting while driving.

Take all the precautions you have to, but once you have secured your home, immerse yourself in life instead of checking the doorknob forty times. Remember that **we handle future adversities way better than we imagine. We also get more support than anticipated. So best to use your energy to prepare and not fear.**

The people who don't mean us well want us to breed excessive fear and destroy our way of life. If they succeed, we will be left with a dry, loveless society in which we will stop trusting Girl Scouts selling cookies. Not a good idea.

ANGER

Our empathic neural response is lower toward those we feel are responsible for their condition (for example, patients who got HIV from drug abuse versus those who received it from a blood transfusion).[910] People we label as strangers or those with a poor reputation also evoke lower empathy.[911, 912] These people are more likely to make us angry.

Anger is a central feature in many psychological disorders and life situations.[913] People vulnerable to anger pay greater attention to hostile social cues, see more hostility in others, and ruminate excessively about previous frustrations.[914] They also spend little time self-regulating their negative thoughts.[915]

Further, **when our heart is beating at 120 beats per minute from anger, our prefrontal cortex stops working**. We stop thinking, become reactive, and are driven mostly by the amygdala. It is in such a state, with its loss of compassion, that we might say or do things that we regret for a very long time, even to the people we love the most.[916] We get internally inflamed.[917] We risk stroke, heart attack, malignant arrhythmias, and sudden death.[918-921] Even in a research laboratory, facial expressions showing anger and smiles that did not show enjoyment correlated with low blood flow to the heart.[922]

Our brain's pre-frontal cortex stops working when our heart starts beating at 120 beats per minute.

After lighting the fire, we sit with our ruminations, thinking and overthinking, and thus perpetuating the anger.[923] The result of these ruminations is that we label others as less informed, stupid, unreasonable, selfish, or awful. We find them unforgiveable. We feel we need to act. The show of anger, in words or actions, is geared to seeking justice as well as deterring future insults or losses.[924]

Much of this either doesn't work or is counterproductive. For example, most customers want to be served well. Many get angry when they experience suboptimal service. A show of anger is just what they feel will fix the problem. But research shows that a **customer's show of anger further decreases employees' ability** to focus and think clearly and also hurts their well-being.[925, 926] Conversely, when customers show positive emotions, employees reciprocate with smiles and efficiency.[927] A smile, particularly a genuine smile, has tremendous value. **People are willing to give up monetary gain in exchange for a genuine (and not just polite) smile.**[928]

Your authentic smile is your gift to the world. It costs you nothing but is priceless for the receiver.

When possible, avoid anger, and if you must get angry, allow your anger to be more controlled and rational by getting angry only with the right person (the one truly at fault), at the right place (avoiding public places or in front of uninvolved others), at the right time (generally not right away and not on special occasions), to the right extent (spilled milk on the dining table doesn't justify yelling), and with the right intention (to help and inspire, not demean and diminish). Choosing to think with greater compassion can help you keep your anger healthy and helpful.[929] Praying for a stranger, a friend, or the person who angered you can decrease anger.[930] **You can put a stop to anger by recognizing that it often originates in a mismatch between expectation and reality.** Reality often can't be changed but expectation is almost always in your control.

You can stop anger in its track by lowering your expectations and assuming positive intent in others.

ENVY

Envy raises its green head at those we believe undeservedly got a better deal than we did. Envy, however, can occur even when the other person is suffering. Our brains have a less empathic response for someone we believe is of superior status.[931] When we see a wealthy person hurting, we do not feel as compassionate. In fact, our reward area may activate seeing a wealthy person struggling.[932] Even oncologists express less empathy toward patients with advanced cancer who they feel have more resources.[933] These predispositions are part of our design.

The more we envy people, the more we notice them.[934] **Envy emerges from our phenomenal ability to notice others' successes much more than their hard work.** This is particularly true for the others who compete with us. I am not envious of the thousands of people whose videos go viral, those whose kids go to Ivy League schools, instant billionaires from an IPO, or any of the Nobel Prize winners. But that list better not include my friend Justin, whom I have competed with all my life, or my cousin Brian, who in my opinion always got the sweet end of the deal. Such envy interferes with our ability to perform.[934] It also incites us to victimize the person we envy.[935]

The reality is that most people have average lives. Their days are not filled with a series of exciting events as might appear from the posts on their Facebook pages. They have fears and struggles similar to mine and yours. **If I could give compassion even a little space that is currently occupied by envy, I would be inspired by others' successes and participate in them instead of feeling left out and drained.**

Realistically, we can't eliminate envy. But if we keep envy in check (often called benign envy), it can inspire us to do better. **Envy is stronger than admiration in spurring us into action.**[936] Just as harboring benign envy can be helpful, feeling envied can boost our self-confidence. This boost, however, often comes at the cost of fear of ill will, particularly for people who value relationships above achievement.[937] Further, unchecked envy can lead to schadenfreude (pleasure in others' misfortune), particularly if we dislike other people, feel inferior, harbor anger, and believe they are undeserving.[393] Schadenfreude is the opposite of compassion.[938]

Unchecked envy can bring out the worst in us.

HATRED

I hate hatred. It often starts with years of simmering fear, anger, and envy. Once these three feelings spend time together in the same container without being diluted by love or mentored by rationality, hatred emerges. Hatred dries up compassion like the midday sun dries up water in the Sahara. From the fire of hatred emerged the Holocaust, the Rwanda Genocide, 9/11, and more. Unfortunately, hatred isn't done yet with hurting us and fracturing our society.

Hatred dehumanizes its target. We have discovered so many ways to dehumanize others: race, religion, country of origin, sexual orientation, political party, even football club.[939] People we call "others" become "things" or "cockroaches" that are dispensable.[940]

We are willing to hurt them and their children, particularly if we perceive their moral values to be different from ours.[941] Such hatred isn't just limited to impoverished or war-torn places. It is common in the civilized world, even in suburban homes. The sad title of a study I recently came across was "Home is where the hatred is."[942]

With respect to hatred, people live in three categories: those who can't hate, those who hate but can overcome their hatred, and those who can't get over hatred.[943] The third kind, those who can't get over their hatred, hurt themselves and others the most. Hatred in their mind is the same as stage-four cancer in the body. Once deeply seated, such hatred doesn't leave the afflicted mind easily, and often it goes to the grave, hurting many lives on its journey. Interestingly, what keeps this hatred alive is a fundamental attributional bias. We ascribe our aggression toward others to our love for our group; we ascribe their aggression toward us to their hatred of us.[944] We thus feel fully justified in our aggression, while we consider others totally unreasonable. This is particularly hurtful to us and our society because crimes motivated by hate are generally more violent and have worse mental-health consequences.[945]

The hatred that seems morally justified leads to the worst immoral and criminal actions.

Not all hatred is avoidable or bad. Loathing for the actions of traitors, terrorists, drunk drivers, corporate thieves, dishonest executives, careless caregivers, and more spurs us into action. We correct these wrongs that hollow our society. But hatred that comes from irrational fear, exaggerated anger, and envy is best avoided. Once we realize that most people, however successful and good-looking, are busy protecting their vulnerable selves—and we also become aware of their hard work, constraints, and losses—anger and envy will stop holding sway over our mind. Even deep-seated hatred can fade if people try. For example, **prevalence of hatred among Kosovo residents dropped from 89 percent in 1999 to 54 percent in 2000, despite all they saw happen in the war**.[946] Many authentic spiritual masters rightly advise us to hate the sin and not the sinner.

PITY

Although the two are confused for each other, pity isn't the same as compassion.[947] **Pity feels uncomfortable at others' distress while having a paternalistic undertone.** When we pity, we think others are lower than we are, even while we notice and acknowledge their pain. Evoking pity doesn't necessarily lead to the compassionate response of helping.[948] Pity is disengaged and can lead to withdrawal from action.

Compassion emerges from a sense of equality.

Feeling superior or inferior makes us feel vulnerable. The greatest joy is in feeling equal.

A lovely Italian proverb comes to my mind: "After the game of chess is over, the king and the pawn go back to the same box." While we may each have a different net worth during this very short earthly journey, we all go to the grave carrying the same set of assets that we came with: nothing. Death is a great equalizer.

YOUR BRAIN, A BUFFET

You can see that the brain is constantly struggling with its multitude of predispositions that promote compassion on the one end and fear, anger, hate, envy, and pity on the other. **Eventually it is up to you which trait you empower.** If you don't intervene, compassion will take a backseat. Don't let that happen to you. If you trust me even a little, take this suggestion: empower your compassion instinct. It will help you and your world in countless ways.

Your brain offers you a buffet of experiences and perspectives. You get to choose what you want for your plate. If your brain's insula and anterior cingulate cortex activate on seeing others in pain, you have the beginning of a compassionate response. If your insula and anterior cingulate cortex activate on seeing others succeed, you have the start of an envious response.[949]

Scientists are trying to influence our responses by using neurochemicals selectively. For example, in a clinical study, intranasal spray of oxytocin enhanced compassion for others.[950] Even in countries troubled by war, oxytocin enhanced empathy toward people belonging to the opposite faction.[951] Researchers are even trying to activate selective areas of the brain with real-time neural feedback using MRI.[952] These are baby steps, that together hopefully are the start of a global movement toward compassion.

We have made fascinating scientific strides in understanding the neuroscience of compassion. We are also discovering neurochemical sprays that can transiently make us more compassionate. But I am not sure to what extent such sprays will change the world. They are not scalable, and to me are akin to taking a nasal spray of a chemical to develop motivation for physical exercise. Eventually the spray will show unintended side effects or an exaggerated and impractical response. The best way, in my mind, is to train the brain for compassion using a combination of insights and skills. In the next chapter, I will present a four-step approach for enhancing compassion.

64

Four Steps to Compassion

A complete compassionate response has four elements: recognizing pain, validating pain, intending to heal, and healing. Let's look at each one of them.

RECOGNIZING PAIN

I don't know you well enough to know your hopes, dreams, concerns, and constraints. But two things I know for sure: you are special, and you have struggles. My personal life has become infinitely simple upon committing myself to this assumption. Every day all day long with each person I meet, I try to remember that the person in front of me is special and struggling. This simple belief and its practice has transformed my days.

And I haven't found this to be a wrong assumption so far. If you agree with the neural vulnerabilities I shared earlier, then you'll agree that we all struggle in our own unique ways. A portion of this struggle is visible, in hospitals, courtrooms, tearful eyes, and therapy sessions. A large part is invisible, though, often beguiled by smiles and superficial celebrations. **The invisible pain goes unrecognized and thus unhealed.**

Many smiles are an effort to hold back tears.
It's good to know that.

Our compassion also depends on our physical and emotional states. **We fail to see the pain of others when we ourselves are hurting.** For example, if you are behind on sleep, you'll struggle with being compassionate.[953] When we are reminded of our mortality, our compassion suffers.[954] Our previous experience with pain also influences our empathic response.[909]

Compassion feasts on our patient presence. When we are hurrying or multitasking, we fail to notice. I have observed that I am less courteous on the road when I am getting late for a meeting. (I promise myself not to let my hurry quash my kindness next time, but I am embarrassed to confess that very often I forget this promise. Curiously, in that moment I feel totally justified in not holding the elevator door long enough so more could come, or not letting someone merge from the side road.)

> *Avoid getting late or packing too much. Time pressure blots away your compassion.*

Further, we are more likely to see the pain of those who we feel are part of the in-group.[955] **Those who are most meaningful to us—our loved ones, close friends, and sometimes those whom we can benefit from—evoke the greatest compassion.**

> *The more diverse our world, the greater the need for compassion.*

Recognizing the pain in others thus takes a lot of effort. That's one reason that cleverness is abundant in our society, while kindness takes effort to find. **If you wish to keep it simple, just assume that everyone you have met so far and will ever meet is special and struggling.** That will be the first and most important step toward compassion.

VALIDATING PAIN

People don't wear their hearts on their faces. We don't know all that is going on in their lives. If someone is walking awkwardly while wearing an ankle brace, we know that he or she has an ankle injury. We don't negatively judge that person. Unfortunately, that isn't true for most emotional hurts. **We are often unkind toward behaviors that we can't ascribe to a visible injury**. Not knowing the full context, we judge people who might be hurting.

One in four homeless people has a mental-health diagnosis, often untreated. One in ten homeless people is a veteran. Almost all of them have a troubled past and many endured childhood abuse. Instead of calling them losers, look at them within their constraints. It doesn't mean you have to start hugging them. All it means is that the next time you see a homeless person, you don't sneer or get angry with the person or our society.

> *See a homeless person as a war veteran. Perhaps we owe our freedom to him.*

Thinking about others' constraints is important for two reasons. First, we feel the pain of those we love greater than we feel even our own pain, particularly if the inflicted pain seems intentional.[882] But **we don't care as much about the pain of those we don't love**.[351]

Second, **compassion is easiest for someone you are sure is struggling**. We don't judge anyone with a sick child, life-limiting diagnosis, abusive partner, toxic work environment, or recent loss. When we feel people deserve their pain, however, because of cynicism, prejudice, or reality, we don't validate their pain. The more we judge and blame others for their misfortunes, the less compassionate we are likely to be,[351] and the greater the need to validate their pain.

While some people sometimes may deserve their pain, this is a dangerous, slippery slope. It is precisely this perspective that leads to the trap of hatred, with its downstream verbal and physical violence. There is a sad surge in violence from parents toward kids who have chronic illness. Even the thought of that makes me want to cry.

Assume people who are hurting are vulnerable and not choosing to be hurting, an assumption that will deepen your compassion.[956] One approach I have often used is that I change the age of the person I am looking at. For someone annoying, I see that person as very young or very old. Either of these perspectives takes away the sting from the other person's behavior, giving me better control over my reactions.

A certain level of sensitivity is needed to validate others. In fact, a research study showed that people who received analgesia had lower empathy for another person in pain.[957] Blocking analgesia restored the pain empathy.[958] This is one of the clearest demonstrations of how **feeling others' emotions to validate them helps develop empathy**.

To keep it simple, just **assume that their pain is their pain; you are in no position to judge it. It is real, and it is hurtful. While someone in the world may be tasked with judging its reality, depth, or rationality, your job is to show compassion, help, and heal.**

Assume that their pain is real and undeserved. Taking any other stance risks becoming cruel and insensitive.

Assume they have constraints that you may never know about. This awareness has helped me become a better person and a better health-care professional. Also assume that they are more similar to you than you can ever imagine; they have similar dreams and similar constraints. **The more similarities you find and the more reasonable you find them, the greater your ability to see and validate their pain**.[959, 960] In a study, an activity as simple as three minutes of synchronous tapping enhanced perception of similarity, which in turn boosted compassionate response.[961]

We are more similar and connected than we can ever imagine or know.

With recognition and validation, you are naturally moved by others' pain. Just as you can't help but feel the thorn stuck in your finger, you can't help but be moved by seeing innocence in pain. The natural next step is a desire to help or heal.

INTENDING TO HELP OR HEAL

Sitting in an airplane, I heard a baby crying a few seats away. Mom and Dad were trying their best, but perhaps the little one's tympanic membrane was too stretched. Some people were politely annoyed. After sitting quietly for a few minutes, I started sending soothing intentions to the baby. I started praying from my deepest place that her pain would ease. Magically, she stopped crying! The scientist in me believes she would have stopped anyway. The dreamer in me likes to believe that my prayerful intention made a difference.

Can thoughts and subtle influences change the outcome? We are still researching this topic. We do know that **priming can have a powerful impact on behavior**.[962] People primed with words related to old age started walking slower; those primed with rudeness started interrupting the experimenter.[963] Children primed with food advertising ate 45 percent more.[964] At a quantum level, physicists know that intention influences the outcome of their experiments. When you set up the experiment to see light as a particle, it behaves as a particle; when you try to see it as a wave, it behaves as a wave.

So, can our healing intention effect actual healing? Wearing a scientist's hat, I can't answer the question conclusively. Personally, I do believe that if I wish someone well from the bottom of my heart, his or her day will likely go (at least a tiny bit) better.

Assume that your healing intentions effect actual healing.

Believing in the converse, that your kind intentions have no effect on the world, paints a dark, callous picture of the world. Such an image will deplete your energy. Further, your actions to help and heal start in your intentions. You will do something only if you believe that your thoughts matter and that you have some power to improve the world around you. The alternative, to sulk in apathy, isn't the most gratifying way to live. It also empowers others who don't mean well to influence your life.

Research shows that **the corrupt and immoral become even more corrupt and immoral when they get power, while those morally aware become more morally aware with power**.[965] If you do not believe in yourself, you'll enable people who can hurt you and your children. It won't be easy. The good people who live with conscience and courage experience more struggles than do the selfish and the greedy.

Here is an important conclusion I have arrived at that I have shared before: **The good people are very good at feeling bad about themselves**. Be good anyway; our world will perish without you. We need good people to engage; let the pious be powerful.

To keep it simple, assume that your intentions have tremendous power and that your words and actions originate in your positive intentions. Further, assume that the other person is part of your own group, an assumption that will bolster your intention to help.[966] **Your compassionate intentions foster compassionate actions.**

HELP/HEAL

Recognizing, validating, and intending lead to the final step: doing something. You can help others with words or with tangible actions. Both are important, and both have their place. **Recognize that not everyone is good with words as well as actions.** Some people can sing; others can dance; a few can do neither even though they appreciate the music. Similarly, some people are good with words, others with actions, and a few, unfortunately, with neither. Those who don't know how to heal with words likely didn't develop the linguistic healing skills early enough. Pick your area of strength and implement it as best as you can. Also appreciate others for the skills they have instead of judging them for the skills they lack.

Some people are good with words, some with actions, and only a rare few with both.

The specifics of your compassionate words and actions will depend on several factors, including your relationship, the situation, your comfort level, and others. Here are a few general ideas that might help:

- **Validate, don't educate**—A common mistake is to provide insight to someone who is hungry for validation and comfort. I once heard a speaker, a father of five, share his experience after he lost a child in an accident. One distant friend came and said, "At least you have four other kids who are alive." The speaker came close to punching him in the nose. **In general, provide insight only when specifically asked.** Insights create hierarchy and may seed fresh regrets, reinjuring a person who is trying to heal. **Compassion is about equality, not hierarchy. The most well-intentioned insights, if delivered unsolicited, can be annoying. Engage people's hearts, not their defenses, particularly with the children and the vulnerable.**

Resist the urge to provide insight to someone hurting. Instead, provide validation and support.

- **Feel to heal.** Earlier I shared research showing that our brains show less neural empathic response to the pain of people of other races. Interestingly, **when participants focus on the other person's pain and take away the race stereotype, empathic response increases.**[967, 968] Further, **greater exposure to people of another race also increases empathic neural response** (newly immigrant Chinese people in Australia had lower neural responses when they saw the locals experiencing pain, compared to the response immigrants had to the same exposure five years later).[969]

- **Bend to mend. Humility keeps close company with kindness.** (We will visit humility shortly). The purity of your compassionate words and actions will be lost with the slightest hint of hubris. Hurry is also best avoided; patience and unhurried presence helps you show that you care. For example, **physicians who chose to sit by the side of the patient were felt to be more compassionate**.[970] Patients also feel that physicians who sit spend more time than do those standing, for the same total time spent.[971] I believe this applies to most professionals, not just in health care.

Show compassion, caring, and humility, in how you carry yourself.

- **Just show up.** Showing up expresses solidarity. Often, you may not know precisely how to help. You may not be able to do much. Just show up with your good intentions, not to enter your name in the log book. Let the person struggling provide you the lead into how best you can help, in his or her own time.
- **Listen.** A sympathetic ear is a phenomenally healing instrument. Sharing information and communicating thoughts and feelings is a source of relief and pleasure even if it doesn't lead to tangible solutions. Scientists have found that **when people share their thoughts and feelings, the reward areas in their brains activate.**[972, 973] **Your engaged listening helps spread happiness in your world. Eventually this happiness will echo back to you.**

Your ears are a powerful organ of healing.

- **Do some homework.** If you feel you could benefit from training your compassion muscles a bit (which I believe all of us can), then consider listening to compassion researchers. Several studies have shown that training in compassion increases compassion,[974] positive affiliation,[975] and altruistic behavior past the training period and improves executive and emotional control and activation of the reward areas of the brain.[236] Further, such training doesn't have to be very elaborate. It could simply be adding a contemplative practice;[976] it could be fun, as in theater classes;[977] and could be obtained online, such as for the busy caregivers of patients with dementia.[978] Finally, only a few hours of training might suffice to make a meaningful difference,[979] although the skills do fade with time and need ongoing reminders.[980] In the appendix I have more fully shared research findings with compassion meditation, which I believe is the meditation with the quickest, most profound, and most lasting benefit.

When I practiced medicine in India, I spent less than 5 percent of my time doing paperwork or working with computers. Almost all my clinical time was with the patients. When I arrived in New York in 1995, I was shocked when I realized that I was spending more than 50 percent of my time working with the numbers in front of a computer screen. If those numbers were right, then I was doing fine. It is only worse now. **Most medicine residents now spend the bulk of the day in front of computers.**[981] We focus more on the computer monitors than on the patients' faces.

Leverage technology to enhance your presence not replace your presence.

As health care begins to center on technology and physicians and patients are pulled apart, it will be very important to remember the definition of health care that I mentioned earlier: **health care is using knowledge and technology to deliver compassion.** When we remember this essence, we will do fine as we integrate technology, and discuss who should or should not be covered. If we forget this basic premise, patients will lose trust in one of the last institutions in our society that still commands a high level of trust.[304]

CELEBRATE TO BE COMPASSIONATE

Your compassion will be tested when others share their happy events. Being truly happy for your work colleague who got promoted while you were not, celebrating with a research colleague who received a large grant while your application got triaged, enjoying selfies of your friend with celebrities—all of these will take superhuman effort. I have faced all of these and many more. I can honestly say that ten years ago, each of these experiences created envy. Today, I am truly happy for someone who is happy. **I see rejoicing in others' success as an act of kindness.**

    Recognize that compassion isn't just diluting sorrow; it is also multiplying joy. When you are truly, deeply happy for others in their success, you are being compassionate. Research shows that just as experiencing good events makes us happier, sharing the good news about our life with others also makes us happier.[982] People sharing their good news aren't showing off; they just want to experience happiness. Further, their happiness multiplies when you receive their news enthusiastically.[983] Independent of the event, you are happy if someone is happy for you. (This is called "capitalization" in the scientific community.)[984]

    Your enthusiastic response will promote trust and improve the relationship. In fact, **response to positive events may have greater influence on relationships than response to negative events**.[985] Some of my best relationships have formed and healed from participating in these celebratory moments.

Training yourself to be happy in others' happiness is an excellent recipe for a lifetime of happiness.

A colleague with whom I had a difficult relationship once won an important award. I immediately sent him a congratulatory e-mail—not just a one-word message but a few sentences with substance. His response was kind. We ran into each other at the elevator a few days later. From his smile, words, and energy, I could tell that our relationship was back to normal.

I surmise that people often are just waiting for the other person to take the initiative. Unfortunately, if no one realizes this, the rift continues. **Whenever you can, show a constructive and active response to others' successes** ("Truly deserving. I am so happy and proud. Tell me more about it!") instead of a destructive and passive response ("That's easy. All you had to do was to apply. In fact, they offered me this position, but I rejected it.").[982]

As you embrace compassion, you reach a point at which limits to your compassion drop, and you become universally compassionate. That is what mindfulness *v*2 strives to accomplish—to help create a world in which every human being cares for every other human being. This is a lofty goal, but it is achievable in our lifetime given how connected we have become. As we march toward this goal, it is good to realize that this is a marathon, not a hundred-meter sprint. Almost invariably, runners who accelerate prematurely in marathons develop fatigue and fall behind. Carefully avoiding compassion fatigue will help your compassion grow, while protecting you from getting personally overwhelmed.

65

Compassion Fatigue

Lisa is a pediatric oncology nurse. It is hard work, taking care of the sickest of the sick little ones. Every week, the staff loses many children to terminal illnesses. I have spoken to this brave group about resilience many times. After a few years, Lisa began to feel exhausted at the end of the workday. She cried, became forgetful, felt lonely, lost hope, and got angry and cynical. Lisa had developed compassion fatigue. Lucky for her, she found a good excuse to leave work for some time—she was pregnant. Now with two children of her own, she can't go back to work, not because she doesn't have the time, but because she is too afraid she will revert to her earlier emotional state. Having her own children also has made her even more sensitive to children's suffering. With a supportive husband who has a good job, Lisa thankfully has a choice. Many others do not, if they are the sole breadwinners for their families.

Fatigue is a protective mechanism built into our body systems; it prevents us from getting injured because of overactivity.

Fatigue is your body's effort to protect itself. Do not blame yourself for your fatigue.

Almost every muscle and gland can get tired if not given optimal rest. The same is true for our emotional machinery. If we are exposed to the suffering of others and we aren't prepared to process it, we get overwhelmed and trapped—fatigued.

FEATURES

No single definition completely captures compassion fatigue. Here are a few ways of looking at it: loss of compassion over time, running on empty, emotionally depleted, tired of caring. Its professional title is "secondary traumatic stress disorder." Almost every caring profession that sees suffering in the people it serves can develop compassion fatigue. It is most commonly seen in health care.

Some of the symptoms of compassion fatigue include: lower sensitivity, emotional exhaustion, inability to focus, physical tiredness, loss of meaning in work, disturbed sleep, loss of morale, loss of self-worth, anger, loss of hope, irritability, impaired judgment, and a pervasive negative attitude.

Of late, a low-grade compassion fatigue is permeating our society because of constant exposure to local and global suffering. This, I believe, is related to an important brain mechanism worth mentioning.

The more news you watch, the greater your stress and compassion fatigue.

COMPASSIONATE INDIFFERENCE

When health-care providers are first exposed to patients' pain, their pain matrices (in the brain) are strongly activated. With repeated exposure, they downregulate their pain response.[986] It frees them up so they can be of greater assistance. Research shows that experience helps decrease their pain matrix activation when they perform potentially painful procedures.[886] This is important and needed. I will be eternally grateful to the emergency-room nurse who inserted the IV in my daughter's dehydrated arm. Unlike her predecessor, who felt the hurt of my daughter, this trained nurse had adjusted to causing short-term pain in service of longer-term meaning. She had developed the much needed "compassionate indifference."

Many of my colleagues who are world renowned for their skills in performing complex procedures notice the same "freedom." A large part of training in professions such as surgery, orthopedics, and invasive radiology is acquiring not just the technical skills and knowledge but also the ability to downregulate the personal pain response. This downregulation needs balance. Although it is helpful for health-care providers doing useful medical procedures, **if numbing becomes a social norm, we will create an insensitive society that stops caring for its members**—exactly the opposite of what we want. This is what concerns me.

INDIFFERENCE

I see many signs that we are pushing in the direction of indifference. College students are getting less compassionate, a trend that has accelerated since the year 2000.[987] In health care, part of this relates to high prevalence of burnout as medical students progress through their training.[988, 989] **The more burned out one feels, the greater the loss of empathy.**[990, 991]

Initially, only the more vulnerable in society catch that bug. These are the people predisposed to experience more stress. For example, people with greater risk of compassion fatigue are those who are low on agreeableness and high on moodiness,[992, 993] have a passive coping style,[993] struggle with a broader perspective, lack social support,[993] are high on self-judgment and low on self-compassion,[994] do not feel meaningfully recognized,[995] have low levels of management support at work,[996] have poor coworker relationships,[997] and are low on emotional intelligence.[998]

Gradually, as our exposure to widespread suffering increases and is coupled with an increase in societal stress, I worry that compassion fatigue, particularly its low-grade version, might globalize, changing how we relate to one another.

Erosion of compassion is one of the greatest risks we face in the world today.

We must work hard to stem this erosion of compassion and proliferation of indifference.

HELPING COMPASSION FATIGUE

The scope of services of many professionals is now expanding beyond their core expertise. Attorneys have to care for victims of trauma, which pushes them to depression, anxiety, and substance abuse. Financial advisers have to spend considerable time handling family disputes.

Given the success of modern medicine in preventing mortality from acute conditions, a high percentage of families now have someone with chronic illness, which includes cancer, dementia, stroke, chronic heart and lung disease, and chronic pain. All of this caring comes at a cost—of time, money, and mental health. The tougher our jobs and the less qualified we are for them, the greater our risk of compassion fatigue.[999] In that sense, I believe, we all have to work with personalities for which we are not trained and don't feel competent at handling. It is fair to say that all professionals are now mental health professionals.

All professionals are now mental health professionals.

Here are a few things you can do to help yourself (in no particular order):

- **Focus on gratitude.** Think about all that you are grateful for, including sunlight, your ability to take a deep breath, the loved ones in your life, and the privilege of supporting them.
- **Avoid excessive news.** I will not be surprised if in a few years watching excessive news will be considered an independent risk factor for heart disease and stroke. We know that excessive television time has already been associated with these risks. **Decrease your dose of daily news to the least amount necessary to keep you informed.**
- **Talk to someone.** Talking to a person who doesn't judge you, is wise, and means well can provide a potent respite and much-needed escape from the confines of the mind.
- **Limit your imaginings.** In a research study, the more participants tried to imagine themselves in another person's situation, the greater was their personal distress.[1000] A healthier response was to think of the other person's feelings and, based on those, look for solutions. **Focusing on how others feel with an intention to heal is healthier than just imagining ourselves experiencing the same suffering.**
- **Optimize your expectations.** I have shared this formula previously:

Happiness = Reality - Expectations.
You can either change the reality or optimize your expectations; the latter is completely in your control (well, almost completely).

- **Learn to accept.** About two-thirds of the earth is covered by clouds at any time. They are bound to wander over your city and neighborhood and make it rain; there is no escaping this reality. Accepting this truth is wisdom.
- **Take care of yourself.** The healthier you are physically, the happier you will be emotionally, both helping your compassion. Pick one of these (whichever you aren't doing right):
    - Eat slower if you eat too fast and notice what you eat (people who remember what they ate during lunch are likely to eat less during rest of the day)[1001-1005]
    - Stand at least once every half an hour if you are sitting a lot (prolonged sitting increases your risk of heart disease, stroke and death even if you work out; in one study, each hour of sitting decreased life span by twenty-two minutes)[1006, 1007]
    - Sleep for at least seven hours (sleep is the time when brain clears itself of toxic chemicals accumulated during the day through a system of channels recently discovered; sleep is like carwash for the brain at the end of a day-long trip)[603, 669, 671, 1008]
    - Know your and your loved one's numbers (cholesterol, blood sugar, blood pressure, BMI, and others appropriate for you).
- **Pursue a hobby.** Do something that nourishes your mind so the stressful part of your day is diluted.
- **Focus on your life's meaning.** Think about your true passion. Do a little something to advance your passion.
- **Cultivate a spiritual practice.** Define spirituality based on your altruistic values and pick a practice that helps you cultivate the spiritual part of your life.

The greater your resilience, the deeper your compassion.

Compassion can simultaneously deplete and replete you. Compassion takes energy, and if it overextends you or isn't compensated by positive meaning, you will feel depleted. Make sure you are physically as good as you can be. It is difficult to have compassion for anyone when you are having a migraine headache. Also try your best to be emotionally in a good place. My six-year-old taught me a beautiful lesson the other day. As she was getting into the car, she said, "I saw a flower in the garden smiling at me." **Wouldn't it be nice if we all, kids and grownups alike, believed that the flowers are smiling for all of us?** That simple awareness would take you on a path to self-acceptance, self-forgiveness, and of course, self-compassion.

66

Self-Compassion

THE THREE RELATIONSHIPS

Three relationships that define a life are with the self, with others, and with what an individual considers sacred. These aren't discrete relationships with tight boundaries. They overlap. Their successful integration is important to fashioning a life worth living.

Of these three relationships, **most of our time is spent with the self**. Unfortunately, the one training we seldom get is how to relate with the self. We are taught how to speak to others, but never are we taught how to speak to ourselves. We are taught to love our neighbors, our loved ones and love and revere the sacred, but seldom are we taught how to love ourselves and discover the sacred within all of us.

We get little or no training to handle the most important relationship: with the self.

As a result, not uncommonly, we relate to the self in a dysfunctional way.

SELF-JUDGMENT

A common dysfunctional relationship with the self involves self-judgment. We fulfill many roles: mom/dad, wife/husband, son/daughter, brother/sister, grandpa/grandma, colleague, employee, supervisor, client, friend, neighbor, and more. We cannot give 100 percent to each role all the time. We cannot be simultaneously at a child's birthday party and on a business dinner two thousand miles away. **Our default instinct is to anchor our self-worth in the role in which we are most underperforming—a recipe for low self-worth.**

Our default instincts predispose us to self-judgment and low self-worth.

Further, we compare ourselves with others. Depending on the situation, we judge whether we are better off or worse off than others. Often, this is a moving target, based on the happenings of the past hour. If that were not the case, you wouldn't have Nobel laureates, fabulously successful entrepreneurs, and Miss Universe contestants struggling with low self-worth about their contribution, success, and looks respectively.

The resulting yo-yo creates moments of high or low self-worth, neither of which are healing.[1009] In this state, we have to feel nicer, better looking, more popular, and more intelligent than others to feel good enough.[1009] This naturally leads to narcissism and selfishness.[1010]

Such a state of self-judgment predisposes us to addictions, lower academic and job performance, and dysfunctional relationships.[1011] We shortchange our potential. In this state, someone is always worse off—either we are or the others are. We feel poorly if we are worse off, but we are on the edge to defend our current state if we feel we are better off. Sometimes we feel guilty when we are better off. This state often leads to self-loathing, in turn predisposing us to depression, lower motivation, fear of failure, and poor performance. This isn't the healthiest way of relating to the self.

The greatest joy is in feeling equal to, not better or worse than, others. That entails compassion for others as well as self-compassion.

SELF-COMPASSION

Self-compassion is applying the Golden Rule to yourself—treating yourself with the same kindness and care with which you treat others. Self-compassion is relating to the self with gentleness, kindness, and patience. **Self-compassion recognizes that you aren't and can't be perfect. Self-compassion, however, isn't lowering standards, indulging, or making excuses.** It isn't self-pity. Self-compassion isn't denying mistakes or critique. It is handling critique wisely. **If the critique is true, use it to learn and grow; if the critique is false, just ignore it, and don't take it to heart.**

Self-compassion isn't lowering standards. It is applying the Golden Rule to yourself.

Do we have research data that shows the value of self-compassion? The answer is a resounding yes. Research shows that self-compassion enhances well-being over the short term as well as the long term.[1012] Self-compassion increases access to positive reappraisal that helps with depressive symptoms[904, 1013] and helps increase optimism and self-efficacy.[1014] People with healthy self-compassion are less likely to have mental-health issues.[1015] **Healthy self-worth leads to humility; humility leads to kindness; and kindness leads to happiness and love.**

Self-compassion also improves binge eating[1016] and body image in young girls.[1017] In a large international study in patients with HIV, self-compassion was associated with lower anxiety, for both men and women.[1018] Further, you don't have to be born with healthy self-compassion. Most of the benefits can be obtained using structured approaches that enhance self-compassion with predictable and lasting results.[1012, 1019]

All the above benefits beg the question of why we aren't more self-compassionate. The obvious reasons are the same as those that increase self-judgment: our tendency to make unhealthy comparisons, trusting negative feedback more than positive feedback, and anchoring self-worth in the outcomes and achievements that aren't always in our control. One less obvious reason is that **we literally fear self-compassion.**[907]

We have been practicing self-loathing and rejection for so long that we have forgotten how to be compassionate with ourselves. We fear that if we are compassionate to the self, we will lower our standards. The hurt of self-loathing multiplies, because those who fear self-compassion also fear receiving compassion from others.[907]

A particularly sad cage is that of self-loathing and rejection. Once we get comfortable in this cage, we languish inside for long, with no hope of escape.

Unfortunately, some of us fear not only compassion but also many other positive emotions, particularly happiness. Research shows that **people who fear happiness are much more likely to develop depression.**[908] They also struggle with forming nurturing relationships.[1020] Many patients with fear of self-compassion develop eating disorders.[1021]

FOUR STEPS TO SELF-COMPASSION
Enhancing self-compassion has the same four steps as compassion for others.

Recognize. Acknowledge your struggles, weaknesses, failures, regrets, and pains and your strengths, successes, and moments of abundance. Try not to suppress or exaggerate them. Look at them as they are, objectively, as an observer of life. Also acknowledge your tendency toward self-judgment.

Validate. Be aware that you can't and don't have to be perfect. You don't have to be better than others to be good enough. Recognize that many different factors, not just your intentions and actions, influence your life. We all work within the constraints that have tremendous influence on our path. **About 50 percent of your resilience depends on your genetic endowment that isn't in your control.**

Also recognize that you aren't alone in your struggles; every one of us are endowed with the same neural traps. We all struggle with life's finiteness and the world's ever-increasing complexity. **Do not judge previous moments of self-judgment; today is a new day, as good as any to change your trajectory.**

Today is a new day…literally.

You can learn from the evergreens. Evergreens withstand harsh, cold winters because their leaves are thick-skinned. **When the world gets cold on you, get tough and thick-skinned like the evergreens.**

Intend. The desire for self-compassion sprouts from awareness and validation. You desire a better relationship with the self, recognizing that how you treat yourself affects how you treat the world. At each heartbeat, your heart first serves itself with blood before nourishing the rest of the body. When it fails in that effort, the patient has a heart attack, which hurts his or her entire being.

Similarly, in order to better serve the world, you intend to be kind to the self and minimize comparisons. You intend to believe in your good intentions. You find no reason to feel superior to others. You do not just celebrate strength or mourn weakness; you **value strength and weakness, and the products, successes, and failures of each, equally as your teachers**.

Help/heal. Make your self-talk intentional and productive. **Empty the space in your brain usurped by self-doubt. Replace it with hope, inspiration, and courage.**

Focus on the positive meaning rather than the minutiae of details. Evaluate yourself by your intentions and effort and not the outcome. Here is one formula I wish for you to know:

$$\text{Outcome} = \text{Intention} + \text{Effort} + X \text{ factor}$$

Intention and effort do not always lead to the desired outcome because of multiple unknown influences that I like to call "the X factor." The X factor could include known external influences (local, national, or international), probability, luck, and more. For people of faith, the divine will influences everything.

The size of the X factor depends on the complexity of the desire. It could be very small for simple actions such as going to a coffee shop and ordering coffee. You have close to a 100 percent chance that your effort and intentions will lead to the outcome of a cup of coffee. But what about the probability of never getting cancer, heart disease, or fibromyalgia? Your intentions and effort will make a difference, but I have seen enough healthy and fit thirty-year-olds with all three conditions to realize that the outcomes are often not in my control. Self-compassion is using your energy wisely. **Focus on the effort and, recognizing the influence of the X factor, accept the outcome.** Internalizing this and bringing it to your daily experience will help you with acceptance, which saves you the energy to bring about the desired change.

The more complex your striving, the greater the uncertainty of achieving it.

Acceptance also includes accepting the self as you are. That'll help you become better than you are. Be willing to forgive yourself. Celebrate small successes and processes perfected; do not wait for the outcomes. Do not fall for fear, hatred, envy, anger, or self-pity. Be willing to face the unpleasant to claim the good. Try not to hide weaknesses or fight with those pointing out your weaknesses. Avoid focusing on differences, superiority, or inferiority. Instead, find meaning in the common humanity. We are all different leaves on the same tree.

Let all these perspectives provide you with a firm foundation of peace so you aren't vulnerable to transient drafts of hardships, losses or failures.

Remember that everyone won't like or adore you. Despite your values and best efforts, some will simply be allergic to you. That's just the way it is. If I am allergic to peanuts, that doesn't make peanuts bad. They are nourishing for the majority of people. Best not to spend too much time with the people in whose company you feel judged or, worse, alone. **If a few people have firmly decided to dislike you, trying to change their opinion will be a waste of time. Focus on the other 7.5 billion.** That's what the trees do. Their roots and leaves draw nourishment from wherever it is coming. We tend to focus more on the places that are drying up. Learn from the trees. If a particular family member is unkind, focus on the rest of the family, friends, neighbors, colleagues, clients, and more.

In this world of infinite personalities and agendas, some people are bound to be allergic to you. Accept this reality and focus on the countless others.

Self-compassion is an expression of wisdom. This wisdom values effort and intention and doesn't anchor self-worth on the outcome. It also looks at the self with the eyes of someone who loves and adores, not someone who judges and reacts.

Self-compassion also remembers that luck is real, and sometimes, despite all your efforts, your flight will be delayed if the tailwind isn't with your wings.

Luck is real.

The self-compassionate judge themselves by their values and effort and not by their achievements. They see common human experience in their own struggles. From such awareness emerges self-acceptance and self-forgiveness. Self-acceptance helps you recognize that the first step in improving the self is to accept yourself as you are, which is a tremendously empowering perspective.

PRESERVING OUR ENERGIES

We spent considerable time talking about compassion. **Without compassion, our species would cease to exist, because we wouldn't be able to raise our babies.** I am sure you know what male lions do to all the cubs when they conquer a pride. They lack compassion. Such behavior is unthinkable for humans. Hence, whatever your goals or beliefs in life, keep compassion in the mix to keep our species alive.

Compassion takes energy. Energy is of two kinds, physical and psychological, and has two sources, inner and outer.

The outer source of physical energy is nature. The inner source of physical energy is the metabolic machinery of the body. This machinery metabolizes the food we eat in the fire of oxygen and generates energy-carrying chemicals (technically called ATPs) to sustain us. Adequate sleep, physical activity, and overall well-being help us generate and use our inner physical energy.

The outer source of our psychological energy is the people in our lives—our role models, the people who love us, and those who inspire us. The inner source of psychological energy comes from gratitude, hope, inspiration, courage, meaning, and faith. We touched on meaning in the previous chapter, and we will briefly visit gratitude in the sixth tenet and hope, inspiration, and courage in the seventh tenet. I will defer faith to a future book.

It is important that we not leak our energy, since it is finite and precious. How do we leak energy? From two forces—unchecked hubris and unhealed hurts. Unchecked hubris starts a chain reaction that puts our energy into thinking, saying, and doing things purely to protect and advance our egos—a waste of energy. Similarly, unhealed hurts create excessive mind wandering and force us to contemplate revenge—another energy trap.

The solutions are simple: humility for hubris and forgiveness for hurts. Let's touch on these in the final two chapters of tenet five.

67

Humility

Before we pointed our telescope at the heavens and became aware of the plurality of the worlds, we bathed in ignorance-fueled hubris. We believed we lived at the center of the universe, based on Ptolemy's geocentric model. The gradual unpeeling of the truth has been humbling. From what we can see of the stars now, the most recent estimate is that the universe has two trillion galaxies.[1022] Every day, our universe spawns three hundred million or more new stars.[238] Our sun is a little dot sitting in an arm of our spiral galaxy, about thirty thousand light years away from the center. The sheer size of the world out there instills within me a sense of awe and humility.

Our universe is bigger than we can ever imagine.

WHAT IS HUMILITY?

I recall an old mango tree in our backyard. One particular season it had hundreds of green mangoes. The tree was literally stooping, bent like a giant sage. When we threw a rock at the tree, it sent fruit in return. That tree represented a good model of humility and kindness.

Humility is having accurate self-awareness with low self-focus. Humble people are willing to accept themselves as they are without the need for comforting illusions that they are somehow better. Humility isn't low self-esteem, putting your interests last, giving all the credit to others, becoming submissive, or letting yourself be trampled. You neither inflate nor deflate your self-worth. Humility is a state of balance. You neither struggle with low self-confidence nor are full of yourself or busy with shameless self-promotion.

To the truly humble, every aspect of nature and every person becomes a teacher. When we are truly thirsty, we care for the water, not the make of the cup. When thirsty for knowledge, we learn from every experience, good or bad. This helps us develop equanimity.

Humility is having accurate self-awareness and low self-focus.

A humble person is aware of and embraces his or her strengths and weaknesses. A humble person is wise and knows that what we know, we know imperfectly; that we don't know what we don't know; and that we don't even know that we don't know. This is self-awareness.[1023] **Not recognizing our ignorance is the primal ignorance** and is dangerous for the individual and the collective. Humble scientists, for example, recognize that most of science is built on theories that are approximate representations of the truth but not the ultimate truth. Such awareness takes away false confidence and instills curiosity,[1023] which helps with growth.

Humility emerges from strength, not weakness. It reflects a secure sense of self. Humble people are honest about their accomplishments and find no reason to exaggerate or decimate their life's work. **Flexibility and an openness to embrace the different, even if that different is not pleasing in the short term, is a hallmark of humility.** Humility thus can be very freeing. When you are freed from the need to always protect your emotional body, you have extra working space in your brain to more fully live your life, including practicing compassion.

Unlike compassion, gratitude, and forgiveness, humility is difficult to measure in research. This is because the humble often don't call themselves humble. The humble are unaware of their humility. They are aware that each person is individually priceless but globally inconsequential.

The humble don't claim they are humble.

It is this ability to hold conflicting and contrary views at the same time, with both the views representing an aspect of the truth, that nurtures wisdom. This ability (to hold conflicting and contrary views) is uniquely human, and it reaches its greatest depth in a humble mind.

WHY HUMILITY?

One reason humility isn't celebrated is because it is often wrongly equated with a self-abasing attitude, a tendency to hide from the limelight, and feelings of shame and submissiveness.[1024] Authentic humility, the kind that helps you celebrate others and delights in healthy pride and optimal self-worth, can be a tremendous source of energy without making you insensitive or depleted of compassion.[1024]

Overconfidence is a dangerous trait. Those who are overconfident and ignorant can hurt themselves and everyone whose lives depend on them. We desperately need more humble, wise, selfless people in the world.

Humility fosters leadership. In his book *Good to Great*, author Jim Collins presents his research findings on traits that are the mark of visionary leaders. These leaders returned profits that beat most other companies. The core attribute wasn't the leader's charisma, brilliance, flamboyance, or vision. It was a combination of intense professional will empowered by extreme personal humility.[1025] Humility, will, ferocious resolve, and the habits of giving credit to others and taking personal responsibility for failures—it was this combination that consistently provided success.[1025] This applies not only to individuals but also to companies, hospitals, and health-care systems.[1026]

Humility opens you to viewpoints that may be very different from yours. You become a student of life. Others feel comfortable sharing their feedback, both positive and negative. This helps you avoid land mines. Humble people have more time to serve others since they don't need as much energy to protect their emotional selves. No wonder that **it is the humble leader, not the flamboyant one, who is the most successful**.

The hallmark of a phenomenal leader is his or her phenomenal humility.

Humility enhances performance. Research shows that humility in a leader enhances team performance, particularly for a competent team. It creates a milieu of shared leadership so everyone is involved and engaged.[1027] In an interesting study, researchers found that humility tempered the negative impact of narcissism on the leaders; leaders with a combination of contrasting narcissistic and humble traits were more effective than the narcissistic ones, and had greater employee engagement and job performance.[1028] Further, humble employees, even when feeling insecure about their jobs, did not engage in destructive work behaviors.[1029]

Humility takes away the need to inflate the ego balloon, which is very freeing. Such freedom saves energy and wins friends.

Humility saves you precious energy to focus on the important and the meaningful.

Humility improves relationships. The opposite of being humble is being narcissistic—harboring a damaged sense of self that needs to be repaired every day by acting superior to others. **Acting superior is a reflection of feeling inferior.** Chasing self-esteem further damages self-esteem. Self-esteem is repaired and enhanced by self-effacement. Humility loves and shares, while arrogance hurts and compares.

The light of your humility shines on others so everyone starts glowing with kindness. **Humility is infectious.** Those who bask in your humble presence feel secure. They no longer need to protect their egos—hence they become humble around you. Such a disposition gives them and their world extra peace. Your humility thus travels further than your physical being. When enough of us embrace humility, the world will change.

Humility makes you resilient. Humility is of particular benefit in the context of adversity. Adversity not only hurts our physical and emotional well-being in the short run but also often changes our worldview. Those with faith become less faithful; those with a just worldview change their view and become more cynical. Research shows these long-term effects are much more prominent in the less humble. **Humility protects you from the harm that adversity does to your worldview.**[1029]

Humility also enhances all four aspects of emotional intelligence: self-awareness, other-awareness, self-compassion, and other-compassion. Leadership and success strongly depend on emotional intelligence.

Humility, which may superficially seem soft, actually makes you stronger than steel on the inside—very much like bamboo shoots, which are indeed stronger than steel.

Humility enhances happiness and contentment. Humble people have fewer mental-health issues. They are better at forgiveness, both of the self and of others.[1030] Humility is also associated with lower anxiety. In a series of studies, researchers found that humble people are more moral even when feeling vulnerable, whereas people low in humility become much more fearful than the humble people when reminded of death. Further, when people were reminded of humility, they maintained self-control even when reminded of mortality.[1031] Humility balances pride in accomplishment, fostering feelings of privilege and gratitude for our ability to serve others.[1023]

In a study assessing the effect of negative church interactions on depressed mood scores, researchers found that humble people had much less negative impact than the less humble.[1032]

Humility helps decrease fear. The dominating and the dominated both live in fear. Joy and fulfillment come from feeling equal and helping others feel equal—the hallmark of humility.

Humility improves health and healthcare. Humility is particularly important in health care, where it is defined as a combination of self-awareness, kind openness to others, and awareness and gratitude for the privilege of caring for sick individuals.[1023] **Research shows that humble health-care providers have better communication with patients and that provider humility might even improve patient outcomes.**[1033]

And if all that were not enough, humility may also help improve physical health, or at least the perception of it. In research, humble people rate their health more favorably.[1034]

The converse of humility, hubris, is dangerous; not recognizing our limits of knowledge and experience can hurt others.[1035] Professionals who lack humility confuse their theories for facts. They don't take help in time, and they undervalue peer review and colleagues' opinions. This attitude causes Wall Street collapses and sinks *Titanic*s.[1035]

―⁂―

Like every other principle discussed here, humility can be cultivated. We all can learn to be a little more humble. Let's see how.

68

How to Be Humble

Some people are born humble. Perhaps they had the right genes, grew up feeling secure about themselves, and found good role models early in life. But most of us struggle with self-worth and thus with humility. **We need to intentionally create the humility habit, since research shows that we don't automatically get humble as we get older.**[1032]

You can train yourself to be humble.

The primary ingredient for humility is a firm conviction that you are loved and accepted for who you are. We search for this love and validation in several domains: from relatives, friends, colleagues, neighbors, and even strangers. Some of us who miss this validation live a vulnerable life. We become hypersensitive to any insult and overreact to the slightest perception of feeling neglected. Overreaction could mean a temper tantrum or much worse.

We sometimes mistakenly expect that the positives will flow from every quarter. We stop noticing all the different sources of love and inordinately focus on that pesky neighbor, colleague or relative who we believe doesn't like us. This is an exercise in futility. Some streams will invariably be dry. Best to pay less attention to the dry streams and instead attend to the sources that are still flowing. If we don't do that, then we will make ourselves and those around us miserable and disappoint those sending their love and appreciation, pushing us into a downward spiral.

Beyond welcoming and receiving the positivity that is already coming our way, we can enhance positivity yet preserve humility in four specific ways captured in these words: truth, openness, habit, and culture.

TRUTH

Truth is sacred. At the core of most spiritual, scientific, and philosophical quests is the pursuit of truth. **When you are willing to look at truth in its eyes and accept it as is, you vanquish fear. A hallmark of humility is seeking the truth.**

Being able to see the truth helps you see your strengths and weaknesses without your biases. You welcome critique and start seeing your critics as your supporters.

Fear not the disturbing truth. Fear the comforting fabrication.

Another level of truth is looking at the purpose of life and the meaning of our existence on this planet. The recognition that we are vulnerable because we intimately depend on nature, started our lives as vulnerable single cells, and will eventually be a vulnerable elder makes us humble. The humble see our planet as just a blue dot, a speck of dust in the vast expanse of the universe; the arrogant are haughty about the little they own.

OPENNESS

Welcoming new and contradictory ideas, ideas that differ from your beliefs or preferences, is a hallmark of humility. Humble people consider themselves to be enrolled in this giant school called life. Their education will continue throughout their lifetimes. Hence, they are open to critique.

When you are humble, you allow others to help you.[1034] You don't have to be the one who has figured it all out. You are comfortable asking for directions. There are many real-life stories in which people hesitated to ask and made a wrong turn that doomed them and their families. **You'll become strong if you aren't afraid to be vulnerable.**

The fear of vulnerability weakens us more than the vulnerability itself.

HABITS

Habits drive most of our days. Nurturing a healthy habit entails trying something new and different, and it needs repetition to create new brain pathways. Try one or more of these to develop the humility habit:

- When you look at others, do not compare yourself to them. Consider everyone to be equal—equally attractive and equally precious.
- Be extra humble toward someone you know struggles with self-worth.
- Help those who work for or under you, feel worthy.
- Hold the elevator door for everyone.
- Include the needs of others, particularly when it comes to minor preferences.
- Be generous in giving credit.

- Share your achievements and connections gingerly.
- Do not name-drop.
- Be truly happy for others' happiness.
- Think and speak with gratitude—for people, luck, and what you consider sacred.
- If you can't decipher an acronym, ask.
- Avoid a sense of entitlement.
- See yourself as a thread in the web, not as the entire web.
- Think about the role models who embody humility. Read about their lives.
- Remember that everything you have is only temporarily leased to you, for a time shorter than you think.

Try and convert your values into habits.

It is particularly important, and difficult, to remain humble in success. **In our default state, success goes to the head while failure goes to the heart. Choose otherwise. Send success to the heart so you are kinder, and send failure to the head so you are wiser.**

Send success to the heart (so you are kinder) and failure to the head (so you are wiser).

CULTURE

Culture is the sum total of social behaviors and norms in a society. Humans have countless cultural units, which range from a family to a religion, country, or continent. Many practices within a culture have historical antecedents, often constraints, that are long forgotten. Why a particular group is vegetarian or shuns beef may have as much to do with spiritual beliefs as it does with the constraints of a time when that practice started. Often the practice passes from one generation to another, and if it gets mixed with religious tradition, disobeying it engenders fear or wrath. That practice is then difficult to shed, even if it's inconvenient or marginally harmful.

Practicing medicine in India, where the rural population, in particular, reveres cows as mothers, I witnessed a common practice of anointing cow dung on the umbilical cord of a newborn. It was considered auspicious and a blessing, and people didn't realize that the practice was causing tetanus. Even now it has not been completely eliminated.

Cultural hubris is easy if we consider the wealthier and more technologically advanced societies to have superior culture. Also, when the other group has completely different attire, eating practices, greetings, and festivals, we can't help but focus on differences. If we don't prioritize humility, then cultural insensitivity leads to bias, avoidance, and ignorance, often resulting in micro-aggressions, which are reported by over 80 percent of racially diverse groups.[1036]

Almost every person feels discriminated these days.

An acquaintance of mine visited India and went to see a shrine. Tens of thousands of people were jostling through crowded stairs for a brief glimpse of the altar. Some had traveled thousands of miles and saved money for several years to take the blessing back to their loved ones—perhaps to a sick child or grandchild. My acquaintance, who is of Indian origin but raised abroad, is now acculturated differently. He saw lack of dignity. He saw poverty and filth. He completely missed the devotees' constraints, love, patience, grit, and piety. Cultural humility can serve us well in avoiding such premature judgments in this increasingly diverse world.

Cultural humility is openness to cultural diversity. It is not only openness but also the expectation of diversity with total understanding and welcoming of such diversity, for one vegetable alone can't make a delicious soup. In an increasingly diverse world, cultural variety expresses itself in many ways, including ethnicity, race, sexual orientation, social status, and professional roles.[1037] We all are different in at least one domain, making the need for cultural humility universal.[1038]

The outcome of cultural humility is mutual respect, learning, partnership, empowerment, and better service. Hospitals with greater cultural humility are considered safer.[1039] I don't know which comes first, humility or quality; nevertheless, research shows that better-performing health-care systems and hospitals are perceived to be humble.[1026]

I wish to remind you of the beautiful Italian proverb I mentioned earlier: "Once the game is over, the king and the pawn go back in the same box." It makes me humble to realize that we all started in this world as few helpless pounds and will all end up immobile and silent. It gives a sense of equality.

That we are all equal is an important realization. Brains can't do what hearts can; hearts can't do what livers can. We are created by collaboration. The same is true for our society. Each member is precious. This awareness takes away from thinking that, compared to others, you have an outsized effect on the world. With equanimity so obtained, the drama becomes less dramatic and more enjoyable.

Collaboration assumes we have different backgrounds and skills. Differences are thus useful.

As you find greater humility through truth, openness, habits, and culture, you'll need one more ingredient: courage. Humility needs courage because the default mind thinks humility will cause vulnerability. I will talk about courage in chapter 78.

HUMBLE THOUGHTS, WORDS AND ACTIONS

Start with humble thoughts. Remember that everything that is yours you have received. Serve all, including those you find different. We have two employers: one who gives the paychecks and second, the people we serve. Consider the customers you serve to be your primary employer. I consider all the world's children as my primary employer.

Be convinced that most of what we achieve and receive is because of sharing. Let your humble thoughts progress to humble words. Use words that help others feel worthy and validated. Gradually, your thoughts and words will transform into actions. Simple actions, such as holding the door for a little longer than you would have done otherwise, give extra pleasure. **Humble actions can be surprisingly pleasing and relationship enhancing.** In a research study, nurses who washed patients' feet felt more connected to them.[1040]

Despite humility, pride will not completely disappear, however. Instead, you'll be humble with occasional moments of pride rather than proud with occasional moments of humility.

With humility, you'll be more secure in love, have better self-control and greater focus on others, and be more grateful, generous, fair, patient, and in awe of the magnificence of creation. You'll recognize that you are because others are, not the other way around.

Humility will decrease your emotional vulnerability. You'll be less likely to get hurt. And if you are hurt, you'll have easier access to forgiveness, our final topic in tenet five. I started talking about forgiveness, particularly the science of it, in the first tenet. Please revisit that information if you wish. Here I will focus on the art of forgiveness.

69

Forgiveness

Even on a day with no dust and no sweat, your clothes get dirty and need a wash. Similarly, **even if you are surrounded by the kindest and most well-meaning people, you'll get hurt**. About two-thirds of us feel discriminated against every day.[1041] More than 90 percent of some demographic groups feels they are discriminated. The emotional hit-and-run—in homes, offices, and neighborhoods—is more common than the physical hit-and-run. We pick up the dirt of unmet expectations, forgotten promises, or, if we are unlucky, purposeful slurs. Our minds need a wash every day so we remain fresh and clean to experience life and share our compassion. The soap in that wash is forgiveness.

Forgiveness clears and cleans your mind and life.

WHAT IS FORGIVENESS?

Forgiveness isn't justifying, condoning, excusing, denying, or enabling. Forgiveness doesn't make you vulnerable or weak. **Forgiveness is intentionally letting go of the desire for retribution despite knowing you were hurt.** Forgiveness could go to the undeserving. **By forgiving, you are helping yourself more than anyone else. Forgiveness is taking the power from the other person and choosing your mindset based on your values. Forgiveness frees you from the trap of negativity built by others that can constrict you for a lifetime.**

Forgiveness often goes to the undeserving.

Forgiveness doesn't exclude the fair meting out of justice. Forgiveness is meant to empower you by freeing your mind from the toxic vitriol of others' indiscretions. These four insights are the key ingredients to succeeding with forgiveness:

- Find the other person more forgivable.
- Rise in your own eyes.

- Find forgiveness meaningful.
- Develop a systematic forgiveness practice.

Let's explore each of these ideas.

FORGIVABLE

You can use several different perspectives and ideas to find the other person more forgivable.

Preemption

The moon seen unaided looks gorgeous, particularly on a full-moon night. Pick a pair of good binoculars, and you start seeing pockmarks. You may have experienced this when seeing your reflection with magnifying mirrors. Whenever I look into one of those lighted mirrors they keep in hotels, a multitude of scars, lines, wrinkles, and unwelcome spots appear on my face. The same thing happens when you get closer to people. **When you get to know people more, you will invariably find blemishes and imperfections you never noticed earlier.** Haven't you noticed that the moment a seemingly almost-perfect person runs for an important government office, investigative reporters suddenly find a lot of skeletons in the closet?

Preemptively accept this reality for the important people in your life. The more you know them, the more you'll know about their imperfections. **The good fades, and the not so good stares you in the face.** It might be easier to forgive if you expect this before it happens and thus keep your expectations in check.

Expectations

One day when I took my daughter, who was four at the time, into my lap and we came face to face, she said, "Daddy, your teeth look yellow!" All I could do was laugh. Thankfully, this wasn't in public. We call her little Yogi Berra. She speaks her mind, in innocence. Her feedback has helped all of us grow. At her age, we don't expect her to be refined in every word she says. With low expectations, the desire for retribution is not even an option. The more you lower intentionality, the greater your ability to forgive.[1042] The bitter rind of orange hides the sweet core. The same is true for some people. **Look past people's bitterness to access their sweetness.**

Too many times I have made the mistake of keeping lofty expectations of friends, colleagues, and loved ones. I get anchored in my expectations, and when they aren't met, I get hurt in the process. Lately, I have found a practical solution. When people don't live up to my expectations, I don't remove them from my heart. I just move them to a different chamber—from the chamber committed to loved ones and close friends to the one in which I keep acquaintances and associates. That way I have been able to preserve many relationships, have kept my expectations reasonable, and have avoided getting hurt.

One of the easiest ways to lower your stress is to lower your expectations of others.

Individual Nature

All dogs aren't created equal. You can't expect a Rottweiler or German shepherd to look or behave like a poodle or Maltese. Each breed has its own predispositions. Some are aggressive and others docile. It is the same with people.

We all have strengths and weaknesses in our personalities. **Many weaknesses are exaggerated strengths.**

With a changed context, our weakness can become our strength, and our strength can become our weakness.

The thoughtful can be labeled lazy, the flexible called noncommittal, the passionate considered to be anxious, and the courageous thought of as reckless. With just a change in words, you can change how you look at others.

Genes

About 50 percent of a person's personality, patience, resilience, and wellness is driven by genes. Given the same stressors, people with a short 5HTTPLR genotype are much more likely to develop posttraumatic stress disorder than are people with a long genotype. A bunch of genes interact with each other, our environment, the way we are raised, and the people we hang out with, and these collectively affect our mindset.

People don't get to pick their genes. Just as we don't judge those with high cholesterol or rheumatoid arthritis, perhaps we shouldn't judge those who get easily nervous or stressed. A more adaptive feeling will be compassion.

Our genes influence 50 percent of our personality that none of us get to choose.

Vulnerable Self

Fear is a powerful emotion. We fear so we can protect our physical as well as emotional bodies. We spend more time during the day protecting our emotional bodies than our physical bodies. In the throes of fear, we sometimes lose rationality. In our efforts to protect ourselves, we hurt others, sometimes unknowingly. **It will help if we can see a hurt hurled at us as someone's effort at self-protection.**

Blind to Blind Spots

Our visual field has a blind spot in each eye. The brain somehow fills the void so we don't see an empty space. As a result, we don't see our blind spots and aren't even aware of them—in essence, we are blind to our blind spots. Similarly, we are blind to many of our biases because we swim in them.

We are blind to our blind spots.

When told that we are biased, we either deny our biases, justify them with far-fetched explanations, or get angry with the accuser. Could I be biased when I am thinking of someone being careless at work? Could I be biased about a certain race, city, state, or even country? If you give these questions a deep thought, sometimes the answers might surprise you.

The more biased we are, the less likely we are to forgive. **Giving the benefit of doubt to others is giving the gift of happiness to yourself.**

Living with the Neural Traps

In the first tenet, I shared our thirteen neural traps. These traps are a part of our design. They support and strengthen each other. Together, they create an extremely strong maze; it is nearly impossible for anyone stuck inside these traps to realize their power. Most people aren't even aware of their neural traps. Unless we intentionally choose to overcome these traps, however, we are predisposed to aggression, cheating, overeating, envy, irrationality, and so much more. That was the state of the world in Uncle Ad's times which Buddha inherited. Fortunately, we now understand ourselves much better, information that is paving the way toward freedom.

Many people endure three strikes.[836] (I discussed this in chapter 56.) The first two are vulnerable genetic endowment and childhood adversities. If, in adulthood, to these two is added a third strike, such as rejection, aggression, failure, or loss, and the person explodes, you might see only the final strike and find the reaction disproportionate. But the iceberg is mostly hidden. It is important to realize that the final factor is preceded by a long story that we might never know. If we knew the full story, forgiveness would be much easier. In the current state, it might be ideal and fair to assume that there is a story that will unravel only with time or that may never unravel.

What Is Important?

The more we value our relationships with the people who hurt us, the easier it is to forgive them.[1043] Forgiveness is easier if the future exploitation risk is low.[1044] One of my loved ones has the perfect personality for getting on anyone's nerves: nosy, rigid, self-focused, judgmental, inconsiderate, demanding, and borderline narcissistic. Spending days with him used to be pure torture. But this is a relationship I can't get out of. One day I asked myself this question: "Let's say I was in severe pain. Would he be happy that I was hurting or want my pain to be relieved as soon as possible?" The answer I got was that without a doubt he would want me to be pain free as soon as possible. That was it. I took a vow to focus on the fact that deep down this person cares for me, because that is more important than his annoying personality traits. I also later realized that he struggled with low self-esteem and multiple insecurities growing up. My anger and frustration have converted to compassion.

The above perspectives have helped me realize this fact: **those closest to us often need our greatest love right when they deserve it the least.** Assume that when they test your patience, they are helping you rise.

The people testing your resilience are giving you a spiritual stress test. They are helping you grow.

RISE

We aren't physical beings having a physical experience; we are spiritual beings having a spiritual experience. The day we all realize this will be the day that forgiveness will become our second nature.

Rise in Your Eyes

When you wake up in the morning and look at your reflection, see kindness in your eyes. The way nature chiseled your nose and lips is less important; more important are the smile, the benevolence, and the blessings your face shares with the world. **When you increase the good in your life, in thoughts, words, and actions, the not so good will naturally fade.**

Increasing the good is easier than decreasing the bad. When you crowd your mind and life with the good, the bad will slowly fade away.

Start your day today convinced that you are a phenomenal person. A bad thought, word, or action is unbecoming of you. The day when we all wake up with this conviction will be the day we will have overcome our neural traps.

Why Am I Here?

Am I here to become the wealthiest person in my city? Am I here to transmit my genes? Am I here to experience every earthly pleasure there is until I am satisfied? Or am I here to help create a world in which every child feels loved? Am I here to learn how to be universally compassionate? Am I here to master the art of forgiveness?

Those with the first three pursuits will leave damage and pain behind and live an unfulfilled life. Even in sacred professions like health care they might act with greed and try to profit by increasing the cost of an essential medicine overnight by 4000 percent. They might abuse the innocent believers who see them as a conduit to God.

The latter three beliefs will help you access the highest possible meaning and live a truly fulfilling life. As a cook, you will be like Brother Lawrence and as a janitor like Adrian (I talked about him in chapter 33).

One of the reasons we all are here is to find happiness through sharing it.

🕊

Who Are My Role Models?

On a foggy day in a new neighborhood, you need GPS to travel safely and arrive on time. Every day in life feels foggy to me. I have a general idea but am not clear on the precise path I should take. Role models help a lot.

People who remain anchored to their values despite extraordinary challenges, the selfless among us, the forgiving, the compassionate, the patriotic, the visionary—I need all of them to fill me with energy. You can find these role models in your family, neighborhood, and workplace. Perhaps your mother or grandmother handled an abusive situation with grace; perhaps your father or grandfather survived the Great Depression; perhaps your sibling fought and vanquished a serious illness, all the while smiling.

Just as a honeybee makes her nectar from many flowers, collect your wisdom from many role models.

🕊

Thinking about our role models helps us rise above ourselves and find the will and energy to forgive. The role models around you will have one or more of the following three characteristics:

1. Other-centric— Their minds are preoccupied with thoughts of how they can be of help to others. Their desire and effort to help others energizes every aspect of their lives.
2. Good stories—They have good stories to tell you about the people who inspire them. They absorb the goodness in the world around them, and when faced with a selfish, cruel person, they use that person as an example of how not to live.
3. Belief—They believe in a truth or power higher than themselves, and this truth fills them with hope and love.

What Will I Regret When I Turn Eighty?

Perhaps the best father-son picture I have seen is of my friend Brian and his elderly father playing golf together. The details are hazy. Twenty-five years earlier, they had a falling-out and stopped talking to each other, although they lived in the same town. Both felt angry and justified. Brian moved out of the house, built a successful career, got married, and had two kids, who as teenagers had never seen their grandpa. I spent considerable time with Brian sharing some of the perspectives I have outlined here, and he softened. Slowly, his father also softened, and finally they decided to meet. When they got together, a few minutes of tears filled up all the remaining cracks. Brian will not have to regret at age eighty that his father left the world harboring anger and animosity toward him.

Ask yourself what will you regret when you are eighty: Apologies given or never asked for? Love shared or love withheld? Help offered or never considered? Mistakes forgiven or revenge nurtured? **When you look forward in life with the art of looking back, kindness becomes easier.**

Thinking of what you might regret will help you act so you don't regret it.

What Will I Be Proud of?

Whom do you hold in higher regard: Hitler or Mother Teresa? Senior executives of Enron or the staff of Doctors Without Borders? Greedy bankers who caused the subprime crisis or altruistic philanthropists? In general, while we may be in awe of the wealthy and the successful, we are truly proud of the kind, the humble, and the selfless.

Forgiveness today may seem like a steep mountain to climb, but once you climb it and reach the other side, you will truly be proud of your sweat and grit. Think of the long-term meaning, not the short-term effort or discomfort.

MEANING IN FORGIVENESS

Two different meanings can help your forgiveness: the effect of forgiveness on relationships and on health and well-being. Further, rethinking hurts as unanticipated opportunities for growth, can also build the case for forgiveness.

Preserving Relationships

One of my cousins is an extreme penny-pincher, another relative has mastered the art of forgetting, a professor deliberately falsified my grades, and someone we believed was a well-wisher and friend tried to bad-mouth my family in the community. Even though we have decreased the dose of these people in our lives, we haven't broken our relationships with any one of them. It would have been easy to fight them and throw them out of our lives. A better approach, though, is to see each person in totality. My penny-pinching cousin is a very caring person, my forgetful relative has always been there in moments of need, the professor who spoiled my grades challenged me to work harder, and the friend who bad-mouthed us was acting on inner insecurities and misconceptions. Our ability to forgive has preserved our relationships.

No one is perfect. You'll have to forgive almost every one at some point.

If you find a part of a person annoying, but the rest of him or her seems acceptable, then try to focus on the rest of that person. Give forgiveness a chance, particularly for people with whom you will have future interactions.[578] If you answer yes to the question, "Is the relationship worth preserving?" then prioritize forgiveness. Otherwise you risk rejecting the vast majority of people who come into your life, since we all have several annoying imperfections.

Can Forgiveness Help Health and Well-Being?

Poison ivy hurts less from its toxin and more from the body's immune reaction to the toxin. Many of our injuries may have started externally but are perpetuated internally. **Every single research study I have evaluated on forgiveness attests to the health benefits of forgiveness.** In young adults, forgiveness predicts better mental and physical health and protects against the damaging effect of stress.[588] Similar results have been found in workers.[586] In workplaces, lack of forgiveness is related to lower productivity.[586]

In a synthesis of several forgiveness studies, forgiveness has been found to have a positive effect on stress, anger, hostility, and depression.[1045] In adolescents who are victims of bullying, a lack of forgiveness is associated with worse mental-health outcomes.[1046] Much of the benefit from forgiveness is likely related to improved relationships and reduced stress.[584] Forgiveness has even been found to enhance longevity.[1047]

Forgiveness has been proposed as a valid therapeutic intervention for a number of chronic medical conditions.[1048] Interestingly, forgiveness of self has been found to have the strongest effect on physical health, followed by forgiveness of others.[1049] **Overall, forgiveness has so many benefits that if it were a pill, we would be taking it three times a day and would not even mind a copay.**

> *I wish a pharmacist could dispense "Rx Forgiveness" for all*
> *of us, three times a day, with refills for life!*

With all these health benefits, consider asking yourself this question: "Is harboring hurt worth the damage it is causing?" If the action is unforgivable or the likelihood of significant future damage is high in a relationship or situation, then do not forgive. But if the likelihood is low, give forgiveness a chance. Simply enter the cost of harboring hurts in the equation and then decide what makes the most sense.

Has My Pain Helped Me?

In a new city, you can travel four different ways: take a cab or public transport, drive yourself using GPS, drive without GPS, or walk. Most of us prefer the first or the second option. As a result, we barely learn the directions, similar to bus drivers in London, whose posterior hippocampus (that helps them remember directions) was found to be smaller than that of taxi drivers.[1050, 1051]

I have found that I learn the best when I ask for directions, mark them on the map and then either drive without GPS or walk. I have to make mistakes, lose my way, and find myself again to really know a place. The same is true in life. Although we may desire to learn life's lessons without losing or experiencing pain, that is well-nigh impossible. **The intention and deeper attention needed to learn best happens when we are faced with difficulty.**

There are two ways our bodies develop immunity to a virus: either by infection or by immunization. If what hurt you didn't break you, consider it a flu shot. It was painful and perhaps caused fever, but it has helped you develop the requisite immunity so you don't get the full-blown flu. **Everyone who has hurt you taught you a lesson about pain so that you could become more compassionate. Material and emotional adversities often bring spiritual gain.**

And then there are situations in which someone's mistake or even intentional harm turns out to be beneficial. A nepotistic leader, a biased manager, a disengaged worker, an incompetent assistant, an envious loved one, an unpredictable friend, a rude neighbor—all of these evoke anger. But consider the possibility that they may have helped you in ways you aren't aware of. I have endured all of the personalities just mentioned at some point in my life, and they have all helped me in ways I couldn't have predicted. Nepotistic, biased, disengaged, and incompetent people pushed me away from the status quo into pursuing newer challenges; envious, unpredictable, and rude people helped me seek newer relationships. Today I truly feel grateful for all the mean people in my life. **Gratitude washes away anger.**

> *Emotional pains can sometimes help us grow. Forgiving those who caused emotional pain will always help us grow.*

I wish I could carry this wisdom from the past for the current and the future mean people in my life. Most likely, I will forget, get upset, and get hurt, but one thing I am sure of is that I will recover faster than I did ten years ago. The principles of mindfulness *v2* provide me the GPS to recover quickly after I take a wrong exit.

I wish to keep upping my offense threshold so compassion replaces the space that was earlier occupied by anger.

THE PROCESS

The process of forgiveness has three steps: make a commitment, take action, and implement a maintenance plan.

Make a Commitment

At the end of my workshops for stress, resilience, or mindfulness, I often ask for commitment—a positive intention to effect a change. We often drill down to the specifics, such as the name of the first person you will send silent gratitude to first thing in the morning.[1052, 1053]

There is some science to commitment. For example, written commitments are better than verbal ones, and a commitment made in a group is better than one made alone.[1054] Publicizing the commitment makes it even stronger. Letting the community know that someone would increase recycling by having his name published in the newspaper increased recycling by 40 percent.[1055] Commitments work best when they are not coerced and are for a behavior the individual values.

Making a commitment helps in two ways: it changes your view of the self and leverages the desire to be seen as good and consistent. Further, **major shifts start with a small commitment.** If you decide to feel grateful for the first five minutes after you wake up, it will slowly start changing your entire morning. If your bumper sticker says, "Be kind," it will have a subtle influence on you while driving.

Commit to doing something good, however small, every day. It will be the start of a transformation.

So, commit to forgiveness. Write a note to yourself. Let someone you can confide in know about your intention to forgive. If socially committing to forgiveness feels awkward, make a more general promise, like I will act with kindness or will focus on the good.

Take Action

The specifics of what you do to forgive will depend on many details of the situation. If you think that formally conveying your forgiveness to someone will bring disdain from him or her or will make you look weak and vulnerable, then it might be best to remain quiet. Formal expression is best applied for a very obvious, proven hurt. In situations in which the slights are subtle and emotional, let your forgiveness be subtle. Reveal your forgiveness by welcoming the other person's kind gesture, accepting invitations, sending invitations, smiling more openly, talking with greater energy, talking less formally, and reminiscing about previous good times.

Remember that forgiving doesn't mean you have to agree with the other person. Also, **assume that most people don't change easily**. Instead, you change your expectation, recognizing that we are all different.

Actions that can help forgiveness include journaling, meditating, and writing an e-mail that expresses your frustration and decision to forgive and then deleting it (make sure you don't put the address in the e-mail in case you accidently press the Send button).

In a research study, a three-minute prayer for one's partner increased forgiveness, compared to focusing on his or her physical features.[1056] **Prayer for your partner has also been shown to increase relationship fidelity, compared with just thinking positive thoughts about him or her.**[715]

Prayer for your partner improves relationship fidelity.

Seeking out stories that inspire you to forgive is another form of action. These could be stories of forgiveness, or they could be stories of vulnerable people beating all odds to make the world a better place. To get out of my ordinary thinking, I just have to go to the pediatric floor of any hospital. It makes me feel small when I realize I am wasting precious time stuck in some minor slur when I could be using that time to do something tangible—work harder, pray, write—to help the children. **With a more mature perspective, the specifics of life don't change, but the life force gets redirected toward pursuing meaning rather than fighting hurts.**

A useful strategy is to allow yourself to be happier. Research shows that **your level of happiness correlates with your ability to forgive.**[1057] Happiness also correlates with success at work, better physical health, and longevity—each of which can put your life on an upward trajectory.[706, 1058, 1059]

The happier you are, the easier it is for you to forgive.

Do not try to forgive when you are grumpy and hungry. Spend some time shopping at your favorite mall, get a massage, take a hot shower, and then, while savoring a bowl of ice cream, think about how to handle your hurt. You'll be much more likely to forgive.

If you are the person needing someone else's forgiveness, remember that seeking an apology and doing something tangible show that you really mean what you're saying. Being fair, just, and considerate, helps with forgiveness.[1060]

Implement a Maintenance Plan

While physical injuries may heal with or without blemishes, emotional injuries always leave a scar. Some scars stay quiet all one's life, while others inflame every so often. Emotional scars inflame because of our wonderful memory, imagination ability, and tendency to catastrophize. We don't willfully choose to inflame our old wounds; inflammation happens because of our neural traps. Every time those scars become painful, or worse, reopen, we have to heal ourselves again. Fortunately, you can do a lot to prevent that from happening.

Forgive in gratitude for the many times you have been forgiven; forgive in honor of those who were hurt worse than you yet still chose to forgive. Forgiveness will be easier if you focus on gratitude for what is right, feel compassion for those around you, find ways to accept imperfections, and live your days with higher meaning. Optimizing expectations, remaining aware of many others who have it worse than you do, and frequently thinking of inspiring role models can help.

Prayer is a powerful antidote to pain, and it opens the door to forgiveness. All of the principles just discussed will lower the dose of your rumination, and that helps with forgiveness.[1061]

As you deepen your presence, you recognize that except for the most egregious hurts, forgiveness was never needed. You preemptively forgive.

You know you have arrived at forgiveness when you realize that forgiveness was never needed.

Recognize that, despite all your good intentions and help, forgiveness for the most egregious, irreparable harms will take a lot of time. You will need a lot of support from others, perhaps even a professional. The more severe the pain, the greater the dose of pain medication needed to relieve it. Often, a combination of a few medications.

In the fifth tenet, we talked about compassion and three practices that support it—patience that creates the space for compassion to find home, and humility and forgiveness that preserve your energy for giving out in compassion.

These are cherished jewels for the mind. Gift your compassion to yourself and the world. Compassion is stronger than gravity and electromagnetic or nuclear forces. It is perhaps one of the strongest forces, if not *the* strongest force, in the world. I believe **a core purpose of human life is to develop universal compassion**. To that effect, mindfulness *v2* leaves no doubt. It doesn't decry non-judgmental stance. Instead, it offers a more actionable and delectable alternative—that of compassion. When compassion pervades every corner of your mind, peace no longer is your goal. Peace becomes the path. You practice not just on the mat but all-day long. Noise becomes silence and silence is filled with melody. The formal practice becomes informal, and informal practice becomes as natural as breath.

Part VII
The Sixth Tenet: Practice

Tenet	Mindfulness v1	Mindfulness v2
Practice	Majority of the practice is formal	Majority of the practice is informal

―⁂―

Long-sitting meditation was easier in the past, when minds were slower and people had more time. In modern times, brief sprinkles of meditation in combination with a kind, grateful, and intentional presence all day long may be more practical and useful.

Mindfulness isn't a practice; mindfulness is a way of life.

70

Fireside Chat #7

"Blaming my genes for my impatience and crediting my good habits for my patience, how did you think of that?"

"Why not? The opposite—blaming yourself for impatience and crediting your genes for patience—isn't very uplifting."

"How do you view genes?"

"We come with a buffet of genes. **We get to choose which genes we activate depending on the choices we make. Your genes are important, but they aren't your destiny.** This viewpoint is based on an established field in science called epigenetics—your ability to affect genetic expression without change in gene sequence."

"Can impatience activate impatience genes?"

"Absolutely. Just as your behavior changes your brain's structure, your behavior changes the set of genes that activate and run your life."

"I see the good and bad in it," Mike said.

"How so?"

"The good is that we have control over our genes. The bad is that this could put us in a loop, with impatience turning on the impatience genes that make us more impatient. This looks like a runaway train."

"It is. It applies to many other aspects. That's why the choices you make are so important."

"How do you deal with people you find impatient and full of hubris?"

"I try to remember that acting superior is a reflection of feeling inferior. First I try compassion for people who I find full of themselves. If that doesn't work, I try my best to decrease their dose in my life."

"How easy is it to be compassionate?"

"Easier than being nonjudgmental. Any time you create an empty space, you create vulnerability. If a non-judgmental stance is a step toward compassion, why not go straight to compassion? It is much easier. In my experience of practicing and teaching these ideas, **acceptance is much more difficult than compassion. And a non-judgmental stance is a very close cousin of acceptance**."

"Talking about compassion, you outlined the difference between empathy and compassion. But many times, I can't do anything about the world's suffering. Should I not then be empathetic?"

"Keep the hope and desire that every person finds his or her way back to the fold, but do not carry the weight of everyone's struggle. Lift only the load that your back will allow."

"What is riskier, lifting no load and living a selfish life, or lifting too much and getting paralyzed by the world's suffering?"

"Both are risky and counterproductive. **If you aren't sure, start with self-compassion. With self-compassion, your capacity will increase, but you will not overload yourself.**"

"I found the neuroscience research on compassion fascinating. Is it that simple? If seeing others' pain activates my reward network, then I am probably not being kind."

"Yes, if you enjoy others' pain, then you are being antisocial. An optimally compassionate response will be activation of your own pain network first and then activation of planning and action areas, along with activation of the reward area on imagining the good you can do. You want to end with the reward-area lighting up, with the satisfaction of the good you were able to do."

"Is this in my control, which networks to activate?"

"Yes, ultimately it is. With repeated intentional thoughts and actions, you can program your brain's networks. Your networks then run on autopilot; compassion becomes as natural to you as breath."

"How does it change my days?"

"What?"

"Compassion becoming natural as breath."

"It transforms your days. Your negative judgments are replaced by positive evaluations. The assumption that most people are struggling isn't far from true. The invisible emotional pain of our veterans who come home with posttraumatic stress disorder can be worse than their physical pain. Another invisible pain is that of veteran caregivers who struggle in silence while trying to support their injured partners. If you expand beyond this group and **assume that every adult is a concerned caregiver for someone and silently suffers in the privacy of his or her mind**, then you can expand compassion for all."

"Have you experienced compassion fatigue?"

"I wish I could say no. I have experienced every negative emotion in the book."

"I am curious how pervasive are our emotions. Is there any research on what proportion of the day do we experience an emotion?"

"Research shows for over 90 percent of the day, you are feeling a feeling.[1061a] While you can't shut down emotions, you can choose which emotion you experience. Our untrained brain, however, isn't very good at regulating our emotions.[1061b] Hence the need to take charge."

"What do you mean by "isn't very good at regulating our emotions"?"

"Do you agree that a good strategy for happiness will be to savor positive emotions and discard unhelpful negative emotions."

"I do."

"But our brain does the opposite. It shuts off supplies to the positive emotions, and keeps refueling the negative ones."

"Remind me why do we do that?"

"Because we are designed to prioritize safety. This instinct was helpful when we were busy, constantly protecting our physical body. It still is a good idea if you are caught in a war zone. But using the same tactic to protect our emotional body could keep us in a combat mode all day long. And the person we are fighting is none other than ourselves. We can cause real hurts while trying to evade imaginary hurts."

"Gets back to taking charge, I mean intentionality."

"They are the same, taking charge and intentionality."

"Give me some examples of taking charge."

"Can you take charge and turn your compassion fatigue into inspiration? Can you play with your fear and turn it into courage and fun? Can you turn anger into a desire to understand? Our default design makes our heart accelerate when we see a police car in the rearview mirror, but we can change that. We can choose to not feel vulnerable for the next hundred miles, and we can choose to turn fear into gratitude and compassion."

"Shifting gears, what is your key message as you try to rethink meditation in the next tenet?"

"**Look at meditation and mindfulness as a way of life, not as a practice.**"

"Why is that?"

"Consider physical fitness, for example. When you consider fitness to be a practice, you work out for thirty minutes three times a week and do not think about fitness the rest of the week. But fitness is really about how you are spending the whole day. Avoiding prolonged sitting, maintaining flexibility, keeping good posture, walking as much as you can, keeping track of your numbers—these are all important. Research shows that if you work out for thirty minutes and sit for the rest of the day, you pretty much undo all the benefits of the workout.[1006] The same holds true for diet. I have met plenty of people who eat two-hundred-calorie salad lunches but snack on chips and cookies all day long. Eating healthy is also a way of life. When you consider that your entire day is your meditation practice, it has a very powerful effect on your well-being."

"Any final thoughts?"

"**If we are privileged enough to be grateful, then we have a responsibility to be compassionate. Breathe in the energy of gratitude; breathe out the energy of compassion.**"

Mike takes a deep breath.

71

Rethinking Meditation

I first learned meditation during a summer vacation as a teenager. I had been practicing yoga for some time, so sitting straight and paying attention to the breath was easy. But I needed the greatest effort to stick with the breath for any longer than a few minutes. Despite considerable mind wandering, I remember feeling calm and renewed at the end of the practice. After continuing for a few months, however, the practice faded as homework, hockey, cricket, and soccer took over. I rediscovered meditation as an adult, but the drive has been anything but smooth.

In my long journey of learning, practicing, and now teaching stress-management and resilience skills, I have found that a very small percentage of people who learn meditation can integrate this practice into their daily routines. Most give up. (Recall the experience with His Holiness the Dalai Lama that I mentioned in chapter 11.) Unless a person is deeply committed, one challenge or another gets in the way. Here are the commonest reasons I have heard:

- "Took too much time."
- "Sitting still was difficult."
- "Couldn't quiet my mind."
- "I got anxious."
- "Didn't work."
- "Seems too new age."
- "Doesn't align with my worldview."

I started with full faith in the benefits of meditation, and I am still a believer. But when I saw that even the most committed practitioners gave up after some time, doubts crept in. Something was amiss. After a good deal of thinking and investigating, I realized my folly. **I was approaching meditation as a practice, while meditation is a way of life.** The same holds true for mindfulness, which is a form of meditation. The reason for this shift is obvious.

The brain now leads a very different life than it did in the BC era. The brain these days spends more than ten hours looking at a screen,[1062] checks a smartphone every ten to fifteen minutes, has 150 undone tasks at any time, and has several dozen user IDs. People spend a meager fifteen seconds with a web page.[1063]

An average person makes over two hundred food-related decisions every day,[530] is sleep deprived half the time, feels lonely and discriminated, and hears about terrorism at least once a day. Many people work twelve-hour days with endless interruptions and frequent disagreements. Conflicts are common, job changes are frequent, and 50 percent of marriages end in divorce. How can fifteen minutes of inhaling and exhaling quiet my mind and undo the toxic load my brain carries every single day? (In the Appendix I provide a synthesis of meditation research to further develop this theme.)

Further, we have a tendency to compensate for our virtuosity. On the days I exercise, I feel entitled to eat more—one reason that exercise alone doesn't work very well for weight loss.[1064] Using standing desks at the office increases standing time at work, but we compensate by sitting more at home.[1065] If we confine spiritual practice to a particular hour on a particular day, we feel entitled to slipups the rest of the week as compensation. I am sure you have heard enough examples of the virtuous and the spiritual doing the most repugnant deeds. Some of them have no guilt. Instead, they feel entitled because of perceived virtuosity.

Just as healthy living isn't a practice but a way of life, meditation isn't a practice, but a way of life.

For all these reasons, it will be better to look at meditation not as a practice, but instead, as a way of life.

INFORMAL PRACTICE IS THE REAL DEAL

I was once helping a significantly overweight gentleman lose weight. I suggested he increase his salad intake and decrease calorie-dense food. But perhaps I didn't communicate the message right; he heard only the salad part and not the calorie-dense-food part. Six weeks later, he came back four pounds heavier. When I asked about his diet, he told me that he had added salad (with rich, thick dressing) to everything else he was eating. He needed an overhaul of his diet, not an addition of more stuff to it.

Quite similarly, the real solution to affect our well-being is to change the way we lead our lives, not to add one more thing to them. We need to find more balance, think thoughts that are pious, speak words that are kind, and act in ways that are rational and prosocial.

Recall that the eightfold path of yoga starts with *yamas* and *niyamas*, which are prescriptions for disciplined and ethical living. Buddha's mindfulness also called for the integration of morality, wisdom, and contemplation and greater emphasis on the informal practice.[74] Somewhere in the translation, we flipped the switch and as a culture became obsessed with the formal practice, hoping that sitting quietly for a bit would open the gates to unending bliss.

For meditation to be a transformative force, we have to rethink the paradigm. In mindfulness *v*2, the bulk of the practice is integrated into our lives so that it transforms the way we experience the world.

Even if you practice a formal program for an hour, you still live with your brain for twenty-three more hours every day. **Making even a slight shift in how you think and connect with others all day long can have a phenomenal impact on your life and the lives of others.** Further, emphasizing the formal practice might create a check-box mentality, in which you check the box once the practice is done and miss out on the deeper purpose.

As for formal practice, we have to make sure that at least as the first step, the practices are short, easy to learn, quickly rewarding, relationship centric, non-ritualistic, and aligned with our worldview. It's the little practices that make a lot of difference, given the energy of time. A redwood tree that can grow to be twenty-five stories tall starts as a tiny seed, a hundred thousand of which weigh just one pound. The constancy of effort over time leads to the graceful giant. The same is true for your personal practices. Make small, workable tweaks and stick with them, rather than trying monumental shifts.

Enjoy and share snacks of intentional kindness, many times during the day.

The emphasis on rituals and myths risks dividing us. More important than a ritualistic practice that is entangled in myths is daily kindness. It might be optimal to look at the formal practice as a tool or a technology. Our goal will be to intelligently integrate the formal and informal practices so they support each other. Let's start with redefining meditation.

72

What Is Meditation?

The practice of meditation has three ingredients: **a**ttention, **i**ntentionality, and **m**indset, the **AIM** model. I like to define meditation as "intentional, grateful, and compassionate attention." Let's explore each word in the AIM model.

ATTENTION

Attention is the gateway to the brain. Your every experience of life will depend on your attention. **At its core, meditation is a technique to strengthen attention.**

When you go to a restaurant, you glance at the menu and then order what you want. Your order becomes your plate. To your mind, the menu is the collection of thoughts and sensory experiences that compete for your attention. Attention picks an extremely small portion of the potential thoughts and sensations and makes them your reality.

Your dinner experience is colored by what's on the table, not what's on the menu. Ideally, attention should order the healthiest and most delicious options from the menu. But that's not what the mind does. I can hear my mind saying something like, "May I have a stale thought, please—one that is negative, will make me feel miserable, and will cost me my peace? Even the one I am allergic to will do." My spontaneous thoughts mostly focus on the discrepancy between my current and desired state.[1065a] A small dose of these thoughts is helpful, but a long train leaves me dissatisfied, sometimes depressed and depleted.

I can't leave me to my instincts. Because of my mind wandering, negativity bias, emotional vulnerability, catastrophizing, tendency to compare, failure of thought suppression, hedonic adaptation, deficits in self-regulation, the habit trap, the unforgiving nature, and brain fatigue, a high percentage of my instinctive thoughts are either negative or neutral. They don't nourish me.

Moments of vulnerability and people who make me feel unworthy occupy a disproportionately large area of my brain. My working memory is also crowded with undone tasks. **Each undone task takes up double the space compared to a completed task or one for which you have a plan.**

For this reason, I have been working hard during the last decade to clear space in my brain and train my attention so that I need less effort to be more intentional.

INTENTIONALITY

Every time I walk in the rain with an umbrella, I look at the experience as reflective of my life. So much in our lives is imperfect. We have colleagues, loved ones, neighbors, and friends who rain uncalled-for, unpredictable showers of unkind words on us. Losses and failures rain on us with predictable certainty. If you wish to walk without getting soaked by all this acidic rain, you have to use the umbrella. This umbrella of principles, values, perspectives, connections, and meaning can protect you from getting drenched.

Your umbrella can neither stop the rain nor completely block you from getting wet. But it will protect you from getting totally drenched. The umbrella will free you to stroll in the rain. Intentionality helps you create the protective umbrella.

We can't stop the rain. But we can use the umbrella.

Intentionality helps you exercise the power of choice. Intentionality gifts you more conscious moments when you are fully alive. It engages your neurons so they host thoughts, words, and actions aligned with your values. It means escaping the default animal mode within you and becoming fully human. Without intentionality, we are only little better than other primates. **Intentionality creates culture and civilization.**

Most sports, educational-training, and self-help programs train your intentionality. Authentic meditation trains your intentionality. You deploy your attention based on your choosing. When your attention falters, you become aware of the faltering and refocus. You keep repeating this until the faltering begins to fade, and your attention begins to flow. This decreases your mind wandering. Further, even the wanderings that happen engender lower inner reactivity.[1065b]

Intentionality, however, is a double-edged sword. For the minds mired in the vitriol of hatred, envy, revenge, and anger, intentionality can train the wrong muscles, leading those minds deeper into the abyss. The corrupt minds contribute greater to headline news these days than do the virtuous ones, hence the need to anchor your intentionality in two timeless values: gratitude and compassion.

Strong and intentional attention alone isn't enough. Intentional attention needs the guidance of gratitude and compassion to preserve its strength and serve an altruistic purpose.

GRATITUDE

Needs, preferences, desires, wants, and greed, combined with concerns, worries, angst, fears, and panic—each of these concepts reflects our three basic instincts: to eat, to not get eaten, and to reproduce. Most of the day, these three instincts color our pursuits and direct our attention. Attention mired in these dispositions remains superficial and wandering. Days, weeks, and years spent stuck in our core animalistic instincts make for an average, dissatisfying life. **Wants cannot be satisfied by acquiring more.** The only plug that can stop up the leaky bottle is that of gratitude.

Material wants are insatiable.

Gratitude is being blessed, knowing that you are blessed, and being thankful for it. Gratitude instills a pause in wanting. Instilling a pause isn't easy, because the mind's eyes constantly look forward, living in a state of programmed dissatisfaction. In many situations, this looking forward is understandable. When we're in pain, we want to be pain-free. When we're pain-free, we want to be happy. When happy, joyous. When joyous, blissful. When blissful, ecstatic. We want to secure this reverie far into the future. Our tendency to inflate the negative, discount the good, and forever compare makes this worse.

Gratitude is the perfect antidote. Unfortunately, we haven't evolved a brain network devoted to gratitude. This is because gratitude isn't essential for survival. Sometimes I look at gratitude as a pizza topping. You can eat the pizza without the topping, but it won't be as delicious. Life without gratitude is similar—still livable but not as delicious.

Life without gratitude is livable, but not deeply enjoyable.

An important point to emphasize is that **gratitude isn't comparing ourselves with others and telling ourselves how much better off we are.**[1066] Gratitude is counting our blessings and being thankful for everything we have received, considering it a privilege and a gift.

Like other skills and sports—from brushing teeth to playing an instrument to swimming—gratitude can be learned. Once learned it can be intentionally cultivated. If we spent one-hundredth of the time that we spend on other activities teaching gratitude to our kids instead, the world would be a much happier place, given all the benefits of feeling and expressing gratitude.[1067]

Wouldn't it be nice for our kids to feel grateful (and not entitled) when receiving Christmas gifts or taking a trip to Mount Rushmore? Wouldn't it be nice for us to feel grateful for the simple and ordinary, such as a glass of water or the ability to walk, talk, touch, feel, smell, and think? Each of these is a phenomenal gift that we usually take for granted. **Being grateful doesn't mean you stop striving for growth and excellence. It means you choose to pause and take a breath as you continue on your climb.**

Teaching our children gratitude and compassion is as important as teaching them math and science.

Gratitude comes in five depths. At level one are people who are ungrateful. I don't call them level zero because even with this state of the mind, there is always hope that they will improve. Level-two people wait for something spectacular to happen to feel grateful. Thankful thoughts visit their minds only when they achieve a phenomenal gain or avert a spectacular loss. They visit happiness and contentment but only occasionally.

Level-three people feel grateful for small things. A glass of water, a deep breath, a smile, the smell of coffee, green grass, a juicy apple—make them feel grateful. If you can take a full, deep breath right now, recognize that millions cannot because of pain, heart or lung disease, or pollution. **What is ordinary is actually precious and special.**

At level four are people who are grateful, period. They need nothing to feel grateful. Gratitude for them is as natural as breath. People at this level realize that just as you can't inhale without exhaling or exhale without inhaling, **every act of receiving entails giving, and every act of giving entails receiving**. They don't focus as much on the specifics as on feeling grateful for the privilege of participating in this exchange. They are among the happiest people on our planet. **They swap "have to" with "get to."** They get to do the laundry, get to take out the trash, get to work, get to help the neighbor, get to mow the lawn, and in Rochester, get to shovel the snow!

As we advance in gratitude, we finally reach level five. Folks at this stage are grateful for even adversities and adversaries. They are zoomed out and can see the good in what seems bad.

Being grateful for the good things in life prepares you to be grateful for the ordinary. Being grateful for the ordinary prepares you to be grateful for adversity. If we can learn to find gratitude even in adversity, then we will not fear failure. We will stop feeling lonely.[1068] We will work hard, find success, make a difference, and thrive through this process.

Gratitude for adversity is the perfect antidote for burnout. The true test of a person is whether he or she can remain grateful not just during the rise but also during the fall.

Gratitude for adversaries takes away their power over us. Just as a scrubber is to dishes, our adversaries are to us. They help us get cleaner and shinier.

Gratitude for adversities and adversaries takes
away their power over us and transforms them into becoming our agents of growth.

Gratitude frees your attention from distracting wants. With gratitude, your attention is free to focus on experiences directed by your core values. A perfect way to start a formal meditation practice is to tell yourself, "I am enough; I have enough." Once you are convinced of this, you spend much less time with could haves, should haves, and what-ifs. Neither formal nor informal meditation is possible without a deep anchor in gratitude, because lack of gratitude will keep you in the seeking mode, causing insuppressible mind wanderings.

Here is one way gratitude has transformed my life. Before meeting family, friends and others, I often pause for a few seconds and remind myself why am I grateful to this person. This little reminder has completely changed how I connect with people. I believe **the best way to prepare for a meeting with someone (at work or home) is to remind yourself why you are grateful to that person.**

The best way to prepare meeting someone is to think about why you are grateful to that person.

❦

The practice of gratitude itself is a form of meditation that elevates you from the ordinary struggles of life to intentional bliss, sometimes even amid a loss or failure. Gratitude clears the deluge of desire, providing a clean slate on which you can write thoughts of your will. Further, gratitude plugs the leak in willpower and thus provides dispensable willpower and attention, which you can use for compassion.

COMPASSION

You can look at your hand as four fingers and a thumb or as one single hand. You can look at your physical body as a skin bag filled with heart, lungs, liver, spleen, kidneys, and other organs, or you can look at it as one single body. You can look at the earth as multiple separate land masses or as one single entity. You can look at the human species as seven and a half billion separate units or as one common humanity. **The more you zoom in, the greater the separation you see; the more you zoom out, the greater the unity you see.**

We need both perspectives. Zooming in and seeing separation allows you to see the uniqueness and value of each person. Zooming out and seeing unity allows you to see how we are related and indivisible. Unfortunately, our instincts make us create silos and separations and seldom allow for flexible zooming in and zooming out. Hence, we need compassion.

We spent considerable time with compassion in chapters 62 through 66, so I will share only a few words here. Compassion helps you recognize others' struggles, validate them from within their perspectives, create intention to help, and take action to relieve their suffering. Compassion is the purest form of love. The practice of compassion provides the deepest joy. I believe **a core purpose of human life is to develop universal compassion.**

Developing universal compassion is a core purpose of human life.

❦

Meditation without compassion is an ordinary attention activity. Meditation with compassion converts an ordinary attention practice into a transformative spiritual force.

Compassion can give meaning to your meditation, focusing both your formal and informal practices. I often dedicate my formal meditation practice to the well-being of all the babies who will be born that day.

In my informal practice, I commit to sending silent good wishes to every person I see throughout the day, remembering that every person is infinitely precious and struggling. Thus, formal and informal practices meld and support each other.

Living the day in such a manner imbues kindness in every experience. **That is the purpose of meditation: to make us more compassionate not just on the mat, but throughout the day.**

Notice that in our definition of meditation we didn't talk about sitting on a couch or floor, folding the legs in a certain way, or even focusing on the breath. Each of these can help some practitioners with the formal practice, but they are not essential. The purpose of the formal meditation practice is to prepare us for the informal practice, which is how we experience each of our waking moments.

73

The Informal Practice

Each day you do hundreds of different things at home, at work, and at leisure. The informal practice influences all aspects of your life and your every relationship—with the self, with others, and with the animate and inanimate world that surrounds you. Here are two questions you can ask yourself for the informal practice:

- Is my presence intentional?
- Is my presence healing?

We have discussed intentionality previously. It boils down to two core questions:

- Am I choosing my thoughts, or is thinking happening to me? and
- Am I choosing my sensory experience, or is my experience happening to me?

You can't choose your every thought and experience, but if you can spend even 10 percent more time in control of how your brain deploys your attention, it will have a phenomenal impact on your creativity, your productivity, your well-being, and the amount of goodness you spread in the world.

During the time that your presence is intentional, the key question to ask is this: Is my presence healing at this moment?

HEALING PRESENCE

I am sure you have experienced that different people carry very different energy. Some carry nervous, fidgety energy, others calm and assured energy. A few, unfortunately, are toxic. Some people drain energy out of you, while others fill you with vitality. Just as an electrically charged particle creates and carries a magnetic field around it, we create and carry energy fields around us. Ask yourself at this moment, "How is my presence right now?" The four major categories are seeking, avoiding, hurting, or healing.

Seeking

When seeking, we are hungry for a thing or an experience. It could be coffee, food, sleep, intimacy, money, recognition, spending, or something else. For a large part of the day, we are seeking one thing or another.[1069]

Avoiding

When avoiding, we are trying to push away a thing or an experience. It could be a loss, a challenge, a person, a fear, or something else.

Hurting

When hurting, we are nursing pain, particularly emotional pain. Emotional pain originates from a feeling of unworthiness, a loss, a regret, an angst, or a mismatched expectation. Such pain often gives birth to feelings of hatred, envy, revenge, and anger.

A large part of the day we are either seeking something, avoiding something, or nursing a hurt.

Healing

With a healing presence, you emanate kindness. **You silently wish others well, you remind people how good they are, you inspire others to be their best selves, and you win them over with love and good humor.** Your healing presence touches not only the people who are kind to you or those you can benefit from but everyone, eventually even those who may not mean well to you. Healing presence can be in words, actions, or silence.

Cultivating and maintaining a consistent healing presence is hard work. With such a presence, you are predictably patient, humble, gentle, flexible, simple, dependable, selfless, forgiving, and difficult to offend. Your compassion crosses the boundaries of your family, neighborhood, ethnic group, city, and country. You care for everyone, all life-forms, even the inanimate. You live in harmony with the world around you.

How many people do you know who always embody such presence? Perhaps you can count them on your fingers. I know several people who claim to spend an hour or more a day in a formal mind-body practice yet are unkind to animals, self-centered, unethical, and even immoral. I have little respect for them. Then again, I have known or heard of several people who never had a formal mind-body practice but who are truly the salt of the earth.

Embodying healing presence day after day is a truly worthy goal. I fully believe that one day we all will embody such presence. Mindfulness *v2* strives to take humanity to that place faster than the forces that are planting the seeds of self-destruction. That will entail changing how we think each thought. This transformation of our inner being is the real calling of meditation. **The purpose of meditation is to be meditative when you are not meditating.**

If you feel you are still a work in progress in terms of embodying a consistent healing presence (which we all are), then look at the next chapter for a few ideas to discover and groom the healer in you.

74

Cultivating Healing Presence

A multitude of perspectives can help you cultivate a healing presence. Here are a few ideas. I am sure you have heard many of these earlier in the book. Hence, I will be brief in their descriptions. You don't have to pick them all, just the ones that make the most sense to you.

Embrace Transience
How many gelatos will you get to eat? How many Thanksgivings will you get to celebrate? How many times will you get to visit your mother? Each moment is unique and precious. **Live your day assuming it's all you have.**

Everything Is a Miracle
Sunrise, hibiscus, dung beetles, even weeds—they are all miracles in the universe. **Notice all the little miracles that surround you.**

The ordinary is miraculous.

Nurture Humility
The elements in the human body are worth only a few dollars. **We all are materially inconsequential yet spiritually priceless.** This realization will help you be humble.

Treat Every Person Equally
The dominating and the dominated both feel vulnerable. We all will have the same final net worth: zero. Honor every person, every life-form. **The greatest power and joy is in feeling equal to others, neither better nor worse.**

Visit Gratitude Often
I have seldom met people who disagree with gratitude. I have also seldom met people who are anchored in gratitude. We all need a reminder to visit gratitude often. Surround yourself with such reminders. **Remind yourself why you are grateful to a person before meeting him or her.**

Re-contextualize

Know that **in almost every good there is bad and that in almost every bad there is good**. Every action, good or bad, has opposite, unintended consequences. Realizing this will soften your attachment to a particular outcome.

> *Finding the good in the bad will keep you cheerful. Finding the not-so-good in the good will keep you composed.*

Value Differences

Don't just tolerate others who are different; truly accept them and find meaning in the differences. If we didn't have differences, we wouldn't have rainbows, soups, and such rich and varied cuisines, cultures, clothes, and fascinating tourist destinations.

Be Patient

People who are serving you—for example, airline agents, telephone operators, grocery clerks, and cab drivers—are all working under phenomenal constraints and have significant struggles. Most likely, they are also carrying family stressors. Do not expect them to work with the speed of an internet search engine. Give them the gift of patience.

Be Flexible

Be a team player. Be flexible about your preferences. Do not impose your desires on others. Flow with life.

Think of Others

The seat assigned to you today was someone else's yesterday and will be someone else's tomorrow. Just as you liked it clean, the next person will like it clean too. Treat the world as honeybees treat the flower. They take the nectar and pollen but leave the flower otherwise undisturbed.

> *Treat rental cars as if you own them.*

Appreciate Humor

Laugh and let laugh. Laugh at yourself. **If you don't laugh at yourself, someone else will.** Elevate the threshold at which you get offended. Recognize that humor is more about connecting socially than about being funny.

Be Dependable

Keep your word. **Let people associate you with quality and dependability.**

Sprinkle Ten Deep Breaths
Every once in a while, pause from planning and problem solving and take ten deep breaths.

Be a Student
The best job in the world is that of being a student. Be curious—a student of life. Recognize that a good sign of growth in wisdom is awareness of ignorance.

Teach Less and Love More
Avoid being a teacher or a lecturer. Instead, be willing to learn, as others educate you about their lives and yours. If you wish them to learn from you then let them know, through words and actions, that you truly deeply care.

Rest Your Brain
Every few hours, give your brain a break from the constant planning and problem solving. I call it my "airplane mode!"

Ask Lots of Whys
The worthiest question to ask is why; the most difficult question to answer is also why.

Think Well of People
It is very difficult to dislike someone who you know likes you. Think and speak well of people, in their presence, as well as when they aren't around you.

If you want others to like you, let them know in ways more than one that you like them.

Remember to Forget (and Forgive)
Let go of the load (to the extent you can) that your mind and your soul find too heavy. Learn the lesson and then opt to forgive as you feel able. Forgetting, however, is very difficult if not impossible.

Forgiving is difficult. Forgetting is near impossible. Be kind to yourself in your journey into forgiveness.

Honor Every Job
Every part of the tree is important; roots and flowers serve distinct and important purposes. Similarly, every worker is important, no matter how his or her job is financially rewarded. Be grateful for the root if you are the flower today, be happy for the flower if you are the root today, knowing someday you also will be a flower.

Some days you are the root, other days you are the flower. Be grateful for the opportunity to participate in the play of nature.

Take Care of Yourself

Eat healthy and fresh food, exercise in moderation, sleep plenty, and engage in appropriate preventive care. Take good care of yourself.

Let's remind ourselves of the definition of meditation. It is intentional, grateful, and compassionate attention. This definition has nothing to do with formal or informal practice. It also has nothing to do with faith or lack of it. It has to do with a way of life. You can live your day as one big meditation.

High-tech biofeedback gadgets can guide you into deep breathing. If you are fascinated by technology and wish to give it a try, that's totally fine. But **make sure, as you breathe intentionally, you breathe in gratitude and breathe out compassion, not just during meditative moments but all-day long**. That is when your whole day will become one big meditation, transforming every aspect of your life. You will become an agent of service and love, helping build a better world for our planet's children. You will spread hope and kindle inspiration as you live your days and years with courage. That's where we are going next—toward hope, inspiration, and courage.

"By their fruits you shall know them" (Matthew 7:16).

Part VIII
The Seventh Tenet: Anchor

Tenet	Mindfulness v1	Mindfulness v2
Anchor	Empty the mind; anchor it in breath	Fill the mind with hope, inspiration, and courage

Instead of emptying the mind, fill it with hope, inspiration, and courage.

75

Fireside Chat #8

"Could you give me one real-life example where you found a better option than a non-judgmental attitude?" Mike asks.

"Sure. In every one of my travels at least one thing goes wrong. I have had delayed flights, cancelled flights, missed flights, flights rerouted, and more. A flat tire, cancelled hotel reservation, lost baggage, tornado warning, sick children, lost USB drive, expired passport—I have seen it all. Until a few years ago I used to get upset. Then I adjusted by saying, it is what it is—a non-judgmental stance."

"That's what I do."

"And that worked a few times. But now I have redefined travel. **Traveling is having a good time, alone or with the person you are traveling with.** Short of illness or accident, I do not allow myself to be stressed by delays and unpredictable snafus. I focus on having a good time. I have also stopped co-piloting the airplane! I let the real pilots do their job. Knowing that in-flight turbulence almost never brings a plane down, I enjoy those moments as a roller coaster. This helps me control the controllable and let go of the rest."

"Traveling is one example. What do you do when you're struggling with self-worth? How do you bring a healing presence when you yourself are hurting?" Mike asks a difficult question.

"That's a good question. You can only give what you have. I try my best to heal myself first, with self-compassion, self-acceptance, and self-forgiveness."

"Could you elaborate?"

"We lose a lot of energy fighting ourselves. **A fight with the self is unwinnable.** Who will defeat whom? When you commit yourself to self-compassion, you stop that fight. You apply the golden rule to yourself. The same applies to self-acceptance and self-forgiveness. All three help you save energy, which you can then use toward meaning. You then have more to give to your relationships."

"Can it become tiring?"

"Being with the self?"

"No, giving more to my relationships."

"It can. But realize that **a candle has to burn to light up the room. You'll have to endure some pain to bring light to people's lives.** In due course, though, you start getting the energy back. Research shows that **the more you appreciate your partner, the greater the appreciation you receive.**[1070] Also, you aren't with others all day long. Most of the day, you have one constant companion, and that is you. When you commit to kindness, you become kinder toward yourself. You are in good company then, all day long."

"I thought you would also mention gratitude here."

"You're right. Gratitude also fills you with positive emotions and warmth for others.[1071] **The two times gratitude can be most productive are right when you wake up and at the end of the work day, before you walk into your home through the garage door.**"

"I know the morning gratitude practice. What is the second one?"

"Let's understand what happens when you reconnect with your family at the end of the workday. There are three ways you can meet them during the first two minutes: cold, lukewarm, or warm.[1072] A cold connection is when you fail to notice them or, worse, display anger or start criticizing the moment you see them. A lukewarm connection is when you acknowledge the other person, and focus mostly on the logistics of the day or what is to come. It's mostly routine and formal."

"How does the warm connection look?"

"With warm connection, you greet and approach each other, say something nice and do something nice."

"As in hug?"

"A hug, kiss, touch, tap, sharing. It depends on your relationship and the details of the moment. Saying something nice could be telling a good story, appropriate humor, or reminding them they were in your thoughts when they were not around you."

"Has someone researched this also?"

"Yes, they have. Most of our connections are lukewarm, occasionally cold or warm."

"Seems like a lost opportunity."

"And sad too. How about if you spend a few seconds in the garage, think about what your loved ones mean to you, bring the feeling of gratitude for them, remind yourself that each day of your connection is precious, and, with that perspective, convert your connection from lukewarm to warm?"

"That would be nice."

"If you remember to pause and think gratitude, the rest will follow."

"Why limit it to immediate family? Can't we do this at every meeting?"

"We can. **If we take ten seconds before meeting someone to remind ourselves of something good that person has done for us, our energy will be very different, and our meeting will go much better**."

"I can see how that could bring a more engaged presence."

"And healing too. **Transition times are the most vulnerable and most powerful. Put extra energy and positivity into those times. In reality, most people we connect with, we meet only for a few minutes. If you pay attention to your energy, you can convert those moments into memorable ones.**"

"It goes back to intentionality."

"It does. Everything does."

"Just to clarify for our audience—are you against meditation?"

"Not at all. I just want to modernize meditation so we can make it more practical and useful, and expand our understanding. I believe the older meditation practices are also excellent, but I see them more as a second step, once we have trained our attention with the ideas I suggest in mindfulness *v2*. Also, it will be helpful to keep realistic expectations from meditation. Most of the phenomenal benefits are seen after years of disciplined practice boosted by intense retreats and careful guidance from a true expert."

"And most of us do not participate in intense retreats or have ongoing access to a meditation Olympian."

"That's right. Given these constraints, I ask myself if by leveraging science, particularly neuroscience, we can develop practices that would bypass these needs. I believe the answer to this very important question is, yes!"

"That's very encouraging. I see that you have hinted at several of the practices in the previous six tenets."

"I will bring them together when I talk about resilience and my personal practice after we discuss the seventh tenet."

"I look forward to the seventh tenet. You are going to talk about our anchors?"

"Yes. I believe less in emptying the mind and more in filling it. Let me tell you why. When researchers put an electrode into the fibrous tissue, they register a blank. You know what happens when they put electrodes on the brain's surface?"

"Isn't it called the EEG?"

"It is. Your brain is humming with electrical activity, whether you are awake or asleep, speaking or silent, sprinting or sitting. Your brain, like your heart, is constantly dancing. The only time our brains stop this dance is when we are ready to be buried. **The nervous system cannot sit quiet. It has to generate electricity, even if it receives no external stimulus.**"

"Why is the brain busy all the time?"

"Let's say you have been sitting for an hour, and a spider crawls on your right shin. What do you do?"

"Shake it off right away before it bites me."

"You're able to shake it off because the brain area that hosts your right leg's movement was idling but not asleep. If that area had shut down, you would have taken some time to awaken it. You may have experienced this when your foot went to sleep from sitting in an awkward posture for too long."

"That is just the nerves asleep, though, not the brain."

"You are right. But if you are a caveman, you can't afford any of that. It may not be a big deal if your legs are asleep facing a spider, but it would be with a rattler, a grizzly, a big cat, or a Neanderthal."

"Aha! Because we couldn't predict the nature and source of the threat at any moment, we had to remain vigilant and ready all the time. That is the reason we have to keep most of the brain networks always ready for launch. Am I getting it right?" Mike is excited at making the connections.

"You are. Although some of the details are speculative since Uncle Ad's ancestors are long gone, it makes sense. I believe we needed to feel safe, at least momentarily, to free up our brains to create, to write *The Iliad* or paint *The Last Supper*. The same rule applies today. The more we can remove fear and focus on meaning, the more creative we'll be."

"What happens when we sleep? We can't feel a thing when we are snoring."

"Your brain doesn't shut down when you sleep. It just scales down its operations. What if, while you were asleep, your brain's pain-sensing areas shut down because they weren't immediately needed? Wouldn't that make you vulnerable?"

"It would. I wouldn't feel if a grizzly was chomping on my scalp."

"Even when our pain areas aren't perceiving pain, they have to be ready and available. The brain thus has learned to keep all its networks ready to go, even if lazing—similar to the idling car engine at the traffic light. Your car's engine doesn't turn off at the traffic light, does it?"

"Of course not, unless it's a hybrid."

"The engine idles so you can put it to work the moment the light turns green. Our brain networks are idling the same way. In fact, this resting activity of the brain accounts for 80 percent of its total energy consumption. It isn't efficient, but it is necessary."

"But that amounts to only a few hundred calories."

"That's true. The brain burns about four hundred calories in a day. You can get that many calories in a slice of pizza or a doughnut. That's not a big deal in this world where even a hardware store has an aisle committed to pre-packaged food. You can go to a hardware store and, if you're not watching, walk away a pound heavier. But getting extra calories was quite a struggle when we were scavengers."

"How does this apply to tenet seven?"

"Let's get to that. In the brain's sensory or motor areas, this activity at rest keeps the brain ready for sensing or moving. In the brain's thought-producing areas, this activity generates thoughts. I suspect many of our low-volume thoughts do not reach conscious awareness. Several "pre-thoughts" compete, and only the highest-volume one registers. Our experience of mind wandering is this constantly running thought train. It is intrinsic to the nature of the nervous system."

"Are you suggesting that the thought train can't be stopped?"

"Given the brain's design and its intrinsic electrical activity, it would take superhuman effort to shut it down. I sure would get an F if I was being judged for stilling my mind. Knowing this science, I don't feel guilty or unaccomplished because of that failure. I used to, but no longer."

"You changed because of all this neuroscience?"

"Yes, the awareness of this science tremendously helped me. I have realized that **my mind wasn't created to be emptied, just as my heart wasn't created to be stopped**. I also realized that suppressing emotions isn't the answer. Emotions assign value to your thoughts and are as important as thoughts in your decision making.[1073] In fact some researchers believe that 70 percent of your decision making is directed by emotions and not rational thinking.

"So **the key is not to try to stop your thoughts or emotions. You will fail in that effort. The key is to choose the content of your thoughts so that your thoughts are filled with the good stuff and allow uplifting emotions to thrive.**

"We have people and things and not emptiness because this is a more desirable state. Similarly, we have thoughts and not silence because that is the more desirable state. Thinking is the crowning achievement of the nervous system's evolution. Silencing your mind would be going back. **But we do not need noise or turbulence; we need music and laminar flow, which for the mind are thoughts laden with wisdom and love.**

"Trying to empty the mind of thoughts is like trying to empty a balloon of air. A balloon is but a potential if not filled with the unseen air. The mind is also a potential. A mind filled with heavy thoughts will feel heavy, a mind filled with hopeful, uplifting, inspiring, courageous thoughts will feel light. Our goal is to fill the mind with uplifting thoughts, that set you free from the negativity the brain generates and the hurts the world sends. Such thoughts power your wings and are the tail wind for your inner hummingbird. **Uplifting thoughts and their related emotions have three flavors: hope, inspiration, and courage.** That is what we will turn to next."

76

Hope

Living in the middle of cornfields, I see hope playing out every spring. With the frost gone and blooms on the horizon, farmers emerge from their thawed driveways to till the soil. This is soon followed by seeding and all the hard work involved in giving each of the thirty-four thousand seeds in an acre the best chance so that they'll convert into ears, silk, and tassel. The energy that drives all this effort is hope, hope that for each acre of soil, the thirty-four thousand seeds will convert into fifteen million at the time of harvesting—a 450-fold return in three months. Not bad.

A few miles from the cornfields, I see a different kind of hope. Each year, about one and a half million people travel from all over the world to Mayo Clinic with their medical records, worries, and presumptive diagnoses, carrying with them the hope of securing health and healing.

Hope is the expectation of a better tomorrow. The unnerving uncertainty of the future has an upside to it: we can choose to fill it with hope. Hope is knowing that the traffic jam will eventually clear, the sun will appear on the presently dark horizon, the baby will grow out of diapers, and the boring meeting will come to an end.

Hope is the feeling that what is desired is possible, that something good will come out of today's struggles, and that it is worthwhile to get out of bed and invest the effort.

Hope powers action.

HOPE IS HELPFUL

Research shows that **hope helps every aspect of personal health and life.** Hope is associated with better self-control and healthier habits.[1074] Hope enhances positive mood, action, coping, and immunity.[1075] People who are more hopeful recover better from injury[1076] and are more likely to continue rehab after surgery or disability.[1077] In patients with recurrent cancer, hope increases quality of life.[1078] A number of outcomes, including heart disease, cancer, pregnancy, and pain, are better in those who have more hope.[1079] **The hopefuls engage in more healthful behavior.**[1080]

Hope is also associated with better caring. When doctors and nurses give up hope, they give up caring.[1081]

Hope generates energy, takes away focus from uncertainty and hopelessness, and thus powers goal-directed action. Hope is associated with better self-esteem.[1074] The hopefuls have better social connections, partly because they work harder at their relationships.[1082] In prisoners, greater hope decreases the rate of reincarceration after release. The hopeful cope by managing, reducing, or eliminating stressors, while the ones with lower hope ignore, avoid, or withdraw.[1083]

If all of the above isn't convincing enough, multiple large studies with a long follow-up have shown that hope is also associated with 30 to 40 percent lower mortality.[1084-1086]

The hopefuls are happier, healthier, and even live longer.

LEFT BRAIN IS OPTIMISTIC

I consider hope and optimism to be very similar constructs. Hope is one trait in which the two sides of the brain behave differently. The hopefuls experience greater activation of the left cerebral cortex compared to the right. People with a dominant left cerebral cortex show a more cheerful attitude, seek the positive aspects of a situation, and anticipate a brighter future.[1087] They make great cheerleaders (but perhaps not the best attorneys, in whom pessimism sometimes correlates with greater success).

A few hard-core neuroscience facts about optimism: Increased volume in the left orbitofrontal cortex has been shown to protect against anxiety through increasing optimism.[1088] In another study, the hopefuls had greater volume in the left thalamus, pulvinar, and parahippocampal gyrus.[1089] On an EEG, greater activity in the left-middle frontal gyrus correlated with greater optimism.[1090]

THREE LEVELS OF HOPE

People exist at three depths with respect to hope. The most vulnerable are people who feel hopeless even when things are going their way. Next are people who feel hopeful when things are going their way but struggle with hope amid adversity. The most hopeful are those who do not give up hope even when things aren't going their way.

While in general hope is healthy, hope will serve you best if it is pragmatic. In particular, be careful about the time frame in which change can happen. Things generally move slower than you desire. Hoping for a person's behavior to change overnight or for a lifetime of chronic pain to melt in a day is as practical as hoping for the corn ears to form the day the crop is seeded. Such hope invariably leads to disappointment, usurping future hope. Expecting the unchangeable to change can also be counterproductive. I used to, but have now stopped fighting subzero temperatures or thunderstorm warnings. A realistic mindset is more helpful in such situations.[1091]

With all those benefits the natural next question is: how can we invite realistic hope into our lives? Here are a few ideas.

BECOMING MORE HOPEFUL

Three groups of factors influence hope: personal, interpersonal, and situational.[1092-1094] **Better physical and emotional health, healthy self-worth, a just model of the world, good memories of the past, control of the controllable (and letting go of the uncontrollable), and a sense of direction (a goal and a path to reach that goal) all enhance hope.** Having people in your life who trust you for who you are and who believe in you increases hope. All things being equal, the greater the opportunities, choices, and control you have and the fewer nonnegotiable obstacles you encounter, the more hopeful you are. In fact, in some studies, situational factors account for 50 percent of hope.[1095]

You can take a number of steps to increase hope.

Self-Care

Take good care of your physical health. **You feel more hopeful when you feel strong.** This doesn't mean you have to be in perfect physical health. Just make an effort to be as healthy as you can be.

Self-Worth

When we feel good about ourselves, we feel good about the world, and life in general. Our self-worth depends on how we value the self and how we perceive others value us. Here is the problem: **others value us not based on who we are but more so on who they are. Giving others the power to influence our self-worth is giving away too much control.** Most people who think they know us in truth barely know us. They don't know our past, our intentions, or our effort. **Anchor your self-worth not in your success or in others' perceptions of you but in your effort and the values you embody every single day.**

Past Memories

If you are sleeping on a bed of rose petals with a thorn sticking into your legs, you'll feel the thorn, not the petals. That's how we are designed. In our default design, the thorn dominates our day. What we don't realize is that we aren't as helpless as we are made to believe. We can always choose to remove the thorn and throw it away. Try to learn from past struggles by interpreting them with self-compassion, gratitude for what was right, acceptance of their imperfections, meaning in what seemed wrong, and forgiveness. A healthy relationship with the past will give you hope that will help you nurture a healthier relationship with the future, which will soon be past.

Model of the World

On a material level, the world isn't just. Bad things happen to good people, and good things happen to bad people. You may try to find valid reasons, but you will struggle, because sometimes newborns start suffering from the first day they open their eyes. About 3 percent of them are born with major birth defects. What wrong could they have possibly done before even being born? I can't understand it, but I get uneasy when I think about it. Instead of believing that it is all chaotic and unjust, I hope that there is rationality beyond what I can see. I don't know the details. I also don't succeed in keeping such hope every day. But more often than not, an effort to nurture hope saves me the energy to pursue my meaning.

Believing in a just model of the world can make you more hopeful.

Control the Controllable

You have finite energy. How you distribute your energy and vitality determines the quality of your day. **Carefully choose which battles you wish to fight.** Instead of fighting the snowstorm, get a snowblower. Instead of lamenting the tornado, go to the basement. Instead of raging over the hurricane, find a shelter. A good warrior knows which wars to pick. You can't easily change your spouse, colleague, supervisor, or neighbor, so for minor annoyances, try to focus on what is right about them and give forgiveness a chance.

If the sun is beating down in your neighborhood, you can choose not to step out, choose to brave the sun and get sunburned, or pick the wiser option of using a good sunscreen. Sunscreen for the mind is the five principles of gratitude, compassion, acceptance, meaning, and forgiveness. I have shared a practical way to integrate these principles into our lives in two previous books.[226, 819]

Sense of Direction

Pick your North Star, the core meaning of your life, and then align the flow of your days, keeping your North Star in sight. The progress will almost always be slower than desirable. But as long as you are traveling in the direction you want to go, you'll feel hopeful. Throughout your journey, don't forget to celebrate short-term successes. If you wait to celebrate until the very end, it could be a very long wait.

People in Your Life

As much as I invite criticism, I do appreciate people who believe in me. It's a long journey, this life. You'll need motivation and uplifting emotions every day, often several times during the day. A good source is the people who believe in you and trust you for who you are. Surround yourself with people who trust your intentions. Be open to their feedback and definitely **do not discount the compliments that come your way. We tend to trust the criticisms but deny the compliments.** That strategy will deplete you very quickly. Take both criticisms and compliments; together they will make a delicious and useful serving. Alone, they are either delicious or useful, not both.

Trust the compliments at least as much as you trust the critique.

Obstacles

The climb uphill is never straight up. You take a few steps forward and then step back for a bit. Just watch an ant walking while carrying a load of bread crumbs. Her journey is all but smooth. But she manages. The obstacles are in place to give your body and mind a little workout. Granted, sometimes those obstacles are mightier than desirable. But if you believe that most obstacles are there to make your life interesting, then you will scale the smaller ones more easily. That will prepare you to deal with the occasional mountain of struggle that is bound to appear at some point. **Whenever you can, look at obstacles as worthy challenges and not as threats.**

See your obstacles as worthy challenges, not threats.

Opportunities

I am often asked to teach students how to develop a research career. Here are the four steps I follow:

1. Ask yourself, "What are some big ideas? What societal needs can I serve? What hurts of the world are amenable to cure or healing?"
2. Of the list you generate, ask yourself, "Which among these challenges am I most capable of tackling?" You'll likely have a few options left at this point.
3. Next ask yourself, "What activities and goals among these do I find most meaningful? What do I get most excited about?" This step will narrow down your choices to what interests you.
4. Finally, ask yourself, "What is feasible? What resources are available to me? What is the low-hanging fruit?" For example, there's no point in doing clinical AIDS research in Antarctica. You won't find too many patients. It is good to dream but also to be practical.

The final answer you get is your opportunity. If it makes sense, align your life's work with that meaning.

Remember that **hope doesn't deny the truth. Hope looks at the truth in its most optimistic version. Hope doesn't mean it won't ever get dark. Hope means that no matter how dark the night, the sun will appear in the morning. It always has and always will.** Hope inspires the birds to start singing each morning even before the horizon is warmed up by our precious, luminous ball of fire. **Befriend hope until your last breath so you remain inspired.**

77

Inspiration

I remember the day I was made line leader of my class for the first time (I had scored well in exams and hadn't been as naughty as before). The admiring look I got from my teacher sustained me for the next several months in my efforts to work hard and be good. I also remember the first time I felt I was a big boy. We had a puddle of water in front of our old home. The kids would jump across the puddle and often end up splashing the water. I was among the first in our group who scaled that jump, handily beating several other boys much taller than I was. My buddies' approval and newfound respect for me put me on a high for several days. I had arrived! I was finally a big boy. These are some of my earliest inspiring moments that are part of my memory bank.

WHAT IS INSPIRATION?

Inspiration is the spontaneous impulse to create beauty, goodness, and value. An inspiring moment is one in which you fall in love—with an idea, object, purpose, or person. **Just as in true love, when you are inspired, you are selfless and just want to do good.** An inspiring moment is often a moment of illumination. You get deep insight, feel you have touched the truth, and wake up to what is important.

Inspiration has three key features:[1096]

- **Inspiration is often spontaneous and can't be willed.** Although it is true that your undistracted presence is essential for the inspiring moments to materialize, the moments that totally change every aspect of your life happen unexplained and unprompted.
- **Inspiration leads you to think beyond yourself**, to be in a state of self-transcendence. Inspiration doesn't create competition; it fosters mastery. A truly inspired person has no desire to best anyone; he or she just wishes to achieve excellence. Such a person transcends the undesirable byproducts of evolutionary human needs—the impulses of fear, greed, and envy.
- **Inspiration is motivating, an impulse to action that fills you with energy.** Inspiration provides the channel that can help direct your energy toward meaning.

Inspired seeking is selfless seeking. Our world depends on the excellence and generosity of the inspired.

WHY BE INSPIRED?

With respect to your enthusiasm, your presence and involvement can be captured in five different words: apathetic, disinterested, interested, engaged, and inspired.

Apathetic describes the state of those who are asked to enter data on a five-year-old project that no one cares about. They just want to keep breathing until it is time to clock out. Apathetic people don't care, and they don't care that they don't care. They see clients as problems. These people are cynical, often have low self-worth, aren't interested in anything, and represent the final stage of burnout. They experience frequent negative emotions because they lose the ability to regulate their amygdala, likely because of a weakened connection between the amygdala and higher executive areas of the brain.[1097]

Slightly better are people who are *disinterested* but not apathetic. They are interested in doing something, but it is different from what they are currently doing. They don't find their current work meaningful or novel.

A step higher are the *interested* ones who enjoy what they are doing as long as it is eight to five, pays a good salary, and isn't too mentally taxing. They are happy to work for a few hours, but then they want to do something else.

Those who are *engaged* are interested, committed, and enthusiastic, and they give all their energy to their work. They give discretionary effort and care about the work, its processes, and the outcomes. Everyone wants them to be on their team.

At the highest level are the truly *inspired*. For inspired people, work is their life's mission. They are filled with energy and spend the bulk of the day in flow. They seek mastery, and work is an end in itself.

No country can expect to be at the pinnacle of success if it doesn't have enough inspired people. Such inspiration cannot come from fear or oppression. It can blossom only when creative freedom is allowed to sprout unencumbered by fear.

Inspiration helps you see the castle as you are laying the brick. Living each day inspired while earning your daily bread is the key to having as much fun as you did at your first lemonade stand or neighborhood car wash.

Inspiration helps creativity, mastery, absorption, competence, optimism, and self-esteem. Inspiration is associated with selflessness and other-centricity. Inspired striving provides lasting happiness. In a series of studies, researchers found that inspiration positively correlated with well-being and life satisfaction.[1098] (Inspiration predicted well-being and not the other way around.) Further, the study showed that **the more inspired you feel in the morning, the happier you are in the evening**.

Inspiration keeps the company of happiness.

In a research study involving 195 student writers and 220 readers, the more inspired the writers were, the greater the inspiration experienced by readers.[1099] Researchers called this "inspiration contagion." In another study, effort predicted the technical merit of the writing, while inspiration predicted the creativity of the writing.[1100]

Inspiration correlates with the number of patents. Inspiration and creativity move together during the day.[1096] Inspiration fosters effort and thus the technical merit of what is created.[1100] In a sense, **inspiration and perspiration are the two wheels on a bicycle. They support and enhance each other, setting the stage for excellence.**[1101]

Inspiration fosters perspiration. Perspiration converts raw inspiration into tangible outcomes.

HOW TO BE INSPIRED

Pause for a second and try to answer this question: What or who is inspiring you today?

If you took more than ten seconds to answer, you are unlikely to have a spectacular day. The first step to being inspired is to recognize the value of living an inspired day.

Inspiration has many sources: nature, music, art, people, and more. Ancient Greeks thought inspiration came from the gods (Muse). Most scriptures of different faiths are believed to be inspired by gods. The gods in heavens, however, aren't accessible to our senses. Instead, we have access to all types of life-forms and the inanimate matter they reside in. Together, they can provide us countless stories for inspiration.

Where the rubber meets the road, two constructs can help bring inspiration to your life: being inspired <u>by someone</u> and being inspired <u>to do something</u>.[1102] Although inspiration is often spontaneous, you can make some choices that can help you create fertile ground for it. The following are three ideas for creating this fertile ground.

Create Your Inspiration List

Go back to early childhood days and recall all the people and experiences that inspired you. When you have a short list, try to revisit those experiences. I have looked at scenes of old movies, searched for my old mentors on the internet, and read old stories. I have used Google Maps to take another look at places where I felt inspired (and am excited to revisit those places in the future with a virtual reality headset). I have thought of the trees working hard today to produce fruit. Who can be more selfless than a tree producing seedless fruits? All of these will help you feel revitalized and younger and fill you with motivation to continue to make a difference.

Be More Open to New Experiences

Novelty draws your attention. When attentive, you infer and make connections you may not have otherwise made. That is the key to inspiration. Try new flavors of ice cream, listen to new music, watch movies you aren't used to, look at different kinds of plants in the nursery, or take up stargazing. Somewhere along the way, a moment will present itself that will fill you with awe and wonder and an impulse to connect and transform.

Strive to Master, Not Compete

Do not try to get better than anyone. Feeling superior and inferior are both uninspired places to be. **The drive for competition is very different from the drive for mastery, even though they might look similar.** You might succeed with either, but competition can burn you, while inspiration can energize you for your entire life.

Inspiration will provide the energy for you to rise after each fall. **If you fall, choose to rise higher than the point from which you fell. That is resilience. Often, the only time we get to rise is when we have fallen.**

Life's falls are sometimes the only real opportunity to rise.

Recognize that although every person can find inspiration, what inspires us varies from person to person. Choose to make your brain a fertile ground for inspiration. Once the sapling of inspiration spreads its roots in your being, you will find that **as you lose yourself in inspiration, you'll find yourself in inspiration**.

Your inspiration will drive you toward meaning, and **when you pursue a higher meaning that you consider sacred, you'll leave fear far behind**. You'll develop an indomitable spirit filled with courage.

78

Courage

Every day, millions of men and women patrol our streets, fight enemies, and work at odd hours, risking life and limb to keep us safe. They embody courage. Many more display courage in different ways. Here are some examples of tremendous courage: Lin Hao, a second-grade student, saving two children after an earthquake; Rosa Parks choosing not to yield her seat; Oscar Schindler saving 1,200 precious lives at personal cost; the sisters of Saint Francis deciding to build a hospital after a devastating tornado in Rochester; a child with a peanut allergy trying a new dish in a foreign country; a five-year-old walking into a dark room alone; a person who has suffered a lifetime of social anxiety speaking from the podium; you sending your thirteen-year-old to the first camp away from home.

You live each day with uncertainty about what is to come. **I have no doubt you have and live with greater courage than you give yourself credit for.**

You are more courageous than you know or can ever know.

Let's understand courage together so we can all discover the courageous beings we are and, of course, increase our courage.

DEFINITION

Courage isn't the absence of fear. In fact, according to some researchers, the presence or absence of fear isn't necessary to define courage.[1103] Nevertheless, after having learned from many experts in the field, here is how I like to define it: **courage is doing the right thing despite the risks.**

Courage means not letting fear or uncertainty prevent you from taking action. The courageous notice fear, refuse to let it paralyze them, and make a choice that takes them toward meaning despite the uncertainty of the outcome. **Courage is recognizing that the meaning that drives you is more powerful than the fears that hold you. Courage means refusing to give up because the meaning you protect by engaging is far greater than the hurt you might avoid by disengaging.**

The courageous don't lack fear; they are skilled at managing fear.

Most acts are considered courageous if they have a prosocial element. Walking into a tiger enclosure at the zoo just for the thrill of it wouldn't be called courageous. Similarly, picking a brawl with someone twice your size because his or her car tailgated yours by mistake also wouldn't be called courageous.

We define courage based on what is moral and meaningful. Further, an action considered ordinary for one person may be a display of phenomenal courage for another. For most people, flying isn't an act of courage, but for someone who is afraid of flying, it is. Similarly, for a person with arachnophobia, looking at a spider is displaying courage, as is someone with a fear of heights climbing on a rooftop to save a child. From that perspective, **people with anxiety who go out and live their daily lives display more courage than many others do**.

The anxious and the underprivileged are often more courageous than those endowed with a calm mind, riches, and choices.

Given this expanded view of courage, we can safely say that the majority of us have acted courageously at some point in our lives. In one study, 94 percent of the children reported doing something that took courage.[1104]

WHY COURAGE?

You dare when you care. Courage enables a fulfilling life. Aristotle remarked, "Courage is the first of human virtues because it makes all others possible." Courage provides the energy for you to do what you are afraid to do. Courage thus helps you live the life of your choosing, with intentionality. Courage is also infectious; it flows to and from you.

More than we believe, know, or can know, our instinct to conform governs many of our actions. Psychologically stable people, when asked to pretend to be prison guards, can become truly cruel toward innocent people acting as prisoners.[1105, 1106] A simple order from an authority figure can be enough for the majority of us to give a fatal 450-volt shock to an innocent research participant. (No one was actually shocked in the research study, but the participants were made to believe that they were shocking the person.)[1107] Interestingly, individuals with conscientious and agreeable personality types were more likely to give high-intensity electric shock.[1108]

Speaking against the authority to defend the truth and the vulnerable is essential to maintaining a just order in the world.

Blindly following the leader hurts. From the Holocaust to Enron, internally insecure but outwardly strong leaders have manipulated the minds of their troops and employees to carry out unethical actions. **It is the courageous who stand for the truth, not just for consensus. Without courage, we would be vulnerable to despots taking over the world.**

Courage is also essential because many threats aren't real. They are like a blown-up puffer fish. **Just a show of courage can scatter away a number of false threats that could have distracted you from your progress and success.**

The loud roar of courage scares away many threats.

Success is of many types: financial, business, scientific, popularity, moral, and more. Courage helps you choose true success. In general, when success in finance, business, science, or gaining celebrity status is associated with moral degeneration, the value of that success is decimated. It is as substantial as the froth on top of your latte. It takes courage to say no to bribes when you see everyone else around you stealing. **Courage helps you take the high road while pursuing excellence. The courageous end their life with fewer regrets.**

The world today needs a different kind of courage than in the past. **We need the courage that allows us to forgive instead of taking revenge**, that releases oxytocin to balance the testosterone. This is because we are no longer throwing spears while riding horseback. Instead, we are shooting e-mails while sitting on leather seats. **Our brains are busy protecting our values as much as our ancestors were busy protecting their cattle.**

NEUROSCIENCE OF COURAGE

To learn the brain mechanisms of fear, researchers conducted an unusual study in which they examined the brain MRI of participants while they chose to move live snakes closer to or farther from their heads.[1109] These participants had already indicated that they were afraid of snakes. Researchers found that fear activated two key areas, the subgenual anterior cingulate cortex (sgACC) and the amygdala. Higher sgACC and lower amygdala activity correlated with courage; lower sgACC and higher amygdala activity correlated with fear.

A key question emerges from this study: Is courage a biological predisposition? Are the courageous wired such that their brains activate sgACC in response to fearful situations? Or does sgACC activate when people choose to be courageous? We do not have definitive answers about which comes first. The important thing to realize is that even the amygdalae of the most courageous people get activated in threatening situations. The question isn't if we develop a fear response; the question is how we manage our fear response. Effective management of the fear response is what makes one courageous. From the perspective of neuroscience, courage isn't the absence of fear; it is the management of fear.

In fact, our goal isn't elimination of fear. **We need our fear in order to be safe.** Damage to the amygdala, which leads to loss of fear, can put us in vulnerable, life-threatening situations. One patient with a damaged amygdala, well-known to neuroscience researchers, is poor at recognizing negative social cues and has an excessive and imbalanced desire to approach others.[1110] This is related to her lack of use of information from her eyes.[1111] Further, she shows no fear response to seeing snakes and spiders, visiting haunted houses, or watching emotionally jarring films.[337] Most of the day she experiences positive emotions which is a good thing, but her inability to see threats has made her vulnerable. She has been the victim of numerous criminal acts and life-threatening situations.

You do not want your amygdalae to be totally quiet. You want your amygdalae to be mentored right.

I need my rational fears to keep me and my loved ones safe.

DISMANTLING STEREOTYPES

Before we look at some ideas to enhance courage, it would be good to revisit some stereotypes we have of courage so we can dismantle them.

Courage and its downstream recognition, heroism, are often equated with fabulously brave and self-sacrificing acts. Exceptional heroism emerges from rare, often once-in-a-lifetime opportunities, like the one faced by Wesley Autrey as he jumped in front of an oncoming train to save the life of a twenty-year-old student who had just had a seizure and was lying helpless on the tracks. Much more widespread than the courage of the superheroes is the courage of the everyday heroes who are just a little more selfless than others, who go the extra mile and are humble, present, and committed to kindness.[1112] These are the courageous people in your family, neighborhood, and workplace. They are the kids who go to class even if they couldn't do the homework. They share their stories of addiction to help colleagues in trouble. They feel comfortable talking about how they failed the test twice before passing it. They let their supervisors know that they are late because they overslept. They could have easily fibbed, but they do the right thing despite the risk. You likely know at least a few of them. Likely, you are one of them.

Courage is often a poor advertiser of itself. Most courageous people are humble. They are thus likely to be courage blind; they will discount their courage. Those announcing their courage to the world probably need some psychological help. The courageous often downplay the accolades coming their way.

Courage keeps the company of humility. You'll often hear the courageous say, "I was just doing my job."

The ancient models of courage would be the brave knights, the gladiators, and the military commanders—mostly men. But research shows that **courage is evenly distributed among men and women**. In fact, in many situations, women may be more courageous. For example, a higher percentage of transplant organ donors are women,[1113, 1114] and most government surveys show that more women volunteer (27.8 percent) than do men (21.8 percent).[1115]

Another stereotype of courage relates to professions. Traditionally, workers in higher-risk jobs have been considered more courageous. But courage isn't limited to these professions. When researchers studied courage using validated surveys (measuring fear and willingness to act), corporate executives tested at least as courageous as police and emergency personnel.[1116] They have a different kind of courage, though. The more courage is paired with selflessness, the closer it reaches the model of heroism.

Courage is less related to the girth of the biceps and more to the strength of the purpose.

Certainly, the point here isn't to inspire a courage contest between different professionals, since courage comes in so many shades. My wife, Richa, can't stand any critters, while the exterminator in our neighborhood has no trouble picking up a spider or beetle. The exterminator can't stand the sight of a bleeding person, which Richa has been trained to handle as an obstetrician. The point is that, similarly to how Howard Gardner defined intelligence, it is **better to assume everyone is courageous and then ask in what particular aspects an individual is courageous.**[1117]

This leads to an important question. Can courage be enhanced? The answer is a definite yes. Let's conclude this chapter by discovering how.

ENHANCING COURAGE

From the brain's perspective, courage is a reflection of relatively greater activation of the sgACC, which is a part of the prefrontal cortex. The sgACC keeps the amygdala in check. Like other prefrontal-cortex activities, courage can also be trained. Here are some things you can do to become more courageous. I have tried all of them and can attest to their value.

Advanced Preparation

The more prepared you are, the more courageous you can be. Fear of the unknown is among the worst fears. We fear the unknown when we are ignorant. Such fear leads to preemptive assaults, cruel actions, and worse. Informing yourself of what's to come and what's at stake helps you prepare, which decreases fear.

When I was applying for a visa for the first time to travel to the United States in 1995, a lot was at stake. My entire career depended on that two-minute interview with a busy official who barely knew me and had to make an on-the-spot decision based on his gut feeling. I knew very little about the United States at that time. But I knew that people here are happier on Fridays! They are also happier after morning coffee. Further, going for the interview when the officials were likely to be hungry and have low brain glucose might have decreased my chances (as was demonstrated in a study that showed that the probability of parole being granted was higher when the judges weren't hungry).[1118] So I went on Friday around nine o'clock in the morning in professional attire. It worked.

You go farther when you know where you are going.

Practicing ahead of time also helps. Research shows that mentally practicing piano notes improves your performance.[1118] Patients with stroke who mentally practice a movement improve in their motor ability.[358] Similarly, practicing bravery in small daily activities works out your courage muscles, helping you become more courageous.

Connection
Animals, particularly the ones that can be prey, herd together. Being alone creates a state of unease and fear. This makes biological sense since gazelles, buffalo, and wildebeests are much more vulnerable as lone prey than they are in large packs.

We have the same instinct. We derive energy and strength from our connections with one another. I grew up hearing that **one and one isn't two; it is eleven**. To cultivate courage, connect with others who trust you, who help you feel worthy, and who serve as a source of strength for you.

One plus one equals eleven.

Believe in Luck
Before any exam, I tell myself, "The good shepherd will help the good shepherd." Somehow, I believe that repeating those words will bring me good luck. It decreases my anxiety. That's what many leading courage researchers believe: magical thinking and believing in luck can enhance courage.

Sneezing behind someone's back is considered a bad omen in some areas of the world. The solution is to offer prayers to calm the spirits. Some believe spilling salt makes you vulnerable, while touching wood or crossing fingers can prevent bad things from happening for others. Since we humans have so little control over the world around us, this sort of magical thinking helps us find at least some aspect we can control. You'll find many elite athletes wearing a talisman or doing rituals to bring them luck. These rituals very likely decrease anxiety and enhance focus.

The World Needs You
Any day you feel weak, think of all those who count on your strength. Also think of all those you could help and inspire by not letting self-doubt get the better of you. **The purpose and people you serve power all your efforts.**

Universe protects the protector.

I shared earlier that I keep the image of a little girl who died in a bomb blast in my office. She reminds me every day about my life's purpose, which is to help build a world in which we treat our little ones better than we treated her. She has never failed in providing me strength.

Do Good Things

The meaning you serve is the primary source of your strength. Courage is typically meant to serve the collective. Courage that lacks morality is cowardice. **Courage is best seen when protecting others.** There are situations in life in which you have no time for fear. You may have heard of grandmas lifting cars and moms resisting men twice their size to protect their young.

In 1947, at the time of the partition of India, Richa's grandfather had to evacuate his home at an hour's notice. As the family was about to leave, he remembered that one of his dear family members was tied to the tree. It was his cow. He knew that if he left the cow tied, she would perish. He could not bring himself to leave her like that. She was family. He ran back to the house to release her, but in the commotion, he wasn't able to rejoin everyone. This must have been an act of tremendous courage driven by meaning. I know for some it may not make sense, but all of you who have loved your pet just as much as another human, will totally understand. Luckily, he was saved by a friend, and he eventually was reunited with his family.

When doing good things, assume that you are the one in charge. The bystander effect is a phenomenon in which shared responsibility means that no one feels responsible to act. It is best to believe that it is up to us to act and no one else.

Embrace Failure

When playing tennis, **even the best players make unforced errors**. Many shots go into the net or outside the line. If by the end of the game you broke a nice sweat and had a good time with the other players, it was all worth it. Don't label failures as failures. Consider failure to be a part of training—the tuition you have to pay to succeed.

Accepting failure doesn't mean welcoming, enjoying, or seeking it. It means recognizing that it is inevitable. If you look at how movies are made, most of the recording is rejected in editing. The shots that are edited out aren't failures. They contribute to the scenes that are placed in the final cut.

Small failures and the lessons learned from them prevent bigger failures. Fear of failure pushes courage away. Finding external excuses for failure or lowering expectations for the self aren't the best responses. The best response is to take failures in stride, recognize their essential role in the totality of your life, learn from them, and keep moving forward.

The lessons learned from small failures prevent bigger failures.

Recognize also the value of fear. Fear blocks self-destructive courage, while courage checks paralyzing fear. In balance, they both help you to be safe and keep growing, through success and failure.

Keep in mind that on some days failure will make you angry, and that's OK. Controlled anger can provide you a sense of control and energy. Anger is better than apathy. Anger sometimes shows you care, are willing to speak up, and won't tolerate being treated like a doormat. Anger has even been associated with optimism.[1119] In fact, some sports, such as boxing, use anger to stimulate courage. Those, however, are exceptions. I would rather be inspired by compassion than aggression!

Part IX
Integration

79

Fireside Chat #9

Mike is now sitting in the audience. I believe he trusts me now, with both my intentions and ideas. I feel good about it. I use this moment to address the audience members who have patiently sat with us all this while. I will count you, the reader, in my audience too. Thank you for being with me so far!

"There is a reason the world has things and bunnies and people instead of nothing. We started with emptiness and silence. They sound good, but they can be deafening after some time. **Better than noise is silence, but better than silence is melody.**

"A melody for the mind is that of hope, inspiration, and courage. **Hope doesn't mean it won't ever get dark. Hope means that no matter how dark the night, you'll find light.** Hope inspires and fills you with courage.

"Mindfulness *v2* recognizes that a species as intelligent and curious as we are, with such a well-developed prefrontal cortex, can't be content with silencing its brain. This brain wants to dance. It wants to travel to the stars. It wants to cure cancer and eradicate poverty and pain.

"Every human being at some point in life experiences a moment of deep intentional presence when the thought cloud clears, the biases fade, and reality appears as it actually is, or at least as close as humanly possible to how it actually is. That is a moment of freedom—from the brain's negative predispositions, the wounds of the past, the chaos of the present, the uncertainty of tomorrow, and the finiteness of time. The circumstances that bring about this event are very individual. It could be related to seeing suffering, experiencing suffering, meeting someone inspiring, praying, or reading a text, or it could happen as a random event with no antecedent. That extraordinary moment of insight stays for a thin slice of time and then passes. Not knowing its preciousness, we let it pass. Life goes on as usual.

"But for a lucky few people, this moment repeats—in a similar or different circumstance. With enough repeats, they pause and think. They start reading what the mystics, philosophers, poets, and scientists have to say about life. They start connecting with like-minded people. A new world emerges for them, one they hadn't previously noticed. They start asking deeper questions, such as 'Who am I? Why am I here? What is this world?'

"Seldom does anyone get conclusive answers. **But the secret isn't in getting the answers. It is in the asking.** A sincere quest points them toward the light. That light has two colors: wisdom and love.

"Wisdom shows timeless truth bereft of individual biases. Love helps people experience the joy of being connected to the whole. This joy and the truth point them in the direction of grace. Grace isn't definable, yet you know when you experience it. Although you can't touch the clouds or taste compassion, they are real. Grace is subtler but every bit as real. **Grace is like the sunlight, but it is up to us to open the windows.**

"You are one of these lucky people. You haven't brushed aside life as one suffering moment after another. You aren't satisfied with the status quo. You wish to walk toward the truth.

"Do not let this moment of clarity be clouded by the fear, ego, and greed that want to block the light. Do not let anyone distract you and weaken your resolve. **Open your eyes and look up when the world wants you to shut your eyes and look down. The brightest stars appear on the darkest nights.**

"The human mind has a tendency to forget. To overcome that tendency, you'll have to remind yourself over and over. **You aren't winning or losing; you are becoming a better human being. How you drive is as important as where you are going. Perhaps you aren't going anywhere; you're just becoming a better driver. The day you wake up and are fully convinced of the truth of this powerful mantra will be the day you'll have plenty. You'll hear yourself say: "I am enough; I have enough.**

"Mindfulness *v2* invites you to wake up with this thought every day so you can overcome your neural vulnerabilities to mind wandering, negativity bias, hedonic adaptation, and more. I have no doubt that we will collectively transcend these vulnerabilities. But leaving that change to nature will take a very long time. How long would it have taken nature to convert silica and metal spontaneously into a computer? Our intentionality accelerated that process. We can do the same with our brains. We can train our brains to adapt to the complexity and speed of the world and transcend the limitations of our control and mortality. It is totally up to us.

"We are slowly but surely moving to a world in which we will all be sages—eight billion sages. I hope that happens in my lifetime. I don't have the patience! I invite your impatience in creating a world in which no hurt is left unhealed and no one is intentionally hurt. That will be a world of freedom, from our brain's negative predispositions, the complexity, the uncertainty, and the trap of time. I pray you find and stay in that freedom, and transform yourself into a force of peace and joy in the world. Thank you."

In the final two chapters, I will respectively summarize the very important topic of resilience and share with you how I live my days as I strive to be a stronger, kinder, and happier person.

80

A Nod to Resilience

Mindfulness *v2* is on a mission—a mission to help you be stronger, kinder, and happier. In this book, you saw many facets of mindfulness *v2*—those of neuroscience, intentional presence, higher principles, courage, hope, inspiration, and more. When these constructs merge together in the mind, with time, they yield a powerful and transformative outcome: resilience. In this penultimate chapter, I wish to share with you what I believe is a key purpose of mindfulness practice—to help you become more resilient.

The two solutions for brain overload that I shared with you in chapter 1 (Setting the stage) are to decrease the load and to increase the brain's capacity to lift the load. Resilience, as we shall soon see, is increasing your brain's capacity to better lift your life's load.

Resilience is extremely important in today's world given the pace of change and concerning research findings that we—grownups and kids alike—are losing resilience. Suicide, drug-related deaths, mental health diagnoses, prevalence of drug use, stress—all are at an all-time or near all-time high. I hope the preceding chapters provided you with insight into why we are struggling and will continue to struggle unless we make a change and take charge, and also the starter kit for a few potential solutions. In the next few pages I will attempt to synthesize the solutions and present them in a compact, structured, and accessible approach that has been found to be effective in several research studies.

Just as fire is to cooked food, mindfulness is to resilience. Resilience is an emergent outcome of disciplined, authentic mindfulness practice, mixed with the key ingredients of deeper connections, healthy lifestyle, meaningful pursuits, altruism, and for many, faith.

Consistent practice of authentic mindfulness leads to resilience.

I'll cover in-depth, the why, what, and how of resilience in a future book. For now, let's dip our toes and get introduced to resilience and the connection between mindfulness *v2* and resilience.

WHAT IS RESILIENCE?
Think of someone you know who has had a lot of rough and tumble in life but no one could diminish this person's spirit or love of life. That person is resilient.

From morning to night, you draw from a well of energy to climb each rung in your life. Resilience is that well. Resilience is the core strength you use to lift the load of life. Experts define resilience as having three parts—your ability to withstand adversity (Resist), to bounce back from adversity (Recover), and to grow despite life's downturns (Rise). The American Heritage Dictionary [2000] definition of resilience is the ability to recover quickly from illness, change, or misfortune. My personal preferred definition is this: **resilience is doing well when you shouldn't be doing well.**

Resilience is doing well when you shouldn't be doing well.

While resilience has as many definitions as there are people defining it,[1120-1125] the best way to understand resilience is through stories. When Marie Curie chose to keep working despite the tragic loss of her husband in an accident, she was demonstrating resilience; the same goes for when Helen Keller chose not to let her disabilities limit her life's work, when Mahatma Gandhi decided to correct the wrong after he was pushed out of the train, and when Mother Teresa chose to walk into the slums despite personal frailty. Throughout this book I have shared many examples of resilience, including the story of my mother, Shashi, who found a path to wellness through illness.

Resilience is the culmination of the successful integration of all the principles discussed in this book—insight, intentional presence, flexible zoom, meaning, curiosity, patience, compassion, humility, forgiveness, gratitude, hope, inspiration, courage, and self-care. The resilience I believe in is kind resilience that is informed by science, powered by altruism, and lives to create a compassionate world.

Resilience is simultaneously an individual's disposition,[1126] a trained skill that effects a process[1127] and a positive outcome.[1128, 1129] Just as mixing fuel, oxygen, and heat creates fire, nurturing deeper connections and practicing authentic mindfulness, sensible self-care, purposeful living, altruism, and, for many, belief in the sacred, creates resilience. I often think of cooking a delicious lentil soup as a good metaphor for nurturing resilience.

THE LENTIL SOUP

My mother-in-law, Kusum, makes the most delicious lentil soup on the planet. If you ask her how she does it, she answers humbly, saying, "Oh, I mix a few things, and it works out." Or she might say, "I just go by my instincts." One day we sat down to capture those instincts into a recipe. We wanted to know how many cups of lentils, how much water, how many tomatoes, and how much salt, curcumin, coriander, chili pepper, and so on. Now that we know the ingredients and the process, we can replicate her success (at least to an extent).

The same applies to resilience. Telling someone who is struggling to just be positive, peaceful, and strong may not be enough. In fact, it may annoy that person. More important and useful is to share the specific ingredients that contribute to a more positive disposition and how we go about mixing the ingredients. Let's talk about the five ingredients that contribute to our resilience. My focus is on the aspects we can influence. For example, geopolitical uncertainties affect our resilience but aren't in our control. That's why they aren't in my equation.

THE FIVE DOMAINS (INGREDIENTS) OF RESILIENCE
The five domains (ingredients) are physical, cognitive, emotional, social, and spiritual.

Physical
Resilient people fall sick less often and recover quicker from illness. They have greater reserve. This is partly because of genetics and partly because of environment. Research shows that 50 percent of our well-being depends on our genes—some people are just lucky and don't fall sick.[1130, 1131] The rest of the 50 percent depends on our life situations and intentional choices. Four important intentional choices are diet, physical activity, adequate sleep, and preventive care.

Half of our wellbeing depends on the choices we make.

Preferring the foods that were available to your grandma (that is, avoiding packaged, refined, calorie-dense food), savoring your meals, being a messenger boy rather than a couch potato all day long (that is, standing and walking more), resting your back in the bed (i.e. sleeping) for about a third of the day, and leveraging technology for early diagnosis and treatment, all contribute to better physical health.

I commonly see patients who struggle with a multitude of symptoms despite normal heart, lungs and other body parts, while others are active and full of energy with 40 percent of their heart damaged. In many situations, science still isn't advanced enough to understand the cause of symptoms among people who have normal labs and scans. Researchers are working on new theories, including central sensitization, to understand some of these symptoms.[1132]

One of our purposes is to not judge those whose back pains can't be explained by an abnormal MRI. Some of the strongest, bravest people I know struggle with these symptoms, including fighter pilots, entrepreneurs, physicians, teachers, and supermoms. In fact, judging them is a grave mistake that can make you insensitive and hurt their healing. Our second job is to find inspiration from those who clearly could have taken to the bed but chose to remain up and about.

***Not every pain can be explained by
an abnormal MRI scan.***

Linda Wortman, a friend and colleague, is one such inspiring person. She had non–smoking related lung cancer and underwent removal of half of her lung. The cancer didn't know what it was up against. Linda not only beat the cancer but also transformed herself, inspiring thousands in the process. With one working lung, she climbs mountains, runs marathons (she has run 5K races in all fifty states), lobbies for altruistic causes, and, with her husband, Jerry, runs a nonprofit to help patients with lung cancer.

Interestingly, recent research shows that **although you cannot change your sequence of inherited genes, you have tremendous control over which genes are expressed**, a phenomenon called epigenetics. So, even the 50 percent of your well-being and resilience that is genetically mediated could be in your control. Perhaps Linda knew this instinctively.

> *Although we can't change our genetic sequence, we can change which genes are expressed. And that may be enough.*

Cognitive

The four important cognitive functions are attention, memory, judgment, and decision making. Attention is the gateway into our mind; memory is your ability to code, store and retrieve information; judgment and decision making is your ability to integrate your personal goals and motivation with information from attention and memory, and translate the resulting insight into a rational view of life and the world. Stress impairs all of these.

If you have struggled finding car keys in the morning while the keys are right in front of you, then you know how stress can impair attention. Or if you have forgotten your password in front of a client or blanked on what you were going to say in an interview or during a talk, you know how stress can affect our memory. Very experienced television reporters have forgotten their lines and experienced a panic attack on live TV.

Stress mediates its effect on cognitive function through changing three critical areas of the brain—the hippocampus, prefrontal cortex, and amygdala. Overall, with ongoing stress, the hippocampus (the memory area) and the prefrontal cortex (the central executive) both atrophy, while the amygdala (the fear processor) increases in activity.[1133, 1134]

> *Excessive stress hurts our ability to focus by causing structural damage to the brain.*

With resilience, we experience less stress and faster recovery, leading to less impairment of our cognitive functions. The example I often share is that of driving. Occasionally, you will veer off and land on the rumble strip. Resilience helps you come back to the highway. With low resilience, though, you might end up in the ditch. Resilience will also prevent you from wandering off onto the rumble strip every other day. Several attention-strengthening skills I discussed in the book and will briefly mention later can help you with cognitive resilience.

Emotional

If you know of people who feel blah for no reason or take a long time to recover from a negative comment, you know what emotional weakness looks like. Emotionally resilient people experience frequent positive emotions and recover quicker from negative emotions. They have balanced optimism and are good at regulating their fear.

The stress-induced brain changes described above (amygdala growth and hippocampus and prefrontal cortex atrophy) also predispose us to emotional vulnerability. Unfortunately, some people show exaggerated changes in the brain and behavior for two reasons—vulnerable genotype and unresolved childhood trauma. An identical stressor is processed differently by people with less resilient versus more resilient genotypes. The same applies to unresolved childhood trauma. Through no fault of theirs, some people are more likely to experience ongoing stress related to an inciting event. They overthink, and their thoughts are often colored by the negative. By morning, they cook up a complex web of thoughts related to a minor comment made the previous evening. Connecting this response with a valid biological reason will help you become kinder. An even more important realization is that all this can be helped by cultivating emotional resilience.

With resilience, you launch a quicker and stronger prefrontal cortex reaction. You thus recover faster. You find humor in the traffic jam, laugh over the stain of spilled milk on your coat, and find meaning relatively quickly if you were skipped over for promotion at work (I hope that never happens). All of this is eminently possible to learn and internalize. Many of the principles I have shared here—including intentionality, flexible zoom, meaning, curiosity, patience, compassion, humility, forgiveness, gratitude, hope, inspiration, and courage—can help you enhance emotional resilience. I will very briefly revisit some of these concepts in the "Mindset" section of the resilience program I mention below.

Social

While physical, cognitive, and emotional resilience are your internal sources of strength, social resilience offers strength from the outside. Social resilience is finding strength through feeling connected and supported. A large body of research shows the benefit of social resilience on physical health, emotional health, performance, and even survival. The opposite of feeling connected and supported is feeling lonely or discriminated against.

It is worthwhile to remind ourselves that loneliness is worse than smoking for its effect on health and longevity.[113, 114, 116] Also, loneliness is a lot about perception. You could be alone, even socially isolated, yet not feel lonely, or you could be surrounded by a hundred people yet feel alone. An important point to realize is that it isn't just the elderly who feel lonely. Loneliness affects all ages, all genders, all races, and all socioeconomic groups.

With respect to discrimination it is important to realize that according to a recent Robert Wood Johnson Foundation and Harvard School of Public Health poll, more than 50 percent people of every single race now feel discriminated in the U.S.[1134b] Those who we feel are discriminating are themselves feeling discriminated. Who will then provide healing? This is a sad statistic that we must reverse by bringing more kindness to our communities.

Those we feel are discriminating, themselves feel discriminated. Who will then heal whom?

In terms of relationships, quality and depth are more important than quantity. That is the reason that a **million likes on social media aren't as powerful as a brother or sister or friend or parent who deeply loves and cares. I so wish every teenager knew that.**

*A million likes on social media are no match to
a deeply loving trusting relationship.*

Spiritual

Spiritual resilience is unique in that its source is both inside and outside. Some believe that deep within them is a source of truth—an infinitely precious, sacred spiritual essence. Some believe in the sacred that is in the heavens or somewhere external. Some believe in both, and some believe in neither. No matter your belief, **the core source of spiritual resilience is nurturing a higher meaning, an altruistic perspective, and a commitment to compassion.** Research shows a strong anchor in the sacred enhances resilience.[1135]

There are many different potential expressions of your spirituality—for example, your desire to help many and hurt none, your passion to make the world a better place for our children, your striving to take care of Mother Earth, your kindness, your selfless work, your faith, and your prayer. Each of these expressions is profound and powerful in its own unique way.

*We all have different models of spirituality. Acceptance of all models as long as
they encourage compassion and the collective good is a path to progress.*

Two additional domains of resilience and well-being are financial and professional. Financial resilience is your ability to live within your means, be prepared for occasional financial jolts, and create a robust long-term plan so you don't have to check the stock market every other day. This needs planning and, given its complexity, help from someone who has knowledge and experience in the financial field.

Professional resilience is pursuing a career that optimally leverages your skills, challenges you, helps you grow, has realistic expectations, rewards fairly, helps your self-worth, and provides a safe and collegial environment. No workplace can consistently provide all of these, but the more the better. Professional resilience is a joint responsibility between you and your employer.

Organizational resilience—the ability of an organization to adapt to change—emerges from your individual work-related resilience combined with well-integrated teams, committed visionary leadership, effective communication systems, leverage of the right technology, and a safe and well-built physical structure.

WHY RESILIENCE?

Exploring the reasons why people struggle is important. Even more important and instructive is why some thrive in the face of adversity. Their secret sauce is resilience. The resilient people look at their obstacles as worthy challenges, focus on what they can control, and find meaning in their difficulties.

Here is a summary of research about the benefits of resilience: *in hundreds of research studies, resilience has been associated with better physical and emotional health, more meaningful relationships, greater success at work, and greater happiness.*

> ***Resilience correlates with better physical and emotional health, more meaningful relationships, greater success at work, and greater happiness.***

Now for some details: The opposite of being resilient is remaining stressed. Your body can handle mild and occasional stress but despises excessive and ongoing stress. The self-help gurus who teach us that stress is good probably aren't thinking about the real-world struggles of countless millions. Try saying that stress is good for you to a mother with an addicted, suicidal teenager; or a person with an adulterous, abusive spouse; or a citizen who lost it all to the hurricane. You will receive a blank stare or, more deservingly, a rebuke. Pick any medical book and scroll through its index, and you will see that every single diagnosis is made worse by stress—from accelerated aging to heart attack to herpes flare, dental caries, and early death. Resilience can protect you—not completely, but to a great extent. What follows is the research evidence, culled from hundreds of research studies.

Physical health

In patients with cancer, resilience correlates with better performance, lower risk of disability, lower fatigue, lower risk of recurrence, and higher survival.[1136-1142] In several other conditions including heart disease,[1143] asthma,[1144] diabetes,[1145, 1146] addictions,[1147] and chronic pain,[1148] resilience correlates with better outcomes. One study reported lower risk of liver and lung cancer among people with higher stress resilience.[1149] In a large study recently completed by our group involving about two thousand participants, resilience correlated with lower frequency and intensity of pain.[1149b]

> ***Resilience is associated with lower frequency and intensity of pain.***

Resilience helps not only in healing illness but also in promoting wellness. The resilient people report higher overall well-being,[1150-1153, 1149b] have fewer health complaints,[1154] and are better protected from the negative effects of aging.[1155-1157] [1158] Resilience also correlates with avoiding high-risk behavior.[1159]

Emotional health

Resilience and good emotional health are identical twins. The more resilient you are, the lower your risk of mental-health diagnoses—depression, anxiety, bipolar disorder, and more.[1160-1172] In one of our studies the prevalence of depression was four times lower among the high resilience group, compared to the low resilience group (4.7 percent versus 19.5 percent).[1149b] In the same study anxiety was three times less likely among the high resilience group compared to the low resilience group (9.1 percent versus 24.7 percent).[1149b]

The resilient people are four times less likely to suffer from depression.

Lack of resilience portends worse outcomes after disasters. After a traumatic event, resilience is protective of developing post-traumatic stress disorder.[1129, 1154, 1173-1176] Police officers with greater resilience have lower prevalence of negative emotions.[1177] Women with adverse childhood experiences who had higher relational resilience (such as sense of security and belongingness) were protected from developing depression.[1178]

The more resilient students on college campuses are likely to be happier and deal more productively with traumatic situations.[1179-1187] If there is one group that sorely needs greater resilience in our society today, it is students on college campuses.

Work

Resilient people have a can-do attitude, lower work-related burnout, and better productivity, and they face their challenges with courage, hope, and determination.[1188-1194] Individual resilience contributes to the evolution of team and community resilience that helps the teams and communities better withstand losses and other external challenges.[1195, 1196] In our study with two thousand participants, compared to the low resilience population, the high resilience group was 62 percent more likely to find meaning in work, 114 percent more likely to have high enthusiasm, and 59 percent more likely to feel that he or she was very successful.[1149b]

The resilient people have remarkably higher enthusiasm and ability to find meaning in their work.

Relationships

People with low resilience have less rewarding relationships, higher risk of divorce, and perceive lower social support. The resilient feel better connected and perceive greater social support.[1197-1199] In our study, the resilient were 56 percent less likely to feel isolated and 51 percent more likely to have close family relationships.[1149b]

Closer personal relationships, less loneliness, higher social support, and lower risk of divorce: these are all the benefits of being more resilient.

Health-care costs

Enhancing resilience among employees has been demonstrated to decrease health-care costs, an important outcome today when health care makes up to 8 percent of the average cost of corporate annual budgets and continues to climb faster than inflation.[1200]

In summary, **pick anything you want in life. You are more likely to succeed at it with greater resilience.**

HOW TO ENHANCE INDIVIDUAL RESILIENCE

Enhancing individual resilience is nurturing a resilient brain in a strong body. Our focus presently is the brain. A resilient brain has good energy, a worthy goal to target its energy, and a well-thought-out path to pursue that goal. Such a brain welcomes challenge, controls the controllable and lets go of the rest, and finds meaning in the gains as well as the losses. A whole host of genes, hormones, neurotransmitters and nerve growth factors work together to fashion a resilient brain, a topic I will more fully explore in future writings.[1201-1203]

Next, I will summarize the core content of a resilience program that I and my colleagues have found effective in over twenty clinical trials and routinely teach at Mayo Clinic and elsewhere to tens of thousands of people every year.[225, 832, 1204-1210, 1210a, 1210b] The program has three parts: *Insight, Attention, and Mindset.*

Insight

Insight is the awareness of how our brains operate. I covered it in the first tenet of this book. The main insight we teach in the program is about three core neural traps—focus (our constant mind wandering), fatigue (the biological need of our brain's neurons to take periodic rest for efficient performance), and fear (our negativity bias). The default operation of our brains makes us very vulnerable to negative emotions and mental fatigue. Educating participants about the brain is perhaps the most important part of helping them carve their personal path to resilience.

Attention

The first set of skills helps you develop deep, sustained, strong, intentional attention. In general, the idea is to externally project the attention and develop intentionality. I have covered these aspects at several places in this and previous books.

Of the many attention practices, the four that I have found most useful and that are core to the resilience program are:

- Morning gratitude. First thing in the morning, before you leave your bed, think about five people in your life who you know care about you (or who you care about) and send them your silent gratitude. This practice helps you develop stronger attention, start your day with positive emotions, feel connected to the people close to you, and take charge of the brain right when you wake up, instead of ceding control to external contingencies.
- Two-minute rule. Meet your family at the end of the work day or at least one person every day as though you haven't seen them for a long time. Starting your evening on a positive note can enhance the quality of your entire evening.
- Curious moments. Notice one new thing or one detail in a familiar thing every day; share that detail with someone. This practice keeps novelty alive in your life.
- Kind attention. Send silent good wishes to people, knowing that everyone is special and has struggles. When you wish others well, you wish yourself well. This is a simple and powerful way to experience positive emotions in the middle of a busy day.

You can access the specifics of these practices in the online (or in-person) Mayo Clinic Healthy Living: Resilient Mind Program or in the previous two Mayo Clinic books. Here are the page numbers and titles under which each of these practices is described in the two books (notice that some of the names of the practices are slightly different):

In the *Mayo Clinic Guide to Stress-Free Living*:[226]

- Morning Gratitude (Start Your Day with Gratitude, pp. 66–69)
- Two-Minute Rule (Finding Novelty in Relationships, pp. 54–62; and Greet Your Loved Ones as if Meeting after a Long Time, pp. 70–71)
- Curious Moments (The World in a Flower, pp. 52–53; and Notice Nature Once a Day and as Needed, pp. 69–70)
- Kind Attention (Practicing Kind Attention with Compassion, Acceptance, Love and Forgiveness, pp. 81–82)

In the *Mayo Clinic Handbook for Happiness*:[819]

- Morning Gratitude (Exercise 1, pp. 48–53)
- Two-Minute Rule (Exercise 3, pp. 55–67)
- Curious Moments (Exercise 2, pp. 53–55)
- Kind Attention (Kind Attention, pp. 76–78).

Resilient Mindset

The insight into neuroscience and strong intentional attention free up extra working space in your brain so you can cultivate deeper thinking and align your thoughts with your core values instead of the instinctive negativity bias. The five core principles of the program are: gratitude, compassion, acceptance, meaning, and forgiveness.

I have discussed each of these and additional principles at multiple places in this book. You can find a structured approach for bringing them to your life in the online (or in-person) Mayo Clinic Healthy Living: Resilient Mind Program or in the previous two Mayo Clinic books (*Mayo Clinic Guide to Stress-Free Living*, parts 3–8, pp. 90–232; *Mayo Clinic Handbook for Happiness*, section 3, "The Second Step," pp. 80–200).

My suggested approach is to pair the principles with a weekday. Here is the sequence I suggest and have used in research studies:

- Monday—Gratitude
- Tuesday—Compassion
- Wednesday—Acceptance
- Thursday—Meaning
- Friday—Forgiveness

None of this is meant to be nerdy. Please don't say on a Thursday that I can't be compassionate today because it is only assigned to Tuesday!

Each of the principles can be practiced in five ways: *reading* about the principle in books or online, *thinking* what the principle means to you, *sharing* it with others, *writing* in your diary or blog, and *practicing*.

By practicing, I am referring to two approaches: *lower the threshold* and *create a discipline*. **If you wait for spectacular news to be grateful, you will have a long wait.** Instead, think gratitude for the water in your faucet, sunlight coming from your window, the taste of food, and a deep breath.

If you have only a few spare minutes during your day, then type the name of the principle for that day along with the search term *quotes* and select images in the internet search engine. Check, for example, "gratitude quotes" or "forgiveness quotes." You will find nice small quotes with beautiful images.

Alternatively, if I am in the mood for a smile, I search with the word *humor*: "gratitude humor" or "forgiveness humor," for example. Enjoy the collective human creativity in the search results. You'll find that some cartoons aren't the most appropriate, but you can easily choose to overlook them.

Integrating

One practical way to integrate the core resilience skills in your life is to incrementally add one skill every week or every few weeks. Here is one suggested approach:

Week 1: Start with morning gratitude
Week 2: Continue week 1 practice + Add two-minute rule or curious moments
Week 3: Continue week 1 and week 2 practices + Add kind attention
Week 4: Continue weeks 1-3 practices + Add resilient mindset
Week 5 onward: Continue weeks 1-4 practices + develop additional ideas

Instead of adding a skill weekly, you can add biweekly or monthly, choose a different sequence, or do whatever works best for you. Also, tweak the skills to your preference and lifestyle.

In the online resilience program, we have two phases: *Train phase* is the initial four weeks of training and practice, and *Sustain phase* entails continuing to deepen and broaden the practice with additional ideas.

The resilience program has two phases: Train and Sustain.

If you're concerned that by the end of the fourth week, you'll be spending six hours every day formally practicing these skills, let me reassure you that **the total time spent in the formal practice is less than ten minutes per day.**

The resilience program can be learned in about three hours and the total formal practice time is less than ten minutes per day.

The reason these skills are so powerful and help you become stronger is that they serve as seeds for an ongoing informal practice that continues long after the brief formal practice is over. Thus, morning gratitude has lifted my entire morning, two-minute rule has added so much more love to our family's evenings, kind attention has deepened every connection with every human, and the principles have helped me reframe most adverse situations. I go deeper in joy and bypass hurts more easily. The hurts still happen but leave fewer scars. Try one of the ideas. Unlike many pharmaceuticals, they are much safer. We have never noticed gratitude causing skin rash, GI upset, or a drop in blood counts!

Further, I have found that I am able to cut down several hours of mind wandering with this trivial time investment. In multiple research studies, my colleagues and I have found that this approach enhances resilience, mindfulness, happiness, quality of life, life satisfaction, and health behaviors, and it decreases stress, anxiety, and burnout.[225, 832, 1204-1210, 1210a, 1210b] In one study with public-school teachers, we found that over 75 percent of teachers reported improved interactions with the students as a result of practicing the program. My team is currently writing this manuscript.

At my workplace, this program is now part of onboarding for all physicians, nurses, and medical students.

ONLY THE THREE DOMAINS

Notice that in terms of the skills in the program, I have mostly focused on cognitive, emotional, and spiritual resilience. I have found that greater cognitive, emotional, and spiritual resilience opens up "space" in your life to enhance all the other resilience domains. Strong attention and healthier emotions help you find the energy to invest in healthy living, putting you into the upward spiral of life.

Enhancing cognitive, emotional and spiritual resilience eventually positively affect all aspects of life.

Further, a better question than asking if one is or isn't resilient, is to ask, in what aspect is one resilient? Everyone is innately resilient in one aspect and not so much in another.

Every person is resilient, in his or her own unique way.

A good strategy is to work on the skills in the domain most interesting to you, and then expand to other aspects as you feel appropriate.

I hope the previous description provided you with a useful summary of resilience. I invite you to connect with me in the online or in-person resilience programs to continue our journey together. I am grateful to you from the deepest place in my heart for your support and for trusting me with your time. Before we close, I wish to share with you how I live my days as I strive to embody a deeper presence, kindness, and resilience.

81

My Personal Practice

This is where the rubber meets the road. In the next few pages, I wish to share with you what I do every day in my struggles to uncage myself from my neural traps, striving to become a better human being.

ALGORITHMS

I struggle with a mind that is wonderful at forgetting. Despite my best intentions to never think thoughts I would be embarrassed to own, such thoughts visit me most days. I will make my confessions in a moment; for now, I wish to share a few perspectives I keep in my back pocket to recover faster. These perspectives are my umbrella. With their protection, even though I still get wet, I don't get drenched. Here are a few algorithms I use to overcome some specific challenges:

If someone seems upset— then I try to remember that **an expression other than love is a call for help.**

If I lose something— then I consider that **I get what I need, not what I want.**

If I face an annoyance— then I remind myself that anything that won't bother me in five years isn't worth fretting about today.

If I am confused about what to do— then I think of my primary employer, the world's children. I do what will help children the most.

If something significantly unpleasant happens— then **I think about what went right within what went wrong.**

If I face several conflicting goals— then I try to remember that **my single goal for myself is to develop universal compassion.**

If I am not able to forgive— then I consider that **forgiveness is for me, not for the other person.**

Create a few such algorithms of your own. Research shows that having these if-then contingencies increases your chance of success with your resolutions.[1211]

SOME CONFESSIONS

Despite keeping these thoughts with me, I struggle with a brain that has all thirteen neural traps I mentioned earlier. Here are some of my imperfections.

- I get envious when I see others being more successful, particularly those who were at the same place I was at some point.
- I get angry (at least internally) when I am slighted.
- I am attracted to money and fame.
- I overeat when served delicious food.
- I would rather be lazy.
- I get irritated by incompetence.
- I struggle with patience.
- I carry stereotypes and biases.
- I am conflicted.
- I have an ego that gets bruised.
- I catastrophize and experience fear.
- I wish I could forgive more easily.
- I judge more quickly than I wish.

That is only a partial list! And this is after at least fifteen years of working hard to discipline my instincts. I am very much a work in progress.

What goes in my favor is that I have good intentions. I am curious and diligent. I truly mean well. I recover quickly from the slights. My ego is small. I am able to convert into compassion many of my feelings that originate in envy, anger, irritation, ego, and biases. I am generally able to convert desires into contentment. I often am able to transform exaggerations into rationality, laziness into energy, impatience into patience, conflicts into commitment, and fear into faith.

Here is how I was about ten years ago: I would have multiple fears, negative and embarrassing thoughts every day, and I would ruminate on these thoughts for hours. I was compassionate to only a few—the ones most meaningful to me.

Here is how I am now: I have occasional negative and embarrassing thoughts, and fears, and I recover quickly from these thoughts—usually within seconds or minutes. I am compassionate to anyone who is struggling, irrespective of whether that person is related to me.

Here is how I want to be before my last breath (hopefully sooner): I will have minimal to no negative and embarrassing thoughts, and I will recover from these thoughts right away. I want to be compassionate to not only every person but also (at least in thought) to every life-form, even those who may have hurt me or might hurt me.

To reach that goal entails changing how I live my entire day, not just ten or fifteen minutes.

MY DAILY PRACTICE

I will list here what I do with my mind every day to keep working toward the goal of developing universal compassion. I am giving a time stamp just to give you an idea.

Upon waking up: The moment I wake up, I send silent gratitude to a few people who I believe care about me or are helping the world become a better place. When I'm in a hurry, I just think about my wife. In addition, I almost never leave the bed until I have thought about one good thing my wife did in the previous twenty-four hours or a few days. I then say a short prayer for peace in the world.

First contact: When I meet my family as I get up, even on a day I didn't sleep enough, I do my best to show I am in a good mood. I know this is infectious. It could be talking in lisps, sharing a joke, engaging in mimicry, or doing something else.

Short workout: After freshening up, I work out for fifteen to twenty minutes, sometimes while watching an inspiring video, such as a good TED talk or listening to good music.

Commute: As I drive to work, I commonly send silent good wishes to drivers on the other side of the road. I continue this practice as I reach my office and often when I see the list of people I have to meet during the day.

10:00 a.m.: Come to my office if you are hungry, because I keep at least ten thousand calories in my room—mostly dark chocolate and almonds. Ten o'clock is the time for my dark-chocolate-and-almond snack. My brain is beginning to get tired now and will soon need some rest.

10:30 a.m.: I have been working for a few hours. My eyes have been strained. My brain has accumulated neurotransmitters that need to be washed away. This is my time to close my eyes and practice deep breathing. I typically do that for five to ten minutes. It has never failed to refresh me.

Lunch: I try to eat before I am very hungry because if I get too hungry, then I invariably overeat or eat unhealthy food. I try to be patient with and savor the first few bites. All of this makes the food more enjoyable.

2:00 p.m.: This is the time for the W3 practice (Wishing Well Walk—few minutes of walking while wishing others well). I step out of my office and take a short stroll while sending a silent good wish to at least twenty people.

4:00 p.m.: Often, I repeat five to ten minutes of deep-breathing practice.

Sprinkled all day long: Several times during the day, I sprinkle a few deep breaths and silent good wishes to others. I also try to bring a smile to my eyes.

Commute: I try to notice something novel as I travel back home, and I send as many silent good wishes as I can.

Meeting family: At the end of each day, I meet my family as though I haven't seen them for a month. I light up, do high fives, show I am in a good mood, share a funny or inspiring story, help them feel worthy, or do something else. Often, before entering the home, I remind myself why I am grateful to my loved ones or how I have only finite moments with them, or anyone else I am about to meet.

Family time: At least once during the day, I try to see the color of my loved ones' eyes. I do work a fair bit after hours, but in between, I try my best to bring my full presence to my family. I have to get better at that.

Bedtime: I often read or create a story for our younger daughter as she is drifting off to sleep. I spend a few minutes in prayer before sleeping at night.

Perspective: I try to keep the perspectives I mentioned earlier (the algorithms) all day long to prevent going into negative thinking and to recover quickly.

While all of this may seem like a lot, I have been working on myself for the last fifteen years. It only takes about ten to fifteen minutes of formal time during the day.

Breathing twenty thousand times a day also sounds like a lot. But because breath is an automatic activity, it is effortless. Similarly, when deep, intentional attention, authentic presence, gratitude, compassion, and forgiveness become ingrained in you, they will become effortless. While you will still experience regrets and hurts, you will recover from them faster—a marker of developing wisdom.[1212] You will find a home in kindness rather than visiting kindness occasionally. Kindness to self and all isn't a luxury. It is an absolute necessity if we are to survive on this planet. Your and my children, grandkids, nephews and nieces deserve it.

THREE BODIES

For most of our evolutionary past, we were busy protecting our *physical bodies*. We had short, violent lives, just long enough to procreate and raise our children but not long enough to play with the grandkids.

A converging set of circumstances helped us build brick houses, alarm systems, hospitals, and more. We learned about our genes and ways to take care of ourselves. We started living longer. Heart disease and cancer replaced external injuries as the commonest causes of death. We got insured for every possible contingency. We graduated from constantly protecting our physical bodies to protecting our emotional bodies.

This is our state right now—sometimes busy protecting our physical bodies but most of the time busy protecting our emotional bodies. In this effort, we experience loneliness, low self-worth, discrimination, anxiety, and depression. We live to collect wealth, forgetting that in this universe of two trillion galaxies, anything that we can acquire on this little planet is so infinitely small that it isn't worth selling our souls over.

We shamelessly self-promote, scheme, and sell our conscience for short-lasting pleasures. The greed of one person can hurt millions. Greed can make us sell our souls to collect worthless goods—not a good bargain. We nurture greed because, collectively, we haven't graduated to protecting the third body—the *spiritual body*.

The spiritual body is the subtlest level of our existence. Its appearance is of integrity; it speaks in the language of gratitude, compassion, patience, humility, and forgiveness. It sees the world as a connected whole. It doesn't know how to lie, deceive, or be selfish. It is busy serving and praying for the well-being of all. It shares others' sorrows and finds joy in sacrificing its joy. It is kind, gentle, flexible, hopeful, bold, and hardworking, and with each breath, it serves the collective.

To think of the right values, consider what values you want your children to embody. **If we all would think, speak, and behave the way we wanted our children to think, speak, and behave, the world would be transformed.** The wisdom of us grown-ups is our childhood innocence repackaged. I was much wiser in kindergarten. I knew to share. I knew how to laugh, hug, and love. I didn't lie, snatch, or steal. I could flow for hours. **Think of what made you happy before you learned to get sad. It'll give you an idea of how to be happy again.**

But as we add years to our lives, we lose our innocence. Thus, in our current state of evolution, we grown-ups are busy protecting all three bodies, but we prioritize the first two—the physical and the emotional. I have no doubt we are slowly but surely evolving toward a state in which we will transcend our selfishness, greed, and fear so we can live each day with timeless values. The day we get busy protecting our spiritual body will be the day when we start speaking the truth for the sake of speaking the truth and start living the values because that is the right thing to do and not because someone is watching. We can progress to that state by revisiting the concept of two lives.

OUR TWO LIVES

You and I are living two lives. When I make multiple trips from Rochester to Minneapolis, a distance of about eighty miles, two things are happening during my commute. First, I am accomplishing the goal of traveling to get some work done. Second, I am becoming a better driver. While each visit may have a slightly different goal, each trip of mine trains me to become a better driver. The same thing is happening in our lives.

Through each experience every day, you are living two lives. In the first, you are accomplishing worldly goals (work, relationships, and more). In the second, you are becoming a better human being.

You have a choice in where you anchor your awareness. Here is my suggestion: consider the second life, the one in which each experience is helping you become a better person, to be at least as important as the real one. Each loss and gain, success and failure, accolade and rejection, help you become a better person. **Success teaches you humility and gratitude; failure teaches you acceptance and compassion.** Learning these lessons is what life is all about.

When you think about this deeper truth, you will start flowing with life. You will zoom out. Kindness will no longer be your second language. It will define your day and take you to freedom.

I like the idea of freedom. In fact, that is how the vision of the hummingbird came to my mind. I woke up one morning and had the vision of a hummingbird trying to find freedom. I felt as if I was seeing the struggle of the entire humanity. That vision inspired me to pick the theme for the book and the subtitle, *Let's Not Cage the Hummingbird*.

It will be befitting our journey, if we conclude it by talking about freedom in the context of mindfulness. I also want to introduce you to a new name and pick your brain about it!

A NEW NAME?

When I think about the last few times I saw a hummingbird, three words come to my mind: grit, grace and freedom. With her strong wings and fast metabolism, she is a role model of how she has overcome the downward pull of gravity, the sideward drafts of the wind, and the hawk eyes of the predators. She has found freedom.

Freedom for me is escaping the trap of my brain's lower predispositions that produce the toxic mix of fear, greed, envy, anger, hatred, hubris, and ignorance. I also seek freedom from the past wounds, present chaos, future worries, the shackles of time, and any rigid constructs that, instead of showing me the blue sky, put me in another cage, even if that cage is slightly bigger and more comfortable.

As our journey through this book comes to a close, I wonder if in leveraging neuroscience to redesign mindfulness, we have come so far from the original idea that it might be helpful to think of a new name. I must confess that the name 'mindfulness *v2*' was a compromise for me. In thinking of a new name, I got stuck in a creativity worm hole! In fact, I (and many others) struggle with the name mindfulness itself, since it is unclear to many what it means, has countless definitions, and perhaps had a different understanding and purpose than we have today.

In the spirit of freedom, here is one suggestion for a new name—**Mindfreeness**. When I close my eyes and think of mindfreeness, I sense lightness, courage, fearlessness, joy, ascent, and becoming untethered. I feel I have the courage to fly because I now have wings and am not afraid of gravity.

My definition of mindfreeness is the same definition as mindfulness *v2*: Living with intentionality, kindness, and gratitude. For me, mindfreeness captures the essence of the seven tenets I have presented in this book. I will love to hear from you if this name and definition makes sense to you, and also if you have another idea.

Mindfreeness: Living with intentionality, kindness, and gratitude.

Perhaps this is a natural stage in our evolution—become aware of our vulnerabilities, gather our attention, cultivate intentionality and kindness, and ascend to a higher state of the mind that is free to soak up deeper wisdom and authentic love. A mind so transformed effortlessly thrives in the realm of the spiritual, where grace resides.

With this ascent, you'll reclaim the freedom and fearlessness you had when you were innocent. The freedom now, however, will bask in the glow of wisdom. Freedom powered by wisdom becomes resilient. This freedom brings with it a phenomenal gift—empowered surrender.

Here is an invitation: spend your next one hour feeling fearless, free, and in empowered surrender. Become a student of life. Create no obstructions in its flow. Live deeper, ascend higher. Exit the dual concepts of good and bad, gain and loss. Instead, look at each experience as one of the infinite ways the world is filling you with patience, humility, gratitude, compassion, forgiveness, courage, hope, and inspiration. Believe, just believe, that your every pure thought, word, and action is helping someone today, someone who is in pain and has no hope. My thought is helping you, and yours is helping me. Thank you.

I can't wait to hear how your hour went. Until then, with love—

Amit

Appendix 1: Curious or Serious?

I wish to continue and deepen the discussion about meditation research here that I started in Chapter 9.

I have met some of the finest human beings whose lives were transformed by meditation. They embody a lightness of spirit and depth of presence that is inspiring. They are grateful, kind, wise, disciplined, selfless, humble, and patient. They have little or no fear, anger, greed, hatred, or envy. They are salt of the earth.

Given that millions of people have tried meditation, a question I wonder about is this—why don't we run into such people every day? Why are the phenomenal benefits of meditation fairly rare? The story of the rice pudding might help us.

THE RICE PUDDING

In the dessert section of most Indian buffets, you'll likely find rice pudding. Rice puddings can be of two types: the mediocre and the magnificent (I know I am being judgmental here!). The mediocre puddings look milky white, with rice having settled at the bottom. When you take a bite, you can taste milk, rice, and sugar separately. The rice is often in small clumps that need to be chewed. The pudding is often very sweet. Most chefs can prepare such pudding in less than an hour.

The magnificent pudding is golden creamy in color. It is lightly sweet, thicker in consistency since the rice and milk have inseparably blended into each other. You don't have to chew the magnificent pudding—it melts into your mouth. The added flavors of grated almonds and cardamom create heaven in each spoon. Don't be shy, go for the seconds!

Why isn't every rice pudding the magnificent kind? Because it takes the right proportion of ingredients, the right temperature, and lots of patience to create. The milk, rice and sugar have to simmer together on slow heat for eight to twenty-four hours for the transformation. I believe the same applies to our meditation practice.

CURIOUS OR SERIOUS?

Andy is in his mid-thirties and works for a startup in San Francisco. He puts in fourteen-hour days, is constantly sleep deprived, and is in and out of several relationships. He takes a supplement for fatigue. He is hoping to make it big through his vested options, once his company launches an IPO. A few months ago, his company offered a weekend course in stress management that included mindfulness meditation. He practices mindfulness meditation a few times a week and finds it relaxing. Mindfulness for him is a temporary escape from life.

Compare Andy to Ananda who is also in mid-thirties. Ananda lives in northern India. He moved to an ashram at age 11 to study meditation. At the ashram, which was a residential facility, he learned ancient scriptures of all major religions. For more than a decade, he has spent six to eight hours every day practicing yoga and meditation. At age twenty-five, he traveled back to his home town to run a branch of the ashram. He thinks of himself as a world citizen. His single purpose in life is to help the betterment of mankind. He has modest possessions, and seeks no fame or fortune. Despite his responsibilities at the ashram, he meditates at least four hours a day. Meditation for him is a way of life.

How fair will it be to compare the outcomes of Andy's and Ananda's practice? Both meditate, but their practices are a class apart. Andy is curious and interested, Ananda is serious and committed. If you perform brain scans of twenty practitioners like Ananda who has already clocked in more than thirty thousand hours of meditation under the guidance of a master, do you think the changes will resemble or be applicable to twenty practitioners like Andy? Probably not, right?

That is the problem with many of the meditation studies. These studies have been done on monks and masters who have been practicing for tens of thousands of hours under close guidance of a grandmaster, a privilege not accessible to the vast majority of us. The reason you are unlikely to access deep open awareness anytime soon is because it takes years and years and years of committed practice.

To be fair, even with his little practice Andy will find some benefit. But as I note below, most of the benefits will be transient. Further, because the practice demands time and discipline and the rewards are further out, Andy is unlikely to continue with it for the long term. Relocation, new partner, new job, personal crisis—any of these can derail his practice. Let's look at what research shows are the benefits for the curious and the serious. I will first talk about the curious.

CURIOUS

The curious practitioners with only a few weeks of practice might notice some improvement in memory, lower mind wandering,[1213, 1214] and improvement in the orienting but not other aspects of attention.[1215]

They might have lower amygdala reactivity and feelings of stress, and with about thirty or more hours of practice, small improvements in markers of cellular aging and inflammation. Short-term improvement in mood, blood pressure and other autonomic variables might accrue. But many of these benefits in research studies disappear when good control groups are introduced.[188] Most of the stronger and lasting benefits, where meditation can change you as a person, accrue after many years and thousands of hours of authentic practice in the right environment and with proper guidance.

SERIOUS

Research with the meditation Olympians totally validates the depth of qualities I have perceived meeting the true meditation masters. Importantly, they demonstrate changes not only during meditation, but also permanently throughout the day. The changes during the "non-meditative" periods of the day perhaps are more important than the transient high of the meditation.[1216]

They show resilience to age-related decline in attention.[1217] Their emotional (insula, cingulate cortex, amygdala) areas are exquisitely sensitive to other's suffering.[976] Nevertheless, they feel less pain, recover quickly from pain, have much lower anxiety about anticipated stressful situations, and use very little neural real estate to focus and sustain focus.[1218]

The brain changes that explain an individual's growth are truly remarkable. Their default mode network (the mind wandering apparatus) is better connected to the intentional part of the brain (the dorso-lateral pre-frontal cortex).[734] Their default network is also much quieter, the basis for lower mind wandering.[734, 1219, 1220] This is particularly true for those practicing compassion meditation.[734] A particular area of the brain, that neuroscientists believe generates the sense of self (posterior cingulate cortex) is less active in the long-term meditators.[1221] Many of these practitioners demonstrate sustained gamma waves on the EEG (capturing the brain's electrical activity), that might imply their heightened sense of awareness and experience of bliss.[1222] These EEG changes can be noticed even during sleep.[1223] To top it all off, long-term meditators at age fifty have a brain that is over seven years younger compared to control non-meditators, and their brain continues to age slower by about two months for each additional year.[1224] Accompanying these changes are lasting improvements in cortisol and inflammatory markers.[1225]

Given meditation's recent global popularity, I believe we haven't had the time in the west for many people to reach the master level. We will, in due course. However, that progress of a few will unlikely impact the population at large given the amount of discipline and time it takes to become a master meditator. Further, it will be difficult to replicate the cultural milieu of ashrams, with the presence of grandmasters from various traditions running the training camps for thousands of years. The pace of the world, increasing stress, and geopolitical drama brought to us every day by 24/7 news creates an anti-meditative culture. Here is one idea that might help.

INTENSITY MATTERS

Very interesting research shows that people who engage in shorter intense meditation practices can start showing lasting changes. For example, in a study involving participants in a three-month intense training practicing five hours of meditation every day, sustained improvement in self-regulation was noticed, up to five months after the training completion.[1226] The same training also showed sustained improvement in attention.[1227]

In another study, even a single day of intense mindfulness meditation enhanced downregulation of inflammatory genes.[1228] Intensive three days of mindfulness practice in a retreat setting increased connection between the dorso-lateral pre-frontal cortex (top-down controlling area of the brain) and default mode network.[101]

Part of the effect of intense practice might be because such practices are often offered in groups. A limited body of research shows that practice in retreats offer unique benefits. For example, in a study assessing the effect of meditation on breathing, retreat hours correlated strongly with slower breathing.[1229]

The retreat-effect may be because the quality of co-participants and teaching has considerable impact on the practice quality.

Research suggests that practice quality may be even more important than practice duration.[1230] This aligns well with data in other fields that are dispelling the ten-thousand-hours myth.[1231]

Finally, the individual who engages in mindfulness practice brings his or her baseline skills to the practice. People who have greater left and right amygdala activation in response to seeing pain in others report greater practice time after compassion meditation training (compared to people with lower amygdala activation).[1232] Limited data supports that people with higher baseline mindfulness might find greater benefit from mindfulness training,[1233] though opposite results have been noted in another study.[1234]

If you don't have the time or resources for an intensive three-month retreat (which most of us don't have), do not have access to a mindfulness grandmaster who has put in over fifty thousand hours of practice (most of them live in the Himalayas) and don't live in an ashram, yet you wish to bring about sustained change in your being, then what are your options? I have two.

A MEDITATION SECRET

I find meditation that focuses on breath, open awareness, or sustained attention toward an object, relatively dry and difficult to sustain beyond a few minutes. Here is the secret—add emotion to your practice, particularly compassion.

A fairly convincing body of research shows that compassion meditation can provide quicker reward and lasting changes. For example, very short-term training in compassion can lead to powerful changes in amygdala reactivity and positive mood, stronger than mindful attention training.[1235] In a research study, only eight hours of compassion training was associated with activation of brain areas that host positive emotions and affiliation with others (medial orbitofrontal cortex, putamen, pallidum, and ventral tegmental area).[885, 975]

An important point here is to recall the difference between empathy and compassion. Empathy is understanding others' pain and/or feeling with their pain.[1236] Empathy alone can be associated with negative emotions (and activation of brain areas that host pain and negative emotions).[885] Compassion, on the other hand, activates reward areas of the brain.[885, 975] And the changes in one's life are fast and lasting.

Just seven minutes of loving kindness practice enhanced feelings of social connection and positivity toward strangers.[1237] Two weeks of compassion training (thirty minutes a day) among fifty-six participants, compared to reappraisal training (that did not involve compassion), increased altruism and enhanced connection between the brain's executive and reward areas.[236] Short training in compassion meditation increased real-money charitable donation.[1238] Loving kindness meditation led to a drop in prejudice against stigmatized groups, compared to discussing compassion or doing nothing.[1239] A twelve-week loving kindness course enhanced self-compassion and lowered symptoms of depression and PTSD.[1239] A recent compilation of multiple studies showed that compassion-based practices continue to show strong benefit even when compared with an active control group, a test which mindfulness based approaches haven't passed yet.[1239a]

Interestingly, compassion meditation produces the same changes in the brain that have been reported in extraordinary altruists (people who donated their kidneys to strangers). They both have a larger right amygdala that responds quicker to fearful feelings among others,[1235, 1240] and active reward circuitry that is able to connect their altruistic intentions with positive feelings.[1241, 885, 975] I find these changes very hopeful, particularly if we can demonstrate that they sustain for the long term.

Today, if you decide to try a contemplative practice, you have a choice. What you choose is important because the outcome of your meditation practice depends on what you practice. In a research study, breath and body scan practice increased internal awareness, loving-kindness enhanced warmth and positive thoughts, and observing one's own thoughts led to greater thought awareness.[161] While the research shows that practicing loving kindness might entail higher initial mental effort, I believe the long-term benefits are worth the initial investment. Further the effort needed plateaus with time.[1242]

I believe our brain comes programmed with the language of kindness and needs just a little reminder to reclaim what is originally ours. That is the reason compassion meditation is the most potent. I have a hunch that the same will apply to gratitude, though we don't have the research data yet.

My second idea to secure the benefits of a long-term meditation practice is to remain in a low-grade meditative state sixteen hours a day by finding a mindful path to resilience, using the ideas and skills I have shared in mindfulness *v2* (mindfreeness).

SIXTEEN-HOUR MEDITATION

Several years ago, I met a monk from New Zealand. He promoted long and deep meditation practice, emphasizing the ten thousand hours philosophy. Talking to him I wondered, as a husband, father, son, brother, physician, researcher, educator, author, colleague, neighbor, and citizen, how would I ever accumulate those many hours. If I practiced an hour a day, which was very ambitious, I might need to practice for about thirty years before I reach the magic number. I don't have that kind of patience. And some say ten thousand hours may not be enough; you really need fifty thousand hours. There goes all my hope for transformation! Then I had an idea.

If I practiced low-intensity meditation sixteen hours a day that emphasizes gratitude and compassion, then I could reach there in only two years instead of needing thirty. But how do I do that?

As a first step, I reminded myself of the definition of meditation: Intentional, grateful, and compassionate attention. *If I could maintain intentional attention for most of the day and keep a disposition of gratitude and compassion, I might arrive there sooner,* I thought. I gave it a try. I experimented with intentional attention for a greater proportion of the day, began noticing novelty in the mundane, started sending silent good wishes to others all day long, woke up with gratitude, tried to remember that everyone I meet is special and struggling, and interpreted my life's struggles and successes with the principles of gratitude, compassion, acceptance, meaning, and forgiveness.

The outcome has been transformative. My apologies for not being humble here. I don't know what the brain scans might show, but I feel I have experienced that cognitively, emotionally and spiritually I got the same outcome as a practitioner with tens of thousands of hours of practice. I haven't had a full-blown cold in ten years (I used to be miserable with them for several weeks at least twice a year prior to that). I feel I am more creative, productive, can think clearer, keep my patience, and reframe adversity much more quickly compared to how I did ten years ago. We have minimal to no arguments in our home, kids are happier, and I believe I have picked up no enemies in a full decade. I feel compassion for most, and have much better control over fear, anger, ego, and envy. There are other benefits and experiences that go beyond the ordinary which I will limit here, given that our present pursuit is mostly scientific and not ethereal.

My suggestion to you is to leverage the wisdom we have gained in the last several thousand years and not limit yourself to just the very old philosophies. Combine your philosophy with scientific findings of the modern sages (the scientists) who are teaching us to create our own recipe. Instead of focusing on transient states, focus on lasting changes. Instead of a meditation high, seek consistent daily calmness and kindness. With time, I have no doubt whichever pursuit you undertake, you will flourish. You'll be the next Marie

Curie, Mother Teresa, Nelson Mandela, or Brother Lawrence. You'll help many. You'll materialize the words of a timeless Indian grandmaster, Ramakrishna Paramhansa, when he inspired his students saying, "Cross the river, not as a lone swimmer, but as a steamer ship, carrying many with you."

In Gratitude

I am grateful to:

- My wife Richa.
- Our children, Gauri and Sia.
- My parents, Shashi and Sahib.
- My in-laws, Kusum and Vinod.
- My sisters, Rajni and Sandhya, and brother, Kishore.
- Our extended family, including Lalit, Sudhir, Preeti, Sundeep, Smita, Poonam, Ritu, Ravi, Arush, Ateev, Arnav, Vardhaman, Prasanna, Anita, Satish, Dhruv, Nidhi.
- Our friends Carla and Russ Paonessa, Neeta and Rakesh Gaur, Seema and Shaji Kumar, Ekta and Prashant Kapoor, Vidya and Prasad Iyer, Riddhi and Sameer Parikh, Lisa and Todd Ustby, Avni Joshi and Vivek Iyer, Ann and Dan Clark, Lisa and Kirk Dalton, Sue Goodin.
- Our many other wonderful friends and extended family.
- My colleagues Drs. Brent Bauer, Alexandra Wolanskyj-Spinner, Jon Tilburt, Tony Chon, Anjali Bhagra, Paul Limburg, Sherry Chesak, Tej Khalsa; Debbie Fuehrer, Sue Cutshall, Angela Martin, Chris Frye, Kathryn Heroff, and Monica Sveen-Ziebell.
- All my other colleagues and leadership at Mayo Clinic.
- All the world's scientists and sages.
- All of you, for working together to build a happier and more hopeful world for our planet's children.

Thank you!
- Amit

Notes

Please access updates to the notes at the following link: Stressfree.org/mindfreeness

1. Rubin DI. Epidemiology and risk factors for spine pain. Neurologic clinics. 2007;25(2):353-71.
2. Neal RS, J. . Workplace Stress on the Rise With 83% of Americans Frazzled by Something at Work2013 July 5th, 2017. Available from: https://globenewswire.com/news-release/2013/04/09/536945/10027728/en/Workplace-Stress on the-Rise-With-83-of-Americans-Frazzled-by-Something-at-Work.html.
3. Wyse R. Seventy-five percent of U.S. employers say stress is their number one workplace health concern2016. Available from: https://globenewswire.com/news-release/2016/06/29/852338/0/en/Seventy-five-percent-of-U-S-employers-say-stress-is-their-number-one-workplace-health-concern.html.
4. Han B, Compton WM, Blanco C, Crane E, Lee J, Jones CM. Prescription Opioid Use, Misuse, and Use Disorders in U.S. Adults: 2015 National Survey on Drug Use and Health. Annals of internal medicine. 2017.
5. Carmichael SG. Everything You Need to Know About Giving Negative Feedback2014 5/8/2017. Available from: https://hbr.org/2014/06/everything-you-need-to-know-about-negative-feedback.
6. Connolly T. Plato: Phaedo5/8/2017. Available from: http://www.iep.utm.edu/phaedo/.
7. Skirry J. René Descartes: The Mind-Body Distinction5/8/2017. Available from: http://www.iep.utm.edu/descmind/.
8. Menon S. Advaita Vedanta5/8/2017. Available from: http://www.iep.utm.edu/adv-veda/.
9. Saraswati SS. A Systematic Course in the Ancient Tantric Techniques of Yoga and Kriya: Yoga Publications Trust/Munger; 2004. 957 p.
10. Ruzsa F. Sankhya5/8/2017. Available from: http://www.iep.utm.edu/sankhya/.
11. Shankardev Saraswati SS, J. Yoga and Samkhya—Purifying the Elements of the Human Being2007 5/8/2017. Available from: http://www.yogajournal.com/article/teach/yoga-and-samkhya-purifying-the-elements-of-the-human-being/.
12. Balasubramaniam M, Telles S, Doraiswamy PM. Yoga on our minds: a systematic review of yoga for neuropsychiatric disorders. Front Psychiatry. 2012;3:117.
13. Chang DG, Holt JA, Sklar M, Groessl EJ. Yoga as a treatment for chronic low back pain: A systematic review of the literature. J Orthop Rheumatol. 2016;3(1):1-8.
14. Chu P, Gotink RA, Yeh GY, Goldie SJ, Hunink MG. The effectiveness of yoga in modifying risk factors for cardiovascular disease and metabolic syndrome: A systematic review and meta-analysis of randomized controlled trials. Eur J Prev Cardiol. 2016;23(3):291-307.
15. Cramer H, Haller H, Lauche R, Steckhan N, Michalsen A, Dobos G. A systematic review and meta-analysis of yoga for hypertension. Am J Hypertens. 2014;27(9):1146-51.
16. Cramer H, Langhorst J, Dobos G, Lauche R. Yoga for metabolic syndrome: A systematic review and meta-analysis. Eur J Prev Cardiol. 2016;23(18):1982-93.
17. Cramer H, Lauche R, Haller H, Dobos G, Michalsen A. A systematic review of yoga for heart disease. Eur J Prev Cardiol. 2015;22(3):284-95.
18. Cramer H, Lauche R, Haller H, Steckhan N, Michalsen A, Dobos G. Effects of yoga on cardiovascular disease risk factors: a systematic review and meta-analysis. Int J Cardiol. 2014;173(2):170-83.
19. Cramer H, Lauche R, Langhorst J, Dobos G. Yoga for depression: a systematic review and meta-analysis. Depress Anxiety. 2013;30(11):1068-83.
20. Cramer H, Lauche R, Langhorst J, Dobos G. Is one yoga style better than another? A systematic review of associations of yoga style and conclusions in randomized yoga trials. Complement Ther Med. 2016;25:178-87.

21. Goode AP, Coeytaux RR, McDuffie J, Duan-Porter W, Sharma P, Mennella H, et al. An evidence map of yoga for low back pain. Complement Ther Med. 2016;25:170-7.
22. Haider T, Sharma M, Branscum P. Yoga as an Alternative and Complimentary Therapy for Cardiovascular Disease: A Systematic Review. J Evid Based Complementary Altern Med. 2016.
23. Hofmann SG, Andreoli G, Carpenter JK, Curtiss J. Effect of Hatha Yoga on Anxiety: A Meta-Analysis. J Evid Based Med. 2016.
24. Innes KE, Selfe TK. Yoga for Adults with Type 2 Diabetes: A Systematic Review of Controlled Trials. J Diabetes Res. 2016;2016:6979370.
25. Jeter PE, Nkodo AF, Moonaz SH, Dagnelie G. A systematic review of yoga for balance in a healthy population. J Altern Complement Med. 2014;20(4):221-32.
26. Jeter PE, Slutsky J, Singh N, Khalsa SB. Yoga as a Therapeutic Intervention: A Bibliometric Analysis of Published Research Studies from 1967 to 2013. J Altern Complement Med. 2015;21(10):586-92.
27. Kan L, Zhang J, Yang Y, Wang P. The Effects of Yoga on Pain, Mobility, and Quality of Life in Patients with Knee Osteoarthritis: A Systematic Review. Evid Based Complement Alternat Med. 2016;2016:6016532.
28. Kim SD. Effects of yoga on chronic neck pain: a systematic review of randomized controlled trials. J Phys Ther Sci. 2016;28(7):2171-4.
29. Klatte R, Pabst S, Beelmann A, Rosendahl JS. The Efficacy of Body-Oriented Yoga in Mental Disorders. Dtsch Arztebl Int. 2016;113(12):195-202.
30. Kumar V, Jagannathan A, Philip M, Thulasi A, Angadi P, Raghuram N. Role of yoga for patients with type II diabetes mellitus: A systematic review and meta-analysis. Complement Ther Med. 2016;25:104-12.
31. Lauche R, Langhorst J, Lee MS, Dobos G, Cramer H. A systematic review and meta-analysis on the effects of yoga on weight-related outcomes. Prev Med. 2016;87:213-32.
32. Liu XC, Pan L, Hu Q, Dong WP, Yan JH, Dong L. Effects of yoga training in patients with chronic obstructive pulmonary disease: a systematic review and meta-analysis. J Thorac Dis. 2014;6(6):795-802.
33. Luu K, Hall PA. Hatha Yoga and Executive Function: A Systematic Review. J Altern Complement Med. 2016;22(2):125-33.
34. Mustian KM. Yoga as Treatment for Insomnia Among Cancer Patients and Survivors: A Systematic Review. Eur Med J Oncol. 2013;1:106-15.
35. Pascoe MC, Bauer IE. A systematic review of randomised control trials on the effects of yoga on stress measures and mood. J Psychiatr Res. 2015;68:270-82.
36. Posadzki P, Cramer H, Kuzdzal A, Lee MS, Ernst E. Yoga for hypertension: a systematic review of randomized clinical trials. Complement Ther Med. 2014;22(3):511-22.
37. Riley KE, Park CL. How does yoga reduce stress? A systematic review of mechanisms of change and guide to future inquiry. Health Psychol Rev. 2015;9(3):379-96.
38. Rioux JG, Ritenbaugh C. Narrative review of yoga intervention clinical trials including weight-related outcomes. Altern Ther Health Med. 2013;19(3):32-46.
39. Sadja J, Mills PJ. Effects of yoga interventions on fatigue in cancer patients and survivors: a systematic review of randomized controlled trials. Explore (NY). 2013;9(4):232-43.
40. Schumann D, Anheyer D, Lauche R, Dobos G, Langhorst J, Cramer H. Effect of Yoga in the Therapy of Irritable Bowel Syndrome: A Systematic Review. Clin Gastroenterol Hepatol. 2016;14(12):1720-31.
41. Sharma M, Lingam VC, Nahar VK. A systematic review of yoga interventions as integrative treatment in breast cancer. J Cancer Res Clin Oncol. 2016;142(12):2523-40.
42. Weaver LL, Darragh AR. Systematic Review of Yoga Interventions for Anxiety Reduction Among Children and Adolescents. Am J Occup Ther. 2015;69(6):6906180070p1-9.
43. Yang ZY, Zhong HB, Mao C, Yuan JQ, Huang YF, Wu XY, et al. Yoga for asthma. Cochrane Database Syst Rev. 2016;4:Cd010346.

44. Youkhana S, Dean CM, Wolff M, Sherrington C, Tiedemann A. Yoga-based exercise improves balance and mobility in people aged 60 and over: a systematic review and meta-analysis. Age Ageing. 2016;45(1):21-9.
45. Cramer H, Ward L, Saper R, Fishbein D, Dobos G, Lauche R. The Safety of Yoga: A Systematic Review and Meta-Analysis of Randomized Controlled Trials. Am J Epidemiol. 2015;182(4):281-93.
46. Satchidananda SS. The Yoga Sutras of Patanjali Integral Yoga Publications; 2012. 272 p.
47. Saraswati SS. Asana Pranayama Mudra Bandha: Bihar School Of Yoga 2013. 544 p.
48. Wikipedia. Gautama Buddha5/8/2017. Available from: https://en.wikipedia.org/wiki/Gautama_Buddha.
49. Grubin D. The Buddha5/8/2017. Available from: http://www.pbs.org/thebuddha/birth-and-youth/.
50. Armstrong K. Buddha (Penguin Lives Biographies): Penguin Lives Biographies; 2004. 240 p.
51. Bodhi B. The Noble Eightfold Path: Way to the End of Suffering: Pariyatti Publishing; 2006. 144 p.
52. Longo O. Hot heads and cold brains. Aristotle, Galen and the "radiator theory". Physis Riv Int Stor Sci. 1996;33(1-3):259-66.
53. Godwin D. Aristotle Thought the Brain Was a Radiator: Scientific American; 2013. Available from: https://www.scientificamerican.com/article/aristotle-thought-the-brain-was-a-radiator/.
54. Wikipedia. Mindfulness5/8/2017. Available from: https://en.wikipedia.org/wiki/Mindfulness.
55. Bhupathiraju SN, Wedick NM, Pan A, Manson JE, Rexrode KM, Willett WC, et al. Quantity and variety in fruit and vegetable intake and risk of coronary heart disease. The American journal of clinical nutrition. 2013;98(6):1514-23.
56. Hjartaker A, Knudsen MD, Tretli S, Weiderpass E. Consumption of berries, fruits and vegetables and mortality among 10,000 Norwegian men followed for four decades. European journal of nutrition. 2015;54(4):599-608.
57. Hung HC, Joshipura KJ, Jiang R, Hu FB, Hunter D, Smith-Warner SA, et al. Fruit and vegetable intake and risk of major chronic disease. Journal of the National Cancer Institute. 2004;96(21):1577-84.
58. Joshipura KJ, Hu FB, Manson JE, Stampfer MJ, Rimm EB, Speizer FE, et al. The effect of fruit and vegetable intake on risk for coronary heart disease. Annals of internal medicine. 2001;134(12):1106-14.
59. Leenders M, Boshuizen HC, Ferrari P, Siersema PD, Overvad K, Tjonneland A, et al. Fruit and vegetable intake and cause-specific mortality in the EPIC study. European journal of epidemiology. 2014;29(9):639-52.
60. Leenders M, Sluijs I, Ros MM, Boshuizen HC, Siersema PD, Ferrari P, et al. Fruit and vegetable consumption and mortality: European prospective investigation into cancer and nutrition. American journal of epidemiology. 2013;178(4):590-602.
61. Nothlings U, Schulze MB, Weikert C, Boeing H, van der Schouw YT, Bamia C, et al. Intake of vegetables, legumes, and fruit, and risk for all-cause, cardiovascular, and cancer mortality in a European diabetic population. The Journal of nutrition. 2008;138(4):775-81.
62. Takata Y, Xiang YB, Yang G, Li H, Gao J, Cai H, et al. Intakes of fruits, vegetables, and related vitamins and lung cancer risk: results from the Shanghai Men's Health Study (2002-2009). Nutrition and cancer. 2013;65(1):51-61.
63. Vieira AR, Abar L, Vingeliene S, Chan DS, Aune D, Navarro-Rosenblatt D, et al. Fruits, vegetables and lung cancer risk: a systematic review and meta-analysis. Annals of oncology : official journal of the European Society for Medical Oncology. 2016;27(1):81-96.
64. Wang X, Ouyang Y, Liu J, Zhu M, Zhao G, Bao W, et al. Fruit and vegetable consumption and mortality from all causes, cardiovascular disease, and cancer: systematic review and dose-response meta-analysis of prospective cohort studies. BMJ (Clinical research ed). 2014;349:g4490.
65. Moore LV, Thompson FE. Adults Meeting Fruit and Vegetable Intake Recommendations - United States, 2013. MMWR Morbidity and mortality weekly report. 2015;64(26):709-13.
66. Bairati I, Meyer F, Jobin E, Gelinas M, Fortin A, Nabid A, et al. Antioxidant vitamins supplementation and mortality: a randomized trial in head and neck cancer patients. Int J Cancer. 2006;119(9):2221-4.

67. Bjelakovic G, Nikolova D, Gluud LL, Simonetti RG, Gluud C. Antioxidant supplements for prevention of mortality in healthy participants and patients with various diseases. Cochrane Database Syst Rev. 2012(3):Cd007176.

68. Greenwald P, Anderson D, Nelson SA, Taylor PR. Clinical trials of vitamin and mineral supplements for cancer prevention. Am J Clin Nutr. 2007;85(1):314s-7s.

69. Myung SK, Ju W, Cho B, Oh SW, Park SM, Koo BK, et al. Efficacy of vitamin and antioxidant supplements in prevention of cardiovascular disease: systematic review and meta-analysis of randomised controlled trials. Bmj. 2013;346:f10.

70. Dreyfus G. Is mindfulness present-centered and non-judgmental? A discussion of the cognitive dimensions of mindfulness. . Contemporary Buddhism. 2011;12:41-54.

71. Dunne J. Toward an understanding of non-dual mindfulness. . Contemporary Buddhism. 2011;12:71-88.

72. Gethin R. On some definitions of mindfulness. . Contemporary Buddhism. 2011;12:263–79.

73. Grossman PVD, N. T. . Mindfulness, by any other name . . . : Trials and tribulations of sati in Western psychology and science. . Contemporary Buddhism. 2011;12:219–39.

74. Bodhi B. What does mindfulness really mean? A canonical perspective. Contemporary Buddhism. 2011;12(1):19-39.

75. Brown KWR, R. M.; Creswell, J. D. Addressing fundamental questions about mindfulness. Psychological Inquiry. 2007;18:211–37.

76. Kabat-Zinn J. *Wherever You Go, There You Are: Mindfulness Meditation in Everyday Life*. 10th Edition ed: Hachette Books; 2005. 304 p.

77. Brown KWR, R. M. . Perils and promise in defining and measuring mindfulness: Observations from experience. Clinical Psychology: Science & Practice, 11(3), 242. . Clinical Psychology: Science & Practice. 2004;11(3):242.

78. Shapiro SL. The integration of mindfulness and psychology. Journal of clinical psychology. 2009;65(6):555-60.

79. Holzel BK, Lazar SW, Gard T, Schuman-Olivier Z, Vago DR, Ott U. How Does Mindfulness Meditation Work? Proposing Mechanisms of Action From a Conceptual and Neural Perspective. Perspectives on psychological science : a journal of the Association for Psychological Science. 2011;6(6):537-59.

80. Malinowski P. Neural mechanisms of attentional control in mindfulness meditation. Frontiers in neuroscience. 2013;7:8.

81. Vago DR, Silberweig DA. Self-awareness, self-regulation, and self-transcendence (S-ART): a framework for understanding the neurobiological mechanisms of mindfulness. Frontiers in human neuroscience. 2012;6:296.

82. Van Dam NT, van Vugt MK, Vago DR, Schmalzl L, Saron CD, Olendzki A, et al. Mind the Hype: A Critical Evaluation and Prescriptive Agenda for Research on Mindfulness and Meditation. Perspectives on psychological science : a journal of the Association for Psychological Science. 2017:1745691617709589.

82a. Davidson RJ, Dahl CJ. Outstanding Challenges in Scientific Research on Mindfulness and Meditation. Perspectives on psychological science : a journal of the Association for Psychological Science. 2017:1745691617718358.

83. Andrasik F, Grazzi L, D'Amico D, Sansone E, Leonardi M, Raggi A, et al. Mindfulness and headache: A "new" old treatment, with new findings. Cephalalgia : an international journal of headache. 2016.

84. Aust J, Bradshaw T. Mindfulness interventions for psychosis: a systematic review of the literature. Journal of psychiatric and mental health nursing. 2017;24(1):69-83.

85. Consedine NS, Butler HF. Mindfulness, health symptoms and healthcare utilization: Active facets and possible affective mediators. Psychology, health & medicine. 2014;19(4):392-401.

86. Guendelman S, Medeiros S, Rampes H. Mindfulness and Emotion Regulation: Insights from Neurobiological, Psychological, and Clinical Studies. Frontiers in psychology. 2017;8:220.

87. MacKenzie MB, Kocovski NL. Mindfulness-based cognitive therapy for depression: trends and developments. Psychology research and behavior management. 2016;9:125-32.
88. McConville J, McAleer R, Hahne A. Mindfulness Training for Health Profession Students-The Effect of Mindfulness Training on Psychological Well-Being, Learning and Clinical Performance of Health Professional Students: A Systematic Review of Randomized and Non-randomized Controlled Trials. Explore (New York, NY). 2017;13(1):26-45.
89. Moskowitz JT, Duncan LG, Moran PJ, Acree M, Epel ES, Kemeny ME, et al. Dispositional Mindfulness in People with HIV: Associations with Psychological and Physical Health. Personality and individual differences. 2015;86:88-93
90. Nitzan Assayag Y, Aderka IM, Bernstein A. Dispositional mindfulness in trauma recovery: Prospective relations and mediating mechanisms. Journal of anxiety disorders. 2015;36:25-32.
91. Rogers JM, Ferrari M, Mosely K, Lang CP, Brennan L. Mindfulness-based interventions for adults who are overweight or obese: a meta-analysis of physical and psychological health outcomes. Obesity reviews : an official journal of the International Association for the Study of Obesity. 2017;18(1):51-67.
92. Ruffault A, Czernichow S, Hagger MS, Ferrand M, Erichot N, Carette C, et al. The effects of mindfulness training on weight-loss and health-related behaviours in adults with overweight and obesity: A systematic review and meta-analysis. Obesity research & clinical practice. 2016.
93. Slonim J, Kienhuis M, Di Benedetto M, Reece J. The relationships among self-care, dispositional mindfulness, and psychological distress in medical students. Medical education online. 2015;20:27924.
94. Spijkerman MP, Pots WT, Bohlmeijer ET. Effectiveness of online mindfulness-based interventions in improving mental health: A review and meta-analysis of randomised controlled trials. Clinical psychology review. 2016;45:102-14.
95. Tang YY, Tang R, Posner MI. Mindfulness meditation improves emotion regulation and reduces drug abuse. Drug and alcohol dependence. 2016;163 Suppl 1:S13-8.
96. Taren AA, Creswell JD, Gianaros PJ. Dispositional mindfulness co-varies with smaller amygdala and caudate volumes in community adults. PloS one. 2013;8(5):e64574.
97. Ulrichsen KM, Kaufmann T, Dorum ES, Kolskar KK, Richard G, Alnaes D, et al. Clinical Utility of Mindfulness Training in the Treatment of Fatigue After Stroke, Traumatic Brain Injury and Multiple Sclerosis: A Systematic Literature Review and Meta-analysis. Frontiers in psychology. 2016;7:912.
98. Zhang J, Xu R, Wang B, Wang J. Effects of mindfulness-based therapy for patients with breast cancer: A systematic review and meta-analysis. Complementary therapies in medicine. 2016;26:1-10.
99. Creswell JD, Irwin MR, Burklund LJ, Lieberman MD, Arevalo JM, Ma J, et al. Mindfulness-Based Stress Reduction training reduces loneliness and pro-inflammatory gene expression in older adults: a small randomized controlled trial. Brain, behavior, and immunity. 2012;26(7):1095-101.
100. Dusek JA, Otu HH, Wohlhueter AL, Bhasin M, Zerbini LF, Joseph MG, et al. Genomic counter-stress changes induced by the relaxation response. PloS one. 2008;3(7):e2576.
101. Creswell JD, Taren AA, Lindsay EK, Greco CM, Gianaros PJ, Fairgrieve A, et al. Alterations in Resting-State Functional Connectivity Link Mindfulness Meditation With Reduced Interleukin-6: A Randomized Controlled Trial. Biological psychiatry. 2016;80(1):53-61.
102. Jacobs TL, Shaver PR, Epel ES, Zanesco AP, Aichele SR, Bridwell DA, et al. Self-reported mindfulness and cortisol during a Shamatha meditation retreat. Health psychology : official journal of the Division of Health Psychology, American Psychological Association. 2013;32(10):1104-9.
103. Hoge EA, Chen MM, Orr E, Metcalf CA, Fischer LE, Pollack MH, et al. Loving-Kindness Meditation practice associated with longer telomeres in women. Brain, behavior, and immunity. 2013;32:159-63.

104. Jacobs TL, Epel ES, Lin J, Blackburn EH, Wolkowitz OM, Bridwell DA, et al. Intensive meditation training, immune cell telomerase activity, and psychological mediators. Psychoneuroendocrinology. 2011;36(5):664-81.

105. Schutte NS, Malouff JM. The Relationship Between Perceived Stress and Telomere Length: A Meta-analysis. Stress and health : journal of the International Society for the Investigation of Stress. 2016;32(4):313-9.

106. Schaufenbuel K. Why Google, Target, and General Mills are investing in mindfulness. 2015 10/16/2017. Available from: https://hbr.org/2015/12/why-google-target-and-general-mills-are-investing-in-mindfulness.

107. Gunderson G. The science is in, and meditation may be the next big business opportunity. 2016 10/16/2017. Available from: http://www.forbes.com/sites/garrettgunderson/2016/06/28/the-science-is-in-and-meditation-may-be-the-next-big-business-opportunity/#2f729c7123c0.

108. Eadicicco L. Americans Check Their Phones 8 Billion Times a Day2015 5/8/2017. Available from: http://time.com/4147614/smartphone-usage-us-2015/.

109. Shapiro Ed; Shapiro D. Why We Find It Hard to Meditate2011 5/8/2017. Available from: http://www.mindful.org/why-we-find-it-hard-to-meditate/.

110. Cacioppo JT, Cacioppo S. Social Relationships and Health: The Toxic Effects of Perceived Social Isolation. Soc Personal Psychol Compass. 2014;8(2):58-72.

111. Hawkley LC, Cacioppo JT. Loneliness matters: a theoretical and empirical review of consequences and mechanisms. Ann Behav Med. 2010;40(2):218-27.

112. Seyfarth RM, Cheney DL. The evolutionary origins of friendship. Annual review of psychology. 2012;63:153-77.

113. Cacioppo JT, Hawkley LC, Norman GJ, Berntson GG. Social isolation. Annals of the New York Academy of Sciences. 2011;1231:17-22.

114. Cacioppo JT, Cacioppo S, Capitanio JP, Cole SW. The neuroendocrinology of social isolation. Annual review of psychology. 2015;66:733-67.

115. Steptoe A, Shankar A, Demakakos P, Wardle J. Social isolation, loneliness, and all-cause mortality in older men and women. Proceedings of the National Academy of Sciences of the United States of America. 2013;110(15):5797-801.

116. Pantell M, Rehkopf D, Jutte D, Syme SL, Balmes J, Adler N. Social isolation: a predictor of mortality comparable to traditional clinical risk factors. American journal of public health. 2013;103(11):2056-62.

117. APA. Stress in America: Paying with our health2015 5/8/2017. Available from: http://www.apa.org/news/press/releases/stress/2014/stress-report.pdf.

118. Luhby T. Americans are wealthier than ever before … can't you tell?2015 5/8/2017. Available from: http://money.cnn.com/2015/09/18/news/economy/americans-wealth/.

119. Sahadi J. The richest 10% hold 76% of the wealth2016 5/8/2017. Available from: http://money.cnn.com/2016/08/18/pf/wealth-inequality/.

120. Wikipedia. Wealth Inequality in the United States5/8/2017. Available from: https://en.wikipedia.org/wiki/Wealth_inequality_in_the_United_States#cite_note-Boyer2014-5.

121. Marsden W. Obama's State of the Union speech will be call to arms on wealth gap2014 5/8/2017. Available from: http://o.canada.com/news/obamas-state-of-the-union-speech-will-be-call-to-arms-on-wealth-gap.

122. Sherman E. America is the richest, and most unequal, country2015 5/8/2017. Available from: http://fortune.com/2015/09/30/america-wealth-inequality/.

123. Miguel E, Camerer C, Casey K, Cohen J, Esterling KM, Gerber A, et al. Social science. Promoting transparency in social science research. Science (New York, NY). 2014;343(6166):30-1.

124. Pashler H, Wagenmakers EJ. Editors' Introduction to the Special Section on Replicability in Psychological Science: A Crisis of Confidence? Perspectives on psychological science : a journal of the Association for Psychological Science. 2012;7(6):528-30.

125. Bawa FL, Mercer SW, Atherton RJ, Clague F, Keen A, Scott NW, et al. Does mindfulness improve outcomes in patients with chronic pain? Systematic review and meta-analysis. The British journal of general practice : the journal of the Royal College of General Practitioners. 2015;65(635):e387-400.

126. Burton A, Burgess C, Dean S, Koutsopoulou GZ, Hugh-Jones S. How Effective are Mindfulness-Based Interventions for Reducing Stress Among Healthcare Professionals? A Systematic Review and Meta-Analysis. Stress and health : journal of the International Society for the Investigation of Stress. 2017;33(1):3-13.

127. Coronado-Montoya S, Levis AW, Kwakkenbos L, Steele RJ, Turner EH, Thombs BD. Reporting of Positive Results in Randomized Controlled Trials of Mindfulness-Based Mental Health Interventions. PloS one. 2016;11(4):e0153220.

128. Crowe M, Jordan J, Burrell B, Jones V, Gillon D, Harris S. Mindfulness-based stress reduction for long-term physical conditions: A systematic review. The Australian and New Zealand journal of psychiatry. 2016;50(1):21-32.

129. Dunne J. Mindfulness in Anorexia Nervosa: An Integrated Review of the Literature. Journal of the American Psychiatric Nurses Association. 2017:1078390317711250.

130. Fish J, Brimson J, Lynch S. Mindfulness Interventions Delivered by Technology Without Facilitator Involvement: What Research Exists and What Are the Clinical Outcomes? Mindfulness. 2016;7(5):1011-23.

131. Geiger PJ, Boggero IA, Brake CA, Caldera CA, Combs HL, Peters JR, et al. Mindfulness-Based Interventions for Older Adults: A Review of the Effects on Physical and Emotional Well-being. Mindfulness. 2016;7(2):296-307.

132. Goldstein KM, Shepherd-Banigan M, Coeytaux RR, McDuffie JR, Adam S, Befus D, et al. Use of mindfulness, meditation and relaxation to treat vasomotor symptoms. Climacteric : the journal of the International Menopause Society. 2017;20(2):178-82.

133. Gong H, Ni CX, Liu YZ, Zhang Y, Su WJ, Lian YJ, et al. Mindfulness meditation for insomnia: A meta-analysis of randomized controlled trials. Journal of psychosomatic research. 2016;89:1-6.

134. Harrison SL, Lee A, Janaudis-Ferreira T, Goldstein RS, Brooks D. Mindfulness in people with a respiratory diagnosis: A systematic review. Patient education and counseling. 2016;99(3):348-55.

135. Hilton L, Hempel S, Ewing BA, Apaydin E, Xenakis L, Newberry S, et al. Mindfulness Meditation for Chronic Pain: Systematic Review and Meta-analysis. Annals of behavioral medicine : a publication of the Society of Behavioral Medicine. 2017;51(2):199-213.

136. Jaffray L, Bridgman H, Stephens M, Skinner T. Evaluating the effects of mindfulness-based interventions for informal palliative caregivers: A systematic literature review. Palliative medicine. 2016;30(2):117-31.

137. Jamieson SD, Tuckey MR. Mindfulness interventions in the workplace: A critique of the current state of the literature. Journal of occupational health psychology. 2017;22(2):180-93.

138. Lever Taylor B, Cavanagh K, Strauss C. The Effectiveness of Mindfulness-Based Interventions in the Perinatal Period: A Systematic Review and Meta-Analysis. PloS one. 2016;11(5):e0155720.

139. Louise S, Fitzpatrick M, Strauss C, Rossell SL, Thomas N. Mindfulness- and acceptance-based interventions for psychosis: Our current understanding and a meta-analysis. Schizophrenia research. 2017.

140. Maglione MA, Maher AR, Ewing B, Colaiaco B, Newberry S, Kandrack R, et al. Efficacy of mindfulness meditation for smoking cessation: A systematic review and meta-analysis. Addictive behaviors. 2017;69:27-34.

141. McLean G, Lawrence M, Simpson R, Mercer SW. Mindfulness-based stress reduction in Parkinson's disease: a systematic review. BMC neurology. 2017;17(1):92.

142. O'Leary K, O'Neill S, Dockray S. A systematic review of the effects of mindfulness interventions on cortisol. Journal of health psychology. 2016;21(9):2108-21.

143. Parsons CE, Crane C, Parsons LJ, Fjorback LO, Kuyken W. Home practice in Mindfulness-Based Cognitive Therapy and Mindfulness-Based Stress Reduction: A systematic review and meta-analysis of participants' mindfulness practice and its association with outcomes. Behaviour research and therapy. 2017;95:29-41.

144. Petterson H, Olson BL. Effects of Mindfulness-Based Interventions in High School and College Athletes for Reducing Stress and Injury, and Improving Quality of Life. Journal of sport rehabilitation. 2016:1-18.
145. Sanada K, Alda Diez M, Salas Valero M, Perez-Yus MC, Demarzo MM, Montero-Marin J, et al. Effects of mindfulness-based interventions on biomarkers in healthy and cancer populations: a systematic review. BMC complementary and alternative medicine. 2017;17(1):125.
146. Sanada K, Montero-Marin J, Alda Diez M, Salas-Valero M, Perez-Yus MC, Morillo H, et al. Effects of Mindfulness-Based Interventions on Salivary Cortisol in Healthy Adults: A Meta-Analytical Review. Frontiers in physiology. 2016;7:471.
147. Shonin E, Van Gordon W, Griffiths MD. Does mindfulness work? BMJ (Clinical research ed). 2015;351:h6919.
148. Stephenson KR, Kerth J. Effects of Mindfulness-Based Therapies for Female Sexual Dysfunction: A Meta-Analytic Review. Journal of sex research. 2017:1-18.
149. Wood K, Lawrence M, Jani B, Simpson R, Mercer SW. Mindfulness-based interventions in epilepsy: a systematic review. BMC neurology. 2017;17(1):52.
150. Johnson C, Burke C, Brinkman S, Wade T. Effectiveness of a school-based mindfulness program for transdiagnostic prevention in young adolescents. Behaviour research and therapy. 2016;81:1-11.
151. Johnson C, Burke C, Brinkman S, Wade T. A randomized controlled evaluation of a secondary school mindfulness program for early adolescents: Do we have the recipe right yet? Behaviour research and therapy. 2017;99:37-46.
152. Anheyer D, Haller H, Barth J, Lauche R, Dobos G, Cramer H. Mindfulness-Based Stress Reduction for Treating Low Back Pain: A Systematic Review and Meta-analysis. Annals of internal medicine. 2017;166(11):799-807.
153. Goyal M, Singh S, Sibinga EMS, Gould NF, Rowland-Seymour A, Sharma R, et al. AHRQ Comparative Effectiveness Reviews. Meditation Programs for Psychological Stress and Well-Being. Rockville (MD): Agency for Healthcare Research and Quality (US); 2014.
154. Foster D. Is mindfulness making us ill? 2016 August 30th, 2017. Available from: https://www.theguardian.com/lifeandstyle/2016/jan/23/is-mindfulness-making-us-ill.
155. Michalak J, Schultze M, Heidenreich T, Schramm E. A randomized controlled trial on the efficacy of mindfulness-based cognitive therapy and a group version of cognitive behavioral analysis system of psychotherapy for chronically depressed patients. Journal of consulting and clinical psychology. 2015;83(5):951-63.
156. Wilson BM, Mickes L, Stolarz-Fantino S, Evrard M, Fantino E. Increased False-Memory Susceptibility After Mindfulness Meditation. Psychological science. 2015;26(10):1567-73.
157. Shaku F, Tsutsumi M, Goto H, Saint Arnoult D. Measuring the effects of Zen training on quality of life and mental health among Japanese monk trainees: a cross-sectional study. Journal of alternative and complementary medicine (New York, NY). 2014;20(5):406-10.
158. Sundquist J, Lilja A, Palmer K, Memon AA, Wang X, Johansson LM, et al. Mindfulness group therapy in primary care patients with depression, anxiety and stress and adjustment disorders: randomised controlled trial. The British journal of psychiatry : the journal of mental science. 2015;206(2):128-35.
159. Farias M, Wikholm C. Has the science of mindfulness lost its mind? BJPsych bulletin. 2016;40(6):329-32.
160. Dahl CJ, Lutz A, Davidson RJ. Reconstructing and deconstructing the self: cognitive mechanisms in meditation practice. Trends in cognitive sciences. 2015;19(9):515-23.
161. Kok BE, Singer T. Phenomenological Fingerprints of Four Meditations: Differential State Changes in Affect, Mind-Wandering, Meta-Cognition, and Interoception Before and After Daily Practice Across 9 Months of Training. Mindfulness. 2017;8(1):218-31.
162. Vollestad J, Nielsen MB, Nielsen GH. Mindfulness- and acceptance-based interventions for anxiety disorders: a systematic review and meta-analysis. The British journal of clinical psychology. 2012;51(3):239-60.

163. Klainin-Yobas P, Cho MA, Creedy D. Efficacy of mindfulness-based interventions on depressive symptoms among people with mental disorders: a meta-analysis. International journal of nursing studies. 2012;49(1):109-21.

164. Shonin E, Van Gordon W, Griffiths MD. Mindfulness-based interventions: towards mindful clinical integration. Frontiers in psychology. 2013;4:194.

165. Davidson RJ, Kaszniak AW. Conceptual and methodological issues in research on mindfulness and meditation. The American psychologist. 2015;70(7):581-92.

166. Goldberg SB, Wielgosz J, Dahl C, Schuyler B, MacCoon DS, Rosenkranz M, et al. Does the Five Facet Mindfulness Questionnaire measure what we think it does? Construct validity evidence from an active controlled randomized clinical trial. Psychological assessment. 2016;28(8):1009-14.

167. Dimidjian S, Segal ZV. Prospects for a clinical science of mindfulness-based intervention. The American psychologist. 2015;70(7):593-620.

167b. Goldberg SB, Tucker RP, Greene PA, Simpson TL, Kearney DJ, Davidson RJ. Is mindfulness research methodology improving over time? A systematic review. PLoS One. 2017 Oct 31; 12(10):e0187298.

168. Luders E, Kurth F, Toga AW, Narr KL, Gaser C. Meditation effects within the hippocampal complex revealed by voxel-based morphometry and cytoarchitectonic probabilistic mapping. Frontiers in psychology. 2013;4:398.

169. Sperduti M, Martinelli P, Piolino P. A neurocognitive model of meditation based on activation likelihood estimation (ALE) meta-analysis. Consciousness and cognition. 2012;21(1):269-76.

170. Hofmann SG, Sawyer AT, Witt AA, Oh D. The effect of mindfulness-based therapy on anxiety and depression: A meta-analytic review. Journal of consulting and clinical psychology. 2010;78(2):169-83.

171. Gaiswinkler L, Unterrainer HF. The relationship between yoga involvement, mindfulness and psychological well-being. Complementary therapies in medicine. 2016;26:123-7.

172. Coyne J. Mindfulness research's huge problem with uninformative control groups2016 5/8/2017. Available from: http://blogs.plos.org/mindthebrain/2016/06/23/mindfulness-researchs-huge-problem-with-uninformative-control-groups/.

173. Chu CS, Stubbs B, Chen TY, Tang CH, Li DJ, Yang WC, et al. The effectiveness of adjunct mindfulness-based intervention in treatment of bipolar disorder: A systematic review and meta-analysis. Journal of affective disorders. 2017;225:234-45.

174. MacCoon DG, MacLean KA, Davidson RJ, Saron CD, Lutz A. No sustained attention differences in a longitudinal randomized trial comparing mindfulness based stress reduction versus active control. PLoS One. 2014;9(6):e97551.

175. Rosenkranz MA, Davidson RJ, Maccoon DG, Sheridan JF, Kalin NH, Lutz A. A comparison of mindfulness-based stress reduction and an active control in modulation of neurogenic inflammation. Brain Behav Immun. 2013;27(1):174-84.

176. MacCoon DG, Imel ZE, Rosenkranz MA, Sheftel JG, Weng HY, Sullivan JC, et al. The validation of an active control intervention for Mindfulness Based Stress Reduction (MBSR). Behaviour research and therapy. 2012;50(1):3-12.

177. Toivonen KI, Zernicke K, Carlson LE. Web-Based Mindfulness Interventions for People With Physical Health Conditions: Systematic Review. Journal of medical internet research. 2017;19(8):e303.

178. Cramer H, Sibbritt D, Park CL, Adams J, Lauche R. Is the practice of yoga or meditation associated with a healthy lifestyle? Results of a national cross-sectional survey of 28,695 Australian women. Journal of psychosomatic research. 2017;101:104-9.

179. Twenge JM, Campbell WK, Carter NT. Declines in trust in others and confidence in institutions among American adults and late adolescents, 1972-2012. Psychological science. 2014;25(10):1914-23.

180. Twenge JM, Donnelly K. Generational differences in American students' reasons for going to college, 1971-2014: The rise of extrinsic motives. The Journal of social psychology. 2016;156(6):620-9.

181. Twenge JM, Kasser T. Generational changes in materialism and work centrality, 1976-2007: associations with temporal changes in societal insecurity and materialistic role modeling. Personality & social psychology bulletin. 2013;39(7):883-97.

182. Twenge JM, Konrath S, Foster JD, Campbell WK, Bushman BJ. Egos inflating over time: a cross-temporal meta-analysis of the Narcissistic Personality Inventory. Journal of personality. 2008;76(4):875-902; discussion 3-28.

183. Topolski RW, J.N.; Martin, Z.; McCoy, J. Choosing between the Emotional Dog and the Rational Pal: A Moral Dilemma with a Tail. ANTHROZOÖS 2013;26(2):253-63.

184. Heide FJ, Borkovec TD. Relaxation-induced anxiety: paradoxical anxiety enhancement due to relaxation training. Journal of consulting and clinical psychology. 1983;51(2):171-82.

185. Adler CC, M.; Barlow, D. Relaxation-induced panic: When resting isn't peaceful. . Integrative Psychiatry. 1987;9:94-112.

186. Jonsson U, Alaie I, Parling T, Arnberg FK. Reporting of harms in randomized controlled trials of psychological interventions for mental and behavioral disorders: a review of current practice. Contemporary clinical trials. 2014;38(1):1-8.

187. Vaughan B, Goldstein MH, Alikakos M, Cohen LJ, Serby MJ. Frequency of reporting of adverse events in randomized controlled trials of psychotherapy vs. psychopharmacotherapy. Comprehensive psychiatry. 2014;55(4):849-55.

188. Goyal M, Singh S, Sibinga EM, Gould NF, Rowland-Seymour A, Sharma R, et al. Meditation programs for psychological stress and well-being: a systematic review and meta-analysis. JAMA internal medicine. 2014;174(3):357-68.

189. Bent S, Padula A, Avins AL. Brief communication: Better ways to question patients about adverse medical events: a randomized, controlled trial. Annals of internal medicine. 2006;144(4):257-61.

190. Walsh R, Roche L. Precipitation of acute psychotic episodes by intensive meditation in individuals with a history of schizophrenia. The American journal of psychiatry. 1979;136(8):1085-6.

191. Van Gordon W, Shonin E, Garcia-Campayo J. Are there adverse effects associated with mindfulness? The Australian and New Zealand journal of psychiatry. 2017:4867417716309.

192. Castillo RJ. Depersonalization and meditation. Psychiatry. 1990;53(2):158-68.

193. Chan-Ob T, Boonyanaruthee V. Meditation in association with psychosis. Journal of the Medical Association of Thailand = Chotmaihet thangphaet. 1999;82(9):925-30.

194. Kuijpers HJ, van der Heijden FM, Tuinier S, Verhoeven WM. Meditation-induced psychosis. Psychopathology. 2007;40(6):461-4.

195. Shonin E, Van Gordon W, Griffiths MD. Do mindfulness-based therapies have a role in the treatment of psychosis? The Australian and New Zealand journal of psychiatry. 2014;48(2):124-7.

196. Yorston G. Mania precipitated by meditation: A case report and literature review. . Mental Health, Religion & Culture. 2001;4:209-14.

197. VanderKooi L. Buddhist teachers' experience with extreme mental states in Western meditators. Journal of Transpersonal Psychology. 1997;29:31-46.

198. Lomas TC, T.; Edginton, T.; Ridge, D. A qualitative analysis of experiential challenges associated with meditation practice. . Mindfulness. 2015;6:848-60.

199. Miller J. The unveiling of traumatic memories and emotions through mindfulness and concentration meditation: Clinical implications and three case reports. . Journal of Transpersonal Psychology. 1993;25:169–80.

200. Leigh J, Bowen S, Marlatt GA. Spirituality, mindfulness and substance abuse. Addictive behaviors. 2005;30(7):1335-41.

201. Lustyk MK, Chawla N, Nolan RS, Marlatt GA. Mindfulness meditation research: issues of participant screening, safety procedures, and researcher training. Advances in mind-body medicine. 2009;24(1):20-30.

202. Dobkin PLI, J. A.; Amar, S. For whom may participation in a mindfulness-based stress reduction program be contraindicated? . Mindfulness. 2011;3:44-50.

203. Tangney JP, Dobbins AE, Stuewig JB, Schrader SW. Is There a Dark Side to Mindfulness? Relation of Mindfulness to Criminogenic Cognitions. Personality & social psychology bulletin. 2017;43(10):1415-26.

204. Shapiro DH, Jr. Adverse effects of meditation: a preliminary investigation of long-term meditators. International journal of psychosomatics : official publication of the International Psychosomatics Institute. 1992;39(1-4):62-7.

205. Kerr CE, Josyula K, Littenberg R. Developing an observing attitude: an analysis of meditation diaries in an MBSR clinical trial. Clinical psychology & psychotherapy. 2011;18(1):80-93.

206. Cebolla A, Demarzo M, Martins P, Soler J, Garcia-Campayo J. Unwanted effects: Is there a negative side of meditation? A multicentre survey. PloS one. 2017;12(9):e0183137.

207. Annels SK, K.; Bridge P. Meditate don't medicate: How medical imaging evidence supports the role of meditation in the treatment of depression. . Radiography. 2016;22:e54-e8.

208. Purser RL, D. Beyond McMindfulness 2013 August 30th, 2017. Available from: http://www.huffingtonpost.com/ron-purser/beyond-mcmindfulness_b_3519289.html.

209. Hagerty B. Are Spiritual Encounters All In Your Head? 2009. Available from: http://www.npr.org/templates/story/story.php?storyId=104291534.

210. Asheim Hansen B, Brodtkorb E. Partial epilepsy with "ecstatic" seizures. Epilepsy & behavior : E&B. 2003;4(6):667-73.

211. Devinsky O, Lai G. Spirituality and religion in epilepsy. Epilepsy & behavior : E&B. 2008;12(4):636-43.

212. McCrae N, Whitley R. Exaltation in temporal lobe epilepsy: neuropsychiatric symptom or portal to the divine? The Journal of medical humanities. 2014;35(3):241-55.

213. Trimble M, Freeman A. An investigation of religiosity and the Gastaut-Geschwind syndrome in patients with temporal lobe epilepsy. Epilepsy & behavior : E&B. 2006;9(3):407-14.

214. Urgesi C, Aglioti SM, Skrap M, Fabbro F. The spiritual brain: selective cortical lesions modulate human self-transcendence. Neuron. 2010;65(3):309-19.

215. Shonin E, Van Gordon W, Griffiths MD. Meditation awareness training (MAT) for improved psychological well-being: a qualitative examination of participant experiences. Journal of religion and health. 2014;53(3):849-63.

216. NCCIH. Use of Complementary Health Approaches in the U.S.: National Health Interview Survey (NHIS)2016 5/8/2017. Available from: https://nccih.nih.gov/research/statistics/NHIS/2012/mind-body/meditation.

217. CDC. Exercise or Physical Activity5/8/2017. Available from: https://www.cdc.gov/nchs/fastats/exercise.htm.

218. Forum P. Frequency of prayer5/8/2017. Available from: http://www.pewforum.org/religious-landscape-study/frequency-of-prayer/.

219. Babauta L. 48 Fun Ways to Exercise2009 5/9/2017. Available from: https://zenhabits.net/48-fun-exercises/.

220. Pikul C. 7 Fun Exercises Your Trainer Doesn't Want You to Know About2011 5/9/2017. Available from: http://www.oprah.com/health/burn-calories-while-having-fun-fun-ways-to-work-out#ixzz4gbnHa4ZG.

221. Vongkhamchanh L. Top 50 Fun Ways to Lose Weight This Spring. Available from: http://www.shape.com/weight-loss/tips-plans/top-50-fun-ways-lose-weight-spring.

222. Heartmath. www.heartmath.org 2017 [

223. Headspace. www.headspace.com; 2017 [Available from: http://www.headspace.com.

224. Choosemuse. Choosemuse.com 2017 [Available from: http://www.choosemuse.com.

225. Sood A. Stress management and resilience training program research2017 July 13th, 2017. Available from: http://stressfree.org/research/.

226. Sood A. The Mayo Clinic Guide to Stress-Free Living: Da Capo Lifelong Books; 2013. 336 p.

227. Sood A. The Mayo Clinic Handbook for Happiness: A Four-Step Plan for Resilient Living: Da Capo Lifelong Books; 2015. 256 p.

228. Sood A. Immerse: A 52-Week Course in Resilient Living: A Commitment to Live With Intentionality, Deeper Presence, Contentment, and Kindness. (Volume 1) Createspace; 2016. 302 p.

229. Sood A. Global Center for Resiliency and Wellbeing; 2017 [Available from: www.stressfree.org.

230. Mayo Clinic. Mayo Clinic Healthy Living: Resilient Mind. Mayo Clinic; 2017 [Available from: resilience.mayoclinic.org.

231. Kopplin J. An Illustrated History of Computers: Part 42002. Available from: http://www.cs.kent.edu/~rothstei/10051/HistoryPt4.htm.

232. History.com. 1903 First airplane flies. Available from: http://www.history.com/this-day-in-history/first-airplane-flies.

233. James G. 3 Words That Create Instant Credibility2013 July 5th, 2017. Available from: http://www.inc.com/geoffrey-james/3-words-that-create-instant-credibility.html.

234. Buchen L. May 29, 1919: A Major Eclipse, Relatively Speaking 2009 July 5th, 2017. Available from: https://www.wired.com/2009/05/dayintech_0529/

235. Engen HG, Singer T. Compassion-based emotion regulation up-regulates experienced positive affect and associated neural networks. Social cognitive and affective neuroscience. 2015;10(9):1291-301.

236. Weng HY, Fox AS, Shackman AJ, Stodola DE, Caldwell JZ, Olson MC, et al. Compassion training alters altruism and neural responses to suffering. Psychological science. 2013;24(7):1171-80.

237. Project TG. Why Am I Neanderthal? 2017 July 5th, 2017. Available from: https://genographic.nationalgeographic.com/neanderthal/.

238. Saintonge A. How many stars are born and die each day? 2015 July 6th, 2017. Available from: http://curious.astro.cornell.edu/about-us/83-the-universe/stars-and-star-clusters/star-formation-and-molecular-clouds/400-how-many-stars-are-born-and-die-each-day-beginner.

239. Ishii A, Tanaka M, Watanabe Y. Neural mechanisms of mental fatigue. Reviews in the neurosciences. 2014;25(4):469-79.

240. Killingsworth MA, Gilbert DT. A wandering mind is an unhappy mind. Science (New York, NY). 2010;330(6006):932.

241. Hamlin JK, Baron AS. Agency attribution in infancy: evidence for a negativity bias. PloS one. 2014;9(5):e96112.

242. Hamlin JK, Wynn K, Bloom P. Three-month-olds show a negativity bias in their social evaluations. Developmental science. 2010;13(6):923-9.

243. Hilgard J, Weinberg A, Hajcak Proudfit G, Bartholow BD. The negativity bias in affective picture processing depends on top-down and bottom-up motivational significance. Emotion (Washington, DC). 2014;14(5):940-9.

244. Sheldon KM, Lyubomirsky S. The challenge of staying happier: testing the Hedonic Adaptation Prevention model. Personality & social psychology bulletin. 2012;38(5):670-80.

245. Diener E, Lucas RE, Scollon CN. Beyond the hedonic treadmill: revising the adaptation theory of well-being. The American psychologist. 2006;61(4):305-14.

246. Chester DS, DeWall CN. The pleasure of revenge: retaliatory aggression arises from a neural imbalance toward reward. Social cognitive and affective neuroscience. 2016;11(7):1173-82.

247. Fredrickson BL, Grewen KM, Algoe SB, Firestine AM, Arevalo JM, Ma J, et al. Psychological well-being and the human conserved transcriptional response to adversity. PloS one. 2015;10(3):e0121839.

248. Statistics BoL. Number of Jobs Held, Labor Market Activity, and Earnings Growth Among the Youngest Baby Boomers: Results from a Longitudinal Survey2015 July 5th, 2017. Available from: https://www.bls.gov/news.release/pdf/nlsoy.pdf.

249. Bernstein J. Survey Says: People Have Way Too Many Passwords To Remember. Joseph Bernstein 2016. Buzzfeed News 2016 July 5th, 2017. Available from: https://www.buzzfeed.com/josephbernstein/survey-says-people-have-way-too-many-passwords-to-remember?utm_term=.qlgPvXXjK#.ibAmBNNQv.

250. Baumeister RFT, J. Willpower: Rediscovering the Greatest Human Strength Penguin books; 2012. 304 p.

251. NFCC. The 2015 Consumer Financial Literacy Survey 2015 July 5th,2017. Available from: https://www.nfcc.org/wp-content/uploads/2015/04/NFCC_2015_Financial_Literacy_Survey_FINAL.pdf.

252. Schooler JW, Smallwood J, Christoff K, Handy TC, Reichle ED, Sayette MA. Meta-awareness, perceptual decoupling and the wandering mind. Trends in cognitive sciences. 2011;15(7):319-26.

253. Smallwood J, Tipper C, Brown K, Baird B, Engen H, Michaels JR, et al. Escaping the here and now: evidence for a role of the default mode network in perceptually decoupled thought. NeuroImage. 2013;69:120-5.
254. Sood A, Jones DT. On mind wandering, attention, brain networks, and meditation. Explore (New York, NY). 2013;9(3):136-41.
255. McMillan RL, Kaufman SB, Singer JL. Ode to positive constructive daydreaming. Frontiers in psychology. 2013;4:626.
256. Andrews-Hanna JR, Smallwood J, Spreng RN. The default network and self-generated thought: component processes, dynamic control, and clinical relevance. Annals of the New York Academy of Sciences. 2014;1316:29-52.
257. Fox KC, Andrews-Hanna JR, Christoff K. The neurobiology of self-generated thought from cells to systems: Integrating evidence from lesion studies, human intracranial electrophysiology, neurochemistry, and neuroendocrinology. Neuroscience. 2016;335:134-50.
258. Fox KC, Spreng RN, Ellamil M, Andrews-Hanna JR, Christoff K. The wandering brain: meta-analysis of functional neuroimaging studies of mind-wandering and related spontaneous thought processes. NeuroImage. 2015;111:611-21.
259. Mittner M, Hawkins GE, Boekel W, Forstmann BU. A Neural Model of Mind Wandering. Trends in cognitive sciences. 2016;20(8):570-8.
260. Lin CT, Chuang CH, Kerick S, Mullen T, Jung TP, Ko LW, et al. Mind-Wandering Tends to Occur under Low Perceptual Demands during Driving. Scientific reports. 2016;6:21353.
261. Raichle ME, MacLeod AM, Snyder AZ, Powers WJ, Gusnard DA, Shulman GL. A default mode of brain function. Proceedings of the National Academy of Sciences of the United States of America. 2001;98(2):676-82.
262. Wilson TD, Reinhard DA, Westgate EC, Gilbert DT, Ellerbeck N, Hahn C, et al. Social psychology. Just think: the challenges of the disengaged mind. Science (New York, NY). 2014;345(6192):75-7.
263. Phillips RC, Salo T, Carter CS. Distinct neural correlates for attention lapses in patients with schizophrenia and healthy participants. Frontiers in human neuroscience. 2015;9:502.
264. Buonomano DV, Merzenich MM. Cortical plasticity: from synapses to maps. Annual review of neuroscience. 1998;21:149-86.
265. Merzenich MM, Nahum M, Van Vleet TM. Neuroplasticity: introduction. Progress in brain research. 2013;207:xxi-xxvi.
266. Shaffer J. Neuroplasticity and Clinical Practice: Building Brain Power for Health. Frontiers in psychology. 2016;7:1118.
267. Gruberger M, Maron-Katz A, Sharon H, Hendler T, Ben-Simon E. The wandering mood: psychological and neural determinants of rest-related negative affect. Frontiers in psychology. 2013;4:961.
268. Coutinho JF, Fernandesl SV, Soares JM, Maia L, Goncalves OF, Sampaio A. Default mode network dissociation in depressive and anxiety states. Brain imaging and behavior. 2016;10(1):147-57.
269. Hamilton JP, Farmer M, Fogelman P, Gotlib IH. Depressive Rumination, the Default-Mode Network, and the Dark Matter of Clinical Neuroscience. Biological psychiatry. 2015;78(4):224-30.
270. Rayner G, Jackson G, Wilson S. Cognition-related brain networks underpin the symptoms of unipolar depression: Evidence from a systematic review. Neuroscience and biobehavioral reviews. 2016;61:53-65.
271. Modi S, Kumar M, Kumar P, Khushu S. Aberrant functional connectivity of resting state networks associated with trait anxiety. Psychiatry research. 2015;234(1):25-34.
272. Pletzer B, Kronbichler M, Nuerk HC, Kerschbaum HH. Mathematics anxiety reduces default mode network deactivation in response to numerical tasks. Frontiers in human neuroscience. 2015;9:202.
273. Tao Y, Liu B, Zhang X, Li J, Qin W, Yu C, et al. The Structural Connectivity Pattern of the Default Mode Network and Its Association with Memory and Anxiety. Frontiers in neuroanatomy. 2015;9:152.
274. Qin LD, Wang Z, Sun YW, Wan JQ, Su SS, Zhou Y, et al. A preliminary study of alterations in default network connectivity in post-traumatic stress disorder patients following recent trauma. Brain research. 2012;1484:50-6.

275. Reuveni I, Bonne O, Giesser R, Shragai T, Lazarovits G, Isserles M, et al. Anatomical and functional connectivity in the default mode network of post-traumatic stress disorder patients after civilian and military-related trauma. Human brain mapping. 2016;37(2):589-99.

276. Russman Block S, King AP, Sripada RK, Weissman DH, Welsh R, Liberzon I. Behavioral and neural correlates of disrupted orienting attention in posttraumatic stress disorder. Cognitive, affective & behavioral neuroscience. 2017;17(2):422-36.

277. Kim BH, Namkoong K, Kim JJ, Lee S, Yoon KJ, Choi M, et al. Altered resting-state functional connectivity in women with chronic fatigue syndrome. Psychiatry research. 2015;234(3):292-7.

278. Hampson JP, Zick SM, Khabir T, Wright BD, Harris RE. Altered resting brain connectivity in persistent cancer related fatigue. NeuroImage Clinical. 2015;8:305-13.

279. Fallon N, Chiu Y, Nurmikko T, Stancak A. Functional Connectivity with the Default Mode Network Is Altered in Fibromyalgia Patients. PloS one. 2016;11(7):e0159198.

280. Napadow V, LaCount L, Park K, As-Sanie S, Clauw DJ, Harris RE. Intrinsic brain connectivity in fibromyalgia is associated with chronic pain intensity. Arthritis and rheumatism. 2010;62(8):2545-55.

281. Nie X, Shao Y, Liu SY, Li HJ, Wan AL, Nie S, et al. Functional connectivity of paired default mode network subregions in primary insomnia. Neuropsychiatric disease and treatment. 2015;11:3085-93.

282. Vatthauer KE, Craggs JG, Robinson ME, Staud R, Berry RB, Perlstein WM, et al. Sleep is associated with task-negative brain activity in fibromyalgia participants with comorbid chronic insomnia. Journal of pain research. 2015;8:819-27.

283. Zhou F, Huang S, Gao L, Zhuang Y, Ding S, Gong H. Temporal regularity of intrinsic cerebral activity in patients with chronic primary insomnia: a brain entropy study using resting-state fMRI. Brain and behavior. 2016;6(10):e00529.

284. Hafkemeijer A, van der Grond J, Rombouts SA. Imaging the default mode network in aging and dementia. Biochimica et biophysica acta. 2012;1822(3):431-41.

285. Petrella JR, Sheldon FC, Prince SE, Calhoun VD, Doraiswamy PM. Default mode network connectivity in stable vs progressive mild cognitive impairment. Neurology. 2011;76(6):511-7.

286. Sheline YI, Raichle ME. Resting state functional connectivity in preclinical Alzheimer's disease. Biological psychiatry. 2013;74(5):340-7.

287. Zhou J, Seeley WW. Network dysfunction in Alzheimer's disease and frontotemporal dementia: implications for psychiatry. Biological psychiatry. 2014;75(7):565-73.

288. Mooneyham BW, Schooler JW. The costs and benefits of mind-wandering: a review. Canadian journal of experimental psychology = Revue canadienne de psychologie experimentale. 2013;67(1):11-8.

289. Smallwood J, Schooler JW. The science of mind wandering: empirically navigating the stream of consciousness. Annual review of psychology. 2015;66:487-518.

290. Eichele T, Debener S, Calhoun VD, Specht K, Engel AK, Hugdahl K, et al. Prediction of human errors by maladaptive changes in event-related brain networks. Proceedings of the National Academy of Sciences of the United States of America. 2008;105(16):6173-8.

291. Dixon ML, Fox KC, Christoff K. A framework for understanding the relationship between externally and internally directed cognition. Neuropsychologia. 2014;62:321-30.

292. Kam JW, Dao E, Stanciulescu M, Tildesley H, Handy TC. Mind wandering and the adaptive control of attentional resources. Journal of cognitive neuroscience. 2013;25(6):952-60.

293. Baird B, Smallwood J, Schooler JW. Back to the future: autobiographical planning and the functionality of mind-wandering. Consciousness and cognition. 2011;20(4):1604-11.

294. Beaty RE, Benedek M, Silvia PJ, Schacter DL. Creative Cognition and Brain Network Dynamics. Trends in cognitive sciences. 2016;20(2):87-95.

295. Beaty RE, Benedek M, Wilkins RW, Jauk E, Fink A, Silvia PJ, et al. Creativity and the default network: A functional connectivity analysis of the creative brain at rest. Neuropsychologia. 2014;64:92-8.

296. Heinonen J, Numminen J, Hlushchuk Y, Antell H, Taatila V, Suomala J. Default Mode and Executive Networks Areas: Association with the Serial Order in Divergent Thinking. PloS one. 2016;11(9):e0162234.

297. Mayseless N, Eran A, Shamay-Tsoory SG. Generating original ideas: The neural underpinning of originality. NeuroImage. 2015;116:232-9.

298. Immordino Yang MH, Christodoulou JA, Singh V. Rest Is Not Idleness: Implications of the Brain's Default Mode for Human Development and Education. Perspectives on psychological science : a journal of the Association for Psychological Science. 2012;7(4):352-64.

299. Christoff K. Undirected thought: neural determinants and correlates. Brain research. 2012;1428:51-9.

300. Bressler SL, Menon V. Large-scale brain networks in cognition: emerging methods and principles. Trends in cognitive sciences. 2010;14(6):277-90.

301. Kidsandcars.org. http://www.kidsandcars.org/how-kids-get-hurt/heat-stroke/ Kidsandcars.org; 2017 [

302. Golchert J, Smallwood J, Jefferies E, Seli P, Huntenburg JM, Liem F, et al. Individual variation in intentionality in the mind-wandering state is reflected in the integration of the default-mode, fronto-parietal, and limbic networks. NeuroImage. 2017;146:226-35.

303. Richardson DS. Everyday Aggression Takes Many Forms. Current Directions in Psychological Science. 2014;23(3).

304. Gallup.com. Confidence in Institutions 2016 July 5th 2017. Available from: http://www.gallup.com/poll/1597/confidence-institutions.aspx.

305. Education USDo. Working to Keep Schools and Communities SafeJuly 5th, 2017. Available from: https://www.ed.gov/school-safety

306. Ingraham C. There's never been a safer time to be a kid in America2015 July 5th, 2017. Available from: https://www.washingtonpost.com/news/wonk/wp/2015/04/14/theres-never-been-a-safer-time-to-be-a-kid-in-america/?utm_term=.fc5dd3707d5b.

307. Pinker S. The Better Angels of Our Nature: Why Violence Has Declined: Penguin Books; 2012. 832 p.

308. Siegrist M, Sutterlin B. Human and nature-caused hazards: the affect heuristic causes biased decisions. Risk analysis : an official publication of the Society for Risk Analysis. 2014;34(8):1482-94.

309. Ro S. Man-Made Disasters Are Way Worse For The Stock Market Than Natural Disasters2012 July 7th, 2017. Available from: http://www.businessinsider.com/man-made-disasters-natural-disasters-and-stocks-2012-11.

310. Siegrist M, Hartmann C, Sutterlin B. Biased perception about gene technology: How perceived naturalness and affect distort benefit perception. Appetite. 2016;96:509-16.

311. Kochanek KD, Murphy SL, Xu JQ, Tejada-Vera B. Deaths: Final data for 2014. National vital statistics reports; vol 65 no 4. Hyattsville, MD: National Center for Health Statistics. 2016.

311b. Xu JQ, Murphy SL, Kochanek KD, Arias E. Mortality in the United States, 2015. NCHS data brief, no 267. Hyattsville, MD: National Center for Health Statistics. 2016.

312. Neihmond P. For Many Americans, Stress Takes A Toll On Health And Family2014 July 5th, 2017. Available from: http://www.npr.org/sections/health-shots/2014/07/07/323351759/for-many-americans-stress-takes-a-toll-on-health-and-family.

313. Association AP. Stress in America [Available from: http://www.apa.org/news/press/releases/stress/index.aspx?tab=6

314. Seppala EC, K. Proof That Positive Work Cultures Are More Productive2015 July 5th, 2017. Available from: https://hbr.org/2015/12/proof-that-positive-work-cultures-are-more-productive.

315. Pratt LAB, D.J. Depression in the U.S. household population, 2009–2012. . NCHS data brief, no 172 [Internet]. 2014 July 5th, 2017. Available from: https://www.cdc.gov/nchs/data/databriefs/db172.htm

316. Pratt L.A.; Brody DJ. Depression in the U.S. household population, 2009–20122014 July 6th 2017; 1NCHS data brief no. 72. Available from: https://www.cdc.gov/nchs/data/databriefs/db172.htm.

317. Kensinger EA, Garoff-Eaton RJ, Schacter DL. How negative emotion enhances the visual specificity of a memory. Journal of cognitive neuroscience. 2007;19(11):1872-87.

318. Peltola MJ, Leppanen JM, Vogel-Farley VK, Hietanen JK, Nelson CA. Fearful faces but not fearful eyes alone delay attention disengagement in 7-month-old infants. Emotion (Washington, DC). 2009;9(4):560-5.

319. Peltola MJ, Leppanen JM, Maki S, Hietanen JK. Emergence of enhanced attention to fearful faces between 5 and 7 months of age. Social cognitive and affective neuroscience. 2009;4(2):134-42.

320. Bishop SJ. Neural mechanisms underlying selective attention to threat. Annals of the New York Academy of Sciences. 2008;1129:141-52.

321. Janak PH, Tye KM. From circuits to behaviour in the amygdala. Nature. 2015;517(7534):284-92.

322. Sears RM, Schiff HC, LeDoux JE. Molecular mechanisms of threat learning in the lateral nucleus of the amygdala. Progress in molecular biology and translational science. 2014;122:263-304.

323. Zheng Z, Gu S, Lei Y, Lu S, Wang W, Li Y, et al. Safety Needs Mediate Stressful Events Induced Mental Disorders. Neural plasticity. 2016; 2016:8058093.

324. Bremner JD, Elzinga B, Schmahl C, Vermetten E. Structural and functional plasticity of the human brain in posttraumatic stress disorder. Progress in brain research. 2008;167:171-86.

325. Mahan AL, Ressler KJ. Fear conditioning, synaptic plasticity and the amygdala: implications for posttraumatic stress disorder. Trends in neurosciences. 2012;35(1):24-35.

326. Chapman HA, Johannes K, Poppenk JL, Moscovitch M, Anderson AK. Evidence for the differential salience of disgust and fear in episodic memory. Journal of experimental psychology General. 2013;142(4):1100-12.

327. Katsyri J, Kinnunen T, Kusumoto K, Oittinen P, Ravaja N. Negativity Bias in Media Multitasking: The Effects of Negative Social Media Messages on Attention to Television News Broadcasts. PloS one. 2016;11(5):e0153712.

328. Baumeister RFB, E.; Finkenauer, C.; Vohs, K.D. Bad Is Stronger Than Good. Review of General Psychology. 2001;5(4):323-70.

329. Vaish A, Grossmann T, Woodward A. Not all emotions are created equal: the negativity bias in social-emotional development. Psychological bulletin. 2008;134(3):383-403.

330. Fredrickson BL. Updated thinking on positivity ratios. The American psychologist. 2013;68(9):814-22.

331. Fredrickson BL, Losada MF. Positive affect and the complex dynamics of human flourishing. The American psychologist. 2005;60(7):678-86.

332. Gottman JM. What Predicts Divorce?: The Relationship Between Marital Processes and Marital Outcomes. 1st edition ed: Psychology Press; 1993.

333. Brown NJ, Sokal AD, Friedman HL. The complex dynamics of wishful thinking: the critical positivity ratio. The American psychologist. 2013;68(9):801-13.

334. Brown NJ, Sokal AD, Friedman HL. Positive psychology and romantic scientism. The American psychologist. 2014;69(6):636-7.

335. Britton JC, Lissek S, Grillon C, Norcross MA, Pine DS. Development of anxiety: the role of threat appraisal and fear learning. Depression and anxiety. 2011;28(1):5-17.

336. Tawakol A, Ishai A, Takx RA, Figueroa AL, Ali A, Kaiser Y, et al. Relation between resting amygdalar activity and cardiovascular events: a longitudinal and cohort study. Lancet (London, England). 2017;389(10071):834-45.

337. Feinstein JS, Adolphs R, Damasio A, Tranel D. The human amygdala and the induction and experience of fear. Current biology : CB. 2011;21(1):34-8.

338. Eisenberger NI. The pain of social disconnection: examining the shared neural underpinnings of physical and social pain. Nature reviews Neuroscience. 2012;13(6):421-34.

339. Kross E, Berman MG, Mischel W, Smith EE, Wager TD. Social rejection shares somatosensory representations with physical pain. Proceedings of the National Academy of Sciences of the United States of America. 2011;108(15):6270-5.

340. Afari N, Ahumada SM, Wright LJ, Mostoufi S, Golnari G, Reis V, et al. Psychological trauma and functional somatic syndromes: a systematic review and meta-analysis. Psychosomatic medicine. 2014;76(1):2-11.

341. Burke NN, Finn DP, McGuire BE, Roche M. Psychological stress in early life as a predisposing factor for the development of chronic pain: Clinical and preclinical evidence and neurobiological mechanisms. Journal of neuroscience research. 2017;95(6):1257-70.

342. Eisenberger NI, Lieberman MD. Why rejection hurts: a common neural alarm system for physical and social pain. Trends in cognitive sciences. 2004;8(7):294-300.

343. Hassett AL, Clauw DJ. The role of stress in rheumatic diseases. Arthritis research & therapy. 2010;12(3):123.

344. Lyon P, Cohen M, Quintner J. An evolutionary stress-response hypothesis for chronic widespread pain (fibromyalgia syndrome). Pain medicine (Malden, Mass). 2011;12(8):1167-78.

345. Cacioppo S, Frum C, Asp E, Weiss RM, Lewis JW, Cacioppo JT. A quantitative meta-analysis of functional imaging studies of social rejection. Scientific reports. 2013;3:2027.

346. Eisenberger NI. Social pain and the brain: controversies, questions, and where to go from here. Annual review of psychology. 2015;66:601-29.

347. Dewall CN, Macdonald G, Webster GD, Masten CL, Baumeister RF, Powell C, et al. Acetaminophen reduces social pain: behavioral and neural evidence. Psychological science. 2010;21(7):931-7.

348. Gershoff ET, Grogan-Kaylor A, Lansford JE, Chang L, Zelli A, Deater-Deckard K, et al. Parent discipline practices in an international sample: associations with child behaviors and moderation by perceived normativeness. Child development. 2010;81(2):487-502.

349. Lilienfeld SOA, H. . Can Positive Thinking Be Negative?2011 July 6th, 2017. Available from: https://www.scientificamerican.com/article/can-positive-thinking-be-negative/.

350. Singer T, Seymour B, O'Doherty J, Kaube H, Dolan RJ, Frith CD. Empathy for pain involves the affective but not sensory components of pain. Science (New York, NY). 2004;303(5661):1157-62.

351. Bucchioni G, Lelard T, Ahmaidi S, Godefroy O, Krystkowiak P, Mouras H. Do we feel the same empathy for loved and hated peers? PloS one. 2015;10(5):e0125871.

352. Lamm C, Decety J, Singer T. Meta-analytic evidence for common and distinct neural networks associated with directly experienced pain and empathy for pain. NeuroImage. 2011;54(3):2492-502.

353. Danziger N, Faillenot I, Peyron R. Can we share a pain we never felt? Neural correlates of empathy in patients with congenital insensitivity to pain. Neuron. 2009;61(2):203-12.

354. Saarela MV, Hlushchuk Y, Williams AC, Schurmann M, Kalso E, Hari R. The compassionate brain: humans detect intensity of pain from another's face. Cerebral cortex (New York, NY : 1991). 2007;17(1):230-7.

355. Lang S, Yu T, Markl A, Muller F, Kotchoubey B. Hearing others' pain: neural activity related to empathy. Cognitive, affective & behavioral neuroscience. 2011;11(3):386-95.

356. Eisenberger NI, Lieberman MD, Williams KD. Does rejection hurt? An FMRI study of social exclusion. Science (New York, NY). 2003;302(5643):290-2.

357. Meister IG, Krings T, Foltys H, Boroojerdi B, Muller M, Topper R, et al. Playing piano in the mind--an fMRI study on music imagery and performance in pianists. Brain research Cognitive brain research. 2004;19(3):219-28.

358. Garcia Carrasco D, Aboitiz Cantalapiedra J. Effectiveness of motor imagery or mental practice in functional recovery after stroke: a systematic review. Neurologia (Barcelona, Spain). 2016;31(1):43-52.

359. Thieme H, Morkisch N, Rietz C, Dohle C, Borgetto B. The Efficacy of Movement Representation Techniques for Treatment of Limb Pain--A Systematic Review and Meta-Analysis. The journal of pain : official journal of the American Pain Society. 2016;17(2):167-80.

360. Beck BD, Hansen AM, Gold C. Coping with Work-Related Stress through Guided Imagery and Music (GIM): Randomized Controlled Trial. Journal of music therapy. 2015;52(3):323-52.

361. Menzies V, Lyon DE, Elswick RK, Jr., McCain NL, Gray DP. Effects of guided imagery on biobehavioral factors in women with fibromyalgia. Journal of behavioral medicine. 2014;37(1):70-80.

362. Mizrahi MC, Reicher-Atir R, Levy S, Haramati S, Wengrower D, Israeli E, et al. Effects of guided imagery with relaxation training on anxiety and quality of life among patients with inflammatory bowel disease. Psychology & health. 2012;27(12):1463-79.

363. Broadbent E, Kahokehr A, Booth RJ, Thomas J, Windsor JA, Buchanan CM, et al. A brief relaxation intervention reduces stress and improves surgical wound healing response: a randomised trial. Brain, behavior, and immunity. 2012;26(2):212-7.

364. Bryant RA, Chan L. Thinking of attachments reduces noradrenergic stress response. Psychoneuroendocrinology. 2015;60:39-45.

365. Geracioti TD, Jr., Jefferson-Wilson L, Strawn JR, Baker DG, Dashevsky BA, Horn PS, et al. Effect of traumatic imagery on cerebrospinal fluid dopamine and serotonin metabolites in posttraumatic stress disorder. Journal of psychiatric research. 2013;47(7):995-8.

366. Ushida T, Ikemoto T, Tanaka S, Shinozaki J, Taniguchi S, Murata Y, et al. Virtual needle pain stimuli activates cortical representation of emotions in normal volunteers. Neuroscience letters. 2008;439(1):7-12.

367. Straube T, Sauer A, Miltner WH. Brain activation during direct and indirect processing of positive and negative words. Behavioural brain research. 2011;222(1):66-72.

368. Richter M, Eck J, Straube T, Miltner WH, Weiss T. Do words hurt? Brain activation during the processing of pain-related words. Pain. 2010;148(2):198-205.

369. Simmons A, Strigo I, Matthews SC, Paulus MP, Stein MB. Anticipation of aversive visual stimuli is associated with increased insula activation in anxiety-prone subjects. Biological psychiatry. 2006;60(4):402-9.

370. Franz VA, Glass CR, Arnkoff DB, Dutton MA. The impact of the September 11th terrorist attacks on psychiatric patients: a review. Clinical psychology review. 2009;29(4):339-47.

371. Bulkeley K, Kahan TL. The impact of September 11 on dreaming. Consciousness and cognition. 2008;17(4):1248-56.

372. Hartmann E, Brezler T. A systematic change in dreams after 9/11/01. Sleep. 2008;31(2):213-8.

373. Hartmann E. The underlying emotion and the dream relating dream imagery to the dreamer's underlying emotion can help elucidate the nature of dreaming. International review of neurobiology. 2010;92:197-214.

374. Revonsuo A. The reinterpretation of dreams: an evolutionary hypothesis of the function of dreaming. The Behavioral and brain sciences. 2000;23(6):877-901; discussion 4-1121.

375. Zadra A, Desjardins S, Marcotte E. Evolutionary function of dreams: A test of the threat simulation theory in recurrent dreams. Consciousness and cognition. 2006;15(2):450-63.

376. Charuvastra A, Cloitre M. Safe enough to sleep: sleep disruptions associated with trauma, posttraumatic stress, and anxiety in children and adolescents. Child and adolescent psychiatric clinics of North America. 2009;18(4):877-91.

377. Levin R, Nielsen TA. Disturbed dreaming, posttraumatic stress disorder, and affect distress: a review and neurocognitive model. Psychological bulletin. 2007;133(3):482-528.

378. Curnoe S, Langevin R. Personality and deviant sexual fantasies: an examination of the MMPIs of sex offenders. Journal of clinical psychology. 2002;58(7):803-15.

379. Howitt D. What is the role of fantasy in sex offending? Criminal behaviour and mental health : CBMH. 2004;14(3):182-8.

380. Hammerbacher J. July 6th, 2017. Available from: http://www.goodreads.com/quotes/747678-the-best-minds-of-my-generation-are-thinking-about-how.

381. Schlanger Z. Forget 2015 - 2050 is the year for predictions2015 July 5th, 2017. Available from: http://www.newsweek.com/forget-2015-2050-year-predictions-296481.

382. Dvash J, Gilam G, Ben-Ze'ev A, Hendler T, Shamay-Tsoory SG. The envious brain: the neural basis of social comparison. Human brain mapping. 2010;31(11):1741-50.

383. Festinger L. A Theory of Social Comparison Processes. Human Relations 1954;7(117).

384. Wang T, Mo L, Mo C, Tan LH, Cant JS, Zhong L, et al. Is moral beauty different from facial beauty? Evidence from an fMRI study. Social cognitive and affective neuroscience. 2015;10(6):814-23.

385. Wen X, Xiang Y, Cant JS, Wang T, Cupchik G, Huang R, et al. The neural correlates of internal and external comparisons: an fMRI study. Brain structure & function. 2017;222(1):563-75.

386. Kedia G, Lindner M, Mussweiler T, Ihssen N, Linden DE. Brain networks of social comparison. Neuroreport. 2013;24(5):259-64.

387. Lyubomirsky S, Ross L. Hedonic consequences of social comparison: a contrast of happy and unhappy people. Journal of personality and social psychology. 1997;73(6):1141-57.

388. Kim J, Hong EK, Choi I, Hicks JA. Companion Versus Comparison: Examining Seeking Social Companionship or Social Comparison as Characteristics That Differentiate Happy and Unhappy People. Personality & social psychology bulletin. 2016;42(3):311-22.

389. Strahan EJ, Wilson AE, Cressman KE, Buote VM. Comparing to perfection: How cultural norms for appearance affect social comparisons and self-image. Body image. 2006;3(3):211-27.

390. Myers TA, Crowther JH. Social comparison as a predictor of body dissatisfaction: A meta-analytic review. Journal of abnormal psychology. 2009;118(4):683-98.

391. Vidyarthi PR, Liden RC, Anand S, Erdogan B, Ghosh S. Where do I stand? Examining the effects of leader-member exchange social comparison on employee work behaviors. The Journal of applied psychology. 2010;95(5):849-61.

392. Takahashi H, Kato M, Matsuura M, Mobbs D, Suhara T, Okubo Y. When your gain is my pain and your pain is my gain: neural correlates of envy and schadenfreude. Science (New York, NY). 2009;323(5916):937-9.

393. van de Ven N, Hoogland CE, Smith RH, van Dijk WW, Breugelmans SM, Zeelenberg M. When envy leads to schadenfreude. Cognition & emotion. 2015;29(6):1007-25.

394. Kross E, Verduyn P, Demiralp E, Park J, Lee DS, Lin N, et al. Facebook use predicts declines in subjective well-being in young adults. PloS one. 2013;8(8):e69841.

395. Chou HT, Edge N. "They are happier and having better lives than I am": the impact of using Facebook on perceptions of others' lives. Cyberpsychology, behavior and social networking. 2012;15(2):117-21.

396. Verduyn P, Lee DS, Park J, Shablack H, Orvell A, Bayer J, et al. Passive Facebook usage undermines affective well-being: Experimental and longitudinal evidence. Journal of experimental psychology General. 2015;144(2):480-8.

397. Holland G, Tiggemann M. A systematic review of the impact of the use of social networking sites on body image and disordered eating outcomes. Body image. 2016;17:100-10.

398. Liu P, Tov W, Kosinski M, Stillwell DJ, Qiu L. Do Facebook Status Updates Reflect Subjective Well-Being? Cyberpsychology, behavior and social networking. 2015;18(7):373-9.

399. Eichstaedt JC, Schwartz HA, Kern ML, Park G, Labarthe DR, Merchant RM, et al. Psychological language on Twitter predicts county-level heart disease mortality. Psychological science. 2015;26(2):159-69.

400. Baker DA, Algorta GP. The Relationship Between Online Social Networking and Depression: A Systematic Review of Quantitative Studies. Cyberpsychology, behavior and social networking. 2016;19(11):638-48.

401. Laranjo L, Arguel A, Neves AL, Gallagher AM, Kaplan R, Mortimer N, et al. The influence of social networking sites on health behavior change: a systematic review and meta-analysis. Journal of the American Medical Informatics Association : JAMIA. 2015;22(1):243-56.

402. Seabrook EM, Kern ML, Rickard NS. Social Networking Sites, Depression, and Anxiety: A Systematic Review. JMIR mental health. 2016;3(4):e50.

403. Chen C, Takahashi T, Yang S. Remembrance of happy things past: positive autobiographical memories are intrinsically rewarding and valuable, but not in depression. Frontiers in psychology. 2015;6:222.

404. Joormann J, Siemer M, Gotlib IH. Mood regulation in depression: Differential effects of distraction and recall of happy memories on sad mood. Journal of abnormal psychology. 2007;116(3):484-90.

405. Pelham B. Affective Forecasting: The Perils of Predicting Future Feelings Psychological Science Agenda [Internet]. 2004 July 6th, 2017. Available from: http://www.apa.org/science/about/psa/2004/04/pelham.aspx

406. Wilson TDG, D.T. Affective forecasting Advances in Experimental Social Psychology. 2003;35:345-411.

407. Gilbert DTW, T. D. Miswanting: Some problems in the forecasting of future affective states. In: Forgas JP, editor. Thinking and feeling: The role of affect in social cognition. Cambridge: Cambridge University Press; 2000. p. 178-97.

408. Sheldon KM, Gunz A, Nichols CP, Ferguson Y. Extrinsic value orientation and affective forecasting: overestimating the rewards, underestimating the costs. Journal of personality. 2010;78(1):149-78.

409. Twenge JM, Campbell WK, Freeman EC. Generational differences in young adults' life goals, concern for others, and civic orientation, 1966-2009. Journal of personality and social psychology. 2012;102(5):1045-62.

410. Stone CT, D.; Sherman, A.; Horton, E. A Guide to Statistics on Historical Trends in Income Inequality2016 July 6th, 2017. Available from: http://www.cbpp.org/research/poverty-and-inequality/a-guide-to-statistics-on-historical-trends-in-income-inequality.

411. Bureau USC. Income Inequality Data Tables2016 July 6th, 2017. Available from: http://www.census.gov/topics/income-poverty/income-inequality/data/data-tables.html

412. Gabay AS, Radua J, Kempton MJ, Mehta MA. The Ultimatum Game and the brain: a meta-analysis of neuroimaging studies. Neuroscience and biobehavioral reviews. 2014;47:549-58.

413. Guo X, Zheng L, Zhu L, Li J, Wang Q, Dienes Z, et al. Increased neural responses to unfairness in a loss context. NeuroImage. 2013;77:246-53.

414. Guroglu B, van den Bos W, Rombouts SA, Crone EA. Unfair? It depends: neural correlates of fairness in social context. Social cognitive and affective neuroscience. 2010;5(4):414-23.

415. Jorm AF, Ryan SM. Cross-national and historical differences in subjective well-being. International journal of epidemiology. 2014;43(2):330-40.

416. Oishi S, Kesebir S. Income Inequality Explains Why Economic Growth Does Not Always Translate to an Increase in Happiness. Psychological science. 2015;26(10):1630-8.

417. Gilbert DT, Malone PS. The correspondence bias. Psychological bulletin. 1995;117(1):21-38.

418. Jones EEH, V.A. . The attribution of attitudes. Journal of Experimental Social Psychology. 1967;3:1-24.

419. Stewart TL, Chipperfield JG, Ruthig JC, Heckhausen J. Downward social comparison and subjective well-being in late life: the moderating role of perceived control. Aging & mental health. 2013;17(3):375-85.

420. Derlega VJ, Greene K, Henson JM, Winstead BA. Social comparison activity in coping with HIV. International journal of STD & AIDS. 2008;19(3):164-7.

421. Alicke MD, LoSchiavo FM, Zerbst J, Zhang S. The person who outperforms me is a genius: maintaining perceived competence in upward social comparison. Journal of personality and social psychology. 1997;73(4):781-9.

422. Gerrard M, Gibbons FX, Lane DJ, Stock ML. Smoking cessation: social comparison level predicts success for adult smokers. Health psychology : official journal of the Division of Health Psychology, American Psychological Association. 2005;24(6):623-9.

423. van de Ven N. Envy and admiration: emotion and motivation following upward social comparison. Cognition & emotion. 2017;31(1):193-200.
424. Lohrenz T, Bhatt M, Apple N, Montague PR. Keeping up with the Joneses: interpersonal prediction errors and the correlation of behavior in a tandem sequential choice task. PLoS computational biology. 2013;9(10):e1003275.
425. Mobbs D, Yu R, Meyer M, Passamonti L, Seymour B, Calder AJ, et al. A key role for similarity in vicarious reward. Science (New York, NY). 2009;324(5929):900.
426. Najmi S, Wegner DM. The gravity of unwanted thoughts: Asymmetric priming effects in thought suppression. Consciousness and cognition. 2008;17(1):114-24.
427. Abramowitz JS, Tolin DF, Street GP. Paradoxical effects of thought suppression: a meta-analysis of controlled studies. Clinical psychology review. 2001;21(5):683-703.
428. Clark DM, Ball S, Pape D. An experimental investigation of thought suppression. Behaviour research and therapy. 1991;29(3):253-7.
429. Clark DM, Winton E, Thynn L. A further experimental investigation of thought suppression. Behaviour research and therapy. 1993;31(2):207-10.
430. Hooper N, McHugh L. The effects of repeated thought suppression attempts on thought occurrence. The American journal of psychology. 2013;126(3):315-22.
431. Lambert AE, Hu Y, Magee JC, Beadel JR, Teachman BA. Thought suppression across time: Change in frequency and duration of thought recurrence. Journal of obsessive-compulsive and related disorders. 2014;3(1):21-8.
432. Malinowski JE. Dreaming and personality: Wake-dream continuity, thought suppression, and the Big Five Inventory. Consciousness and cognition. 2015;38:9-15.
433. Wegner DM, Schneider DJ, Carter SR, 3rd, White TL. Paradoxical effects of thought suppression. Journal of personality and social psychology. 1987;53(1):5-13.
434. Giuliano RJ, Wicha NY. Why the white bear is still there: electrophysiological evidence for ironic semantic activation during thought suppression. Brain research. 2010;1316:62-74.
435. Carew CL, Milne AM, Tatham EL, MacQueen GM, Hall GB. Neural systems underlying thought suppression in young women with, and at-risk, for depression. Behavioural brain research. 2013;257:13-24.
436. Mitchell JP, Heatherton TF, Kelley WM, Wyland CL, Wegner DM, Neil Macrae C. Separating sustained from transient aspects of cognitive control during thought suppression. Psychological science. 2007;18(4):292-7.
437. Wyland CL, Kelley WM, Macrae CN, Gordon HL, Heatherton TF. Neural correlates of thought suppression. Neuropsychologia. 2003;41(14):1863-7.
438. Aso T, Nishimura K, Kiyonaka T, Aoki T, Inagawa M, Matsuhashi M, et al. Dynamic interactions of the cortical networks during thought suppression. Brain and behavior. 2016;6(8):e00503.
439. Brewin CR, Beaton A. Thought suppression, intelligence, and working memory capacity. Behaviour research and therapy. 2002;40(8):923-30.
440. Gillie BL, Vasey MW, Thayer JF. Individual differences in resting heart rate variability moderate thought suppression success. Psychophysiology. 2015;52(9):1149-60.
441. Petkus AJ, Gum A, Wetherell JL. Thought suppression is associated with psychological distress in homebound older adults. Depression and anxiety. 2012;29(3):219-25.
442. Marcks BA, Woods DW. Role of thought-related beliefs and coping strategies in the escalation of intrusive thoughts: an analog to obsessive-compulsive disorder. Behaviour research and therapy. 2007;45(11):2640-51.
443. McLaren S, Crowe SF. The contribution of perceived control of stressful life events and thought suppression to the symptoms of obsessive-compulsive disorder in both non-clinical and clinical samples. Journal of anxiety disorders. 2003;17(4):389-403.
444. Garland EL, Brown SM, Howard MO. Thought suppression as a mediator of the association between depressed mood and prescription opioid craving among chronic pain patients. Journal of behavioral medicine. 2016;39(1):128-38.

445. Garland EL, Roberts-Lewis A. Differential roles of thought suppression and dispositional mindfulness in posttraumatic stress symptoms and craving. Addictive behaviors. 2013;38(2):1555-62.
446. Collins B, Fischer S, Stojek M, Becker K. The relationship of thought suppression and recent rape to disordered eating in emerging adulthood. Journal of adolescence. 2014;37(2):113-21.
447. Rosenthal MZ, Cheavens JS, Lynch TR, Follette V. Thought suppression mediates the relationship between negative mood and PTSD in sexually assaulted women. Journal of traumatic stress. 2006;19(5):741-5.
448. Riley B. Experiential avoidance mediates the association between thought suppression and mindfulness with problem gambling. Journal of gambling studies. 2014;30(1):163-71.
449. Ferreira C, Palmeira L, Trindade IA, Catarino F. When thought suppression backfires: its moderator effect on eating psychopathology. Eating and weight disorders : EWD. 2015;20(3):355-62.
450. Wenzel A, Barth TC, Holt CS. Thought suppression in spider-fearful and nonfearful individuals. The Journal of general psychology. 2003;130(2):191-205.
451. Zeitlin SB, Netten KA, Hodder SL. Thought suppression: an experimental investigation of spider phobics. Behaviour research and therapy. 1995;33(4):407-13.
452. Erskine JA, Georgiou GJ, Kvavilashvili L. I suppress, therefore I smoke: effects of thought suppression on smoking behavior. Psychological science. 2010;21(9):1225-30.
453. Barnes RD, Tantleff-Dunn S. Food for thought: examining the relationship between food thought suppression and weight-related outcomes. Eating behaviors. 2010;11(3):175-9.
454. Neufeind J, Dritschel B, Astell AJ, MacLeod MD. The effects of thought suppression on autobiographical memory recall. Behaviour research and therapy. 2009;47(4):275-84.
455. Pettit JW, Temple SR, Norton PJ, Yaroslavsky I, Grover KE, Morgan ST, et al. Thought suppression and suicidal ideation: preliminary evidence in support of a robust association. Depression and anxiety. 2009;26(8):758-63.
456. Amstadter AB, Vernon LL. A Preliminary Examination of Thought Suppression, Emotion Regulation, and Coping in a Trauma Exposed Sample. Journal of aggression, maltreatment & trauma. 2008;17(3):279-95.
457. Vazquez C, Hervas G, Perez-Sales P. Chronic thought suppression and posttraumatic symptoms: data from the Madrid March 11, 2004 terrorist attack. Journal of anxiety disorders. 2008;22(8):1326-36.
458. Hulsebusch J, Hasenbring MI, Rusu AC. Understanding Pain and Depression in Back Pain: the Role of Catastrophizing, Help-/Hopelessness, and Thought Suppression as Potential Mediators. International journal of behavioral medicine. 2016;23(3):251-9.
459. Chapman BP, Fiscella K, Kawachi I, Duberstein P, Muennig P. Emotion suppression and mortality risk over a 12-year follow-up. Journal of psychosomatic research. 2013;75(4):381-5.
460. Ishii H, Nagashima M, Tanno M, Nakajima A, Yoshino S. Does being easily moved to tears as a response to psychological stress reflect response to treatment and the general prognosis in patients with rheumatoid arthritis? Clinical and experimental rheumatology. 2003;21(5):611-6.
461. Westin V, Ostergren R, Andersson G. The effects of acceptance versus thought suppression for dealing with the intrusiveness of tinnitus. International journal of audiology. 2008;47 Suppl 2:S112-8.
462. Wegner DM. Setting free the bears: escape from thought suppression. The American psychologist. 2011;66(8):671-80.
463. Hooper N, Davies N, Davies L, McHugh L. Comparing thought suppression and mindfulness as coping techniques for spider fear. Consciousness and cognition. 2011;20(4):1824-30.

464. Marcks BA, Woods DW. A comparison of thought suppression to an acceptance-based technique in the management of personal intrusive thoughts: a controlled evaluation. Behaviour research and therapy. 2005;43(4):433-45.
465. Ju YJ, Lien YW. Better control with less effort: The advantage of using focused-breathing strategy over focused-distraction strategy on thought suppression. Consciousness and cognition. 2016;40:9-16.
466. Robinson TE, Berridge KC. The neural basis of drug craving: an incentive-sensitization theory of addiction. Brain research Brain research reviews. 1993;18(3):247-91.
467. Sinha R. The clinical neurobiology of drug craving. Current opinion in neurobiology. 2013;23(4):649-54.
468. Castro DC, Berridge KC. Advances in the neurobiological bases for food 'liking' versus 'wanting'. Physiology & behavior. 2014;136:22-30.
469. Esch T, Stefano GB. The neurobiological link between compassion and love. Medical science monitor : international medical journal of experimental and clinical research. 2011;17(3):Ra65-75.
470. Fattore L, Melis M, Fadda P, Pistis M, Fratta W. The endocannabinoid system and nondrug rewarding behaviours. Experimental neurology. 2010;224(1):23-36.
471. Drugabuse.gov. Drugs and the brain2014 July 6th, 2017. Available from: https://www.drugabuse.gov/publications/drugs-brains-behavior-science-addiction/drugs-brain
472. Berridge KC, Robinson TE. Liking, wanting, and the incentive-sensitization theory of addiction. The American psychologist. 2016;71(8):670-9.
473. Ballas D, Dorling D. Measuring the impact of major life events upon happiness. International journal of epidemiology. 2007;36(6):1244-52.
474. Brickman P, Coates D, Janoff-Bulman R. Lottery winners and accident victims: is happiness relative? Journal of personality and social psychology. 1978;36(8):917-27.
475. Henriksson A, Carlander I, Arestedt K. Feelings of rewards among family caregivers during ongoing palliative care. Palliative & supportive care. 2015;13(6):1509-17.
476. Umass.edu. Ramesh Sitaraman's research shows how poor online video quality impacts viewers2013 July 6th, 2017. Available from: https://www.cics.umass.edu/news/latest-news/research-online-videos
477. Frost R, McNaughton N. The neural basis of delay discounting: A review and preliminary model. Neuroscience and biobehavioral reviews. 2017;79:48-65.
478. Fields SA, Lange K, Ramos A, Thamotharan S, Rassu F. The relationship between stress and delay discounting: a meta-analytic review. Behavioural pharmacology. 2014;25(5-6):434-44.
479. Amlung M, Vedelago L, Acker J, Balodis I, MacKillop J. Steep delay discounting and addictive behavior: a meta-analysis of continuous associations. Addiction (Abingdon, England). 2017;112(1):51-62.
480. Barlow P, Reeves A, McKee M, Galea G, Stuckler D. Unhealthy diets, obesity and time discounting: a systematic literature review and network analysis. Obesity reviews : an official journal of the International Association for the Study of Obesity. 2016;17(9):810-9.
481. McClelland J, Dalton B, Kekic M, Bartholdy S, Campbell IC, Schmidt U. A systematic review of temporal discounting in eating disorders and obesity: Behavioural and neuroimaging findings. Neuroscience and biobehavioral reviews. 2016;71:506-28.
482. Anokhin AP, Golosheykin S, Grant JD, Heath AC. Heritability of delay discounting in adolescence: a longitudinal twin study. Behavior genetics. 2011;41(2):175-83.
483. Anokhin AP, Grant JD, Mulligan RC, Heath AC. The genetics of impulsivity: evidence for the heritability of delay discounting. Biological psychiatry. 2015;77(10):887-94.
484. Amlung M, MacKillop J. Clarifying the relationship between impulsive delay discounting and nicotine dependence. Psychology of addictive behaviors : journal of the Society of Psychologists in Addictive Behaviors. 2014;28(3):761-8.

485. MacKillop J, Amlung MT, Few LR, Ray LA, Sweet LH, Munafo MR. Delayed reward discounting and addictive behavior: a meta-analysis. Psychopharmacology. 2011;216(3):305-21.
486. Reynolds B. A review of delay-discounting research with humans: relations to drug use and gambling. Behavioural pharmacology. 2006;17(8):651-67.
487. Stea JN, Hodgins DC, Lambert MJ. Relations between delay discounting and low to moderate gambling, cannabis, and alcohol problems among university students. Behavioural processes. 2011;88(3):202-5.
488. Katz J. Drug Deaths in America Are Rising Faster Than Ever 2017 July 6th, 2017. Available from: https://www.nytimes.com/interactive/2017/06/05/upshot/opioid-epidemic-drug-overdose-deaths-are-rising-faster-than-ever.html?_r=0
489. Olds JM, P. Positive reinforcement produced by electrical stimulation of septal area and other regions of rat brain. Journal of Comparative and Physiological Psychology. 1954;47(6):419-27.
490. Cohort study finds that impatience and hostility in young adults are linked with long-term risk of hypertension. Evidence-based cardiovascular medicine. 2004;8(1):34-5; discussion 6-7.
491. Aghababaei N, Tabik MT. Patience and Mental Health in Iranian Students. Iranian journal of psychiatry and behavioral sciences. 2015;9(3):e1252.
492. Mischel W, Ayduk O, Berman MG, Casey BJ, Gotlib IH, Jonides J, et al. 'Willpower' over the life span: decomposing self-regulation. Social cognitive and affective neuroscience. 2011;6(2):252-6.
493. Reach G, Michault A, Bihan H, Paulino C, Cohen R, Le Clesiau H. Patients' impatience is an independent determinant of poor diabetes control. Diabetes & metabolism. 2011;37(6):497-504.
494. Mischel W, Shoda Y, Rodriguez MI. Delay of gratification in children. Science (New York, NY). 1989;244(4907):933-8.
495. Schlam TR, Wilson NL, Shoda Y, Mischel W, Ayduk O. Preschoolers' delay of gratification predicts their body mass 30 years later. The Journal of pediatrics. 2013;162(1):90-3.
496. Shoda YM, W.; Peake, P. K. . Predicting Adolescent Cognitive and Self-Regulatory Competencies from Preschool Delay of Gratification: Identifying Diagnostic Conditions Developmental Psychology. 1990;26(6):978-86.
497. Righetti F, Finkenauer C. If you are able to control yourself, I will trust you: the role of perceived self-control in interpersonal trust. Journal of personality and social psychology. 2011;100(5):874-86.
498. R.L. K. Personal decisions are the leading cause of death. Operations Research. 2008;56(6):1335-47.
499. Tryon MS, DeCant R, Laugero KD. Having your cake and eating it too: a habit of comfort food may link chronic social stress exposure and acute stress-induced cortisol hyporesponsiveness. Physiology & behavior. 2013;114-115:32-7.
500. Tryon MS, Carter CS, Decant R, Laugero KD. Chronic stress exposure may affect the brain's response to high calorie food cues and predispose to obesogenic eating habits. Physiology & behavior. 2013;120:233-42.
501. Mischel W, Ebbesen EB, Zeiss AR. Cognitive and attentional mechanisms in delay of gratification. Journal of personality and social psychology. 1972;21(2):204-18.
502. Murray J, Theakston A, Wells A. Can the attention training technique turn one marshmallow into two? Improving children's ability to delay gratification. Behaviour research and therapy. 2016;77:34-9.
503. Callan DE, Naito E. Neural processes distinguishing elite from expert and novice athletes. Cognitive and behavioral neurology : official journal of the Society for Behavioral and Cognitive Neurology. 2014;27(4):183-8.
504. Kim W, Chang Y, Kim J, Seo J, Ryu K, Lee E, et al. An fMRI study of differences in brain activity among elite, expert, and novice archers at the moment of optimal aiming. Cognitive and behavioral neurology : official journal of the Society for Behavioral and Cognitive Neurology. 2014;27(4):173-82.
505. Lappi O. The Racer's Brain - How Domain Expertise is Reflected in the Neural Substrates of Driving. Frontiers in human neuroscience. 2015;9:635.

506. Ashby FG, Turner BO, Horvitz JC. Cortical and basal ganglia contributions to habit learning and automaticity. Trends in cognitive sciences. 2010;14(5):208-15.
507. Jog MS, Kubota Y, Connolly CI, Hillegaart V, Graybiel AM. Building neural representations of habits. Science (New York, NY). 1999;286(5445):1745-9.
508. Wood W, Runger D. Psychology of Habit. Annual review of psychology. 2016;67:289-314.
509. Wood W, Quinn JM, Kashy DA. Habits in everyday life: thought, emotion, and action. Journal of personality and social psychology. 2002;83(6):1281-97.
510. Neal DT, Wood W, Wu M, Kurlander D. The pull of the past: when do habits persist despite conflict with motives? Personality & social psychology bulletin. 2011;37(11):1428-37.
511. Wansink B. From mindless eating to mindlessly eating better. Physiology & behavior. 2010;100(5):454-63.
512. Psychology SfPaS. How we form habits, change existing ones Science Daily [Internet]. August 8, 2014 July 6th, 2017. Available from: <www.sciencedaily.com/releases/2014/08/140808111931.htm>
513. Gardner B, Lally P, Wardle J. Making health habitual: the psychology of 'habit-formation' and general practice. The British journal of general practice : the journal of the Royal College of General Practitioners. 2012;62(605):664-6.
514. Lally P, Chipperfield A, Wardle J. Healthy habits: efficacy of simple advice on weight control based on a habit-formation model. International journal of obesity (2005). 2008;32(4):700-7.
515. Wood W, Witt MG, Tam L. Changing circumstances, disrupting habits. Journal of personality and social psychology. 2005;88(6):918-33.
516. Lin PY, Wood W, Monterosso J. Healthy eating habits protect against temptations. Appetite. 2016;103:432-40.
517. Quinn JM, Pascoe A, Wood W, Neal DT. Can't control yourself? Monitor those bad habits. Personality & social psychology bulletin. 2010;36(4):499-511.
518. Neal DT, Wood W, Drolet A. How do people adhere to goals when willpower is low? The profits (and pitfalls) of strong habits. Journal of personality and social psychology. 2013;104(6):959-75.
519. Love T, Laier C, Brand M, Hatch L, Hajela R. Neuroscience of Internet Pornography Addiction: A Review and Update. Behavioral sciences (Basel, Switzerland). 2015;5(3):388-433.
520. Rothman AJ, Gollwitzer PM, Grant AM, Neal DT, Sheeran P, Wood W. Hale and Hearty Policies: How Psychological Science Can Create and Maintain Healthy Habits. Perspectives on psychological science : a journal of the Association for Psychological Science. 2015;10(6):701-5.
521. Eyar NHR. Hooked: How to Build Habit-Forming Products: Portfolio; 2014. 256 p.
522. Bourgeois A, Chelazzi L, Vuilleumier P. How motivation and reward learning modulate selective attention. Progress in brain research. 2016;229:325-42.
523. Leigh SJ, Morris MJ. The role of reward circuitry and food addiction in the obesity epidemic: An update. Biological psychology. 2016.
524. Moriguchi Y, Hiraki K. Prefrontal cortex and executive function in young children: a review of NIRS studies. Frontiers in human neuroscience. 2013;7:867.
525. Volkow ND, Baler RD. NOW vs LATER brain circuits: implications for obesity and addiction. Trends in neurosciences. 2015;38(6):345-52.
526. Koob GF, Volkow ND. Neurobiology of addiction: a neurocircuitry analysis. The lancet Psychiatry. 2016;3(8):760-73.
527. Gibbs N. Sex, Lies, Arrogance: What Makes Powerful Men Behave So Badly?2011 July 6th, 2017. Available from: http://content.time.com/time/magazine/article/0,9171,2072641,00.html.
528. Sherwood CC, Bauernfeind AL, Bianchi S, Raghanti MA, Hof PR. Human brain evolution writ large and small. Progress in brain research. 2012;195:237-54.
529. Teffer K, Semendeferi K. Human prefrontal cortex: evolution, development, and pathology. Progress in brain research. 2012;195:191-218.
530. Wansink BS, J. Mindless Eating: The 200 daily food decisions we overlook Environment and behavior. 207;39(1):106-23.

531. Hsu M, Bhatt M, Adolphs R, Tranel D, Camerer CF. Neural systems responding to degrees of uncertainty in human decision-making. Science (New York, NY). 2005;310(5754):1680-3.
532. Schwartz B. The Paradox of Choice: Why More Is Less Harper Perennial; 2005. 304 p.
533. Karg K, Schmelz M, Call J, Tomasello M. Chimpanzees strategically manipulate what others can see. Animal cognition. 2015;18(5):1069-76.
534. Hare B, Call J, Tomasello M. Chimpanzees deceive a human competitor by hiding. Cognition. 2006;101(3):495-514.
535. Hodge G. The Ugly Truth of Online Dating: Top 10 Lies Told by Internet Daters2012 July 6th, 2017. Available from: http://www.huffingtonpost.com/greg-hodge/online-dating-lies_b_1930053.html.
536. Waugh R. 'Natural blonde, age 21, size 8': Study reveals 80% of online daters lie in their profiles - but leave clues that give them away 2012 July 6th, 2017. Available from: http://www.dailymail.co.uk/sciencetech/article-2100981/Eighty-cent-online-daters-lie-profiles--clues-hidden-in.html
537. WADA. Antidoping testing figures2016 July 6th, 2017. Available from:https://www.wada-ama.org/en/resources/laboratories/anti-doping-testing-figures
538. White MC. You won't believe how many people lie on their resume2015 July 6th, 2017. Available from: http://time.com/money/3995981/how-many-people-lie-resumes/.
539. John LK, Loewenstein G, Prelec D. Measuring the prevalence of questionable research practices with incentives for truth telling. Psychological science. 2012;23(5):524-32.
540. Mazar N, Ariely D. Dishonesty in scientific research. The Journal of clinical investigation. 2015;125(11):3993-6.
541. Mazar N, Aggarwal P. Greasing the palm: can collectivism promote bribery? Psychological science. 2011;22(7):843-8.
542. Mann H, Garcia-Rada X, Houser D, Ariely D. Everybody else is doing it: exploring social transmission of lying behavior. PloS one. 2014;9(10):e109591.
543. Gino F, Ayal S, Ariely D. Contagion and differentiation in unethical behavior: the effect of one bad apple on the barrel. Psychological science. 2009;20(3):393-8.
544. Pearsall MJ, Ellis AP. Thick as thieves: the effects of ethical orientation and psychological safety on unethical team behavior. The Journal of applied psychology. 2011;96(2):401-11.
545. Gino F, Ayal S, Ariely D. Self-Serving Altruism? The Lure of Unethical Actions that Benefit Others. Journal of economic behavior & organization. 2013;93.
546. Gino F, Norton MI, Ariely D. The counterfeit self: the deceptive costs of faking it. Psychological science. 2010;21(5):712-20.
547. Gino F, Ariely D. The dark side of creativity: original thinkers can be more dishonest. Journal of personality and social psychology. 2012;102(3):445-59.
548. Gino F, Wiltermuth SS. Evil genius? How dishonesty can lead to greater creativity. Psychological science. 2014;25(4):973-81.
549. Lammers J, Stapel DA, Galinsky AD. Power increases hypocrisy: moralizing in reasoning, immorality in behavior. Psychological science. 2010;21(5):737-44.
550. Mead NL, Baumeister RF, Gino F, Schweitzer ME, Ariely D. Too Tired to Tell the Truth: Self-Control Resource Depletion and Dishonesty. Journal of experimental social psychology. 2009;45(3):594-7.
551. Williams EF, Pizarro D, Ariely D, Weinberg JD. The Valjean effect: Visceral states and cheating. Emotion (Washington, DC). 2016;16(6):897-902.
552. Kouchaki M, Desai SD. Anxious, threatened, and also unethical: how anxiety makes individuals feel threatened and commit unethical acts. The Journal of applied psychology. 2015;100(2):360-75.
553. Reinders Folmer CP, De Cremer D. Bad for me or bad for us? Interpersonal orientations and the impact of losses on unethical behavior. Personality & social psychology bulletin. 2012;38(6):760-71.
554. Garrett N, Lazzaro SC, Ariely D, Sharot T. The brain adapts to dishonesty. Nature neuroscience. 2016;19(12):1727-32.

555. Welsh DT, Ordonez LD, Snyder DG, Christian MS. The slippery slope: how small ethical transgressions pave the way for larger future transgressions. The Journal of applied psychology. 2015;100(1):114-27.

556. Burgoon JK. When is Deceptive Message Production More Effortful than Truth-Telling? A Baker's Dozen of Moderators. Frontiers in psychology. 2015;6:1965.

557. Yin L, Reuter M, Weber B. Let the man choose what to do: Neural correlates of spontaneous lying and truth-telling. Brain and cognition. 2016;102:13-25.

558. Abe N, Suzuki M, Mori E, Itoh M, Fujii T. Deceiving others: distinct neural responses of the prefrontal cortex and amygdala in simple fabrication and deception with social interactions. Journal of cognitive neuroscience. 2007;19(2):287-95.

559. DePaulo BM, Kashy DA, Kirkendol SE, Wyer MM, Epstein JA. Lying in everyday life. Journal of personality and social psychology. 1996;70(5):979-95.

560. Abe N, Greene JD. Response to anticipated reward in the nucleus accumbens predicts behavior in an independent test of honesty. The Journal of neuroscience : the official journal of the Society for Neuroscience. 2014;34(32):10564-72.

561. Ruedy NE, Moore C, Gino F, Schweitzer ME. The cheater's high: the unexpected affective benefits of unethical behavior. Journal of personality and social psychology. 2013;105(4):531-48.

562. Kouchaki M, Gino F. Memories of unethical actions become obfuscated over time. Proceedings of the National Academy of Sciences of the United States of America. 2016;113(22):6166-71.

563. Shu LL, Gino F, Bazerman MH. Dishonest deed, clear conscience: when cheating leads to moral disengagement and motivated forgetting. Personality & social psychology bulletin. 2011;37(3):330-49.

564. Shu LL, Gino F. Sweeping dishonesty under the rug: how unethical actions lead to forgetting of moral rules. Journal of personality and social psychology. 2012;102(6):1164-77.

565. Chance Z, Norton MI, Gino F, Ariely D. Temporal view of the costs and benefits of self-deception. Proceedings of the National Academy of Sciences of the United States of America. 2011;108 Suppl 3:15655-9.

566. Cohen TR, Panter AT, Turan N, Morse L, Kim Y. Moral character in the workplace. Journal of personality and social psychology. 2014;107(5):943-63.

567. Ayal S, Gino F, Barkan R, Ariely D. Three Principles to REVISE People's Unethical Behavior. Perspectives on psychological science : a journal of the Association for Psychological Science. 2015;10(6):738-41.

568. Treasury UDo. Update on Reducing the Federal Tax Gap and Improving Voluntary Compliance. 2009 July 6th, 2017. Available from: http://www.irs.gov/pub/newsroom/tax_gap_report_-final_version.pdf. .

569. FBI.gov. Insurance FraudJuly 6th, 2017. Available from: https://www.fbi.gov/stats-services/publications/insurance-fraud.

570. Day MV, Bobocel DR. The weight of a guilty conscience: subjective body weight as an embodiment of guilt. PloS one. 2013;8(7):e69546.

571. Shu LL, Mazar N, Gino F, Ariely D, Bazerman MH. Signing at the beginning makes ethics salient and decreases dishonest self-reports in comparison to signing at the end. Proceedings of the National Academy of Sciences of the United States of America. 2012;109(38):15197-200.

572. Ariely D. The Honest Truth About Dishonesty: How We Lie to Everyone--Especially Ourselves: Harper Perennial; 2013. 336 p.

573. Bryan CJ, Adams GS, Monin B. When cheating would make you a cheater: implicating the self prevents unethical behavior. Journal of experimental psychology General. 2013;142(4):1001-5.

574. Gino F, Mogilner C. Time, money, and morality. Psychological science. 2014;25(2):414-21.

575. Peer E, Acquisti A, Shalvi S. "I cheated, but only a little": partial confessions to unethical behavior. Journal of personality and social psychology. 2014;106(2):202-17.

576. McCullough ME, Pedersen EJ, Tabak BA, Carter EC. Conciliatory gestures promote forgiveness and reduce anger in humans. Proceedings of the National Academy of Sciences of the United States of America. 2014;111(30):11211-6.

577. Singer T, Seymour B, O'Doherty JP, Stephan KE, Dolan RJ, Frith CD. Empathic neural responses are modulated by the perceived fairness of others. Nature. 2006;439(7075):466-9.
578. Billingsley J, Losin EAR. The Neural Systems of Forgiveness: An Evolutionary Psychological Perspective. Frontiers in psychology. 2017;8:737.
579. Kramer UM, Jansma H, Tempelmann C, Munte TF. Tit-for-tat: the neural basis of reactive aggression. NeuroImage. 2007;38(1):203-11.
580. Chester DS, DeWall CN. Combating the sting of rejection with the pleasure of revenge: A new look at how emotion shapes aggression. Journal of personality and social psychology. 2017;112(3):413-30.
581. Carlsmith KM, Wilson TD, Gilbert DT. The paradoxical consequences of revenge. Journal of personality and social psychology. 2008;95(6):1316-24.
582. McCullough ME. Beyond Revenge: The Evolution of the Forgiveness Instinct 1st Edition. San Francisco, CA: Jossey-Bass; 2008. 320 p.
583. Ricciardi E, Rota G, Sani L, Gentili C, Gaglianese A, Guazzelli M, et al. How the brain heals emotional wounds: the functional neuroanatomy of forgiveness. Frontiers in human neuroscience. 2013;7:839.
584. Toussaint LL, Shields GS, Slavich GM. Forgiveness, Stress, and Health: a 5-Week Dynamic Parallel Process Study. Annals of behavioral medicine : a publication of the Society of Behavioral Medicine. 2016;50(5):727-35.
585. Seawell AH, Toussaint LL, Cheadle AC. Prospective associations between unforgiveness and physical health and positive mediating mechanisms in a nationally representative sample of older adults. Psychology & health. 2014;29(4):375-89.
586. Toussaint L, Worthington EL, Jr., Van Tongeren DR, Hook J, Berry JW, Miller AJ, et al. Forgiveness Working: Forgiveness, Health, and Productivity in the Workplace. American journal of health promotion : AJHP. 2016.
587. Dezutter J, Toussaint L, Leijssen M. Forgiveness, Ego-Integrity, and Depressive Symptoms in Community-Dwelling and Residential Elderly Adults. The journals of gerontology Series B, Psychological sciences and social sciences. 2016;71(5):786-97.
588. Toussaint L, Shields GS, Dorn G, Slavich GM. Effects of lifetime stress exposure on mental and physical health in young adulthood: How stress degrades and forgiveness protects health. Journal of health psychology. 2016;21(6):1004-14.
589. Davis DE, Ho MY, Griffin BJ, Bell C, Hook JN, Van Tongeren DR, et al. Forgiving the self and physical and mental health correlates: a meta-analytic review. Journal of counseling psychology. 2015;62(2):329-35.
590. Ermer AE, Proulx CM. Unforgiveness, depression, and health in later life: the protective factor of forgivingness. Aging & mental health. 2016;20(10):1021-34.
591. Worthington EL, Jr., Witvliet CV, Pietrini P, Miller AJ. Forgiveness, health, and well-being: a review of evidence for emotional versus decisional forgiveness, dispositional forgivingness, and reduced unforgiveness. Journal of behavioral medicine. 2007;30(4):291-302.
592. Wade NG, Hoyt WT, Kidwell JE, Worthington EL. Efficacy of psychotherapeutic interventions to promote forgiveness: a meta-analysis. Journal of consulting and clinical psychology. 2014;82(1):154-70.
593. Majolo BA, F.; Schino, G. Meta-analysis and animal social behaviour. Evol Ecol. 2012;26(5):1197-2011.
594. Ma WJ, Husain M, Bays PM. Changing concepts of working memory. Nature neuroscience. 2014;17(3):347-56.
595. Faber LG, Maurits NM, Lorist MM. Mental fatigue affects visual selective attention. PloS one. 2012;7(10):e48073.
596. Hopstaken JF, van der Linden D, Bakker AB, Kompier MA. The window of my eyes: Task disengagement and mental fatigue covary with pupil dynamics. Biological psychology. 2015;110:100-6.
597. Tanaka M, Mizuno K, Tajima S, Sasabe T, Watanabe Y. Central nervous system fatigue alters autonomic nerve activity. Life sciences. 2009;84(7-8):235-9.
598. Tanaka M, Mizuno K, Yamaguti K, Kuratsune H, Fujii A, Baba H, et al. Autonomic nervous alterations associated with daily level of fatigue. Behavioral and brain functions : BBF. 2011;7:46.

599. Mizuno K, Tajima K, Watanabe Y, Kuratsune H. Fatigue correlates with the decrease in parasympathetic sinus modulation induced by a cognitive challenge. Behavioral and brain functions : BBF. 2014;10:25.
600. Hopstaken JF, van der Linden D, Bakker AB, Kompier MA, Leung YK. Shifts in attention during mental fatigue: Evidence from subjective, behavioral, physiological, and eye-tracking data. Journal of experimental psychology Human perception and performance. 2016;42(6):878-89.
601. Boksem MA, Meijman TF, Lorist MM. Mental fatigue, motivation and action monitoring. Biological psychology. 2006;72(2):123-32.
602. Boksem MA, Tops M. Mental fatigue: costs and benefits. Brain research reviews. 2008;59(1):125-39.
603. Jessen NA, Munk AS, Lundgaard I, Nedergaard M. The Glymphatic System: A Beginner's Guide. Neurochemical research. 2015;40(12):2583-99.
604. Ataka S, Tanaka M, Nozaki S, Mizuma H, Mizuno K, Tahara T, et al. Effects of oral administration of caffeine and D-ribose on mental fatigue. Nutrition (Burbank, Los Angeles County, Calif). 2008;24(3):233-8.
605. Kennedy DO, Scholey AB. A glucose-caffeine 'energy drink' ameliorates subjective and performance deficits during prolonged cognitive demand. Appetite. 2004;42(3):331-3.
606. van Duinen H, Lorist MM, Zijdewind I. The effect of caffeine on cognitive task performance and motor fatigue. Psychopharmacology. 2005;180(3):539-47.
607. Holtzer R, Shuman M, Mahoney JR, Lipton R, Verghese J. Cognitive fatigue defined in the context of attention networks. Neuropsychology, development, and cognition Section B, Aging, neuropsychology and cognition. 2011;18(1):108-28.
608. Wascher E, Rasch B, Sanger J, Hoffmann S, Schneider D, Rinkenauer G, et al. Frontal theta activity reflects distinct aspects of mental fatigue. Biological psychology. 2014;96:57-65.
609. Xiao Y, Ma F, Lv Y, Cai G, Teng P, Xu F, et al. Sustained attention is associated with error processing impairment: evidence from mental fatigue study in four-choice reaction time task. PloS one. 2015;10(3):e0117837.
610. Boksem MA, Meijman TF, Lorist MM. Effects of mental fatigue on attention: an ERP study. Brain research Cognitive brain research. 2005;25(1):107-16.
611. Matthews G, Desmond PA. Task-induced fatigue states and simulated driving performance. The Quarterly journal of experimental psychology A, Human experimental psychology. 2002;55(2):659-86.
612. van der Linden D, Frese M, Meijman TF. Mental fatigue and the control of cognitive processes: effects on perseveration and planning. Acta psychologica. 2003;113(1):45-65.
613. MacMahon C, Schucker L, Hagemann N, Strauss B. Cognitive fatigue effects on physical performance during running. Journal of sport & exercise psychology. 2014;36(4):375-81.
614. Marcora SM, Staiano W, Manning V. Mental fatigue impairs physical performance in humans. Journal of applied physiology (Bethesda, Md : 1985). 2009;106(3):857-64.
615. Van Cutsem J, Marcora S, De Pauw K, Bailey S, Meeusen R, Roelands B. The Effects of Mental Fatigue on Physical Performance: A Systematic Review. Sports medicine (Auckland, NZ). 2017.
616. Smith MR, Coutts AJ, Merlini M, Deprez D, Lenoir M, Marcora SM. Mental Fatigue Impairs Soccer-Specific Physical and Technical Performance. Medicine and science in sports and exercise. 2016;48(2):267-76.
617. Veness D, Patterson SD, Jeffries O, Waldron M. The effects of mental fatigue on cricket-relevant performance among elite players. Journal of sports sciences. 2017:1-7.
618. Mizuno K, Tanaka M, Yamaguti K, Kajimoto O, Kuratsune H, Watanabe Y. Mental fatigue caused by prolonged cognitive load associated with sympathetic hyperactivity. Behavioral and brain functions : BBF. 2011;7:17.

619. Iwasaki K, Takahashi M, Nakata A. Health problems due to long working hours in Japan: working hours, workers' compensation (Karoshi), and preventive measures. Industrial health. 2006;44(4):537-40.
620. Ke DS. Overwork, stroke, and karoshi-death from overwork. Acta neurologica Taiwanica. 2012;21(2):54-9.
621. Rosenfield M. Computer vision syndrome: a review of ocular causes and potential treatments. Ophthalmic & physiological optics : the journal of the British College of Ophthalmic Opticians (Optometrists). 2011;31(5):502-15.
622. Chu CA, Rosenfield M, Portello JK. Blink patterns: reading from a computer screen versus hard copy. Optometry and vision science : official publication of the American Academy of Optometry. 2014;91(3):297-302.
623. Gowrisankaran S, Sheedy JE. Computer vision syndrome: A review. Work (Reading, Mass). 2015;52(2):303-14.
624. Hockey GR, Earle F. Control over the scheduling of simulated office work reduces the impact of workload on mental fatigue and task performance. Journal of experimental psychology Applied. 2006;12(1):50-65.
625. Berset M, Semmer NK, Elfering A, Amstad FT, Jacobshagen N. Work characteristics as predictors of physiological recovery on weekends. Scandinavian journal of work, environment & health. 2009;35(3):188-92.
626. Zeng EQ, Zeng BQ, Tian JL, Du B, Tian XB, Chen H. Perceived Social Support and Its Impact on Mental Fatigue in Patients with Mild Traumatic Brain Injury. Balkan medical journal. 2016;33(2):152-7.
627. Blanchfield AW, Hardy J, De Morree HM, Staiano W, Marcora SM. Talking yourself out of exhaustion: the effects of self-talk on endurance performance. Medicine and science in sports and exercise. 2014;46(5):998-1007.
628. Blanchfield A, Hardy J, Marcora S. Non-conscious visual cues related to affect and action alter perception of effort and endurance performance. Frontiers in human neuroscience. 2014;8:967.
629. Hopstaken JF, van der Linden D, Bakker AB, Kompier MA. A multifaceted investigation of the link between mental fatigue and task disengagement. Psychophysiology. 2015;52(3):305-15.
630. van der Linden D, Frese M, Sonnentag S. The impact of mental fatigue on exploration in a complex computer task: rigidity and loss of systematic strategies. Human factors. 2003;45(3):483-94.
631. Akerstedt T, Knutsson A, Westerholm P, Theorell T, Alfredsson L, Kecklund G. Mental fatigue, work and sleep. Journal of psychosomatic research. 2004;57(5):427-33.
632. Gobin CM, Banks JB, Fins AI, Tartar JL. Poor sleep quality is associated with a negative cognitive bias and decreased sustained attention. Journal of sleep research. 2015;24(5):535-42.
633. Martin K, Staiano W, Menaspa P, Hennessey T, Marcora S, Keegan R, et al. Superior Inhibitory Control and Resistance to Mental Fatigue in Professional Road Cyclists. PloS one. 2016;11(7):e0159907.
634. Blikman LJ, Huisstede BM, Kooijmans H, Stam HJ, Bussmann JB, van Meeteren J. Effectiveness of energy conservation treatment in reducing fatigue in multiple sclerosis: a systematic review and meta-analysis. Archives of physical medicine and rehabilitation. 2013;94(7):1360-76.
635. Gross S, Semmer NK, Meier LL, Kalin W, Jacobshagen N, Tschan F. The effect of positive events at work on after-work fatigue: they matter most in face of adversity. The Journal of applied psychology. 2011;96(3):654-64.
636. Blasche G, Pasalic S, Baubock VM, Haluza D, Schoberberger R. Effects of Rest-Break Intention on Rest-Break Frequency and Work-Related Fatigue. Human factors. 2017;59(2):289-98.
637. Chen C, Xie Y. The impacts of multiple rest-break periods on commercial truck driver's crash risk. Journal of safety research. 2014;48:87-93.
638. Dababneh AJ, Swanson N, Shell RL. Impact of added rest breaks on the productivity and well being of workers. Ergonomics. 2001;44(2):164-74.
639. Hallbeck MS, Lowndes BR, Bingener J, Abdelrahman AM, Yu D, Bartley A, et al. The impact of intraoperative microbreaks with exercises on surgeons: A multi-center cohort study. Applied ergonomics. 2017;60:334-41.

640. Hunter EM, Wu C. Give me a better break: Choosing workday break activities to maximize resource recovery. The Journal of applied psychology. 2016;101(2):302-11.

641. Neri DF, Oyung RL, Colletti LM, Mallis MM, Tam PY, Dinges DF. Controlled breaks as a fatigue countermeasure on the flight deck. Aviation, space, and environmental medicine. 2002;73(7):654-64.

642. Park AE, Zahiri HR, Hallbeck MS, Augenstein V, Sutton E, Yu D, et al. Intraoperative "Micro Breaks" With Targeted Stretching Enhance Surgeon Physical Function and Mental Focus: A Multicenter Cohort Study. Annals of surgery. 2017;265(2):340-6.

643. Sianoja M, Syrek CJ, de Bloom J, Korpela K, Kinnunen U. Enhancing Daily Well-Being at Work Through Lunchtime Park Walks and Relaxation Exercises: Recovery Experiences as Mediators. Journal of occupational health psychology. 2017.

644. Evans L. The exact amount of time you should work every day 2014 July 6th, 2017. Available from: https://www.fastcompany.com/3035605/how-to-be-a-success-at-everything/the-exact-amount-of-time-you-should-work-every-day.

645. Finkbeiner KM, Russell PN, Helton WS. Rest improves performance, nature improves happiness: Assessment of break periods on the abbreviated vigilance task. Consciousness and cognition. 2016;42:277-85.

646. Gentes EL, Ruscio AM. A meta-analysis of the relation of intolerance of uncertainty to symptoms of generalized anxiety disorder, major depressive disorder, and obsessive-compulsive disorder. Clinical psychology review. 2011;31(6):923-33.

647. Wilbert-Lampen U, Leistner D, Greven S, Pohl T, Sper S, Volker C, et al. Cardiovascular events during World Cup soccer. The New England journal of medicine. 2008;358(5):475-83.

648. Khairy LT, Barin R, Demoniere F, Villemaire C, Billo MJ, Tardif JC, et al. Heart Rate Response in Spectators of the Montreal Canadiens Hockey Team. The Canadian journal of cardiology. 2017.

649. Marmot MG, Smith GD, Stansfeld S, Patel C, North F, Head J, et al. Health inequalities among British civil servants: the Whitehall II study. Lancet (London, England). 1991;337(8754):1387-93.

650. Wall M. Big Data: Are you ready for blast-off? 2014 July 6th, 2017. Available from: http://www.bbc.com/news/business-26383058.

651. Pullen JPC, J.. 116 Teen Text Terms Decoded for Confused Parents 2016 July 6th, 2017. Available from: http://time.com/4373616/text-abbreviations-acronyms/

652. Hamilton J. Bingeing On Bad News Can Fuel Daily Stress 2014 July 6th, 2017. Available from: http://www.npr.org/sections/health-shots/2014/07/10/323355132/binging-on-bad-news-can-fuel-daily-stress

653. Mauss IB, Savino NS, Anderson CL, Weisbuch M, Tamir M, Laudenslager ML. The pursuit of happiness can be lonely. Emotion (Washington, DC). 2012;12(5):908-12.

654. Dunn EW, Aknin LB, Norton MI. Spending money on others promotes happiness. Science (New York, NY). 2008;319(5870):1687-8.

655. Quoidbach J, Dunn EW, Hansenne M, Bustin G. The price of abundance: how a wealth of experiences impoverishes savoring. Personality & social psychology bulletin. 2015;41(3):393-404.

656. Quoidbach J, Dunn EW, Petrides KV, Mikolajczak M. Money giveth, money taketh away: the dual effect of wealth on happiness. Psychological science. 2010;21(6):759-63.

657. Whillans AV, Dunn EW, Smeets P, Bekkers R, Norton MI. Buying time promotes happiness. Proceedings of the National Academy of Sciences of the United States of America. 2017.

658. Van Boven L, Gilovich T. To do or to have? That is the question. Journal of personality and social psychology. 2003;85(6):1193-202.

659. Matz SC, Gladstone JJ, Stillwell D. Money Buys Happiness When Spending Fits Our Personality. Psychological science. 2016;27(5):715-25.

660. Caprariello PA, Reis HT. To do, to have, or to share? Valuing experiences over material possessions depends on the involvement of others. Journal of personality and social psychology. 2013;104(2):199-215.

661. Aknin LB, Sandstrom GM, Dunn EW, Norton MI. It's the recipient that counts: spending money on strong social ties leads to greater happiness than spending on weak social ties. PloS one. 2011;6(2):e17018.
662. Aknin LB, Barrington-Leigh CP, Dunn EW, Helliwell JF, Burns J, Biswas-Diener R, et al. Prosocial spending and well-being: cross-cultural evidence for a psychological universal. Journal of personality and social psychology. 2013;104(4):635-52.
663. Vanderhasselt MA, De Raedt R, Dillon DG, Dutra SJ, Brooks N, Pizzagalli DA. Decreased cognitive control in response to negative information in patients with remitted depression: an event-related potential study. Journal of psychiatry & neuroscience : JPN. 2012;37(4):250-8.
664. Mueller EM, Hofmann SG, Santesso DL, Meuret AE, Bitran S, Pizzagalli DA. Electrophysiological evidence of attentional biases in social anxiety disorder. Psychological medicine. 2009;39(7):1141-52.
665. Dai Q, Feng Z. More excited for negative facial expressions in depression: evidence from an event-related potential study. Clinical neurophysiology : official journal of the International Federation of Clinical Neurophysiology. 2012;123(11):2172-9.
666. Dai Q, Feng Z. Deficient inhibition of return for emotional faces in depression. Progress in neuro-psychopharmacology & biological psychiatry. 2009;33(6):921-32.
667. Chen J, Ma W, Zhang Y, Wu X, Wei D, Liu G, et al. Distinct facial processing related negative cognitive bias in first-episode and recurrent major depression: evidence from the N170 ERP component. PloS one. 2014;9(10):e109176.
668. Iliff JJ, Wang M, Liao Y, Plogg BA, Peng W, Gundersen GA, et al. A paravascular pathway facilitates CSF flow through the brain parenchyma and the clearance of interstitial solutes, including amyloid beta. Science translational medicine. 2012;4(147):147ra11.
669. Iliff JJ, Lee H, Yu M, Feng T, Logan J, Nedergaard M, et al. Brain-wide pathway for waste clearance captured by contrast-enhanced MRI. The Journal of clinical investigation. 2013;123(3):1299-309.
670. Xie L, Kang H, Xu Q, Chen MJ, Liao Y, Thiyagarajan M, et al. Sleep drives metabolite clearance from the adult brain. Science (New York, NY). 2013;342(6156):373-7.
671. Lee H, Xie L, Yu M, Kang H, Feng T, Deane R, et al. The Effect of Body Posture on Brain Glymphatic Transport. The Journal of neuroscience : the official journal of the Society for Neuroscience. 2015;35(31):11034-44.
672. Allison A. Many Americans Say Doing Taxes Is Easier Than Eating Right2012 July 6th, 2017. Available from: http://www.npr.org/sections/thesalt/2012/05/23/153416865/many-americans-saying-doing-taxes-is-easier-than-eating-right.
673. Mankins M. Is Technology Really Helping Us Get More Done? 2016 July 6th, 2017. Available from: https://hbr.org/2016/02/is-technology-really-helping-us-get-more-done.
674. Harari YN. Sapiens: A Brief History of Humankind: HarperCollins 2015. 469 p.
675. Yeh CS. The power and prevalence of loneliness2017 July 6th, 2017. Available from: http://www.health.harvard.edu/blog/the-power-and-prevalence-of-loneliness-2017011310977.
676. Victor CR, Yang K. The prevalence of loneliness among adults: a case study of the United Kingdom. The Journal of psychology. 2012;146(1-2):85-104.
677. Janiak A. Kant's Views on Space and Time 2016 July 6th, 2017. Available from: https://plato.stanford.edu/archives/win2016/entries/kant-spacetime/.
678. DeVoe SE, Pfeffer J. Time is tight: how higher economic value of time increases feelings of time pressure. The Journal of applied psychology. 2011;96(4):665-76.
679. Brunye TT, Wood MD, Houck LA, Taylor HA. The path more travelled: Time pressure increases reliance on familiar route-based strategies during navigation. Quarterly journal of experimental psychology (2006). 2017;70(8):1439-52.
680. DA AL, Rotgans JI, Mamede S, I AL, Magzoub ME, Altayeb FM, et al. Does Time Pressure Have a Negative Effect on Diagnostic Accuracy? Academic medicine : journal of the Association of American Medical Colleges. 2016;91(5):710-6.

681. Roxburgh S. 'There just aren't enough hours in the day': the mental health consequences of time pressure. Journal of health and social behavior. 2004;45(2):115-31.
682. Wahlstrom J, Hagberg M, Johnson PW, Svensson J, Rempel D. Influence of time pressure and verbal provocation on physiological and psychological reactions during work with a computer mouse. European journal of applied physiology. 2002;87(3):257-63.
683. Chen CY, Muggleton NG, Juan CH, Tzeng OJ, Hung DL. Time pressure leads to inhibitory control deficits in impulsive violent offenders. Behavioural brain research. 2008;187(2):483-8.
684. Frank A. Is Time An Illusion? From The Buddha To Brian Greene 2011 July 6th, 2017. Available from: http://www.npr.org/sections/13.7/2011/11/08/142118441/is-time-an-illusion-from-the-buddha-to-brian-greene.
685. Mastin L. Special theory of relativityJuly 6th, 2017. Available from: http://www.physicsoftheuniverse.com/topics_relativity_special.html.
686. Natu V, O'Toole AJ. The neural processing of familiar and unfamiliar faces: a review and synopsis. British journal of psychology (London, England : 1953). 2011;102(4):726-47.
687. Freeman JB, Stolier RM, Ingbretsen ZA, Hehman EA. Amygdala responsivity to high-level social information from unseen faces. The Journal of neuroscience : the official journal of the Society for Neuroscience. 2014;34(32):10573-81.
688. Huang S, Han S. Shared beliefs enhance shared feelings: religious/irreligious identifications modulate empathic neural responses. Social neuroscience. 2014;9(6):639-49.
689. Xu X, Zuo X, Wang X, Han S. Do you feel my pain? Racial group membership modulates empathic neural responses. The Journal of neuroscience : the official journal of the Society for Neuroscience. 2009;29(26):8525-9.
690. Jarvinen A, Korenberg JR, Bellugi U. The social phenotype of Williams syndrome. Current opinion in neurobiology. 2013;23(3):414-22.
691. Haas BW, Hoeft F, Searcy YM, Mills D, Bellugi U, Reiss A. Individual differences in social behavior predict amygdala response to fearful facial expressions in Williams syndrome. Neuropsychologia. 2010;48(5):1283-8.
692. Rakel DP, Hoeft TJ, Barrett BP, Chewning BA, Craig BM, Niu M. Practitioner empathy and the duration of the common cold. Family medicine. 2009;41(7):494-501.
693. Stormer VS, Alvarez GA. Attention Alters Perceived Attractiveness. Psychological science. 2016;27(4):563-71.
694. Hawthorne D. What's the body worth? 2010 July 6th, 2017. Available from: https://liblog.mayo.edu/2010/01/14/whats-the-body-worth/
695. Barraza JA, Zak PJ. Empathy toward strangers triggers oxytocin release and subsequent generosity. Annals of the New York Academy of Sciences. 2009;1167:182-9.
696. Holt-Lunstad J, Birmingham WA, Light KC. Influence of a "warm touch" support enhancement intervention among married couples on ambulatory blood pressure, oxytocin, alpha amylase, and cortisol. Psychosomatic medicine. 2008;70(9):976-85.
697. Grewen KM, Anderson BJ, Girdler SS, Light KC. Warm partner contact is related to lower cardiovascular reactivity. Behavioral medicine (Washington, DC). 2003;29(3):123-30.
698. Inagaki TK, Eisenberger NI. Shared neural mechanisms underlying social warmth and physical warmth. Psychological science. 2013;24(11):2272-80.
699. Hertenstein MJ, Holmes R, McCullough M, Keltner D. The communication of emotion via touch. Emotion (Washington, DC). 2009;9(4):566-73.
700. Kraus MW, Huang C, Keltner D. Tactile communication, cooperation, and performance: an ethological study of the NBA. Emotion (Washington, DC). 2010;10(5):745-9.
701. Howes MJ, Hokanson JE, Loewenstein DA. Induction of depressive affect after prolonged exposure to a mildly depressed individual. Journal of personality and social psychology. 1985;49(4):1110-3.
702. Fowler JH, Christakis NA. Dynamic spread of happiness in a large social network: longitudinal analysis over 20 years in the Framingham Heart Study. BMJ (Clinical research ed). 2008;337:a2338.

703. Goncalves B, Perra N, Vespignani A. Modeling users' activity on twitter networks: validation of Dunbar's number. PloS one. 2011;6(8):e22656.

704. Papa A, Bonanno GA. Smiling in the face of adversity: the interpersonal and intrapersonal functions of smiling. Emotion (Washington, DC). 2008;8(1):1-12.

705. Surakka V, Hietanen JK. Facial and emotional reactions to Duchenne and non-Duchenne smiles. International journal of psychophysiology : official journal of the International Organization of Psychophysiology. 1998;29(1):23-33.

706. Barreto SM. Why does happiness matter? Understanding the relation between positive emotion and health outcomes. Social science & medicine (1982). 2017;191:61-4.

707. Hamlin JK, Wynn K. Young infants prefer prosocial to antisocial others. Cognitive development. 2011;26(1):30-9.

708. Hamlin JK, Wynn K, Bloom P. Social evaluation by preverbal infants. Nature. 2007;450(7169):557-9.

709. Holvoet C, Scola C, Arciszewski T, Picard D. Infants' preference for prosocial behaviors: A literature review. Infant behavior & development. 2016;45(Pt B):125-39.

710. Bratman GN, Hamilton JP, Hahn KS, Daily GC, Gross JJ. Nature experience reduces rumination and subgenual prefrontal cortex activation. Proceedings of the National Academy of Sciences of the United States of America. 2015;112(28):8567-72.

711. Beauchemin KM, Hays P. Sunny hospital rooms expedite recovery from severe and refractory depressions. Journal of affective disorders. 1996;40(1-2):49-51.

712. Capaldi CA, Dopko RL, Zelenski JM. The relationship between nature connectedness and happiness: a meta-analysis. Frontiers in psychology. 2014;5:976.

713. Beauchemin KM, Hays P. Dying in the dark: sunshine, gender and outcomes in myocardial infarction. Journal of the Royal Society of Medicine. 1998;91(7):352-4.

713b. Montori, V. Why we revolt: A patient revolution for careful and kind care. The patient revolution, 2017.

714. Buhle JT, Silvers JA, Wager TD, Lopez R, Onyemekwu C, Kober H, et al. Cognitive reappraisal of emotion: a meta-analysis of human neuroimaging studies. Cerebral cortex (New York, NY : 1991). 2014;24(11):2981-90.

715. Fincham FD, Lambert NM, Beach SR. Faith and unfaithfulness: can praying for your partner reduce infidelity? Journal of personality and social psychology. 2010;99(4):649-59.

716. Cain MS, Mitroff SR. Distractor filtering in media multitaskers. Perception. 2011;40(10):1183-92.

717. Minear M, Brasher F, McCurdy M, Lewis J, Younggren A. Working memory, fluid intelligence, and impulsiveness in heavy media multitaskers. Psychonomic bulletin & review. 2013;20(6):1274-81.

718. Ophir E, Nass C, Wagner AD. Cognitive control in media multitaskers. Proceedings of the National Academy of Sciences of the United States of America. 2009;106(37):15583-7.

719. Uncapher MR, M KT, Wagner AD. Media multitasking and memory: Differences in working memory and long-term memory. Psychonomic bulletin & review. 2016;23(2):483-90.

720. Gradus JL. Prevalence and prognosis of stress disorders: a review of the epidemiologic literature. Clinical epidemiology. 2017;9:251-60.

721. Nilsen C, Andel R, Fritzell J, Kareholt I. Work-related stress in midlife and all-cause mortality: can sense of coherence modify this association? European journal of public health. 2016;26(6):1055-61.

722. Prior A, Fenger-Gron M, Larsen KK, Larsen FB, Robinson KM, Nielsen MG, et al. The Association Between Perceived Stress and Mortality Among People With Multimorbidity: A Prospective Population-Based Cohort Study. American journal of epidemiology. 2016;184(3):199-210.

723. Schocker L. This is your body on stress2013 July 6th, 2017. Available from: http://www.huffingtonpost.com/2013/03/19/body-stress-response_n_2902073.html.

724. Hill JL, Martinowich K. Activity-dependent signaling: influence on plasticity in circuits controlling fear-related behavior. Current opinion in neurobiology. 2016;36:59-65.

725. Izquierdo I, Furini CR, Myskiw JC. Fear Memory. Physiological reviews. 2016;96(2):695-750.

726. Johnson DC, Casey BJ. Easy to remember, difficult to forget: the development of fear regulation. Developmental cognitive neuroscience. 2015;11:42-55.

727. Clarke TC, Black LI, Stussman BJ, Barnes PM, Nahin RL. Trends in the use of complementary health approaches among adults: United States, 2002-2012. National health statistics reports. 2015(79):1-16.

728. Lipka M. 5 Facts About Prayer2016 July 6th, 2017. Available from: http://www.pewresearch.org/fact-tank/2016/05/04/5-facts-about-prayer/.

729. Draganski B, May A. Training-induced structural changes in the adult human brain. Behavioural brain research. 2008;192(1):137-42.

730. Hyde KL, Lerch J, Norton A, Forgeard M, Winner E, Evans AC, et al. Musical training shapes structural brain development. The Journal of neuroscience : the official journal of the Society for Neuroscience. 2009;29(10):3019-25.

731. Mackey AP, Miller Singley AT, Bunge SA. Intensive reasoning training alters patterns of brain connectivity at rest. The Journal of neuroscience : the official journal of the Society for Neuroscience. 2013;33(11):4796-803.

732. Hasenkamp W, Wilson-Mendenhall CD, Duncan E, Barsalou LW. Mind wandering and attention during focused meditation: a fine-grained temporal analysis of fluctuating cognitive states. NeuroImage. 2012;59(1):750-60.

733. Garrison KA, Zeffiro TA, Scheinost D, Constable RT, Brewer JA. Meditation leads to reduced default mode network activity beyond an active task. Cognitive, affective & behavioral neuroscience. 2015;15(3):712-20.

734. Brewer JA, Worhunsky PD, Gray JR, Tang YY, Weber J, Kober H. Meditation experience is associated with differences in default mode network activity and connectivity. Proceedings of the National Academy of Sciences of the United States of America. 2011;108(50):20254-9.

735. Taren AA, Gianaros PJ, Greco CM, Lindsay EK, Fairgrieve A, Brown KW, et al. Mindfulness Meditation Training and Executive Control Network Resting State Functional Connectivity: A Randomized Controlled Trial. Psychosomatic medicine. 2017;79(6):674-83.

736. Vestergaard-Poulsen P, van Beek M, Skewes J, Bjarkam CR, Stubberup M, Bertelsen J, et al. Long-term meditation is associated with increased gray matter density in the brain stem. Neuroreport. 2009;20(2):170-4.

737. Luders E, Toga AW, Lepore N, Gaser C. The underlying anatomical correlates of long-term meditation: larger hippocampal and frontal volumes of gray matter. NeuroImage. 2009;45(3):672-8.

738. Luders E, Thompson PM, Kurth F, Hong JY, Phillips OR, Wang Y, et al. Global and regional alterations of hippocampal anatomy in long-term meditation practitioners. Human brain mapping. 2013;34(12):3369-75.

739. Luders E, Phillips OR, Clark K, Kurth F, Toga AW, Narr KL. Bridging the hemispheres in meditation: thicker callosal regions and enhanced fractional anisotropy (FA) in long-term practitioners. NeuroImage. 2012;61(1):181-7.

740. Luders E, Kurth F, Mayer EA, Toga AW, Narr KL, Gaser C. The unique brain anatomy of meditation practitioners: alterations in cortical gyrification. Frontiers in human neuroscience. 2012;6:34.

741. Lazar SW, Kerr CE, Wasserman RH, Gray JR, Greve DN, Treadway MT, et al. Meditation experience is associated with increased cortical thickness. Neuroreport. 2005;16(17):1893-7.

742. Kang DH, Jo HJ, Jung WH, Kim SH, Jung YH, Choi CH, et al. The effect of meditation on brain structure: cortical thickness mapping and diffusion tensor imaging. Social cognitive and affective neuroscience. 2013;8(1):27-33.

743. Hernandez SE, Suero J, Barros A, Gonzalez-Mora JL, Rubia K. Increased Grey Matter Associated with Long-Term Sahaja Yoga Meditation: A Voxel-Based Morphometry Study. PloS one. 2016;11(3):e0150757.

744. Grant JA, Duerden EG, Courtemanche J, Cherkasova M, Duncan GH, Rainville P. Cortical thickness, mental absorption and meditative practice: possible implications for disorders of attention. Biological psychology. 2013;92(2):275-81.

745. Grant JA, Courtemanche J, Duerden EG, Duncan GH, Rainville P. Cortical thickness and pain sensitivity in zen meditators. Emotion (Washington, DC). 2010;10(1):43-53.

746. Young KS, van der Velden AM, Craske MG, Pallesen KJ, Fjorback L, Roepstorff A, et al. The impact of mindfulness-based interventions on brain activity: A systematic review of functional magnetic resonance imaging studies. Neuroscience and biobehavioral reviews. 2017.

747. Fox KC, Nijeboer S, Dixon ML, Floman JL, Ellamil M, Rumak SP, et al. Is meditation associated with altered brain structure? A systematic review and meta-analysis of morphometric neuroimaging in meditation practitioners. Neuroscience and biobehavioral reviews. 2014;43:48-73.

748. Giron EC, McIsaac T, Nilsen D. Effects of kinesthetic versus visual imagery practice on two technical dance movements: a pilot study. Journal of dance medicine & science : official publication of the International Association for Dance Medicine & Science. 2012;16(1):36-8.

749. Lotze M. Kinesthetic imagery of musical performance. Frontiers in human neuroscience. 2013;7:280.

749a. Scheibner HJ, Bogler C, Gleich T, Haynes JD, Bermpohl F. Internal and external attention and the default mode network. Neuroimage. 2017 Mar 1;148:381-389. doi: 10.1016/j.neuroimage.2017.01.044. Epub 2017 Jan 18.

750. James W. Talks to Teachers on Psychology: And to Students on Some of Life's Ideals. New York: Henry Holt & Company; 1899.

751. Gottlieb J, Oudeyer PY, Lopes M, Baranes A. Information-seeking, curiosity, and attention: computational and neural mechanisms. Trends in cognitive sciences. 2013;17(11):585-93.

752. Oudeyer PY, Kaplan F. What is Intrinsic Motivation? A Typology of Computational Approaches. Frontiers in neurorobotics. 2007;1:6.

753. Loewenstein G. The Psychology of Curiosity: A Review and Reinterpretation. Psychological bulletin. 1994;116(1):75-98.

754. Berlyne DE. A theory of human curiosity. British journal of psychology (London, England : 1953). 1954;45(3):180-91.

755. Engel S. Children's Need to Know: Curiosity in Schools. Harvard Educational Review. 2011;81(4):625-45.

756. Najemnik J, Geisler WS. Optimal eye movement strategies in visual search. Nature. 2005;434(7031):387-91.

757. Kidd C, Hayden BY. The Psychology and Neuroscience of Curiosity. Neuron. 2015;88(3):449-60.

758. Jepma M, Verdonschot RG, van Steenbergen H, Rombouts SA, Nieuwenhuis S. Neural mechanisms underlying the induction and relief of perceptual curiosity. Frontiers in behavioral neuroscience. 2012;6:5.

759. Hughes BL, Zaki J. The neuroscience of motivated cognition. Trends in cognitive sciences. 2015;19(2):62-4.

760. Scoville WB, Milner B. Loss of recent memory after bilateral hippocampal lesions. Journal of neurology, neurosurgery, and psychiatry. 1957;20(1):11-21.

761. Kang MJ, Hsu M, Krajbich IM, Loewenstein G, McClure SM, Wang JT, et al. The wick in the candle of learning: epistemic curiosity activates reward circuitry and enhances memory. Psychological science. 2009;20(8):963-73.

762. Nevill AM, Holder RL. Home advantage in sport: an overview of studies on the advantage of playing at home. Sports medicine (Auckland, NZ). 1999;28(4):221-36.

763. Musich S, Wang SS, Kraemer S, Hawkins K, Wicker E. Purpose in Life and Positive Health Outcomes Among Older Adults. Population health management. 2017.

764. Krause N. Meaning in life and mortality. The journals of gerontology Series B, Psychological sciences and social sciences. 2009;64(4):517-27.

765. Mujcic R, A JO. Evolution of Well-Being and Happiness After Increases in Consumption of Fruit and Vegetables. American journal of public health. 2016;106(8):1504-10.

766. Kim ES, Sun JK, Park N, Kubzansky LD, Peterson C. Purpose in life and reduced risk of myocardial infarction among older U.S. adults with coronary heart disease: a two-year follow-up. Journal of behavioral medicine. 2013;36(2):124-33.

767. Grant A. In the company of givers and takers. Harvard business review. 2013;91(4):90-7, 142.

768. van der Meulen M, Kamping S, Anton F. The role of cognitive reappraisal in placebo analgesia: an fMRI study. Social cognitive and affective neuroscience. 2017.

769. Rath TH, J. . Your friends and your social wellbeing 2010 July 6th, 2017. Available from: http://www.gallup.com/businessjournal/127043/friends-social-wellbeing.aspx

770. Barger SD. Social integration, social support and mortality in the US National Health Interview Survey. Psychosomatic medicine. 2013;75(5):510-7.

771. Ertcl KA, Glymour MM, Berkman LF. Effects of social integration on preserving memory function in a nationally representative US elderly population. American journal of public health. 2008;98(7):1215-20.

772. Cole SW, Levine ME, Arevalo JM, Ma J, Weir DR, Crimmins EM. Loneliness, eudaimonia, and the human conserved transcriptional response to adversity. Psychoneuroendocrinology. 2015;62:11-7.

773. Amabile TM, Kramer SJ. Inner work life: understanding the subtext of business performance. Harvard business review. 2007;85(5):72-83, 144.

774. Nohria N, Groysberg B, Lee LE. Employee motivation: a powerful new model. Harvard business review. 2008;86(7-8):78-84, 160.

775. Loehr J, Schwartz T. The making of a corporate athlete. Harvard business review. 2001;79(1):120-8, 76.

776. Schwartz TP, C. Why you hate work 2014 July 6th, 2017. Available from: https://www.nytimes.com/2014/06/01/opinion/sunday/why-you-hate-work.html?_r=3.

777. Adkins A. Employee engagement in U.S. stagnant in 2015 2016 July 6th, 2017. Available from: http://www.gallup.com/poll/188144/employee-engagement-stagnant-2015.aspx.

778. Weyburnthisweek. Two thirds of Canadians stressed by work 2016 July 6th, 2017. Available from: http://www.weyburnthisweek.com/news/two-thirds-of-canadians-stressed-by-work-1.2235743.

779. Stress.org. Workplace stress: Stress.org; 2017. Available from: https://www.stress.org/workplace-stress/.

780. Brooks D. Should you live for your resume or your eulogy? David Brooks. TED.com, 2014 TED.com; 2014.

781. Taubert M, Villringer A, Ragert P. Learning-related gray and white matter changes in humans: an update. The Neuroscientist : a review journal bringing neurobiology, neurology and psychiatry. 2012;18(4):320-5.

782. Ditye T, Kanai R, Bahrami B, Muggleton NG, Rees G, Walsh V. Rapid changes in brain structure predict improvements induced by perceptual learning. NeuroImage. 2013;81:205-12.

783. Cohen S, Janicki-Deverts D, Doyle WJ, Miller GE, Frank E, Rabin BS, et al. Chronic stress, glucocorticoid receptor resistance, inflammation, and disease risk. Proceedings of the National Academy of Sciences of the United States of America. 2012;109(16):5995-9.

784. Gouin JP, Glaser R, Malarkey WB, Beversdorf D, Kiecolt-Glaser J. Chronic stress, daily stressors, and circulating inflammatory markers. Health psychology : official journal of the Division of Health Psychology, American Psychological Association. 2012;31(2):264-8.

785. Sin NL, Graham-Engeland JE, Almeida DM. Daily positive events and inflammation: findings from the National Study of Daily Experiences. Brain, behavior, and immunity. 2015;43:130-8.

786. Sin NL, Graham-Engeland JE, Ong AD, Almeida DM. Affective reactivity to daily stressors is associated with elevated inflammation. Health psychology : official journal of the Division of Health Psychology, American Psychological Association. 2015;34(12):1154-65.

787. Kim SH, Vincent LC, Goncalo JA. Outside advantage: can social rejection fuel creative thought? Journal of experimental psychology General. 2013;142(3):605-11.

788. Benjet C, Bromet E, Karam EG, Kessler RC, McLaughlin KA, Ruscio AM, et al. The epidemiology of traumatic event exposure worldwide: results from the World Mental Health Survey Consortium. Psychological medicine. 2016;46(2):327-43.

789. Gallup.com. Gallup Daily: U.S. Employee Engagement: Gallup; [Available from: http://www.gallup.com/poll/180404/gallup-daily-employee-engagement.aspx.

790. Sorenson S. How employee engagement drives growth2013 July 6th, 2017. Available from: http://www.gallup.com/businessjournal/163130/employee-engagement-drives-growth.aspx.

791. Kliisel T. Improving A Leading Indicator of Financial Performance: Employee Engagement2011 July 6th, 2017. Available from: https://www.forbes.com/sites/tykiisel/2011/12/14/improvinga-leading-indicator-of-financial-performance-employee-engagement/#39467623754b.

792. Highhouse S, Zickar MJ, Yankelevich M. Would you work if you won the lottery? Tracking changes in the American work ethic. The Journal of applied psychology. 2010;95(2):349-57.

793. Mann AH, J. The worldwide employee engagement crisis, 2016, Gallup 2016 July 6th, 2017. Available from: http://www.gallup.com/businessjournal/188033/worldwide-employee-engagement-crisis.aspx.

794. Hensley SH, A. Stressed Out: Americans Tell Us About Stress In Their Lives2014 July 6th, 2017. Available from: http://www.npr.org/sections/health-shots/2014/07/07/327322187/stressed-out-americans-tell-us-about-stress-in-their-lives.

795. Lawrence B. The Practice of the Presence of God: Whitaker House; 1982. 85 p.

796. Csikszentmihalyi M. Flow: The psychology of optimal experience: Harper Collins; 2008. 322 p.

797. Csikszentmihalyi M, LeFevre J. Optimal experience in work and leisure. Journal of personality and social psychology. 1989;56(5):815-22.

798. Dietrich A. Neurocognitive mechanisms underlying the experience of flow. Consciousness and cognition. 2004;13(4):746-61.

799. Lane RD. Neural substrates of implicit and explicit emotional processes: a unifying framework for psychosomatic medicine. Psychosomatic medicine. 2008;70(2):214-31.

800. Limb CJ, Braun AR. Neural substrates of spontaneous musical performance: an FMRI study of jazz improvisation. PloS one. 2008;3(2):e1679.

801. Lee EM, Klement KR, Ambler JK, Loewald T, Comber EM, Hanson SA, et al. Altered States of Consciousness during an Extreme Ritual. PloS one. 2016;11(5):e0153126.

802. Del Giorno JM, Hall EE, O'Leary KC, Bixby WR, Miller PC. Cognitive function during acute exercise: a test of the transient hypofrontality theory. Journal of sport & exercise psychology. 2010;32(3):312-23.

803. Dietrich A. Transient hypofrontality as a mechanism for the psychological effects of exercise. Psychiatry research. 2006;145(1):79-83.

804. Dietrich A, Sparling PB. Endurance exercise selectively impairs prefrontal-dependent cognition. Brain and cognition. 2004;55(3):516-24.

805. Radel R, Brisswalter J, Perrey S. Saving mental effort to maintain physical effort: a shift of activity within the prefrontal cortex in anticipation of prolonged exercise. Cognitive, affective & behavioral neuroscience. 2017;17(2):305-14.

806. Wang CC, Chu CH, Chu IH, Chan KH, Chang YK. Executive function during acute exercise: the role of exercise intensity. Journal of sport & exercise psychology. 2013;35(4):358-67.

807. Tempest GD, Davranche K, Brisswalter J, Perrey S, Radel R. The differential effects of prolonged exercise upon executive function and cerebral oxygenation. Brain and cognition. 2017;113:133-41.

808. Wollseiffen P, Schneider S, Martin LA, Kerherve HA, Klein T, Solomon C. The effect of 6 h of running on brain activity, mood, and cognitive performance. Experimental brain research. 2016;234(7):1829-36.

809. Harmat L, de Manzano O, Theorell T, Hogman L, Fischer H, Ullen F. Physiological correlates of the flow experience during computer game playing. International journal of psychophysiology : official journal of the International Organization of Psychophysiology. 2015;97(1):1-7.

810. Kotler S. The science of peak human performance Time; 2014. Available from: http://time.com/56809/the-science-of-peak-human-performance/.

811. Cranston SK, S. Increasing the 'meaning quotient' of work2012 July 6th, 2017. Available from: http://www.mckinsey.com/business-functions/organization/our-insights/increasing-the-meaning-quotient-of-work.

812. McKinley RA, McIntire L, Bridges N, Goodyear C, Bangera NB, Weisend MP. Acceleration of image analyst training with transcranial direct current stimulation. Behavioral neuroscience. 2013;127(6):936-46.
813. Beilock SL, Carr TH, MacMahon C, Starkes JL. When paying attention becomes counterproductive: impact of divided versus skill-focused attention on novice and experienced performance of sensorimotor skills. Journal of experimental psychology Applied. 2002;8(1):6-16.
814. Kashdan TB, Rottenberg J. Psychological flexibility as a fundamental aspect of health. Clinical psychology review. 2010;30(7):865-78.
815. Kuhbandner C, Spitzer B, Pekrun R. Read-out of emotional information from iconic memory: the longevity of threatening stimuli. Psychological science. 2011;22(5):695-700.
816. Roskes M, De Dreu CK, Nijstad BA. Necessity is the mother of invention: avoidance motivation stimulates creativity through cognitive effort. Journal of personality and social psychology. 2012;103(2):242-56.
817. Roskes M, Elliot AJ, Nijstad BA, De Dreu CK. Time pressure undermines performance more under avoidance than approach motivation. Personality & social psychology bulletin. 2013;39(6):803-13.
818. Byron K, Khazanchi S. Rewards and creative performance: a meta-analytic test of theoretically derived hypotheses. Psychological bulletin. 2012;138(4):809-30.
819. Sood A. The Mayo Clinic Handbook for Happiness: A Four-Step Plan for Resilient Living: Da Capo Lifelong Books; 2015.
820. Gilbert DT. Stumbling on happiness: Vintage; 2007. 336 p.
821. Thaker PH, Lutgendorf SK, Sood AK. The neuroendocrine impact of chronic stress on cancer. Cell cycle (Georgetown, Tex). 2007;6(4):430-3.
822. Sood AK, Lutgendorf SK. Stress influences on anoikis. Cancer prevention research (Philadelphia, Pa). 2011;4(4):481-5.
823. Moreno-Smith M, Lutgendorf SK, Sood AK. Impact of stress on cancer metastasis. Future oncology (London, England). 2010;6(12):1863-81.
824. Lutgendorf SK, Sood AK. Biobehavioral factors and cancer progression: physiological pathways and mechanisms. Psychosomatic medicine. 2011;73(9):724-30.
825. Cole SW, Nagaraja AS, Lutgendorf SK, Green PA, Sood AK. Sympathetic nervous system regulation of the tumour microenvironment. Nature reviews Cancer. 2015;15(9):563-72.
826. Chida Y, Hamer M, Wardle J, Steptoe A. Do stress-related psychosocial factors contribute to cancer incidence and survival? Nature clinical practice Oncology. 2008;5(8):466-75.
827. Armaiz-Pena GN, Lutgendorf SK, Cole SW, Sood AK. Neuroendocrine modulation of cancer progression. Brain, behavior, and immunity. 2009;23(1):10-5.
828. Antoni MH, Lutgendorf SK, Cole SW, Dhabhar FS, Sephton SE, McDonald PG, et al. The influence of bio-behavioural factors on tumour biology: pathways and mechanisms. Nature reviews Cancer. 2006;6(3):240-8.
829. Stagl JM, Lechner SC, Carver CS, Bouchard LC, Gudenkauf LM, Jutagir DR, et al. A randomized controlled trial of cognitive-behavioral stress management in breast cancer: survival and recurrence at 11-year follow-up. Breast cancer research and treatment. 2015;154(2):319-28.
830. Stagl JM, Bouchard LC, Lechner SC, Blomberg BB, Gudenkauf LM, Jutagir DR, et al. Long-term psychological benefits of cognitive-behavioral stress management for women with breast cancer: 11-year follow-up of a randomized controlled trial. Cancer. 2015;121(11):1873-81.
831. McGregor BA, Dolan ED, Murphy KM, Sannes TS, Highland KB, Albano DL, et al. Cognitive Behavioral Stress Management for Healthy Women at Risk for Breast Cancer: a Novel Application of a Proven Intervention. Annals of behavioral medicine : a publication of the Society of Behavioral Medicine. 2015;49(6):873-84.
832. Loprinzi CE, Prasad K, Schroeder DR, Sood A. Stress Management and Resilience Training (SMART) program to decrease stress and enhance resilience among breast cancer survivors: a pilot randomized clinical trial. Clinical breast cancer. 2011;11(6):364-8.

833. Lengacher CA, Reich RR, Paterson CL, Ramesar S, Park JY, Alinat C, et al. Examination of Broad Symptom Improvement Resulting From Mindfulness-Based Stress Reduction in Breast Cancer Survivors: A Randomized Controlled Trial. Journal of clinical oncology : official journal of the American Society of Clinical Oncology. 2016;34(24):2827-34.

834. Hermelink K, Buhner M, Sckopke P, Neufeld F, Kaste J, Voigt V, et al. Chemotherapy and Post-traumatic Stress in the Causation of Cognitive Dysfunction in Breast Cancer Patients. Journal of the National Cancer Institute. 2017;109(10).

835. Andersen BL, Yang HC, Farrar WB, Golden-Kreutz DM, Emery CF, Thornton LM, et al. Psychologic intervention improves survival for breast cancer patients: a randomized clinical trial. Cancer. 2008;113(12):3450-8.

836. Daskalakis NP, Bagot RC, Parker KJ, Vinkers CH, de Kloet ER. The three-hit concept of vulnerability and resilience: toward understanding adaptation to early-life adversity outcome. Psychoneuroendocrinology. 2013;38(9):1858-73.

837. Caspi A, Sugden K, Moffitt TE, Taylor A, Craig IW, Harrington H, et al. Influence of life stress on depression: moderation by a polymorphism in the 5-HTT gene. Science (New York, NY). 2003;301(5631):386-9.

838. Cruz-Fuentes CS, Benjet C, Martinez-Levy GA, Perez-Molina A, Briones-Velasco M, Suarez-Gonzalez J. BDNF Met66 modulates the cumulative effect of psychosocial childhood adversities on major depression in adolescents. Brain and behavior. 2014;4(2):290-7.

839. Klengel T, Binder EB. Gene-environment interactions in major depressive disorder. Canadian journal of psychiatry Revue canadienne de psychiatrie. 2013;58(2):76-83.

840. Lopizzo N, Bocchio Chiavetto L, Cattane N, Plazzotta G, Tarazi FI, Pariante CM, et al. Gene-environment interaction in major depression: focus on experience-dependent biological systems. Frontiers in psychiatry. 2015;6:68.

841. Garmezy N. Children in poverty: resilience despite risk. Psychiatry. 1993;56(1):127-36.

842. Werner EE. Children and war: risk, resilience, and recovery. Development and psychopathology. 2012;24(2):553-8.

843. University CotDCaH. Supportive Relationships and Active Skill-Building Strengthen the Foundations of Resilience: Working Paper No. 13. 2015 July 6th, 2017. Available from: http://46y5eh11fhgw3ve3ytpwxt9r.wpengine.netdna-cdn.com/wp-content/uploads/2015/05/The-Science-of-Resilience2.pdf.

844. Luby JL, Barch DM, Belden A, Gaffrey MS, Tillman R, Babb C, et al. Maternal support in early childhood predicts larger hippocampal volumes at school age. Proceedings of the National Academy of Sciences of the United States of America. 2012;109(8):2854-9.

845. Luby J, Belden A, Botteron K, Marrus N, Harms MP, Babb C, et al. The effects of poverty on childhood brain development: the mediating effect of caregiving and stressful life events. JAMA pediatrics. 2013;167(12):1135-42.

846. Slopen N, Loucks EB, Appleton AA, Kawachi I, Kubzansky LD, Non AL, et al. Early origins of inflammation: An examination of prenatal and childhood social adversity in a prospective cohort study. Psychoneuroendocrinology. 2015;51:403-13.

847. Miller GE, Chen E, Parker KJ. Psychological stress in childhood and susceptibility to the chronic diseases of aging: moving toward a model of behavioral and biological mechanisms. Psychological bulletin. 2011;137(6):959-97.

848. McCrory C, Dooley C, Layte R, Kenny RA. The lasting legacy of childhood adversity for disease risk in later life. Health psychology : official journal of the Division of Health Psychology, American Psychological Association. 2015;34(7):687-96.

849. Fagundes CP, Glaser R, Kiecolt-Glaser JK. Stressful early life experiences and immune dysregulation across the lifespan. Brain, behavior, and immunity. 2013;27(1):8-12.

850. Folkman S. Personal control and stress and coping processes: a theoretical analysis. Journal of personality and social psychology. 1984;46(4):839-52.

851. Folkman S, Lazarus RS, Dunkel-Schetter C, DeLongis A, Gruen RJ. Dynamics of a stressful encounter: cognitive appraisal, coping, and encounter outcomes. Journal of personality and social psychology. 1986;50(5):992-1003.

852. Gruen RJ, Folkman S, Lazarus RS. Centrality and individual differences in the meaning of daily hassles. Journal of personality. 1988;56(4):743-62.

853. Kilpatrick DG, Resnick HS, Milanak ME, Miller MW, Keyes KM, Friedman MJ. National estimates of exposure to traumatic events and PTSD prevalence using DSM-IV and DSM-5 criteria. Journal of traumatic stress. 2013;26(5):537-47.

854. WHO. Suicide DataJuly 6th, 2017. Available from: http://www.who.int/mental_health/prevention/suicide/suicideprevent/en/.

855. WHO. Preventing Suicide: A Global Imperative2014 July 6th, 2017. Available from: http://apps.who.int/iris/bitstream/10665/131056/1/9789241564779_eng.pdf?ua=1&ua=1.

856. Seery MD, Holman EA, Silver RC. Whatever does not kill us: cumulative lifetime adversity, vulnerability, and resilience. Journal of personality and social psychology. 2010;99(6):1025-41.

857. Ford BQ, Shallcross AJ, Mauss IB, Floerke VA, Gruber J. DESPERATELY SEEKING HAPPINESS: VALUING HAPPINESS IS ASSOCIATED WITH SYMPTOMS AND DIAGNOSIS OF DEPRESSION. Journal of social and clinical psychology. 2014;33(10):890-905.

858. Mauss IB, Tamir M, Anderson CL, Savino NS. Can seeking happiness make people unhappy? [corrected] Paradoxical effects of valuing happiness. Emotion (Washington, DC). 2011;11(4):807-15.

859. McNulty JK, Fincham FD. Beyond positive psychology? Toward a contextual view of psychological processes and well-being. The American psychologist. 2012;67(2):101-10.

860. Santos S, Almeida I, Oliveiros B, Castelo-Branco M. The Role of the Amygdala in Facial Trustworthiness Processing: A Systematic Review and Meta-Analyses of fMRI Studies. PloS one. 2016;11(11):e0167276.

861. Vanderveldt A, Oliveira L, Green L. Delay discounting: Pigeon, rat, human--does it matter? Journal of experimental psychology Animal learning and cognition. 2016;42(2):141-62.

862. Gianotti LR, Figner B, Ebstein RP, Knoch D. Why Some People Discount More than Others: Baseline Activation in the Dorsal PFC Mediates the Link between COMT Genotype and Impatient Choice. Frontiers in neuroscience. 2012;6:54.

863. Meyer-Lindenberg A, Weinberger DR. Intermediate phenotypes and genetic mechanisms of psychiatric disorders. Nature reviews Neuroscience. 2006;7(10):818-27.

864. Tost H, Bilek E, Meyer-Lindenberg A. Brain connectivity in psychiatric imaging genetics. NeuroImage. 2012;62(4):2250-60.

865. van den Bos W, Rodriguez CA, Schweitzer JB, McClure SM. Adolescent impatience decreases with increased frontostriatal connectivity. Proceedings of the National Academy of Sciences of the United States of America. 2015;112(29):E3765-74.

866. Yan LL, Liu K, Matthews KA, Daviglus ML, Ferguson TF, Kiefe CI. Psychosocial factors and risk of hypertension: the Coronary Artery Risk Development in Young Adults (CARDIA) study. Jama. 2003;290(16):2138-48.

867. Nyberg L, Bohlin G, Hagekull B. Assessing Type A behavior in children: a longitudinal exploration of the overlap between Type A behavior and hyperactivity. Scandinavian journal of psychology. 2004;45(2):145-56.

868. Wacogne C, Lacoste JP, Guillibert E, Hugues FC, Le Jeunne C. Stress, anxiety, depression and migraine. Cephalalgia : an international journal of headache. 2003;23(6):451-5.

869. Yim OS, Zhang X, Shalev I, Monakhov M, Zhong S, Hsu M, et al. Delay discounting, genetic sensitivity, and leukocyte telomere length. Proceedings of the National Academy of Sciences of the United States of America. 2016;113(10):2780-5.

870. Mendes de Leon CF, Powell LH, Kaplan BH. Change in coronary-prone behaviors in the recurrent coronary prevention project. Psychosomatic medicine. 1991;53(4):407-19.

871. Reimers SM, E.A.; Stewart, N.; Chater, N. . Associations between a one-shot delay discounting measure and age, income, education and real-world impulsive behavior. Personality and individual differences. 2009;47(8):973-8.

872. Barling J, Bluen S, Moss V. Type A behavior and marital dissatisfaction: disentangling the effects of achievement striving and impatience-irritability. The Journal of psychology. 1990;124(3):311-9.
873. Nabi H, Consoli SM, Chastang JF, Chiron M, Lafont S, Lagarde E. Type A behavior pattern, risky driving behaviors, and serious road traffic accidents: a prospective study of the GAZEL cohort. American journal of epidemiology. 2005;161(9):864-70.
874. Perry AR, Baldwin DA. Further evidence of associations of type a personality scores and driving-related attitudes and behaviors. Perceptual and motor skills. 2000;91(1):147-54.
875. Day AL, Jreige S. Examining Type A behavior pattern to explain the relationship between job stressors and psychosocial outcomes. Journal of occupational health psychology. 2002;7(2):109-20.
876. DeSteno D, Li Y, Dickens L, Lerner JS. Gratitude: a tool for reducing economic impatience. Psychological science. 2014;25(6):1262-7.
877. Eaton K. How One Second Could Cost Amazon $1.6 billion in Sales.2012 July 6th, 2017. Available from: https://www.fastcompany.com/1825005/how-one-second-could-cost-amazon-16-billion-sales.
878. Zhong CB, Devoe SE. You are how you eat: fast food and impatience. Psychological science. 2010;21(5):619-22.
879. Rosati AG, Stevens JR, Hare B, Hauser MD. The evolutionary origins of human patience: temporal preferences in chimpanzees, bonobos, and human adults. Current biology : CB. 2007;17(19):1663-8.
880. Stevens JR, Hallinan EV, Hauser MD. The ecology and evolution of patience in two New World monkeys. Biology letters. 2005;1(2):223-6.
881. Bernhardt BC, Singer T. The neural basis of empathy. Annual review of neuroscience. 2012;35:1-23.
882. Akitsuki Y, Decety J. Social context and perceived agency affects empathy for pain: an event-related fMRI investigation. NeuroImage. 2009;47(2):722-34.
883. Lamm C, Batson CD, Decety J. The neural substrate of human empathy: effects of perspective-taking and cognitive appraisal. Journal of cognitive neuroscience. 2007;19(1):42-58.
884. Valeriani M, Betti V, Le Pera D, De Armas L, Miliucci R, Restuccia D, et al. Seeing the pain of others while being in pain: a laser-evoked potentials study. NeuroImage. 2008;40(3):1419-28.
885. Klimecki OM, Leiberg S, Ricard M, Singer T. Differential pattern of functional brain plasticity after compassion and empathy training. Social cognitive and affective neuroscience. 2014;9(6):873-9.
886. Cheng Y, Lin CP, Liu HL, Hsu YY, Lim KE, Hung D, et al. Expertise modulates the perception of pain in others. Current biology : CB. 2007;17(19):1708-13.
887. Conradt L, Roper TJ. Consensus decision making in animals. Trends in ecology & evolution. 2005;20(8):449-56.
888. Conradt L, Roper TJ. Democracy in animals: the evolution of shared group decisions. Proceedings Biological sciences. 2007;274(1623):2317-26.
889. Conradt L, Roper TJ. Deciding group movements: where and when to go. Behavioural processes. 2010;84(3):675-7.
890. Couzin ID, Ioannou CC, Demirel G, Gross T, Torney CJ, Hartnett A, et al. Uninformed individuals promote democratic consensus in animal groups. Science (New York, NY). 2011;334(6062):1578-80.
891. Arch JJ, Brown KW, Dean DJ, Landy LN, Brown KD, Laudenslager ML. Self-compassion training modulates alpha-amylase, heart rate variability, and subjective responses to social evaluative threat in women. Psychoneuroendocrinology. 2014;42:49-58.
892. Stellar JE, Cohen A, Oveis C, Keltner D. Affective and physiological responses to the suffering of others: compassion and vagal activity. Journal of personality and social psychology. 2015;108(4):572-85.
893. Breines JG, Thoma MV, Gianferante D, Hanlin L, Chen X, Rohleder N. Self-compassion as a predictor of interleukin-6 response to acute psychosocial stress. Brain, behavior, and immunity. 2014;37:109-14.

894. Pace TW, Negi LT, Dodson-Lavelle B, Ozawa-de Silva B, Reddy SD, Cole SP, et al. Engagement with Cognitively-Based Compassion Training is associated with reduced salivary C-reactive protein from before to after training in foster care program adolescents. Psychoneuroendocrinology. 2013;38(2):294-9.

895. Rakel D, Barrett B, Zhang Z, Hoeft T, Chewning B, Marchand L, et al. Perception of empathy in the therapeutic encounter: effects on the common cold. Patient education and counseling. 2011;85(3):390-7.

896. Poole AD, Sanson-Fisher RW. Long-term effects of empathy training on the interview skills of medical students. Patient counselling and health education. 1980;2(3).125-7.

897. Batson CD, Polycarpou MP, Harmon-Jones E, Imhoff HJ, Mitchener EC, Bednar LL, et al. Empathy and attitudes: can feeling for a member of a stigmatized group improve feelings toward the group? Journal of personality and social psychology. 1997;72(1):105-18.

898. Gini G, Albiero P, Benelli B, Altoe G. Does empathy predict adolescents' bullying and defending behavior? Aggressive behavior. 2007;33(5):467-76.

899. Pollak KI, Ostbye T, Alexander SC, Gradison M, Bastian LA, Brouwer RJ, et al. Empathy goes a long way in weight loss discussions. The Journal of family practice. 2007;56(12):1031-6.

900. Castillo R, Salguero JM, Fernandez-Berrocal P, Balluerka N. Effects of an emotional intelligence intervention on aggression and empathy among adolescents. Journal of adolescence. 2013;36(5):883-92.

901. Shen L. Targeting smokers with empathy appeal antismoking public service announcements: a field experiment. Journal of health communication. 2015;20(5):573-80.

902. Smith DD, Kellar J, Walters EL, Reibling ET, Phan T, Green SM. Does emergency physician empathy reduce thoughts of litigation? A randomised trial. Emergency medicine journal : EMJ. 2016;33(8):548-52.

903. Kemper KJ, Mo X, Khayat R. Are Mindfulness and Self-Compassion Associated with Sleep and Resilience in Health Professionals? Journal of alternative and complementary medicine (New York, NY). 2015;21(8):496-503.

904. Diedrich A, Grant M, Hofmann SG, Hiller W, Berking M. Self-compassion as an emotion regulation strategy in major depressive disorder. Behaviour research and therapy. 2014;58:43-51.

905. Fogarty LA, Curbow BA, Wingard JR, McDonnell K, Somerfield MR. Can 40 seconds of compassion reduce patient anxiety? Journal of clinical oncology : official journal of the American Society of Clinical Oncology. 1999;17(1):371-9.

906. Wohlleben P. The Hidden Life of Trees: What They Feel, How They Communicate—Discoveries from a Secret World: Greystone books; 2016. 288 p.

907. Gilbert P, McEwan K, Matos M, Rivis A. Fears of compassion: development of three self-report measures. Psychology and psychotherapy. 2011;84(3):239-55.

908. Gilbert P, McEwan K, Gibbons L, Chotai S, Duarte J, Matos M. Fears of compassion and happiness in relation to alexithymia, mindfulness, and self-criticism. Psychology and psychotherapy. 2012;85(4):374-90.

909. Hein G, Singer T. I feel how you feel but not always: the empathic brain and its modulation. Current opinion in neurobiology. 2008;18(2):153-8.

910. Decety J, Echols S, Correll J. The blame game: the effect of responsibility and social stigma on empathy for pain. Journal of cognitive neuroscience. 2010;22(5):985-97.

911. Meyer ML, Masten CL, Ma Y, Wang C, Shi Z, Eisenberger NI, et al. Empathy for the social suffering of friends and strangers recruits distinct patterns of brain activation. Social cognitive and affective neuroscience. 2013;8(4):446-54.

912. Zheng L, Wang Q, Cheng X, Li L, Yang G, Sun L, et al. Perceived reputation of others modulates empathic neural responses. Experimental brain research. 2016;234(1):125-32.

913. Fernandez E, Johnson SL. Anger in psychological disorders: Prevalence, presentation, etiology and prognostic implications. Clinical psychology review. 2016;46:124-35.

914. Owen JM. Transdiagnostic cognitive processes in high trait anger. Clinical psychology review. 2011;31(2):193-202.

915. Wilkowski BM, Robinson MD. The anatomy of anger: an integrative cognitive model of trait anger and reactive aggression. Journal of personality. 2010;78(1):9-38.

916. Birkley EL, Eckhardt CI. Anger, hostility, internalizing negative emotions, and intimate partner violence perpetration: A meta-analytic review. Clinical psychology review. 2015;37:40-56.

917. Suls J. Anger and the heart: perspectives on cardiac risk, mechanisms and interventions. Progress in cardiovascular diseases. 2013;55(6):538-47.

918. Lampert R. Anger and ventricular arrhythmias. Current opinion in cardiology. 2010;25(1):46-52.

919. Mostofsky E, Penner EA, Mittleman MA. Outbursts of anger as a trigger of acute cardiovascular events: a systematic review and meta-analysis. European heart journal. 2014;35(21):1404-10.

920. Rosa PB, Orquiza B, Rocha FB, Donadel RW, Diniz RP, Beloni TM, et al. Anger and stroke: a potential association that deserves serious consideration. Acta neuropsychiatrica. 2016;28(6):346-51.

921. Eaker ED, Sullivan LM, Kelly-Hayes M, D'Agostino RB, Sr., Benjamin EJ. Anger and hostility predict the development of atrial fibrillation in men in the Framingham Offspring Study. Circulation. 2004;109(10):1267-71.

922. Rosenberg EL, Ekman P, Jiang W, Babyak M, Coleman RE, Hanson M, et al. Linkages between facial expressions of anger and transient myocardial ischemia in men with coronary artery disease. Emotion (Washington, DC). 2001;1(2):107-15.

923. Denson TF, Moulds ML, Grisham JR. The effects of analytical rumination, reappraisal, and distraction on anger experience. Behavior therapy. 2012;43(2):355-64.

924. McCullough ME, Kurzban R, Tabak BA. Cognitive systems for revenge and forgiveness. The Behavioral and brain sciences. 2013;36(1):1-15.

925. Rafaeli A, Erez A, Ravid S, Derfler-Rozin R, Treister DE, Scheyer R. When customers exhibit verbal aggression, employees pay cognitive costs. The Journal of applied psychology. 2012;97(5):931-50.

926. Fisk GM, Neville LB. Effects of customer entitlement on service workers' physical and psychological well-being: a study of waitstaff employees. Journal of occupational health psychology. 2011;16(4):391-405.

927. Kim E, Yoon DJ. Why does service with a smile make employees happy? a social interaction model. The Journal of applied psychology. 2012;97(5):1059-67.

928. Shore DM, Heerey EA. The value of genuine and polite smiles. Emotion (Washington, DC). 2011;11(1):169-74.

929. Szasz PL, Szentagotai A, Hofmann SG. The effect of emotion regulation strategies on anger. Behaviour research and therapy. 2011;49(2):114-9.

930. Bremner RH, Koole SL, Bushman BJ. "Pray for those who mistreat you": effects of prayer on anger and aggression. Personality & social psychology bulletin. 2011;37(6):830-7.

931. Feng C, Li Z, Feng X, Wang L, Tian T, Luo YJ. Social hierarchy modulates neural responses of empathy for pain. Social cognitive and affective neuroscience. 2016;11(3):485-95.

932. Guo X, Zheng L, Zhang W, Zhu L, Li J, Wang Q, et al. Empathic neural responses to others' pain depend on monetary reward. Social cognitive and affective neuroscience. 2012;7(5):535-41.

933. Pollak KI, Arnold R, Alexander SC, Jeffreys AS, Olsen MK, Abernethy AP, et al. Do patient attributes predict oncologist empathic responses and patient perceptions of empathy? Supportive care in cancer : official journal of the Multinational Association of Supportive Care in Cancer. 2010;18(11):1405-11.

934. Hill SE, DelPriore DJ, Vaughan PW. The cognitive consequences of envy: attention, memory, and self-regulatory depletion. Journal of personality and social psychology. 2011;101(4):653-66.

935. Kim E, Glomb TM. Victimization of high performers: the roles of envy and work group identification. The Journal of applied psychology. 2014;99(4):619-34.

936. van de Ven N, Zeelenberg M, Pieters R. Why envy outperforms admiration. Personality & social psychology bulletin. 2011;37(6):784-95.

937. Rodriguez Mosquera PM, Parrott WG, Hurtado de Mendoza A. I fear your envy, I rejoice in your coveting: on the ambivalent experience of being envied by others. Journal of personality and social psychology. 2010;99(5):842-54.

938. Jankowski KF, Takahashi H. Cognitive neuroscience of social emotions and implications for psychopathology: examining embarrassment, guilt, envy, and schadenfreude. Psychiatry and clinical neurosciences. 2014;68(5):319-36.

939. Cabeldue MK, Cramer RJ, Kehn A, Crosby JW, Anastasi JS. Measuring Attitudes About Hate: Development of the Hate Crime Beliefs Scale. Journal of interpersonal violence. 2016.

940. Ilibagiza I. Left to Tell: Discovering God Amidst the Rwandan Holocaust: Hay House; 2014. 256 p.

941. Weisel O, Bohm R. "Ingroup love" and "outgroup hate" in intergroup conflict between natural groups. Journal of experimental social psychology. 2015;60:110-20.

942. Shepherd S. Domestic violence. Home is where the hatred is. The Health service journal. 2009;119(6151):22-4.

943. Galdston R. The longest pleasure: a psychoanalytic study of hatred. The International journal of psycho-analysis. 1987;68 (Pt 3):371-8.

944. Waytz A, Young LL, Ginges J. Motive attribution asymmetry for love vs. hate drives intractable conflict. Proceedings of the National Academy of Sciences of the United States of America. 2014;111(44):15687-92.

945. Hein LC, Scharer KM. Who cares if it is a hate crime? Lesbian, gay, bisexual, and transgender hate crimes--mental health implications and interventions. Perspectives in psychiatric care. 2013;49(2):84-93.

946. Lopes Cardozo B, Kaiser R, Gotway CA, Agani F. Mental health, social functioning, and feelings of hatred and revenge of Kosovar Albanians one year after the war in Kosovo. Journal of traumatic stress. 2003;16(4):351-60.

947. Boleyn-Fitzgerald P. Care and the problem of pity. Bioethics. 2003;17(1):1-20.

948. Kamenetsky SB, Dimakos C, Aslemand A, Saleh A, Ali-Mohammed S. Eliciting Help Without Pity: The Effect of Changing Media Images on Perceptions of Disability. Journal of social work in disability & rehabilitation. 2016;15(1):1-21.

949. Cikara M, Fiske ST. Bounded empathy: neural responses to outgroup targets' (mis)fortunes. Journal of cognitive neuroscience. 2011;23(12):3791-803.

950. Hurlemann R, Patin A, Onur OA, Cohen MX, Baumgartner T, Metzler S, et al. Oxytocin enhances amygdala-dependent, socially reinforced learning and emotional empathy in humans. The Journal of neuroscience : the official journal of the Society for Neuroscience. 2010;30(14):4999-5007.

951. Shamay-Tsoory SG, Abu-Akel A, Palgi S, Sulieman R, Fischer-Shofty M, Levkovitz Y, et al. Giving peace a chance: oxytocin increases empathy to pain in the context of the Israeli-Palestinian conflict. Psychoneuroendocrinology. 2013;38(12):3139-44.

952. Yao S, Becker B, Geng Y, Zhao Z, Xu X, Zhao W, et al. Voluntary control of anterior insula and its functional connections is feedback-independent and increases pain empathy. NeuroImage. 2016;130:230-40.

953. Guadagni V, Burles F, Ferrara M, Iaria G. The effects of sleep deprivation on emotional empathy. Journal of sleep research. 2014;23(6):657-63.

954. Luo S, Shi Z, Yang X, Wang X, Han S. Reminders of mortality decrease midcingulate activity in response to others' suffering. Social cognitive and affective neuroscience. 2014;9(4):477-86.

955. Tarrant M, Dazeley S, Cottom T. Social categorization and empathy for outgroup members. The British journal of social psychology. 2009;48(Pt 3):427-46.

956. Wikstrom BM. A picture of a work of art as an empathy teaching strategy in nurse education complementary to theoretical knowledge. Journal of professional nursing : official journal of the American Association of Colleges of Nursing. 2003;19(1):49-54.

957. Rutgen M, Seidel EM, Riecansky I, Lamm C. Reduction of empathy for pain by placebo analgesia suggests functional equivalence of empathy and first-hand emotion experience. The Journal of neuroscience : the official journal of the Society for Neuroscience. 2015;35(23):8938-47.

958. Rutgen M, Seidel EM, Silani G, Riecansky I, Hummer A, Windischberger C, et al. Placebo analgesia and its opioidergic regulation suggest that empathy for pain is grounded in self pain. Proceedings of the National Academy of Sciences of the United States of America. 2015;112(41):E5638-46.

959. Hein G, Silani G, Preuschoff K, Batson CD, Singer T. Neural responses to ingroup and outgroup members' suffering predict individual differences in costly helping. Neuron. 2010;68(1):149-60.

960. Young SG, Hugenberg K. Mere social categorization modulates identification of facial expressions of emotion. Journal of personality and social psychology. 2010;99(6):964-77.

961. Valdesolo P, Desteno D. Synchrony and the social tuning of compassion. Emotion (Washington, DC). 2011;11(2):262-6.

962. Sheeran P, Gollwitzer PM, Bargh JA. Nonconscious processes and health. Health psychology : official journal of the Division of Health Psychology, American Psychological Association. 2013;32(5):460-73.

963. Bargh JA, Chen M, Burrows L. Automaticity of social behavior: direct effects of trait construct and stereotype-activation on action. Journal of personality and social psychology. 1996;71(2):230-44.

964. Harris JL, Bargh JA, Brownell KD. Priming effects of television food advertising on eating behavior. Health psychology : official journal of the Division of Health Psychology, American Psychological Association. 2009;28(4):404-13.

965. DeCelles KA, DeRue DS, Margolis JD, Ceranic TL. Does power corrupt or enable? When and why power facilitates self-interested behavior. The Journal of applied psychology. 2012;97(3):681-9.

966. Sturmer S, Snyder M, Kropp A, Siem B. Empathy-motivated helping: the moderating role of group membership. Personality & social psychology bulletin. 2006;32(7):943-56.

967. Sheng F, Han S. Manipulations of cognitive strategies and intergroup relationships reduce the racial bias in empathic neural responses. NeuroImage. 2012;61(4):786-97.

968. Sheng F, Liu Q, Li H, Fang F, Han S. Task modulations of racial bias in neural responses to others' suffering. NeuroImage. 2014;88:263-70.

969. Cao Y, Contreras-Huerta LS, McFadyen J, Cunnington R. Racial bias in neural response to others' pain is reduced with other-race contact. Cortex; a journal devoted to the study of the nervous system and behavior. 2015;70:68-78.

970. Bruera E, Palmer JL, Pace E, Zhang K, Willey J, Strasser F, et al. A randomized, controlled trial of physician postures when breaking bad news to cancer patients. Palliative medicine. 2007;21(6):501-5.

971. Swayden KJ, Anderson KK, Connelly LM, Moran JS, McMahon JK, Arnold PM. Effect of sitting vs. standing on perception of provider time at bedside: a pilot study. Patient education and counseling. 2012;86(2):166-71.

972. Tamir DI, Zaki J, Mitchell JP. Informing others is associated with behavioral and neural signatures of value. Journal of experimental psychology General. 2015;144(6):1114-23.

973. Tamir DI, Mitchell JP. Disclosing information about the self is intrinsically rewarding. Proceedings of the National Academy of Sciences of the United States of America. 2012;109(21):8038-43.

974. Leiberg S, Klimecki O, Singer T. Short-term compassion training increases prosocial behavior in a newly developed prosocial game. PloS one. 2011;6(3):e17798.

975. Klimecki OM, Leiberg S, Lamm C, Singer T. Functional neural plasticity and associated changes in positive affect after compassion training. Cerebral cortex (New York, NY : 1991). 2013;23(7):1552-61.

976. Lutz A, Brefczynski-Lewis J, Johnstone T, Davidson RJ. Regulation of the neural circuitry of emotion by compassion meditation: effects of meditative expertise. PloS one. 2008;3(3):e1897.

977. Dow AW, Leong D, Anderson A, Wenzel RP. Using theater to teach clinical empathy: a pilot study. Journal of general internal medicine. 2007;22(8):1114-8.

978. Hattink B, Meiland F, van der Roest H, Kevern P, Abiuso F, Bengtsson J, et al. Web-Based STAR E-Learning Course Increases Empathy and Understanding in Dementia Caregivers: Results from a Randomized Controlled Trial in the Netherlands and the United Kingdom. Journal of medical internet research. 2015;17(10):e241.

979. Riess H, Kelley JM, Bailey RW, Dunn EJ, Phillips M. Empathy training for resident physicians: a randomized controlled trial of a neuroscience-informed curriculum. Journal of general internal medicine. 2012;27(10):1280-6.

980. Lor KB, Truong JT, Ip EJ, Barnett MJ. A randomized prospective study on outcomes of an empathy intervention among second-year student pharmacists. American journal of pharmaceutical education. 2015;79(2):18.

981. Sinsky C, Colligan L, Li L, Prgomet M, Reynolds S, Goeders L, et al. Allocation of Physician Time in Ambulatory Practice: A Time and Motion Study in 4 Specialties. Annals of internal medicine. 2016;165(11):753-60.

982. Gable SL, Reis HT, Impett EA, Asher ER. What do you do when things go right? The intrapersonal and interpersonal benefits of sharing positive events. Journal of personality and social psychology. 2004;87(2):228-45.

983. Reis HT, Smith SM, Carmichael CL, Caprariello PA, Tsai FF, Rodrigues A, et al. Are you happy for me? How sharing positive events with others provides personal and interpersonal benefits. Journal of personality and social psychology. 2010;99(2):311-29.

984. Demir M, Dogan A, Procsal AD. I am so happy 'cause my friend is happy for me: capitalization, friendship, and happiness among U.S. and Turkish college students. The Journal of social psychology. 2013;153(2):250-5.

985. Gable SL, Gonzaga GC, Strachman A. Will you be there for me when things go right? Supportive responses to positive event disclosures. Journal of personality and social psychology. 2006;91(5):904-17.

986. Decety J, Yang CY, Cheng Y. Physicians down-regulate their pain empathy response: an event-related brain potential study. NeuroImage. 2010;50(4):1676-82.

987. Konrath SH, O'Brien EH, Hsing C. Changes in dispositional empathy in American college students over time: a meta-analysis. Personality and social psychology review : an official journal of the Society for Personality and Social Psychology, Inc. 2011;15(2):180-98.

988. Elkins C, Plante KP, Germain LJ, Morley CP. Burnout and Depression in MS1 and MS3 Years: A Comparison of Cohorts at One Medical School. Family medicine. 2017;49(6):456-9.

989. Dyrbye LN, Harper W, Durning SJ, Moutier C, Thomas MR, Massie FS, Jr., et al. Patterns of distress in US medical students. Medical teacher. 2011;33(10):834-9.

990. Brazeau CM, Schroeder R, Rovi S, Boyd L. Relationships between medical student burnout, empathy, and professionalism climate. Academic medicine : journal of the Association of American Medical Colleges. 2010;85(10 Suppl):S33-6.

991. Thomas MR, Dyrbye LN, Huntington JL, Lawson KL, Novotny PJ, Sloan JA, et al. How do distress and well-being relate to medical student empathy? A multicenter study. Journal of general internal medicine. 2007;22(2):177-83.

992. O'Mahony S, Ziadni M, Hoerger M, Levine S, Baron A, Gerhart J. Compassion Fatigue Among Palliative Care Clinicians. The American journal of hospice & palliative care. 2017:1049909117701695.

993. Yu H, Jiang A, Shen J. Prevalence and predictors of compassion fatigue, burnout and compassion satisfaction among oncology nurses: A cross-sectional survey. International journal of nursing studies. 2016;57:28-38.
994. Beaumont E, Durkin M, Hollins Martin CJ, Carson J. Compassion for others, self-compassion, quality of life and mental well-being measures and their association with compassion fatigue and burnout in student midwives: A quantitative survey. Midwifery. 2016;34:239-44.
995. Kelly L, Runge J, Spencer C. Predictors of Compassion Fatigue and Compassion Satisfaction in Acute Care Nurses. Journal of nursing scholarship : an official publication of Sigma Theta Tau International Honor Society of Nursing. 2015;47(6):522-8.
996. Hunsaker S, Chen HC, Maughan D, Heaston S. Factors that influence the development of compassion fatigue, burnout, and compassion satisfaction in emergency department nurses. Journal of nursing scholarship : an official publication of Sigma Theta Tau International Honor Society of Nursing. 2015;47(2):186-94.
997. Hinderer KA, VonRueden KT, Friedmann E, McQuillan KA, Gilmore R, Kramer B, et al. Burnout, compassion fatigue, compassion satisfaction, and secondary traumatic stress in trauma nurses. Journal of trauma nursing : the official journal of the Society of Trauma Nurses. 2014;21(4):160-9.
998. Zeidner M, Hadar D, Matthews G, Roberts RD. Personal factors related to compassion fatigue in health professionals. Anxiety, stress, and coping. 2013;26(6):595-609.
999. Sinclair S, Raffin-Bouchal S, Venturato L, Mijovic-Kondejewski J, Smith-MacDonald L. Compassion fatigue: A meta-narrative review of the healthcare literature. International journal of nursing studies. 2017;69:9-24.
1000. Batson CDE, S.; Salvarani, H. Perspective taking: imagining how another feels versus imagining how you would feel. Pers Soc Psychol Bull. 1997;23:751-8.
1001. Higgs S, Donohoe JE. Focusing on food during lunch enhances lunch memory and decreases later snack intake. Appetite. 2011;57(1):202-6.
1002. Higgs S, Jones A. Prolonged chewing at lunch decreases later snack intake. Appetite. 2013;62:91-5.
1003. Higgs S, Woodward M. Television watching during lunch increases afternoon snack intake of young women. Appetite. 2009;52(1):39-43.
1004. Robinson E, Aveyard P, Daley A, Jolly K, Lewis A, Lycett D, et al. Eating attentively: a systematic review and meta-analysis of the effect of food intake memory and awareness on eating. The American journal of clinical nutrition. 2013;97(4):728-42.
1005. Robinson E, Kersbergen I, Higgs S. Eating 'attentively' reduces later energy consumption in overweight and obese females. The British journal of nutrition. 2014;112(4):657-61.
1006. Diaz KM, Howard VJ, Hutto B, Colabianchi N, Vena JE, Safford MM, et al. Patterns of Sedentary Behavior and Mortality in U.S. Middle-Aged and Older Adults: A National Cohort Study. Annals of internal medicine. 2017.
1007. Veerman JL, Healy GN, Cobiac LJ, Vos T, Winkler EA, Owen N, et al. Television viewing time and reduced life expectancy: a life table analysis. British journal of sports medicine. 2012;46(13):927-30.
1008. Benveniste H, Lee H, Volkow ND. The Glymphatic Pathway. The Neuroscientist : a review journal bringing neurobiology, neurology and psychiatry. 2017:1073858417691030.
1009. Neff KD. The Role of Self-Compassion in Development: A Healthier Way to Relate to Oneself. Human development. 2009;52(4):211-4.
1010. Neff KD, Vonk R. Self-compassion versus global self-esteem: two different ways of relating to oneself. Journal of personality. 2009;77(1):23-50.
1011. Baumeister RF, Campbell JD, Krueger JI, Vohs KD. Does High Self-Esteem Cause Better Performance, Interpersonal Success, Happiness, or Healthier Lifestyles? Psychological science in the public interest : a journal of the American Psychological Society. 2003;4(1):1-44.
1012. Neff KD, Germer CK. A pilot study and randomized controlled trial of the mindful self-compassion program. Journal of clinical psychology. 2013;69(1):28-44.

1013. Diedrich A, Hofmann SG, Cuijpers P, Berking M. Self-compassion enhances the efficacy of explicit cognitive reappraisal as an emotion regulation strategy in individuals with major depressive disorder. Behaviour research and therapy. 2016;82:1-10.

1014. Smeets E, Neff K, Alberts H, Peters M. Meeting suffering with kindness: effects of a brief self-compassion intervention for female college students. Journal of clinical psychology. 2014;70(9):794-807.

1015. MacBeth A, Gumley A. Exploring compassion: a meta-analysis of the association between self-compassion and psychopathology. Clinical psychology review. 2012;32(6):545-52.

1016. Kelly AC, Carter JC. Self-compassion training for binge eating disorder: a pilot randomized controlled trial. Psychology and psychotherapy. 2015;88(3):285-303.

1017. Toole AM, Craighead LW. Brief self-compassion meditation training for body image distress in young adult women. Body image. 2016;19:104-12.

1018. Kemppainen J, Johnson MO, Phillips JC, Sullivan KM, Corless IB, Reid P, et al. A multinational study of self-compassion and human immunodeficiency virus-related anxiety. International nursing review. 2013;60(4):477-86.

1019. Germer CK, Neff KD. Self-compassion in clinical practice. Journal of clinical psychology. 2013;69(8):856-67.

1020. Gilbert P, McEwan K, Catarino F, Baiao R, Palmeira L. Fears of happiness and compassion in relationship with depression, alexithymia, and attachment security in a depressed sample. The British journal of clinical psychology. 2014;53(2):228-44.

1021. Kelly AC, Vimalakanthan K, Carter JC. Understanding the roles of self-esteem, self-compassion, and fear of self-compassion in eating disorder pathology: an examination of female students and eating disorder patients. Eating behaviors. 2014;15(3):388-91.

1022. Castelvecchi D. Universe has ten times more galaxies than researchers thoughtOctober 2016 July 6th, 2017. Available from: http://www.nature.com/news/universe-has-ten-times-more-galaxies-than-researchers-thought-1.20809.

1023. Coulehan J. On humility. Annals of internal medicine. 2010;153(3):200-1.

1024. Weidman AC, Cheng JT, Tracy JL. The Psychological Structure of Humility. Journal of personality and social psychology. 2016.

1025. Collins J. Level 5 leadership. The triumph of humility and fierce resolve. Harvard business review. 2001;79(1):66-76, 175.

1026. Hofmann PB, Yates GR. The Power of Humility. Trustee : the journal for hospital governing boards. 2015;68(9):27-8.

1027. Chiu CC, Owens BP, Tesluk PE. Initiating and utilizing shared leadership in teams: The role of leader humility, team proactive personality, and team performance capability. The Journal of applied psychology. 2016;101(12):1705-20.

1028. Owens BP, Wallace AS, Waldman DA. Leader narcissism and follower outcomes: The counterbalancing effect of leader humility. The Journal of applied psychology. 2015;100(4):1203-13.

1029. Chirumbolo A. The Impact of Job Insecurity on Counterproductive Work Behaviors: The Moderating Role of Honesty-Humility Personality Trait. The Journal of psychology. 2015;149(6):554-69.

1030. Krause N. Assessing the relationships among race, religion, humility, and self-forgiveness: A longitudinal investigation. Advances in life course research. 2015;24:66-74.

1031. Kesebir P. A quiet ego quiets death anxiety: humility as an existential anxiety buffer. Journal of personality and social psychology. 2014;106(4):610-23.

1032. Krause N. Exploring the relationships among humility, negative interaction in the church, and depressed affect. Aging & mental health. 2014;18(8):970-9.

1033. Ruberton PM, Huynh HP, Miller TA, Kruse E, Chancellor J, Lyubomirsky S. The relationship between physician humility, physician-patient communication, and patient health. Patient education and counseling. 2016;99(7):1138-45.

1034. Krause N. Religious Involvement, Humility, and Self-Rated Health. Social indicators research. 2010;98(1):23-39.

1035. Gruppen LD. Humility and respect: core values in medical education. Medical education. 2014;48(1):53-8.

1036. Hook JN, Farrell JE, Davis DE, DeBlaere C, Van Tongeren DR, Utsey SO. Cultural humility and racial microaggressions in counseling. Journal of counseling psychology. 2016;63(3):269-77.
1037. Foronda C, Baptiste DL, Reinholdt MM, Ousman K. Cultural Humility: A Concept Analysis. Journal of transcultural nursing : official journal of the Transcultural Nursing Society. 2016;27(3):210-7.
1038. Yeager KA, Bauer-Wu S. Cultural humility: essential foundation for clinical researchers. Applied nursing research : ANR. 2013;26(4):251-6.
1039. Hook JN, Boan D, Davis DE, Aten JD, Ruiz JM, Maryon T. Cultural Humility and Hospital Safety Culture. Journal of clinical psychology in medical settings. 2016;23(4):402-9.
1040. de Vries K. Humility and its practice in nursing. Nursing ethics. 2004;11(6):577-86.
1041. APA. Discrimination Linked to Increased Stress, Poorer Health, American Psychological Association Survey Finds2016 July 7th, 2017. Available from: http://www.apa.org/news/press/releases/2016/03/impact-of-discrimination.aspx.
1042. McCullough ME, Fincham FD, Tsang JA. Forgiveness, forbearance, and time: the temporal unfolding of transgression-related interpersonal motivations. Journal of personality and social psychology. 2003;84(3):540-57.
1043. McCullough ME, Luna LR, Berry JW, Tabak BA, Bono G. On the form and function of forgiving: modeling the time-forgiveness relationship and testing the valuable relationships hypothesis. Emotion (Washington, DC). 2010;10(3):358-76.
1044. Burnette JL, McCullough ME, Van Tongeren DR, Davis DE. Forgiveness results from integrating information about relationship value and exploitation risk. Personality & social psychology bulletin. 2012;38(3):345-56.
1045. Akhtar S, Barlow J. Forgiveness Therapy for the Promotion of Mental Well-Being: A Systematic Review and Meta-Analysis. Trauma, violence & abuse. 2016.
1046. Barcaccia B, Howard Schneider B, Pallini S, Baiocco R. Bullying and the detrimental role of un-forgiveness in adolescents' wellbeing. Psicothema. 2017;29(2):217-22.
1047. Toussaint LL, Owen AD, Cheadle A. Forgive to live: forgiveness, health, and longevity. Journal of behavioral medicine. 2012;35(4):375-86.
1048. Elliott BA. Forgiveness therapy: a clinical intervention for chronic disease. Journal of religion and health. 2011;50(2):240-7.
1049. Webb JR, Hirsch JK, Visser PL, Brewer KG. Forgiveness and health: assessing the mediating effect of health behavior, social support, and interpersonal functioning. The Journal of psychology. 2013;147(5):391-414.
1050. Maguire EA, Gadian DG, Johnsrude IS, Good CD, Ashburner J, Frackowiak RS, et al. Navigation-related structural change in the hippocampi of taxi drivers. Proceedings of the National Academy of Sciences of the United States of America. 2000;97(8):4398-403.
1051. Maguire EA, Woollett K, Spiers HJ. London taxi drivers and bus drivers: a structural MRI and neuropsychological analysis. Hippocampus. 2006;16(12):1091-101.
1052. McKenzie-Mohr D. Fostering sustainable behavior through community-based social marketing. The American psychologist. 2000;55(5):531-7.
1053. Lee NRK, P. Social Marketing: Changing Behaviors for the Good (5th ed.). California: Sage Publications; 2008. 584 p.
1054. McKenzie-Mohr D. Fostering sustainable behavior: An introduction to community based social marketing Canada: New Society Publishers; 2011. 192 p.
1055. Lehman PKG, E. S. Behavior analysis and environmental protection: Accomplishments and potential for more. Behavior and Social Issues,. 2004;13(1):13-32.
1056. Toussaint L, Kamble S, Marschall JC, Duggi DB. The effects of brief prayer on the experience of forgiveness: An American and Indian comparison. International journal of psychology : Journal international de psychologie. 2016;51(4):288-95.
1057. Jiang F, Yue X, Lu S, Yu G. Can you forgive? It depends on how happy you are. Scandinavian journal of psychology. 2015;56(2):182-8.

1058. Lyubomirsky S, King L, Diener E. The benefits of frequent positive affect: does happiness lead to success? Psychological bulletin. 2005;131(6):803-55.

1059. Lawrence EM, Rogers RG, Wadsworth T. Happiness and longevity in the United States. Social science & medicine (1982). 2015;145:115-9.

1060. Tabak BA, McCullough ME, Luna LR, Bono G, Berry JW. Conciliatory gestures facilitate forgiveness and feelings of friendship by making transgressors appear more agreeable. Journal of personality. 2012;80(2):503-36.

1061. McCullough ME, Bono G, Root LM. Rumination, emotion, and forgiveness: three longitudinal studies. Journal of personality and social psychology. 2007;92(3):490-505.

1061a. Trampe D, Quoidbach J, Taquet M. Emotions in Everyday Life. PLoS One. 2015 Dec 23;10(12):e0145450. doi: 10.1371/journal.pone.0145450. eCollection 2015. PubMed PMID: 26698124; PubMed Central PMCID: PMC4689475.

1061b. Heiy JE, Cheavens JS. Back to basics: a naturalistic assessment of the experience and regulation of emotion. Emotion. 2014 Oct;14(5):878-91. doi: 10.1037/a0037231. Epub 2014 Jul 7. PubMed PMID: 24999913.

1062. Howard J. Americans devote more than 10 hours a day to screen time, and growing 2016 July 7th, 2017. Available from: http://www.cnn.com/2016/06/30/health/americans-screen-time-nielsen/.

1063. Haile T. What You Think You Know About the Web Is Wrong 2014 July 7th, 2017. Available from: http://time.com/12933/what-you-think-you-know-about-the-web-is-wrong/.

1064. Pontzer H, Durazo-Arvizu R, Dugas LR, Plange-Rhule J, Bovet P, Forrester TE, et al. Constrained Total Energy Expenditure and Metabolic Adaptation to Physical Activity in Adult Humans. Current biology : CB. 2016;26(3):410-7.

1065. Mansoubi M, Pearson N, Biddle SJ, Clemes SA. Using Sit-to-Stand Workstations in Offices: Is There a Compensation Effect? Medicine and science in sports and exercise. 2016;48(4):720-5.

1065a. Marchetti I, Koster EHW, Klinger E, Alloy LB. Spontaneous thoughts and vulnerability to mood disorders. The dark side of the wandering mind. Clin Psychol Sci. 2016 Sep;4(5):835-857. doi: 10.1177/2167702615622383. Epub 2016 Feb 8.

1065b. Seli P, Carriere JS, Smilek D. Not all mind wandering is created equal. dissociating deliberate from spontaneous mind wandering. Psychol Res. 2015 Sep;79(5):750-8. doi: 10.1007/s00426-014-0617-x. Epub 2014 Oct 5.

1066. Emmons RA, McCullough ME. Counting blessings versus burdens: an experimental investigation of gratitude and subjective well-being in daily life. Journal of personality and social psychology. 2003;84(2):377-89.

1067. McCullough ME, Emmons RA, Tsang JA. The grateful disposition: a conceptual and empirical topography. Journal of personality and social psychology. 2002;82(1):112-27.

1068. Caputo A. The Relationship Between Gratitude and Loneliness: The Potential Benefits of Gratitude for Promoting Social Bonds. Europe's journal of psychology. 2015;11(2):323-34.

1069. Hofmann W, Baumeister RF, Forster G, Vohs KD. Everyday temptations: an experience sampling study of desire, conflict, and self-control. Journal of personality and social psychology. 2012;102(6):1318-35.

1070. Gordon AM, Impett EA, Kogan A, Oveis C, Keltner D. To have and to hold: gratitude promotes relationship maintenance in intimate bonds. Journal of personality and social psychology. 2012;103(2):257-74.

1071. Williams LA, Bartlett MY. Warm thanks: gratitude expression facilitates social affiliation in new relationships via perceived warmth. Emotion (Washington, DC). 2015;15(1):1-5.

1072. Campos B, Graesch AP, Repetti R, Bradbury T, Ochs E. Opportunity for interaction? A naturalistic observation study of dual-earner families after work and school. Journal of family psychology : JFP : journal of the Division of Family Psychology of the American Psychological Association (Division 43). 2009;23(6):798-807.

1073. Bechara A. The role of emotion in decision-making: evidence from neurological patients with orbitofrontal damage. Brain and cognition. 2004;55(1):30-40.

1074. Dekhtyar M, Beasley CR, Jason LA, Ferrari JR. Hope as a Predictor of Reincarceration Among Mutual-Help Recovery Residents. Journal of offender rehabilitation. 2012;51(7):474-83.

1075. Richardson RL. Where there is hope, there is life: toward a biology of hope. Journal of pastoral care. 2000;54(1):75-83.

1076. Warwick A. Recovery following injury hinges upon expectation and hope. Journal of trauma nursing : the official journal of the Society of Trauma Nurses. 2012;19(4):251-4.

1077. Kortte KB, Stevenson JE, Hosey MM, Castillo R, Wegener ST. Hope predicts positive functional role outcomes in acute rehabilitation populations. Rehabilitation psychology. 2012;57(3):248-55.

1078. Herth K. Enhancing hope in people with a first recurrence of cancer. Journal of advanced nursing. 2000;32(6):1431-41.

1079. Rasmussen HN, Scheier MF, Greenhouse JB. Optimism and physical health: a meta-analytic review. Annals of behavioral medicine : a publication of the Society of Behavioral Medicine. 2009;37(3):239-56.

1080. Schiavon CC, Marchetti E, Gurgel LG, Busnello FM, Reppold CT. Optimism and Hope in Chronic Disease: A Systematic Review. Frontiers in psychology. 2016;7:2022.

1081. Hockley J. The concept of hope and the will to live. Palliative medicine. 1993;7(3):181-6.

1082. Carver CS, Scheier MF. Dispositional optimism. Trends in cognitive sciences. 2014;18(6):293-9.

1083. Nes LS, Segerstrom SC. Dispositional optimism and coping: a meta-analytic review. Personality and social psychology review : an official journal of the Society for Personality and Social Psychology, Inc. 2006;10(3):235-51.

1084. Brummett BH, Helms MJ, Dahlstrom WG, Siegler IC. Prediction of all-cause mortality by the Minnesota Multiphasic Personality Inventory Optimism-Pessimism Scale scores: study of a college sample during a 40-year follow-up period. Mayo Clinic proceedings. 2006;81(12):1541-4.

1085. Giltay EJ, Geleijnse JM, Zitman FG, Hoekstra T, Schouten EG. Dispositional optimism and all-cause and cardiovascular mortality in a prospective cohort of elderly dutch men and women. Archives of general psychiatry. 2004;61(11):1126-35.

1086. Kim ES, Hagan KA, Grodstein F, DeMeo DL, De Vivo I, Kubzansky LD. Optimism and Cause-Specific Mortality: A Prospective Cohort Study. American journal of epidemiology. 2017;185(1):21-9.

1087. Hecht D. The neural basis of optimism and pessimism. Experimental neurobiology. 2013;22(3):173-99.

1088. Dolcos S, Hu Y, Iordan AD, Moore M, Dolcos F. Optimism and the brain: trait optimism mediates the protective role of the orbitofrontal cortex gray matter volume against anxiety. Social cognitive and affective neuroscience. 2016;11(2):263-71.

1089. Yang J, Wei D, Wang K, Qiu J. Gray matter correlates of dispositional optimism: a voxel-based morphometry study. Neuroscience letters. 2013;553:201-5.

1090. De Pascalis V, Cozzuto G, Caprara GV, Alessandri G. Relations among EEG-alpha asymmetry, BIS/BAS, and dispositional optimism. Biological psychology. 2013;94(1):198-209.

1091. Bortolotti L, Antrobus M. Costs and benefits of realism and optimism. Current opinion in psychiatry. 2015;28(2):194-8.

1092. Coulehan J. Deep hope: a song without words. Theoretical medicine and bioethics. 2011;32(3):143-60.

1093. Ebright PR, Lyon B. Understanding hope and factors that enhance hope in women with breast cancer. Oncology nursing forum. 2002;29(3):561-8.

1094. Nekolaichuk CL, Jevne RF, Maguire TO. Structuring the meaning of hope in health and illness. Social science & medicine (1982). 1999;48(5):591-605.

1095. Stevens EB, Buchannan B, Ferrari JR, Jason LA, Ram D. An Investigation of Hope and Context. Journal of community psychology. 2014;42(8):937-46.

1096. Thrash TM, Elliot AJ. Inspiration as a psychological construct. Journal of personality and social psychology. 2003;84(4):871-89.

1097. Golkar A, Johansson E, Kasahara M, Osika W, Perski A, Savic I. The influence of work-related chronic stress on the regulation of emotion and on functional connectivity in the brain. PloS one. 2014;9(9):e104550.

1098. Thrash TM, Elliot AJ, Maruskin LA, Cassidy SE. Inspiration and the promotion of well-being: tests of causality and mediation. Journal of personality and social psychology. 2010;98(3):488-506.

1099. Thrash TM, Maruskin LA, Moldovan EG, Oleynick VC, Belzak WC. Writer-Reader Contagion of Inspiration and Related States: Conditional Process Analyses Within a Cross-Classified Writer x Reader Framework. Journal of personality and social psychology. 2016.

1100. Thrash TM, Maruskin LA, Cassidy SE, Fryer JW, Ryan RM. Mediating between the muse and the masses: inspiration and the actualization of creative ideas. Journal of personality and social psychology. 2010;98(3):469-87.

1101. Oleynick VC, Thrash TM, LeFew MC, Moldovan EG, Kieffaber PD. The scientific study of inspiration in the creative process: challenges and opportunities. Frontiers in human neuroscience. 2014;8:436.

1102. Thrash TM, Elliot AJ. Inspiration: core characteristics, component processes, antecedents, and function. Journal of personality and social psychology. 2004;87(6):957-73.

1103. Woodard CP, C.L.S. . The Construct of Courage: Categorization and Measurement. Consulting Psychology Journal: Practice and Research. 2007;59(2):135-47.

1104. Muris P. Fear and Courage in Children: Two Sides of the Same Coin? Journal of child and family studies. 2009;18(4):486-90.

1105. Haney C, Zimbardo PG. Persistent dispositionalism in interactionist clothing: fundamental attribution error in explaining prison abuse. Personality & social psychology bulletin. 2009;35(6):807-14; author reply 15-8.

1106. Haney CB, W. C.; Zimbardo, P. G. Study of prisoners and guards in a simulated prison Naval Research Reviews, Washington, DC: Office of Naval Research. 1973;9:1-17.

1107. Milgram S. BEHAVIORAL STUDY OF OBEDIENCE. Journal of abnormal psychology. 1963;67:371-8.

1108. Begue L, Beauvois JL, Courbet D, Oberle D, Lepage J, Duke AA. Personality predicts obedience in a Milgram paradigm. Journal of personality. 2015;83(3):299-306.

1109. Nili U, Goldberg H, Weizman A, Dudai Y. Fear thou not: activity of frontal and temporal circuits in moments of real-life courage. Neuron. 2010;66(6):949-62.

1110. Adolphs R, Tranel D, Damasio H, Damasio A. Impaired recognition of emotion in facial expressions following bilateral damage to the human amygdala. Nature. 1994;372(6507):669-72.

1111. Adolphs R, Gosselin F, Buchanan TW, Tranel D, Schyns P, Damasio AR. A mechanism for impaired fear recognition after amygdala damage. Nature. 2005;433(7021):68-72.

1112. Keczer Z, File B, Orosz G, Zimbardo PG. Social Representations of Hero and Everyday Hero: A Network Study from Representative Samples. PloS one. 2016;11(8):e0159354.

1113. Ge F, Huang T, Yuan S, Zhou Y, Gong W. Gender issues in solid organ donation and transplantation. Annals of transplantation. 2013;18:508-14.

1114. Thiel GT, Nolte C, Tsinalis D. Gender imbalance in living kidney donation in Switzerland. Transplantation proceedings. 2005;37(2):592-4.

1115. Statistics BoL. Volunteering in the United States, 20152016 July 6th, 2017. Available from: https://www.bls.gov/news.release/volun.nr0.htm.

1116. Biswas-Diener R. The Courage Quotient: How Science Can Make You Braver Jossey-Bass; 2012. 208 p.

1117. Gardner HE. Multiple Intelligences: New Horizons in Theory and Practice: Basic Books; 2006. 320 p.

1118. Danziger S, Levav J, Avnaim-Pesso L. Extraneous factors in judicial decisions. Proceedings of the National Academy of Sciences of the United States of America. 2011;108(17):6889-92.

1119. Lerner JS, Keltner D. Fear, anger, and risk. Journal of personality and social psychology. 2001;81(1):146-59.

1120. Southwick SM, Bonanno GA, Masten AS, Panter-Brick C, Yehuda R. Resilience definitions, theory, and challenges: interdisciplinary perspectives. Eur J Psychotraumatology. 2014;October 1: 5

1121. Chmitorz A, Kunzler A, Helmreich I, Tuscher O, Kalisch R, Kubiak T, Wessa M, Lieb K. Intervention studies to foster resilience – A systematic review and proposal for a resilience framework in future intervention studies. Clinical Psychology Review. 2017; November 10.

1122. Ungar M, Ghazinour M, Richter J. Annual Research Review: What is resilience within the social ecology of human development? J Child Psychology Psychiatry. 2013; 54(4): 348-66

1123. Rutter M. Psychosocial resilience and protective mechanisms. Am J Orthopsychiatry. 1987;57(3):316-31.

1124. Masten AS, Obradovic J. Competence and resilience in development. Annals of the New York Academy of Sciences. 2006;1094:13-27.

1125. Connor KM, Davidson JR. Development of a new resilience scale: the Connor-Davidson Resilience Scale (CD-RISC). Depression and anxiety. 2003;18(2):76-82.

1126. Pietrzak RH, Goldstein MB, Malley JC, Rivers AJ, Johnson DC, Southwick SM. Risk and protective factors associated with suicidal ideation in veterans of Operations Enduring Freedom and Iraqi Freedom. Journal of affective disorders. 2010;123(1-3):102-7.

1127. Masten AS. Ordinary magic. Resilience processes in development. The American psychologist. 2001;56(3):227-38.

1128. Maguen S, Turcotte DM, Peterson AL, Dremsa TL, Garb HN, McNally RJ, et al. Description of risk and resilience factors among military medical personnel before deployment to Iraq. Military medicine. 2008;173(1):1-9.

1129. Bonanno GA, Galea S, Bucciarelli A, Vlahov D. Psychological resilience after disaster: New York City in the aftermath of the September 11th terrorist attack. Psychological science. 2006;17(3):181-6.

1130. Bouchard TJ, Jr., Lykken DT, McGue M, Segal NL, Tellegen A. Sources of human psychological differences: the Minnesota Study of Twins Reared Apart. Science (New York, NY). 1990;250(4978):223-8.

1131. Bouchard TJ, Jr. Genes, environment, and personality. Science (New York, NY). 1994;264(5166):1700-1.

1132. Cagnie B, Coppieters I, Denecker S, Six J, Danneels L, Meeus M. Central sensitization in fibromyalgia? A systematic review on structural and functional brain MRI. Seminars in arthritis and rheumatism. 2014;44(1):68-75.

1133. McEwen BS. Neurobiological and Systemic Effects of Chronic Stress. Chronic stress (Thousand Oaks, Calif). 2017;1.

1134. McEwen BS, Nasca C, Gray JD. Stress Effects on Neuronal Structure: Hippocampus, Amygdala, and Prefrontal Cortex. Neuropsychopharmacology : official publication of the American College of Neuropsychopharmacology. 2016;41(1):3-23.

1134b. Neel, J. You, Me and Them: Experiencing Discrimination in America. NPR. October 28th, 2017.

1135. Manning LK, Miles A. Examining the Effects of Religious Attendance on Resilience for Older Adults. Journal of religion and health. 2017.

1136. Matzka M, Mayer H, Kock-Hodi S, Moses-Passini C, Dubey C, Jahn P, et al. Relationship between Resilience, Psychological Distress and Physical Activity in Cancer Patients: A Cross-Sectional Observation Study. PloS one. 2016;11(4):e0154496.

1137. Eicher M, Matzka M, Dubey C, White K. Resilience in adult cancer care: an integrative literature review. Oncology nursing forum. 2015;42(1):E3-16.

1138. Gotay CC, Isaacs P, Pagano I. Quality of life in patients who survive a dire prognosis compared to control cancer survivors. Psycho-oncology. 2004;13(12):882-92.

1139. Groenvold M, Petersen MA, Idler E, Bjorner JB, Fayers PM, Mouridsen HT. Psychological distress and fatigue predicted recurrence and survival in primary breast cancer patients. Breast cancer research and treatment. 2007;105(2):209-19.

1140. Strauss B, Brix C, Fischer S, Leppert K, Fuller J, Roehrig B, et al. The influence of resilience on fatigue in cancer patients undergoing radiation therapy (RT). Journal of cancer research and clinical oncology. 2007;133(8):511-8.

1141. Schumacher A, Sauerland C, Silling G, Berdel WE, Stelljes M. Resilience in patients after allogeneic stem cell transplantation. Supportive care in cancer : official journal of the Multinational Association of Supportive Care in Cancer. 2014;22(2):487-93.

1142. Rosenberg AR, Syrjala KL, Martin PJ, Flowers ME, Carpenter PA, Salit RB, et al. Resilience, health, and quality of life among long-term survivors of hematopoietic cell transplantation. Cancer. 2015;121(23):4250-7.

1143. Lu W, Wang Z, You X. Physiological Responses to Repeated Stress in Individuals with High and Low Trait Resilience. Biological psychology. 2016.

1144. Hopkins KD, Shepherd CC, Taylor CL, Zubrick SR. Relationships between Psychosocial Resilience and Physical Health Status of Western Australian Urban Aboriginal Youth. PloS one. 2015;10(12):e0145382.

1145. Nawaz A, Malik JA, Batool A. Relationship between resilience and quality of life in diabetics. Journal of the College of Physicians and Surgeons--Pakistan : JCPSP. 2014;24(9):670-5.

1146. Pesantes MA, Lazo-Porras M, Abu Dabrh AM, Avila-Ramirez JR, Caycho M, Villamonte GY, et al. Resilience in Vulnerable Populations With Type 2 Diabetes Mellitus and Hypertension: A Systematic Review and Meta-analysis. The Canadian journal of cardiology. 2015;31(9):1180-8.

1147. Hodder RK, Daly J, Freund M, Bowman J, Hazell T, Wiggers J. A school-based resilience intervention to decrease tobacco, alcohol and marijuana use in high school students. BMC public health. 2011;11:722.

1148. Alschuler KN, Kratz AL, Ehde DM. Resilience and vulnerability in individuals with chronic pain and physical disability. Rehabilitation psychology. 2016;61(1):7-18.

1149. Kennedy B, Fang F, Valdimarsdottir U, Udumyan R, Montgomery S, Fall K. Stress resilience and cancer risk: a nationwide cohort study. Journal of epidemiology and community health. 2017;71(10):947-53.

1149b. Kermott C, Sood A, et al. Correlation of resilience with physical, emotional, social and occupational health among corporate executives. Manuscripts in preparation.

1150. Losoi H, Waljas M, Turunen S, Brander A, Helminen M, Luoto TM, et al. Resilience is associated with fatigue after mild traumatic brain injury. The Journal of head trauma rehabilitation. 2015;30(3):E24-32.

1151. Tempski P, Santos IS, Mayer FB, Enns SC, Perotta B, Paro HB, et al. Relationship among Medical Student Resilience, Educational Environment and Quality of Life. PloS one. 2015;10(6):e0131535.

1152. Innes SI. The relationship between levels of resilience and coping styles in chiropractic students and perceived levels of stress and well-being. The Journal of chiropractic education. 2016.

1153. Lavoie J, Pereira LC, Talwar V. Children's Physical Resilience Outcomes: Meta-Analysis of Vulnerability and Protective Factors. Journal of pediatric nursing. 2016.

1154. Green KT, Calhoun PS, Dennis MF, Beckham JC. Exploration of the resilience construct in posttraumatic stress disorder severity and functional correlates in military combat veterans who have served since September 11, 2001. The Journal of clinical psychiatry. 2010;71(7):823-30.

1155. Moore RC, Eyler LT, Mausbach BT, Zlatar ZZ, Thompson WK, Peavy G, et al. Complex interplay between health and successful aging: role of perceived stress, resilience, and social support. The American journal of geriatric psychiatry : official journal of the American Association for Geriatric Psychiatry. 2015;23(6):622-32.

1156. Duan-Porter W, Cohen HJ, Demark-Wahnefried W, Sloane R, Pendergast JF, Snyder DC, et al. Physical resilience of older cancer survivors: An emerging concept. Journal of geriatric oncology. 2016.

1157. Manning LK, Carr DC, Kail BL. Do Higher Levels of Resilience Buffer the Deleterious Impact of Chronic Illness on Disability in Later Life? The Gerontologist. 2016;56(3):514-24.

1158. Faye C, McGowan JC, Denny CA, David DJ. Neurobiological mechanisms of stress resilience and implications for the aged population. Current neuropharmacology. 2017.

1159. McNair OS, Gipson JA, Denson D, Thompson DV, Sutton MY, Hickson DA. The Associations of Resilience and HIV Risk Behaviors Among Black Gay, Bisexual, Other Men Who Have Sex with Men (MSM) in the Deep South: The MARI Study. AIDS and behavior. 2017.

1160. Min JA, Yoon S, Lee CU, Chae JH, Lee C, Song KY, et al. Psychological resilience contributes to low emotional distress in cancer patients. Supportive care in cancer : official journal of the Multinational Association of Supportive Care in Cancer. 2013;21(9):2469-76.

1161. Shin JI, Chae JH, Min JA, Lee CU, Hwang SI, Lee BS, et al. Resilience as a possible predictor for psychological distress in chronic spinal cord injured patients living in the community. Annals of rehabilitation medicine. 2012;36(6):815-20.

1162. Kim KR, Song YY, Park JY, Lee EH, Lee M, Lee SY, et al. The relationship between psychosocial functioning and resilience and negative symptoms in individuals at ultra-high risk for psychosis. The Australian and New Zealand journal of psychiatry. 2013;47(8):762-71.

1163. Cohen M, Baziliansky S, Beny A. The association of resilience and age in individuals with colorectal cancer: an exploratory cross-sectional study. Journal of geriatric oncology. 2014;5(1):33-9.

1164. Lim JW, Shon EJ, Paek M, Daly B. The dyadic effects of coping and resilience on psychological distress for cancer survivor couples. Supportive care in cancer : official journal of the Multinational Association of Supportive Care in Cancer. 2014;22(12):3209-17.

1165. Tian J, Hong JS. Assessment of the relationship between resilience and quality of life in patients with digestive cancer. World journal of gastroenterology. 2014;20(48):18439-44.

1166. Duan W, Guo P, Gan P. Relationships among Trait Resilience, Virtues, Post-traumatic Stress Disorder, and Post-traumatic Growth. PloS one. 2015;10(5):e0125707.

1167. Gouzman J, Cohen M, Ben-Zur H, Shacham-Shmueli E, Aderka D, Siegelmann-Danieli N, et al. Resilience and psychosocial adjustment in digestive system cancer. Journal of clinical psychology in medical settings. 2015;22(1):1-13.

1168. Simpson GK, Dall'Armi L, Roydhouse JK, Forstner D, Daher M, Simpson T, et al. Does Resilience Mediate Carer Distress After Head and Neck Cancer? Cancer nursing. 2015;38(6):E30-6.

1169. Wu WW, Tsai SY, Liang SY, Liu CY, Jou ST, Berry DL. The Mediating Role of Resilience on Quality of Life and Cancer Symptom Distress in Adolescent Patients With Cancer. Journal of pediatric oncology nursing : official journal of the Association of Pediatric Oncology Nurses. 2015;32(5):304-13.

1170. Cuhadar D, Tanriverdi D, Pehlivan M, Kurnaz G, Alkan S. Determination of the psychiatric symptoms and psychological resilience levels of hematopoietic stem cell transplant patients and their relatives. European journal of cancer care. 2016;25(1):112-21.

1171. Pakalniskiene V, Viliuniene R, Hilbig J. Patients' resilience and distress over time: Is resilience a prognostic indicator of treatment? Comprehensive psychiatry. 2016;69:88-99.

1172. Tian X, Gao Q, Li G, Zou G, Liu C, Kong L, et al. Resilience is associated with low psychological distress in renal transplant recipients. General hospital psychiatry. 2016;39:86-90.

1173. Bonanno GA. Loss, trauma, and human resilience: have we underestimated the human capacity to thrive after extremely aversive events? The American psychologist. 2004;59(1):20-8.

1174. Bonanno GA, Diminich ED. Annual Research Review: Positive adjustment to adversity--trajectories of minimal-impact resilience and emergent resilience. Journal of child psychology and psychiatry, and allied disciplines. 2013;54(4):378-401.

1175. Bonanno GA, Westphal M, Mancini AD. Resilience to loss and potential trauma. Annual review of clinical psychology. 2011;7:511-35.

1176. Norris FH, Friedman MJ, Watson PJ, Byrne CM, Diaz E, Kaniasty K. 60,000 disaster victims speak: Part I. An empirical review of the empirical literature, 1981-2001. Psychiatry. 2002;65(3):207-39.

1177. McCanlies EC, Gu JK, Andrew ME, Burchfiel CM, Violanti JM. Resilience mediates the relationship between social support and post-traumatic stress symptoms in police officers. Journal of emergency management (Weston, Mass). 2017;15(2):107-16.

1178. Howell KH, Miller-Graff LE, Schaefer LM, Scrafford KE. Relational resilience as a potential mediator between adverse childhood experiences and prenatal depression. Journal of health psychology. 2017:1359105317723450.

1179. Rahimi B, Baetz M, Bowen R, Balbuena L. Resilience, stress, and coping among Canadian medical students. Canadian medical education journal. 2014;5(1):e5-e12.

1180. Campbell-Sills L, Cohan SL, Stein MB. Relationship of resilience to personality, coping, and psychiatric symptoms in young adults. Behaviour research and therapy. 2006;44(4):585-99.

1181. Arrogante O, Perez-Garcia AM, Aparicio-Zaldivar EG. [Psychological well-being in nursing: relationships with resilience and coping]. Enfermeria clinica. 2015;25(2):73-80.

1182. Shi M, Wang X, Bian Y, Wang L. The mediating role of resilience in the relationship between stress and life satisfaction among Chinese medical students: a cross-sectional study. BMC medical education. 2015;15:16.

1183. Li Y, Cao F, Cao D, Liu J. Nursing students' post-traumatic growth, emotional intelligence and psychological resilience. Journal of psychiatric and mental health nursing. 2015;22(5):326-32.

1184. Kemper KJ, Khirallah M. Acute Effects of Online Mind-Body Skills Training on Resilience, Mindfulness, and Empathy. Journal of evidence-based complementary & alternative medicine. 2015;20(4):247-53.

1185. Gloria CT, Steinhardt MA. Relationships Among Positive Emotions, Coping, Resilience and Mental Health. Stress and health : journal of the International Society for the Investigation of Stress. 2016;32(2):145-56.

1186. Bacchi S, Licinio J. Resilience and Psychological Distress in Psychology and Medical Students. Academic psychiatry : the journal of the American Association of Directors of Psychiatric Residency Training and the Association for Academic Psychiatry. 2016.

1187. Vieselmeyer J, Holguin J, Mezulis A. The Role of Resilience and Gratitude in Posttraumatic Stress and Growth Following a Campus Shooting. Psychological trauma : theory, research, practice and policy. 2016.

1188. Robertson HD, Elliott AM, Burton C, Iversen L, Murchie P, Porteous T, et al. Resilience of primary healthcare professionals: a systematic review. The British journal of general practice : the journal of the Royal College of General Practitioners. 2016;66(647):e423-33.

1189. Hartley MT. Examining the relationships between resilience, mental health, and academic persistence in undergraduate college students. Journal of American college health : J of ACH. 2011;59(7):596-604.

1190. Cora-Bramble D, Zhang K, Castillo-Page L. Minority faculty members' resilience and academic productivity: are they related? Academic medicine : journal of the Association of American Medical Colleges. 2010;85(9):1492-8.

1191. Pereira JA, Barkham M, Kellett S, Saxon D. The Role of Practitioner Resilience and Mindfulness in Effective Practice: A Practice-Based Feasibility Study. Administration and policy in mental health. 2016.

1192. Rees CS, Heritage B, Osseiran-Moisson R, Chamberlain D, Cusack L, Anderson J, et al. Can We Predict Burnout among Student Nurses? An Exploration of the ICWR-1 Model of Individual Psychological Resilience. Frontiers in psychology. 2016;7:1072.

1193. Rios-Risquez MI, Carrillo-Garcia C, Sabuco-Tebar EL, Garcia-Izquierdo M, Martinez-Roche ME. An exploratory study of the relationship between resilience, academic burnout and psychological health in nursing students. Contemporary nurse. 2016:1-22.

1194. Secades XG, Molinero O, Salguero A, Barquin RR, de la Vega R, Marquez S. Relationship Between Resilience and Coping Strategies in Competitive Sport. Perceptual and motor skills. 2016;122(1):336-49.

1195. Bowers C, Kreutzer C, Cannon-Bowers J, Lamb J. Team Resilience as a Second-Order Emergent State: A Theoretical Model and Research Directions. Frontiers in psychology. 2017;8:1360.

1196. Lee J, Blackmon BJ, Cochran DM, Kar B, Rehner TA, Gunnell MS. Community Resilience, Psychological Resilience, and Depressive Symptoms: An Examination of the Mississippi Gulf Coast 10 Years After Hurricane Katrina and 5 Years After the Deepwater Horizon Oil Spill. Disaster medicine and public health preparedness. 2017:1-8.

1197. Pietrzak RH, Cook JM. Psychological resilience in older U.S. veterans: results from the national health and resilience in veterans study. Depression and anxiety. 2013;30(5):432-43.

1198. Rosenberg AR, Wolfe J, Bradford MC, Shaffer ML, Yi-Frazier JP, Curtis JR, et al. Resilience and psychosocial outcomes in parents of children with cancer. Pediatric blood & cancer. 2014;61(3):552-7.

1199. Schaan VK, Vogele C. Resilience and rejection sensitivity mediate long-term outcomes of parental divorce. European child & adolescent psychiatry. 2016.

1200. Creating a mentally healthy workplace: Return on investment analysis2014:[1-38 pp.]. Available from: https://www.headsup.org.au/docs/default-source/resources/beyondblue_workplaceroi_finalreport_may-2014.pdf.

1201. McEwen BS. In pursuit of resilience: stress, epigenetics, and brain plasticity. Annals of the New York Academy of Sciences. 2016;1373(1):56-64.

1202. McEwen BS, Bowles NP, Gray JD, Hill MN, Hunter RG, Karatsoreos IN, et al. Mechanisms of stress in the brain. Nature neuroscience. 2015;18(10):1353-63.

1203. McEwen BS. Allostasis and the Epigenetics of Brain and Body Health Over the Life Course: The Brain on Stress. JAMA psychiatry. 2017.

1204. Chesak SS, Bhagra A, Schroeder DR, Foy DA, Cutshall SM, Sood A. Enhancing resilience among new nurses: feasibility and efficacy of a pilot intervention. The Ochsner journal. 2015;15(1):38-44.

1205. Kashani K, Carrera P, De Moraes AG, Sood A, Onigkeit JA, Ramar K. Stress and burnout among critical care fellows: preliminary evaluation of an educational intervention. Medical education online. 2015;20:27840.

1206. Magtibay DL, Chesak SS, Coughlin K, Sood A. Decreasing Stress and Burnout in Nurses: Efficacy of Blended Learning With Stress Management and Resilience Training Program. The Journal of nursing administration. 2017;47(7-8):391-5.

1207. Prasad K, Wahner-Roedler DL, Cha SS, Sood A. Effect of a single-session meditation training to reduce stress and improve quality of life among health care professionals: a "dose-ranging" feasibility study. Alternative therapies in health and medicine. 2011;17(3):46-9.

1208. Sharma V, Sood A, Prasad K, Loehrer L, Schroeder D, Brent B. Bibliotherapy to decrease stress and anxiety and increase resilience and mindfulness: a pilot trial. Explore (New York, NY). 2014;10(4):248-52.

1209. Sood A, Sharma V, Schroeder DR, Gorman B. Stress Management and Resiliency Training (SMART) program among Department of Radiology faculty: a pilot randomized clinical trial. Explore (New York, NY). 2014;10(6):358-63.

1210. Stonnington CM, Darby B, Santucci A, Mulligan P, Pathuis P, Cuc A, et al. A resilience intervention involving mindfulness training for transplant patients and their caregivers. Clinical transplantation. 2016;30(11):1466-72.

1210a. Werneburg, BL, Jenkins SL, Friend JL, Berkland BE, Clark MM, Rosedahl JK, Preston HR, Daniels DC, Riley BA, Olsen KD, Sood A. Improving Resiliency in Healthcare Employees. American Journal of Health Behavior. 2018;42(1):39-50

1210b. Berkland BE, Werneburg, BL, Jenkins SL, Friend JL, Clark MM, Rosedahl JK, Limburg PJ, Riley BA, Lecy DR, Sood A. A Worksite Wellness Intervention: Improving Happiness, Life Satisfaction and Gratitude in Health Care Workers. Mayo Clinic Proceedings: IQ&O. In Press.

1211. Achtziger A, Gollwitzer PM, Sheeran P. Implementation intentions and shielding goal striving from unwanted thoughts and feelings. Personality & social psychology bulletin. 2008;34(3):381-93.

1212. Brassen S, Gamer M, Peters J, Gluth S, Buchel C. Don't look back in anger! Responsiveness to missed chances in successful and nonsuccessful aging. Science (New York, NY). 2012;336(6081):612-4.

1213. Mrazek MD, Franklin MS, Phillips DT, Baird B, Schooler JW. Mindfulness training improves working memory capacity and GRE performance while reducing mind wandering. Psychological science. 2013;24(5):776-81.

1214. Mrazek MD, Smallwood J, Schooler JW. Mindfulness and mind-wandering: finding convergence through opposing constructs. Emotion (Washington, DC). 2012;12(3):442-8.

1215. Jha AP, Krompinger J, Baime MJ. Mindfulness training modifies subsystems of attention. Cognitive, affective & behavioral neuroscience. 2007;7(2):109-19.

1216. Lacaille J, Sadikaj G, Nishioka M, Carriere K, Flanders J, Knauper B. Daily Mindful Responding Mediates the Effect of Meditation Practice on Stress and Mood: The Role of Practice Duration and Adherence. Journal of clinical psychology. 2017.

1217. van Leeuwen S, Muller NG, Melloni L. Age effects on attentional blink performance in meditation. Consciousness and cognition. 2009;18(3):593-9.

1218. Grant JA, Courtemanche J, Rainville P. A non-elaborative mental stance and decoupling of executive and pain-related cortices predicts low pain sensitivity in Zen meditators. Pain. 2011;152(1):150-6.

1219. Taylor VA, Daneault V, Grant J, Scavone G, Breton E, Roffe-Vidal S, et al. Impact of meditation training on the default mode network during a restful state. Social cognitive and affective neuroscience. 2013;8(1):4-14.

1220. Taylor VA, Grant J, Daneault V, Scavone G, Breton E, Roffe-Vidal S, et al. Impact of mindfulness on the neural responses to emotional pictures in experienced and beginner meditators. NeuroImage. 2011;57(4):1524-33.

1221. Garrison KA, Santoyo JF, Davis JH, Thornhill TAt, Kerr CE, Brewer JA. Effortless awareness: using real time neurofeedback to investigate correlates of posterior cingulate cortex activity in meditators' self-report. Frontiers in human neuroscience. 2013;7:440.

1222. Lutz A, Greischar LL, Rawlings NB, Ricard M, Davidson RJ. Long-term meditators self-induce high-amplitude gamma synchrony during mental practice. Proceedings of the National Academy of Sciences of the United States of America. 2004;101(46):16369-73.

1223. Ferrarelli F, Smith R, Dentico D, Riedner BA, Zennig C, Benca RM, et al. Experienced mindfulness meditators exhibit higher parietal-occipital EEG gamma activity during NREM sleep. PloS one. 2013;8(8):e73417.

1224. Luders E, Cherbuin N, Gaser C. Estimating brain age using high-resolution pattern recognition: Younger brains in long-term meditation practitioners. NeuroImage. 2016;134:508-13.

1225. Rosenkranz MA, Lutz A, Perlman DM, Bachhuber DR, Schuyler BS, MacCoon DG, et al. Reduced stress and inflammatory responsiveness in experienced meditators compared to a matched healthy control group. Psychoneuroendocrinology. 2016;68:117-25.

1226. Sahdra BK, MacLean KA, Ferrer E, Shaver PR, Rosenberg EL, Jacobs TL, et al. Enhanced response inhibition during intensive meditation training predicts improvements in self-reported adaptive socioemotional functioning. Emotion (Washington, DC). 2011;11(2):299-312.

1227. MacLean KA, Ferrer E, Aichele SR, Bridwell DA, Zanesco AP, Jacobs TL, et al. Intensive meditation training improves perceptual discrimination and sustained attention. Psychological science. 2010;21(6):829-39.

1228. Kaliman P, Alvarez-Lopez MJ, Cosin-Tomas M, Rosenkranz MA, Lutz A, Davidson RJ. Rapid changes in histone deacetylases and inflammatory gene expression in expert meditators. Psychoneuroendocrinology. 2014;40:96-107.

1229. Wielgosz J, Schuyler BS, Lutz A, Davidson RJ. Long-term mindfulness training is associated with reliable differences in resting respiration rate. Scientific reports. 2016;6:27533.

1230. Goldberg SB, Del Re AC, Hoyt WT, Davis JM. The secret ingredient in mindfulness interventions? A case for practice quality over quantity. Journal of counseling psychology. 2014;61(3):491-7.

1231. Ericsson AP, R. Peak: Secrets from the New Science of Expertise. 1 ed: Eamon Dolan/Houghton Mifflin Harcourt; 2016.

1232. Mascaro JS, Rilling JK, Negi LT, Raison CL. Pre-existing brain function predicts subsequent practice of mindfulness and compassion meditation. NeuroImage. 2013;69:35-42.

1233. Shapiro SL, Brown KW, Thoresen C, Plante TG. The moderation of Mindfulness-based stress reduction effects by trait mindfulness: results from a randomized controlled trial. Journal of clinical psychology. 2011;67(3):267-77.

1234. Gawrysiak MJ, Grassetti SN, Greeson JM, Shorey RC, Pohlig R, Baime MJ. The many facets of mindfulness and the prediction of change following mindfulness-based stress reduction (MBSR). Journal of clinical psychology. 2017.

1235. Desbordes G, Negi LT, Pace TW, Wallace BA, Raison CL, Schwartz EL. Effects of mindful-attention and compassion meditation training on amygdala response to emotional stimuli in an ordinary, non-meditative state. Frontiers in human neuroscience. 2012;6:292.

1236. Decety J. The neurodevelopment of empathy in humans. Developmental neuroscience. 2010;32(4):257-67.

1237. Hutcherson CA, Seppala EM, Gross JJ. Loving-kindness meditation increases social connectedness. Emotion (Washington, DC). 2008;8(5):720-4.

1238. Ashar YK, Andrews-Hanna JR, Yarkoni T, Sills J, Halifax J, Dimidjian S, et al. Effects of compassion meditation on a psychological model of charitable donation. Emotion (Washington, DC). 2016;16(5):691-705.

1239. Kang Y, Gray JR, Dovidio JF. The nondiscriminating heart: lovingkindness meditation training decreases implicit intergroup bias. Journal of experimental psychology General. 2014;143(3):1306-13.

1239a. Kirby JN, Tellegen CL, Steindl SR. A Meta-Analysis of Compassion-Based Interventions: Current State of Knowledge and Future Directions. Behavior Therapy. 2017;48(6):778-792.

1240. Marsh AA, Stoycos SA, Brethel-Haurwitz KM, Robinson P, VanMeter JW, Cardinale EM. Neural and cognitive characteristics of extraordinary altruists. Proceedings of the National Academy of Sciences of the United States of America. 2014;111(42):15036-41.

1241. Shdo SM, Ranasinghe KG, Gola KA, Mielke CJ, Sukhanov PV, Miller BL, et al. Deconstructing empathy: Neuroanatomical dissociations between affect sharing and prosocial motivation using a patient lesion model. Neuropsychologia. 2017.

1242. Lumma AL, Kok BE, Singer T. Is meditation always relaxing? Investigating heart rate, heart rate variability, experienced effort and likeability during training of three types of meditation. International journal of psychophysiology : official journal of the International Organization of Psychophysiology. 2015;97(1):38-45.

About Dr. Sood

Dr. Amit Sood is married to his lovely wife of 25 years, Dr. Richa Sood. They have two girls, Gauri age 13 and Sia age 7.

Dr. Sood holds the rank of professor of medicine at Mayo Clinic. He serves as chair of the Mind Body Medicine Initiative and director of student wellness for Mayo Clinic College of Medicine. He is the creator and lead instructor of the Mayo Clinic Healthy Living: Resilient Mind Program. He provides resiliency and stress management consults to patients at Mayo Clinic.

Dr. Sood completed his residency in internal medicine at the Albert Einstein School of Medicine, an integrative medicine fellowship at the University of Arizona and earned a master's degree in clinical research from Mayo Clinic College of Medicine. He has received several National Institutes of Health grants and foundation awards to test and implement integrative and mind-body approaches within medicine.

Dr. Sood has developed an innovative approach toward mind-body medicine by incorporating concepts from neuroscience, evolutionary biology, psychology, philosophy and biomedical research. His resulting program, Stress Management and Resiliency Training (SMART©) has now been adapted as Mayo Clinic Healthy Living: Resilient Mind. The program reaches approximately 50,000 patients and learners each year. The program has been tested in 20 completed clinical trials.

Dr. Sood's programs are offered for a wide variety of patients and learners including to improve resiliency; decrease stress and anxiety; enhance well-being, happiness and mindfulness; improve health behaviors; enhance coping in patients with chronic illness; and wellness solutions for caregivers, corporate executives, health care professionals, parents, and students. At Mayo Clinic, SMART© program is now available enterprise-wide to the staff and integrated within the leadership and burnout curriculum for physicians, nurses, and medical students.

Dr. Sood has authored or co-authored over 70 peer-reviewed articles, editorials, book chapters, abstracts, and letters. He has developed award-winning patient education DVDs on topics within integrative medicine ranging from paced breathing meditation and mindfulness to wellness solutions for obesity, insomnia, and fibromyalgia. He developed the first Mayo Clinic iPhone app for meditation training. Dr. Sood is author of the books *The Mayo Clinic Guide to Stress-Free Living*, *The Mayo Clinic Handbook for Happiness*, and *Immerse: A 52-Week Course in Resilient Living*.

As an international expert in his field, Dr. Sood's work has been widely cited in the press including – *The Atlantic Monthly, USA Today, Wall Street Journal, New York Times, Forbes, NPR, Reuters Health, Time Magazine (online), Good Housekeeping, Parenting, Real Simple, Shape, US News, Huffington Post, Mens Health Magazine, AARP, The Globe and Mail, CBS News, and Fox News*. He served as one of the 2015 Health care pioneer for the Robert Wood Johnson Foundation.

He is highly sought after as a speaker on resilience, stress management, mindfulness and happiness, presenting more than 100 workshops each year. Some of his most popular videos include his TEDx talk – *Happy Brain: How to Overcome Our Neural Predispositions to Suffering*, and an animation, *A Very Happy Brain*.

Dr. Sood has received several awards for his work, including the Mayo's 2010 Distinguished Service Award, Mayo's 2010 Innovator of the Year Award, Mayo's 2013 outstanding physician scientist award, and Mayo's 2016 Faculty of the Year Award. He was selected as one among the top 20 intelligent optimists "helping the world be a better place" by *Ode Magazine*. In 2016, Dr. Sood was voted as the top impact maker in healthcare in Rochester, MN.